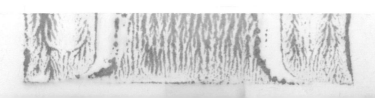

Fundamentals of Good Writing

By Robert Penn Warren

ALL THE KING'S MEN

CIRCUS IN THE ATTIC

AT HEAVEN'S GATE

NIGHT RIDER

JOHN BROWN: THE MAKING OF A MARTYR

SELECTED POEMS, 1923-1934

By Cleanth Brooks

THE WELL WROUGHT URN

MODERN POETRY AND THE TRADITION

Fundamentals of Good Writing

A HANDBOOK OF MODERN RHETORIC

Cleanth Brooks
Robert Penn Warren

Harcourt, Brace & World, Inc. · New York

TO DAVID M. CLAY

CONTENTS

Introduction

THE MAIN CONSIDERATIONS	1
THE MOTIVATION OF THE WRITER	3
THE NATURE OF THE READER	5
THE RELATIONSHIP BETWEEN READER AND WRITER	5
THE FUSION OF MEDIUM, SUBJECT AND OCCASION	6
YOUR BACKGROUND FOR SUCCESSFUL WRITING	7

I. SOME GENERAL PROBLEMS

FINDING A TRUE SUBJECT	11
UNITY	13
COHERENCE	15
EMPHASIS	19
THE MAIN DIVISIONS OF A DISCOURSE	23
PROPORTIONING THE MAIN DIVISIONS	25
THE OUTLINE	26

2. THE KINDS OF DISCOURSE

THE MAIN INTENTION	29
THE FOUR KINDS OF DISCOURSE	30
MIXTURE OF THE KINDS OF DISCOURSE	30
OBJECTIVE AND SUBJECTIVE DISCOURSE	31

3. EXPOSITION

INTEREST   38

THE METHODS OF EXPOSITION   41

IDENTIFICATION   41

EXPOSITORY DESCRIPTION: TECHNICAL DESCRIPTION   42

THE RELATION BETWEEN THE TECHNICAL-SUGGESTIVE DISTINCTION

     AND THE OBJECTIVE-SUBJECTIVE DISTINCTION   53

THE USES OF TECHNICAL AND SUGGESTIVE DESCRIPTION   55

EXPOSITORY NARRATION   57

ILLUSTRATION   57

COMPARISON AND CONTRAST   61

CLASSIFICATION AND DIVISION   67

DEFINITION   83

EXTENDED DEFINITION   91

ANALYSIS: THE TWO KINDS   98

ANALYSIS AND STRUCTURE   99

ANALYSIS: RELATION AMONG PARTS   100

ANALYSIS AND EXPOSITORY DESCRIPTION   101

EXPOSITORY METHODS AND THEIR USES   119

SUMMARY   120

4. ARGUMENT

THE APPEAL OF ARGUMENT   125

ARGUMENT AND CONFLICT   125

ARGUMENT AND THE UNDERSTANDING   127

WHAT ARGUMENT IS ABOUT   128

THE PROPOSITION: TWO KINDS   131

THE STATEMENT OF THE PROPOSITION   131

HISTORY OF THE QUESTION   134

ISSUES   135

PROPOSITIONS OF FACT   146

EVIDENCE   148

KINDS OF EVIDENCE: FACT AND OPINION 148

REASONING 154

INDUCTION: GENERALIZATION 155

DEDUCTION 159

FALLACIES 167

FALLACIES AND REFUTATION 170

THE IMPLIED SYLLOGISM 170

EXTENDED ARGUMENT: THE BRIEF 172

ORDER OF THE BRIEF AND ORDER OF THE ARGUMENT 183

PERSUASION 183

SUMMARY 189

5. DESCRIPTION

RELATION OF SUGGESTIVE DESCRIPTION TO OTHER KINDS
OF DISCOURSE 195

THE DOMINANT IMPRESSION 200

PATTERN AND TEXTURE IN DESCRIPTION 200

TEXTURE: SELECTION IN DESCRIPTION 211

DESCRIPTION OF FEELINGS AND STATES OF MIND 220

FIGURATIVE LANGUAGE IN THE DESCRIPTION OF FEELINGS
AND STATES OF MIND 223

CHOICE OF WORDS IN THE TEXTURE OF DESCRIPTION 226

SUMMARY 229

6. NARRATION

MOVEMENT 237

TIME 238

MEANING 239

NARRATIVE AND NARRATION 240

NARRATION AND THE OTHER KINDS OF DISCOURSE 242

PATTERN IN NARRATION 250

EXAMPLES OF NARRATIVE PATTERN 255

PROPORTION 262

TEXTURE AND SELECTION 264

POINT OF VIEW 267

SCALE 273

DIALOGUE 275

CHARACTERIZATION 281

SUMMARY 285

7. THE PARAGRAPH

THE PARAGRAPH AS A CONVENIENCE TO THE READER 290

THE PARAGRAPH AS A UNIT OF THOUGHT 291

THE STRUCTURE OF THE PARAGRAPH 292

SOME TYPICAL STRUCTURAL PRINCIPLES 294

LINKING PARAGRAPHS TOGETHER 299

USE OF THE PARAGRAPH TO INDICATE DIALOGUE 302

SUMMARY 302

8. THE SENTENCE

RHETORIC AND GRAMMAR 304

THE FIXED WORD ORDER OF THE NORMAL SENTENCE 307

POSITION OF THE MODIFIERS 311

GENERAL PRINCIPLES OF SENTENCE STRUCTURE 318

SENTENCE LENGTH AND SENTENCE VARIATION 323

SUMMARY 327

9. STYLE

GENERAL DEFINITION OF STYLE 329

THREE ASPECTS OF LITERARY STYLE 330

STYLE AS AN INTERPLAY OF ELEMENTS 331

THE PLAN OF THE FOLLOWING CHAPTERS ON STYLE 332

10. DICTION

DENOTATION AND CONNOTATION 335

LANGUAGE GROWTH BY EXTENSION OF MEANING 342

THE COMPANY A WORD KEEPS: COLLOQUIAL, INFORMAL,

   AND FORMAL 348

HOW CONNOTATIONS CONTROL MEANINGS 349

WORN-OUT WORDS AND CLICHÉS 353

SUMMARY 359

11. METAPHOR

METAPHOR DEFINED 361

IMPORTANCE OF METAPHOR IN EVERYDAY LANGUAGE 362

THE FUNCTION OF METAPHOR 371

METAPHOR AS ESSENTIAL STATEMENT 374

WHAT MAKES A "GOOD" METAPHOR? 378

METAPHOR AND SYMBOL 385

METAPHOR AND THE CREATIVE IMAGINATION 386

SUMMARY 388

12. SITUATION AND TONE

TONE AS THE EXPRESSION OF ATTITUDE 390

THE IMPORTANCE OF TONE 391

WHAT DETERMINES TONE? 392

TONE AS A QUALIFICATION OF MEANING 397

SOME PRACTICAL DON'TS 401

SOME PRACTICAL APPLICATIONS 402

TONE: FAMILIAR AND FORMAL 411

COMPLEXITY OF TONE: WHEN, AND WHY, IT IS NECESSARY 416

SUMMARY 422

13. THE FINAL INTEGRATION

RHYTHM 425

RHYTHM AS A DEVICE OF EXPRESSION 428

STYLE AS HARMONIOUS INTEGRATION 432

THE INSEPARABILITY OF FORM AND CONTENT 435

STYLE AS AN EXPRESSION OF PERSONALITY   438
STYLE CULTIVATED BY READING   455
SUMMARY   457
A MORE CONCRETE SUMMARY   459

14. READING: WHAT DOES IT MEAN TO A WRITER? 461

APPENDIXES   473

Appendix 1. CAUSAL ANALYSIS   475

Appendix 2. THE SYLLOGISM   481

Appendix 3. THE OUTLINE, SUMMARY, AND PRÉCIS; NOTES;
                RESEARCH PAPER; AND BOOK REPORT   486

INDEX   519

Fundamentals of Good Writing

THERE is no easy way to learn to write. There is no certain formula, no short cut, no bag of tricks. It is not a matter of memorizing rules or of acquiring a few skills. To write well is not easy for the simple reason that to write well you must think straight. And thinking straight is never easy.

Straight thinking is the basis of all good writing. It does not matter whether you are planning to write fiction, poetry, news reports, magazine articles, essays, or sermons. What is common to all kinds of good writing is more important than what distinguishes one kind from another. This is a fundamental point, and this book is an attempt to deal with the fundamentals of writing.

THE MAIN CONSIDERATIONS

What is it that we must think straight about if we are to write well? Unfortunately there is no simple answer to this. A writer, as Robert Louis Stevenson says in his "Essay on Style," is like a juggler who must keep several balls in the air at once.

What are the several balls? What are the considerations that a writer must simultaneously think straight about? This book is an attempt to answer that question; but even when this book is finished the answer will not be a complete one. For the present, however, we may try to reduce the considerations to three general types. We may define them in reference to various aspects of the act of writing:

1. The medium
2. The subject
3. The occasion

These terms, as we are using them, require some explanation.

THE MEDIUM

A writer writes in a language, the substance, as it were, through which he exerts his force, the medium through which he communicates his ideas and feelings. This language operates in terms of certain principles and usages which a writer must observe if he is to exercise his full force or even, in some instances, to be understood at all. For example, grammar is an aspect of the medium itself. Rhythm is another aspect, and it may exercise a very powerful effect on the reader, even if he is not aware of it. Another aspect is diction—the qualities of the individual words even beyond their bare dictionary definitions.

These topics, and others related to them, will be discussed in the course of this book, but for the present it is important only that we understand them as representing aspects of the medium, of language itself.

THE SUBJECT

A writer writes about something. The something may be his own feelings, his love or his hate, or again it may be the theory of aerodynamics. But in either instance he has a subject—and one that can be distinguished from all other possible subjects.

The nature of the subject will, in some respects, dictate the nature of the treatment. For instance, if a writer is interested in explaining a process of some kind, the running of an experiment in physics or the building of a log cabin, he will have to organize his material with some reference to the chronological order of the process. If he is trying to explain why he loves or hates someone, he will probably be concerned with the analysis of traits of character which have no necessary reference to chronology; therefore, his ordering of the material may well be in terms of degrees of importance and not in terms of time sequence.

Furthermore, the subject may dictate differences in diction. For instance, if the writer is trying to explain the process of an experiment in physics, his diction will be dry and technical, clear and factual; but if he is trying to define the grief experienced at the death of a friend, his diction may well be chosen to convey emotional effects.

Or the type of rhythm may vary according to the subject. The explanation of the experiment in physics will probably involve a rather flat rhythm, or at least an unobtrusive rhythm, but the attempt to define the grief at the death of the friend will probably depend to a considerable degree for its success on the rhythm employed, for the rhythm of language, even in prose, is of enormous importance in the communication of feelings.

THE OCCASION

Third, a writer writes out of a special situation, the occasion. We may say that this situation involves three basic elements: the motivation of the writer; the nature of the reader; and the relationship between writer and reader.

THE MOTIVATION OF THE WRITER

As for motivation, two general types may be distinguished: expression and communication. The writer may be primarily concerned to affirm his own feelings, to clarify his own mind, to define for himself his own sense of the world. When he writes from some such motivation, the urge to expression may be said to be dominant, and he has, on such an occasion, more in common with a man singing in the bath, with the child uttering the spontaneous cry of pain, or with the cat purring on the rug than he has with the judge handing down a decision from the bench, a teacher explaining a point of grammar from the platform, or a woman giving her daughter a recipe for pie. For the judge, the teacher, and the cook are not primarily concerned to express but to communicate something.

It may be said, however, that, in the ultimate sense, we never have a case of pure expression or pure communication. Even the cry of pain, which seems to be pure expression, may be said to presuppose a hearer; the hurt child redoubles its screams when it sees the mother approaching. And the poet who has written his poem without a conscious thought of the reader, who has been concerned with the effort of getting his own feelings and ideas into form, hurries to the post office to mail his finished poem to a magazine through which it can reach a number of readers.

Conversely, even the most objective presentation of an idea or analysis of a situation may involve an expressive element. To take an extreme instance, we may say that a man may take pleasure in the accuracy and tidiness of his working out of a mathematical demonstration and feel that those qualities "express" him.

If it is true that we can never find an example of pure expression or of pure communication, if we have to regard expression and communication as, shall we say, the poles of the process of writing or speaking, we can still see that a great deal of variation in the relative proportions of communication and expression may exist.

ACCENT ON EXPRESSION

When the writer is primarily concerned with expression, he does not pay attention to his audience; if, under such circumstances, he thinks of the audience, it is only to assume that there will be people enough like himself to have an interest in his work. Yet even then, even when the writer is primarily concerned with expression, his private and individual intentions will have to be represented in a medium that has public and general standards. When the writer accepts language as his medium of expression, he also accepts the standards of communication.

ACCENT ON COMMUNICATION

When the writer is primarily concerned with communication rather than expression, he must, however, give special attention to the audience which he wishes to reach. He must consider the reader's interests and attitudes. Even if the writer wishes to give the reader a new interest, he must work in terms of the interests that already exist. When the writer does not, in some way, appeal to the already existing interests, the reader will not even bother to finish the book or article. Or if the writer wishes to make the reader change his attitude on some issue, he must work in terms of already existing attitudes. Unless the writer can discover that he and the reader have *some* attitudes in common, he can have no hope of convincing the reader about the matter on which they disagree.

THE NATURE OF THE READER

Just as the writer must concern himself with the reader's interests and attitudes, so he must concern himself with the reader's training and capacities. Every piece of writing is addressed to a more or less limited audience. It is perfectly logical that a piece of writing addressed to the specialist will not be understood by the layman. Articles in professional medical journals or law journals employ a language and a treatment largely incomprehensible to the ordinary reader. But the same thing holds true, though less obviously, in regard to all differences of education or capacity. Because of differences in education, the housewife is not likely to understand the article on international finance that may be perfectly clear to the banker or businessman who is her husband. Or one housewife, because of innate intelligence and sensitivity, can understand and enjoy a certain novel, while another woman in the same block, who has been educated at the same school, is merely confused and annoyed by the book.

It is true that there are types of writing which have a relatively broad appeal—the novels of Dickens or the plays of Shakespeare—but we must remember that even their appeal is only relatively broad, and that there are a great number of people who infinitely prefer the sports page of the daily paper or the financial section or the comic strip to Dickens or Shakespeare. And remembering this, the writer must concern himself with the level of education and intelligence of the special group which he wishes to address.

THE RELATIONSHIP BETWEEN READER AND WRITER

Just as the writer must consider his own motivation and the nature of his intended reader as components of the "occasion," so must he consider the relationship between himself and that reader. For instance, does he feel that he must speak down to his reader? If he does speak down, shall he take the tone of a man laying down the law from some position of authority—like a judge on a bench—or shall he take a tone of good-natured condescension? Or if he does not wish to speak down to his reader but regards the reader as on the same level with himself, shall he take a tone of friendly discussion or of serious, life-and-death argument? The possible variations on this score are almost numberless, too, and the writer, if he is to be most effective, must take them into consideration. Is he, for instance, addressing a reader who is hostile and suspicious? If so, he must try to discover the approach which will mollify the hostility and allay the suspicions. Or if his reader is assumed to be friendly but unserious, how shall he adapt himself to that situation? Is he writing to a student who is anxious to learn or to a casual reader who must be lured into the subject under discussion? Obviously the writer must, if he wishes to succeed with his reader, study the relationship existing between himself and his intended reader and adapt his tone to that aspect of the occasion.

TONE

The writer's relationship to his reader and to his subject may be summed up in the word *tone* (see Chapter 12). Just as the tone of voice indicates what the speaker's attitude is to his subject and his listener, so certain qualities of a piece of writing may indicate the attitude of the writer. Rhythms may be harsh and abrupt or lingering and subtle. Diction may be homely and direct or elaborate and suggestive. Sentence structure may be simple and downright or complicated by modifying and qualifying elements. Appeal may be made through logic or through persuasion. These and many other factors are related to the writer's conception of the relation between himself and the reader.

THE FUSION OF MEDIUM, SUBJECT AND OCCASION

Under the headings of (1) medium, (2) subject, and (3) occasion, we have briefly discussed some of the basic considerations which the writer must keep in mind—the balls which the juggler of Stevenson's essay must keep simultaneously in the air. The word *simultaneously* is important here, for though we have necessarily had to discuss our topics in order, we are not to assume that the order is one of either importance or of time sequence. Can one say that a knowledge of the subject under discussion is more or less important than a knowledge of the principles and usages of the language in which the subject is to be discussed? Or that a knowledge of the principles and usages of the language is more or less important than the sense of the nature of the occasion?

In the process of writing there is no one consideration to which the writer must give his attention first. His mind, in so far as he is a conscious craftsman, will play among the various considerations in the attempt to produce a piece of writing which will fulfill at the same time the demands of the medium, the subject, and the occasion. In this book we shall take up various topics individually, and you may find it helpful when you are revising a piece of writing to consider one question at a time. But the final piece of writing is always a fusion.

YOUR BACKGROUND FOR SUCCESSFUL WRITING

The foregoing remarks, with their emphasis on the complicated demands that a good piece of writing must fulfill, have perhaps made the business of writing seem enormously difficult. And it is true that the simplest piece of writing, when well done, *is* the fruit of a great deal of effort. But you are not, with this book, starting your career as a writer from scratch. You already have behind you many years of effort which can be made to apply on the writing you now do. You are already the beneficiary of a long training.

LANGUAGE AND EXPERIENCE

In the first place, you command a working knowledge of the English language. You began the process of learning that language when you were an infant, and the process has been a continuous one ever since. Books have helped you and they can be made to help you even more. They can broaden your vocabulary, and can give you a sense of the subtleties and shadings of words. But already —books aside—you are the master of very considerable resources in your native tongue.

A CAPACITY FOR STRAIGHT THINKING

In the second place, your experience has given you a great range of subjects, and a capacity for thinking logically about them. As for the subjects, almost any event of your day, any sport or craft which you understand, any skill or technique which you possess, any scene which you have witnessed, any book or article which you have read, any person whom you know—all these are potential subjects. And any one of them can become interesting in so far as it is actually important to you and in so far as you can think straight about it.

As for logical thinking, demands for the exercise of this faculty are made on you every day. You are constantly under the necessity of adjusting means to ends, of correcting errors in your calculations, of planning in terms of cause and effect, of estimating possibilities. To manage your simplest affairs you must have some capacity for straight thinking. When you come to the business of writing, you need merely to apply this capacity to the subject in hand—to see what is important about it for your interests and purposes, to stick to your point, to make one sentence follow from the previous sentence and lead to the next, to make one paragraph follow from the previous paragraph and lead to the next, to make one idea follow from another, to state the relations between things in terms of time, space, or causality, to emphasize the important item and subordinate the unimportant, to proportion your discourse so that it will have an introduction, a development, and a conclusion. All of these problems of analysis and organization are problems which you may have to confront when you start any piece of writing, but you confront them with the aid of all the straight thinking that you have ever done.

A BROAD SOCIAL EXPERIENCE

In the third place, all of your experiences with other people in the past have provided a training that will help you adjust yourself to your intended reader. Your social experience, from your early childhood, has given you a training in tact, in grasping the truth about a human relationship, in adjusting your manner to the mood or prejudice of another person in order to convince, persuade, entertain, or instruct him. Every child is aware that, when he wants something from his mother or father, there is a right way to go about asking for it and a wrong way. And he knows that what is the right way for asking the mother may very well be the wrong way for asking the father. No doubt, the child never puts it to himself in these terms, but he acts on the truth behind these terms when he actually deals with mother or father. He develops early a sense of the occasion and a sensitivity to what we shall call problems of tone.

The discussion in this section comes to this: All of your experience in the past can be said, without too much wrenching of fact, to be a training for the writing which you wish to do. Your problem is, in part, to learn to use the resources which you already possess. For unless you learn to use those resources, you will not be able to acquire new resources.

Some General
Problems

WHERE should the study of writing begin? With considerations of the medium? Of the subject? Of the occasion? It is impossible to say that one of these is more important than the others, and it is impossible to say that one should logically precede the others.

It might be argued that, since the word is the smallest unit in composition, we should begin with the study of diction and move by easy stages through the study of the sentence and the paragraph to the study of the general problem of organization, with attention finally given to questions of the occasion.

But we could reply that when we choose words we choose them in relation to other words, in relation to some general subject and our general intention concerning that subject, and in relation to our attitude toward the reader. In the same way we could say that the study of the sentence, important as it is, should not necessarily precede the study of problems of more general organization. For it is the pattern of the sentences, not the individual sentence, which gives the thrust of our thought and defines the progression of our ideas. We are first, and finally, concerned with the nature of our complete utterance, our over-all idea, our main intention. And perhaps we should, therefore, be first concerned with general problems of organization.

FINDING A TRUE SUBJECT

Your first problem will always be to define for yourself what your central idea is. Your second problem will always be to develop that idea clearly and forcefully. In other words, you must think before you write. And you must think as you write. For writing is both the expression of thought and an instrument of thought.

What constitutes a subject? As we have already observed, anything can be a subject—your autobiography, George Washington, a house, war, religion, boats, a picnic, chemical research. This answer is true as far as it goes. But if we put down the subject "George Washington" and then simply assemble various facts, ideas, and speculations about him, we find that we do not have a true subject. It is too vague, too inclusive; and the writer feels like a man trying to grab a handful of fog. The subject must be limited and fixed if it is to be manageable.

To limit and fix a subject we must think of it with reference to a basic interest—an interest dictated by an occasion assigned to us, or discovered for ourselves. The subject is not in and of itself a subject—George Washington, a house, war, religion, and so forth—but is so created by some mind. Even an idea as such is not a subject, say the idea of goodness or the idea of infinity. To become a true subject, a mind must work on that idea, define it, take some attitude toward it.

The true subject is a topic brought to focus. If we take, for instance, the topic "George Washington," we can think of various possible interests which might give us true subjects: "George Washington as the Type of the Colonial Planter," "The Development of Leadership in George Washington," "What the Frontier Taught George Washington," "George Washington as a Statesman," "The Influence of George Washington on American Political Thought," "Myths about George Washington," "The Courtships of George Washington," "George Washington as a Strategist." But this would be only the beginning of a list of true subjects. Whatever about George Washington might interest anybody would be a possible subject. So the true subject is something *about* a subject.

It may be objected that a large work on George Washington, say a biography, might contain many of the items listed above. That is true. But even in a large work there would be some fundamental line of interest and interpretation to which the other interests would be related and subordinated.

Before you undertake any piece of composition, you should try to frame the real subject, the central concern. You do not write about a house. You write about its appearance, the kind of life it suggests, its style of architecture, or your associations with it. You do not write about chemical research. You write about the method of chemical research, the achievements of chemical research, or the opportunities for chemical research. You do not write about goodness. You write about the different views of goodness which have been held by different societies or religions at different times, about the Christian idea of goodness, about goodness as exemplified by people you know or know about, or about the definition of goodness which you personally accept. You must search your own thoughts and feelings to find your true subject.

UNITY

Once the writer has his true subject, he must not lose sight of it as he pursues various related ideas. A good piece of writing has UNITY. The fundamental interest, which is his subject, must permeate the whole composition. The composition must be *one* thing, and not a hodgepodge.

Unity is not arbitrary, something imposed from the outside. It is simply the indication that the writer's own mind can work systematically and can therefore arrive at a meaning. To put it another way, the unity of the composition is an indication that his mind has unity—that he is not scatterbrained.

Let us look at a composition which is not well unified.

WHY I WISH TO BE AN ENGINEER

(1) I suppose that one reason I want to be an engineer and have made my college plans in that direction is that my father is an engineer. He was a student here at the State University back in 1909-1914. He began his college career with the intention of being a doctor, but he soon changed his mind. He finished his course in 1914, and worked as a draftsman for two years in Chicago in an engineering firm. But World War I got him into the army, and he wound up a major in the Engineering Corps. It was a valuable experience for him in more ways than one, for he says it taught him how to deal with men of all kinds and to get work done under

pressure. Also it meant that he was to get a taste for action and adventure. After the war, he went to Mexico and worked on building a railroad in the mountains. He had many difficult construction problems to solve. I was born in Mexico, and I was raised in a family where they talked engineering all the time, for my mother was interested in my father's work.

(2) There is a great future for an engineer in this country. It makes me tired to hear people talk of the lack of opportunity in that line. It is true that during the Depression many engineers were out of work, but that applied to many occupations and professions. Besides, many of the engineers out of work were not well trained to begin with. If you are really well trained and are willing to put out your best efforts you can almost always get along. There is a great future for engineering here, for we are on the verge of a great technological revolution which will mean the rebuilding of much of the industrial plant and the development of new transport facilities. Besides, land reclamation and the expansion of public works are long-range programs. This country is an engineer's paradise, for we are the most mechanical-minded people in the world. They say that that is the great talent of America, and I see nothing to be ashamed of in that. Engineers make the world easier to live in for everybody. Think of things like the great bridges and dams, the highways and airports. What would we do without them?

(3) I like the life of action, and that is another reason I plan to be an engineer. My father had a very interesting life in Mexico. After five years there he went to Argentina. He had learned the language in Mexico, and had made a name for himself there. So he got a good offer in Argentina. He sent my mother and me back to the U. S. until I grew up a little, but he came to see us at the end of the first year and took us back to Argentina with him. We lived there four years. Then he went to India, and supervised the building of some bridges there. But he did not take us to India with him. He understood that the climate was too bad. And he was right, because he almost died there of dysentery. He never left America again, but his talk about his adventures gave me a desire for an active life, and he has never discouraged me.

(4) I make my best marks in mathematics. Mathematics is the basis of engineering, and I think that a man should follow his best talent. I like other things, too, history for instance, and I read a good many novels and stories. But I cannot see myself making a profession of any of these things. Business would be too confining for me. I have an uncle who is a lawyer, and it seems to me that he never gets out of his office except to come home at night.

Taking everything together, I think that engineering is the right profession for me.

The writer here has a subject, which is expressed in the title. And if we examine the theme carefully we can dig out the reasons for his choice of a career: family background, the opportunity to make a good living, the appetite for action, and the aptitude for mathematics. These four reasons should give him the outline for his theme.

But he is constantly bringing in material which does not bear directly on the subject or which is developed without reference to the main line of interest. For instance, he is so much impressed with his father's life that he devotes far too much attention to it: most of the first and third paragraphs. For present purposes we only need to know the barest facts about the father's career. The last part of the second paragraph, too, is not relevant. The writer may have two points here—that an engineer feels himself characteristically American and that the engineer has the sense of being a useful member of society. But he does not state these points, and they are lost in his general remarks. If we get them at all, we get them by implication only. In the fourth paragraph, too, we find some irrelevant material—the reference to the writer's interest in history and fiction, and the remark about his uncle's occupation.

COHERENCE

An effective discourse must have unity. And it must also have COHERENCE. That is, the elements of the discourse must stick together. This seems to be another way of saying that a discourse must have unity, and in one sense that is true. The distinction may be stated thus: When we speak of unity we are referring primarily to the nature of the materials as related to the subject, and when we speak of coherence we are referring primarily to the way the materials are organized to give a continuous development of the subject. A discourse which lacks coherence will, in the larger sense, seem to lack unity, for even if the materials individually relate to the subject, we will not be able to see how they relate to each other.

We can consider coherence in two respects: (1) as involving overall organization of the discourse, and (2) as involving local transitions within the discourse.

COHERENCE THROUGH OVER-ALL ORGANIZATION

There is no one principle by which the materials of a discourse are to be organized. Obviously, a principle of organization good for describing a woman's face would not be good for telling the story of a baseball game or a battle, for explaining the causes of the Russian Revolution, or for arguing against the abolition of Greek letter fraternities. Different intentions involve different principles of organization. We shall study the basic intentions and some of their characteristic methods when we come to the chapters on description, narrative, exposition, and argument, but for the present we can content ourselves with the common-sense principle: One thing should lead to another.

The following piece of writing is coherent.

THE PERSON I ADMIRE MOST

(1) I suppose that my uncle Conroy is the person I admire most in the world. This statement would probably seem strange to a person who happened to visit in our house and see the old man who sits at a corner of the hearth, hunched over, shabbily dressed, and not saying much. He looks like the complete failure, and by ordinary standards he is. He has no money. He has no children. He is old and sick. But he has made his own kind of success, and I think he is happy.

(2) At one time in his life he was a success by ordinary standards. He was the son of a poor Methodist minister (my mother's father), but he ran away from home in Illinois to Oklahoma back in the days when things were beginning to boom out there. He had a fine house in Oklahoma City and a ranch. He was a hail-fellow-well-met, and men and women liked him. He was a sportsman, kept good horses, and took long hunting trips to Mexico and Canada. Then one day, on his own ranch, his horse stumbled in a gopher hole and threw him. He was badly hurt and was in the hospital for many months. While he was still in the hospital the Depression came on. If he had been well and able to take care of his affairs, he might have saved some of his money from the crash. But as it was he lost everything. So he came back to Illinois, and my mother and father took him in.

(3) It must have been an awful come-down for a man like that to be living on charity. But the worst was yet to happen, for he developed arthritis in a very painful form. I remember the first year or so, even though I was a very small child. He even tried to commit suicide with

gas from the stove. But my mother saved him, and after that he began to change.

(4) The first thing was that he began to take an interest in us children. He would read to us and talk to us. He helped us with our lessons. That relieved mother a great deal and made her life easier. My father was an insurance man and had a lot of paper work to do. It got so that my uncle took an interest in that, and before long he was helping my father by doing reports and writing letters. He helped my father tide over the bad time of the Depression. Then when my mother was ill for a long time, he learned to do some of the housework, as much as his strength would permit, and even dressed the two smaller children.

(5) What he did was important, but more important was the way he did things. He was so natural about it. You never got the impression he was making any effort or sacrifice. We all got so we didn't notice what he did, and I am sure that that was what he wanted.

(6) As I look back now, or when I go home and see Uncle Conroy, the biggest achievement, however, seems to be the kind of example he gave us all. He was often in pain, but he was always cheerful. If he felt too bad he simply hid away from the family for a while in his room —what he called his "mope-room." He even made a joke out of that. And he didn't act like a man who had failed. He acted like a man who had found what he could do and was a success at it. And I think that he is a success. We all admire success, and that is why I admire my uncle Conroy.

We can see how each section of this theme fits into the general pattern. The main business of the writer is to tell *why* he admires his uncle, but he does not immediately set up the reasons. First, by way of introduction, he gives a brief sketch of the man as he now appears—the man who is to be interpreted. The appearance of failure in contrast to the reality of success gives dramatic interest, and excites the reader's curiosity. In the second paragraph he tells of the uncle's days of outward success. This topic does not get into the theme merely because the uncle, as a matter of fact, had such success. Many things that happened to him are certainly omitted here. Instead, it gets in because the taste of worldly success makes the uncle's achievement and shift of values more impressive. The third paragraph presents the despair of the uncle—a normal response to bankruptcy and illness. This topic has a place in the general organization, for it states the thing that the uncle must fight against. The fourth, fifth, and sixth paragraphs define the nature of the uncle's achievement. The order here is one of ascending importance, toward a climax—the special practical things he did, the attitude he took toward the doing, the long-range effect of his example on others. (There is one small defect in the organization here. The reference to the uncle's cheerfulness in the sixth paragraph probably should go back into the fifth paragraph, for it really belongs under the heading of the uncle's attitude.) The sixth paragraph not only states the uncle's most important achievement, but serves as a kind of summary of the preceding material.

COHERENCE THROUGH LOCAL TRANSITIONS

Thus far we have been talking about what is involved in the over-all organization of a piece of writing. But the question of local transitions within the discourse is also extremely important. How do we get from one section to another, one paragraph to another, one sentence to another?

Obviously there must be an intrinsic continuity: what one section, paragraph, or sentence presents must bear some relation to the whole subject and to what has just preceded. But even when there is this intrinsic continuity, we may have to help the reader by using certain devices of connection and transition, by giving him links or signposts.

We can begin a section, paragraph, or sentence with some reference to what has gone before. The repetition or rephrasing of something in the preceding unit will provide a link. For example, let us look at the link which ties together these two paragraphs:

. . . All of these factors result in a condition of *social unrest and economic uncertainty*, which seems to presage the end of our civilization.

Social unrest and economic uncertainty, however, are not always an unhealthy condition. Actually, that condition may be the prelude, not to ruin, but to great revolutionary gains. . . .

The repetition of the phrase "social unrest and economic uncertainty" at the beginning of the second paragraph provides the link between the two. But pronouns and other words of reference (like *such, similar,* and so forth) may serve the same purpose.

. . . All of these factors result in a condition of *social unrest and economic uncertainty*, which seems to presage the end of our civilization.

This situation, however, need not fill us with alarm. . . .

or:

Such a situation, however, is not unhealthy. . . .

Furthermore, there are words whose function is to indicate specific relations: conjunctions, conjunctive adverbs, and some adverbs. These words say what they mean. *And, or, nor* establish a coordinate connection. *But, however, nevertheless* establish a contrast. *So, therefore, consequently* establish a result. *Moreover* and *furthermore* indicate additions or elaborations. Notice how the word *however* is used in the example above.

Another way to establish continuity is found in a large group of more or less conventional phrases. Such phrases are self-explanatory: "in addition," "as has been said," "that is to say," "that is," "by consequence," "for example," "for instance," "as a result," "on the contrary."

None of these lists is complete. They are merely suggestive. But they may serve to indicate the function of such words and phrases so that the writer can by his reading build up his own resources.

We must not use such transitional words and phrases unless they are necessary. They are not ornaments, and they impede the reader rather than help him if the sense is clear without them.

EMPHASIS

A piece of writing may be unified and coherent and still not be effective if it does not observe the principle of EMPHASIS. When this principle is properly observed the intended scale of importance of elements in the discourse is clear to the reader. All cats are black in the dark, but all things should not look alike in the light of a reasonable writer's interest in his subject. To change our metaphor, there is a foreground and a background of interest, and the writer should be careful to place each item in its proper location. Like unity and coherence, emphasis is a principle of organization.

How do we emphasize an element in a piece of writing?

EMPHASIS BY FLAT STATEMENT

The first and most obvious way is for the writer to state quite flatly his own view on the importance of a matter. If we turn back to the theme "The Person I Admire Most," we find that paragraphs 4, 5, and 6 represent a scale of importance.

(4) The first thing was that he began to take an interest in us children. . . .

(5) What he did was important, but *more important* was the way he did things. . . .

(6) As I look back now, or when I go home and see Uncle Conroy, tho *biggest achievement,* however, seems to be the kind of example he gave us all. . . .

In depending on his own statement for emphasis the writer should remember that the actual content must justify the statement. Before he makes the statement, he must think through the subject and be sure that he really believes in his own statement.

EMPHASIS BY POSITION

A second way is by position. "First or last" is a fairly sound rule for emphasis by position. This rule corresponds to two general methods for treating a subject. The main idea can be presented and then discussed or proved, or discussion or proof can lead up to the main idea. Ordinarily the second method is better, and the end is the most emphatic position, for the last impression on a reader is what counts most. But some rather conventionalized forms of writing, like news stories, put the most important material first. In any case, the middle is the least emphatic position.

EMPHASIS BY PROPORTION

Proportion in itself is a means of emphasis. The most important topic in a discussion reasonably receives the fullest treatment. This principle, however, is more flexible than the preceding. In some writings the last and most important topic may have been so well prepared for by the foregoing discussion that it does not require elaborate treatment. The writer must decide each case on its own merits and be sure that he is not indulging in elaboration merely for the sake of elaboration.

EMPHASIS BY STYLE

Even when there is no emphasis by proportion or position, the way of saying a thing may make it emphatic and memorable.

So we have emphasis by style. Sharpness or vividness of phrasing, an illuminating comparison, an air of seriousness, a rhythm that sticks in the ear—any of these things or several of them in combination may give emphasis.

It is hard to say exactly what constitutes sharpness of phrasing, though we certainly recognize the dull phrase.

Suppose Patrick Henry had said: "Liberty is a very important thing for a man to have. It means that he can pursue his own designs and develop his own fortunes and seek his own happiness so long as he does not interfere with the rights of other people. Therefore liberty is a very important thing. I had rather have liberty than anything else, for it is the basis of everything else. I had rather die than lose liberty."

His audience would have yawned in his face. But what he actually said was, "I know not what course others may take; but as for me, give me liberty or give me death!" and the words have come a long way from the room in colonial Virginia where they were spoken. The dramatic quality of the statement, the swelling balance of the rhythm, the economy of language—these things make the statement memorable, when the mere idea, stated otherwise, would have been forgotten.

Or suppose that John Randolph had said about a fellow-politician: "Henry Clay seems to be a very brilliant man, but his apparent brilliance is really just superficial cleverness. He is vain and strutting. He is also very corrupt." Nobody would remember the remark. But he actually said, "So brilliant, yet so corrupt, which, like a rotten mackerel by moonlight, shines and stinks." The comparison sums up all he meant, vividly and unforgettably, and we have one of the most savage insults in the language.

Or suppose Lincoln had said at the end of his Second Inaugural Address: "We want to finish this war and have a fair peace. We do not want a vindictive peace but one that will restore the country to unity. We believe that we are right and are determined to win and have a fair peace. And after the war we must not forget to take care of the veterans and the dependents of those who were killed or wounded in the struggle." The sentiments would have done him credit, perhaps, but the sentiments would probably have vanished with the words spoken. What he actually said was:

With malice toward none, with charity for all, with firmness in the right as God gives us to see the right, let us strive on to finish the work we are in, to bind up the nation's wounds, to care for him who shall have borne the battle and for his widow and his orphan, to do all which may achieve and cherish a just and lasting peace among ourselves and with all nations.

Here again it is style which makes the difference—the precision and economy of statement, the concreteness and simplicity of expression, the full, sonorous, sustained rhythm.

Not many writers or speakers have the gift exhibited in these examples, but the principle exemplified here should apply to anything we write; the well-said thing is the memorable thing. No matter how important an idea is, it is lost if the words are blundering. And almost anyone can, by practice and attention, gain enough skill to write honestly and cleanly.

MINOR DEVICES OF EMPHASIS

Flat statement, order of importance, proportion, and style are major means of emphasis, but there are certain minor ones. For instance, repetition of an idea can give it prominence. The danger here is that the repetition may become merely mechanical and therefore dull. To be effective, repetition must be combined with some variety and some progression in the treatment of the subject. Or there is the device of the short, isolated paragraph. The thing set off by itself strikes the eye. But not all short paragraphs are in themselves emphatic. The content and phrasing of the short paragraph must in itself appear worthy of the special presentation.

FAULTY DEVICES OF EMPHASIS

There are certain devices of emphasis which often occur but which are frequently worse than useless. Irresponsible exaggeration always repels the reader. Catchwords and hackneyed phrases like "awfully," "terribly," "tremendously," "the most wonderful thing I ever saw," "you never saw anything like it," "I can't begin to tell you," make a claim on the reader's attention that he is rarely prepared to grant. Random underlining and italicizing, or the use of capitals and exclamation points usually defeat their own purpose. Writers use these devices when they aren't sure that what they have to say will stand on its own merits. To insist that what you have to say is important does not prove the point. And the writer's business is to prove that point.

In applying any of these means of emphasis the writer must first of all be sure that the thing emphasized is worth emphasizing. Common sense must help him here. Nothing else can.

THE MAIN DIVISIONS OF A DISCOURSE

There are three main divisions into which any rounded discourse will fall: INTRODUCTION, BODY or DISCUSSION, and CONCLUSION. What should each accomplish, and what should be their relations to each other?

THE INTRODUCTION

The introduction must really introduce. At some stage it must let the reader know the business in hand. Occasionally the title can be explicit enough to give the reader a good idea of that business, but usually the introduction must limit and fix the subject. It must state the precise question with which the discussion is to be concerned.

Sometimes the introduction can properly concern itself with the background of the subject. If the subject, for example, is a new process in industrial chemistry, and the audience is composed of general readers, it may be necessary to inform them about the function of such a process and about the nature of the old process before they can understand the significance of the new one. If you are explaining why a certain novel is good, you may properly introduce your remarks by saying what qualities you prize in fiction. Or if you are explaining the greatness of Galileo, you may not be able to make your point unless you describe the condition of science before he accomplished his work. But here, as when limiting and fixing the subject itself, you must have some idea of the audience. How much preparation is needed to make them get your point?

An introduction may tell the reader what method of investigation has provided the material for the discussion or what method of discussion you intend to pursue. This element in an introduction is ordinarily confined to more or less technical discussions. For instance, a physicist might describe the nature of his method of investigation before he analyzes his findings. Or an economist might tell what evidence he had assessed. As for the forecast of the method of discussion, this is only desirable when the method itself is of some importance. If, for instance, you are writing in defense of J. E. B. Stuart's cavalry operations at the time of the Battle of Gettysburg, your introduction might very well include a statement of your method. You might say that the points to be determined are: (1) Was Stuart acting under orders? (2) Was he acting against orders? (3) Was he acting at discretion? (4) If he was acting at discretion, what information was available to him? (5) On the grounds of information available to him, were his operations consistent with reason and military science? Then you might say that you propose to investigate these questions and rest your case upon the answers. Such an introduction is sometimes very useful when the material to be treated is complicated and the reader's interest might easily be distracted by some incidental matter. It serves as a blueprint or a signpost.

One other job may be performed by an introduction. It may be used to catch the reader's interest and lure him into the subject. When an audience is already interested in the subject, this is superfluous. But when you are writing for the general reader, this part of the work of the introduction may be very important. If you check through feature articles in newspapers or magazines, you will find that the introduction usually makes some bid for the reader's attention. It explains why the subject should interest the reader, how it touches his life, if only indirectly, or it presents some incident of dramatic interest, some suggestive anecdote, or some provocative question.

Of these four general functions of an introduction, the first is the only essential one: The introduction must always lead the reader to the subject and must show him clearly what it is. The other functions are to be performed only when the occasion demands.

THE MAIN BODY OF THE WRITING

It is difficult to make any significant generalizations concerning the main body of a piece of writing. Different subjects and interests call for different methods, and several of our subsequent chapters will be devoted to such questions. But this much may be insisted on now: The body of the discussion should not betray the promise of the introduction. It should really develop the introduction. If the body does betray the introduction but seems good in itself, then you must go back and rewrite the introduction. The two things must be geared together.

THE CONCLUSION

The conclusion gives you your last chance at your reader. If you fail there, you have probably failed throughout your work.

Occasionally, a formal conclusion is not necessary, especially in short pieces where the reader can easily carry the whole business in his head. But when there is no conclusion, it is usually a good idea to make the last part of the main body of the theme the most important part, the climax, so that your strongest point will be freshest for the reader when he leaves you. As we have already said, the end is the most emphatic position.

In more elaborate pieces of writing some formal conclusion is necessary to give the reader a perspective on the whole discussion. It may involve a summary of things the body of the discussion has established, but it should do more than summarize. It must also show how those things fit together to support your position or the effect you desire. It may be that you want to explain something, to convince the reader of the truth of something, to persuade him to a course of action, to make him think for himself about something. Whatever your dominant purpose may be, the conclusion should bring it into clear focus. The worst effect of all is for the reader, as he puts down your pages, to have only a hazy notion of what you meant to say. He should, rather, have a clear idea.

PROPORTIONING THE MAIN DIVISIONS

In talking about emphasis we mentioned the problem of proportion. But in that connection it was a matter of local concern. What of proportion in relation to the big main divisions?

Our answer cannot take the form of a mathematical ratio—the body five times longer than the introduction, or something of the sort, and six times longer than the conclusion. But we must remember that the introduction is just an introduction, a preparation for the main business, and that the main business is to be transacted in the body of the piece. If the introduction is long and cumbersome, and the body brief, then the reader gets the impression that the mountain has labored and brought forth a mouse. Likewise, if there is a formal conclusion, that conclusion should seem to be the blow that sinks the nail head in the wood. In short, it should "conclude" the theme—not start fresh considerations. If the conclusion is long and cumbersome, then the reader has another unfortunate impression. It is preposterous, too, for the mouse to labor and try to bring forth the mountain. Or to apply another saying, the tail should not wag the dog. As a kind of rule of thumb, we may venture that the body should be at least several times longer than the introduction or conclusion.

To think of the matter mechanically, however, is not the way to get at it. If the writer has a subject worthy of discussion, and if he understands the proper function of the introduction and conclusion, the problem of proportion is apt to take care of itself.

THE OUTLINE

A person writing into a subject blind may come out, by luck or instinct, with a well-organized and well-proportioned composition. But ordinarily the safe procedure is to think through the subject beforehand and set up a plan, an outline, of the projected discourse.

There are various types of outlines ranging from the formal sentence outline down to a scratch outline composed of jottings as they come to mind in the first survey of the subject. For the moment, however, we shall concern ourselves with a simple topic outline.

In our analysis of the theme "The Person I Admire Most" (p. 16), we have already indicated what such a preliminary outline might be. Let us now set it up.

Statement of the subject: Why I admire my uncle Conroy

Introduction:

    I. My uncle as he now appears—apparent failure and real success

Body:

    II. The background of my uncle's achievement
        A. His worldly success and ruin (paragraph 2)
        B. His illness and despair (paragraph 3)

III. The nature of my uncle's achievement
    A. His practical achievements (paragraph 4)
        1. Help with the children
        2. Help with my father's business
        3. Help with my mother's illness
    B. His achievement in self-control (paragraph 5)
        1. Naturalness of his actions
        2. Cheerfulness in the face of pain
          (Now in paragraph 6; should be in paragraph 5)
    C. His greatest achievement, an example to others—the summary of his other achievements (paragraph 6)

Conclusion:

    IV. My uncle as a type of success and my admiration for him (paragraph 6)

The writer of the theme probably should have made topic IV into a separate paragraph, a conclusion giving a statement of the author's definition of success and the application to his uncle's case. Nevertheless, he has written a theme which is fundamentally systematic, which builds continuously toward its point. The outline defines the stages in that progression.

A preliminary outline is a help in the actual writing of a theme, but it should not be followed slavishly. In the process of writing, new thoughts may come and new material may be suggested. The writer should always be ready to take advantage of these. He may have to stop the writing and go back to do a new outline, or he may be able to incorporate the new thoughts or new material in the actual body of the theme. In any event, it is a good idea to go back after the writing is completed and check against the original outline or, if necessary, make a new outline. When the bare bones are laid out, the writer can criticize the organization of his work.

It is always a question, too, how fully the outline can predict the scale of a piece of writing. If the author of "The Person I Admire Most" made an outline, he might not have been able to predict exactly how much space each topic would take. For instance, topic III-A might have developed into three paragraphs instead of one, or topics II-A and II-B might have been managed in one paragraph instead of two. Such problems usually have to be settled in the course of actual composition when the writer discovers the scale on which he is working. But the matter of scale and proportion in itself is something which we shall come to a little later.

The outline we have constructed for "The Person I Admire Most" is relatively simple. It should be adequate for the preliminary study of such a subject. But a writer who has trouble in organizing his material may do well to consult the Appendix on the Outline in this book (p. 486). A little practice in making sentence outlines may increase his power to deal with a body of material. But there is no virtue in outlining for its own sake. It is a means to an end, a help to straight thinking and well-organized writing. It is not an end in itself.

The Kinds
of Discourse

THE MAIN INTENTION

WHEN a writer sets out to write he has some main intention, some central purpose. Let us look at this matter as an aspect of communication, and not as an aspect of expression. That is, let us suppose that the writer wishes to communicate something to a reader, to work some effect on him.

First, his main intention may be to explain something, to make clear to the reader some idea, to analyze a character or a situation, to define a term, to give directions. He may wish, in other words, to inform him.

Second, he may wish to make the reader change his mind, his attitude, his point of view, his feelings. He may appeal to the reader's powers of logic in a perfectly objective and impersonal fashion, or he may appeal to his emotions, but in either case the intention is to work a change in him.

Third, he may wish to make the reader see or hear something as vividly as the writer himself has seen or heard it, to make him get the feel of the thing, the quality of a direct experience. The thing in question may be a natural scene, a city street, a cat or a race horse, a person's face, the odor of a room, a piece of music.

Fourth, he may wish to tell the reader about an event—what happened and how it happened. The event may be grand or trivial, a battle or a ball game, a presidential campaign or a picnic, but whatever it is, the writer will be anxious to give the sequence in time and perhaps to give some notion of how one thing led to another. And above all his chief concern will be to give an immediate impression of the event, to give the sense of witnessing it.

THE FOUR KINDS OF DISCOURSE

We can see, with only a moment of reflection, that these four types of intention correspond to the four basic kinds of discourse: EXPOSITION, ARGUMENT, DESCRIPTION, and NARRATION. Exposition embodies the wish to inform the reader, argument the wish to make the reader change his mind or attitude, description the wish to make the reader perceive something, narration the wish to make the reader grasp the movement of an event.

What is important here is to understand that these traditional kinds of discourse are not arbitrary divisions of the subject of writing, but that each corresponds to a main intention, a fundamental wish on the part of the writer. Each fulfills one of his needs. And it is important, too, to see that this main intention, this fundamental wish, relates both to the nature of the subject and the nature of the occasion. That is, one begins a piece of writing by asking himself what kind of treatment is natural to the subject and what kind of effect he wants to work on the reader.

MIXTURE OF THE KINDS OF DISCOURSE

Thinking back over various articles and books you have read, you may remark that none of these kinds of discourse often appears in a pure form. For instance, a novel will describe as well as narrate, it will give sections of exposition, it may even present argument. A magazine article on international affairs may very well employ narrative, as in an illustrative anecdote, or description, as in presenting the statesmen on whose decisions the settlement of affairs depends. Both exposition and argument may be intertwined in a most complicated fashion: the writer must make clear to the reader the state of affairs, and that calls for exposition, and he will probably have in mind some convictions which he wants to see put into action by his reader, and that calls for argument. Even class reports, which tend to be almost pure exposition, may involve narrative. For instance, a report on a chemistry experiment may involve the presentation of an event—the setting up of the apparatus, the sequence of occurrences. In fact, the form of exposition which deals with such a process is sometimes called expository narration because it is necessarily bound to a sequence in time.

All of this does not mean that in a good and effective piece of writing the mixture of the kinds of discourse is irresponsible. There will always be a *main intention*, a fundamental wish. The class report will always be, by the nature of the case, an example of exposition. The novel, no matter how much exposition, description, and argument it contains, will always be an example of narration. Other instances may not be so clear-cut, but in any instance, a good writer knows for what purpose he is using a given type of discourse. He will use it to support his main intention.

Though most writing involves a mixture of the kinds of discourse, we can best study them in isolation, one by one. This study will mean the systematic analysis of relatively pure examples in order to observe the various types of organization appropriate to any one kind. It is only after one understands the kinds of discourse in a pure form that one can make them work together to give unity to a larger discourse.

OBJECTIVE AND SUBJECTIVE DISCOURSE

Before we discuss at length the four kinds of discourse that we have distinguished, we may make some other distinctions that will be useful to us.

First, we shall distinguish the SUBJECTIVE and the OBJECTIVE use of language. Compare these two statements: "The girl had beautiful hair," and "The girl had black hair." The first statement is "subjective." It represents a perceiving *subject's* impression of, and interpretation of, a fact. The second statement is, by comparison, quite objective. It presents a fact objectively—that is, without personal interpretation and judgment. The fact presented is true, whether we think black hair is beautiful or not beautiful, or whether this head of black hair impresses us as beautiful or ugly. Subjective is inner and private; objective is outer and public. We tend to have quite different standards of beauty; we tend to have rather general standards of what is black.

But the statement that the girl has black hair is not wholly objective. The girl's hair may be a dark brown and the person who claims that it is black may not have as keen a discrimination of colors as another. By comparison the statement "The girl weighs 116 pounds" is more nearly objective. For unless the scales are wrong or the person who reads them has made an error, that statement depends upon a universal standard. The Bureau of Weights and Measures at Washington furnishes us with a very precise standard of what a pound is.

To sum up, the subjective represents the response of a subject who perceives, a response that reveals all the individuality of standard and bias and preconception and emotional coloring that attach to personal judgment. The objective represents an appeal to general standards with the elimination of personal bias and impression.

SCIENTIFIC INTENTION

Here are some further examples of objective and subjective statements. We may write, "The water was 31 per cent saturated with filterable solids," or we may write, "The water was stained a muddy brown." We may write, "The man was 5 ft. 3½ in. tall," or we may write, "He was a runty little fellow." We may write, "The animal caught was a mature male of the species *Rattus norvegicus* weighing 1 lb. 3½ oz.," or we may write, "We caught a fat brown rat."

Now *all* these statements report facts, not merely the first members of each pair of statements. How then do the first members of each pair differ from the second members of the pair? They differ in making use of a defined and agreed-upon set of classifications and measurements. That is why we call them objective. The word *rat* may suggest something loathsome, furtive, and destructive. *Rattus norvegicus* does not. Muddy water may call up happy memories of the old swimming pool or unpleasant associations of dirt. The author interested in cold and scientific fact finds these associations, whether pleasant or unpleasant, quite irrelevant to his purpose; moreover, how muddy is muddy? On the other hand, 31 per cent saturation provides an accuracy with which he is very much concerned. What is a runt? What is a runty man? That will depend upon the point of view; moreover, it implies a judgment, a disparaging judgment. The measurement 5 ft. 3½ in. is an accurate statement and it gives us the fact quite apart from whether we think that it represents a satisfactory or an unsatisfactory height for a man.

Scientific statement, of course, represents our nearest approach to complete objectivity. Scientific statements make use of some agreed-upon scheme of reference: an accepted classification of mammals, or Mendelyeev's Periodic Table, or the metric system of weights and measures, and so on. A very important consequence follows from this fact: scientific statements make reference to *abstractions*. To illustrate, *Rattus norvegicus* is not any particular member of the brown rat family. It is the family itself: that compound of characteristics which defines the particular species called the brown rat. *Rattus norvegicus* is an *ideal* rat. The personal equation has been eliminated. Any competent biologist can say whether the specimen in question belongs to the family or not.

We can say, then, that when the writer's main purpose is scientific his language tends to be technical and objective. It is technical in that it consists of special terms used strictly with reference to an agreed-upon scheme. It is objective in that the emotional coloring of a particular observer has been eliminated. A strictly scientific purpose obviously demands an emotionally neutral vocabulary of this sort.

ARTISTIC INTENTION

The strictly scientific intention, however, represents an extreme. Very little of our writing turns out to be purely scientific. Moreover, important as the scientific intention is, it is not the sole intention of the writer. Let us consider the other intention, and to make the contrast as sharp as possible, let us take this other intention in its most extreme form. We might call it an "artistic" intention, though in using the term "artistic" we do not mean to limit it to the higher and more serious forms of literature. As we shall use it here, "artistic intention" includes the purpose that directs the telling of a good joke or the description of an exciting boxing match, or the writing of a warm letter to an intimate friend, and many other kinds of discourse which we use in our everyday life. The writer with this intention insists that we "see" the object, feel the experience, respond imaginatively to the whole scene portrayed. He uses terms which are particular and concrete and which invite the reader's reaction. Moreover, such a writer tends to deal with objects in their immediacy and concreteness. He does not abstract certain qualities and characteristics as the scientist does; he tends to fuse and combine them. It is easy to see why.

A moment's reflection will show us that our actual experience of a thing comes to us with more fullness and richness than any single adjective, tied to the single sense, will indicate. We look at an apple and see the patch of red, and say, "The apple is red." But we are also prepared to say that it is, for example, "glossy" and "juicy-looking." Even though we have not touched this particular apple or tasted it, other senses than sight become involved in our experience of the apple. Our past experiences with apples are operating at the moment in our experience of the present apple. We see the apple and sense the special complex of qualities which mean "appleness"—the color, the texture of the skin, the fragrance, the juiciness. So when we come to describe something, in ordinary speech, we may not merely assemble adjectives with the intention of making them indicate the qualities to be perceived by a single sense. Our ordinary use of language indicates something of the complication of the perception. When, for example, we say "glossy" of the apple, we are, in a way, fusing two senses, sight and touch. Or when we look at the frozen lake and say, "The ice is glassy," we evoke, with the word *glassy*, a whole complex of qualities which are fused in the single word—slickness, hardness, transparency, and brightness.

The kind of richness and fullness about which we have been talking may involve also the element of interpretation. When we say, as above, "The ice is glassy," we attribute certain qualities to the ice, though, of course, our statement implies a person who perceives. But when we say, "The music is soothing," the reference to a person who perceives is much more positively and intimately involved in the statement. For here the music is described only in terms of its effect upon a hearer. The soothing effect may take place because the music is soft, or has a certain type of melody and rhythm, or for some other reason, but the statement as given does not even mention those qualities; it mentions only the effect on a hearer. In other words, here the subjective reference of the description is extremely important, for it is through the subjective reference, the effect on a hearer, that the person who reads the description becomes aware of the nature of the music in question.

Subjectivity, in the light of the artistic intention, becomes a virtue, not a vice. We want terms which suggest qualities, not bare technical terms which bar all but one meaning. The thing to be avoided is technical dryness, since the reader is to respond powerfully to the experience set forth.

What is the relation between the scientific-artistic distinction and the distinction of the four kinds of discourse?

In an offhand way we tend to think that exposition and argument employ language that is objective, logical, scientific, and that description and narration employ language that is subjective, emotional, artistic. Within limits, this is true, but only within limits. Exposition giving us information about an automobile motor would use objective, logical, scientific language, but exposition setting forth the motives of a human act might very well have to resort to the other kind of language. Or even if the main intention of argument is to convince by appealing to the logical faculties, we may have to resort to persuasion, to emotional appeals, to get a hearing for our argument, to present it with the right tone. Description may as well concern itself with the floor plan of a house as with a beautiful woman or the effect of a sonata. Narration may give us the stages of a laboratory experiment or the experience of a courtship or a prize fight.

We may regard the four kinds of discourse as representing different basic intentions, but any one of these intentions may use either or both of the two kinds of appeals (objective, logical, scientific or subjective, emotional, artistic).

In making the distinction between the two kinds of appeals we have deliberately used extreme examples. The extreme examples may make the difference come clear and sharp. In actual practice, however, our basic intention is not often purely scientific or purely artistic. And we must warn ourselves against a misleading oversimplification: we must not assume that all thinking can be conducted in a terminology that is technical and objective, and that all emotional language is vague and confused. To take extremes again, the poet may use language as precisely in his kind of discourse as the physicist in his.

Furthermore, though we have contrasted objective language with subjective language, and technical terms with suggestive and imaginative terms, we go badly astray if we assume that, since the scientific intention makes use of objective and technical language, the artistic intention makes use *merely* of suggestive and subjective language. Far from it. Even a novel may include description which is rather studiedly objective and a poem, on occasion, may make use of highly technical language.

Perhaps the best way to see the relation of these terms to the writer's intention is to return to our account of the nature of scientific language. It achieves its objectivity, as we have seen (p. 33), by using accepted terms and schemes of reference, and we have observed that these are arrived at by a process of abstraction. The individual's response is cut away from the term so as to leave it fixed and unchanging. But only abstractions (that is, generalized qualities and ideas) are fixed and unchanging. We get, not any individual rat, half-grown, mangy, dead in the trap, scuttling through the walls of a house, or the pet rat named "Jim," but rather *Rattus norvegicus,* that is, ratness—an abstract rat.

In other words, technical and objective terms represent a *reduced* language, core-meanings from which personal interpretation and implied meanings and suggestions have been removed. It is a specialized language which is developed by abstracting—cutting away —from the richer and more complex language of our ordinary experience all but the general qualities and characteristics.

Instead, therefore, of arranging our terms in neat oppositions thus:

SCIENTIFIC	ARTISTIC
objective	subjective
technical	suggestive

we must see them arranged in this way:

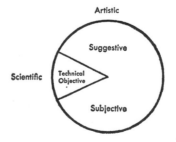

The segment of the circle represents a specialized intention with its appropriate devices. The circle as a whole represents our general intention of which the segment is a part. This may explain why in realizing the more general intention, we may use, not only a language which goes beyond the specialized techniques of the pure scientific intention, but also on occasion the specialized language as well.

Finally, we need to remind ourselves once more that in the discussion thus far we have dealt with extremes: that objective, for example, is not an absolute term but a relative term. *Beautiful* is more subjective than *white*, but *white* is more subjective than "the color without hue at one extreme end of the scale of grays, opposite to black." So with the other terms which we have used, such as subjective, technical, and so on. They are relative terms, not absolute. In actual practice we rarely make an appeal that is purely scientific or purely artistic, just as the four kinds of presentation rarely exist pure and unmixed. But it is necessary to make the distinction sharply, for in the chapters that follow we shall need to refer to the "objective" and "technical" as contrasted in direction with the "subjective" and the "suggestive."

Exposition

EXPOSITION is the kind of discourse which explains or clarifies a subject. That is, as the word *exposition* quite literally means, it sets forth a subject. Its appeal is to the understanding. Description and narration may lead to understanding, but they lead to it by presenting the qualities and movement of their subject. Exposition, however, leads to understanding by explaining something about its subject. Argument involves understanding in that it aims to convince of the truth or desirability of something, but its aim is to convince, not merely to explain.

Exposition is the most common kind of writing, for it is applicable to anything which challenges the understanding—the definition of a word, the way to a street address, the structure of a plant, the mechanism of a watch, the meaning of a historical event. the motive of an act, the significance of a philosophical system.

INTEREST

A piece of exposition may be regarded as the answer to a question about a subject. If the question has actually been asked us— "How do I get to the Court House?" or "What were the causes of the American Revolution?"—it is easy to frame an answer that does not waver from the point. But if we set out to write a piece of exposition without the benefit of a real, leading question, simply because we feel that a subject is interesting or important, we are very apt to give a confused account of the subject. We should always try to decide what INTEREST we want to appeal to.

An informal list may suggest the kind of interests to which exposition appeals:

What is it?
What does it mean?
How is it put together?
How does it work?
Why is it the way it is?
How did it come to be this way?
When did it occur or exist?
What is it worth?
What is its importance?
How well does it fulfill its intended function?

We can ask other questions, of course, about a thing, whatever that thing may be, but these are among the most usual.

Naturally, not all of these questions would be appropriate for the same subject. If we are trying to explain the nature of a triangle, we would scarcely ask when it occurred, for the nature of a triangle —what makes a figure a triangle and not something else—has no reference to time at all. Or if we are discussing the French Revolution, we would scarcely ask how well it fulfilled its intended function, for the Revolution was a complex event answering to no single intention. It would be appropriate, however, to ask about its causes or its importance.

Already, in an earlier chapter (p. 12), we have discussed the problem of locating the real subject in a general topic, the concern that will give unity to a composition. The problem here is the same, but narrowed to apply to the methods of exposition. The interest we wish to appeal to determines the line we will follow in our discussion and will give that discussion its proper unity. We may, for instance, want to define a word, either to instruct our reader or to clarify our own thinking. We may want to describe a subject—to tell what its qualities are and relate those qualities to those of another subject. We may want to account for a subject—tell how it came to exist. We may want to evaluate or criticize a subject. Any one of these endeavors would provide us with a unified discussion.

A writer, however, may appeal to more than one interest in the same composition, and in any extended discussion he is almost certain to appeal to more than one interest. But in doing so he must be careful to keep them distinct. He must not mix up the answer to one question with the answer to another. He must see the interests as representing different stages in his single over-all treatment. Furthermore, if he does appeal to more than one interest, he must be sure that some relation is established among them, and that there is a logical progression from one to another. In other words, there must be clear division among the parts, and significant relation among the parts.

Let us take an example. A writer wishes to write a review of Dickens's *Oliver Twist*. He knows that it is a novel, and he has a pretty good notion of what a novel is and can assume that his reader, too, has such a notion. But what kind of a novel is it? He decides that it is a novel of social protest. He is not so sure that his reader knows exactly what a novel of social protest is. So he sets out to define the term "novel of social protest," and decides that it is a novel in which the author's primary interest is to show the injustice in society. So far he has classified the novel and given a definition of the class into which it falls.

Next he may summarize the story, present the characters, and comment on Dickens's attitude expressed in them. Now he is answering the question, "How is it put together?" He is explaining the organization of the book.

Next, he may tell how Dickens drew on previous novels for suggestions in method, and on his own life and observation for material. Now he is answering the question, "Why is it the way it is?" He is giving an account of how the novel came to be.

He may conclude by saying that the novel is good because the plot keeps the reader in suspense and because the reader sympathizes with little Oliver. And he may add that the novel served a useful purpose by helping to bring about social reform. In the first statement he would be evaluating the novel purely as a novel—how well it fulfills certain requirements of fiction. In the second he would be evaluating the novel as a social force. In other words, he would be considering two different meanings of the question, "What is it worth?"

This would not be the only line of discussion possible for a review of *Oliver Twist*, but it will illustrate how a writer may appeal to more than one interest and still be systematic.

THE METHODS OF EXPOSITION

We shall now take up the study of the most usual methods of exposition—the ways we go about answering questions that demand exposition. This is not to say that there is a method to correspond to each question on our list. Some methods may be used in answering more than one question, and the answer to a single question may sometimes be made by more than one method or by a combination of methods. It is useful, however, to remember that the methods arc ways of answering questions, of appealing to interests.

The same discourse—for example, an editorial, an essay, a theme, a chapter in a text book—may use more than one expository method. Often we do not find a method in its pure state. But here, where we are trying to understand the nature of each method, we shall be concerned with relatively pure examples.

IDENTIFICATION

IDENTIFICATION is one of the simplest methods of exposition. It is one of the ways of answering the question, "What is it?" In one way, it is a kind of pointing by means of language. "Who is Mrs. Bertrand Smith?" somebody asks, and the answer is, "Oh, she is the blond woman in the black dress, sitting to the right of the white-haired old man." The reply has worked like pointing a finger. But perhaps Mrs. Smith is not there to be pointed at so easily. So the answer may be, "She is the woman who won the city golf tournament last year and then married the son of old Jason Smith, the banker." In either case the answer places the subject, Mrs. Smith, in such a context that she can be identified.

We constantly use such casual forms of identification. But we are using the same method if we begin an article on the Carmel Mission by writing: "The Carmel Mission stands just outside the village of Monterey, California. It was founded by Padre Junipero Serra who had come up from San Diego in the year 1770." We have tried to locate the subject.

The same principle may apply if the thing we are trying to identify, unlike Mrs. Smith or the Carmel Mission, has no concrete existence—if, for instance, it is Scholastic philosophy. To identify it we might begin: "Scholastic philosophy is that system of thought developed in the late Middle Ages in Western Europe by the Catholic Church. The most famous philosopher associated with this system is Saint Thomas Aquinas." Here, again, we are in the process of locating.

If identification becomes elaborate it tends to absorb other expository methods; it begins, for example, to use analysis, comparison, or contrast; and the simple intention of identification may be lost in other and perhaps more interesting intentions in the discussion. Even so, we can distinguish this intention, and see that it has a method appropriate to itself, the method of locating, or placing, of making recognition possible.

EXPOSITORY DESCRIPTION: TECHNICAL DESCRIPTION

As identification may absorb other expository methods, so exposition itself may absorb other kinds of discourse and use them for its purpose. Description, for instance, is frequently used for an expository purpose. In fact, the kind of description usually associated with exposition is so different from ordinary description that it has a special name, EXPOSITORY DESCRIPTION or TECHNICAL DESCRIPTION.

We can distinguish between technical description and ordinary description by considering the different types of occasion from which they arise. First, there is the occasion that demands *information about* the thing described. Second, there is the occasion that demands an immediate impression of the thing described. The first kind is expository, or technical, in so far as it aims to enlarge the understanding. But the second type—the type we ordinarily think of when we use the word description—aims to suggest the qualities of the object as though it were immediately perceived. It aims to give an experience of the object through the imagination. We shall call this type SUGGESTIVE DESCRIPTION.

A full discussion of suggestive description will be reserved for a later chapter,[1] but for the present it is necessary to contrast it with technical description that we may better understand the use of description for exposition. Let us begin with some examples.

[1] See Chapter 5, pp. 195-199, below.

TECHNICAL:

FOR QUICK SALE

Wellington Boulevard

Attractive Cape Cod cottage, lge. liv. rm., 13 x 25, knotty pine, stone fireplace; din. rm., sunny, 12 x 14; small den or libr., fireplace; kitchen, modern, elec. stove, lge. gas refrig., dishwasher, all practically new; med.-size, concrete basement, gas furn., ht. watr.; 2 bedrms., 14 x 16, 15 x 18; 2 baths, lge. and small; roof white oak shingle. Lot well planted, landscaped, brook, 2 acres; heated garage, 2 cars; small greenhouse. Built by owner, 1930. Excellent condition. Take reasonable offer. Call: BE-1632.

SUGGESTIVE:

Dear Mother:

We have found a place at last, and we love it, Jack just as much as I. I must tell you about it, so you can have some notion before you come to see us here. Well, you don't see it from the highway, for there is a high hedge across the front of the property with just a little gap that lets you into the lane, a winding lane among a grove of white oaks, like a lane going down to a pasture on somebody's farm. That's the whole impression—just like a farm, a million miles away from town. When you pass the oaks you see a dip down to a brook, lined with willows, and a stone bridge, and just beyond the bridge the house on a slight rise that the brook curves around. The house is white and trim, two stories, but rather low, just seeming to crop out of the ground, with a couple of enormous oaks behind to give a background for it. You have the feeling that once you cross that bridge and enter that door you'll be safe and sound and the world will never come to bother you.

When you do enter, you know that your feeling is right. There is a long room with a big fireplace, and windows to the east for the morning sun. It is a perfect room for the furniture which Grandmother left me, just the sort of room she would have loved, peaceful and old-fashioned. The instant you come in, you think of a fire crackling on the hearth, and a kettle humming to heat water for tea, and you see the copper glinting on the andirons. . . .

The motives behind the two pieces of description are very different. The seller of the house wants to give information about the house. The buyer of the house, writing to her mother, wants to give the feel, the atmosphere, of the house.

The advertisement is an instance of technical description. Except in so far as we know the general type of Cape Cod cottage, we have no basis for visualizing the actual house. The writer of the advertisement has not been concerned that we should get an impression of his house; the only attempt in this direction is his use of the word *sunny* about the dining room. But if the writer has not been concerned to give us the picture and atmosphere of his house, he has been greatly concerned to give us a systematic and complete body of information about the house considered from a technical point of view as a shelter and a machine for living.

We should find the same motive behind a naturalist's description of a species of bird, a mechanic's description of the ignition system of an automobile, or a physiologist's description of the structure of the human brain. In none of these examples would there be any attempt to make us perceive the thing described except in so far as that attempt would enlarge our understanding.

In the excerpt from the letter above, however, the situation is reversed. The writer is concerned to make an appeal to her reader's senses, to establish the impression of the place, its quietness and isolation, its old-fashioned charm. The details she has selected for comment all contribute to this impression. The suggestive description does not, as does the technical, give a systematic and relatively complete body of information concerning the object. Instead, it simply presents the details that support the sensory and emotional effect the writer wishes to communicate. The technical description *tends* to be enumerative; the suggestive description *tends* to be selective and impressionistic.

There is another and very important distinction between the technical and the suggestive description. In the strictly technical description there is no place for interpretation by the writer. It is concerned only with the facts about the object, facts that can be observed by anyone. For example, when the writer of the advertisement of the Cape Cod cottage lists six rooms, or says that the living room is of knotty pine, he is stating a fact, something objective and beyond dispute. He is being strictly technical. But when he says that the cottage is "attractive" he is not being strictly technical. He is interpreting the situation according to his own idea of what constitutes attractiveness. Likewise when the buyer writes her letter and says that the house is peaceful and charming, she is interpreting.

To another person with different tastes the place might not seem peaceful but depressing.

This is not to say that the suggestive description does not use facts. It must use facts if it is to give any sense of the reality of the thing described. But it uses its facts as related to some impression it wishes to communicate. The facts are interpreted.

Let us take another pair of examples, examples in which the difference is not so immediately obvious but is equally as important.

TECHNICAL:

The West Indies stand in a warm sea, and the trade winds, warmed and moistened by this sea, blow across all of them. These are the two great primary geographic facts about this group of islands whose area is but little larger than that of Great Britain.

These trade winds, always warm, but nevertheless refreshing sea breezes, blow mostly from the east or the northeast. Thus one side of every island is windward, and the other side is leeward. The third great geographical fact about these islands is that most of them are mountainous, giving to the windward sides much more rain than the leeward sides receive. This makes great differences in climate within short distances, a thing quite unknown in the eastern half of the United States, where our slowly whirling cyclonic winds blow in quick succession from all directions upon every spot of territory. Thus both sides of the Appalachian Mountains are nearly alike in their rainfall, forest growth, and productive possibilities. On the contrary, the West Indian mountains have different worlds on their different slopes. The eastern or windward side, cloud-bathed and eternally showered upon, is damp and dripping. There are jungles with velvety green ferns, and forests with huge trees. The rainbow is a prominent feature of the tropic landscape. On the windward side one receives a striking impression of lush vegetation. On the leeward side of the very same ridge and only a few miles distant there is another kind of world, the world of scanty rainfall, with all its devastating consequences to vegetation. A fourth great geographic fact is the division of these islands into two great arcs, an outer arc of limestone and an inner arc of volcanic islands. The limestone areas are low. The volcanic areas are from moderately high to very high. Some islands have both the limestone and the volcanic features.—J. RUSSELL SMITH and M. OGDEN PHILLIPS: *North America*, Chap. 40.[2]

[2] From *North America* by J. Russell Smith and M. Ogden Phillips, copyright, 1940, by Harcourt, Brace and Company.

SUGGESTIVE:

Take five-and-twenty heaps of cinders dumped here and there in an outside city lot; imagine some of them magnified into mountains, and the vacant lot the sea; and you will have a fit idea of the general aspect of the Encantadas, or Enchanted Isles. A group rather of extinct volcanoes than of isles; looking much as the world at large might, after a penal conflagration.

It is to be doubted whether any spot on earth can, in desolation, furnish a parallel to this group. Abandoned cemeteries of long ago, old cities by piecemeal tumbling to their ruin, these are melancholy enough; but like all else which has once been associated with humanity they still awaken in us some thoughts of sympathy, however sad. Hence, even the Dead Sea, along with whatever other emotions it may at times inspire, does not fail to touch in the pilgrim some of his less unpleasurable feelings. . . .

But the special curse, as one may call it, of the Encantadas, that which exalts them in desolation above Idumea and the Pole, is that to them change never comes; neither the change of seasons nor of sorrows. Cut by the Equator, they know not autumn and they know not spring; while already reduced to the lees of fire, ruin itself can work little more upon them. The showers refresh the deserts, but in these isles, rain never falls. Like split Syrian gourds, left withering in the sun, they are cracked by an everlasting drought beneath a torrid sky. "Have mercy upon me," the wailing spirit of the Encantadas seems to cry, "and send Lazarus that he may dip the tip of his finger in water and cool my tongue, for I am tormented in this flame." . . .

In many places the coast is rock-bound, or more properly, clinker-bound; tumbled masses of blackish or greenish stuff like the dross of an iron-furnace, forming dark clefts and caves here and there, into which a ceaseless sea pours a fury of foam; overhanging them with a swirl of grey, haggard mist, amidst which sail screaming flights of unearthly birds heightening the dismal din. However calm the sea without, there is no rest for these swells and those rocks, they lash and are lashed, even when the outer ocean is most at peace with itself. On the oppressive, clouded days such as are peculiar to this part of the watery Equator, the dark vitrified masses, many of which raise themselves among white whirlpools and breakers in detached and perilous places off the shore, present a most Plutonian sight. In no world but a fallen one could such lands exist.—HERMAN MELVILLE: "The Encantadas, or Enchanted Isles," *The Piazza Tales.*

The first of these passages is from a geography of North America. Though it is not as brutally synoptic as the advertisement for the sale of the Cape Cod cottage, it has essentially the same kind of organization; it is an enumeration of facts pertinent to the special technical interest involved. Four "great geographic" facts are listed, and the consequences in terms of climate, vegetation, and appearance are indicated. There are occasional, and feeble, attempts to make the reader see the islands, as for instance in the phrases "cloud-bathed," and "velvety-green ferns," but the tendency is toward generalized information, toward abstraction. For instance, instead of giving us the sight of the rainbow in terms of images which would stir our imaginations, the writers simply say, "The rainbow is a prominent feature of the tropic landscape." Or instead of picturing for us the arid slopes of the leeward side of the mountains, they simply offer the phrase, "all its devastating consequences to vegetation."

The second passage, like the first, is the description of a group of tropic islands. But Melville, the author, is not concerned to give us a list of the great geographic facts and their consequences. His description involves some of these facts, but the passage is not organized about an enumeration of them. It is organized in such a way as to return the reader continually to the sense of loneliness, ruin, and desolation which characterizes the islands.

The passage begins with the comparison to heaps of cinders in a dumping ground, with that association of the used-up, the finished, the valueless, the dreary. The first paragraph ends with the phrase "penal conflagration," which implies ideas not merely of ruin and waste but also of sin and punishment—sin and punishment on a universal scale. The next paragraph is based on the ideas of the unhuman desolation, the blankness. The third is based on the idea of changelessness, the terrible monotony; but this monotony is presented as a "special curse," and is finally defined by the cry of Dives in Hell. In other words, in both the curse and the Biblical reference, we find an echo of the notion of sin and punishment, a continuation of the idea in the first paragraph. In the last paragraph appears again the image of the wasteland of cinders in the phrases "clinker-bound" and "like the dross of an iron-furnace." And also in the constant tumult of the sea, in the phrase "lash and are lashed," appears the idea of punishment and suffering, which becomes explicit in the last sentence, "In no world but a fallen one could such lands exist."

In other words, the whole passage is based on two things, the image of the cinder heap and the idea of sin and punishment, which combine to give the notion of a world after the Judgment, the final desolation. And it is this notion that provides the organizing principle for the description. It is the key to the interpretation that Melville gives to his facts.

Since the purpose of technical description is to give information about its object, the kind of description called GENERALIZED DESCRIPTION is one form it sometimes assumes. Generalized description presents the characteristics of a type rather than of a particular individual. If we set out to write a theme about the collie as a type, giving the points and qualities of the breed, we are using generalized description. If, on the other hand, we set out to write a theme about Old Buck, our favorite dog, we are using suggestive description, for we want to make clear to the reader what qualities the particular dog has.

The following description of the North American Indian, from an old work on the subject, is obviously an example of generalized description.

The general appearance of a North American Indian can be given in few words. . . . They are about of the average height which man attains when his form is not cramped by premature or excessive labor, but their erect posture and slender figure give them the appearance of a tall race. Their limbs are well formed, but calculated rather for agility than strength, in which they rarely equal the more vigorous of European nations. They generally have small feet.

The most distinguishing peculiarities of the race are, the reddish or copper color of the skin; the prominence of the cheek-bone; and the color and quality of the hair. This is not absolutely straight, but somewhat wavy, and has not inaptly been compared to the mane of the horse —less from its coarseness than from its glossy hue and the manner in which it hangs. Their eyes are universally dark. The women are rather short, with broader faces, and a greater tendency to obesity than the men, but many of them possess a symmetrical figure, with an agreeable and attractive countenance.—CHARLES DE WOLF BROWNELL: *The Indian Races of North and South America,* Chap. 1.

The following description, however, is obviously particular and suggestive.

He had the spare, alert and jaunty figure that one often finds in army men, an almost professional military quality that somehow seemed to set his figure upon a horse as if he had grown there or had spent a lifetime in the cavalry. His face also had the same lean, bitter, professional military quality; his speech, although good-natured and very friendly, was clipped, incisive, jerky, and sporadic, his lean weather-beaten face was deeply, sharply scarred and sunken in the flanks, and he wore a small cropped mustache, and displayed long frontal teeth when he smiled—a spare, gaunt, toothy, yet attractive smile.

His left arm was withered, shrunken, almost useless; part of his hand and two fingers had been torn away by the blast or explosion which had destroyed his arm; but it was not this mutilation of the flesh that gave one the sense of a life that had been ruined, lost, and broken irretrievably. In fact, one quickly forgot his physical injury; his figure looked so spare, lean, jaunty, well-conditioned in its energetic fitness that one never thought of him as a cripple, nor pitied him for any disability. No: the ruin that one felt in him was never of the flesh, but of the spirit. Something seemed to have been exploded from his life—it was not the nerve-centers of his arms, but of his soul, that had been destroyed. There was in the man somewhere a terrible dead vacancy and emptiness, and that spare, lean figure that he carried so well seemed only to surround this vacancy like a kind of shell.—THOMAS WOLFE: *Of Time and the River*, Chap. 70.[3]

Let us summarize the distinction between technical description and suggestive description. The technical gives information about the object. The suggestive gives an immediate impression of the object. The technical *tells us something about* the object; the suggestive *gives* us the object in our imagination, almost as though it were before us. The technical tends to be abstract; the suggestive tends to be concrete. The technical tends to completeness in listing qualities of the object (with reference to the special interest that motivates the description); the suggestive tends to selectivity (with reference to the main impression desired). The technical employs a schematic organization defined by the special interest involved in the description (the listing of rooms, etc., in the first example, the

---

[3] From *Of Time and the River* by Thomas Wolfe, copyright. 1935, by Charles Scribner's Sons.

listing of the four great geographical facts, etc., in the second). The suggestive employs an organization defined by the main impression and response desired (peacefulness and charm in the letter, burned-out desolation in the essay by Melville). In addition, technical description may be generalized and not particular.

We can list the distinctions:

TECHNICAL	SUGGESTIVE
information	impression
about the object	the object
abstract	concrete
completeness	selectivity
schematic organization	impressionistic organization
no interpretation	interpretation
(general)	particular

OBJECTIVE AND SUBJECTIVE DESCRIPTION

Another distinction may be useful in our thinking about description, the distinction we have already made (p. 31) between OBJECTIVE and SUBJECTIVE.

When we say, "The apple is red," we point to a quality which the apple possesses. There is no reference here to any observer of the apple. This is a simple case of objective description. It is concerned only with the object being described.

But when we say, "The music is soothing," we refer to the effect of the music upon a listener. The soothing effect may occur because the music is soft, and has a certain kind of melody and rhythm, but our statement as given does not mention those qualities objectively. It only mentions the effect on the person who experiences the music, on the "subject" as he is called. The statement, then, is a simple example of subjective description.

Let us take some examples somewhat more complicated than our statements about the apple and the music.

(1) If anyone wants to exemplify the meaning of the word "fish," he cannot choose a better animal than a herring. The body, tapering to each end, is covered with thin, flexible scales, which are very easily rubbed off. The taper head, with its underhung jaw, is smooth and scaleless on the top; the large eye is partly covered by two folds of transparent skin, like eyelids—only immovable and with the slit between

them vertical instead of horizontal; the cleft behind the gill-cover is very wide, and, when the cover is raised, the large red gills which lie underneath it are freely exposed. The rounded back bears the single moderately long dorsal fin about its middle.—THOMAS HENRY HUXLEY: "The Herring."

In this passage we find a clear instance of description without reference to any observer. Information is given about the object with no interpretation: the facts are the facts.

Let us turn to an example, however, in which an observer is specified, a passage in which Gulliver, a man of normal size who has been captured by the tiny Lilliputians, describes the house assigned to him.

(2) At the place where the carriage stopped, there stood an ancient temple, esteemed to be the largest in the whole kingdom, which having been polluted some years before by an unnatural murder, was, according to the zeal of those people, looked upon as profane, and therefore had been applied to common uses, and all the ornaments and furniture carried away. In this edifice it was determined I should lodge. The great gate fronting to the north was about four foot high, and almost two foot wide, through which I could easily creep. On each side of the gate was a small window not above six inches from the ground: into that on the left side, the King's smiths conveyed fourscore and eleven chains, like those that hang to a lady's watch in Europe, and almost as large, which were locked to my left leg with six and thirty padlocks. Over against this temple, on t'other side of the great highway, at twenty foot distance, there was a turret at least five foot high. Here the Emperor ascended with many principal lords of his court, to have an opportunity of viewing me, as I was told, for I could not see them.—JONATHAN SWIFT: *Gulliver's Travels*, Chap. 1.

An observer is introduced into this scene, but the observer is a mere observer, a kind of device for registering the facts, and no reference is made to the effect of the scene upon him. The facts are presented objectively in themselves and the items mentioned (such as measurement, shape, color) are items about which objective agreement would be relatively easy. So we see that the mere presence of an observer does not mean that a description may not be objective. The description is apparently subjective but is really objective.

Our next example also gives an observer:

(3) I know not how it was—but, with the first glimpse of the building, a sense of insufferable gloom pervaded my spirit. I say insufferable; for the feeling was unrelieved by any of that half-pleasurable, because poetic, sentiment, with which the mind usually receives even the sternest natural images of the desolate or terrible. I looked upon the scene before me— upon the mere house, and the simple landscape features of the domain, upon the bleak walls, upon the vacant eye-like windows, upon a few rank sedges, and upon a few white trunks of decayed trees—with an utter depression of soul which I can compare to no earthly sensation more properly than to the after-dream of the reveler upon opium: the bitter lapse into every-day life, the hideous dropping off of the veil.— EDGAR ALLAN POE: "The Fall of the House of Usher."

The observer here, unlike Gulliver, is not a mere observer. What is important here is his reaction, his gloom, his depression. We get an impression of the scene, it is true, but the reaction is more important than the scene itself. We have only a small amount of factual information about the scene; there are the vacant windows in the building, there is the growth of sedge, there are the few decayed trees gone white. Everything else in the passage is devoted, directly or indirectly, to indicating a response to the scene. Not only is this true of the parts of the passage in which the narrator definitely states his personal reactions. It is also true of words like "bleak" and "eye-like" which pretend to describe the object but in reality indicate a response to the object. For example, the phrase "vacant eye-like windows" is really giving the morbid comparison of the house to a fleshless skull—is really implying that the house is a house of death.

What are we to make, however, of description in which no observer appears, but which indicates a very definite response for the reader? With this question in mind let us look at the following passage:

(4) The waters are out in Lincolnshire. An arch of the bridge in the park has been sapped and sopped away. The adjacent low-lying ground, for half a mile in breadth, is a stagnant river, with melancholy trees for islands in it, and a surface punctured all over, all day long, with falling rain. My Lady Dedlock's "place" has been extremely dreary. The weather, for many a day and night, has been so wet that the trees seem wet through, and the soft loppings and prunings of the woodsman's axe

can make no crack or crackle as they fall. The deer, looking soaked, leave quagmires where they pass. The shot of a rifle loses its sharpness in the moist air, and its smoke moves in a tardy little cloud towards the green rise, coppice-topped, that makes a background for the falling rain. The view from my Lady Dedlock's own windows is alternately a lead-coloured view, and a view in Indian ink. The vases on the stone terrace in the foreground catch the rain all day; and the heavy drops fall, drip, drip, drip, upon the broad flagged pavement, called, from old time, the Ghost's Walk, all night. On Sundays, the little church in the park is mouldy; the oaken pulpit breaks out into a cold sweat; and there is a general smell and taste as of the ancient Dedlocks in their graves.— CHARLES DICKENS: *Bleak House*, Vol. I, Chap. 2.

As we have said, no observer is officially introduced into this scene, but a certain response to it is strongly indicated, a certain mood is developed. All details are presented to reinforce the impression of dampness, depression, and gloom. The river is "stagnant," the blows of the ax make only "soft loppings," the report of the rifle "loses its sharpness in the moist air," the heavy drops "drip, drip, drip," the church is "mouldy," the pulpit "breaks out into a cold sweat," there is the general taste and smell of a tomb. Notice how the phrase "breaks out in a cold sweat," though applied to the damp wood of the pulpit actually serves to remind us of a situation that would make a human being do the same thing, and leads us up to the taste and smell of the Dedlocks in their graves. We can see that, though Dickens has apparently maintained an objective method (he has put no observer in the scene), the effect of the passage is actually much closer to that from Poe than to the objective passage by Huxley with which we started.

THE RELATION BETWEEN THE TECHNICAL-SUGGESTIVE DISTINCTION AND THE OBJECTIVE-SUBJECTIVE DISTINCTION

What is the relation between the technical-suggestive distinction and the objective-subjective distinction? We can best answer this question by remembering that technical description does not interpret its material and the suggestive description does. Then we can set up a scheme to answer our question:

TECHNICAL	SUGGESTIVE

Without an observer

(1) Without observer and with strictly objective method. (Huxley: "The Herring")

(4) Without observer, apparently objective in method, but with interpretation of material. (Dickens: *Bleak House*)

With an observer

(2) With observer, apparently subjective in method, but with no reference to the observer's responses and with no interpretation. (Swift: *Gulliver's Travels*)

(3) With observer and with strictly subjective method. (Poe: "The Fall of the House of Usher")

We cannot let this scheme stand, however, without some modifying comment.

First, technical description of the strictest kind, such as the description of a device in a handbook of mechanics ordinarily uses type 1.

Second, even when suggestive description puts the greatest emphasis on the interpretation of material, on the response of a specified observer or of the reader, it must still give an impression of the object itself. It is not a mere presentation of responses. In the description of the House of Usher, for instance, we do have a picture of the landscape. The point is that such physical items are used as will support the interpretation.

Third, even in a composition where the over-all intention is suggestive, elements of technical description may appear. For example, the writer may want to give some general information about an object or a class of objects. In his novel *Moby Dick,* Herman Melville is not primarily interested in writing a technical study of whaling and whaling ships, but we find in it such a description as the following, in which he is not trying to give us a vivid impression but to make us understand technically the characteristic structure of the tryworks of a whaler. So he uses a description which is objective and is essentially of type 1.

Besides her hoisted boats, an American whaler is outwardly distinguished by her try-works. She presents the curious anomaly of the most solid masonry joining with oak and hemp in constituting the completed ship. It is as if from the open field a brick-kiln were transported to her planks.

The try-works are planted between the foremast and mainmast, the most roomy part of the deck. The timbers beneath are of a peculiar strength, fitted to sustain the weight of an almost solid mass of brick and mortar, some ten feet by eight square, and five in height. The foundation does not penetrate the deck, but the masonry is firmly secured to the surface by ponderous knees of iron bracing it on all sides, and screwing it down to the timbers. On the flanks it is cased with wood, and at top completely covered by a large, sloping, battened hatchway. Removing this hatch we expose the great try-pots, two in number, and each of several barrels' capacity. When not in use, they are kept remarkably clean. Sometimes they are polished with soapstone and sand, till they shine within like silver punch-bowls.—HERMAN MELVILLE: *Moby Dick*, Chap. 46.

Another use of technical description in a composition where the over-all intention is suggestive may appear when the writer wants the reader to take a cool, detached, almost scientific attitude toward what is being presented. For example, *Gulliver's Travels* is a fantastic narrative, a set of absolutely impossible events, but the fact that Swift adopts an unemotional attitude, that he makes his description technical, tends to lead the reader to accept the fantasy. The reader, of course, knows that the events are not true, that no such creatures as the Lilliputians ever existed, but he is willing to accept the illusion.

With these reservations, our scheme of the relation of the technical-suggestive distinction to the objective-subjective distinction may be useful. What we must remember is that such distinctions and relations are not always mathematically clear-cut, that the mind may carry more than one interest at a time. And this idea may lead us to a more general consideration of the uses of technical and suggestive description.

THE USES OF TECHNICAL AND SUGGESTIVE DESCRIPTION

We cannot say that either type of description is better than the other. Each has its uses, and at one time we find need for one and at another time the need for the other. In one department of our living we are concerned with information about the world; in another department, with the direct experience of the world; and the two types of description may be said to correspond to those two kinds of interest, to two kinds of motivation. The advertisement of the Cape Cod cottage is concerned with information about the object, the letter of the buyer, with her direct experience of the cottage and her feelings about it.

We have already referred to this distinction (p. 42), but we may return to it here in considering the distinction between the two kinds of description and remember that scientists appeal to our interest in information about the world and in explanation of the world, and that artists (of all kinds, painters, poets, novelists, musicians, and so forth) appeal to our interest in direct experience of the world. This means that we find technical description characteristically in scientific writing and suggestive description characteristically in the work of literary artists, poets or essayists or fiction writers. For instance, the geographers, describing the West Indies, are writing as scientists, and Melville, describing the Encantadas, is writing as an artist.

Most of us are neither scientists nor artists and never shall be, but we all have a little of the scientist and a little of the artist in us. We want to know about the world and we want to extend our experience of the world. At the same time, these two kinds of interest lead us, in so far as we become well-developed human beings, to the use of the two kinds of description. In so far as we are scientists we find a use for technical description, and in so far as we are artists we find a use for suggestive description.

All of this does not mean that we find technical description only in scientific works or suggestive description only in artistic works. Technical description may occur in a letter, an essay, a guidebook, a history, an advertisement—wherever and whenever the impulse appears to give information about the qualities of an object. By the same token, suggestive description may occur in any piece of writing which embodies the impulse for immediacy and vividness. Sometimes, as we have said, both types may appear in the same work, whether its prevailing temper is scientific or artistic.

EXPOSITORY NARRATION

As we can make a distinction between expository description and ordinary description we can make one between EXPOSITORY NARRATION and ordinary narration. Ordinary narration, as we shall see when we come to discuss it as a basic kind of discourse, is concerned with presenting an action. It aims to give the sense of the event as experienced, and it involves an appeal to the imagination. But narration may be employed merely to give information, to enlarge the understanding. If we give directions as to how to build a boat or make a cake, we are treating a sequence of events in time, and we are forced to use a form of narration. If we tell how radar works, we are again using a kind of narration. An instructor in military history lecturing on the First Battle of the Marne in World War I is concerned to make his class understand the stages of the event and the problems of tactics, but is not necessarily concerned to bring the event into the imagination of his audience. So he, too, is using expository narration.

Expository narration, like expository description, may take a generalized form. The lecturer on the First Battle of the Marne is not using generalized narration, for he is dealing with an individual event, but if he were to give instructions as to the proper method of executing a certain maneuver, he would be using generalized narration, for he would be concerned with a type of event, not with a particular event. So if we undertake to tell how a bill becomes a law or to give an account of fraternity rushing day, we should be using generalized narration. We would be concerned with a type of event.

ILLUSTRATION

Generalized description, as we have seen, is concerned with the qualities of a type, class, or group. ILLUSTRATION also aims to explain a type, class, or group, but it does so by presenting an example. It explains the general by presenting the particular.

Here is an example (and by our own phrase, "here is an example," we announce that we are here about to use the method of illustration) of the explanation of a class by presenting one member of it, a "Handsome Sailor":

In the time before steamships, or then more frequently than now, a stroller along the docks of any considerable seaport would occasionally have his attention arrested by a group of bronzed marines, man-of-war's men or merchant sailors in holiday attire ashore on liberty. In certain instances they would flank, or, like a bodyguard, quite surround some superior figure of their own class, moving along with them like Aldebaran among the lesser lights of his constellation. The signal object was the "Handsome Sailor," of the less prosaic time alike of the military and merchant navies. With no perceptible trace of the vainglorious about him, rather with the off-hand unaffectedness of natural regality, he seemed to accept the spontaneous homage of his shipmates. A somewhat remarkable instance recurs to me. In Liverpool, now half a century ago, I saw under the shadow of the great dingy street-wall of Prince's Dock (an obstruction long since removed) a common sailor, so intensely black that he must needs have been a native African of the unadulterate blood of Ham. A symmetric figure much above the average height. The two ends of a gay silk handkerchief thrown loose about the neck danced upon the displayed ebony of his chest; in his ears were big hoops of gold, and a Scotch Highland bonnet with a tartan band set off his shapely head.

It was a hot noon in July; and his face, lustrous with perspiration, beamed with barbaric good-humor. In jovial sallies right and left, his white teeth flashing into view, he rollicked along, the center of a company of his shipmates. . . . At each spontaneous tribute rendered by the wayfarers to this black pagod of a fellow—the tribute of a pause and stare, and less frequent an exclamation—the motley retinue showed that they took that sort of pride in the evoker of it which the Assyrian priests doubtless showed for their grand sculptured Bull when the faithful prostrated themselves.—HERMAN MELVILLE: *Billy Budd*, Chap. 1.

In the following parable told by Jesus we find a general idea illustrated by a particular instance:

And he began again to teach by the seaside: and there was gathered unto him a great multitude, so that he entered into a ship, and sat in the sea; and the whole multitude was by the sea on the land.

And he taught them many things by parables, and said unto them in his doctrine,

Hearken; Behold, there went out a sower to sow:

And it came to pass, as he sowed, some fell by the wayside, and the fowls of the air came and devoured it up.

ILLUSTRATION   59

And some fell on stony ground, where it had not much earth; and immediately it sprang up, because it had no depth of earth:

But when the sun was up, it was scorched; and because it had no root, it withered away.

And some fell among thorns, and the thorns grew up, and choked it, and it yielded no fruit.

And other fell on good ground, and did yield fruit that sprang up and increased; and brought forth, some thirty, some sixty, and some an hundred.

And he said unto them, He that hath ears to hear, let him hear.

And when he was alone, they that were about him with the twelve asked of him the parable.

And he said unto them, Unto you it is given to know the mystery of the kingdom of God: but unto them that are without, all *these* things are done in parables:

That seeing they may see, and not perceive; and hearing they may hear, and not understand; lest at any time they should be converted, and *their* sins should be forgiven them.

And he said unto them, Know ye not this parable? and how then will ye know all parables?

The sower soweth the word.

And these are they by the wayside, where the word is sown; but when they have heard, Satan cometh immediately, and taketh away the word that was sown in their hearts.

And these are they likewise which are sown on stony ground; who, when they have heard the word, immediately receive it with gladness;

And have no root in themselves, and so endure for a time: afterward, when affliction or persecution ariseth for the word's sake, immediately they are offended.

And these are they which are sown among thorns; such as hear the word,

And the cares of this world, and the deceitfulness of riches, and the lusts of other things entering in, choke the word, and it becometh unfruitful.

And these are they which are sown on good ground; such as hear the word, and receive *it*, and bring forth fruit, some thirty-fold, some sixty, and some an hundred.—Mark 4:1-20.

The same method of giving the particular instance to explain the general idea appears here:

A good neighbor, as the term was understood in the days when as a little girl I lived on a farm in Southern Michigan, meant all that nowadays is combined in corner store, telephone, daily newspaper, and radio. But your neighbor was also your conscience. You had to behave yourself on account of what the neighbors would think.

A good neighbor knew everything there was to know about you—and liked you anyway. He never let you down—as long as you deserved his good opinion. Even when you failed in that, if you were in trouble he would come to your rescue. If one of the family was taken sick in the night, you ran over to the neighbors' to get someone to sit up until the doctor arrived. Only instead of sending for the doctor, you went for him. Or one of the neighbors did.

The Bouldrys were that kind of neighbors. Lem Bouldry was a good farmer and a good provider. Mis' Bouldry kept a hired girl and Lem had two men the year round. They even had a piano, while the most the other neighbors boasted was an organ or a melodeon. Mis' Bouldry changed her dress every afternoon (my mother did too; she said she thought more of herself when she did), and they kept the front yard mowed.

But the Covells were just the opposite—the most shiftless family the Lord ever let set foot on land. How they got along my father said he didn't know, unless it was by the grace of God. Covell himself was ten years younger than my father, yet everybody called him "Old Covell." His face and hands were like sole leather and if his hair had ever been washed, it was only when he got caught in a rainstorm. Father said Old Covell would borrow the shirt off your back, then bring it around to have it mended; Mother said, well, one thing certain, he wouldn't bring it around to be washed.

Yet the time Mis' Covell almost died with her last baby—and the baby did die—Mis' Bouldry took care of her; took care of the rest of the children too—four of them. She stayed right there in the Covell house, just going home to catch a little sleep now and then. She had to do that, for there wasn't so much as an extra sheet in the house, much less an extra bed. And Mis' Bouldry wasn't afraid to use her hands even if she did keep a hired girl—she did all the Covells' washing herself.

But even Old Covell, despite his shiftlessness, was a good neighbor in one way: he was a master hand at laying out the dead. Of course, he wasn't worth a cent to sit up with the sick, for if it was Summer he'd go outside to smoke his pipe and sleep; and if it was Winter he'd go into the kitchen and stick his feet in the oven to warm them and go to sleep there. But a dead man seemed to rouse some kind of pride and responsibility in him. There was no real undertaker nearer than ten miles, and often the roads were impassable. Folks sent for my mother when a child or woman died, but Old Covell handled all the men. Though he

ILLUSTRATION   61

never wore a necktie himself, he kept on hand a supply of celluloid collars and little black bow ties for the dead. When he had a body to lay out, he'd call for the deceased's best pants and object strenuously if he found a hole in the socks. Next, he'd polish the boots and put on a white shirt, and fasten one of his black ties to the collar button. All in all, he would do a masterly job.

Of course, nobody paid Old Covell for this. Nobody ever thought of paying for just being neighborly. If anybody had ever offered to, they'd have been snubbed for fair. It was just the way everybody did in those half-forgotten times.—DELLA T. LUTES: "Are Neighbors Necessary?" [4]

It is clear that in the excerpt from Melville description is used, in the parable narration is used, and in the essay on neighborliness both description and narration are used. But here we must observe that the description is not, strictly speaking, expository description. Taken in itself, it is suggestive description. It is used, however, for an expository purpose, to illustrate. The same situation prevails in regard to the narration. The parable, for instance, is an example of ordinary narration, and is not, in itself, expository narration. But it is used here for an expository purpose. In each of these instances, an expository intention dominates and gives unity to the composition.

COMPARISON AND CONTRAST

In COMPARISON, as a method of exposition, we clarify a subject by indicating similarities between two or more things; in CONTRAST, by indicating differences. We constantly and instinctively use comparison and contrast, but they are not always used for expository purposes. For example, the poet making a comparison in a poem, or a painter making a contrast of two forms in planning the composition of a picture, may not be doing so for an expository purpose. The poet or the painter is acting with an appreciative or artistic motivation (see p. 33), as contrasted with an expository or scientific one, and all of us, even though we may not write poems or paint pictures, sometimes make comparisons and contrasts out of a similar motivation to gain vividness, to appeal to the imagination.

We also use comparison constantly and instinctively for exposi-

4 From "Are Neighbors Necessary?" by Della T. Lutes. Reprinted by permission of the *American Mercury* and Mrs. Cecily I. Dodd.

tory purposes. A child asks, "What is a zebra?" And we are apt to reply, "Oh, a zebra—it's an animal sort of like a mule, but it's not as big as a mule. And it has stripes like a tiger, black and white stripes all over. But you remember that a tiger's stripes are black and orange." Here we have used both comparison and contrast. We have compared the shape of the zebra to that of the mule, but have contrasted the two animals in size. And we have compared the stripes of the zebra to the stripes of a tiger, but have contrasted them in color. If the child knows what mules and tigers are like, he now has a pretty good idea of a zebra. But our instinctive application of comparison and contrast can be made more useful if we are systematic.

To be systematic means, for one thing, to understand the purpose for which a comparison or contrast is made. We may distinguish three types of purpose. In the first place our purpose may be to inform the reader about one item, and we may do so by relating it to another item with which the reader is already familiar. Second, we may wish to inform the reader about both items involved, and do so by comparing or contrasting them in relation to some general principle with which the reader is already familiar and which would apply to both. For example, if we are reviewing two novels we may compare and contrast them by reference to what we assume our reader knows about the principles of fiction. Third, we may compare and contrast items with which the reader is already familiar for the purpose of informing him about some general principle or idea. For example, a student of political science, already well acquainted with the governmental systems of the United States and England, might undertake to compare and contrast those systems for the purpose of understanding, or of explaining to others, the nature of democratic government.

To be systematic means, also, to understand the area of interest involved in a comparison or contrast. Mere differences and mere similarities are not very instructive. To compare and contrast a hawk and a handsaw would not be very profitable. No common area of interest brings them together and makes them worth treating. A zoologist might, however, profitably compare a hawk and a wren, for his interest in them as living creatures would embrace both. Or a student of the laws of flight might compare a hawk and an airplane.

WAYS OF ORGANIZING MATERIAL

When we come to apply comparison and contrast in extended form we find that there are two general ways of organizing the material. First, we can fully present one item and then fully present the other. Second, we can present a part of one item and then a part of the other, until we have touched on all the parts relevant to our comparison or contrast.

Each of these methods of organization has its utility. The first method is, generally speaking, appropriate when the two items treated are relatively uncomplicated, or when the points of comparison and contrast are fairly broad and obvious. It is clear that in a very extended and complicated presentation the reader could not carry enough detail in his mind to be properly aware of all the points of comparison and contrast. When a great many details are involved the second method is more apt to be useful. It is possible, of course, to work out a sort of compromise. One can present the first of the items in full, and then in presenting the second refer the reader, point by point, to the earlier treatment for comparison or contrast.

Here is an example of the first type of organization:

My father died when I was a small child, and I do not even remember him. I was raised by my mother and my maternal grandfather, in whose house we lived until I came to college. My mother loved her father and I have no reason to think he did not love her, but they were so different that I was aware from the first of a conflict between them. Or, if it was not a direct conflict between them, it was a conflict between what they stood for. And both of them exerted a strong influence over me. Therefore, as I grow up, I think more and more about their contrasting personalities and values and try to detect in myself the traces of each of them. I do this because I am trying to understand myself.

My grandfather, whose name was Carruthers McKenzie, was of Scotch-Irish blood, and belonged to the Presbyterian Church. He looked like those pictures of pre-Civil War statesmen who had long, bony faces, sunken cheeks, and straggly beards, like John C. Calhoun, for instance. He was a man with an iron will if I ever saw one, and all of his way of life was one long discipline for himself and everybody about him. But it was a discipline chiefly for himself. He never spent a day in bed in his life until his last illness, and yet he was probably ill a good part of his life. I used to see him spit blood when I was a child. After he died—and he died of a cancer of the stomach—the doctor told us that he could not understand how any man could keep on his feet so long without giving in to the pain which he must have suffered before his collapse. There was discipline enough left over for my mother and me and the two Negroes who worked about the place. We had morning prayers and evening prayers. I had to read the Bible an hour a day and learn long passages by heart. My grandfather was a prosperous man, but I never had a nickel to spend which I had not earned, and his rates of payment for my chores were not generous. I was never allowed to speak in the presence of my elders unless I could show some great practical reason for it. From the time I was eight on, I had to study three hours in the afternoon and at least two hours at night, except for week ends. My grandfather never uttered a word of praise to me except now and then the statement, "You have done your duty." As one could guess, my grandfather never told jokes, was scrupulous about all kinds of obligations, never touched an alcoholic beverage or even soft drinks, and wore sober black, winter and summer.

My mother must have taken after her own mother, who was of South German parentage, and a Catholic by training. Her people had come to this country just before her birth. My mother's mother had given up her religion to marry my grandfather, and had taken on his way of life, but she died very young. My mother looked like her pictures. My mother was rather short in stature and had a rather full but graceful figure, the kind they call "partridge-y." She had round, pink cheeks and a complexion like a child's. She had blue eyes, very large. They always seemed to be laughing. My mother loved to laugh and joke, and spent a great deal of time in the kitchen with Sally, the Negro cook. They laughed and talked together a great deal. My mother was a good mother, as the phrase goes; she loved me and she was careful of all my wants. But she also liked idleness. She would sit on the veranda half the afternoon and look across the yard, just rocking in her chair and enjoying the sunshine. And she went to bridge parties and even took an occasional glass of wine or, as I imagine, a highball.

She was made for a good time and noise and people, and when my grandfather was out of the house, she used to romp and play with me or take me on long walks in the country back of our place. I am now sure that she would have got married very soon if she had not felt it best to keep me in my grandfather's house and with the advantages which his prosperity would give me. For after I grew up, when I was eighteen and went off to college, she got married.

She married the kind of man you would expect her to pick. He was big and strong-looking, with a heavy black mustache with a little gray in it. He smokes cigars and he likes fine whisky. He has a Packard agency in the city and he keeps a little plane out at the airport. He loves sports and a good time. My mother has married exactly the man for her, I think, and I am enough like my mother to think he is fine, too. But as I look back on my grandfather—he died three years ago when I was seventeen—I have a great admiration for him and a sneaking affection.

What follows is an example of the mixed type of organization. We can see how in the second paragraph the contrasting characteristics leads even to the use of balanced sentences treating a single point of contrast.

We have divided men into Red-bloods and Mollycoddles. "A Red-blood man" is a phrase which explains itself; "Mollycoddle" is its opposite. We have adopted it from a famous speech by Mr. Roosevelt,[5] and redeemed it—perverted it, if you will—to other uses. A few examples will make the notion clear. Shakespeare's Henry V is a typical Red-blood; so was Bismarck; so was Palmerston; so is almost any business man. On the other hand, typical Mollycoddles were Socrates, Voltaire, and Shelley. The terms, you will observe, are comprehensive and the types very broad. Generally speaking, men of action are Red-bloods. Not but what the Mollycoddles may act, and act efficiently. But, if so, he acts from principle, not from the instinct for action. The Red-blood, on the other hand, acts as the stone falls, and does indiscriminately anything that comes to hand. It is thus that he carries on the business of the world. He steps without reflection into the first place offered him and goes to work like a machine. The ideals and standards of his family, his class, his city, his country, his age, he swallows as naturally as he swallows food and drink. He is therefore always "in the swim"; and he is bound to "arrive," because he has set before him the attainable. You will find him everywhere in all the prominent positions. In a military age he is a soldier, in a commercial age a business man. He hates his enemies, and he may love his friends; but he does not require friends to love. A wife and children he does require, for the instinct to propagate the race is as strong in him as all other instincts. His domestic life, however, is not always happy; for he can seldom understand his wife. This is part of his general incapacity to understand any point of view but his own. He is incapable of an idea and contemptuous of a principle. He is the Samson, the blind force, dearest to Nature of her children. He neither looks back nor looks ahead. He lives in present action. And when he can no longer act, he loses his reasons for existence. The Red-blood is happiest if he dies in the prime of life; otherwise, he may easily end with suicide. For he has no inner life; and when the outer life fails, he can only fail with it. The instinct that animated him being dead, he dies too. Nature, who has blown through him, blows elsewhere. His stops are dumb; he is dead wood on the shore.

The Mollycoddle, on the other hand, is all inner life. He may indeed act, as I said, but he acts, so to speak, by accident; just as the Red-blood may reflect, but reflects by accident. The Mollycoddle in action is the Crank; it is he who accomplishes reforms; who abolished slavery, for example, and revolutionized prisons and lunatic asylums. Still, primarily, the Mollycoddle is a critic, not a man of action. He challenges all standards and all facts. If an institution is established, that is a reason why he will not accept it; if an idea is current, that is a reason why he should repudiate it. He questions everything, including life and the universe. And for that reason Nature hates him. On the Red-blood she heaps her favors; she gives him a good digestion, a clear complexion, and sound nerves. But to the Mollycoddle she apportions dyspepsia and black bile. In the universe and in society the Mollycoddle is "out of it" as inevitably as the Red-blood is "in it." At school, he is a "smug" or a "swat," while the Red-blood is captain of the Eleven. At college, he is an "intellectual," while the Red-blood is in the "best set." In the world, he courts failure while the Red-blood achieves success. The Red-blood sees nothing; but the Mollycoddle sees through everything. The Red-blood joins societies; the Mollycoddle is a non-joiner. Individualist of individualists, he can only stand alone, while the Red-blood requires the support of a crowd. The Mollycoddle engenders ideas, and the Red-blood exploits them. The Mollycoddle discovers and the Red-blood invents. The whole structure of civilization rests on foundations laid by Mollycoddles; but all the building is done by Red-bloods. The Red-blood despises the Mollycoddle, but, in the long run, he does what the Mollycoddle tells him. The Mollycoddle also despises the Red-blood, but he cannot do without him. Each thinks he is master of the other, and, in a sense, each is right. In his lifetime the Mollycoddle may be the slave of the Red-blood; but after his death, he is his master, though the Red-blood may know it not.

Nations, like men, may be classified roughly as Red-blood and Mollycoddle. To the latter class belong clearly the ancient Greeks, the Italians, the French and probably the Russians; to the former the Romans, the Germans, and the English. But the Red-blood nation *par excellence* is the American; so that in comparison with them, Europe as a whole might almost be called Mollycoddle. This characteristic of Americans is reflected in the predominant physical type—the great jaw and chin, the huge teeth, the predatory mouth; in their speech, where beauty and distinction are sacrificed to force; in their need to live and feel and act in masses. To be born a Mollycoddle in America is to be born to a hard fate. You must either emigrate or succumb. This, at least hitherto, has been the alternative practiced. Whether a Mollycoddle will ever be produced strong enough to breathe the American atmosphere and live, is a crucial question for the future. It is the question whether America will ever be civilized. For civilization, you will have perceived, depends on a just balance of Red-bloods and Mollycoddles. Without the Red-blood there would be no life at all, no stuff, so to speak, for the Mollycoddle to work upon; without the Mollycoddle, the stuff would remain shapeless and chaotic. The Red-blood is the matter, the Mollycoddle the form; the Red-blood the dough, the Mollycoddle the yeast. On these two poles turns the orb of human society. And if, at this point, you choose to say that the poles are points and have no dimensions, that strictly neither the Mollycoddle nor the Red-blood exist, and that real men contain elements of both mixed in different proportions, I have no quarrel with you except such as one has with the man who states the obvious. I am satisfied to have distinguished the ideal extremes between which the Actual vibrates. The detailed application of the conception I must leave to more patient researchers.—G. LOWES DICKINSON: "Red-bloods and Mollycoddles," *Appearances.*[6]

CLASSIFICATION AND DIVISION

CLASSIFICATION and DIVISION are ways of thinking in terms of a system of classes.

By a class we mean a group whose members have significant characteristics in common. What constitutes a significant characteristic may vary according to the interest involved. For example, a maker of cosmetics may think of women in groups determined by complexion, and the secretary of a Y.W.C.A. may think in groups determined by religious affiliations. What is significant for the maker of cosmetics is not significant for the Y.W.C.A. secretary. Or, to take another example, the registrar of a college may group

[6] From: *Appearances* by G. Lowes Dickinson. Copyright 1914 by G. Lowes Dickinson. Reprinted by permission of Doubleday & Company, Inc.

students according to grades, and the gymnasium instructor according to athletic ability. The registrar and the gymnasium instructor have different interests in classifying the same body of students.

By a system we mean a set of classes ranging from the most inclusive down through the less inclusive. Let us set up a simple example of such a system:

(I)

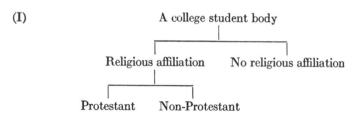

A college student body

Religious affiliation   No religious affiliation

Protestant   Non-Protestant

Here the group *student body* is the most inclusive class. Under it we find classes less and less inclusive.

What is the difference between classification and division? Our most useful way of thinking about this question is to regard them as opposite movements, one down and one up, within a system. In division we start with a class and divide it into subclasses by reference to whatever characteristic is dictated by the interest prompting the division. If, however, we start with the individuals, arrange them in groups and then relate those groups to a more inclusive group or a set of more inclusive groups, we have performed a classification.

Suppose we wish to classify the books we own. We may begin by sorting out the individual items into classes, let us say (1) short stories, (2) novels, (3) lyric poetry, (4) narrative poetry, (5) prose drama, (6) verse drama, (7) critical essays, (8) informal essays, (9) ethics, (10) logic, (11) political history, (12) economic history, (13) social history, (14) literary history, (15) geometry, (16) algebra. We see immediately that some of the classes are related to each other in terms of superior classes—more inclusive classes. For instance, we see that short stories and novels belong in a class together, the class of fiction, and we see that there are several kinds of history represented. Next, we observe that several classes, even more inclusive, are involved—literature, for example. So we can set up a scheme which covers this particular collection of books.

(II)

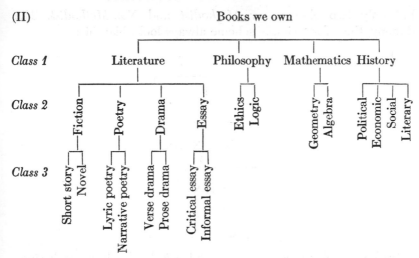

This scheme indicates the classification of the books in this particular collection. But we understand that we do not have examples of all kinds of books. For example, in class 1 we do not have science or theology. In class 2 under philosophy we have only ethics and logic, and under mathematics, only geometry and algebra. In class 3 under poetry, we have only lyric and narrative poetry, and under the essay, only critical and informal essays. So we find many classes blank in our particular scheme, classes which would not be blank in the scheme for the classification of books for a great library having copies of all kinds of books. The method of classification for our little collection and for the great library would be, however, the same.

The scheme which we have set up by classifying the books in our collection would indicate equally well a division, for the difference is not in the kind of scheme we arrive at but in the way we go about setting up the scheme.

In general, there are two kinds of schemes. Scheme I above is an example of the SIMPLE and scheme II an example of the COMPLEX.

In the simple scheme we recognize, at any stage, only two classes, which we can indicate by X and Non-X, for example, the class *Protestant* and the class *Non-Protestant*. No matter how far we carry such a scheme, we use this same method. For example, under the class *Protestant*, we would not put the various denominations, but only two classes, say *Methodist* and *Non-Methodist*. The dummy, then, for a simple scheme always looks like this:

(III)

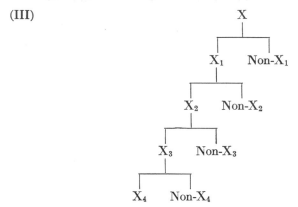

In the complex scheme we recognize individually at each stage all the classes available. For example, in scheme II we indicate at the first stage four classes (*literature, philosophy, mathematics, history*) and would recognize other such general groups if they were represented in the collection with which we are dealing. At the second stage we indicate various groups under each head. For example, under the head of *literature* we indicate four classes (*fiction, poetry, drama, essay*). That is, we are prepared to indicate as many classes at any stage as we can distinguish on the basis of whatever interest is determining the process. The dummy for a complex scheme, then, varies from instance to instance, but is of this general type:

(IV)

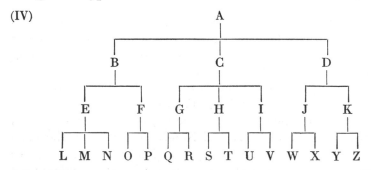

In dealing with such schemes it is customary to use the two terms GENUS (plural: GENERA) and SPECIES (plural: SPECIES) to indicate the superior and the inferior class in a system. The upper class is called the genus and each subclass immediately under it is called a species. For example, in the dummy above, D is a species of the genus A, and G is a species of the genus C. Or to return to scheme II the class *fiction* is a species of the genus *literature,* and the class *lyric poetry* is a species of the genus *poetry.* But we must remember that what is regarded as a species at one stage is regarded at the next stage below as a genus. The class *fiction,* for example, is regarded as a species of the genus *literature,* but as the genus including the species *short story* and the species *novel.* A class may be regarded as species or genus, according to whether we look above or below it.

To be useful a scheme must fulfill certain requirements:

I. There can be only one principle of division applied at each stage.

II. The subclass under any class must exhaust that class.

Rule I: We can best understand what is at stake here by looking at an extreme and ridiculous instance. Suppose we try to divide a student body into tall and short, men and women. Here two principles of division would be employed at the same time, namely, height and sex. But obviously these two principles cannot be applied at the same time, for they are at cross purposes with each other. They result in what is called a CROSS DIVISION. A member of the student body would necessarily be either a man or a woman, and at the same time would be classifiable with reference to height. Two competing principles are involved.

But can we ever apply more than one principle to a class without getting the nonsense of a cross division? We can do so if we apply the principles in sequence and not at the same time. Let us take an example. Suppose that we want to discover or exhibit the proportion of Protestant veterans in a college student body. We have here two principles, *veteran* and *religious affiliation.* First, we might divide the student body on the basis of religious affiliation in general. This would give the first stage. Then we might divide the class *religious affiliation* into the classes *Protestant* and *non-Protestant.* Thus, at the second stage, we have isolated the class *Protestant,* the particular religious affiliation we are concerned with. At this point we can introduce our second principle. So now we divide the class *Protestant* into the classes *veteran* and *nonveteran* for a third stage. So we get the following scheme:

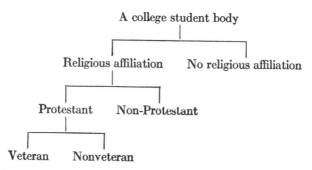

A college student body

Religious affiliation   No religious affiliation

Protestant   Non-Protestant

Veteran   Nonveteran

The thing to remember is to avoid applying the second principle until the first has been worked out to its conclusion. We do not apply the principle *veteran* until we have worked out the principle *religious affiliation* as far as our interest dictates. It may be said, of course, that when we apply the second principle *veteran* we are really beginning a new system. And in one sense this is true. But, in any case, the over-all scheme gives us exactly what we need.

Rule II: To restate this rule, the sum of the members of the subclasses under a class must equal the sum of the members of the class. In other words, we must account in the subclasses for all members of the class. For example, dividing a student body into Methodists, Baptists, Jews, and Catholics does not account for all members of the student body if there are also in it some atheists and Presbyterians. This problem of accounting for all the members of a group does not arise in a simple system as indicated by scheme III. At any stage we have only X and Non-X as subgroups, and the formula necessarily takes all members into account. The problem does arise in a complex system. If in scheme II we had forgotten to include the class *philosophy* we would not have accounted for all the books in the collection being classified. And of course scheme II as it now stands would be shockingly defective in this regard if it were regarded as applying to the books of a large general library, which would have dozens of classes of books not accounted for here.

In an essay or some other type of discussion we may find a very elaborate system running through several stages, but ordinarily

there are only one or two stages. The following selection is a classification of the kinds of thinking.

We do not think enough about thinking, and much of our confusion
is the result of current illusions in regard to it. Let us forget for the
moment any impressions we may have derived from the philosophers,
and see what seems to happen in ourselves. The first thing that we notice
is that our thought moves with such incredible rapidity that it is almost
impossible to arrest any specimen of it long enough to have a look at it.
When we are offered a penny for our thoughts we always find that we
have recently had so many things in mind that we can easily make a
selection which will not compromise us too nakedly. On inspection we
shall find that even if we are not downright ashamed of a great part of
our spontaneous thinking it is far too intimate, personal, ignoble, or trivial
to permit us to reveal more than a small part of it. I believe this must be
true of everyone. We do not, of course, know what goes on in other
people's heads. They tell us very little and we tell them very little. The
spigot of speech, rarely fully opened, could never emit more than driblets
of the ever renewed hogshead of thought—*noch grösser wie's Heidel-
berger Fass* [even larger than the Heidelberg vat]. We find it hard to
believe that other people's thoughts are as silly as our own, but they
probably are.

We all appear to ourselves to be thinking all the time during our
waking hours, and most of us are aware that we go on thinking while we
are asleep, even more foolishly than when awake. When uninterrupted
by some practical issue we are engaged in what is now known as a
reverie. This is our spontaneous and favorite kind of thinking. We allow
our ideas to take their own course and this course is determined by our
hopes and fears, our spontaneous desires, their fulfillment or frustration;
by our likes and dislikes, our loves and hates and resentments. There is
nothing else anything like so interesting to ourselves as ourselves. All
thought that is not more or less laboriously controlled and directed will
inevitably circle about the beloved Ego. It is amusing and pathetic to
observe this tendency in ourselves and in others. We learn politely and
generously to overlook this truth, but if we dare to think of it, it blazes
forth like the noontide sun.

The reverie or "free association of ideas" has of late become the subject of scientific research. While investigators are not yet agreed on the
results, or at least on the proper interpretation to be given to them,
there can be no doubt that our reveries form the chief index to our
fundamental character. They are a reflection of our nature as modified by
often hidden and forgotten experiences. We need not go into the matter

further here, for it is only necessary to observe that the reverie is at all times a potent and in many cases an omnipotent rival to every other kind of thinking. It doubtless influences all our speculations in its persistent tendency to self-magnification and self-justification, which are its chief preoccupations, but it is the last thing to make directly or indirectly for honest increase of knowledge. Philosophers usually talk as if such thinking did not exist or were in some way negligible. This is what makes their speculations so unreal and often worthless.

The reverie, as any of us can see for himself, is frequently broken and interrupted by the necessity of a second kind of thinking. We have to made practical decisions. Shall we write a letter or no? Shall we take the subway or a bus? Shall we have dinner at seven or half-past? Shall we buy U. S. Rubber or a Liberty Bond? Decisions are easily distinguishable from the free flow of reverie. Sometimes they demand a good deal of careful pondering and the recollection of pertinent facts; often, however, they are made impulsively. They are a more difficult and laborious thing than the reverie, and we resent having to "make up our mind" when we are tired, or absorbed in a congenial reverie. Weighing a decision, it should be noted, does not necessarily add anything to our knowledge, although we may, of course, seek further information before making it.

A third kind of thinking is stimulated when anyone questions our belief and opinions. We sometimes find ourselves changing our minds without any resistance or heavy emotion, but if we are told that we are wrong we resent the imputation and harden our hearts. We are incredibly heedless in the formation of our beliefs, but find ourselves filled with an illicit passion for them when anyone proposes to rob us of their companionship. It is obviously not the ideas themselves that are dear to us, but our self-esteem, which is threatened. We are by nature stubbornly pledged to defend our own from attack, whether it be our person, our family, our property, or our opinion. A United States Senator once remarked to a friend of mine that God Almighty could not make him change his mind on our Latin-American policy. We may surrender, but rarely confess ourselves vanquished. In the intellectual world at least peace is without victory.

Few of us take the pains to study the origin of our cherished convictions; indeed, we have a natural repugnance to so doing. We like to continue to believe what we have been accustomed to accept as true, and the resentment aroused when doubt is cast upon any of our assumptions leads us to seek every manner of excuse for clinging to them. *The result is that most of our so-called reasoning consists in finding arguments for going on believing as we already do.*

I remember years ago attending a public dinner to which the Governor of the state was bidden. The chairman explained that His Excellency could not be present for certain "good" reasons; what the "real" reasons were the presiding officer said he would leave us to conjecture. This distinction between "good" and "real" reasons is one of the most clarifying and essential in the whole realm of thought. We can readily give what seem to us "good" reasons for being a Catholic or a Mason, a Republican or a Democrat, an adherent or opponent of the League of Nations. But the "real" reasons are usually on quite a different plane. Of course the importance of this distinction is popularly, if somewhat obscurely, recognized. The Baptist missionary is ready enough to see that the Buddhist is not such because his doctrines would bear careful inspection, but because he happened to be born in a Buddhist family in Tokio. But it would be treason to his faith to acknowledge that his own partiality for certain doctrines is due to the fact that his mother was a member of the First Baptist Church of Oak Ridge. A savage can give all sorts of reasons for his belief that it is dangerous to step on a man's shadow, and a newspaper editor can advance plenty of arguments against the Bolsheviki. But neither of them may realize why he happens to be defending his particular opinion.

The "real" reasons for our beliefs are concealed from ourselves as well as from others. As we grow up we simply adopt the ideas presented to us in regard to such matters as religion, family relations, property, business, our country, and the state. We unconsciously absorb them from our environment. They are persistently whispered in our ear by the group in which we happen to live. Moreover, as Mr. Trotter has pointed out, these judgments, being the product of suggestion and not of reasoning, have the quality of perfect obviousness, so that to question them "is to the believer to carry skepticism to an insane degree, and will be met by contempt, disapproval, or condemnation, according to the nature of the belief in question. When, therefore, we find ourselves entertaining an opinion about the basis of which there is a quality of feeling which tells us that to inquire into it would be absurd, obviously unnecessary, unprofitable, undesirable, bad form, or wicked, we may know that that opinion is a non-rational one, and probably, therefore, founded upon inadequate evidence." [7]

Opinions, on the other hand, which are the result of experience or of honest reasoning do not have this quality of "primary certitude." I remember when as a youth I heard a group of businessmen discussing the question of the immortality of the soul, I was outraged by the sentiment of doubt expressed by one of the party. As I look back now I see that

[7] *Instincts of the Herd*, p. 44.

I had at the time no interest in the matter, and certainly no least argument to urge in favor of the belief in which I had been reared. But neither my personal indifference to the issue, nor the fact that I had previously given it no attention, served to prevent an angry resentment when I heard *my* ideas questioned.

This spontaneous and loyal support of our preconceptions—this process of finding "good" reasons to justify our routine beliefs—is known to modern psychologists as "rationalizing"—clearly only a new name for a very ancient thing. Our "good" reasons ordinarily have no value in promoting honest enlightenment, because, no matter how solemnly they may be marshaled, they are at bottom the result of personal preference or prejudice, and not of an honest desire to seek or accept new knowledge.

In our reveries we are frequently engaged in self-justification, for we cannot bear to think ourselves wrong, and yet have constant illustrations of our weaknesses and mistakes. So we spend much time finding fault with circumstances and the conduct of others, and shifting on to them with great ingenuity the onus of our own failures and disappointments. *Rationalizing is the self-exculpation which occurs when we feel ourselves, or our group, accused of misapprehension or error.*

The little word *my* is the most important one in all human affairs, and properly to reckon with it is the beginning of wisdom. It has the same force whether it is *my* dinner, *my* dog, and *my* house, or *my* faith, *my* country, and *my* God. We not only resent the imputation that our watch is wrong, or our car shabby, but that our conception of the canals of Mars, of the pronunciation of "Epictetus," of the medicinal value of salicine, or the date of Sargon I, are subject to revision.

Philosophers, scholars, and men of science exhibit a common sensitiveness in all decisions in which their *amour propre* is involved. Thousands of argumentative works have been written to vent a grudge. However stately their reasoning, it may be nothing but rationalizing, stimulated by the most commonplace of all motives. A history of philosophy and theology could be written in terms of grouches, wounded pride, and aversions, and it would be far more instructive than the usual treatments of these themes. Sometimes, under Providence, the lowly impulse of resentment leads to great achievements. Milton wrote his treatise on divorce as a result of his troubles with his seventeen-year-old wife, and when he was accused of being the leading spirit in a new sect, the Divorcers, he wrote his noble *Areopagitica* to prove his right to say what he thought fit, and incidentally to establish the advantage of a free press in the promotion of Truth.

All mankind, high and low, thinks in all the ways which have been described. The reverie goes on all the time not only in the mind of the mill hand and the Broadway flapper, but equally in weighty judges and godly bishops. It has gone on in all the philosophers, scientists, poets, and theologians that have ever lived. Aristotle's most abstruse speculations were doubtless tempered by highly irrelevant reflections. He is reported to have had very thin legs and small eyes, for which he doubtless had to find excuses, and he was wont to indulge in very conspicuous dress and rings and was accustomed to arrange his hair carefully.[8] Diogenes the Cynic exhibited the impudence of a touchy soul. His tub was his distinction. Tennyson in beginning his "Maud" could not forget his chagrin over losing his patrimony years before as the result of an unhappy investment in the Patent Decorative Carving Company. These facts are not recalled here as a gratuitous disparagement of the truly great, but to insure a full realization of the tremendous competition which all really exacting thought has to face, even in the minds of the most highly endowed mortals.

And now the astonishing and perturbing suspicion emerges that perhaps almost all that had passed for social science, political economy, politics, and ethics in the past may be brushed aside by future generations as mainly rationalizing. John Dewey has already reached this conclusion in regard to philosophy.[9] Veblen [10] and other writers have revealed the various unperceived presuppositions of the traditional political economy, and now comes an Italian sociologist, Vilfredo Pareto, who, in his huge treatise on general sociology, devotes hundreds of pages to substantiating a similar thesis affecting all the social sciences.[11] This conclusion may be ranked by students of a hundred years hence as one of the several great discoveries of our age. It is by no means fully worked out, and it is so opposed to nature that it will be very slowly accepted by the great mass of those who consider themselves thoughtful. As a historical student I am personally fully reconciled to this newer view. Indeed, it seems to me inevitable that just as the various sciences of nature were, before the opening of the seventeenth century, largely masses of rationalizations to suit the religious sentiments of the period, so the social sciences have continued even to our own day to be rationalizations of uncritically accepted beliefs and customs.

[8] *Diogenes Laertius*, Book V.
[9] *Reconstruction in Philosophy.*
[10] *The Place of Science in Modern Civilization.*
[11] *Traité de Sociologie Générale, passim.* The author's term *"derivations"* seems to be his precise way of expressing what we have called the "good" reasons, and his *"residus"* correspond to the "real" reasons. He well says, *"L'homme éprouve le besoin de raisonner, et en outre d'étendre une voile sur ses instincts et sur ses sentiments"*—hence, rationalization. (p. 788.) His aim is to reduce sociology to the "real" reasons. (p. 791.)

It will become apparent as we proceed that the fact that an idea is ancient and that it has been widely received is no argument in its favor, but should immediately suggest the necessity of carefully testing it as a probable instance of rationalization.

This brings us to another kind of thought which can fairly easily be distinguished from the three kinds described above. It has not the usual qualities of the reverie, for it does not hover about our personal complacencies and humiliations. It is not made up of the homely decisions forced upon us by everyday needs, when we review our little stock of existing information, consult our conventional preferences and obligations, and make a choice of action. It is not the defense of our own cherished beliefs and prejudices just because they are our own—mere plausible excuses for remaining of the same mind. On the contrary, it is that peculiar species of thought which leads us to *change* our mind.

It is this kind of thought that has raised man from his pristine, sub-savage ignorance and squalor to the degree of knowledge and comfort which he now possesses. On his capacity to continue and greatly extend this kind of thinking depends his chance of groping his way out of the plight in which the most highly civilized peoples of the world now find themselves. In the past this type of thinking has been called Reason. But so many misapprehensions have grown up around the word that some of us have become very suspicious of it. I suggest, therefore, that we substitute a recent name and speak of "creative thought" rather than of Reason. *For this kind of meditation begets knowledge, and knowledge is really creative inasmuch as it makes things look different from what they seemed before and may indeed work for their reconstruction.*

In certain moods some of us realize that we are observing things or making reflections with a seeming disregard of our personal preoccupations. We are not preening or defending ourselves; we are not faced by the necessity of any practical decision, nor are we apologizing for believing this or that. We are just wondering and looking and mayhap seeing what we never perceived before.

Curiosity is as clear and definite as any of our urges. We wonder what is in a sealed telegram or in a letter in which someone else is absorbed, or what is being said in the telephone booth or in low conversation. This inquisitiveness is vastly stimulated by jealousy, suspicion, or any hint that we ourselves are directly or indirectly involved. But there appears to be a fair amount of personal interest in other people's affairs even when they do not concern us except as a mystery to be unraveled or a tale to be told. The reports of a divorce suit will have "news value" for many weeks. They constitute a story, like a novel or play or moving picture. This is not an example of pure curiosity, however, since we readily identify ourselves with others, and their joys and despair then become our own.

We also take note of, or "observe," as Sherlock Holmes says, things which have nothing to do with our personal interests and make no personal appeal either direct or by way of sympathy. This is what Veblen so well calls "idle curiosity." And it is usually idle enough. Some of us when we face the line of people opposite us in a subway train impulsively consider them in detail and engage in rapid inferences and form theories in regard to them. On entering a room there are those who will perceive at a glance the degree of preciousness of the rugs, the character of the pictures, and the personality revealed by the books. But there are many, it would seem, who are so absorbed in their personal reverie or in some definite purpose that they have no bright-eyed energy for idle curiosity. The tendency to miscellaneous observation we come by honestly enough, for we note it in many of our animal relatives.

Veblen, however, uses the term "idle curiosity" somewhat ironically, as is his wont. It is idle only to those who fail to realize that it may be a very rare and indispensable thing from which almost all distinguished human achievement proceeds, since it may lead to systematic examination and seeking for things hitherto undiscovered. For research is but diligent search which enjoys the high flavor of primitive hunting. Occasionally and fitfully, idle curiosity thus leads to creative thought, which alters and broadens our own views and aspirations and may in turn, under highly favorable circumstances, affect the views and lives of others, even for generations to follow. An example or two will make this unique human process clear.

Galileo was a thoughtful youth and doubtless carried on a rich and varied reverie. He had artistic ability and might have turned out to be a musician or painter. When he had dwelt among the monks at Vallombrosa he had been tempted to lead the life of a religious. As a boy he busied himself with toy machines and he inherited a fondness for mathematics. All these facts are on record. We may safely assume also that, along with many other subjects of contemplation, the Pisan maidens found a vivid place in his thoughts.

One day when seventeen years old he wandered into the cathedral of his native town. In the midst of his reverie he looked up at the lamps hanging by long chains from the high ceiling of the church. Then something very difficult to explain occurred. He found himself no longer thinking of the building, worshipers, or the services; of his artistic or religious interests; of his reluctance to become a physician as his father wished. He forgot the question of a career and even the *graziosissime donne*. As he watched the swinging lamps he was suddenly wondering if mayhap their oscillations, whether long or short, did not occupy the same time. Then he tested this hypothesis by counting his pulse, for that was the only timepiece he had with him.

This observation, however remarkable in itself, was not enough to produce a really creative thought. Others may have noticed the same thing and yet nothing came of it. Most of our observations have no assignable results. Galileo may have seen that the warts on a peasant's face formed a perfect isosceles triangle, or he may have noticed with boyish glee that just as the officiating priest was uttering the solemn words, *Ecce agnus Dei,* a fly lit on the end of his nose. To be really creative, ideas have to be worked up and then "put over," so that they become a part of man's social heritage. The highly accurate pendulum clock was one of the later results of Galileo's discovery. He himself was led to reconsider and successfully to refute the old notions of falling bodies. It remained for Newton to prove that the moon was falling, and presumably all the heavenly bodies. This quite upset all the consecrated views of the heavens as managed by angelic engineers. The universality of the laws of gravitation stimulated the attempt to seek other and equally important natural laws and cast grave doubts on the miracles in which mankind had hitherto believed. In short, those who dared to include in their thought the discoveries of Galileo and his successors found themselves in a new earth surrounded by new heavens.

On the 28th of October, 1831, two hundred and fifty years after Galileo had noticed the isochronous vibrations of the lamps, creative thought and its currency had so far increased that Faraday was wondering what would happen if he mounted a disk of copper between the poles of a horseshoe magnet. As the disk revolved an electric current was produced. This would doubtless have seemed the idlest kind of experiment to the stanch businessmen of the time, who, it happened, were just then denouncing the child-labor bills in their anxiety to avail themselves to the full of the results of earlier idle curiosity. But should the dynamos and motors which have come into being as the outcome of Faraday's experiment be stopped this evening, the businessman of today, agitated over labor troubles, might, as he trudged home past lines of "dead" cars, through dark streets to an unlighted house, engage in a little creative thought of his own and perceive that he and his laborers would have no modern factories and mines to quarrel about if it had not been for the strange practical effects of the idle curiosity of scientists, inventors and engineers.

The examples of creative intelligence given above belong to the realm of modern scientific achievement, which furnishes the most striking instances of the effects of scrupulous, objective thinking. But there are, of course, other great realms in which the recording and embodiment of acute observation and insight have wrought themselves into the higher life of man. The great poets and dramatists and our modern story-tellers have found themselves engaged in productive reveries, noting and artistically presenting their discoveries for the delight and instruction of those who have the ability to appreciate them.

The process by which a fresh and original poem or drama comes into being is doubtless analogous to that which originates and elaborates so-called scientific discoveries; but there is clearly a temperamental difference. The genesis and advance of painting, sculpture, and music offer still other problems. We really as yet know shockingly little about these matters, and indeed very few people have the least curiosity about them.[12] Nevertheless, creative intelligence in its various forms is what makes man. Were it not for its slow, painful, and constantly discouraged operations through the ages man would be no more than a species of primate living on seeds, fruit, roots, and uncooked flesh, and wandering naked through the woods and over the plains like a chimpanzee.

The origin and progress and future promotion of civilization are ill understood and misconceived. These should be made the chief theme of education, but much hard work is necessary before we can construct our ideas of man and his capacities and free ourselves from innumerable persistent misapprehensions. There have been obstructionists in all times, not merely the lethargic masses, but the moralists, the rationalizing theologians, and most of the philosophers, all busily if unconsciously engaged in ratifying existing ignorance and mistakes and discouraging creative thought. Naturally, those who reassure us seem worthy of honor and respect. Equally naturally those who puzzle us with disturbing criticisms and invite us to change our ways are objects of suspicion and readily discredited. Our personal discontent does not ordinarily extend to any critical questioning of the general situation in which we find ourselves. In every age the prevailing conditions of civilization have appeared quite natural and inevitable to those who grew up in them. The cow asks no questions as to how it happens to have a dry stall and a supply of hay. The kitten laps its warm milk from a china saucer, without knowing anything about porcelain; the dog nestles in the corner of

[12] Recently a re-examination of creative thought has begun as a result of new knowledge which discredits many of the notions formerly held about "reason." See, for example, *Creative Intelligence*, by a group of American philosophic thinkers: John Dewey, *Essays in Experimental Logic* (both pretty hard books): and Veblen, *The Place of Science in Modern Civilization*. Easier than these and very stimulating are Dewey, *Reconstruction in Philosophy*, and Woodworth, *Dynamic Psychology*.

a divan with no sense of obligation to the inventors of upholstery and the manufacturers of down pillows. So we humans accept our breakfasts, our trains and telephones and orchestras and movies, our national Constitution, our moral code and standards of manners, with the simplicity and innocence of a pet rabbit. We have absolutely inexhaustible capacities for appropriating what others do for us with no thought of a "thank you." We do not feel called upon to make any least contribution to the merry game ourselves. Indeed, we are usually quite unaware that a game is being played at all.

We have now examined the various classes of thinking which we can readily observe in ourselves and which we have plenty of reasons to believe go on, and always have been going on, in our fellow men. We can sometimes get quite pure and sparkling examples of all four kinds, but commonly they are so confused and intermingled in our reverie as not to be readily distinguishable. The reverie is a reflection of our longings, exultations, and complacencies, our fears, suspicions, and disappointments. We are chiefly engaged in struggling to maintain our self-respect and in asserting that supremacy which we all crave and which seems to us our natural prerogative. It is not strange, but rather quite inevitable, that our beliefs about what is true and false, good and bad, right and wrong, should be mixed up with the reverie and be influenced by the same considerations which determine its character and course. We resent criticisms of our views exactly as we do of anything else connected with ourselves. Our notions of life and its ideals seem to us to be *our own* and as such necessarily true and right, to be defended at all costs.

We very rarely consider, however, the process by which we gained our convictions. If we did so, we could hardly fail to see that there was usually little ground for our confidence in them. Here and there, in this department of knowledge or that, some one of us might make a fair claim to have taken some trouble to get correct ideas of, let us say, the situation in Russia, the sources of our food supply, the origin of the Constitution, the revision of the tariff, the policy of the Holy Roman Apostolic Church, modern business organization, trade unions, birth control, socialism, the League of Nations, the excess-profits tax, preparedness, advertising in its social bearings; but only a very exceptional person would be entitled to opinions on all of even these few matters. And yet most of us have opinions on all these, and on many other questions of equal importance, of which we may know even less. We feel compelled, as self-respecting persons, to take sides when they come up for discussion. We even surprise ourselves by our omniscience. Without taking thought we see in a flash that it is most righteous and expedient to discourage birth control by legislative enactment, or that one who decries intervention in Mexico is clearly wrong, or that big advertising is essential to big business and that big business is the pride of the land. As godlike beings why should we not rejoice in our omniscience?

It is clear in any case, that our convictions on important matters are not the result of knowledge or critical thought, nor, it may be added, are they often dictated by supposed self-interest. Most of them are *pure prejudices* in the proper sense of that word. We do not form them ourselves. They are the whispering of "the voice of the herd." We have in the last analysis no responsibility for them and need assume none. They are not really our own ideas, but those of others no more well informed or inspired than ourselves, who have got them in the same humiliating manner as we. It should be our pride to revise our ideas and not to adhere to what passes for respectable opinion, for such opinion can frequently be shown to be not respectable at all. We should, in view of the considerations that have been mentioned, resent our supine credulity. As an English writer has remarked:

"If we feared the entertaining of an unverifiable opinion with the warmth with which we fear using the wrong implement at the dinner table, if the thought of holding a prejudice disgusted us as does a foul disease, then the dangers of man's susceptibility would be turned into advantages."—JAMES HARVEY ROBINSON: *The Mind in the Making*, Chap. 2.[13]

DEFINITION

In one sense we can say that DEFINITION answers the question, "What is it?" A small child asks, "What is a zebra?" and the grownup replies, very unscientifically, that a zebra is a kind of horse, but not as big as a real horse, with black and white stripes. The grownup has given a description of the animal.

In another and stricter sense, however, it can be said that a definition is not of a thing, but of the word referring to the thing. Its function is to tell how to use the word. It sets the bound or limit within which the word will apply—as the derivation of the word *definition* implies (it comes from two Latin words, *de* meaning *concerning*, and *finis* meaning *limit*). This idea of definition as the limiting of a word is illustrated in the demand frequently made

[13]From *The Mind in the Making* by James Harvey Robinson. Copyright, 1921, by Harper & Brothers. Copyright, 1949, by Bankers Trust Company.

during an argument: "Define your terms." And by TERM we mean any word or group of words that constitutes a unit of meaning—that refers to one thing or idea.

We shall discuss definition as the definition of a term, but it is clear that we cannot define a term without some knowledge of the thing to which the term refers. So the process of making a definition involves knowledge. It is not a mere game of words. Not only may definition enlarge the understanding of the person who receives a definition, but the process of definition may lead the maker of the definition to clarify his own mind on the subject involved.

PARTS OF A DEFINITION

A definition falls into two parts, the element to be defined and the element which does the defining. The two elements form an equation, that is, one can be substituted for the other in a statement without changing the sense in any respect.

For example, we may define a *slave* as a human being who is the legal property of another, and then set this up as an equation:

The *to-be-defined* = the *definer*
Slave is human being who is the legal property of another.

Now if we make a statement using the word *slave,* we may substitute the *definer* ("human being who is the legal property of another") for that word without any change of sense. The statement,

1. To be a slave is worse than death.

has exactly the same meaning as the statement,

2. To be the legal property of another is worse than death.

We must remember that the adequacy of the original definition is not the point here. We may have given an inadequate definition, but in so far as we are willing to stand by our definition we are willing to substitute the *definer* for the *to-be-defined* in any statement. Furthermore, the truth or falsity of any particular statement is not relevant. What is relevant is that the two elements form an equation, are CONVERTIBLE.

When the elements are not convertible, we do not have a real definition.

THE PROCESS OF DEFINITION

To get a notion of the process of definition let us take a very simple situation. A small child who has never seen a cat receives one as a pet. The father tells the child that the animal is a cat— a kitty. The proud parent now assumes that the child knows what the word *cat* means, but he may be surprised one day to find the child pointing at a Pekingese and calling, "Kitty, kitty." It is obvious that the child is using the word to mean any small, furry animal, and when the father takes him to the park the child is very apt to call a squirrel a kitty, too.

The father now undertakes to give the child a definition of *cat*. To do so he must instruct the child in the differences between a cat, a Pekingese, and a squirrel. In other words, he undertakes to break up the group the child has made (all small, furry animals) into certain subgroups (cats, Pekingese, squirrels) by focusing attention upon the differences, the DIFFERENTIA.

If the child understands his father, he now has the knowledge to give a definition of the word *cat*—a very inadequate definition but a kind of definition. If we question the child we may elicit a definition.

Questioner: What does *cat* mean?

Child: It's a little-bitty animal, and it's got fur.

Questioner: But dogs have fur, too, and dogs aren't cats.

Child: Yes, but dogs bark. Cats don't bark. Cats me-ow. And cats climb trees.

Questioner: But squirrels have fur, and they climb trees and are little-bitty.

Child: Yes, but squirrels don't just climb trees like cats. They live in trees. And they don't me-ow like cats.

The child has put *cat* into a group (small, furry animals) and then has distinguished the subgroup of cats from other subgroups of Pekingese and squirrels.

If we chart the child's reasoning we get something like this:

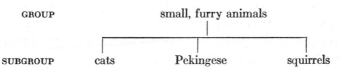

GROUP	small, furry animals	
SUBGROUP	cats	Pekingese	squirrels

The pattern of the child's definition is the pattern of all definition. It involves, we see, the kind of scheme we have already studied
under classification and division. Here the class *small, furry animals*
is the genus, and the classes *cats, Pekingese,* and *squirrels* are the
species. Definition involves placing the relevant species under its
genus and then indicating the characteristics which distinguish it
from other species of the same genus. So we get the formula:

Definition of species = genus + differentia

The pattern of the child's definition of *cat* is the pattern of all
definition, but the particular definition will not serve in an adult
world. The classifications the child is using are not significant, since
smallness and furriness are not sufficiently particularized traits. A
zoologist would go about the business differently.

He might begin by saying: "A cat—*Felis domestica,* we call it—is
a digitigrade, carnivorous mammal, of the genus *Felis,* which includes the species tiger (*Felis tigris*), the species ocelot (*Felis par-
dalis*), the species lion (*Felis leo*), the species cougar (*Felis concolor*),
and several other species. All the species of the genus *Felis* have
lithe, graceful, long bodies, relatively short legs, with soft, padded
feet, strong claws which are retracted into sheaths when not in
use, powerful jaws with sharp teeth, and soft, beautifully marked
fur. The cat is the smallest species of the genus, usually measuring
so-and-so. It is the only species easily domesticated. . . ."

Like the child, the zoologist has set up a group (which he calls
a genus), and has given the characteristics of the group. Then he
has broken up the group into several subgroups (each of which he
calls a species). Last he has set about pointing out the differences
between the species *cat* and the other species of the same genus.
Set up as a scheme, his thinking has this form:

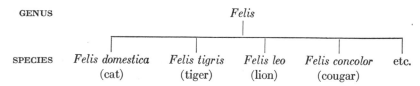

GENUS   *Felis*

SPECIES   *Felis domestica*   *Felis tigris*   *Felis leo*   *Felis concolor*   etc.
           (cat)   (tiger)   (lion)   (cougar)

The form used by the zoologist is, we see, the same as that used
by the child. The difference is that the zoologist thinks in significant
classes. It is true that for him the words *genus* and *species* have a

somewhat different meaning from the meanings we use in referring to classification and division. For the zoologist the word *genus* means a group of species closely related structurally and by origin, and the word *species* means a group whose members possess numerous characteristics in common and do or may interbreed to preserve those characteristics. This difference comes from the fact that the zoologist is dealing with living forms. But despite these differences in the meaning of genus and species he uses them in his pattern of definition in the same way we have used them.

Though our thinking may follow the pattern of genus and species, we do not ordinarily use those terms in framing a definition. To define *bungalow* we may say that the species falls under the genus *house* and give the differentia distinguishing it from other species, other types of houses. Set up formally the scheme would be this:

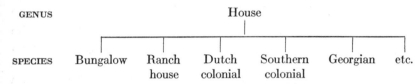

GENUS			House			
SPECIES	Bungalow	Ranch house	Dutch colonial	Southern colonial	Georgian	etc.

Ordinarily, however, we would not use the technical terms. We might say: "A bungalow is a kind of house. It differs from some kinds, like the Dutch colonial, the Georgian, and the Southern colonial, in that it has only one story. But it differs from other one-story types, like the ranch house, in that its floor plan is so-and-so." The important thing is the pattern of thought.

DEFINITION AND THE COMMON GROUND

If we are not content with a definition given us—for instance, the definition of *cat* given by the zoologist—we may push the giver back by asking more about the genus in which he has located the species under discussion. If we ask the zoologist about the genus *Felis*, he may say that it is a group under the family *Felidae*, which contains another genus, the genus *Lynx*. If, after he has established the differentia here between the genera *Felis* and *Lynx*, we are still not satisfied, he may patiently repeat the process, going up the scale to another group, for instance, mammals, and on above that to vertebrates, and on above that to animals. We would conclude with some very elaborate scheme, roughly as follows:

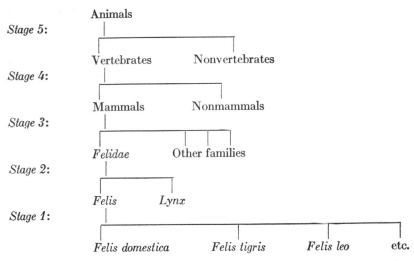

If we keep forcing the zoologist upward from stage to stage, he will in each instance give us a new definition by the same method. The only difference will be that what has been the main group in Stage 1, for example, becomes the subgroup in Stage 2, and so on up the scale. Here he is seeking a point where the questioner will feel at home, where he and the questioner will have common ground.

Common ground is necessary for an effective definition. Such common ground may be difficult to discover in a transaction between a scientist, for instance a zoologist, who employs a highly technical language and a highly technical scheme based on the structures of living creatures, and a layman who deals in language and in appearances in a rough-and-ready way. But if the scientist wishes to communicate with the layman he must find a common ground and a common language.

This principle of the common ground for a definition is very important, for it implies that a definition is not only *of some term* but is *for somebody*. The giver of the definition can only define by reference to what his particular audience already knows or is willing to learn.

This knowledge must be of two kinds.

First, since any definition must be in words, the giver of the definition must use words that his audience is, or can readily become, acquainted with. For instance, when the zoologist refers to the cat as a "digitigrade mammal," and so on, he is using words that no small child and few adults would know. In such cases, the zoologist would have to explain further that *digitigrade* means "walking on the toes" the way a cat does, as opposed to "walking on the whole foot" (plantigrade) the way a man does. In this way the zoologist would provide the common ground in words which would make the definition effective.

Second, the giver of a definition must appeal to information which his audience has or can readily get. For instance, there is no use in trying to define the color beige to a man blind from birth. If you say that beige is a light grayish color, the natural color of wool, you have really said nothing to him. For he has had no experience of color. It will do no good to continue and say that gray is a mixture of black and white. If you go on and give the physicist's definition of color, referring to wave lengths of light, you run into the same difficulty. He can grasp the notion of wave length, but he has no basis for knowing what light is. You run into a defect in his experience, in his knowledge.

PRINCIPLES OF DEFINITION

Assuming, however, that the giver of the definition finds the common ground in regard to both words and knowledge, there are still certain principles to be observed if the *definer* is truly to enlarge the audience's understanding of the *to-be-defined*.

I. The *to-be-defined* must be equivalent to the *definer*.

II. The *to-be-defined* must not be part of the *definer*.

III. The *definer* must not be negative unless the *to-be-defined* is negative.

I. We see immediately that in principle I we are repeating the notion that a definition involves an equation, the possibility of substitution of one element of the definition for the other. But it may be useful to break this notion down:

1. The *definer* must not be broader than the *to-be-defined*.

2. The *definer* must not be narrower than the *to-be-defined*.

We have an example of the violation of principle 1 if we define *table* as a piece of furniture on which we put dishes, lamps, ashtrays, books, or knickknacks. The *definer* is here too broad because it would equally well apply to sideboards, chests of drawers, buffets, or what-nots—on which we put dishes, lamps, and so forth. The *definer* says some things that are true, but these true things apply too widely. To put it another way, we can say that the definition does not properly consider the differentia which would distinguish the various species under the genus furniture.

We have an example of the violation of principle 2 if we define *table* as the piece of furniture on which we serve our meals. Here the *definer* is too narrow, because it would not apply to some types of tables, such as end tables, study tables, bedside tables, or sewing tables. It really only applies to a subspecies of the species *table*, and not to the species. Yet the species *table* is what is involved in the definition.

II. The *to-be-defined* is part of the *definer* when it is defined in whole, or in part, in terms of itself. This occurs in two sorts of cases:

1. When a word or phrase of the *to-be-defined*, or a variation of a word or phrase, is significantly repeated in the *definer*.

2. When an idea of the *to-be-defined*, though in different words, is significantly repeated in the *definer*.

We get an example of the first when we define the word *statistician* by saying it means anyone who makes a profession of compiling and studying statistics. The trouble here is that *statistics* is a mere variation of *statistician*. The essential question, "What kind of thing does a statistician do?" is left unanswered because we have not yet defined statistics. Or if we define *man* as a human being, we commit the same error. In these cases the *definer* tells a truth, but it is not a new truth. It is a truth already implicit in the *to-be-defined*. There has been no real enlargement of understanding. To state the matter another way, there has been a circle in the definition: you come back to your starting point.

In the first type of circular definition, it is clear that when we repeat in the *definer* a word or words of the *to-be-defined* we repeat an idea already expressed. But it is possible to repeat an idea in different words, and this, too, gives a circle in the definition. For example, we have a circle in the definition when we say that *fast* means having a rapid rate of motion. The *definer* does not really enlarge our notion of the *to-be-defined* because the word *rapid*, the key word in the *definer*, really repeats the idea of *fast*, the word to be defined.

III. If we define a positive *to-be-defined* by a negative *definer* we may wind up with something like this: "Tiffin is what the English in India call a meal not eaten in the morning." Now it is perfectly true that tiffin is not eaten in the morning. It is eaten at noon. But the trouble with the negative statement is that it does not exclude other possibilities than morning. According to the definition given above, tiffin might just as well be eaten in the afternoon or the evening. The truth in the *definer* is not the whole truth, and the definition fails to establish the necessary equation between the elements of the definition.

When, however, the *to-be-defined* is negative—when its nature involves some deficiency—it is correct to use a negative *definer*. For example, it is correct to define the word *widow* as a woman who has lost her husband by death, for here the idea of loss, of deficiency, is the essential notion in the *to-be-defined*.

EXTENDED DEFINITION

Early in the discussion of definition we said that definition not only is useful to a person who receives it but may also be useful to the person who makes it. It is a way of thinking, a way of clarifying one's own views. This consideration is not very important in dealing with a word like *house*. With a little information we can make a workable definition. But sometimes a little information is not all we need. We may need to think through a very complicated set of relations. We may need a discussion and not a simple definition. Let us take for an example the following discussion of the meaning of the word *labor*.

It is easy to meet with definitions or at least descriptions of the term labour, especially among non-British economists. We need hardly notice the definition of Cicero, who says, "*Labor est functio quaedam vel animi vel corporis.*" If we are thus to make labour include all action of mind or body, it includes all life. . . . Malthus expressly defines labour as follows: "The exertions of human beings employed with a view to remuneration. If the term be applied to other exertions, they must be particularly specified." In this proposition, however, the word remuneration is very uncertain in meaning. Does it mean only wages paid by other persons than the labourer, or does it include the benefit which a labourer may gain directly from his own labour? . . .

It is plain that labour must consist of some energy or action of the body or mind, but it does not follow that every kind of exertion is to be treated in economics. Lay has restricted the term by the following concise definition: *"Travail; action suivie, dirigée vers un but."* The action here contemplated excludes mere play and sport, which carries its whole purpose with it. There must be some extrinsic benefit to be purchased by the action, which moreover must be continued, consistent action, directed steadily to the same end. This correctly describes the great mass of economic labour which is directed simply to the earning of wages and the producing of the commodities which eventually constitute wages. But there is nothing in this definition to exclude the long-continued exertions of a boat's crew training for a race, the steady practice of a company of cricketers, or even the regular constitutional walk of the student who values his good health. Moreover, no considerable continuity of labour is requisite to bring it under economic laws. A poor man who gathers groundsell in the morning and sells it about the streets the same afternoon may complete the circle of economic action within twenty-four hours. . . .

Senior has given a definition of the term in question, saying, "Labour is the voluntary exertion of bodily or mental faculties for the purpose of production." Here the term production is made the scapegoat. Does production include the production of pleasure or prevention of pain in every way? Does it include the training of the cricketer? The word "voluntary," again, excludes the forced labour of slaves and prisoners, not to speak of draught animals. Yet many economic questions arise about the productiveness of the exertions of such agents. . . .

Some later economists consider pain or disagreeableness to be a necessary characteristic of labour, and probably with correctness. Thus Mill defines labour as "muscular or nervous action, including all feelings of a disagreeable kind, all bodily inconvenience or mental annoyance connected with the employment of one's thoughts or muscles, or both, in a particular occupation." He seems to intend that only what is disagreeable, inconvenient or annoying, shall be included. Professor Hearn also says that such effort as the term labour seems to imply is "more or less troublesome." It may be added that in all the dictionaries pain seems to be regarded as a necessary constituent of labour.

Nevertheless it cannot possibly be said that all economic labour is simple pain. Beyond doubt a workman in good health and spirits, and fresh from a good night's rest actually enjoys the customary exertion of his morning task. To a man brought up in the steady round of daily trade and labour, inactivity soon becomes tedious. Happiness has been defined as the reflex of unimpeded energy, and whatever exactly this may mean, there can be no doubt that any considerable degree of pleasure can be attained only by setting up some end to be worked for and then working. The real solution of the difficulty seems to be this—that, however agreeable labour may be when the muscles are recruited and the nerves unstrained, the hedonic condition is always changed as the labour proceeds. As we shall see, continued labour grows more and more painful, and when long-continued becomes almost intolerable. However pleasurable the beginning, the pleasure merges into pain. Now when we are engaged in mere sport, devoid of any conscious perception of future good or evil, exertion will not continue beyond the point when present pain and pleasure are balanced. No motive can exist for further action. But when we have any future utility in view the case is different. The mind of the labourer balances present pain against future good, so that the labour before it is terminated becomes purely painful. Now the problems and theorems of economics always turn upon the point where equality or equilibrium is attained; when labour is itself pleasurable no questions can arise about its continuance. There is the double gain—the pleasure of the labour itself and the pleasure of gaining its produce. No complicated calculus is needed where all is happy and certain. It is on this ground that we may probably dismiss from economic science all sports and other exertions to which may be applied the maxim—leave off as soon as you feel inclined. But it is far otherwise with that advanced point of economic labour when the question arises whether more labour will be repaid by the probability of future good.

I am by no means sure that it is possible to embody in a single definition the view here put forward. If obliged to attempt a definition, I should say that labour includes all exertion of body and/or mind eventually becoming painful if prolonged, and not wholly undertaken for the sake of immediate pleasure. This proposition plainly includes all painful exertion which we undergo in order to gain future pleasures or to ward off pains, in such a way as to leave a probable hedonic balance in our favor; but it does not exclude exertion which, even at the time of exertion, is producing such a balance.—WILLIAM STANLEY JEVONS: *The Principles of Economics*, Chap. 14.[14]

The author ends by putting labor in the general group of "exertion of body and/or mind," and by distinguishing it from other possible types of exertion. He has used the formula of definition. But he arrives at his own definition by a discussion of previous definitions. He criticizes them and indicates his reason for rejecting

[14] From *The Principles of Economics* by William Stanley Jevons. Reprinted by permission of The Macmillan Company.

them. It is through this criticism that he sets up the differentia for his own definition.

Let us take another word, *liberty*, which is probably even more difficult to define than *labor*. Offhand, we think we have a very clear notion of its meaning, but when we try to define it we may become aware of our own ignorance or vagueness. We have some notion, no doubt, that *liberty* means being able to do what one likes. But reflection shows us that we cannot mean that if we hold that the word has any reference to the real world we live in. For no one is free to do what he likes. All sorts of things thwart us, our physical limitations, our intellectual limitations, our economic limitations, social pressures, laws. We can say, of course, that we choose to use the word *liberty* to refer to the state of being able to do what one likes; and that statement, if we are consistent in our use of the word, will constitute a kind of definition. But if we wish to use the word as having some reference to the actual situation of human beings, we must explore the concept more fully.

Such an exploration would undoubtedly lead us very far afield. We would find that we had gone far beyond the kind of vest-pocket definition which appears in a dictionary. We would write an essay or a book. And innumerable essays and books have been written in the attempt to define *liberty*.

How might we go about framing a definition of *liberty?*

The word *liberty* is used to refer to several different things. It may refer to the theological question of the relation of the human will in relation to God's will and foreknowledge. It may refer to the psychological question of whether the human being makes choices or is a very complicated mechanism that responds but does not choose. It may refer to the question of the relation of the individual to society. Before we attempt a definition of the word we obviously must decide which reference here is our concern.

John Stuart Mill begins his famous essay "On Liberty" by indicating the particular aspect of the subject which he intends to treat. "The subject of this Essay is not the so-called Liberty of the Will, so unfortunately opposed to the misnamed doctrine of Philosophical Necessity; but Civil or Social Liberty: The nature and limits of the power which can be legitimately exercised by society over the individual."

Having in this fashion confined his interest to social liberty, Mill

then proceeds to distinguish the different conceptions of social liberty
which have prevailed at different times and places: (1) immunities
under a "governing One, or a governing tribe or caste" who did
not govern "at the pleasure of the governed"; (2) constitutional
checks under the same type of government as above; (3) the right
to elect rulers; (4) the right to protection against the will of the
majority as expressed through government; (5) the right to protection against social pressure. Set up as a scheme we have this:

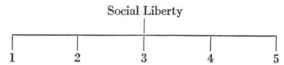

Mill then goes on to point out that in the modern world conceptions 1, 2, and 3 are outmoded, for the historical situations accounting for them no longer prevail. Thus conceptions 4 and 5 are left
as the special content of his subject—which may be called Social
Liberty in its modern reference.

But Social Liberty in its modern reference has various areas of
application, which must be distinguished from each other. These
various areas of application are: (a) liberty of "consciousness"—
liberty of conscience, of thought, and of opinion, and by extension, of expression; (b) liberty of "tastes and pursuits"—liberty
of framing the "plan of our life to suit our own character"; (c)
liberty of "combination"—liberty of individuals to unite, the individuals combining "being supposed to be of full age, and not forced
or deceived." So we can develop our scheme:

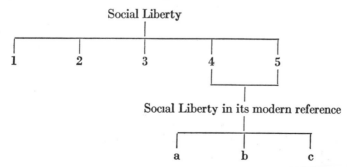

By making this series of distinctions Mill has limited and explained the area of his discussion. He can now proceed to frame

his definition with some assurance that his audience will see where the definition can be applied and by what line of thought it was developed.

All the way through his discussion Mill is conscious of the fact that the liberty of one individual cannot be thought of apart from the liberty of other individuals, for all are members of a society. Therefore, if one individual, in pursuing what he takes to be his liberty, infringes upon or limits the liberty of another individual, he is not exercising his liberty but is doing something else. That is, liberty must be understood as meaning the maximum liberty of all individuals and not the mere opportunity of one individual to do what he pleases.

Having developed that thought, Mill can now define Social Liberty in its modern reference as the pursuit of "our own good in our own way, so long as we do not attempt to deprive others of theirs, or impede their efforts to obtain it." It may be said, of course, that Mill is really defining the term *justifiable liberty* and not the term *liberty*. But this, he says, is the only liberty that "deserves the name." That is, he would use the term *liberty* only to apply to the situation just described, and his definition means something to us because of the discussion that has preceded it.

Let us turn to another famous essay, "What is a University?" by John Henry Newman, as an example of extended definition. This is the first paragraph:

If I were asked to describe as briefly and popularly as I could, what a University was, I should draw my answer from its ancient designation of a *Studium Generale,* or "School of Universal Learning." This description implies the assemblage of strangers from all parts in one spot;—*from all parts;* else, how will you find professors and students for every department of knowledge? and *in one spot;* else, how can there be any school at all? Accordingly, in its simple and rudimental form, it is a school of knowledge of every kind, consisting of teachers and learners from every quarter. Many things are requisite to complete and satisfy the idea embodied in this description; but such as this a University seems to be in its essence, a place for the communication and circulation of thought, by means of personal intercourse, through a wide extent of country.

We remember that both Jevons and Mill move toward a definition through a discussion, but here we see that Newman starts with a definition. The definition is the basis for a discussion, the discussion being a development of the implications of the original definition.

CHANGED USE OF A TERM

We can see another difference between the essay by Mill and that by Newman. Mill looks back over history to see what has been understood by liberty at different times in the past, but the definition he finally gives is for his own time and not for any past time. Newman, too, looks back to the past, and begins his first paragraph by referring to an earlier notion. But he does not contrast the earlier notion with a modern notion. Instead, he uses the old notion to help him define the word *university* in a modern reference. What he draws from the old term *Studium Generale* he applies to the new term *university*.

A study of the use of a term in the past may be useful, then, because of either continuity or contrast. For example, if we are asked to define the term *American democracy*, we may very profitably raise the historical question. Do we understand the same thing by it as the Founding Fathers did? What must we make of the fact that the Founding Fathers did not believe in universal suffrage and that we may? Are there any elements of continuity?

DERIVATION OF A TERM TO BE DEFINED

As it is sometimes useful to know the history of the use of a term, it is sometimes useful to know the derivation of a term. Every word has a history, and the history of the word itself may lead to a fuller notion of its meaning. For instance, it helps us to understand the meaning of the word *philosophy* to learn that it derives from a Greek word meaning the love of wisdom. The derivation may indicate or explain some basic meaning. For instance, an article on asceticism begins as follows:

ASCETICISM: the theory and practice of bodily abstinence and self-mortification, generally religious. The word is derived from a Greek word (ἀσκέω) meaning "to practice," or "to train," and it embodies a metaphor taken from the ancient wrestling place, where victory rewarded those who had best trained their bodies.—*Encyclopaedia Britannica,* 14th edition.

Here the derivation of the word really enlightens us about the significance of self-denial for the religious person: it is like the training of an athlete.

METHODS OF EXTENDED DEFINITION

We begin to see some of the ways in which the simple definition may be extended. We may start by looking into the derivation of the term to be defined. We may follow Newman's method of defining a present term by reference to an old usage. We may look at the history of various meanings of a term as a background for a present meaning, as Mill looks at the history of *liberty*. We may extend the discussion through several stages as Mill does, to locate the precise area in which the definition will apply. We may develop a definition by a series of illustrations, comparisons, and contrasts, as Newman does in the body of his essay. We may do any or all of these things. We may, in fact, do anything that will really help to make our definition clear.

In writing an extended definition we may find, of course, that we are running away from the strict concern of definition into illustrations, for example, or comparisons and contrasts. Other intentions may become dominant over the intention to define. If we are setting out to write a definition, and *only* a definition, this wavering of intention may confuse us and our readers. But definition may be merely the beginning of a piece of exposition, and may be subordinate to other intentions. Then, what is important is to be able to use the method of definition as far as it is fruitful for understanding the subject. Definition is, in the end, a device for reaching understanding.

ANALYSIS: THE TWO KINDS

ANALYSIS is the method of dividing into component parts. The word means loosening into parts. The method can be applied to anything that can be thought of as having parts. We can analyze an object such as a dog, a house, a tree, a picture. We can analyze an idea such as nationalism, religion, or treachery. We can analyze an organization such as a church, a corporation, a university, or a government.

We must make a distinction between PHYSICAL ANALYSIS and CON-
CEPTUAL ANALYSIS.

In physical analysis some object is spatially separated into its
components. If a clockmaker takes a clock apart, he performs a
physical analysis. If a student of zoology dissects a pickled dogfish,
he performs a physical analysis. If a chemist makes a chemical
analysis of a sample of butter, he performs a physical analysis.

Obviously an idea cannot be separated into parts like cogs and
springs or chemical elements. An idea can be analyzed only into
other ideas. For instance, the idea of nationalism can be analyzed
only in terms of human motives, attitudes, and interests. Nor can
an organization be analyzed by spatial separation. For example, a
corporation cannot be analyzed by physically grouping the individual chairs, desks, typewriters, and filing cabinets which appear
in various departments. These objects do not constitute the departments, nor do the physical persons employed in the respective
departments. We can analyze a corporation only by understanding
what constitutes the function of a department.

In dealing with nationalism or a corporation, then, we must perform the analysis in our minds, by the use of our reason. This is
conceptual analysis. It must be remembered, however, that conceptual analysis may be used to report on subjects which have
physical existence. For instance, when the chemist, instead of performing a chemical analysis before his class, describes the composition of a substance, he is giving a conceptual analysis. The fact
that he has earlier made a chemical analysis of the substance in
his laboratory does not mean that the present analysis is physical.

Conceptual analysis is the kind which concerns us here, the kind
which we can perform in our minds and report in words, in a
discourse.

ANALYSIS AND STRUCTURE

Analysis, as we have said, is a method of dividing into parts. In
this statement we should emphasize the word *method*. An analysis
does not take place by accident, but by design, in the light of
some principle. A baby tearing up the morning paper can scarcely
be said to perform an analysis.

We can propose an analysis only if we regard the thing analyzed as constituting a determinate structure. A thing constitutes a structure when its components may be regarded not as assembled at random but as being organized, as having necessary relations to each other. For example, we do not regard a pile of bricks as a structure, but we do so regard a brick wall. We regard an automobile as a structure, a human body, a corporation, a textbook, a tree. In each of these things some principle determines the relation among the parts.

According to our different interests, we may regard the same object as having various kinds of structure. For example, the botanist would regard an apple as one kind of structure, and therefore would analyze it into, shall we say, stem, skin, flesh, seeds, and so forth, whereas a chemist would regard it as another kind and would analyze it into certain chemical elements, or a painter would regard it as still another kind and would analyze it into a pattern of color. Each man would perform his analysis in terms of a particular interest, and the interest prompting his analysis would decide the kind of structure which he took the object to be, and the kind of structure which he took it to be would determine what might be regarded as a part of the structure.

In illustrating the fact that the same thing may be regarded as having different kinds of structure, we have used an example having physical existence, an apple. But the same thing may hold good of something with no physical existence, say a short story. We may regard it as a grammatical structure, for it is made up of words. Or we may regard it as a fictional structure, that is, as being composed of plot, of characters, of theme—things which we can think of and discuss as separate elements. Or an institution may be regarded as having different kinds of structure. For instance, we may regard the family as an educational structure, an economic structure, or a moral structure. Each of these structures implies different relationships among the members of a family.

ANALYSIS: RELATION AMONG PARTS

We have said that a thing may be regarded as a structure when its parts may be regarded not as assembled at random but as being organized, as having necessary relations to each other. So a complete analysis does not merely specify the parts of the thing analyzed but indicates the relation among parts. It tells how the parts fulfill their individual functions in composing the structure in which they participate. It tells what principle binds them together. For instance, a lecturer in political science analyzing the structure of our government would not only name the three main divisions—legislative, judicial, and executive—but would indicate the significance of each in the government. Otherwise, his audience would learn little from him. Or if we analyze a theme into its parts—introduction, discussion, and conclusion—we make our analysis intelligible by telling what constitutes an introduction, what it is supposed to accomplish.

We have said that in making an analysis it is useful to indicate the relation among the parts distinguished. In fact, we may go even further and say that a part is to be distinguished as an element which has some significant relation to the whole. In analyzing the ignition system of an automobile we are not concerned with the color of the insulation on the wires. The color has no significant relation. Or in analyzing a corporation we can scarcely be concerned with the age of the second vice-president or his taste in cigars. We are concerned only with his relation to the corporation as a corporation, not with his individual qualities in so far as they have no bearing on his job.

ANALYSIS AND EXPOSITORY DESCRIPTION

Such analysis as we have been discussing—analysis which divides a thing into its parts—can be regarded as a form of expository description (p. 42). It is a way of explaining the thing analyzed. It is technical in its method, and aims, not at giving a vivid immediate impression, but at leading to an understanding of the thing analyzed. When the analysis is concerned with a type, we have generalized description. In the example below we see that the analysis is of a type of mechanism, not of a particular set of radar equipment. It is concerned with the parts which must be present in any radar set if that set is to fulfill its proper function. We notice that, though the primary intention is to distinguish the parts, there is also a clear indication of the use of each part in the structure.

Practically every radar set is made up of the following major parts or components:

1, A modulator; 2, A radio-frequency oscillator; 3, An antenna with suitable scanning mechanism; 4, A receiver; and 5, An indicator.

While the physical form for each of these components may vary widely from one kind of radar set to another, each radar must have this complement of parts in order to function.

1. The *modulator* is a device for taking power from the primary source (which may be the commercial power line, a special engine or motor-driven generator, or storage batteries) and forming suitable voltage pulses to drive the r-f oscillator in its bursts of radio-frequency oscillations. In other words, it is the modulator which turns on the radio-frequency oscillator to oscillate violently for a millionth of a second or so, turns it off sharply and keeps it in repose until time for the next burst.

2. The *radio-frequency oscillator* is a vacuum tube of suitable design, or a group of such tubes, which will oscillate at the desired radio frequency and give the desired bursts of radio-frequency power when connected to the modulator. The development of suitable oscillator tubes has been one of the major achievements of the radar art. It is a relatively simple job to produce a radio-frequency oscillator which will give oscillations of any desired frequency provided one is satisfied with a power of only a few thousandths of a watt. In the receiving part of a radar circuit this amount of power is adequate. A practical radar transmitter, however, must generate during its momentary bursts of oscillation a power which may run into hundreds of kilowatts. Since the oscillator is turned on a small fraction of the time, the average power is usually hundreds of times less than the peak power, but even the average power may run up to the order of one kilowatt. Thus, practical radar equipment requires extremely high frequency oscillators running at powers thousands of times greater than was thought possible a few years ago.

3. The problem of *antenna* design is also one of the major problems in radar, incomprehensible as this may seem to the operator of a home radio receiver, who finds a few yards of wire strung up on his roof adequate for his purpose. A suitable radar antenna must have the following characteristics:

  a. It must be directional; that is, it must concentrate the radio energy into a definitely defined beam, since this is the method by which the direction to the objects detected is determined.

  b. It must be highly efficient. All of the generated power must go into

the beam and none must leak off into "side lobes" in other directions, since such side lobes may often be fatally confusing; and,

c. The radar antenna must be capable of being directed or scanned
from one point in space to another, and on shipboard and in air-
craft it must frequently be stabilized to take out the motions of the
ship or airplane itself.

An antenna may be made directional either by building it up of an
array of small antennas or dipoles, suitably spaced and phased to concentrate the energy in one direction, or it may be built on the searchlight principle of spraying the energy into a large parabolic "mirror,"
which focuses the energy into a beam. In either case, the larger the
antenna, the sharper the beam for any given wave length. Sometimes
antennas may be longer in one direction than the other, giving a beam
which is sharper in the first direction and thus fan shaped.

The *scanning* of the portion of space which the radar set is intended
to cover must usually be done by mechanical movement of the antenna
structure itself. This means that the structure, whatever its size, must
swing around or up and down to direct the beam in the necessary
direction. In certain cases where one needs to scan only a small sector,
techniques have been worked out for rapid electrical scanning not requiring the motion of the whole antenna structure itself. So far, however, there has been no method for extending this rapid electrical
scanning to cover more than a relatively small sector. Radars for directing
guns which need accurate and fast data in a small sector are making
use, however, of this valuable technique.

To carry the radio-frequency energy from the oscillator to the antenna, and the echo from the antenna to the receiver, wires and coaxial
cables are used at ordinary wave lengths. For microwaves, however, it
is more efficient to use wave guides, which essentially are carefully proportioned hollow pipes—and the transmission system hence is often
called "plumbing."

4. The problem of the *receiver* for radar is also a complex one. In
practically all radars the superheterodyne principle is employed, which
involves generating at low power a radio frequency fairly close to that
received, and "beating" this against the received signals, forming an
intermediate frequency, which is then amplified many times. Curiously
enough the crystal, used as a detector and mixer, has again come into
its own in microwave receivers. The peculiar characteristics of pulse signals require that receivers be built with extremely fast response, much
faster even than that required in television. The final stages must prepare
the signals for suitable presentation in the indicator. The receiver nor-

mally occupies a relatively small box in the complete radar set, and yet this box represents a marvel of engineering ingenuity. A particularly difficult piece of development is concerned with a part closely connected with the receiver. This is a method of disconnecting the receiver from the antenna during intervals when the transmitter is operating so that the receiver will not be paralyzed or burned out by the stupendous bursts of radio-frequency energy generated by the transmitter. Within a millionth of a second after the transmitter has completed its pulse, however, the receiver must be open to receive the relatively weak echo signals; but now the transmitter part of the circuit must be closed off so it will not absorb any of this energy.

5. It is the *indicator* of a radar that presents the information collected in a form best adapted to efficient use of the set. Nearly (but not quite) all radar indicators consist of one or more cathode-ray tubes. In the simplest or "A" type of presentation the electron beam is given a deflection proportional to time in one direction—say, horizontally—and proportional to the strength of the echo pulse in the other—say, vertically. If no signals are visible, then one sees a bright horizontal line (the "time base") across the tube face, the distance along this line representing time elapsed after the outgoing pulse. A returning echo then gives a V-shaped break in the line at the point corresponding to the time it took the echo to come back. The position of the "pip" along this line measures the distance to the reflecting object. There are many variations of this type of indicator for special purposes, but most radars have an A-scope, even when other types are also provided.

Many types of radar whose antennas "scan" various directions employ the PPI tube. Here the time base starts from the center of the tube and moves radially outward in a direction corresponding to that in which the antenna is pointing. This time base rotates in synchronism with the antenna. The returning signal, instead of causing a break in the time base, simply intensifies its brilliance for an instant. Hence each signal appears as a bright spot of light at a position corresponding to the range and bearing of the target. Thus a maplike picture of all reflecting objects appears in the cathode-ray tube face.

Since the antenna can usually be rotated only slowly (e.g., from 1 to 20 r.p.m.) and since the light from an ordinary cathode-ray tube fades away almost instantly, one might expect not to see a "map" at all, but only bright flashes at various spots as the antenna revolves. Some way had to be found to make the brightness of these flashes persist for many seconds after they were produced. Special screens were developed which continue to glow for some time after being lighted by a signal. Thus the whole map is displayed at once.—OFFICE OF WAR INFORMATION: *Radar: A Report on Science at War.*[15]

FUNCTIONAL ANALYSIS

The kind of analysis which we have been discussing provides the answer to such a question as, "How is it put together?" But when we undertake to answer the question, "How does it work?" we give what is called FUNCTIONAL ANALYSIS. We have to say how the parts of a thing, whatever that thing is, relate to each other in action so that that thing fulfills its characteristic function. We are, furthermore, concerned with the stages of a process. We have to explain how something comes about, and this means that our analysis will be in a time sequence.

Since it is in time sequence, this kind of analysis is a form of expository narration. It may be of a particular event, say the stages by which an inventor arrived at the solution of a problem, or it may be of an event which is characteristically repeated, say the manufacture of hydrochloric acid or the training of a football squad. In the latter instance, the analysis of the stages of an event characteristically repeated, we get generalized narration.

It is easiest to understand functional analysis if we think of it as applied to some mechanism. If we take an alarm clock, for instance, we can see how the spring provides power, how this power is controlled by a system of reducing gears and a checking device so that it does not expend itself in one spurt, how the pace of expenditure is evenly controlled so that the movement of the hands serves as a register of time, and how at a certain fixed point the alarm is released. We are concerned with the parts here, but only in so far as they relate to the special function of the mechanism. In so far as we undertake to explain the process by which the special function is fulfilled, we are giving a functional analysis. In other words, our primary concern is with stages in a process, and the parts are interesting to us only in so far as they are associated with stages. To take another example, it is not functional analysis to list the components of apple pie and describe their relation to each other,

15 From *Radar: A Report on Science at War,* issued by the Office of War Information, sponsored by the Office of Scientific Research and Development, the War Department and the Navy Department, obtainable from the Superintendent of Documents, U. S. Government Printing Office.

but it is functional analysis to tell how to make a pie. When we give these directions, we are dealing with stages in a process.

The same general principle, the concern with stages, applies when we are dealing, not with a mechanism or with directions for making or doing something, but with an organization or institution. It is one thing, for instance, to describe the organization of our government, and it is quite another to tell how a bill becomes law, how legality may be tested in the Supreme Court, and how the law may be enforced. In telling how the bill becomes law, and so on, we are giving a functional analysis.

Functional analysis, then, is the method by which we distinguish the stages in a process which may be regarded as having a characteristic function or purpose. Though we use the word *functional* to describe the particular kind of analysis, we may distinguish between the characteristic function and the characteristic purpose of whatever is analyzed. An example may enlighten us. If we are discussing a university, we can treat the subject in terms of purpose, for it is an institution created by men to gain certain ends. But if we are discussing the circulation of the blood, we can treat the subject only in terms of a characteristic function. We cannot say that purpose is involved. Or to take another contrasted pair of examples, if we give directions for making an apple pie, we are treating our subject in terms of purpose, but if we discuss the stages of development of an apple, we are treating the subject in terms of function. In both instances we can, of course, observe a regular pattern, but in one case we interpret the pattern as representing purpose and in the other as representing function.

Sometimes we can fruitfully distinguish both function and purpose in a thing which we wish to analyze. For instance, it might be said that we give an analysis of a radar set in terms of function: it operates because of certain natural laws which cannot be said to represent purpose. But at the same time the equipment is constructed to use those natural laws for a purpose. Man has a purpose in constructing the equipment. To construct the set man has manipulated certain materials in terms of natural laws (the only way he could manipulate the materials) to achieve a certain purpose. He cannot manipulate his circulatory system. So we may take the fact of manipulation as the point of distinction.

What is the significance of this distinction for purposes of exposition? It is a way of defining our subject, of knowing exactly what sort of structure we are dealing with. And that in itself is a step toward understanding.

Below is an example of functional analysis applied to a mechanism, something created by man to fulfill a certain purpose, a radar set. Contrast the method used here with the previous analysis of the set into its parts.

In radar, unlike communications, the transmitter and the receiver are located at the same place, and more often than not have a common antenna. The transmitter is actually sending out energy only a very small part of the time; it sends out this energy in very intense bursts of small duration, called pulses. These pulses may be only a millionth of a second long. After each pulse, the transmitter waits a relatively long time—a few thousandths of a second—before sending out the next pulse. During the interval between pulses, the receiver is working and the signals it receives are the echoes of the powerful transmitted pulse from nearby objects. The nearest objects will give echoes coming very soon after the transmitter pulse is finished; those farther away give later returns. The elapsed time between the transmission of the pulse and the reception of its echo measures the distance of the object giving that echo—ship, airplane, mountain, or building—from the place where the radar set is located. This is possible because the elapsed time is just that required for the pulse, which travels with the speed of light, to get there and back. Light travels very fast, as everybody knows, hence these intervals are very small. Their exact measurement is one of the technical triumphs of modern radar. Since light goes 186,000 miles a second, or 328 yards each millionth of a second, and since it must travel twice—out and back—the distance from radar to target, an object 1,000 yards from the radar will give an echo only six-millionths of a second later than the transmitted pulse. This is a rather short time, by prewar standards, but we have learned how to measure time like this with an accuracy which corresponds to only 5 or 10 yards range, or about one-thirtieth of a millionth of a second.

The use of pulses, as we have seen, gives a simple means of measuring the range. How, then, is the direction in which a target lies determined? This is done by providing the radar with a directional antenna, which sends out the pulses in a narrow beam, like a searchlight. This antenna may be rotated as the pulses are sent out, and we get back a "pip" (radar slang for a target indication) when the antenna is pointed toward its target. We get the strongest pip when the beam of energy sent out by the radar is pointed directly at the target. The bearing of the antenna

—which is also the bearing of the target—may then be read off and used to point a warship's guns, or set the course of a bomber, or direct a fighter to intercept an enemy plane, or for other use the particular purpose of the equipment dictates.

An even more spectacular indication of the direction and range of the target is obtained with the use of the PPI—Plan Position Indicator. In this case, the radar echoes are caused to draw a map on the face of a cathode-ray tube. The radar operator could imagine himself suspended high above the set, whether on a ship or plane or on the ground, looking down on the scene spread out below. No matter how many targets surround the radar set, each is indicated by a blob of light on the tube face—the direction of the blob from the center indicating the target's range. The whole picture is there. It is not like television; the blobs do not actually look like ships or planes, but are interpretable to a trained operator.

Still other ways of displaying radar echoes are used. On a battleship, for example, where exact range is desired to lay the 16-inch guns, the radar echoes are so displayed that the operator can read a range scale down to a few yards. In the case of Army antiaircraft fire, the radar antenna actually moves automatically so that it always points at the plane without help from an operator, and the guns follow automatically by remote control. Other types of radar use other types of displays, designed to perform one or another special purpose.

What we may call the sharpness of vision of a radar set—its ability to distinguish separately the echoes from two targets close together and at the same distance from the radar—depends on the sharpness of the radar beam. With an antenna of given size, the beam will become sharper and sharper as the wave length decreases. In fact, for a given antenna size, the beam width is just proportional to the wave length. The earliest radar worked on wave lengths of several meters, with correspondingly broad beams, unless large antennas were used. Then there was a great flowering of equipment working near a meter and a half, which was, at the beginning of the war, about the shortest wave length at which radio techniques had been worked out. The wartime period of development has witnessed an intensive exploitation of shorter and shorter wave lengths.
—OFFICE OF WAR INFORMATION: *Radar: A Report on Science at War.*

Here is an example of functional analysis applied to an organization, our financial system. This is not a very orderly piece of exposition as compared with the analysis of radar. But we can reduce it to order by extracting the answers to several questions: (1) What would be the four functions of a financial system in our society?

(2) How were these functions related to each other to produce the present system? (3) How would these functions be related in what Brandeis calls a beneficent system?

How the masters of credit-financing gradually, through processes of interlocking directorates, achieved their complete overlordship of finance, industry, insurance, communication, and transportation is a long story— too long to be told here. The interested reader can get it most vividly in Louis (now Justice) Brandeis' *Other People's Money*. In that book he declares:

"The dominant element in our financial oligarchy is the investment banker. Associated banks, trust companies and life insurance companies are his tools. Controlled railroads, public service and industrial corporations are his subjects. Though properly but middlemen, these bankers bestride as masters America's business world, so that practically no large enterprise can be undertaken successfully without their participation or approval."

It is well to ponder these words: "practically no large enterprise can be undertaken successfully without their participation or approval." They are an ironic commentary upon the statement so often made by the defenders of the economic *status quo* that the present system is one which encourages the utmost freedom of initiative. "These bankers bestride as masters America's business world."

"The key to their power," Brandeis continues, "is combination." In the first place, there was the legal consolidation of banks and trust companies; then there were affiliations brought about by stockholders, voting trusts, and interlocking directorates in banking institutions which were not legally connected; and finally, there were the gentlemen's agreements, joint transactions, and "banking ethics," which unofficially eliminated competition among the investment bankers.

In the second place, the organization of railroads into huge systems, the large consolidations of public service corporations, and the creation of industrial trusts directly played into the hands of the associated New York bankers, for these businesses were so vast that no local, independent bank could supply the necessary funds.

These factors alone, however, "could not have produced the Money Trust . . . another and more potent factor of combination was added." It is this third factor that is most astounding.

Investment bankers were dealers in stocks, bonds, and notes. As such, they performed one necessary function in our kind of society. In order that they should possess the public's confidence, they had to be able, with complete objectivity, to estimate the soundness of what they sold. Hence they could not themselves, properly, have an interest in the investments. They had to be middlemen pure and simple.

But not so. Through the purchases of voting stock they became the directing power in the very enterprises—railroads, public service and industrial corporations—that were the *issuers* of the securities they sold.

But more than this. They purchased voting stock in the great enterprises, like life insurance companies and other corporate reservoirs of the people's savings, that were the buyers of securities. So they made for themselves a ready market for the securities which they themselves issued.

And finally, they became the governing power in banks and trust companies. These were the depositories of the savings of the people. As holders of these savings they were able to make loans to (their own) corporations; these in turn could issue securities that the investment bankers could readily sell to their own corporations as well as buy at figures acceptable to themselves and sell at conveniently higher prices to their own depositors and the public.

"Thus four distinct functions, each essential to business, and each exercised, originally, by a distinct set of men became united in the investment banker. It is to this union of business functions that the existence of the Money Trust is mainly due."

And Brandeis concludes his analysis with this ominous observation:

"The development of our financial oligarchy followed, in this respect, lines with which the history of political despotism has familiarized us: usurpation, proceeding by gradual encroachment rather than by violent acts; subtle and often long-concealed concentration of distinct functions, which are beneficent when separately administered, and dangerous only when combined in the same persons. It was by such processes as these that Caesar Augustus became master of Rome."—H. A. OVERSTREET: *A Declaration of Interdependence,* Chap. 3.[16]

CHRONOLOGICAL ANALYSIS

Sometimes we are called upon to deal with a subject which we cannot easily treat with reference to function or purpose. For instance, a historical event.

It is true that a historical event may involve human purposes, many human purposes, but the event itself cannot be understood merely by reference to those purposes. The individual purposes

[16] Reprinted from *A Declaration of Interdependence* by H. A. Overstreet, by permission of W. W. Norton & Company, Inc. Copyright 1937 by the publishers. The late Justice Brandeis is quoted by permission of Susan Brandeis.

may be too numerous, too various, and too confused. By the same token we cannot find a characteristic function. Or different people may find different functions, as it were, according to their interpretation of history. For example, it is hardly precise to say that the French Revolution had a function in our sense of the word, in the sense that the human heart has a function in the circulation of the blood.

If we cannot discuss an event, however, with reference to a purpose or function, we may, at least, try to distinguish the stages in the process. We can sort out the steps. Our concern is to establish the facts in their chronological order and to arrange them so that they can be grasped as some sort of pattern. We may want to do this as a preliminary to further study, but if we can do no more we can at least try to see the pattern of sequence in time. This kind of analysis we may call CHRONOLOGICAL ANALYSIS.

For example, in an article on the last days of General Rommel, who was in command of the German forces supposed to defend France against the British and American landings on D-Day, June 6, 1944, the author analyzes the complex event into its stages:

> There were to be five acts in the swift concluding drama of Rommel's career—and of his world. Roughly stated, their themes in sequence were: initial stupefaction, improvisation, frustration, desperation, and final liquidation.—WILLIAM HARLAN HALE: "The End of Marshal Rommel."

Then the author proceeds to discuss each stage. The chronological analysis gives him the frame for his treatment, for his interpretation.

CAUSAL ANALYSIS

We often want to go beyond a mere sequence in time. One way to do this is to consider cause and effect. CAUSAL ANALYSIS is concerned with two questions: "What caused this?" and "Given this set of circumstances, what effect will follow?" In answering the first we must reason from effect back to cause, and in answering the second, from cause forward to effect. Again, as with chronological analysis, this kind of analysis usually takes the form of expository narration. We are accustomed to think of cause and effect in a time sequence, a chain of happenings.

CAUSE

What do we understand by cause? We all have a rough-and-ready notion. We have to have a notion of it in order to manage our daily lives. The burnt child shuns the fire only after he has learned that a certain act, putting his finger in the flame, is followed by a certain unpleasant effect, a burn. He has made a connection between events.

Cause is a certain kind of connection between events. It is the kind of connection that enables us to say that without event A, event B would not have come about, and whenever you have A you will have B.[17]

IMMEDIATE CONNECTION

The connection between cause and effect, between our A and our B, is relatively immediate. Sometimes we encounter an idea of cause that ignores the immediate connection—that regards as a cause of B whatever goes to provide, however remotely, the conditions that have resulted in the existence of B. In the poem "Flower in the Crannied Wall," by Tennyson, we see that idea:

> Flower in the crannied wall,
> I pluck you out of the crannies,
> I hold you here, root and all, in my hand,
> Little flower—but *if* I could understand
> What you are, root and all, and all in all,
> I should know what God and man is.

The poet says that if he could explain the flower he could explain God and man. He is here thinking of a tissue of relationships binding the whole universe so that to know the "cause" of the flower would be to know the entire universe.

To take another example, one might say, by this wide use of the

[17] The use of the word *event* here may be objected to. It may be said, for instance, that the word *thing* might be substituted, at least on some occasions, for the word *event*. We may say that a nail is the cause of the fact that the picture hangs on the wall, and that a nail is a thing. But it is not the nail as a thing that sustains the picture. It is its state of being in the wall that causes the picture to be sustained, and its state of being in the wall is an event. There must be things, of course, for there to be events, but the event is what we are concerned with. The state of a thing is an event, in the meaning of the word in our discussion.

word *cause*, that the birth of the grandfather (A) is the "cause" of the death of the grandson (B)—for had the grandfather not existed, the grandson would not have existed, and had the grandson not existed, he could not have died.

In our discussion, however, we are concerned with a more immediate idea of cause: the death of the grandson is in our ordinary view caused by, shall we say, a fall from a stepladder and not by the birth of the grandfather. By and large, the more immediate the relation between A and B the more certainly it can be discussed as cause.

CAUSE AND INTEREST

What we take to be the cause of an event is, in one way, dictated by our special interest in the event. When the little grandson falls from the stepladder and is killed, a neighbor, commenting on the event, would be satisfied by the fact of the fall from the ladder as the cause. But the mother might take her own carelessness as the cause: she left the stepladder standing on the edge of the back porch instead of putting it away in the closet where it belonged. Or a physiologist might take a more scientific view of the cause and say that death was the result of a fracture of the skull of such and such a nature.

In its own perspective, in relation to the special interest brought to bear on the event, each of these statements may be true. What is important is to know what we are doing when we take a particular line of interest to explain an event.

A CONDITION

An event does not take place in complete isolation. It takes place in the world, and many factors constitute its setting. To study the cause of something we must give some attention to the setting, the situation in which it occurs.

Let us take a simple instance, one that could be set up as an experiment. To a clockwork device which will sway back and forth when hung on a string, we attach a little bell. The bell will ring as the device oscillates on its string. The whole thing is hung inside a large glass jar. When the mechanism swings, we can hear the bell ring. But let us pump the air out of the jar. The bell will continue to swing back and forth and the clapper will strike the sides of the bell, but now we can hear no sound. The bell does not ring.[18]

We know why. For there to be a sound, there must be a medium in which the sound waves can travel to our ears. When there was air in the jar there was a sound because the air was the medium for the waves. But when there is no air, there is no sound.

In this situation we may call the air a CONDITION. And a condition, as we use the word, is whatever factor existing in a situation will permit the effect to appear. It is a factor that we regard as a kind of background to the event being considered. Yet it must be a significant background. Some background factors are not significant. For instance, in our experiment the color of the glass of the jar is not significant. It has no relation to the event. A change in the color of the glass will not alter the event.[19]

[18] This account of the experiment is paraphrased from L. S. Stebbing, *A Modern Introduction to Logic*, 2nd ed., London, 1933, pp. 270-71.

[19] How do we distinguish a condition from a cause? If, in our jar experiment, we are thinking of cause in its most immediate connection, we may take the stroke of the clapper against the side of the bell to be the cause of the sound. In that case, we regard the motion generated by the clockwork mechanism to be, like the presence of the air, a condition. But we might take the motion of the mechanism to be the cause, and regard the free-swinging clapper as a condition, a factor that permits the event to take place.

So we cannot make an absolute distinction between condition and cause. We must return to our notion that the interest we bring to bear on a situation is significant in our taking one factor rather than another to be the cause. We focus our interest on one factor, and assume the presence of the others. For instance, Tennyson, looking at his flower in the crannied wall, might have said that the cause was the fact that a bird had dropped a seed there. But without the conditions of nutrition, moisture, heat, and light, he would not have had the flower. When he selected one factor as the cause of the event, he was assuming the presence of the others. In a fuller sense, then, *the* cause of the flower is the complex of factors, of conditions. And so it may be said of any event.

What is important in thinking about cause is to know what we are doing if we take some single factor to be the cause of an event. We must try to know how the factor we have selected is related to other factors. Or if we take a group of factors to be the cause, we must try to know what relation they bear to each other and to the event. And this leads us to the distinction, discussed above, between two kinds of condition.

SUFFICIENT CONDITION AND NECESSARY CONDITION

There are two kinds of condition, SUFFICIENT CONDITION and NECESSARY CONDITION.

Let us take a situation in which the event B occurs. In this situation X is a factor, a condition. The condition X is a sufficient condition if, other things being the same, B occurs whenever X is present. But suppose that B occurs on some occasions when X is not present. For example, the bell of our experiment might be heard when some other gas than air was present in the jar. In that case the air is a sufficient condition, but it is not necessary: some other gas will do. Or to take another example, we may say that whenever we do not bank the furnace at night, the fire goes out. Not banking the furnace is, then, a sufficient condition. But it is not a necessary condition. The furnace may also go out if the damper is closed or if there is not enough fuel.

To illustrate a necessary condition, we may take a situation in which B never occurs when the condition Y is absent. It is necessary for Y to be present for B to occur. Thus we may say that nutrition is a necessary condition of human life, or that fuel is a necessary condition for the functioning of the furnace.

But we can have a condition that is necessary and not sufficient. To have the spark plugs in order is a necessary condition for the running of our automobile. But this is not a sufficient condition. Among other things, we must have the battery connected. Nor is nutrition a sufficient condition of human life. Many other conditions must prevail at the same time for life to exist.

THE PRINCIPLE OF UNIFORMITY

When we say that A is the cause of B, we are not merely referring to the particular case of a particular A and a particular B. We are also implying that a general principle exists, that under the same circumstances any A would cause a B. We imply a principle of uniformity behind the particular case. Let us take a simple instance:

Tom asks, "Why did Jane behave so strangely last night at dinner?"

Jack replies, "Because she was mad at her husband."

Tom asks, "How do you know?"

Jack replies, "That's the way she always behaves when she gets mad at him."

Tom asks, "You must have been around the family a lot?"

Jack replies, "Sure, I lived in the house for a year."

When Jack says that the cause of Jane's conduct was her anger at her husband he is not merely commenting on the particular instance. And Tom's further question elicits the fact that a principle of uniformity is involved: Jane behaves this way *every* time she gets angry with her husband. The principle here may not be one on which we can depend with any great degree of certainty. On some future occasion she may not merely be short with her husband at dinner but may kick the cat, get a divorce, or shoot her husband in the shoulder with a Smith and Wesson .38. But past observation gives us some degree of probability that when Jane is angry with her husband she merely behaves in a certain way at dinner, that a principle of uniformity is involved.

The same principle is involved in what we call a law of nature. A chemist says that when we ignite hydrogen in the presence of oxygen we will get water, H_2O. The element hydrogen and the element oxygen will always behave the same way under specified conditions. At least we believe that to be true because the two elements have always behaved that way in the past. We must appeal to experience and to a number of instances.

Furthermore, the principle of uniformity refers only to the essential characteristics of the situation. For instance, it doesn't matter whether the laboratory worker igniting hydrogen in the presence of oxygen is a Catholic or a Jew, a Republican or a Democrat, a Chinese or a Greek. Or to take Charles Lamb's story of the boy who accidentally discovered how to roast a pig by burning down a house, the boy had not isolated the essential characteristic of the situation: he had not learned that he didn't have to burn down a house every time he wanted roast pig but could make a small fire in the yard. He had not isolated the essential characteristic of fire that would do the roasting.

Or let us examine the treatment of the sick in a certain primitive tribe. The medicine man undertakes to cure the patient by a draught of a brew, the sacrifice of three cocks, and a dance around the pallet. In a fair number of instances the patient recovers. A modern physician examining the situation regards the sacrifice and dancing as irrelevant to a cure. But he analyzes the brew and discovers that one of the plants always present has a purgative effect. He has located the essential characteristic, and now only has to persuade the tribe that a dose of castor oil is cheaper, quicker, and better for stomach-ache than the medicine man's ritual. The principle of uniformity applies to the essential characteristic, the effect of castor oil on the human body.

REASONING ABOUT CAUSE

How do we reason about the cause-and-effect relation in a situation?

To begin with we must keep in mind two primary notions:

1. A cannot be the cause of B if A is ever absent when B is present.

2. A cannot be the cause of B if B is ever absent when A is present.

This is but another way of saying that, under a given set of circumstances, A and B are uniformly related.

Let us notice the phrase, "under a given set of circumstances." It is relatively easy in a laboratory to control the circumstances of an experiment, and to repeat the experiment any number of times in the same circumstances. This gives the experimenter the chance to try different combinations of factors until he has isolated the one factor or the group of factors which he can regard as a cause. If, for example, his situation has factors A, X, Y, and Z as possible causes for the effect B, he can show by a process of elimination that A will cause B, and that X, Y, and Z will not.

But it is hard to control the circumstances outside of the laboratory. And many events in the outside world that we want to explain cannot be repeated at will. We must examine the cases we have and try to make sense of them. Furthermore, many events are enormously complicated. More than one factor contributes to the effect, and we have a complex and not a simple cause. Situations involving human behavior are difficult to treat in terms of cause and effect, but we are constantly making the effort despite the complexity of factors involved. The advertising man, the politician, the teacher, the mother of a family, the sociologist, the historian—they are all trying to reason about human behavior. We must make the

effort, even if we know that we can scarcely hope for a full measure
of success.

Even if we cannot hope for full success in dealing with complicated situations we can at least reduce our margin of error by
remembering certain things. First, we can examine the situation to
try to see what is essential in it. In every event there are certain
factors that are not relevant to the event, things that are merely
associated with it. We must rule those factors out of our consideration.

For an example, we can take the following passage:

Whenever I see the movement of a locomotive I hear the whistle and
see the valves opening and wheels turning; but I have no right to conclude that the whistling and the turning of wheels are the cause of the
movement of the engine.

The peasants say that a cold wind blows in late spring because the
oaks are budding, and really every spring cold winds do blow when
the oak is budding. But I do not know what causes the cold winds to
blow when the oak buds unfold, I cannot agree with the peasants that
the unfolding of the oak buds is the cause of the cold wind, for the force
of the wind is beyond the influence of the buds. I see only a coincidence
of occurrences such as happens with all the phenomena of life, and I
see that however much and however carefully I observe the hands of the
watch, and the valves and wheels of the engine, and the oak, I shall
not discover the cause of the bells ringing, the engine moving, or of the
winds of spring. To do that I must entirely change my point of view and
study the laws of the movement of steam, of the bells, and of the wind.
—LEO TOLSTOY: *War and Peace*, Book XI, Chap. 1.

The fact that something is merely associated with something else
in time does not mean that it is to be regarded as either cause or
effect of the thing. In fact, one of the commonest failures in reasoning about cause and effect is to assume that if something comes
after something else it is to be regarded as the effect. The Russian
peasant in Tolstoy's novel thinks the cold wind is the effect of the
budding of the oak because it comes after it. To avoid such an
error, we must try to find the essential characteristic in the situation we are studying.

We must remember, too, that we are concerned with a principle
of uniformity. That means that we must consider more than one
case. We must check other situations which seem similar to our

situation in order to find what is constant from one to the other. For example, if a historian should wish to find what situations provoke revolutions, he would study as many revolutions as possible to locate the common factors. Then he might venture a conclusion. But studying one revolution would scarcely give him grounds for a conclusion. When we try to find the cause of a given effect, we appeal to what we know about uniformities beyond the particular situation.

We must remember that we are dealing with a complex of factors. Therefore we must not be too ready to seize on one factor as *the* cause. We must analyze as fully as possible the factors involved and try to see what group of factors must be present for our effect to take place. In situations involving human behavior, for example, a historical event, we may have difficulty distinguishing between factors that are relevant to the event and factors that are present as mere background. If we can accomplish this much, we have done a great deal. Then if we discuss some single factor or group of factors as cause, we must remember the relation of that factor or group of factors to the other factors present.

One last caution: in studying a situation we must try to be systematic. In the foregoing discussion of cause many of the ideas have probably struck the reader as something he already knew. He *has* known them. He has been making judgments of cause and effect all his life—in fishing and hunting, in games, in gardening, in laboratory work, in crossing the street. Being acquainted with the ideas is not, however, quite enough. One must make a practice of applying them systematically to a situation. If the reader can think straight about a problem of cause and effect, then it will be easy for him to write well about it. And to think straight, he must be systematic in applying ideas (see Appendix on Causal Analysis, p. 475).

EXPOSITORY METHODS AND THEIR USES

In this chapter we have considered various expository methods in relatively pure form, for example, definition by itself, or illustration by itself. But in actual practice the methods are often mixed. We move from one to another as the occasion demands. This is only natural, for the methods are methods of thought and in treating the same subject we may be compelled to use different kinds of thinking to reach a full understanding. Or in appealing to a single interest we may have to use different methods. Suppose we are dealing with the question, "What is it worth?" We have to make an evaluation of whatever the "it" happens to be. But to make an evaluation we may have to classify the thing, then analyze it, then think of its effects, then compare it with a standard we set up for the kind of thing it is.

We must not be bound by the methods. We must see them as tools which we use. And at any moment we should be able to use whatever will accomplish the purpose at hand.

SUMMARY

EXPOSITION is the kind of discourse which explains or clarifies a subject. It appeals to the understanding, and can be applied to anything which challenges the understanding.

A piece of exposition may be regarded as the answer to a question, whether or not the question has in reality been asked. In giving a piece of exposition one should know what question, or questions, he wishes to answer, what INTEREST he wishes to appeal to. For example, "What is it?" "What does it mean?" "How is it put together?" "How does it work?" "When did it exist or occur?" "What is it worth?" If a writer wishes to appeal to more than one interest, he should keep these various interests distinct and should establish the relationship among them.

IDENTIFICATION and ILLUSTRATION are simple ways of answering the question, "What is it?"

Identification is a kind of pointing by language, a way of locating the subject in time and place, or in relation to some system. When it becomes elaborate it tends to move over into other types of exposition, such as comparison or classification.

Illustration is the method employed when some class or group is identified by giving a particular instance of the class or group. The particular instance may be an object, an event, a person, an idea—anything which may be conceived of as belonging to a certain class or group.

EXPOSITORY DESCRIPTION or TECHNICAL DESCRIPTION is the kind of description which does not aim at presenting a vivid impression of its subject, as does ordinary or SUGGESTIVE DESCRIPTION, but aims at giving information about its subject. It is scientific rather than artistic in its nature. GENERALIZED DESCRIPTION is expository description applied to a class.

EXPOSITORY NARRATION corresponds to ordinary narration as expository description corresponds to ordinary description. It is narration used to give information, and may be applied to a class to give GENERALIZED NARRATION.

In COMPARISON we clarify a subject by indicating similarities between two or more things, in CONTRAST by indicating differences. Comparison and contrast as methods of exposition are most effective when used systematically. This means that they should represent some purpose and should be undertaken in some area of interest. Comparison and contrast may be organized in either of two ways. We may fully present one item, and then fully present another. Or we may present one part of one item and then a part of the other, until we have touched on all the parts relevant to our comparison or contrast. The methods, of course, may sometimes be mixed.

CLASSIFICATION and DIVISION are ways of thinking in terms of a system of classes. A class is a group whose members have significant characteristics in common. What constitutes a significant characteristic, however, may vary according to the interest involved. For instance, a cosmetic-maker may classify women by complexion and the secretary of a Y.W.C.A. by religious affiliation. A system is a set of classes ranging from a most inclusive class down through less and less inclusive classes. Division represents a downward movement of subdivision by classes from a most inclusive class through less and less inclusive classes. Classification, however, starts with individuals, arranges them in groups, and then relates those groups to more inclusive groups above. To be useful a scheme of classes must conform to the following rules of division:

I. There can be only one principle of division applied at each stage.

II. The subgroups under any group must exhaust that group.

III. The same principle of division that is applied in the first stage must be continued through successive stages if such exist.

DEFINITION is one way to answer the question, "What is it?" But strictly speaking, definition is of a word, or phrase, and not of the thing indicated by the word or phrase. It is a way of telling how properly to use the word or phrase. It sets the limit of meaning. But a definition cannot be made without knowledge of the thing behind the word. So the process of definition may lead to an enlargement of understanding not only of the word but of the thing referred to.

A definition has two parts, the element to be defined and the element that defines. The elements are parts of an equation. That is, one may be used for the other in a discourse without changing the meaning.

The process of definition is the placing of the *to-be-defined* in a group (called the GENUS) and the differentiating of it from other members of the same group (SPECIES) by pointing out the qualities which distinguish it (DIFFERENTIA).

Definition is not only of some term but is for somebody. The audience must be considered, and the definition must refer to what the audience knows or is willing to learn. The language and the experience of the audience must be regarded. There must be a common ground for the definition.

Once the common ground is established, there are certain principles to be regarded:

I. The *to-be-defined* must be equivalent to the *definer*.

II. The *to-be-defined* must not be part of the *definer*.

III. The *definer* must not be negative unless the *to-be-defined* is negative.

For a complicated *to-be-defined* the simple definition may not be satisfactory. It is sometimes impossible to appeal to a generally accepted notion, and the writer must develop his own definition in detail. For example, a word like *democracy* or *liberty* cannot be defined simply. It requires an EXTENDED DEFINITION, a discussion.

The DERIVATION of a word is sometimes helpful in setting up a definition, even when the application of the word has changed during its history.

ANALYSIS is the method of dividing into component parts. It can be applied to anything that can be thought of as having parts. There are two kinds of analysis, PHYSICAL ANALYSIS and CONCEPTUAL ANALYSIS. In physical analysis some object is spatially separated into its components, as when a clockmaker takes a clock apart. But things like ideas and institutions cannot be dealt with except in the mind, by the use of reason, as when we analyze the organization of a government. Conceptual analysis, the kind which is performed in the mind and can be reported in words, is what concerns us here.

We can propose an analysis only if we regard the thing to be analyzed as having a structure. A thing has a structure when its components may be regarded not as assembled at random but as being organized, as having necessary relations to each other. The same thing may be regarded as being different kinds of structures. The botanist regards the apple as one kind of structure, and the chemist, as another. The same principle may apply to things which cannot be physically analyzed, such as ideas or organizations.

Analysis when fully realized not only divides into parts but indicates the relation among parts, their place in the structure. In fact, we may regard a part as whatever can be described as having a necessary place in a structure.

FUNCTIONAL ANALYSIS answers the question, "How does it work?" It is concerned not primarily with the parts of a thing analyzed but with the stages of some sequence. This means that functional analysis is a kind of expository narration.

Functional analysis can be applied to anything which involves a process: to the working of a mechanism or the working of an institution, to natural processes, such as the growth of a seed, or to human processes, such as making or doing something.

CHRONOLOGICAL ANALYSIS is concerned with determining the stages of an event when the event is one which cannot be treated as having a function, for example, a historical event. It is a preliminary step toward fuller understanding and interpretation.

CAUSAL ANALYSIS deals with the relation of cause and effect.

CAUSE is the kind of connection between events that enables us to say that without event A, event B would not have come about, and whenever you have A, you will have B.

The connection must be considered as relatively IMMEDIATE. In one sense, the whole universe is a tissue of relationships and anything, however remote, may be taken to be a "cause" of something else. But only immediate connections tell us very much.

What we take to be the cause of an event may be dictated by our INTEREST. A coroner investigating the death of a child would state the cause as a fall from a stepladder, whereas the mother might take her negligence to be the cause.

An event does not take place in complete isolation. Various factors constitute a setting for the event. A factor which, existing in the situation, will permit the effect to appear is called a CONDITION.

There are two kinds of condition, SUFFICIENT CONDITION and NECESSARY CONDITION.

For example, take a situation in which the event B occurs and in which the factor X is present as a condition. The condition X is sufficient if, whenever X is present, B occurs. But in such an example, if B still occurs with X absent and some other factor taking its place, then X is not a necessary condition. A necessary condition is one which must be present for the effect to take place.

When we speak of a cause we refer to some PRINCIPLE OF UNIFORMITY. Under the same circumstances the A would always cause the B. This is the principle involved in what is called a law of nature. Hydrogen ignited in the presence of oxygen *always* gives us water.

To reason about cause, we must keep in mind two principles:

1. A cannot be the cause of B if A is ever absent when B is present.

2. A cannot be the cause of B if B is ever absent when A is present. That is, A and B are uniformly related.

Argument

ARGUMENT is the kind of discourse used to make the audience (reader or listener) think or act as the arguer desires. It is sometimes said that the purpose of argument is not double, as just stated, but single—in other words, that its purpose is to lead the audience to act. In the final analysis there is justification for this view, for a way of thinking means by implication a way of acting, and acting is the fulfillment of a way of thinking. As Justice Holmes says, "Every idea is an incitement." But in practice we can distinguish between the two purposes.

THE APPEAL OF ARGUMENT

It is sometimes said that argument may make either or both of two appeals, the appeal to understanding and the appeal to emotions, and that in appealing to the understanding, argument aims to CONVINCE, and in appealing to the emotions, aims to PERSUADE. Here we shall take a stricter view, and treat argument as an appeal to the understanding. How, then, does it differ from other forms of discourse, which also involve, in various ways, an appeal to the understanding?

ARGUMENT AND CONFLICT

Argument differs from the other kinds of discourse because of the basic situation in which it originates. Argument implies conflict or the possibility of conflict. We do not argue with a person who

already agrees with us, but with a person who is opposed to us or
who is undecided. Furthermore, argument implies a conflict between positions. We do not argue about a subject if only one position can possibly be taken in regard to it. The arguer presumably
believes that his position is the only reasonable position, but by the
fact of arguing at all he recognizes that another position, no matter
how mistakenly, is held or may be held. The purpose of argument
is to resolve the conflict in which the argument originates. The
arguer argues to convince, to win.

The situation of conflict distinguishes argument from the other
kinds of discourse, but in the course of achieving his purpose of
resolving the conflict the arguer may resort to the other kinds of
discourse, especially to exposition. In fact, if a dispute is really
based on the misunderstanding of a set of facts, mere exposition
may be enough to win the argument. Argument, like the other
kinds of discourse, rarely appears in an absolutely pure form. Here,
as in the other kinds of discourse, we define a particular piece of
speaking or writing in terms of its dominant intention. The dominant intention of a piece of argument, no matter how much description, narration, or exposition it may use, is to make the audience
change its mind or conduct.

Argument, either as the dominant intention or a subsidiary intention, may appear in many forms. It appears in conversation, in
public addresses, in the lawyer's presentation of his case, in feature
articles, in editorials, in textbooks on any subject, in essays, in
poetry, in history, in drama, in fiction. It properly appears wherever
the possibility of conflict between positions appears. The salesman
trying to sell a car uses argument. The historian trying to prove
that a certain event took place at a certain time uses argument.
The congressman speaking on behalf of a bill uses argument. The
dramatist setting two characters into conflict may use argument.
But no matter what form argument takes, the general principles
involved remain the same. In this chapter we shall try to examine
some of the principles. With many of them we are already acquainted, for in so far as we have been able to argue reasonably
we have always been thinking in accordance with them.

ARGUMENT AND THE UNDERSTANDING

Argument gains its ends by an appeal to the understanding, to man's reasoning nature. We ordinarily recognize this fact when we say of a speaker, "He didn't really have an argument; he merely carried the audience by appealing to their emotions." Such a speaker has persuaded but he has not convinced. The advertiser who puts the picture of a sweet-faced, gray-haired grandmother beside the picture of his ice box is not appealing to reason but to emotion. He may have a good sales argument in favor of his ice box on grounds of economy, efficiency, or convenience, but he is not presenting it. The political speaker who screams, "Every red-blooded American will vote for John Jones, the friend of the people!" is not offering an argument any more than the defense lawyer who points to the accused murderer and, with tears in his voice, demands of the jury, "This man before you, this simple man who loves his children, who prays for them every night—would you send him to the gallows? You fathers and mothers, would you make those poor babes fatherless?" The advertiser may sell the ice box, the politician may get the votes, the lawyer may get an acquittal for the accused by the appeal to the emotions, but in no case has an argument been offered.

The objection may be raised: "What does it matter if the advertiser or politician or lawyer didn't offer an argument? The ice box *was* good—or the politician *was* honest and able—or the accused *was* innocent." If the ice box was good, etc., then the question is merely a practical one: Is the simple appeal to the emotions the best and safest way of achieving the good purpose? Perhaps not, for if an audience becomes aware that no real argument is being offered, that there is only an attempt to play on its emotions, it may feel that it is being treated like a child, that proper respect is not being paid to its powers of reason, that it is being duped and betrayed. So the appeal to the emotions may backfire, and regardless of the merits of the case there may be blind resentment instead of blind agreement.

But another objection may be raised: "Suppose the advertiser or politician or lawyer did gain his purpose, no matter what the merit of the case. He won, didn't he? And isn't the object to win?"

If the ice box was not good, the question now becomes a moral one: Is a man entitled to practice a fraud merely because he has the ability to do so—in this instance to sway people by the appeal to the emotions? But the same question would apply if the man did not appeal to the emotions of his audience but offered them misleading arguments.

If the appeal to the understanding is the appeal of argument, then what becomes of the appeal to the emotions? Nothing becomes of it. It is still a very important consideration. It remains important even in relation to argument. If we have a good case on logical grounds, we may still lose it because we present it untactfully, because we do not know how to make the most of the temperament and attitude of the audience. Frequently the problem may be to "persuade" the audience to give our logical case an examination. Persuasion begins in the attempt to find common ground in attitudes, feelings, sentiments. And only if we find such common ground as a starting point can we ordinarily hope, in the end, to win an agreement about the matter of argument. Persuasion is very important in the strategy of argument, and at the end of this chapter we shall discuss it. But for the present we shall consider questions arising from the consideration of argument as an appeal to the understanding.

WHAT ARGUMENT IS ABOUT

What is argument about? People argue about anything, we may answer. But that is not a specific answer.

To illustrate:

John comes upon a group obviously engaged in a heated argument. "What are you arguing about?"

Jack answers: "Football."

John asks: "What about football?"

Jack answers: "About who won the Army-Navy game in 1936."

John laughs and says: "For the Lord's sake, what are you wasting your breath for? Why don't you telephone the information bureau at the newspaper and find out?"

John is right. When a fact can be established by investigation, there is no need to establish it by argument. Why argue about the length of a piece of string if there is a ruler handy?

Or again suppose John asks his first question, and Jack replies, "Football."

John asks: "What about football?"

Jack answers: "Which is the better game, football or basketball?"

John laughs again, and says: "For the Lord's sake, what are you wasting your breath for? You can't settle that. A guy just likes the game he likes. Take me, I like tennis better than either of them."

John is right again. An argument about a matter of mere taste is useless, and in so far as the word "better" [1] in the above conversation merely means what one happens to like, there is no proper matter for argument.

Anyone sees immediately the absurdity of an argument between two children about whether candy is better than pie. Such a disagreement permits of no conclusion. No process of reason can lead to an agreement between the taste buds of Sally's mouth and the taste buds of Susie's mouth, for both sets of taste buds give "truth" for the person to whom they belong. But a doctor could argue that spinach is better than either candy or pie for the child. He can do so because he has a definite objective standard, the child's health, to which he can appeal.

In other words, a matter of absolute taste is not a matter for argument. Only a matter of judgment is a matter for argument. We must remember, however, that there is no single sharp and fast line

---

[1] Expressions like "better," "more desirable," "to be preferred," "greater," "good," "acceptable," and so forth, may indicate mere preference, an unarguable question of taste, and in ordinary usage this is frequently so. When dealing with such an expression, one should ask questions which will determine whether or not the word has an objective content. Take the simple statement: "That is a good horse." We immediately have to ask, "Good for what?" For draying, for racing, for the bridle path, for the show ring, for the range? Or does the speaker merely mean that the horse is gentle, responsive, and affectionate, a sort of pet? By forcing the question we may discover the real meaning behind the original statement. But sometimes there is no meaning beyond the question of taste. Somebody says: "Jake is a good guy." If you force the question here and get the reply, "Oh, he's just regular, I like to be around him," you discover that the statement has no objective content. It tells you nothing about Jake. As the philosopher Spinoza puts it, Paul's opinion about Peter tells more about Paul than about Peter.

Useful forcing questions to apply to such expressions are: What is *it* good, desirable, etc. for? What is *it* good in relation to? Is the standard invoked objective and therefore worth discussing?

between matters of taste and matters of judgment. In between obvious extremes, there is a vast body of matters about which it is difficult to be sure, and each question must be examined on its own merits.

Let us take, for example, an argument about whether Wordsworth or Longfellow is the finer poet. Are we dealing with a matter of taste or a matter of judgment?

If one person says, "I don't care what other people think, I just like Longfellow better," he is treating the whole business as a matter of taste. He is making no appeal to reason. But if another person tries to set up a standard for poetic excellence in general and tests the poets by that standard, he is making an appeal to judgment. He might say, for instance, that Wordsworth has greater originality in subject matter, has more serious ideas, has had more influence on later poets, and uses fresher and more suggestive metaphors. He might not win agreement, but he is at least using the method of argument, is trying to appeal to reason in terms of an objective standard.

But let us come back to our original illustration. We notice that in both instances when Jack says that he and his friends are arguing about football, John asks: "What about football?"

John is bound to ask this question if he has any real curiosity about the argument. For football, in itself, is no matter for argument. It may provide the material for an argument, but that is all. There must be something "about" football which is the matter for argument. So John asks the question.

Jack answers: "Oh, about the Michigan-Purdue game last Saturday."

John says: "Gosh, but you are thick-headed. What *about* the game?"

Jack answers: "About Randall and Bolewiensky."

John says: "Well, I give up! What *about* Randall and Bolewiensky?"

Jack answers: "About who is the more useful player."

John says: "Well, it is sure time you were telling me."

John's thick-headed friend has finally managed to state what the argument is about. If there is an argument here, somebody holds that Randall is a more useful player than Bolewiensky and somebody denies it. In other words, the argument is about a PROPOSITION.

A proposition is what an argument is about, and is the only thing
an argument can be about. The argument develops when somebody affirms a proposition and somebody else denies it.

THE PROPOSITION: TWO KINDS

A proposition is the declaration of a judgment. It is a statement
that can be believed, doubted, or disbelieved. A proposition states
something as a fact or states that some line of action should or
should not be followed. So we have PROPOSITIONS OF FACT and
PROPOSITIONS OF POLICY. A lawyer arguing that his client has an
alibi for a certain time is dealing with a proposition of fact. A bond
salesman trying to sell a bond to an investor is dealing with a
proposition of policy. The typical statement of a proposition of fact
is *is* or *does*. The typical statement of a proposition of policy is
should.

The mere presence in a statement, however, of *is* or *does* cannot
be taken to indicate a proposition of fact. For instance, the following statement uses *is:*

It is desirable to abolish the poll tax.

But the statement means that the poll tax *should* be abolished. It
indicates a line of action. Therefore, it is a proposition of policy.

Likewise, the mere presence of *should* does not necessarily indicate a proposition of policy. For instance:

Any experienced reader of poetry should regard Wordsworth as
a better poet than Longfellow.

This statement really means that any experienced reader of poetry
does regard Wordsworth as a better poet than Longfellow. It is a
statement of fact that may be believed, doubted, or disbelieved.

So the typical form of a proposition can be disguised, and one
must look to the fundamental intention of a statement and not to
its accidental phrasing.

THE STATEMENT OF THE PROPOSITION

In formal debate the proposition is ordinarily given as a resolution: *Resolved,* That the United States should adopt free trade.

Or: *Resolved,* That the language requirements for the B.A. degree should be abolished.

Formal debates, however, make up only a fraction of all argument. We find argument in a hundred other places—wherever anyone is trying to lead us to accept something as a fact or to accept a line of action. Ordinarily the proposition underlying an argument is not formally stated, and sometimes may not be stated at all. For instance, the arguer may refrain from giving the proposition because he is sure the audience already grasps it, or because he wishes to lead the audience by degrees to discover it for themselves. In certain kinds of propaganda, for example, the arguer deliberately conceals the proposition in order to deceive the audience.

If an arguer wishes to think straight he ought to be able to state his proposition. If he is to be effective he must know exactly what is at stake in the argument, and the best way to be sure that he knows what is at stake is to frame the proposition, at least for himself. And the proposition should be single, clear, and unprejudiced.

THE SINGLE PROPOSITION

A proposition should be single. It should not express more than one idea for argument. We must fix here on the phrase, "one idea for argument." Even the proposition, "This rose is red," expresses more than one idea. It says that the "this" is a rose, and it says that the "this" is red. But obviously it intends to present only one point for argument—the redness. Presumably the idea that the "this" is a rose is expected to pass without question.

It is always possible, of course, that someone may challenge an idea which is not put forward for argument but is implied in the proposition. In such a case the argument then turns on a new proposition. For instance, suppose I say, "The whale is the most intelligent fish." Obviously, I intend the argument to turn on the question of the intelligence of the whale. But a zoologist may challenge another idea of my proposition by saying that a whale is not a fish. This may start another argument based on the idea in my original proposition that a whale is a fish. Or I may take the zoologist's word that the whale is a mammal, and restate my original proposition: "A whale is the most intelligent creature living in water."

To say that a proposition should be single does not mean that a total argument may not involve more than one arguable idea.

Many arguable ideas may appear in the course of an argument. But each idea should be treated separately to avoid confusion. The discussion of this question will be postponed, however, until we treat the organization of argument.

THE CLEAR PROPOSITION

A clear proposition says what we mean. But it is not easy to say what we mean. Most words as we ordinarily use them do not have very precise limits. Even words which refer to an objective physical situation may be vague. How "tall" is a tall man? Five feet, eleven? Six feet? Six feet, three? Any of these men would be well above average height, but there is a great range here. So we may say "tallish," "tall," or "very tall" to indicate the scale; but even then we might hesitate about the choice of a word. Or take the word "bald." How much hair must be lacking before we can say that a man is bald? The word does not fix an objective standard although it does refer to an objective situation.

The problem is even more complicated when we come to words like "good," "cute," or "progressive" which do not refer to objective physical situations. What is really said in the proposition, "Mary is the cutest girl in town"? The word "cute" indicates some laudatory or appreciative attitude on the part of the speaker, but it does not tell us very much about Mary. Or if we hear, "Mr. Black is a progressive citizen," what are we to understand? That Black works hard, pays his taxes, treats his family decently, saves money, and stays out of jail? Or that he is interested in improving the local school, bringing new factories to town, and planting flowers in the park? Or that he has a certain political philosophy? Such a word tells us very little about Mr. Black. It seems to indicate some general approval on the part of the speaker, but we don't know exactly what, and the odds are that he does not know either. The word is vague.

Let us take another example of vagueness, the proposition, "Soviet Russia is more democratic than England."

A person defending the above proposition might argue that Russia is more democratic than England because in its system there are no hereditary titles, because great fortunes cannot be accumulated, and because the worker is glorified. A person attacking the proposition might argue that England is more democratic

because actual political power is in the hands of leaders chosen by
the majority of voters in free elections, because there is freedom
of speech, and because a man can choose his occupation. The word
"democratic" is vague, and the two disputants are using it in different senses. They can have no argument on the original proposition until they have agreed on a definition of democracy. And this,
of course, may mean that the argument shifts to a new proposition:
"Democracy is so-and-so."

Many words, like "democracy," have no generally accepted
meaning to which we can refer. Even the dictionary does not help
us much with such a word. It can give us authority for a word like
"horse," for to zoology a horse is a horse wherever we find it. As
for "democracy," the dictionary may give us some idea of several
more or less well-accepted senses and may start us on the way to
a clear statement, but the dictionary definition can rarely be full
enough to cover the meaning of such a word as it will appear in
an argument. In framing a proposition we should try to fix the
definition (pp. 83-91) of any significant word, to determine exactly
what we mean by it, and then we should stick to that definition.
Until both parties to an argument agree about terms, there can be
no fruitful meeting, indeed, no meeting.

THE UNPREJUDICED PROPOSITION

A proposition should not only be single and clear. It should also
be unprejudiced. That is, it should not smuggle into the proposition
anything which implies a foregone conclusion to the argument.
The following is not an unprejudiced proposition: "The unsanitary
condition of the slaughter pens at Morgansville is detrimental to
the public health." It is prejudiced, for the adjective *unsanitary*
really means "detrimental to the public health." If we accept that
word into the proposition, there is nothing arguable: the point of
the argument has been already settled. The question has been
begged, to use the phrase ordinarily applied to such a situation.

HISTORY OF THE QUESTION

We have to understand our proposition before we can argue
about it. Some propositions can be understood immediately, but
some can only be understood if we go into the HISTORY OF THE

QUESTION—that is, if we inform ourselves about the circumstances which brought the argument into being. For instance, in a debate about tariffs some knowledge of how they have worked in this country and elsewhere would be almost essential to a full understanding of what is really at stake at the present moment. Even a matter of definition of words in a proposition may depend on our knowledge of the history of the question. For similar reasons it is important to understand the OCCASION OF THE DISCUSSION—that is, what makes the argument significant at the present moment.

ISSUES

But once we understand our proposition we are still not ready to argue it. Common sense tells us that there may be many arguments for and against a given proposition. Though the proposition properly stated is single, reasons for and against it may be plural. The single idea of the proposition may raise various questions for controversy. When a question is ESSENTIAL to the proposition, we call it an ISSUE. And any question is essential if its defeat means the defeat of the proposition. An issue, then, is a point of fundamental importance in the argument, and the affirmative side, the side supporting the proposition, must win on all issues in order to win on the proposition.

Let us take a simple example. The constitution of a certain college honor society, which we shall call the Corinthians, specifies that a student to be eligible for membership must (1) have a scholastic average of *B* or above, (2) have won a letter in at least one college sport, (3) have made some substantial contributions to the general good of the college community, and (4) have conducted himself as a gentleman during the period of his college career. William Smith is proposed for election. His sponsor argues that Smith has made an *A*-average, has won the state junior championship in swimming, has brought about a reform of the student council system by his editorials in the college paper, and is a person of high character and good manners. Smith seems certain of election until one Corinthian refers to the constitution and regretfully points out that Smith cannot fulfill requirement 2. "But he is an excellent athlete," the sponsor retorts; "he can out-swim anybody in this school."

"That's not the point," the other Corinthian replies. "The constitution explicitly states that to be eligible a student must have won a letter in at least one sport. And Rutherford College has no swimming team, and therefore does not give a letter for swimming."

If the constitution is taken seriously, Smith's eligibility must be denied. The proposition is that Smith is eligible for membership in the Corinthians, and the constitution is the source of authority for the requirements for eligibility. Each of those requirements is *essential*, and in the argument about Smith's eligibility would therefore properly be an issue.

ADMITTED ISSUES AND CRUCIAL ISSUES

It is important to notice here that the opposition does not contest Smith's eligibility on every point. It admits that Smith has made a scholastic average of *B* or above, has made some substantial contribution to the general good of the college community, and has conducted himself as a gentleman. The proposition really depends on the college letter in athletics. Now in most arguments, some issues are uncontested. These are called ADMITTED ISSUES. The remaining issues (or issue) are called CRUCIAL ISSUES. They are the points on which the real argument takes place.

LOCATING THE ISSUES: ANALYSIS OF THE PROPOSITION

Let us return for a moment to the case of Smith's eligibility. Suppose someone says: "Well, Smith ought to be elected, and if a man like Smith can't get in under the present constitution, then the constitution ought to be changed." That may be true, but that is another problem, and would have to be considered on its own merits. This situation is similar to certain cases at law in which one may feel that the letter of the law defeats justice. For example, a defending lawyer in a first-degree murder case may argue that his client had suffered intolerable provocation, that the victim had grievously slandered the defendant's wife, and that the defendant, a simple man raised in rather primitive surroundings, had thought killing the slanderer to be the only course of honor and decency. The prosecution argues that this is no issue in the case, because the legal definition of murder is such and such, and makes no recognition of the provocation of slander, or of the personal background of the accused. The prosecutor is, of course, right. The law defines the issues by which the proposition, that so-and-so is guilty of murder in the first degree, must stand or fall. If the jury does acquit the defendant, it does so out of sentiment, prejudice, or some notion of justice which is inconsistent with the law.

The case of William Smith or of the murderer is very simple, for the issues are defined beforehand by a document—eligibility for membership by the constitution of the Corinthians, or murder by the law. In many arguments, however, we must locate the issues for ourselves. We do this by making an ANALYSIS of the proposition.

In making the analysis of a proposition we do not arbitrarily decide that certain questions are issues. They are implied in the proposition, and we must locate them, or discover them. In a rough-and-tumble argument, undertaken without preparation, two reasonably intelligent opponents will eventually isolate at least some of the issues; but in the clash of argument, issues develop more or less hit-or-miss. If there is time for preparation, as there usually is in writing a theme or an article, we should try to determine the issues beforehand.

The first step in this process is to set up all the possible arguments on each side of the proposition. In first draft such a list may be a very crude affair, with important and unimportant items jumbled together, but it will give a kind of preview of the problem. Even in this form, however, we can see that arguments tend to go in pairs, a negative as opposed to an affirmative. Not all arguments may, however, be paired. The negative may admit certain points, and naturally does not offer arguments in regard to them.

Let us set up such a preliminary list for the proposition of policy that the United States should adopt universal military training.

AFFIRMATIVE (A)	NEGATIVE (N)
1. There is a dangerous international situation and the United States has no clearly defined policy to meet it.	
2. The present army of the United States will be inadequate for a major conflict as soon as the atomic bomb is possessed by other nations.	

AFFIRMATIVE (A)   NEGATIVE (N)

3. Within a few years our trained
   reserves will be over-age.

4. The next war will probably
   move rapidly to a decision and
   will give no time to train and
   equip an army.

5. The tensions in international   No nation can now afford to under-
   relations at present are serious   take a war, least of all the nations
   and a war may come within a   which might be arrayed against
   few years.   us. Further, there are no insupera-
                                         ble difficulties to peace.

6. Our possible enemies are main-   If other nations are assured of our
   taining large armies.   good faith by our relative dis-
                                         armament, they will reduce their
                                         own forces.

7. Military training gives young   The time spent in military train-
   men a sense of responsibility   ing seriously impairs the education
   and discipline which is valu-   of young men, and reduces their
   able in any occupation of   efficiency in later life.
   later life.

8. The United Nations does not   The United Nations has not been
   guarantee our safety.   given a fair trial; we must show
                                         our good faith in it.

9. No cost is too great to pay for   The country is burdened with a
   our national safety.   great national debt and needs to
                                         practice economy if our system is
                                         to survive.

10. Military training does not fos-   Military life fosters immorality.
    ter immorality.

11. Military training will produce   The next war will be a war of
    specialists and even if the next   specialists, and a large body of
    war is a war fought with   ordinary troops would be useless.
    atomic bombs, robot planes,
    etc., trained men are required
    to operate such mechanisms
    and ground troops will always
    be required to occupy and
    hold territory.

AFFIRMATIVE (A)	NEGATIVE (N)
12. Universal military training does not aggravate the international situation. Instead our preparedness would tend to prevent a conflict.	Universal military training would signify to the world that we had no faith in the possibility of peace and would precipitate an armament race.
13. Victory would be possible in a future war, for there is reason to believe that defenses can be developed against the new methods of attack.	The next war, if it comes, will be a war of total destruction; therefore the only hope of survival for civilization is to bend every effort for peace by developing a world federation or a world government.

This list is not systematic. The items are jotted down as they occur in a first survey of the subject. So in revising the list we must try to put things together that are closely related in meaning. For instance, if we finally keep 7 and 10, we must put them in some relation to each other, for they both bear on the effect of military training on the education and the morality of young men.

Order, however, is not the only thing we must consider. There are four other considerations which we can introduce at this stage.

I. Are the arguments all significant?

II. Do they cover the subject?

III. Do they overlap each other?

IV. Does any really include more than one idea?

With these considerations in mind we can see that 7, 9, and 10 do not bear on the proposition. They raise questions concerning the effects on education (7) and morality (10) of military training, and of the cost (9) of the military training. Obviously, if the national survival is at stake (and that is what is implied in the word *should* of the proposition), these questions are not significant.

Upon inspection we may discover that the issues do not cover the subject. First, we may notice that, though 2, 3, and 4 imply the need for military policy, no such argument is stated. And certainly such an important point should be stated. Second, we discover that the question of pacifism is nowhere mentioned. Pacifism is a sweeping and important argument, either when grounded on the notion that all war is sinful and is never justifiable or when grounded on the idea that nonviolence eventually defeats violence. A person arguing the negative side might not believe in pacifism and therefore would not wish to raise the objection, but anyone intending to support the affirmative side would have to include the argument for the sake of completeness. He cannot be sure what arguments may appear.

As for overlapping among arguments, we find several instances. Items 1A and 5A overlap, for they both affirm the danger in the existing situation. Furthermore, 2A, 3A, and 4A might be fused, for they are closely related as arguments for the notion that a military policy is needed. And if items 7 and 10 had not already been excluded as not significant, they should be fused.

Last we find that item 1A really includes two ideas, one concerning the danger in the international situation and the other concerning the lack of any policy, either political or military, to combat the danger. The same is true of 13N, which states two ideas, one that another war would destroy all civilization, the other that the hope for survival lies in a world federation or a world government.

If now we try to systematize what we have, we get something like the following:

AFFIRMATIVE	NEGATIVE
1. There is a dangerous international situation.	
2. The United States has no policy to meet the danger, either political or military. (1, 8) [2]	
3. There is need for a military policy, for (a) as soon as the secret of the atomic bomb is in the hands of other nations, our present force will be inadequate for a major conflict, (b) within a few years our trained reserves will be over-age, and (c) the speed with which the next war would move to a decision would give no time to train and equip an army. (2, 3, 4)	The need is for a political policy.

[2] Numbers in parentheses refer to numbers in first draft of possible issues.

AFFIRMATIVE

NEGATIVE

4. Our possible enemies are maintaining large armies. (6)

If other nations are assured of our good faith, they will reduce their armaments. (6)

5. Military training would help to prepare specialists, and even if the next war is fought with atomic bombs, robot planes, etc., large numbers of men are required to operate such mechanisms and ground troops will always be required to occupy and hold territory. (11)

The next war will be a war of specialists, and military training would not produce them. Furthermore, in such a war, large bodies of troops would be useless.

6. Our preparedness would tend to prevent a conflict.

Universal military training would signify that we had no faith in peace and would precipitate an armament race. (12)

7. Victory would be possible in a future war, for there is reason to believe that defenses can be developed against the new methods of attack. (13)

The next war, if it comes, will be a war of total destruction for all involved. (13)

8. We can hope for the development of international safeguards, but we cannot be sure of them at this date. (8)

The only hope for survival lies in world federation or world government. (13)

9. There are theoretical arguments against pacifism even on religious grounds. (For instance, most churches do not preach pacifism as such.) If we take the argument that nonviolence always conquers violence in the end, we find no evidence for this in history. In any case the argument for pacifism is irrelevant on practical grounds because in neither this country nor any other are there many pacifists.

War is morally wrong and should not be resorted to for any reason. But even if war were not wrong on moral grounds, pacifism would still be a good policy, for nonviolence always conquers violence in the end.

We see here that some new material has been introduced. Since a statement has emerged that there is need for a military policy (3), the negative counters by stating the need for a political policy instead. And the arguments for and against pacifism now appear in the list. We also see that there are no negative arguments for items 1 and 2. The negative admits these points.

STOCK QUESTIONS

The second draft is more systematic and complete than the first. But we can further simplify the treatment and more definitely locate the issues. We need to carry on our analysis and find the big, main issues under which merely particular arguments can be organized. We are here dealing with what is called a proposition of policy, which means that the argument is about the best way of accomplishing some end; and in arguments of this sort there are certain STOCK QUESTIONS which can be applied to the material as a kind of guide for locating issues. These stock questions help us, first, to simplify our material, and second, to establish the essentiality of our issues.[3]

    I. Is there a need for some change?
    II. Will the policy suggested by the proposition be effective?
   III. Are the possible benefits of this policy greater than any new disadvantage which it may create?
   IV. Is the proposed policy better than any alternative policy?

Upon reflection we may see that I includes 1, 2, 3, and 4; that II includes 5 and 7; that III includes 6;[4] and that IV includes 8 and 9.

   [3] See essential issues, p. 135.

   [4] It might be said that 6 really belongs under II, and that there is no III to be considered in the present argument. There is some ground for this view, for if, as 6A states, preparedness would help prevent a conflict, then that policy would be effective in maintaining national safety. But if, as in 6N, emphasis is on the new, or increased danger, which preparedness would create by precipitating an armament race, then we can consider this as a definite disadvantage—it *increases* the danger already existing. It will be found that in practice II and III often overlap to a degree, but the difference in emphasis between them is important. We can find, however, perfectly clear-cut cases of difference between II and III. For example, a farmer might decide that a dam on a creek would stop erosion on his land—would be an effective policy for

We should now be prepared to set up the issues. When formally stated, issues appear as questions so phrased that the affirmative must answer *yes* to them if the proposition is to stand.

STOCK QUESTION	ISSUE
I. ————	1. Is there a dangerous international situation? (1) [5]
	2. Is there need for a military policy? (2, 3, 4)
II. ————	3. Would the universal military training be an effective military policy? (5, 6, 7)
III. ————	4. Would the advantages of universal military training outweigh the dangers that it might create or aggravate? (6)
IV. ————	5. Is universal military training better than any alternative policy? (8, 9)

To summarize what we have done thus far: First, we have set up, more or less at random, opposed particular arguments. Whenever we have found a pairing of an affirmative and a negative argument, we have located a point of collision, a possible issue. Second, we have analyzed these possible issues to see that they (1) are relevant and essential, (2) cover the subject, and (3) do not overlap each other or do not individually include more than one possible issue. Third, after the analysis we have drawn a revised list of affirmative and negative arguments. Fourth, to the revised list we have applied the four stock questions as a guide: (1) Is there a need for change? (2) Will the policy suggested by the proposition be effective? (3) Are the possible benefits of this policy greater than any new disadvantages which it might create? (4) Is the proposed policy better than any alternative policy? We have given each issue thus defined the form of a question which demands an affirmative

---

that purpose (II). But he then might discover that the dam would flood some of his best pasture land further up the creek. This would be a new disadvantage, and would raise a new question (III).

It might also be said that 5 belongs under IV, for the negative, by implication at least, suggests an alternative policy, the creation of an army of specialists. But this really raises the question of the effectiveness of the policy suggested by the proposition. So II and IV overlap on this point.

[5] Numbers in parentheses refer to numbers in the second draft of possible issues.

answer if the proposition is to be supported. These questions are the issues.

We may note that the first issue, since it is not contested by the negative on our list, is an admitted issue. We may note also that under each issue we have indicated the particular arguments from the revised list which should be discussed under the general head provided by that issue. For instance, under issue 2, we have placed arguments 2, 3, and 4 from the revised list.

If we have done our work well, we now have the material organized for our argument. This does not mean that the arguments need follow this order. We might, for example, want to dispose of the question of pacifism and to point out reasons for pessimism concerning a system of international arrangements (topic 5 in our final list of issues) before arguing the specific merits of universal training. Or the strategy of persuasion for a particular audience might make us take a very indirect approach to the whole subject. We might, for instance, want to paint a vivid picture of the destruction our cities would suffer if we were caught unprepared. But the arrangement of issues as set up provides a reasonable scheme for treating the subject. A student, in the theme given below, has followed this scheme in arguing on the affirmative side. (The numbers in parentheses refer to the steps in the revised draft.)

SHOULD THE UNITED STATES ADOPT UNIVERSAL MILITARY TRAINING?

(1) No thinking person can deny that the world at this date is in terrible confusion. While World War II was going on, many of us thought that victory over the evil forces of Nazism and Fascism would bring in a new day and give us a happier world than man had ever known. Those of us who were really in the show had to feel that way to keep on going. We had to feel that or we had to be sure we didn't feel anything at all. But in May, 1947, now that we are back home and in school or holding jobs, we find that what we expected has not come true. Any newspaper we pick up tells us that much.

There are several things making for this terrible confusion. The conquered countries are in a desperate condition and some of those on the winning side are not much better. France, Greece, and China are suffering from many shortages and actual hunger, at times to the point of starvation. In the conquered countries there are many people who are just waiting for a chance to avenge their defeat, and they are ready to sign on with anybody who may help them. Behind this confusion there is the struggle between two very different notions of how the world ought to be run. Soviet Russia stands for one notion, and the United States stands for the other. In other countries, France, Germany, Italy, China, and even England, those two notions divide the people into parties and even into armed camps. The two notions are communism and democracy. There is the making here of a war which would make previous war look like a Boy Scout jamboree.

(2) The United States has no clear policy in international affairs to meet this crisis. The loan to Greece and Turkey is something, but nobody could say that it is a long-range policy and answers all our questions. We do not even know what we want to do about the United Nations.

(3) It is certainly important to get a foreign policy and work for peace, but it is also important to get a military policy. When the war was over everybody wanted to get home, and this was only human. Also the atomic bomb made us feel safe. But the result is that right now we are a disarmed nation, and (3a) soon the atomic bomb will be in the hands of other nations. (3b) Within a few years, too, most of our trained reserves will be a little too old to make the best soldiers. (3c) And if another war comes, it will move so fast there will not be time to train and equip forces. (4) Our possible enemies are not making this mistake, for they are maintaining large armies and are training new men. As soon as they get the secret of the bomb, our edge will be gone.

Universal military training is something that we need to safeguard our future. I know that there are arguments against this, but I do not believe that they will stand up against the facts.

(5) The first argument which you often hear is that universal military training would not be desirable because the new type of war will be a war of specialists which universal military training would not produce. But this depends on the kind of training which is given. The training can be adapted to changing military needs. But in any case, there is good reason to believe that there will always be a place for the guy in the mud. I was one of them myself, and I know that they always had to send us in sooner or later. Large bodies of troops will be required to occupy and hold territory.

(6) The second argument [6] is that universal military training would provoke an armament race. The answer is that the race is already on,

[6] This argument is not placed according to the scheme. It really concerns a disadvantage which might be created by the proposed policy (stock question III), but here it is placed between two arguments for the effectiveness of universal military training (stock question II).

but at the present is merely a one-sided race. The other countries are racing to get what we have got—the A-bomb. But they are also building up big armies. If we showed that we mean to be strong, it might discourage other countries and make them want to come to an understanding.

(7) The third argument is that the next war, if it comes, will be a war of general suicide. It is said that nobody will survive except a few starved and diseased people among the ruins. This picture is too pessimistic. I do not want to deny what horrors of war can be, for I have seen some of them in West Germany when we went in. But the history of war shows that for every weapon of offense a weapon of defense develops sooner or later. Our scientists and military men should develop defenses just as they should develop weapons of offense. We have to do all we can to be sure that we are prepared if the war comes. And one of the things necessary is to adopt universal military training.

(8) Even people who admit that a strong military policy might be effective in itself sometimes argue that a better plan is to try to set up a world system of some kind. Any sensible person wants to avoid war, and one way to do that is to work for international understanding. But we are a long way from a system which we can depend on, and there is no reason why we should commit suicide as a nation in trying to get one. If we are strong we can enter into any international arrangements with a good bargaining position.

(9) There is one other argument which sometimes crops up in discussions about military training. That is the pacifist argument. People say that war is sinful and that you should never fight. Now I respect some of the people who argue that way. One of my best high school buddies was a pacifist, and when war came he went to a C.O. camp. I respect him, but I think that he was a crackpot. It is against human nature to take everything lying down, and that is really what pacifism amounts to. The man who lies down gets stepped on. History shows that. But there really aren't enough pacifists in this country or any other to make the subject worth arguing about.

To sum up, I say, "Work for peace, but prepare for war." Teddy Roosevelt's idea of walking softly and carrying a big stick still makes sense, for the world has not changed much since his day. And one big stick that the United States can carry is universal military training.

PROPOSITIONS OF FACT

The proposition argued above is, of course, a proposition of policy. But how do we go about establishing the issue, or issues, in a proposition of fact? In the case of the eligibility of William Smith for membership in the Corinthians, the issues were defined beforehand by a document—the constitution of the society. But there are propositions of fact in which the issues are not established beforehand by any such definition.

Let us take a very simple instance, one in which there can be only a single issue. If two men in the wilderness wish to cross a stream, one of them may propose that they drop a tree across it. The other objects that the available tree is too short. They can establish the height of the tree by geometric calculation, but they cannot establish the width of the stream. Therefore the proposition (the tree is long enough) is a matter of judgment, and is subject to argument. Several arguments, good or bad, may be offered on either side, but there is only one issue: Is the tree long enough? In such cases of simple fact, the proposition itself establishes the issue. But in other cases the fact may not be simple, and there may be no prior definition of the issues (as in the case of William Smith and the Corinthians).

Let us take such an example: John did right in leaving his fortune to the Ashford Medical Foundation.

First, are we sure that this is a proposition of fact? At first glance it may look like a proposition of policy, for it contains the phrase "did right"—which seems to imply policy. Certainly, we would have a proposition of policy if it were stated: John will do right to. . . . Or: John should leave. . . . But in its original form, the proposition concerns an event that has already taken place, and concerns the nature of the event, not a course of action to be pursued. This becomes clear if we translate the proposition into the standard form: John's conduct in leaving his fortune to the Ashford Medical Foundation *is* (or *was*) right. So we have an *is* proposition, not a *should* proposition.

Second, how can we establish the issues? To do so, we must decide what we mean by the word "right"—the predicate of the proposition. Suppose the opponents agree that a deed is morally right *only* if it fulfills *all* of the following requirements: (1) the doer is responsible, (2) the doer undertakes the deed for a laudable motive, and (3) the consequences of the deed are beneficial. The issues then become:

1. Was John of sound mind when he made his will?
2. Was his motive laudable?
3. Will the money be used for a beneficial activity?

The affirmative must establish all of these points in order to win the argument. Suppose that there is no doubt of John's sanity, and no doubt that the money will be used for a good purpose. Suppose that these facts are admitted. Yet if the negative establishes that John, in a fit of fury at his daughter for making a marriage without his consent, changed his will, then the motive is a bad one, for the deed comes out of spite and offended vanity. Therefore the proposition would be lost.

In such propositions of fact, where the fact is complex, the locating of the issues becomes a matter of analyzing the fact. In practice this may mean defining the key word (or words) in the proposition, as *right* in the example that we have just discussed.

EVIDENCE

When you get into an argument, you may be pretty sure that your opponent will be from Missouri. He will say, "Seeing is believing," and what he wants is the EVIDENCE. Without evidence you can only offer your own unsupported views, which you already know the opponent will not accept—for if he did accept them there would have been no argument in the first place.

Evidence is whatever can be offered as support for a proposition.

KINDS OF EVIDENCE: FACT AND OPINION

What constitutes evidence? People constantly appeal to facts, or try to appeal to facts, to support argument. "The facts of the case" are important as evidence, but they are not the only thing which can be used as evidence. People also appeal to opinions of other people who are supposed to have authority. "Expert testimony" is offered in the courtroom as evidence to support a case. The murder trial may bring out the alienist, the ballistics expert, the medical examiner, and any number of other experts whose opinions are to be considered by the jury. Presumably they base their testimony on facts, but what the jury is asked to accept is their *opinion,* their judgment of the facts.

The expert may be wrong, and experts frequently disagree among themselves; and what they disagree about is ordinarily not the facts but their interpretation of the facts. Opinion, therefore, appears as evidence. But not only the so-called expert opinion may appear as evidence. Even before the law we find what is called the character witness, and what the character witness finally offers is his opinion. In ordinary argument people constantly invoke opinion of all sort— "Mr. Allen says so, and I should think he would know," or "The New York *Times* says so." The author of the student theme on universal military training invokes the opinion of Teddy Roosevelt: Roosevelt's opinion about carrying the big stick is used as evidence.

Fact or opinion may constitute evidence. What tests can we apply to them to satisfy ourselves that they are worth admitting into an argument?

FACTS AS EVIDENCE

A fact must be made to stick. That is, the fact must be a fact. What is offered as a fact may turn out to be merely a mistaken opinion. We know this pattern well from detective stories. A "fact" points to the guilt of a certain character. He is arrested by the stupid police sergeant. The clever detective proves that the "fact" was not a fact at all. The true criminal had worn the hooded raincoat which everybody at the house party associated with Miss Perkins, and he had been mistaken for her in the mist on the beach. The "fact"—that Miss Perkins was observed near the scene of the crime at a certain hour—turns out to be not a fact at all, and justice is done.

To stick, a fact must be (1) verifiable or (2) attested by a reliable source.

VERIFICATION

Certain facts can be established by referring to some regularity in nature—that a certain type of cord would not support a certain weight, that potassium permanganate will explode under certain conditions, that the robin's egg is a certain shade of blue with brown markings, that a certain night of the year did not have a full moon, that *rigor mortis* sets in at a certain time after death. Such facts belong to a pattern in nature which is observable, and to test a particular fact we refer it to the pattern. We have an example in a story about one of Abraham Lincoln's law cases. A witness testified that he had observed a certain event. Lincoln asked him how, and he replied that he had seen it by moonlight. By producing an almanac, Lincoln showed that there had been no moon on the night in question. Lincoln tested the fact by referring it to a natural pattern. We shall here use the word *verifiable* in this sense.

FACT ESTABLISHED BY TESTIMONY

Suppose, however, Lincoln had not been able to check the witness by an almanac. What questions could he have asked to determine the reliability of the evidence offered by the witness? Four questions are relevant in such cases:

1. Was there opportunity for the witness to observe the event?

2. Was the witness physically capable of observing the event?

3. Was the witness intellectually capable of understanding the event and reporting accurately?

4. Was the witness honest?

The first question is clear enough, but the others are a little more complicated. For instance, if a blind newsman attests that Bill Sims was present in a railway station at such a time, how good is his evidence? Was he capable of observing the event? If it can be demonstrated that the blind man is capable of recognizing a step and was acquainted with the step of Bill Sims, who stopped at his newsstand every day to buy cigarettes, then it can be assumed that the newsman is capable of recognizing Bill Sims' presence at a certain time. If, furthermore, it can be accepted that the newsman has common sense, is not given to delusions, flights of fancy, or exaggerations, and has a good memory, then it can be assumed that he is intellectually capable of understanding and reporting the event. What remains is the question of honesty. If the newsman has no connection with the case, if no malice, profit, or other special interest is involved, then it can be readily assumed that his report is an honest one. But if some motive which might make him color or falsify the report can be established, then this fact must be assessed in relation to what is known about the newsman's general character. Generally speaking, an interested witness is a poor witness. Even if he is honest, his report does not carry prompt conviction, especially to a hostile or indifferent audience.

The case we have given for reliability here—the blind newsman's testimony—is a relatively simple one. But it illustrates the kind of questions that must be raised in all situations involving testimony. A historian trying to determine the truth about an event long past, a Congressional committee conducting a hearing on an economic situation, a farmer shopping for a new tractor are all engaged in assessing the reliability of testimony, and must ask the same questions.

To sum up: only facts that are verifiable or reliably attested should be admitted into the argument.

OPINION AS EVIDENCE

We can set up a parallel set of tests for the admission of opinion into the argument. Corresponding to the first requirement for the admission of a fact, we find the authority of an opinion. There is no use in introducing an opinion to support our argument if the opinion will carry little or no weight. For instance, no lawyer would want to introduce as expert a witness who had no reputation for competence in his particular field. The manufacturer of athletic supplies wants a champion, not a dud, to endorse his tennis racquet, and the manufacturer of cosmetics wants a lady of fashion or a famous actress to give a testimonial for the facial cream. We should be as sure as possible that any authority which we invoke in an argument is a real authority: a second-rate navy is no navy, and a second-rate authority is no authority, when the moment of combat comes.

TESTS OF AUTHORITY

How do we find out if an authority is real authority? "Ask the man who owns one," a famous advertising slogan suggests; and the maker of a washing machine shows the picture of a happy housewife standing by her prized contraption. The advertisers here appeal to authority on the principle that the proof of the pudding is in the eating: ask the eater, for he is an authority. This is a kind of rough-and-ready authority based on experience, useful but very limited in the degree of conviction which it can carry. Very probably the automobile buyer has not used many different makes of cars and the housewife has not used many different kinds of washing machines. The opinion of an impartial technical expert who had tested many makes of car or washing machine for efficiency, durability, and so forth, would carry much more authority. Here we appeal to experience too, but to the experience of the expert.

Authority is very often based on an appeal to success. The rich man is supposed to know how to make money, the famous painter how to paint pictures, the heavyweight champion how to fight. Success carries prestige and predisposes us to accept the pronouncement of the successful man. But we should still scrutinize each case. Perhaps the rich man got rich by luck—he *happened* to get into business at a time of expansion and rising markets. No doubt he himself attributes his success to his own sterling character, shrewdness, and indefatigable industry, but we may be more inclined to trust the evidence of the economic situation of his time. Or the famous painter may have struck a prejudice and a fashion of his time, and history is littered with the carcasses of artists of all kinds whose success was the accident of the moment. The heavyweight gives us a better case, for it is a simpler case—he merely had to square off with one man at one moment and slug it out. But perhaps a granite jaw, a fighting heart, and an explosive punch gave him the championship, and all that he has to say about training, footwork, and strategy may be wrong. He didn't succeed by luck, like the businessman or the painter—he really did flatten the opponent by his own force—but he may give the wrong reasons for his success. The fact of success doesn't mean that the successful man really knows the conditions of his success. And he can speak with authority only if at that point he knows. Many successful people are like the man who lived to be a hundred and revealed his secret for long life: "I never read less than one chapter of the Holy Writ a day or drink more than three slugs of likker a night."

Not infrequently we encounter an appeal to what, for lack of a better phrase, we may call authority by transference. Because a man is considered an authority in one field, it is assumed that he is an authority on anything. The famous musician is used as an authority on statesmanship, the great mathematician is appealed to as an authority on morality, and the great physicist on religion; the All-America fullback endorses a certain breakfast food, and a debutante prefers such-and-such a cigarette. This sort of reasoning is obviously nonsensical and pernicious, for it is simply a means of imposing on the gullibility of the audience. And because it is a means of imposing on gullibility, it is very common.

Authority, too, has some relation to time. What was acceptable as authority at one time may not be acceptable at another. In any field where the body of knowledge is constantly being enlarged and revised, timeliness is very important. A book on chemistry or physics written ten years ago may now lack authority in certain respects, or a history of the American Civil War written in 1875 may now be considered very misleading. Or should George Washington's views on foreign policy influence our own? We want the best authority of *our* time.

What tests, in the end, can we apply? There are no ready-made tests. We must, in the end, use our own judgment to select the authority by which we wish to support our argument. This seems to leave us where we started; but that is not quite true. Finding the man who might know is, after all, different from finding out for ourselves what he knows. If we are dealing with authority presumably based on experience, we can ask about the nature of the experience (one washing machine or ten washing machines?) and the intelligence and training of the person who has had the experience. If we are dealing with authority based on success, we can inquire into the nature of the success (how much was luck?) and into the capacity of the successful person for analyzing the means to success. And we should not forget to ask if the authority of the successful man is being used as authority by transference. Furthermore, we have to ask if our authority is timely.

Let us suppose that we wish to find an authority on some point of American history. It will not do to go to the library and take down the first book on the subject. The mere fact of print bestows no authority, for every error is somewhere embalmed between boards. We have to find out something about the author. Is he of recent date? (That is, would he have available the latest research on the subject?) Does he have any special bias or prejudice which must be discounted? Does he occupy a responsible position or has he had other professional recognition? (That is, is he on the faculty of some important university, have his works been favorably reviewed, and so forth?) How do his views compare with the views of some other historians of recognized importance? And all this means that we have to find out something about the field of American history, even if we are not capable of settling the particular point in question by our own investigation.

AUTHORITY AND THE AUDIENCE

One more thing must be considered. The authority is going to be used for a particular audience, and is intended to be effective for that audience—if not the opponent, at least some listener. Effective authority is authority which is acceptable to the particular audience. The Mohammedan *Koran* carries no authority to a Catholic, the Pope carries no authority to a Methodist, and the first chapter of Genesis carries no authority to a geologist. If we can use an authority our audience already knows and respects, we have an initial advantage. If this is not possible, then we must establish the prestige of the authority. We can sometimes do this merely by informing the audience, but sometimes we must resort to persuasion. And, as we have said, the discussion of persuasion will be postponed.

REASONING

Once we have our evidence we must know how to reason about it if it is to support our position. So reasoning is essential to argument.

The whole process of living, from first to last, is a long education in the use of reason. Fire burns, cats scratch, pulling things off tables brings a frown or a spanking—we learn these great truths early. Later on we learn other truths—a stitch in time saves nine, honesty is the best policy, to be good is to be happy. We say we learn from experience (or from somebody else's experience), but that is not quite true. Experience would teach nothing if we could not reason about experience.

Reasoning, therefore, is not something which we learn from books. The race learned it the hard way over a long time: if your powers of reason failed you too often you were liquidated by the falling tree, a saber-toothed tiger, or a neighbor who had *reasoned* out that a sharp stone tied to the end of a stout stick gave him certain advantages in a dispute. But we can train our powers of reason by learning something about the reasoning process.

SUBJECT AND ATTRIBUTE

Reasoning is the process by which the mind moves from certain data (the evidence) to a conclusion which was not given. We can make this progress from data to conclusion because we recognize some regularity in the world we are dealing with. We recognize a regularity of cause and effect, and a regularity of subject and attribute.

The cause-and-effect relationship has already been discussed at some length in the chapter on Exposition.[7] We continually use the cause-and-effect relationship in our ordinary reasoning. But we also continually use the subject-attribute relationship. For instance, we know that green apples are sour. Therefore we do not eat the green apple we find on the bough. Here green apples (subject) are affirmed to have a certain attribute (sour), and when we encounter the subject we conclude that the attribute is present. Or we believe that a sales tax is unfair. So we vote against such-and-such a tax because it is a sales tax.

INDUCTION: GENERALIZATION

Let us examine two examples of reasoning, examples of the kind of reasoning called INDUCTION. A businessman has hired five boys at different times from the Hawkins School and has found them all honest, well mannered, and well educated. Therefore, when the sixth boy comes along for a job the man will be inclined to hire him. In other words, the man has generalized from the five instances to the conclusion that all boys from Hawkins School are honest, well mannered, and well educated. The man has made a GENERALIZATION, moving from a number of particular instances to the general conclusion that all instances of the type investigated will be of this same sort.

To take a second example of generalization, after long observation men have concluded that water always freezes at a certain temperature, 32 degrees. Behind this conclusion, as behind the conclusion about the boys of Hawkins School, lies the assumption that a certain regularity exists. In regard to the water, we assume that

[7] Pages 111-119. A further discussion appears in the Appendix on Cause (pp. 475 ff.).

the same kind of thing in nature always behaves the same way under the same conditions—metal expands when heated; in a vacuum falling bodies, no matter what their mass, move at the same rate. Without this assumption of regularity we could not accept the conclusion we arrive at from examining the individual instances, and in fact, all science is based upon this assumption.

The principle of regularity also applies in the reasoning about the boys from Hawkins School. We assume that certain intellectual standards are maintained, that certain manners are insisted upon, that honesty is inculcated, and that the stupid, idle, boorish, or dishonest boy is not graduated. It does not matter that the conclusions we reach in these two instances compel different degrees of assent. We scarcely doubt that the next pail of water we leave out will freeze at a certain temperature, but we do doubt that absolutely all graduates of Hawkins School are models of education, manners, and honesty. We recognize here that the principle of regularity (Hawkins' standards) in human nature is scarcely as dependable as the principle of regularity in nature. The school has tried to weed out the incompetent, the boorish, and the dishonest, but human nature is very complicated and human organizations are very fallible.

THE INDUCTIVE LEAP

We recognize that the conclusion we reach about the boys from Hawkins School is only a probability, but students of logic tell us that from the strictly logical standpoint the conclusion that water always freezes at 32 degrees is also a probability. This is true because no argument which moves from *some* to *all* can give more than a probability. Undoubtedly millions of instances of water freezing at 32 degrees have been observed, but *all* instances—past, present, and future—have not been observed. After examining a certain number of instances we take the leap from the some to the all, the INDUCTIVE LEAP. We cannot be sure about the all. It does no good to appeal to the principle of regularity in nature by saying that water is water and will always behave the same way, for that principle is itself simply derived from the inspection of a number of instances and itself represents a leap from some to all.

What tests can we apply to reduce the risk of error in making the inductive leap?

First, a fair number of instances must be investigated. An instance or two proves nothing. Somebody says: "All Chinese are short and slender. Why, I used to know one out in Wyoming, and he wasn't more than five feet tall and I bet he didn't weigh more than a hundred pounds." Or: "All boys from St. Joseph's College are snobs. There was a fellow from home. . . ." We all know this type of reasoning, and can see that it proves nothing. A fair number of instances have not been examined. But there is no way to determine certainly what is a fair number of instances. We simply have to use the evidence possible to us under the given circumstances and remember that only the untrained mind is rash enough to leap without looking.

Second, the instances investigated must be typical. In a laboratory the scientist may be able to test a substance to be sure it is typical of its kind. He could detect alcohol in a sample of water and would, therefore, not use that sample in an experiment to demonstrate the freezing point of water.

But sometimes we have to assume, without testing the fact, that the instances available are typical. For example, the businessman who has hired five boys from Hawkins School assumes that they are typical—that other boys from the school will be like them. At other times, however, when we are making out a case, we can choose from among a number of instances for our investigation; in such a situation we should be sure that the instances chosen are representative. Let us consider the problem of a sociologist who, for some purpose, wishes to give a description of the life in the southern Appalachians. The sociologist picks three settlements, investigates the pattern of life there, and concludes that life (in general) in the southern Appalachians is such-and-such. But an opponent may point out that the settlements chosen are not typical, that the people are of Swiss descent and maintain a good many Swiss customs. The sociologist's generalization, then, may be worthless because his instances are not typical.

Third, if negative instances occur they must be explained. Obviously, any negative instance occurring among those which we are using as a basis for a generalization will reduce the validity of the generalization unless we can demonstrate that the negative instance is *not* typical, and therefore need not be considered. For example, if the businessman who has hired five Hawkins boys and found them all honest, hires a sixth and finds that he is pilfering in the stock room, the businessman may decide that he must give up the generalization that the Hawkins graduates are desirable employees. But he discovers that the boy who did the pilfering is a very special case, that he is really unbalanced, is a kleptomaniac, and consequently cannot be taken as typical. Therefore, the businessman returns to his generalization that Hawkins graduates are desirable employees.

To summarize, the tests for making a generalization are:

1. A fair number of instances must be investigated.

2. The instances investigated must be typical.

3. All negative instances must be explained.

INDUCTION: ANALOGY

Another type of induction is by ANALOGY. This type of reasoning is based on the idea that if two instances are alike in a number of important points they will be alike in the point in question. For example, a board of directors might argue that Jim Brown would make a good corporation executive because he has been a colonel in the army. The analogy here is between the requirements for a good army officer and a good business executive. The points of similarity might be taken as the ability to deal with men, the ability to make and execute policy, the willingness to take responsibility. Then if Brown has been successful as a colonel it may be assumed that he will be successful as a business executive.

We can arrive at certain tests for analogy similar to those for generalization:

1. The two instances compared must be similar in important respects.

2. Differences between the two instances must be accounted for as being unimportant.

In addition to these tests, we must remember that increasing the number of similar instances tends to strengthen our argument. For example, if Brown, the man being considered for an executive position in the corporation, has been a successful division chief in a government bureau as well as a successful colonel, his case is strengthened in the eyes of the board. But in the case of analogy, as of generalization, we can arrive only at probability.

DEDUCTION

On this point of probability we can distinguish the two types of induction (generalization and analogy) from the type of reasoning known as DEDUCTION. Deduction does not give probability; it gives certitude.

The most familiar example of deduction is found in ordinary geometry, the geometry we studied in high school. The system starts with certain axioms. For instance: "Things that are equal to the same thing are equal to each other." Or: "If equals be added to equals the wholes are equal."

There is no attempt in the system of geometry to prove these axioms. They are the starting point we accept. (They are LOGICALLY PRIMITIVE in the deductive system of geometry.) Once we accept them, the whole system *necessarily* follows. Accepting the axioms we can deduce our first theorem. Then, having thus obtained the first theorem, we can prove the second, and so on throughout the system generated by the axioms. Once we have the axioms the system must necessarily follow. It cannot be otherwise.

THE SYLLOGISM

Deductive reasoning appears, however, in other forms than geometry. Let us take an example of the type of reasoning called the SYLLOGISM:

All men are mortal.
Socrates was a man.
∴ Socrates was mortal.

We are reasoning here about a relation among three classes, mortal creatures, men, and Socrates. It may help us to think of the matter as a series of concentric circles, one small (Socrates), one medium-size (men), and one large (mortal creatures). We put the medium-size circle in the large one, and then the small circle in the medium-size circle. Then, obviously, the small circle is included in the large circle. We see this from the following chart:

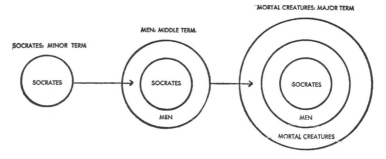

Each class is indicated by a TERM in the syllogism, the small class by the MINOR TERM, the medium-size class by the MIDDLE TERM, and the large class by the MAJOR TERM. The syllogism itself is composed of three propositions, the first two called PREMISES, and the third called the CONCLUSION. The proposition containing the major term is called the MAJOR PREMISE and that containing the minor term the MINOR PREMISE.

All men are mortal.   (major premise)
Socrates was a man.   (minor premise)
∴ Socrates was mortal. (conclusion)

The minor term is, we see, the subject of the conclusion, the major term the predicate of the conclusion, and the middle term the term that has made their relation in the conclusion possible.

Let us take another piece of reasoning that seems to have the same form:

Some soldiers are corporals.
All sergeants are soldiers.
∴ All sergeants are corporals.

We sense immediately that there has been a slip in the reasoning. And we can see why if we chart the relations among the classes in the syllogism:

The major premise (Some soldiers are corporals) says that the class *corporals* falls within the class *soldiers,* but the word *some* tells us that part of the class *soldiers* falls outside the class *corporals.* So for this premise we get Fig. 1.

The minor premise (All sergeants are soldiers) says that the class *sergeants* falls within the class *soldiers,* but this means that some of the class *soldiers* falls outside the class *sergeants.* So we get Fig. 2.

The conclusion (All sergeants are corporals) says that the class *sergeants* falls within the class *corporals*. It pretends to make the same kind of figure we had for Socrates in the end, but it cannot do so. For it is clear that the premises have given us no ground for any relation between the class *sergeants* and the class *corporals*. The premises have merely put the two classes within the third class *soldiers*. So the only figure we could reasonably get would be Fig. 3.

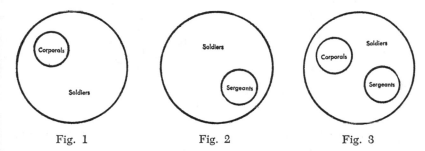

Fig. 1   Fig. 2   Fig. 3

The argument is not VALID. There has been a slip in the reasoning.

This is not the only kind of slip in reasoning that we may make in dealing with classes. Let us take another example:

All banks are financial institutions.
Some building and loan companies are not banks.
∴ Some building and loan companies are not financial institutions.

The major premise (All banks are financial institutions) says that the class *banks* falls within the class *financial institutions*. So we get Fig. 4.

The minor premise (Some building and loan companies are not banks) says that part of the class *building and loan companies* falls outside the class *banks*. This gives Fig. 5.

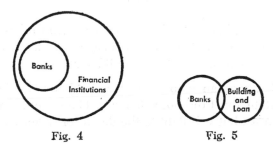

Fig. 4   Fig. 5

The conclusion (Some building and loan companies are not financial institutions) tells us that some of the class *building and loan companies* falls outside the class *financial institutions*. But this does not follow. We know that the class *banks* falls inside the class financial institutions, and the part of the class *building and loan*

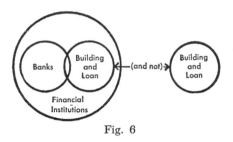

Fig. 6

companies which falls outside of the class *banks* may still fall inside the class *financial institutions,* as would be the case with Fig. 6.

In either one of the faulty arguments given above we know at a glance that the conclusion is wrong, because we know the facts of the case. We know that sergeants are not corporals and that all building and loan companies are financial institutions. But some-

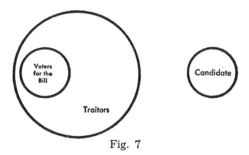

Fig. 7

times we may not know the facts; then we have to depend on the correctness of the reasoning. For instance, are we impressed by the following argument of a political candidate?

"Every Congressman who voted for the Jones-Higgins Bill betrayed this state. But I did not vote for it. Therefore, I am no traitor to your interests, but will fight to the death for them. . . ."

We are not impressed, for the candidate has not offered any finally convincing argument that he is not a traitor to the public interest. Voting for the Jones-Higgins Bill is not the only way a Congressman can betray the public interest.

What he wants his conclusion to look like is represented in Fig. 7. But all we are sure of is that the candidate belongs outside the class of those who voted for the Jones-Higgins Bill. For all he has proved, he may still be inside the class of traitors to the public interest, and we may have Fig. 8.

In any reasoning about relations among classes, it is necessary for us to look behind the words and see what and how much is said to be included within what. And it is some-times helpful to use charts such as we have made above, at least until one is experienced in dealing with this type of reasoning. And when we make a chart if, in diagramming the second premise, we automatically diagram the conclusion, then the argument is valid. This is the case, we recall, with the chart about Socrates. We diagram the major premise by putting the class *men* into the class mortal *creatures*.

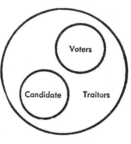

Fig. 8

Then when we diagram the minor premise by putting the class *Socrates* into the class *men* we find that we have automatically diagrammed the conclusion: Socrates was mortal. Socrates is put into the class of mortal creatures.[8]

VALID SYLLOGISM AND TRUE CONCLUSION

We have spoken of valid syllogisms, those in which the process of reasoning is correct. But we may reason correctly and still not have a true conclusion if we start with a mistaken assumption, a premise which is not true. For instance, let us look at this syllogism:

All legless creatures that crawl are snakes.
Worms are legless creatures that crawl.
∴ Worms are snakes.

In this the reasoning is correct: *If* all legless creatures that crawl were snakes, then worms, which are legless, crawling creatures,

[8] For a more detailed discussion see the Appendix on the Syllogism, p. 481.

would be snakes. But we know that the major premise (All legless creatures that crawl are snakes) is not true. Therefore, no matter how correct the reasoning may be, we cannot depend upon it to give us a true conclusion.

In other words, a syllogism may be valid (correct in its reasoning) and its conclusion may be untrue. But we always want true conclusions. Therefore, we must be careful to inspect our premises. Truth of the premises is as necessary as correct reasoning.

KINDS OF PROPOSITIONS

We can make four basic kinds of propositions about relations among classes:

1. All X is in Y. *All men are mortal.*
2. All X is excluded from Y. (Or: No X is in Y.) *No whales are fish.*
3. Some X is in Y. *Some women are cruel.*
4. Some X is excluded from Y. *Some heroes are not recognized.*

Many propositions about relations among classes do not come to us, however, in such simple forms. When that is true, our first step must be to see into which of these basic kinds the proposition is translatable. Often we can do this almost instinctively. There is no difficulty, for instance, in seeing that the proposition, "Warm gases ascend," can be translated into the form, "All warm gases are in the class of things that ascend." But some instances are more difficult and require careful analysis. Propositions containing restrictive and exclusive terms such as *all but, only,* and *all except* are especially apt to give trouble.

For example, the proposition, "None but the brave deserve the fair," seems at first glance to mean, "All the brave deserve the fair." But a little reflection shows us that such is not the case, and that it really means, "All who deserve the fair are some of the brave," and is an example of type 1. Or to take another proposition, to say, "Only students willing to work will pass this course," does not mean, "All students willing to work will pass this course." Rather, it means, "All who pass this course will be in the class of those who are willing to work." Students who are badly prepared or are stupid may not pass even if they are willing to work.

REASONING BY *EITHER–OR*

In addition to the ordinary syllogism, there are two kinds of syllogism which we shall look at briefly. The first we shall call reasoning by *either–or*, though it has a technical name, the DISJUNCTIVE SYLLOGISM.

Let us set up an example. Upon going into the kitchen and finding the steak off the table and on the floor under the sink, we think that either the cat or the dog has pulled it down. Then we discover that the cat is locked in the barn to catch rats. Therefore the dog must have committed the crime. The formula is simple. We decide on two possibilities. We exclude one. Naturally the other becomes our conclusion.

To get a true conclusion, we must be sure, as with the ordinary syllogism, that our starting point is dependable.

First, the *either–or* premise must really cover the case. The alternatives must be exhaustive. In the example of the cat and dog, if the cat was locked in the barn and the dog was out chasing rabbits, the premise simply does not cover the case. We have to investigate further to cover the possibilities. We find that, after all, it was curly-headed little Willie who pulled the steak off the table and deserves the licking.

Second, we must really mean the *either–or*. The possibilities must be distinct with no overlap between them. They must be exclusive. Let us examine a piece of reasoning which may be faulty because there is an overlap between the possibilities set up.

> To maintain peace we must have either the United Nations or a
> system of international police.
> But a system of international police is undesirable.
> ∴ We must have the United Nations.

If we take it in fact that the United Nations does *not* involve a basic system of international police, then the conclusion is valid. But if we take it that the United Nations does involve a system of international police, then the conclusion is not acceptable. It is not because the two items of the *either–or* are not distinct: international police occurs in both of them, stated in one and implied in the other. The result is that in one premise we say that international police is undesirable, and then say it is desirable (under another name) in the conclusion. But this makes nonsense.

To be sure that our starting point for reasoning by *either–or* is satisfactory we have to know what we are talking about. We must examine the facts and use our common sense to be sure that the *either–or* covers the case and that there is no overlap between the items.

REASONING BY *IF–THEN*

Reasoning by *if–then* deals with a condition and a result. The condition being fulfilled, the result follows. The technical name of this kind of reasoning is the HYPOTHETICAL SYLLOGISM.

We constantly use reasoning of this kind, as in the statement, "If you had banked the furnace, we would have had heat this morning." Fully stated, the argument would go like this:

If you do not bank the furnace, the fire will die.
But you did not bank the furnace.
∴ The fire died.

The reasoning above is correct. We have affirmed the *if*, the condition, and therefore the result necessarily follows. But the reasoning is also correct if we deny the *then*, as in the following instance:

If you do not bank the furnace, the fire will die.
But the fire has not died.
∴ You did bank the furnace.

The following example does not, however, give us correct reasoning:

If you do not bank the furnace, the fire will die.
The fire died.
∴ You did not bank the furnace.

The conclusion here is not *necessarily* acceptable. The fire may have died because the furnace was not banked, but it also may have died from other causes. For instance, there may not have been enough fuel. That is, not banking the furnace is a sufficient but not a necessary condition of the fire's going out. (See the discussion of sufficient and necessary conditions, p. 115.) For the reasoning in this last example to be valid, the *if* would have to mean *only if*. Most errors in reasoning of the type of *if–then* come about because we interpret an *if* as an *only if*. Of course, there are instances where the *if* is legitimately to be interpreted as *only if*. But this is a matter of the truth of the premise with which we start, and if we mean *only if* we should say so in the premise.

FALLACIES

In discussing each type of reasoning, inductive or deductive, we have tried to indicate the characteristic errors into which we may fall. An argument that does not follow the course of reason—an argument that involves such an error—is called a FALLACY. In induction a generalization based on too few instances is a fallacy (p. 157). Or an analogy based on instances different in important respects is a fallacy (pp. 157-58). And again, in deduction when the major and the minor terms are not properly related in the syllogism we have a fallacy (pp. 159-63).

There are fallacies which we have not touched on, at least not directly, which are all too common in argument. They are EQUIVO-CATION, BEGGING THE QUESTION, IGNORING THE QUESTION, and NON SEQUITUR (Latin for "it does not follow").

EQUIVOCATION

Equivocation is the fallacy of using the same term in different meanings in the same argument. Here is a well-known example:

Even scientists recognize a power beyond nature, for they speak of "natural law"; and if there is law, there must be a power to make the law; such a power beyond nature is called God; therefore scientists believe in God.

Here the word *law* is used equivocally, in two meanings. In the sense in which scientists use it when they speak of "natural law" it means the recognition of regularity in natural process—the law of gravity, for example. Here the sense is descriptive. But in the second sense it means what is ordinarily meant in government, a command given by a superior authority. Here the sense is prescriptive. Since the whole argument is based on the word *law*, it does not make sense *as an argument* if the word shifts its meaning. It may be true that a number of scientists do believe in God, but that does not make this a good argument.

BEGGING THE QUESTION

Begging the question occurs when the arguer assumes something to be true which really needs proof. We have already seen (p. 134) how this occurs in prejudiced propositions, such as "This unjust tax should be repealed." To say that the tax is unjust is equivalent to saying that it should be repealed. Yet the repeal is what the argument is supposed to be about. The word *unjust* smuggles into the proposition as already accepted what is supposed to be at stake and under debate.

The same principle appears on a larger scale whenever we argue in a circle. For example:

A: I admire Rembrandt's painting "The Night Watch."
B: Why?
A: Because it is a great painting.
B: How do you know?
A: All the best critics say it is.
B: How do you know who are the best critics?
A: Why, the best critics are those who recognize great painting.

Here speaker A gives a circle in the proof. He sets out to prove that the painting is great by appealing to the best critics, and then identifies the best critics as those who recognize great painting. This instance is very simple, but sometimes the begging may be concealed in a very elaborate argument. We must always be on the watch for it, for such question-begging is an attempt to establish a thing *by itself*.

IGNORING THE QUESTION

An arguer ignores the question when he introduces any consideration that will distract from what is really at stake. There are numberless ways of doing this. A competing question may be set up so that argument is shifted to new ground. Or an appeal may be made to some emotional attitude having nothing to do with the logic of the case. For instance, if a man arguing for a Republican candidate shifts the issue from the candidate's qualifications to the praise of Lincoln, the great hero of the party, he is ignoring the question. Or if a Democrat leaves a present question and begins to discuss the glorious achievements of Thomas Jefferson, he is ignoring the question. Or if a lawyer defending a man accused of murder does not deal with the question of guilt, but argues that the victim was a wicked man or that the family of the accused is worthy of pity, we have the same situation.

One of the commonest forms of ignoring the question is to shift from the question to the character or personality of the opponent. We get an instance when the husband criticizes his wife and she replies, "Well, you aren't so perfect yourself!" She has ignored the rights and wrongs of the question, her own burnt bread or bad arithmetic or overbid at bridge, and has begun to discuss his shortcomings. Or we get an instance when we argue that we cannot endorse a certain political measure because the Congressman who proposes it is divorced or drinks. We have shifted from the measure to the man.

NON SEQUITUR

Non sequitur, as we have said, means, "It does not follow." In one sense, of course, any fallacy is a *non sequitur,* because by the very nature of the case the conclusion does not follow from fallacious reasoning. But here we shall use the term to cover certain more special kinds of argument.

For instance, it may be argued: "William Brown doesn't drink or smoke, and so he ought to make a good husband." But it is obvious that a man who does not drink or smoke may still make a bad husband. He may gamble, or loaf, or beat his wife. Or it may be argued: "Harry Thompson would make a good governor, because he belongs to the upper classes." We know, however, that belonging to a certain social class proves nothing about a man's ability or integrity. So the conclusion that Thompson would make a good governor does not follow. A connection has been asserted which does not exist.

A somewhat more complicated form of *non sequitur* appears in a piece of parental reasoning like this: "As soon as I increased Billie's allowance, his grades at school began to fall. Therefore we ought to reduce his allowance since having extra money makes him idle." But Billie may have been suffering from eye strain, or may have fallen in love, or may now be taking up a subject for which he is badly prepared. Or let us take another example: "Just after Herbert Hoover was elected President we had the greatest depression in history. How can you respect a man like that?"

In the argument about Billie and the argument about Hoover the same thing has happened. It is argued that because A (an increase in Billie's allowance or the election of Hoover) precedes B (Billie's bad grades or the depression), A must necessarily be the cause of B. This occurs when the arguer does not understand the nature of a cause (pp. 117-19) or does not take the trouble to analyze the situation. He simply assumes that if one thing precedes another, it is the cause of that other.

FALLACIES AND REFUTATION

Some understanding of fallacies is useful to help us reason straight, but it is also useful to help us locate defects in an opposing argument. If we can point out a fallacy in an opposing argument, we can REFUTE that argument, and REFUTATION is a powerful secondary weapon for maintaining our own position. Even if we are not engaged in a debate but are simply writing a piece of argument, we often find that we have to refute certain arguments—arguments which we can anticipate. Or we may want to refute certain arguments already made in order to clear the ground for our own views.

It is not necessary to memorize a list of fallacies to discover defects in reasoning or to reason straight. Many people who have never heard the word *fallacy* can reason straight or locate defects in the reasoning of another person. When we meet the example of a fallacy in cold type on the page of a textbook, we are inclined to say, "Nobody with common sense would commit such an error." That is true. But common sense is not so common, after all, and sometimes we have to work for it.

THE IMPLIED SYLLOGISM

When we first study the syllogism we are inclined to feel that to do so is a waste of time because in actual practice we rarely use or encounter it. It seems so remote from the texture of living argument and reasoning that we think it impractical, nothing but a schoolbook exercise.

Now it is true that we rarely encounter the syllogism in the form which we have treated here. But that does not mean that it may not lie behind many arguments which we make or attend to. As a matter of fact, syllogistic reasoning is often embedded in the body of a discourse like the bones in the flesh—and it may serve the same purpose as the bones. This may be so even when part of the syllogism is never stated at all, when it is assumed that the audience will supply the unstated part. We may say that such a piece of reasoning is an implied syllogism. But it has a technical name, ENTHYMEME ("in the mind").

A hunter says: "This setter has not been well trained. It is gun-shy." Behind his remark lies a syllogism, which we can formally set up:

A gun-shy setter is not well trained. (major premise)
This setter is gun-shy. (minor premise)
∴ This setter is not well trained.

We see immediately that in the hunter's remark the major premise does not appear. It is assumed that his audience has it in mind. So in his statement we have an implied, and not a developed, syllogism.

Similarly, a minor premise or a conclusion may be suppressed. In the following example the conclusion is suppressed: "A girl who is selfish with her mother and father probably won't make a good wife, and Susie certainly imposes on her parents. Now that ought to give you something to think about if you continue to go around with her." Set up formally, the syllogism appears:

A girl who is selfish, etc., probably won't make a good wife.
Susie is selfish (imposes on her parents).
∴ Susie will not make a good wife (what you had better think about).

These examples are very simple, and we seize on their meaning in a flash without the necessity of framing the argument in full. But sometimes the basic argument is more deeply embedded in the midst of evidence, examples, and other material. Here is a paragraph from an editorial:

Nobody denies that our economic situation is desperate and that we are facing a crisis, and nobody denies that there is great need for wise legislation in all matters affecting the business of the nation. We must scrutinize with redoubled attention every bill which comes before Congress and try to see what its effect will be in this sphere of activity. This is undoubtedly necessary with the present bill to lower taxes. If it is passed it will have an inflationary effect. What attitude shall we take toward the present bill?

The main point here concerns the tax reduction bill. It is assumed that the present situation is desperate and that good legislation is needed. All of that is background. The argument to follow can really be divided into two syllogisms linked together:

Tax reduction promotes inflation.
The present bill would reduce taxes.
∴ The present bill would promote inflation.

The conclusion of this syllogism provides a premise for the next one, the link in the argument.

Whatever produces inflation is bad.
The present bill would promote inflation.
∴ The present bill is bad.

Neither the major premise nor the conclusion of this syllogism is stated in the editorial. The editorial writer feels that his reader knows that inflation is bad, and he feels that the conclusion about this particular bill will strike the reader more powerfully if the reader is forced to come to it himself. The reader will himself answer the question: "What attitude shall we take toward the present bill?"

An extended argument may be a tissue or chain of implied syllogisms, the conclusion of one becoming a premise in the next. The writer trusts his reader to grasp the line of reasoning without the full statement. But a chain is no stronger than its weakest link, and if we are making an argument we must be careful not to insert a link that will not bear the strain of the argument. A good way to avoid this danger is to go back over an argument to inspect each implied syllogism and to make sure that in its developed form it would be valid.

EXTENDED ARGUMENT: THE BRIEF

The composition of an extended argument calls for very careful planning. One point must lead to another, effect must be traced to cause, premise must give conclusion. Random thoughts, no mat-

ter how important in themselves, will not carry conviction. Therefore it is a good idea to think through an argument before beginning the actual writing. To prepare a systematic outline of the argument is the best way to be sure that the subject is covered and the
relationship among the parts is clear.

When a lawyer prepares the BRIEF of a case, he does just this.
The brief is not a set of jottings and suggestions. It is the full outline of an argument. *The brief is the arrangement in logical sequence and in logical relationship of the evidence and the argument
on one side of the dispute. The brief makes complete sense in itself,
even to a reader who is not previously familiar with the dispute.*

The process of drawing a brief in the law or for a formal debate
of any sort is a very complicated one. But for ordinary purposes
we can dispense with some of the subtleties and refinements useful
to the lawyer or debater. We cannot, however, dispense with the
requirements listed above: logical sequence, logical relationship,
completeness.

PARTS OF THE BRIEF

The brief is divided into three general sections: INTRODUCTION,
ARGUMENT or DISCUSSION, and CONCLUSION.

The introduction should give whatever information is necessary
for an understanding of the situation: proposition, definition of
terms, history of the question, immediate occasion of the dispute,
statement of admissions and issues. Not all of these items are necessary in all briefs, but the proposition and the statement of issues
are always demanded. In any event, *nothing not acceptable to both
sides* should appear in the introduction. The argument presents all
the evidence and the inferences drawn from that evidence step by
step to lead to the single conclusion desired. When such are demanded it also presents refutations of opposing views and answers
possible objections to its own. The conclusion summarizes the fundamental points of the argument and when necessary shows how
they relate to the question at stake.

ORGANIZATION OF THE BRIEF

It is important so to arrange the items of the brief on the page
that the relationship among them is immediately clear. Each of the
three main sections should be treated independently, with a system

of numbering complete under that section. Main headings under a section should be given Roman numerals, the subdivisions scaling down in importance marked *A, 1, a.* A dummy form will make the system clear.

I. _____
   A. _____
      1. _____
         a. _____   _____
         b. _____
      2. _____
         a. _____
   B. _____
      1. _____
         a. _____
II. _____
   A. etc.,

It is important to keep the indentations on the left margin consistent in each class and to be sure that a class of lower importance is more deeply indented than the class just above it. If more subdivisions are needed than are indicated here, the system can be begun over again with the key numerals and letters in parentheses. For instance, if subdivisions are needed under *a*, we can use *(I)*, *(A)*, *(1)*, and so forth. But for ordinary purposes such an extension is rarely necessary.

In the second section of the brief (the argument), a new element is introduced that is not shown in the dummy above. Here we have to indicate the relation of evidence to the inferences drawn from the evidence. That is, *I* is true *because* of *A*, and *A* is true *because* of *1* and *2*, and *1* is true *because* of *a* and *b*. We give the conclusion (as *I*) and work back through a chain of reasons.

So for the argument we can fill out the dummy thus:

I. _____ *because* (or *for*) [9]
   A. _____ *because*
      1. _____ *because*
         a. _____ *and*
         b. _____

[9] We may make a distinction for this purpose of a brief between *because*

Thus all the relationships are indicated as a chain of proof. If we need to interrupt the chain of proof to refute an opposing view or to answer an objection, we can do it as follows:

c (following *b* above). The view that (so-and-so) is true can be refuted because

(I) ——————————————————————— *and*

(II) ———————————————————————

or:

c. The objection that (so-and-so) is not valid because

(I) ———————————————————————

(II) ———————————————————————

Such a form can be used at any necessary level, and not merely at the level of *a*, *b*, and so on.

EXAMPLE OF THE BRIEF

Let us see how we would go about using a brief in preparing a theme. Suppose we have been given the proposition: "Scientists should refuse to participate in research which may lead to the production of military weapons."

We may have an immediate, almost instinctive reaction to the proposition, either for or against it, or we may not be able to reach a conclusion without further consideration. In either case, we feel it worth while to get some acquaintance with the literature on the subject. If we have not made up our own mind, the arguments by others may help us. If we have made up our own mind, we may

———

and *for*, using *because* to mean the *cause of*, and *for* to mean the *reason for believing the truth of*. Let us take a simple example:

Because:
 I. Three people died in Morgansville in traffic accidents this week, *because*
   A. The driver, in one instance, was intoxicated, *and*
   B. The streets, in the other instances, were slick with ice.

For:
 I. Three people died in Morgansville in traffic accidents this week, *for*
   A. I saw one person die, *and*
   B. The Morgansville *Herald* reported the deaths of two other persons in the issue of May 21.

The point here is to indicate clearly what is being asserted, the cause of an event or the reason for believing the event to have occurred.

find arguments in support of our view, and we shall certainly encounter arguments against our view which we should be prepared to refute.

If we went to the library to investigate the question we might find a considerable body of material on the subject. After reading such material we might have reached an opinion of our own. Let us suppose that we wish to attack the proposition, to take the negative side.

Sometimes the history of a question is important, and that is true here. The events of the past war make the question very important. So we may begin our brief with the "History of the Question." Then we may move on to a statement of the "Occasion for Discussion." That is, the immediate discussion is provoked by a general debate going on over the country. Then we want to be sure that we know exactly what the real issues are. So we set up a section on "Issues." Then we are ready to give the body of the argument.

We might make a brief like the following:

Introduction:

I. Proposition: Scientists should refuse to participate in research which may lead to the production of military weapons.
II. History of the Question
    A. The atomic bomb made clear the destructive power of modern science.
        1. Scientists realize this power.
            a. Dr. Kistiakowsky, who witnessed the Alamogordo explosion called it "the nearest thing to doomsday." (William L. Laurence, *Dawn over Zero: The Story of the Atomic Bomb,* New York, Alfred A. Knopf, 1946, p. 11)
            b. Albert Einstein says that atomic war might destroy two-thirds of mankind. ("Einstein on the Atomic Bomb," as told to Raymond Swing, *Atlantic Monthly,* CLXXVI, November 1945, 43)
        2. Laymen realize this power.
            a. The press has been full of information on this point, and there have been numerous articles and books, like John Hersey's *Hiroshima* (New York, Alfred A. Knopf, 1946), and Norman Cousins's *Modern Man is Obsolete* (New York, Macmillan, 1946).

B. Efforts have been made to curb the use of atomic energy for war.
1. The Atomic Commission has been set up in this country.
2. The United Nations are trying to reach an agreement to bar the bomb.
III. Occasion for Discussion
A. There has been debate among scientists about their responsibility.
1. Norbert Wiener refused to give information about research having military significance. ("A Scientist Rebels," *Atlantic Monthly*, CLXXIX, January 1947, 46)
2. Louis N. Ridenour attacked Dr. Wiener's position. ("The Scientist Fights for Peace," *Atlantic Monthly*, CLXXIX, May 1947, 80-83)
3. *The American Scholar* published a forum on the relation of scientists to war (XVI, Spring 1947, 213-225) and a set of letters in reply ("Should the Scientists Resist Military Intrusion?" XVI, Summer 1947, 353-360).
IV. Issues
A. Does the scientist behave morally by refusing to participate?
B. Does the refusal to participate practically serve the cause of peace?

Argument:

I. To refuse is not moral, *for*
A. In so far as the scale of war is a determining factor, the refusal is morally meaningless, *for*
1. The fact of killing constitutes the moral question without reference to the number of victims. (Louis N. Ridenour, *op. cit.*, p. 82)
B. The scientist who refuses neglects some of the broader moral issues, *for*
1. If he believes that this system of government has moral value, it is worth defending in war, *and*
2. If in case of such a war he had not assisted in preparation or refused to participate in research, after the commencement of war, he would want victory at somebody else's expense.
II. To refuse is not practical, *for*
A. No distinction can now be drawn between research which may have a military value and research which may not, *for*
1. Scientific advance depends on a number of individual discoveries and ideas, the importance of no one of which by itself can be predicted, *for*

a. No one scientist or discovery made the atomic bomb possible. (William L. Laurence, *op. cit.*)

    2. A scientific discovery may lead to both a peaceful and a warlike purpose, *for*

      a. An airplane may drop a bomb or carry serum.

B. In total war the "whole range of industrial and technical know-how in the world becomes a military factor." (William Yandell Elliott, "Facts and Values," *American Scholar*, XVI, Summer 1947, 358)

C. The idea that the scientist is a special case to be distinguished from the farmer, factory worker or manager, mother, and so forth, can be refuted, *for*

    1. Food, manufactured goods, and manpower are all necessary in war.

D. If scientists did refuse to participate, the cause of peace would not necessarily be advanced, *for*

    1. If the scientists in this country should refuse, the policy in other countries would not be affected, *and*

    2. If scientists everywhere refused to work, war could still be carried on with the weapons which can now be manufactured.

E. The problem of maintaining peace is not a scientific one, *for*

    1. Science does not define values (Christian Gauss, "The Threat of Science," *Scribner's*, LXXXVII, May 1930, 467-478), *and*

    2. Peace must be maintained at the practical level of applied values, *for*

      a. World-wide economic adjustments would promote peace, *and*

      b. Political arrangements are necessary to set up the machinery of peace.

Conclusion:

I. It follows that the scientist would serve no moral or practical purpose by refusing to continue his research.

We notice that in such a brief every item is a complete sentence making its own point, and that if we read the argument through the relationship of each item to the chain of proof is clear. Furthermore, whenever a reference is given for some printed piece of evidence, the reference is given full bibliographical form.[10]

[10] See Appendix 3, pp. 486-516 for information about bibliographical forms.

When such a brief has been completed, most of the work for an argument has been done. All that remains is to develop the material so that it will be attractive reading. Here is a theme developed from the preceding brief.

SHOULD THE SCIENTISTS STRIKE?

INTRODUCTION   The scientists of the world are in a peculiar position. For a long time, almost ever since the beginning of modern science, people have been looking to the scientists for a better world for them to live in. And in our time we were all taught from childhood that the scientists would not only bring plenty to the world but would also bring peace. Many of the scientists themselves must have believed this too. But now science has just shown everybody how powerful it is to destroy as well as to create, and some of the scientists are afraid of

[1] I   what they have done. [1] Some of them have gone so far as to say that they will refuse to engage in any research leading to the invention of military weapons.

[2] II, A   [2] The day the atomic bomb fell on Hiroshima science became the central fact for warfare. Science has always been used to improve weapons, but this time it provided *the* weapon which in a single instant destroyed a city and conquered an empire.

[3] II, A, 1   [3] The scientists were the first to realize that this was a new period in history. William L. Laurence in his book *Dawn over Zero: The Story of the Atomic Bomb* * tells

[4] II, A, 1, a   how [4] Dr. Kistiakowsky, one of the scientists watching the trial explosion at Alamogordo, New Mexico, said it was "the nearest thing to doomsday that one could pos-

[5] II, A, 1, b   sibly imagine." And [5] Albert Einstein, the great scientist whose work made the bomb possible, has said that the bomb may destroy two-thirds of mankind. †

[6] II, A, 2   [6] Ordinary people, too, are aware of the danger as we can tell by picking up any newspaper or magazine. Al-

[7] II, A, 2, a   most everybody has read [7] John Hersey's story of Hiroshima ‡ and the horrible effects of the bomb, and many

* New York, Alfred A. Knopf, 1946, p. 11.

† "Einstein on the Atomic Bomb," as told to Raymond Swing, *Atlantic Monthly,* CLXXVI, November 1945, 43.

‡ New York, Alfred A. Knopf, 1946.

people have read the book by Cousins called *Modern Man is Obsolete.* *

⁸ II, B

⁹ II, B, 1

¹⁰ II, B, 2

[8] Some things have been done to curb the use of atomic energy for war. For example, [9] the Atomic Commission has been set up in this country, and the [10] United Nations are trying to control the use of atomic energy.

¹¹ III, A

[11] It is only natural that scientists, who made the bomb, should try to do something about the use of

¹² III, A, 1

science for war. When [12] Norbert Wiener, who is a prominent mathematician and who did research for World War II, was asked for some information about his work, he wrote a letter refusing to have anything more to do with creating armaments. His letter was published under the title "A Scientist Rebels." † This letter caused a long debate among scientists which is still going on. The scientists cannot agree about Dr. Wiener's course

¹³ III, A, 2

¹⁴ III, A, 3

of action. For instance, [13] Louis N. Ridenour ‡ attacked Dr. Wiener's position, and the [14] *American Scholar* § published a forum on the relation of scientists to war with letters in reply in a later issue.

¹⁵ IV

[15] Since this is a problem that concerns everybody, we should all think about it. I am not a scientist or a politician, but I do have my views on the subject for what they are worth. It seems to me that Dr. Wiener is wrong. I shall try to argue my views on two main points.

¹⁶ IV, A

¹⁷ IV, B

[16] First, is the refusal of a scientist to participate in any research that may be used for military purposes morally good? [17] Second, if he refuses, does he really serve the cause of peace? I do not mean to say that these two questions can be completely separated, but for the sake of this discussion I shall try to keep them separate.

ARGUMENT

¹⁸ I, A

There are several objections to the idea that a refusal to participate in such research is morally good. [18] First, it seems clear to me that on moral grounds there is no difference between an old-fashioned war and a new-

* New York, Macmillan, 1946.

† *Atlantic Monthly,* CLXXIX, January 1947, 46.

‡ "The Scientist Fights for Peace," *Atlantic Monthly,* CLXXIX, May 1947, 80-83.

§ XVI, Spring 1947, 213-225, Summer 1947, 353-360.

¹⁹ I, A, 1

fashioned one. ¹⁹ The number of people killed, and whether they are soldiers in the field or civilians in cities, does not change the moral question. That has been there all the time. I shall quote from the article by Louis N. Ridenour, who has written an answer to Dr. Wiener. On this point he says: "God told Moses, 'Thou shalt not kill'—not 'Thou shalt not kill with atomic energy, for that is so effective as to be sinful.' " *

²⁰ I, B

²⁰ Second, the scientist who refuses research on Dr. Wiener's grounds does not see some of the broader moral issues.

²¹ I, B, 1

²¹ If he believes that this country gives a moral way of life, with more liberty than some other, he might have to admit that war would be necessary under some circumstances to defend it. But this would contradict his other opinion.

²² I, B, 2

²² And if he still held to his refusal to participate in research, he would still want to share in the benefits of victory in such a war. This means that he would want somebody else to do the scientific work and the fighting so that he could keep his own hands clean and his conscience clear. But that does not seem moral to me, to make somebody else do the dirty work for you.

²³ II

²³ I shall turn now to the question, does the scientist's refusal do any practical good? Does it serve the cause of peace? I believe that Dr. Wiener has made this matter appear too simple just as he has made the matter of morality appear too simple. There are several objections that occur to me.

²⁴ II, A

²⁴ First, how can the scientist tell which piece of research may serve a military purpose and which will not?

²⁵ II, A, 1

²⁵ Scientific advance depends on a number of individual discoveries and ideas. Anybody who reads *Dawn over Zero*, which I have already mentioned,

²⁶ II, A, 1, a

²⁶ will see how many single pieces of research lay behind the atomic bomb. And nobody could have guessed that many of them would ever be used to kill human beings.

²⁷ II, A, 2

²⁷ Furthermore, when the scientific discovery does lead to a machine or a process, that machine or process may be used

²⁸ II, A, 2, a

for either a peaceful or a warlike purpose. ²⁸ An airplane dropped the bomb on Hiroshima and an airplane may be used to carry serum to a baby dying of diphtheria.

---

* Ridenour, *op. cit.*, p. 82.

²⁹ When we think about what is required to carry on a modern war, we see another objection. Food, all sorts of manufactured goods, and man power are necessary, as well as weapons. The farm, the factory and the nursery are just as important from one point of view as the laboratory. William Yandell Elliott, Professor of Government at Harvard University, has made this point in writing about science and war: * "The whole range of industrial and technical know-how in the world be-

²⁰ II, C

comes a military factor." ³⁰ Would Dr. Wiener want every farmer to quit raising corn, every worker to quit making automobiles or playing cards, and every woman

³¹ II, C, 1

to stop having children? ³¹ To be consistent he would have to demand that, for food, manufactured goods, and man power are all necessary in war.

³² II, D

³² For a third objection, I can suggest that even if Dr. Wiener's view were adopted by all the scientists in this country peace would not be guaranteed. ³³ There is no

³³ II, D, 1

reason to believe that all other nations would stop research. ³⁴ Furthermore, even if all scientists everywhere

³⁴ II, D, 2

refused to work, war could still be carried on with the weapons which people already know how to make.

³⁵ II, E

³⁵ This leads to my last objection, that the problem of maintaining peace is not a scientific one at all. Science gives us the technical know-how, as Dr. Elliott calls it, but it does not tell us what to do with that know-how.

³⁶ II, E, 1

³⁶ We have to figure out the good and the bad for ourselves. I can refer to an essay by Christian Gauss on this point. He says: "Quite evidently there are certain questions which the scientist can answer and certain others which he cannot. Among these latter are questions as important as the following: Is this holy or is this obscene? Is this beautiful or is this ugly? Is this good or is this evil?" †

³⁷ II, E, 2

³⁷ When we get around to figuring out the good and bad for ourselves, we find that we are involved in things

³⁸ II, E, 2, a

like economics and politics and not in science. ³⁸ If scientific methods were applied to producing food and goods all over the world, many of the causes for war

* "Facts and Values," *American Scholar,* XVI, Summer 1947, 358.

† "The Threat of Science," *Scribner's,* LXXXVII, May 1930, 470.

would be removed. But that is an economic problem.
[39] II, E, 2, b   [39] And it is by political arrangements at home and abroad that we can set up the actual machinery for peace.

CONCLUSION   If my line of argument is sound, then the refusal of a scientist to participate in any research which might have military value is not admirable morally and does no practical good. And if that is true, the scientist should continue to follow his chosen occupation. He can work for peace in other ways which we hope will be more effective than his laboratory strike.

ORDER OF THE BRIEF AND ORDER OF THE ARGUMENT

We notice that the author of the theme has very closely followed the brief, step by step. This is not always necessary. Sometimes the author may want to plunge into the very middle of his argument, at what he considers the crucial point, and then later set up the background of the question. Or he may move to the question by anecdote or illustration and thus catch the interest of his audience. Or he may state his conclusion first, and then give his reasons. We rarely find an article or essay which sticks slavishly to the line of the brief.

But the ability to draw up a brief remains important. It is a very good way for the author to clear his own mind. After he has cleared his own mind, he can then more readily adapt his method to his audience. And in any event, it is advisable for the inexperienced writer to follow very closely the line of the brief when he comes to the actual composition of his argument.

The theme given above is rather elaborate and runs to nearly 2,000 words. It is really a "readings" theme in the form of an argument. But the same method can be used on a theme of any scale. Even in a very short theme involving an argument, it is well to brief the material before beginning the actual writing.

PERSUASION

In the beginning of this chapter we said that, though argument makes the appeal to reason and aims at conviction, the appeal to the emotions, persuasion, may be very important as the strategy of presenting an argument. The appeal to reason and the appeal to emotion can be distinguished, but both may appear in the same discourse.

The human being is a unit, after all, and his reason and his emotions are but different aspects of that unity. Even the most rigorously impersonal and logical mathematician is driven to his work by some *desire*—he feels that knowledge is good in itself, that using his faculties is good, that to satisfy his curiosity is good. He is not thinking what his work is good *for*, merely that it is good.

Though all our reasoning is undertaken in the broad context of our emotional life and in the end we want it to lead to satisfactions of the emotional life, the emotions may locally, at a given moment, get in the way of the exercise of reason. Then we get a kind of short circuit, and the short-range satisfaction of the emotions will defeat the long-range satisfaction. So Tom Smith votes Republican (or Democratic) against his long-range interests, just because his grandfather fought under General Sherman (or General Lee). So Jack Brown hits the bottle to avoid a problem instead of facing the problem and trying to solve it. So Susie Perkins makes a joke at the expense of a friend just to please her own vanity in her wit, and loses a friend.

Reason should serve to show us the way to long-run satisfaction; but sometimes, human nature being what it is, we have to appeal to short-range satisfactions in order to lead someone to see the long-range satisfaction. We have to make a person feel that the immediate effort is worth while. Our problem is to find the way to establish fruitful contact with him. That is the problem of persuasion in argument.

We cannot expect our ideas, no matter how good they are, to make their way readily if we do not know how to present them. Even the scientist is irritated and put off if he does not find clarity in the discussion he is attending to—no matter how valuable the ideas may be in that discussion; and mathematicians talk about "elegance" in a proof just as a woman might speak of style in a dress or a painter about the execution of a picture. And when we get away from the cold, accurate language of mathematics and science into the warm and confused language of the ordinary world, the way of presenting an idea becomes even more important. The right way may predispose our audience to hear us out, to listen with sympathy, to give us the benefit of the doubt.

THE OCCASION AND THE "RIGHT WAY"

What is the "right way"? There is no single right way, for what is right for one subject and one audience is wrong for another. But the right way always accomplishes one basic thing: it catches the attention of the audience, and it defines a common ground for speaker or writer and audience.

The good writer or speaker is aware of his occasion (p. 3), and the occasion involves (1) the speaker, (2) the subject, and (3) the audience. All three are interrelated, and we have to ask several questions about them:

1. What is the attitude of the audience toward the subject?
2. What is the speaker's attitude toward the subject?
3. What kinds of treatment will the subject permit?
4. What is the audience's attitude toward the speaker?
5. What is the speaker's attitude toward his audience?

The right way to catch and hold the attention of the audience and to find common ground with them depends on the answers to these five questions.

If we are addressing an audience already specially interested in our subject, half our battle is won. The writer of an article in a scientific journal can assume that his reader is interested; he is addressing the specialist. The speaker addressing a mass meeting to protest a particular tax bill can depend on his audience. But the writer of an article on a scientific subject or on some theory of taxation in a popular magazine like the *Atlantic Monthly* or *Collier's* has to capture his audience, and capture it quickly.

What catches the eye? The moving object or the bright object, not the fixed or the dull. And what catches the eye catches the mind. So drama and vividness are important. The sharp anecdote, the interesting or shocking scene, the memorable phrase, the disturbing question—all of these devices may be used to catch the attention. We know them all from the pages of magazines, the platform, and the pulpit. When they are really relevant to the topic under discussion—when the anecdote makes a point or the question truly leads into the discussion—such devices are effective. When they are not relevant, the audience may feel that it is being patronized and imposed upon.

Sometimes, however, the writer can dispense with devices like scenes or anecdotes, and catch the attention of the audience by showing immediately that the topic which the audience had felt was very remote from its concerns is really of great importance. For instance, Tibet is fairly remote from the concerns of the ordinary citizen, but if the writer can show that Tibet may become very significant in the general political picture of the Orient and that world stability depends on stability in the Orient, then the ordinary citizen realizes that he has some interest in Tibet. The problem, then, is to move fast enough; you have to prove to the reader immediately that what you are talking about really concerns him and may affect his life.

Once the audience's attention has been caught, the game is merely begun. Vividness remains important, even though the vividness may no longer concern scenes or anecdotes but phrasing or apt similes and metaphors, and the drama may not involve people but the clash of ideas and opinions. The audience must be constantly aware of what is going on, what issues are at stake, how the argument moves from one point to another, and that ground has been gained. It must catch the sense of impending climax, the sense of an objective. Without clarity of language and organization this is not possible: we cannot then hold the attention of the audience.

These considerations are relative to a particular situation—to the answers we would have to give to our first three questions in the particular situation. We might, for instance, catch the attention of an audience which had a neutral attitude toward our subject, but then find that in doing so we had falsified our own attitude toward the subject. The anecdote that might be right for a political article might be wrong for the pulpit simply because in the pulpit it would falsify the basic attitude of the speaker toward the subject. If the speaker is urgent and serious about his subject and wants to impress that fact upon his audience, he cannot use devices which contradict his own basic attitude, or if he does so he must use great skill in making the transition back to the effect he fundamentally desires. And for some subjects certain methods of treatment are inapplicable. Even clarity is a relative matter, for what is clear to some people is not clear to others, and some subjects cannot be simplified beyond a certain point. The question is always, "Clear for whom and clear about what?"

THE COMMON GROUND

So far we have been concerned with the problem of catching and holding the attention of the audience. But there is the problem of finding the common ground. This is the final problem, for if we do not find this common ground, everything else is meaningless. We have already touched on this question in speaking of the possibility of catching the interest of the audience by showing that a subject—like Tibet—which had seemed to be of no concern is really of great concern. In such attempts we try to find the common ground between the audience and the subject.

But there remains the problem of finding the common ground between audience and speaker or writer. Without finding this, it is impossible to convince the audience. As we have said earlier, in the most impersonal and technical piece of argument, it is assumed that there is the common ground of definition and reason. This common ground must always be found, but most often this is not enough. We have to overcome prejudices, personal hostilities, habits of feeling and thinking, inherited attitudes. And to do this we must find a starting point acceptable to the audience. Let us take an example.

Suppose Mr. Brown has a strong anti-Semitic attitude and Mr. Smith is arguing against that view.

SMITH: Look here, I know how you feel, but I'm just curious to know how it squares with your other views. It just doesn't seem consistent with what I know about you.
BROWN: What do you mean?
SMITH: Well, just the way you manage your affairs, the way you treat people.
BROWN: What's that got to do with it?
SMITH: Well, nobody ever said you aren't a straight shooter, or didn't believe in justice, or any of these things. Like that time when you—
BROWN: That hasn't got anything to do with it.
SMITH: You don't deny that you believe in people getting justice.
BROWN: Sure, I don't deny that, but—

Smith has tried to locate the common ground. He has made Brown admit that he has a notion of justice. Now he has the job of making Brown see what justice would mean in a particular situation. That may be a hard job, but at least there is a starting point in the common agreement that justice is desirable. But suppose that Brown denies that he is interested in justice.

BROWN: Look here, I know justice is all right, by and large. But, buddy, this is a tough world and a man's got to look out for himself. He's got to watch his interests.

SMITH: OK, let's forget that justice stuff. A man's got to watch his own interests. That's right. It's a good practical point of view.

BROWN: I'm a practical man.

SMITH: Well, the question just boils down to what a man's interests are, doesn't it?

BROWN: Sure.

SMITH: Now on the Jewish question, maybe our interests aren't as simple as they sometimes seem—

Smith has here accepted the common ground of practical self-interest. Now his job is to show that in the light of self-interest anti-Semitism may be a short-sighted policy in any society. Again, he may not convince his friend, but at least he has a starting point.

We have to find the starting point. If there is no starting point possible, argument is not possible. There remains only the resort to force if a question is to be resolved.

To find the common ground we must know our audience and know ourselves. And when we are sure about what we do agree on we must say to the audience: "We disagree about the question before us, but we really agree on something more important than the question before us, something that lies deeper than the question. And since we do agree on that deeper question, I can show you that we ought to agree on the present question." We do not say that in so many words, but that is what we mean to convey.

We must convey this if we are to overcome the hostile attitude of the audience. By and large, we must convince the audience that our own attitude toward it is friendly. There are times when a brutal shock may bring an audience to its senses and may startle it into thought, but even then the audience, in the end, must come to feel that the motive behind giving the shock is a responsible one. Hard words mean nothing to a man unless he respects or likes the speaker of the hard words. So tact, fair-mindedness, patience, and respect for the audience are essential. They are not only essential for persuasion in argument. They are important for many kinds of writing. And all of this comes down to a matter of TONE. The chapter on Tone will discuss this subject at length.

SUMMARY

Argument is the kind of discourse used to make the audience (reader or listener) think or act as the arguer desires. It appeals to the understanding, and aims to CONVINCE. It differs from the other forms of discourse in that it arises, directly or indirectly, from a situation of conflict in ideas or attitudes.

An argument cannot be about a subject considered as a vague generality, or about a question of mere taste. An argument must be about a PROPOSITION, a statement that can be believed, doubted, or denied. A proposition represents a judgment.

There are two kinds of propositions, Propositions of FACT and propositions of POLICY. The proposition of fact asserts that something is true. The proposition of policy asserts that a certain line of action is desirable.

A proposition should be SINGLE. It should not express more than one idea for argument. Even though an extended argument involves several propositions, each one must still be single, and must be argued individually.

A proposition should be CLEAR. That is, it should not contain terms which are not understood, and the accepted terms should be understood in a single sense for the purpose of that argument. An argument cannot proceed unless all concerned accept the definition of the terms involved.

A proposition should be UNPREJUDICED. The wording should not smuggle in anything which would imply a foregone conclusion to the argument, anything that "begs the question."

Some propositions can be understood immediately, but for some we must know the HISTORY OF THE QUESTION in order to know exactly what is at stake. And for similar reasons it is sometimes necessary to know the OCCASION OF THE DISCUSSION. The particular circumstances may modify the meaning.

The single idea of the proposition may raise several reasons for and against it. We should study the proposition to determine what are the points on which controversy may focus. An essential point is called an ISSUE.

A point is essential if its defeat means the defeat of the proposition. The supporter of a proposition must win on all the issues to win on the proposition. A whole argument can hinge on one point, or issue.

There are two kinds of issues, ADMITTED and CRUCIAL. An issue on which both parties to an argument are in agreement is admitted. The issue (or issues) on which they are not in agreement is crucial.

We arrive at the issues by making an ANALYSIS of the proposition. To analyze a proposition, all possible arguments on both sides are listed, the affirmative facing its negative, when such pairing is possible. There is no pair for an admitted issue. That is, there is nothing on the opposing side against it. The next step is to reduce the points of argument to the fundamental ones.

When the proposition is one of policy certain STOCK QUESTIONS may help to reduce the arguments to order. These stock questions, which can be applied to the individual points, are:

1. Is there a need for change?

2. Will the policy suggested be effective?

3. Are the possible benefits of the suggested policy greater than any new disadvantages?

4. Is there any alternative policy better than the proposed one?

In a proposition of fact the location of the issues becomes a problem of defining the fact, or facts, by which the proposition stands or falls.

The actual process of argument involves EVIDENCE, whatever can be offered as support for an argument. Evidence is of two kinds, FACT and OPINION.

To be accepted as fact a piece of evidence must be VERIFIABLE or ATTESTED by a reliable source.

Verifiable evidence, as we use the phrase here, is the kind that can be established by referring to some regularity in nature. For instance, it can be verified by a test that a certain cord will support a certain weight or that water will freeze at a certain temperature. Or it can be verified that the moon was full on a certain night.

Evidence by testimony can be subjected to the following tests:

1. Was there opportunity for the witness to observe the event?

2. Was the witness physically capable of observing the event?

3. Was the witness intellectually capable of understanding and reporting?

4. Was the witness honest?

But neither verifiable evidence nor attested evidence is valuable if it is not truly relevant to the issue in question.

The reliability of evidence of opinion depends on the AUTHORITY of the person giving the opinion. Experience and success are generally taken to signify authority, but neither is reliable unless the person who is experienced or successful is capable of analyzing his experience or the means of his success. Authority, too, must be considered in relation to time. What is acceptable as authority at one time may not be accepted at another. The authority of a physicist of 1850 would not necessarily be accepted today. Furthermore, what is acceptable as authority for one audience may not be acceptable for another.

In evidence of opinion, as in evidence of fact, the question of relevance must be considered.

Once evidence is available it must be reasoned about in an argument. Reasoning is the process by which the mind moves from certain given data (evidence) to a conclusion that was not given.

There are two types of reasoning, INDUCTION and DEDUCTION.

There are two types of induction, GENERALIZATION and ANALOGY.

Generalization is the process of moving from a number of particular instances to a general conclusion that all instances of the type being investigated will be the same. For example, if five boys from the Hawkins School prove honest we generalize that all boys from that school will prove honest. But there is always a risk in generalization. At the best it can only give probability. There is an INDUCTIVE LEAP.

To reduce the risk of error, the following rules can be applied:

1. A fair number of instances must be investigated. One or two instances indicate nothing.

2. The instances investigated must be typical of the class being investigated.

3. If negative instances occur they must be explained.

Analogy is the type of reasoning based on the idea that if two

instances are alike in a number of particulars they will be alike in
the point in question. For example, it may be reasoned that a man
who has made a success as a high officer in the army will make a
success as a business executive, for both things involve the ability
to organize and to command.

As in generalization, there is always a risk in analogy. To reduce
the risk, the following rules can be applied:

1. The two instances compared must be alike in important respects.

2. Differences between the two instances must be accounted for.

Whereas induction can give only probability, deduction can give
certitude. A deduction starts from certain assumptions, like the
axioms in geometry, which if accepted *necessarily* generate the
system that follows.

Deductive reasoning appears in the SYLLOGISM. The syllogism
consists of two propositions, called premises, and a conclusion, as
follows:

All men are mortal.   (major premise)
Socrates was a man.   (minor premise)
∴. Socrates was mortal.   (conclusion)

The premises involve three terms, the MAJOR TERM, the MINOR
TERM, and the MIDDLE TERM. The major term is the term that constitutes the predicate of the conclusion (*mortal*), the minor term the
subject of the conclusion (*Socrates*), the middle term the link
between the major and minor terms (*man, men*). The process establishes relations among classes. We can chart the syllogism above
by thinking of a nest of boxes: a small box (Socrates) placed in a
medium-size box (men), and that placed in a large box (mortal
creatures).

When the process of reasoning is correct in a syllogism, the syllogism is said to be VALID. But a valid syllogism may not give a true
conclusion if the premises are not true. Therefore, to be sure of
getting a true conclusion the premises must be inspected.

In addition to the ordinary syllogism there are two other types,
the EITHER–OR (called the DISJUNCTIVE) syllogism, and the IF–THEN
(called the HYPOTHETICAL) syllogism.

In reasoning by *either–or,* two possibilities are set up, one is ruled
out, and therefore the second must be accepted. The two items of

the *either–or* must really cover the case—cover all possibilities. And the two items must not have any overlap.

Reasoning by *if–then* deals with a condition and a result. If the condition is fulfilled, the result follows. Most errors in this form of reasoning come from misinterpreting the *if* of the condition to mean *only if.*

An argument, either inductive or deductive, that does not follow the course of reason is called a FALLACY. There are numerous fallacies, but four of common occurrence are EQUIVOCATION, BEGGING THE QUESTION, IGNORING THE QUESTION, and NON SEQUITUR (Latin for "it does not follow").

Equivocation occurs when a significant word in an argument is used in two senses.

Begging the question occurs when the arguer assumes something to be true which really needs proof, as in a prejudiced proposition or in arguing in a circle.

An arguer ignores the question when he introduces any consideration which will distract from what is really at stake, as when he shifts the interest of the argument or makes an appeal to the emotions and prejudices of the audience.

Non sequitur occurs when an arguer asserts a connection between two items which does not exist; for example, when a thing is taken to be the cause of another simply because it comes before it in time or is associated with it.

Some understanding of fallacies is useful to straight thinking, but it is also useful for REFUTATION, the attack on an opposing argument.

Syllogisms in developed form rarely appear in extended argument, but the implied syllogism, called ENTHYMEME, is common. A syllogism is implied when one of the three elements, major premise, minor premise, or conclusion, is suppressed, and it is assumed that the audience can supply it. Often an extended argument is a chain of enthymemes.

The composition of an extended argument calls for careful planning. The systematic outline for an extended argument is called a BRIEF. It is the arrangement in logical sequence and in logical relationship of the evidence and the argument on one side of a dispute. The brief makes complete sense in itself, even to a reader who is not previously acquainted with the dispute.

The brief is divided into three parts, INTRODUCTION, ARGUMENT or DISCUSSION, and CONCLUSION. The introduction gives whatever is necessary for an understanding of the situation, certainly the proposition and the statement of admissions and issues, and sometimes the definition of terms, the history of the question, and the immediate occasion of the dispute. Each of the three main sections of the brief is to be treated independently. Within the section, main headings are indicated by Roman numerals, with subdivisions indicated in descending importance by A, 1, a. In the section of argument the relation between evidence and inference is indicated. For example, I is true *because* of A, and A is true *because* of 1 and 2, and 1 is true *because* of a and b. The brief moves down from statement through a chain of proof.

After the brief is made, the arguer may not necessarily follow its order. He may, for instance, begin his actual presentation at what he considers a crucial point. But the brief does provide him with the skeleton of the argument.

It has been said that argument, strictly considered, appeals to the reason. But PERSUASION, the appeal to the emotions, is very useful in leading the audience to the content of the argument.

Persuasion depends to a large extent upon VIVIDNESS of presentation and upon discovering the COMMON GROUND between the arguer and his audience. The quality of vividness catches interest, and the discovery of a common ground overcomes hostility or indifference. For persuasion, it is necessary to exhibit tact, fair-mindedness, patience, and respect for the audience.

5 Description

DESCRIPTION, as we shall understand the word in this discussion, is the kind of discourse concerned with the appearance of the world. It tells what qualities a thing has, what impression it makes on our senses. It aims to suggest to the imagination the thing as it appears immediately before an observer. We call this kind of description SUGGESTIVE to distinguish it from another kind, expository description, or technical description, which is really a form of exposition, and has already been discussed.[1]

RELATION OF SUGGESTIVE DESCRIPTION TO OTHER KINDS OF DISCOURSE

Even suggestive description may appear in close association with other kinds of discourse. It may be used in connection with exposition [2] or with argument,[3] but more often, in fact quite commonly, it appears in connection with narration. When we are telling a story, we must, if we wish our audience to grasp it as real, give some impression of the scene and of the persons involved. In neither conversation nor writing do we ordinarily set up the necessary description as a long, separate, preliminary part of the whole composition; instead, we tend to weave it into the body of the narrative as the occasion demands. The vivid stroke of description, small in itself

[1] Page 42. Review the section on the distinction between suggestive description and technical description.
[2] See Chap. 3, p. 61.
[3] See Chap. 4, p. 185.

and apparently unimportant, may lend the touch of reality and may stir the imagination so that the reader is ready to accept and respond to the whole composition.

Here is a piece of narrative which has been stripped of all its descriptive elements:

> The other waved the cigar, the other hand in Horace's face. Horace shook it, and freed his hand. "I thought I recognized you when you got on at Oxford," Snopes said, "but I— May I set down?" he said, already shoving at Horace's knee with his leg. He flung the overcoat on the seat and sat down as the train stopped. "Yes, sir, I'm always glad to see any of the boys, any time . . ." He leaned across Horace and peered out the window at a station. " 'Course you ain't in my county no longer, but what I say a man's friends is his friends, whichever way they vote. Because a friend is a friend, and whether he can do anything for me or not . . ." He leaned back, the cigar in his fingers.

Here is the passage in its original form, with the descriptive elements italicized. Notice how they give the sense of reality, or the immediately observable world, to what otherwise would be a bare synopsis of events.

> The other waved the cigar, the other hand, *palm-up, the third finger discolored faintly at the base of a huge ring,* in Horace's face. Horace shook it and freed his hand. "I thought I recognized you when you got on at Oxford," Snopes said, "but I— May I set down?" he said, already shoving at Horace's knee with his leg. He flung the overcoat—*a shoddy blue garment with a greasy velvet collar*—on the seat and sat down as the train stopped. "Yes, sir, I'm always glad to see any of the boys, any time . . ." He leaned across Horace and peered out the window at a *small dingy station with its cryptic bulletin board chalked over, an express truck bearing a wire chicken coop containing two forlorn fowls, at three or four men in overalls gone restfully against the wall, chewing.* " 'Course you ain't in my county no longer, but what I say a man's friends is his friends, whichever way they vote. Because a friend is a friend, and whether he can do anything for me or not . . ." He leaned back, the *unlighted* cigar in his fingers.—WILLIAM FAULKNER: *Sanctuary,* Chap. 19.[4]

It is clear that in the passage above description is subordinate to narrative. As a matter of fact, description is usually subordinate

[4] From *Sanctuary* by William Faulkner, copyright, 1931, by Random House, Inc.

when it appears mixed with some other kind of discourse, and it rarely appears alone in any very extended form. This is only to be expected, for description, which has to do with the appearance of the world, cannot satisfy us very long. We are constantly straining beyond the appearance of things; we want to see what they do and know what they mean, or we are interested in our own responses to and ideas about them. Therefore, though description can present us with the vivid appearance of things, it is constantly moving over, in ordinary use, into narrative and exposition and, even, argument, the kinds of discourse which express our fuller interests.

This is not to say, however, that a capacity for description is not important for any writer. Without the resources of description most kinds of composition would be very bare and unconvincing—fiction, poetry, letters, feature articles, reporting, history, essays, biography, speeches, and even certain kinds of philosophical writing. Description is far more important than its mere proportion in what we read would seem to indicate. And furthermore, any attempt to understand its principles will sharpen our own perceptions and increase our pleasure in both literature and the real world we live in.

SUGGESTIVE DESCRIPTION AND THE SENSES

Description, and particularly suggestive description, is the kind of discourse that has primarily to do with the appearance of the world, with the way things present themselves to our sense. We say, "The apple is red," and we refer to what the sense of sight tells us about the apple. But we also say, "The tweed is rough," or "The music is loud," or "The milk is sweet," or "The lilies are fragrant," and in so doing appeal to other senses, touch, hearing, taste, smell. We are also aware of the world in terms of heat and cold, and weight, pressure, and strain, and we have a language to describe that awareness, too.

The descriptive sentences just given are crude and general. They do not make us vividly aware of the thing described. A good writer is not satisfied with such crude and general descriptions. He is interested in making close discriminations and in indicating slight differences. Therefore, he must be a good observer. Even if he is writing a description of an imagined object rather than one really before his eyes, he can be successful only if his mind is stored with impressions drawn from actual experience.

Therefore, a person who wants to become a good writer should make some effort to train his powers of observation and to expand his vocabulary, especially in words that indicate differences in perception. He must tie his perceptions and his words together. The loud noise must cease to be loud noise for him, and must become the crash, the bang, the thud, the clatter, the clash, the boom, the bong, the clang, the howl, the wail, the scream, or whatever most vividly presents the thing he has heard. And the same for the other senses, for all the senses are important to the writer who wants to give a clear picture of the world.

Here are three bits of description, each one primarily concerned with impressions of a single sense. Note the discriminations made in each passage and the language used to record the close observation.

To tell when the scythe is sharp enough this is the rule. First the stone clangs and grinds against the iron harshly; then it rings musically to one note; then, at last, it purrs as though the iron and stone were exactly suited. When you hear this, your scythe is sharp enough; and I, when I heard it that June dawn, with everything quite silent except the birds, let down the scythe and bent myself to mow.—HILAIRE BELLOC: "The Mowing of a Field," *Hills and the Sea.*[5]

He knew the inchoate sharp excitement of hot dandelions in young Spring grass at noon; the smell of cellars, cobwebs, and built-on secret earth; in July, of watermelons bedded in sweet hay, inside a farmer's covered wagon; of cantaloupe and crated peaches; and the scent of orange rind, bitter-sweet, before a fire of coals.—THOMAS WOLFE: *Look Homeward, Angel,* Chap. 8.

When I think of hills, I think of the upward strength I tread upon. When water is the object of my thought, I feel the cool shock of the plunge and the quick yielding of the waves that crisp and curl and ripple about my body. The pleasing changes of rough and smooth, pliant and rigid, curved and straight in the bark and branches of a tree give the truth to my hand. The immovable rock, with its juts and warped surfaces, bends beneath my fingers into all manner of grooves and hollows. The bulge of a watermelon and the puffed-up rotundities of squashes that sprout, bud, and ripen in that strange garden planted some-

[5] From *Hills and the Sea* by Hilaire Belloc, copyright, 1935, by Charles Scribner's Sons.

where behind my finger-tips are the ludicrous in my tactual memory and imagination.—HELEN KELLER: *The World I Live In*, Chap. 1.[6]

In the first of these selections the sense of hearing is dominant, in the second the sense of smell, and in the third, the sense of touch. But in the third selection, which comes from a remarkable book written by a woman blind and deaf almost from birth, we also find temperature and pressure and strain: the coolness of the water and the "upward strength" of the hill.

As we can see from the quotations above, especially from the first two, a single sense may be dominant in a piece of description. But generally speaking, we may limit ourselves far too much if we insist on making the impression of a single sense dominant. This is certainly true if we think of description as a business of tying the single adjective to the single sense impression, as we do when we say, "The apple is red." When we observe the apple we observe much more than the color, and if we describe only the color, even if we find the exact word or phrase—such as "tawny-freckled" instead of the general word *red*—we still leave out, as we have said earlier, a great deal that we have observed.[7]

We have observed not only color. We are prepared to say that the apple is, for example, "slick-looking," or "juicy-looking," and many other things besides. Other senses than sight are involved in our experience of the apple. Our past experiences with apples are operating in our experience of the present apple. We are not touching the present apple, but we are prepared to say that it is slick-looking. And so on. We see the apple and sense the complex of qualities which mean "appleness"—the color, the texture, the fragrance, the juiciness. That is to say, our experience of the apple is more massive than the response of one sense. A good writer often tries to indicate something of the massiveness of perception.

Our ordinary use of language illustrates this massiveness. When we say "slick-looking" of the apple, we are, in a way, fusing two senses, sight and touch. Or when we look at a frozen lake and say, "The ice is glassy," we evoke with the word *glassy* a whole complex of qualities which are fused in the single word—slickness, hard-

[6] From *The World I Live In* by Helen Keller, copyright, 1908, by the Century Company. Reprinted by permission of Appleton-Century-Crofts, Inc.

[7] See p. 34 above.

ness, transparency, brightness. Though description may sometimes confine itself to the report of a single sense, it frequently tries to fuse the report of several senses to give impression of the fullness of the experience, the unity of perception.

THE DOMINANT IMPRESSION

We have already seen how the facts selected by Melville in his description of the volcanic islands (p. 46), by Poe in his description of the House of Usher (p. 52), and by Dickens in his description of the Dedlock estate (p. 52) are all related to the single effect the writer desires to create. Each writer wishes to leave his reader with a single DOMINANT IMPRESSION, a single attitude, a single feeling.

A writer should try to select and organize his material so that such a single impression is dominant. Vividness of detail is important, for without that the reader does not really grasp the object in his imagination, but vividness alone is not enough to insure a good description. There must be the basic line of feeling, the unifying idea, to make it memorable for him. Contradictory and irrelevant items in a description disturb the reader and leave him at a loss. In such a case he may not even understand why the description is given in the first place.

For example, if Dickens had presented in some detail the roaring fires on the hearths in the Dedlock mansion and the steaming roasts and puddings on the table, he would have distracted from the interpretation he wishes the scene to bear. Undoubtedly the Dedlock family had roaring fires and steaming roasts, but that is not the point. The point is what the writer wants a description to work on the reader.

PATTERN AND TEXTURE IN DESCRIPTION

Even if a writer knows what dominant impression he wishes to give and knows what items will contribute to his effect, he still has to settle certain questions of method. No one can lay down formulas that will assure the writer of success, but the understanding of certain principles will help him avoid confusion and will sharpen his effects.

We can consider the problem under two general heads: PATTERN and TEXTURE. The first, pattern, has to do with the general organization; the second, texture, has to do with the nature of the details, and their interrelation.

PATTERN

Under pattern we are here concerned with the various principles by which a piece of description may be organized. If one observes a person, an object, or a scene, it has its proper unity—in a flash we recognize a friend, a tree, a familiar room, a meadow with woods beyond. But if, when we set out to describe one of these things, we give a mere catalogue of unrelated details, a mere enumeration of this, that, and the other, the sense of vital unity is gone.

The reason is not far to seek. In fact, when we look at something, even though our attention is focused on some one aspect, we are constantly aware of the totality; it is all there before us at one time. In description, however, the details are presented to us one after another; instead of the simultaneous presentation which we find in fact, we now have presentation in sequence. Since simultaneous presentation is impossible in description, the writer must provide some pattern into which the reader can fit the details if he is to give them a proper unity.

1. PATTERN FROM FIXED POINT OF VIEW

The most obvious method of ordering details is dictated by the arrangement of the details in the object; we describe from left to right, or from top to bottom, giving each item as it comes. But as it comes to whom? There must be an observer, specified or implied. And that observer occupies, as it were, a certain fixed point of view, specified or implied, from which he can read off the details.

Study the following description of an English cathedral:

Let us go together up the more retired street, at the end of which we can see the pinnacles of one of the towers, and then through the low, grey gateway with its battlemented top and small latticed window in the center, into the inner private-looking road or close, where nothing goes in but the carts of the tradesmen who supply the bishop and the chapter, and here there are little shaven grassplots, fenced in by neat rails, before old-fashioned groups of somewhat diminutive and excessively trim houses, with little oriel and bay windows jutting out here

and there, and deep wooden cornices and eaves painted cream colour
and white, and small porches to their doors in the shape of cockleshells,
or little, crooked, thick, indescribable, wooden gables warped a little on
one side; and so forward till we come to the larger houses, also old-
fashioned, but of red brick, and with gardens behind them, and fruit
walls, which show here and there, among the nectarines, the vestiges
of an old cloister arch or shaft; and looking in front on the cathedral
square itself, laid out in rigid divisions of smooth grass and gravel walk,
yet not uncheerful, especially on the sunny side, where the canons'
children are walking with their nurserymaids. And so, taking care not to
tread on the grass, we will go along the straight walk to the west front,
and there stand for a time, looking up at its deep-pointed porches and
the dark places between their pillars where there were statues once,
and where the fragments, here and there, of a stately figure are still
left, which has in it the likeness of a king, perhaps indeed a king on
earth, perhaps a saintly king long ago in heaven; and so higher and
higher up to the great mouldering wall of rugged sculpture and confused arcades, shattered, and grey, and grisly with heads of dragons
and mocking fiends, worn by the rain and swirling winds into yet un-
seemlier shape, and coloured on their stony scales by the deep russet-
orange lichen, melancholy gold; and so, higher still, to the bleak towers,
so far above that the eye loses itself among the bosses of their traceries,
though they are rude and strong, and only sees, like a drift of eddying
black points, now closing, now scattering, and now settling suddenly into
invisible places among the bosses and flowers, the crowd of restless birds
that fill the whole square with that strange clangour of theirs, so harsh
and yet so soothing, like the cries of birds on a solitary coast between
the cliffs and sea.—JOHN RUSKIN: *The Stones of Venice*, Vol. I, Chap. 4.

In this passage, the author has very carefully specified the observer, in this case the reader, who is invited to go with him.
And he specifies even more carefully the point in space from which
the cathedral is to be viewed; he even conducts the reader to that
point on the west side. The order of the details in the description
then follows the order in which the observer would meet those
details as he raised his eyes slowly upward. The items given us in
the earlier part of the passage belong to the ground level; the last
item is the birds above the tower.

2. PATTERN FROM MOVING POINT

Sometimes, however, the observer, specified or implied, does not
occupy a fixed point in space, but moves from one point to another.

Then another principle of sequence comes into play, a principle well illustrated by the following passage:

Our path took us between the Sakhara and the Sukhur by a narrow gorge with sandy floor and steep bare walls. Its head was rough. We had to scramble up shelves of coarse-faced stone, and along a great fault in the hill-side between two tilted red reefs of hard rock. The summit of the pass was a knife-edge, and from it we went down an encumbered gap, half-blocked by one fallen boulder which had been hammered over with the tribal marks of all the generations of men who had used this road. Afterwards there opened tree-grown spaces, collecting grounds in winter for the sheets of rain which poured off the glazed sides of the Sukhur. There were granite outcrops here and there, and a fine silver sand underfoot in the still damp water-channels. The drainage was towards Heiran.—T. E. LAWRENCE: *Seven Pillars of Wisdom*, Chap. 31.[8]

3. PATTERN OF FRAME IMAGE

Sometimes, however, the object of a description is too large or unwieldy for unity of impression to be achieved by either of the methods involving, as specified or implied, a "real" point of view. In such a case, the writer may give unity by means of what we may call a FRAME IMAGE; he can compare the whole object to some smaller object which can be visualized, and which will serve as a frame into which the reader's imagination can fit the necessary details of the object being described. For instance, let us take the following example:

The nether sky opens and Europe is disclosed as a prone and emaciated figure, the Alps shaping like a backbone, and the branching mountain-chains like ribs, the peninsular plateau of Spain forming a head. Broad and lengthy lowlands stretch from the north of France across Russia like a grey-green garment hemmed by the Ural mountains and the glistening Arctic Ocean.—THOMAS HARDY: *The Dynasts*, Part I.[9]

In this example, the writer has begun by providing the frame image and then giving the details which are to be set in the frame. But sometimes the writer will reverse the process; that is, he will

[8] From: *Seven Pillars of Wisdom* by T. E. Lawrence. Copyright 1926, 1935 by Doubleday & Company, Inc.

[9] From Thomas Hardy: *The Dynasts*. Copyright, 1904 by The Macmillan Company and used with their permission.

first give the details, perhaps a swarm of them which stimulate and baffle the reader's imagination, and then give the frame image which will suddenly reduce all to order. Here is a very simple example of the method:

I studied M. de Charlus. The tuft of his grey hair, the eye, the brow of which was raised by his monocle to emit a smile, the red flowers in his buttonhole formed, so to speak, the three mobile apices of a convulsive and striking triangle.—MARCEL PROUST: *The Guermantes Way*, Part I, Chap. 1.

4. PATTERN BY MOOD

In the types of pattern thus far discussed, the position of an observer, specified or implied, determines the organization of the details, but his reactions and interests are irrelevant. We shall now turn, however, to examples in which the emphasis is subjective, in which the reactions and interests of the observer, specified or implied, provide the basic principle for ordering and unifying the details.

The first of these patterns based on the observer we may call pattern by mood. We have already had examples of this. The passage from Poe's "The Fall of the House of Usher" (p. 52) gives us an example with the observer specified, and the passage from Dickens's *Bleak House* (p. 52) gives us an example with the observer implied. In neither of these descriptions does the writer follow a mechanical order. Instead, he arranges the items of the scene to build toward the subjective effect desired. At the end Poe describes the effect of his scene as the horrible dropping off of a veil, and Dickens concludes with the general taste and smell of the Dedlocks in their graves. In each of these passages the mood is established very early and pervades the whole, though with mounting intensity.

In some instances of effective description, however, the mood does not so definitely pervade the whole passage. Rather, it may appear early as a kind of lead and then be dropped or be presented only by implication. Or the description may begin with an accumulation of details which seem to be collected almost at random but are brought to focus in the end by the emergence of a dominant mood.

The following passage is an example of the last type of pattern:

Except for the Marabar Caves—and they are twenty miles off—the city of Chandrapore presents nothing extraordinary. Edged rather than washed by the river Ganges, it trails for a couple of miles along the bank, scarcely distinguishable from the rubbish it deposits so freely. There are no bathing-steps on the river front, as the Ganges happens not to be holy here; indeed there is no river front, and bazaars shut out the wide and shifting panorama of the stream. The streets are mean, the temples ineffective, and though a few fine houses exist they are hidden away in gardens or down alleys whose filth deters all but the invited guest. Chandrapore was never large or beautiful, but two hundred years ago it lay on the road between Upper India, then imperial, and the sea, and the fine houses date from that period. The zest for decoration stopped in the eighteenth century, nor was it ever democratic. There is no painting and scarcely any carving in the bazaars. The very wood seems made of mud, the inhabitants of mud moving. So abased, so monotonous is everything that meets the eye, that when the Ganges comes down it might be expected to wash the excrescence back into the soil. Houses do fall, people are drowned and left rotting, but the general outline of the town persists, swelling here, shrinking there, like some low but indestructible form of life.—E. M. FORSTER: *A Passage to India*, Chap. 1.[10]

5. PATTERN BY INTEREST

Just as mood may give the principle of unity, so a special interest may provide it. If a man out to shoot quail and a man out to paint a landscape look at the same field, their different interests mean different kinds of observation. The hunter focuses attention on the clump of brush as possible cover for a covey; the painter looks at it merely as one form in his total composition and as a patch of color in relation to other colors, the tawny of the dry sage and the blackness of the tree trunks beyond.

In the following passage there are many details which would be vivid in any description, but we notice that what holds the whole passage together is the special interest with which the scene is regarded. Here a soldier is inspecting a bridge which he intends to dynamite. The structure of the bridge and the location of the enemy defenses are what finally concern him.

[10] From *A Passage to India* by E. M. Forster, copyright, 1924, by Harcourt, Brace and Company, Inc.

The late afternoon sun that still came over the brown shoulder of the mountain showed the bridge dark against the steep emptiness of the gorge. It was a steel bridge of a single span and there was a sentry box at each end. It was wide enough for two motor cars to pass and it spanned, in solid-flung metal grace, a deep gorge at the bottom of which, far below, a brook leaped in white water through rocks and boulders down to the main stream of the pass.

The sun was in Robert Jordan's eyes and the bridge showed only in outline. Then the sun lessened and was gone and looking up through the trees at the brown, rounded height that it had gone behind, he saw, now, that he no longer looked into the glare, that the mountain slope was a delicate new green and that there were patches of old snow under the crest.

Then he was looking at the bridge again in the sudden short trueness of the little light that would be left, and studying its construction. The problem of its demolition was not difficult. As he watched he took out a notebook from his breast pocket and made several quick line sketches. As he made the drawings he did not figure the charges. He would do that later. Now he was noting the points where the explosive should be placed in order to cut the support of the span and drop a section of it back into the gorge. It could be done unhurriedly, scientifically and correctly with a half dozen charges laid and braced to explode simultaneously; or it could be done roughly with two big ones. They would need to be very big ones, on opposite sides and should go at the same time.—ERNEST HEMINGWAY: *For Whom the Bell Tolls*, Chap. 3.[11]

It does not greatly matter what the nature of the interest is. The dynamiter's interest in the bridge holds this passage together, and makes the bridge serve as a focus for the scene. But in the following passage the comparison which Huckleberry Finn draws between houses in town and the house of the Grangerford plantation provides the unifying interest:

It was a mighty nice family, and a mighty nice house, too. I hadn't seen no house out in the country before that was so nice and had so much style. It didn't have an iron latch on the front door, nor a wooden one with a buckskin string, but a brass knob to turn, the same as houses in a town. There warn't no bed in the parlor, nor a sign of a bed; but heaps of parlors in town has beds in them. There was a big fireplace that was bricked on the bottom, and the bricks was kept clean and red by

[11] From *For Whom the Bell Tolls* by Ernest Hemingway, copyright, 1940, by Charles Scribner's Sons.

pouring water on them and scrubbing them with another brick; sometimes they wash them over with red water-paint that they call Spanish-brown, same as they do in town. They had big brass dog-irons that could hold up a saw-log. There was a clock on the middle of the mantelpiece, with a picture of a town painted on the bottom half of the glass front, and a round place in the middle of it for the sun, and you could see the pendulum swinging behind it.—SAMUEL CLEMENS: *The Adventures of Huckleberry Finn,* Chap. 17.

6. IMPRESSIONISTIC PATTERN

In the examples of pattern by mood and pattern by interest given above, we find more than a mere listing of things or the qualities of things. Something is said about the things; we find fully formed sentences, one leading to another to give a unified paragraph. But it is possible to list things or qualities with relation to a dominant mood or interest and successfully give an impression of unity by enumeration without formal organization. This method is called impressionistic. Here is an example of it, the description of the main street in a small Middlewestern town.

From a second-story window the sign, "W. P. Kennicott, Phys. & Surgeon," gilt on black sand.

A small wooden motion-picture theater called "The Rosebud Movie Palace." Lithographs announcing a film called, "Fatty in Love."

Howland & Gould's Grocery. In the display window, black, overripe bananas and lettuce on which a cat was sleeping. Shelves lined with red crepe paper which was now faded and torn and concentrically spotted. Flat against the wall of the second story the signs of the lodges—the Knights of Pythias, the Maccabees, the Woodmen, the Masons.

Dahl & Oleson's Meat Market—a reek of blood.—SINCLAIR LEWIS: *Main Street,* Chap. 4.[12]

7. PATTERN OF ABSORBED DESCRIPTION

As has already been pointed out, description is frequently used in conjunction, almost in fusion, with other modes. It is difficult sometimes to say of a passage whether it is primarily descriptive or narrative or expository or argumentative in its emphasis. But sometimes we observe passages which, we feel, are primarily descriptive in emphasis but which are organized in terms of, for

[12] From *Main Street* by Sinclair Lewis, copyright, 1920, by Harcourt, Brace and Company, Inc.

instance, a narrative element. In such passages the descriptive details, if given in isolation, would be merely an enumeration of items with only a slight degree of unity of impression. But the line of action or explanation or argument holds them together, gives them their focus, so that the reader gets an effect of unity. It is difficult to find an appropriate name for this method, but perhaps the phrase "absorbed description" will serve.

Here is an example of absorbed description:

They called a special meeting of the Board of Aldermen. A deputation waited upon her, knocked at the door through which no visitor had passed since she ceased giving china-painting lessons eight or ten years earlier. They were admitted by the old Negro into a dim hall from which a stairway mounted into still more shadow. It smelled of dust and disuse—a close, dank smell. The Negro led them into the parlor. It was furnished in heavy, leather-covered furniture. When the Negro opened the blinds of one window, they could see that the leather was cracked; and when they sat down, a faint dust rose sluggishly about their thighs, spinning with slow motes in the single sun-ray. On a tarnished gilt easel before the fireplace stood a crayon portrait of Miss Emily's father.

They rose when she entered—a small, fat woman in black, with a thin gold chain descending to her waist and vanishing into her belt, leaning on an ebony cane with a tarnished gold head. Her skeleton was small and spare; perhaps that was why what would have been merely plumpness in another was obesity in her. She looked bloated, like a body long submerged in motionless water, and of that pallid hue. Her eyes, lost in the fatty ridges of her face, looked like two small pieces of coal pressed into a lump of dough as they moved from one face to another while the visitors stated their errand.

She did not ask them to sit. She just stood in the door and listened quietly until the spokesman came to a stumbling halt. Then they could hear the invisible watch ticking at the end of the gold chain.—WILLIAM FAULKNER: "A Rose for Emily." [13]

In the passage above we can readily isolate the parts which are purely descriptive. For instance, in the second paragraph, except for the first part of the first sentence and the last part of the last sentence, there is nothing but description. But in the following passage the description is much more completely absorbed; it is a

[13] From "A Rose for Emily," *These Thirteen* by William Faulkner, copyright, 1931, by Random House, Inc.

matter of words and phrases, and not of sentences and sections of paragraphs, and yet the scene is very fully suggested.

In the square bedroom with the big window Mama and Papa were lolling back on their pillows handing each other things from the wide black tray on the small table with the crossed legs. They were smiling and they smiled even more when the little boy, with the feeling of sleep still in his skin and hair, came in and walked up to the bed. Leaning against it, his bare toes wriggling in the white fur rug, he went on eating peanuts which he took from his pajama pocket. He was four years old.

"Here's my baby," said Mama. "Lift him up, will you?"

He went limp as a rag for Papa to take him under the arms and swing him up over a broad, tough chest. He sank between his parents like a bear cub in a warm litter, and lay there comfortably. He took another peanut between his teeth, cracked the shell, picked out the nut whole and ate it.—KATHERINE ANNE PORTER: "The Downward Path to Wisdom." [14]

8. MIXED PATTERNS

We have tried to distinguish several typical methods for unifying description, but in actual practice these methods may often be combined. Sometimes the most vivid effects can be obtained by the mixed method. Here is an example:

About four in the morning, as the captain and Herrick sat together on the rail, there arose from the midst of the night, in front of them, the voice of the breakers. Each sprang to his feet and stared and listened. The sound was continuous, like the passing of a train; no rise or fall could be distinguished; minute by minute the ocean heaved with an equal potency against the invisible isle; and as time passed, and Herrick waited in vain for any vicissitude in the volume of that roaring, a sense of the eternal weighed upon his mind. To the expert eye, the isle itself was to be inferred from a certain string of blots along the starry heaven. And the schooner was laid to and anxiously observed till daylight.

There was little or no morning bank. A brightening came in the east; then a wash of some ineffable, faint, nameless hue between crimson and silver; and then coals of fire. These glimmered awhile on the sealine, and seemed to brighten and darken and spread out; and still the night and the stars reigned undisturbed. It was as though a spark should catch and glow and creep along the foot of some heavy and almost incom-

[14] From *The Leaning Tower and Other Stories* by Katherine Anne Porter, copyright, 1944, by Katherine Anne Porter. Reprinted by permission of Harcourt, Brace and Company, Inc.

bustible wall-hanging, and the room itself be scarcely menaced. Yet a little after, and the whole east glowed with gold and scarlet, and the hollow of heaven was filled with the daylight.

The isle—the undiscovered, the scarce believed in—now lay before them and close aboard; and Herrick thought that never in his dreams had he beheld anything more strange and delicate. The beach was excellently white, the continuous barrier of trees inimitably green; the land perhaps ten feet high, the trees thirty more. Every here and there, as the schooner coasted northward, the wood was intermitted; and he could see clear over the inconsiderable strip of land (as a man looks over a wall) to the lagoon within; and clear over that, again, to where the far side of the atoll prolonged its pencilling of trees against the morning sky. He tortured himself to find analogies. The isle was like the rim of a great vessel sunken in the waters; it was like the embankment of an annular railway grown upon with wood. So slender it seemed amidst the outrageous breakers, so frail and pretty, he would scarce have wondered to see it sink and disappear without a sound, and the waves close smoothly over its descent.—ROBERT LOUIS STEVENSON: *The Ebb Tide*, Chap. 7.[15]

In the passage by Stevenson we notice that we have a location and an observer specified. At one time in the course of the description (the view across the atoll) we find the method of simple spatial ordering used. At another time, the principle of sequence comes into play. In fact, it comes into play in two different ways. First, we have the principle of sequence in time (in the coming of dawn) and then we have it in space, with the moving point of view, as the schooner coasts northward along the island. But we also find the frame image used to give us a clearer notion of the island: Herrick, the observer, "tortured himself to find analogies," and to describe the atoll we find the frame image of the "rim of a great vessel sunken in the waters," or of the "embankment of an annular railway grown upon with wood." We may notice, furthermore, that a certain mood, the response to a fragile and dreamlike beauty, dominates the whole description—Herrick's response to the scene, and we may notice that there is an organization in terms of climax, for only at the end of the passage as given here do we get the full statement of the frame image and of the basic mood.

If the passage were read in its full context, we should be able

[15] From *The Ebb Tide* by Robert Louis Stevenson, copyright, 1905, by Charles Scribner's Sons.

to observe that the method of unity in terms of interest is employed throughout, for the schooner is seeking an entrance to the harbor inside the atoll, and the final concern, in reference to the narrative, is to find anchorage.

The use of a mixed method, certainly of a mixed method which employs as many individual methods as the above passage, offers certain difficulties to the inexperienced writer. By and large, it is better for the inexperienced writer to try the simpler approaches to his material, at least until he is confident that he understands the principles involved in the various methods and has acquired some skill in adapting them.

TEXTURE: SELECTION IN DESCRIPTION

Pattern, as we have seen, is concerned with the ordering of the details of description. Texture, which we shall now discuss, is concerned with the nature of the details presented.

How are the details actually presented in a description selected from among all the details which might have been presented? Already, in discussing the difference between technical and suggestive description and in explaining what is meant by a dominant impression, we have touched on the problem of SELECTION (pp. 42-53, 200), but we have not explored it.

It is clear that no one can hope to render all of the details of an object to be described, and it is also clear that if one could render all of the details we should have a mere enumeration, tedious and mechanical, without giving the unified impression the object actually makes upon an observer. But what the writer wants to do is to give his reader such a unified impression. To do this he must select the details which will suggest the whole object and set the reader's imagination to work.

But what are the grounds on which selection is to be made? We may break this question down into two other questions:

1. What details are vivid in the object?
2. What details are significant for the impression the writer considers dominant?

Vividness and significance—these are the two considerations which should govern selection of details. It is possible that the same detail may be both vivid and significant, but for the purpose of discussion we can consider these qualities independently.

VIVIDNESS

A descriptive detail is vivid if it is striking, if it can set the imagination to work so that the reader calls up the object in his mind's eye. In the following description the most obvious quality of the scene, the contrast between brilliant light and black shadow, is emphasized. The writer does not give a detailed description of the town. Instead, he gives what would be the most obvious and striking characteristic, the light effect which would blur out other aspects of the Arab town when the observer first encountered it.

But when at last we anchored in the outer harbor, off the white town hung between the blazing sky and its reflection in the mirage which swept and rolled over the wide lagoon, then the heat of Arabia came out like a drawn sword and struck us speechless. It was midday; and the noon sun in the East, like moonlight, put to sleep the colors. There were only lights and shadows, the white houses and black gaps of streets; in front, the pallid lustre of the haze shimmering upon the inner harbors; behind, the dazzle of league after league of featureless sand, running up to an edge of low hills, faintly suggested in the far away mist of heat.— T. E. LAWRENCE: *Seven Pillars of Wisdom*, Chap. 8.[16]

This seizing on the most striking and obvious characteristic is a very natural method. Time after time we encounter a bit of description introduced by some such statement as, "The most impressive feature of his face was his wide, innocent, childlike blue eyes which seemed to offer trust to all the world," or, "The first thing you noticed as you topped the hill was a pond lying in the cup of the valley, reflecting the brilliance of the sky." The writer indicates what feature in the object would first catch attention.

Vividness, however, may be gained by indicating some detail which might escape ordinary observation. In such a case, it is the precision and subtlety of the description which makes the object come alive for us. John Burroughs, the naturalist, in a passage on the art of observation, gives a list of vivid details which would

[16] From: *Seven Pillars of Wisdom* by T. E. Lawrence. Copyright 1926, 1935 by Doubleday & Company, Inc.

escape most observers but which present a vivid sense of a series of scenes and moments:

His senses are so delicate that in his evening walk he feels the warm and cool streaks in the air, his nose detects the most fugitive odors, his ears the most furtive sounds. As he stands musing in the April twilight, he hears that fine, elusive stir and rustle made by the angleworms reaching out from their holes for leaves and grasses; he hears the whistling wings of the wood-cock as it goes swiftly by him in the dusk; he hears the call of the killdee come down out of the March sky; he hears far above him in the early morning the squeaking cackle of the arriving blackbirds pushing north; he hears the soft, prolonged, lulling call of the little owl in the cedars in the early spring twilight; he hears at night the roar of the distant waterfall, and the rumble of the train miles across country when the air is "hollow"; before a storm he notes how distant objects stand out and are brought near on those brilliant days that we call "weather-breeders." When the mercury is at zero or lower, he notes how the passing trains hiss and simmer as if the rails or wheels were red-hot.—JOHN BURROUGHS: *Leaf and Tendril*, Chap. 1.[17]

The rustling of the angleworms gives a vivid and immediate sense of the stillness; more vivid and immediate than any number of more usual and easily observable details. Or take the squeaking cackle of the blackbirds; it is the absolutely right phrase to describe the sound, and because of the accuracy of the observation, our imagination fills the sky with the flock of birds passing over.

Were it not for the detail of the dyed hand, we would have only a vague sense of the presence of the handsome young sailor in the following description:

Cast in a mould peculiar to the finest physical examples of those Englishmen in whom the Saxon strain would seem not at all to partake of any Norman or other admixture, he showed in face that humane look of reposeful good nature which the Greek sculptor in some instances gave to his heroic strong man, Hercules. But this again was subtly modified by another and pervasive quality. The ear, small and shapely, the arch of the foot, the curve in the mouth and nostril, even the indurated hand dyed to the orange-tawny of the toucan's bill, a hand telling of the halyards and tar-buckets; but above all, something in the mobile expression, and every chance attitude and movement, something

---

[17] From *Leaf and Tendril* by John Burroughs, through the courtesy of Houghton Mifflin Company.

suggestive of a mother eminently favored by Love and the Graces; all this strangely indicated a lineage in direct contradiction to his lot.— HERMAN MELVILLE: *Billy Budd,* Chap. 2.

And in the following portrait it is the detail of the pimples that makes the person come alive to the reader's imagination:

Complicated, but light, transparent, and innocently immodest was the dress of his daughter, tall and slender, with magnificent hair gracefully combed; her breath was sweet with violet-scented tablets, and she had a number of tiny and most delicate pink pimples near her lips and between her slightly powdered shoulder blades.—IVAN BUNIN: "The Gentleman from San Francisco." [18]

The process of seizing on either the striking characteristic or the small, sharply perceived detail may lead to exaggeration and caricature. The detail, as it were, becomes the whole object. In the first of the following passages, Dickens takes the obvious oiliness of Mr. Chadband as the key to the description of his appearance and, finally, of his character:

Mr. Chadband is a large yellow man, with a fat smile, and a general appearance of having a good deal of train oil in his system. Mrs. Chadband is a stern, severe-looking, silent woman. Mr. Chadband moves softly and cumbrously, not unlike a bear who has been taught to walk upright. He is very much embarrassed about the arms, as if they were inconvenient to him, and he wanted to grovel; is very much in a perspiration about the head; and never speaks without first putting up his great hand, as delivering a token to his hearers that he is going to edify them. —CHARLES DICKENS: *Bleak House,* Chap. 19.

Dickens uses a striking detail and exaggerates it into the whole person, but in the following passage the writer uses the trivial detail of Miss Plimsoll's nose, and the little drop of moisture at its tip, as the main feature of the comic portrait of the poor old maid.

Miss Plimsoll's nose was sharp and pointed like that of Voltaire. It was also extremely sensitive to cold. When the thermometer fell below 60° it turned scarlet; below 50° it seemed a blue tinge with a little white morbid circle at the end; and at 40° it became sniffly and bore a permanent though precarious drop below its pointed tip. I remember with what interest I watched that drop as we drove from the station at Sofia.

[18] Reprinted from *The Gentleman from San Francisco* by Ivan Bunin, by permission of Alfred A. Knopf, Inc. Copyright 1923 by Alfred A. Knopf, Inc.

My parents went in front in the first carriage and Miss Plimsoll and I
followed in the brougham. The night was cold and we drove along an
endless wind-swept boulevard punctuated by street lamps. With the
approach of each successive lamp Miss Plimsoll's pinched little face
beside me would first be illuminated frontways, and then as we came
opposite the lamp, spring into a sharp little silhouette, at the point of
which the drop flashed and trembled like a diamond.—HAROLD NICOL-
SON: "Miss Plimsoll," *Some People*.[19]

SIGNIFICANCE

By significance in the selection of detail we mean the quality
which contributes to the dominant impression of a description. And
by the dominant impression we mean the mood the writer intends
to communicate, the attitude he intends to create in the reader, or
idea about the object he wishes to suggest.

We have already touched on this topic in our discussion of the
dominant impression (p. 200) and in our remarks on the passage
from Poe's "The Fall of the House of Usher" (p. 52), the description of the Dedlock estate from Dickens's *Bleak House* (p. 52),
and the passage from Melville's "The Encantadas" (p. 46). In each
of these examples, as we have seen, the selection is made to build
up a certain mood or to indicate a certain idea. In each example,
the writer refrains from introducing any item which might distract
from the dominant impression.

In the following description of the Arab town, Jidda, we can see
how the writer uses details that contribute to the effect of stealth
and sinister, brooding quiet:

The style of architecture was like crazy Elizabethan half-timber work,
in the elaborate Cheshire fashion, but gone gimcrack to an incredible
degree. House-fronts were fretted, pierced and pargetted till they looked
as though cut out of cardboard for a romantic stage-setting. Every storey
jutted, every window leaned one way or other; often the very walls
sloped. It was like a dead city, so clean underfoot, and so quiet. Its
winding, even streets were floored with damp sand solidified by time
and as silent as the tread of any carpet. The lattices and wall-returns
deadened all reverberation of voice. There were no carts, nor any street
wide enough for carts, no shod animals, no bustle anywhere. Everything was hushed, strained, even furtive. The doors of houses shut softly

[19] From *Some People* by Harold Nicolson. Reprinted by permission of the
author and Constable and Company.

as we passed. There were no loud dogs, no crying children; indeed, except in the bazaar, still half asleep, there were few wayfarers of any kind; and the people we did meet, all thin, and as it were wasted by disease, with scarred, hairless faces and screwed up eyes, slipped past us quickly and cautiously, not looking at us. Their skimp, white robes, shaven polls with little skull-caps, red cotton shoulder shawls, and bare feet were so same as to be almost a uniform.—T. E. LAWRENCE: *Seven Pillars of Wisdom*, Chap. 9.[20]

The same method can be used in description to give an impression of the character of a person. The following portrait of Eustacia Vye, the heroine of Thomas Hardy's novel *The Return of the Native*, deals ostensibly with appearance of the young woman, but all the details of her appearance are really chosen, as Hardy himself indicates rather explicitly now and then, to give us an impression of her inner nature.

She was in person full-limbed and somewhat heavy; without ruddiness, as without pallor; and soft to the touch as a cloud. To see her hair was to fancy that a whole winter did not contain darkness enough to form its shadow: it closed over her forehead like nightfall extinguishing the western glow.

Her nerves extended into those tresses, and her temper could always be softened by stroking them down. When her hair was brushed she would instantly sink into stillness and look like the Sphinx. If, in passing under one of the Egdon banks, any of its thick skeins were caught, as they sometimes were, by a prickly tuft of the large *Ulex Europaeus*—which will act as a sort of hairbrush—she would go back a few steps, and pass against it a second time.

She had Pagan eyes, full of nocturnal mysteries, and their light, as it came and went, and came again, was partially hampered by their oppressive lids and lashes; and of these the under lid was much fuller than it usually is with English women. This enabled her to indulge in reverie without seeming to do so: she might have been believed capable of sleeping without closing them up. Assuming that the souls of men and women were visible essences, you could fancy the color of Eustacia's soul to be flame-like. The sparks from it that rose into her dark pupils gave the same impression. . . .

Her presence brought memories of such things as Bourbon roses, rubies, and tropical midnights; her moods recalled lotus-eaters and the march

[20] From: *Seven Pillars of Wisdom* by T. W. Lawrence. Copyright 1926, 1935 by Doubleday & Company, Inc.

in "Athalie"; her motions, the ebb and flow of the sea; her voice, the viola. In a dim light, and with a slight rearrangement of her hair, her general figure might have stood for that of either of the higher female deities. The new moon behind her head, an old helmet upon it, a diadem of accidental dew-drops round her brow, would have been adjuncts sufficient to strike the note of Artemis, Athene, or Hera respectively, with as close an approximation to the antique as that which passes muster on many respected canvases.—THOMAS HARDY: *Return of the Native,* Chap. 7.

In the following description of a Mexican revolutionist who is both sentimental and cruel, energetic and self-indulgent, lazy and sinister, the explicit definition of the character does not appear, but is suggested by the details selected:

Braggioni catches her glance solidly as if he had been waiting for it, leans forward, balancing his paunch between his spread knees, and sings with tremendous emphasis, weighing his words. He had, the song relates, no father and no mother, nor even a friend to console him; lonely as a wave of the sea he comes and goes, lonely as a wave. His mouth opens round and yearns sideways, his balloon cheeks grow oily with the labor of song. He bulges marvellously in his expensive garments. Over his lavender collar, crushed upon a purple necktie, held by a diamond hoop; over his ammunition belt of tooled leather worked in silver, buckled cruelly around his gaping middle: over the tops of his glossy yellow shoes Braggioni swells with ominous ripeness, his mauve silk hose stretched taut, his ankles bound with the stout leather thongs of his shoes.

When he stretches his eyelids at Laura she notes again that his eyes are the true tawny yellow cat's eyes.—KATHERINE ANNE PORTER: "Flowering Judas." [21]

As the details of description may be used to suggest the character of a person described, so they may be used to indicate the attitude the writer wishes the reader to take toward a scene or event. The following passage gives a battle scene, but the writer uses certain descriptive touches to play down ironically the violence or the event. We know that horror and excitement and suffering are involved here, and the writer knows it too. But he takes a certain

[21] From *Flowering Judas and Other Stories* by Katherine Anne Porter, copyright, 1935, by Katherine Anne Porter. Reprinted by permission of Harcourt, Brace and Company, Inc.

actual and emotional distance from the scene—the flags "laugh," the cannon merely "denounce," the "jaunty" brigade marches "airily," there is a calm white house beyond. The impression of distance, of unreality, and of triviality actually works to suggest to us, by contract, the real violence.

In another direction he saw a magnificent brigade going with the evident intention of driving the enemy from a wood. They passed in out of sight, and presently there was a most awe-inspiring racket in the wood. The noise was unspeakable. Having stirred this prodigious uproar and, apparently, finding it too prodigious, the brigade, after a little time, came marching airily out again with its fine formation in nowise disturbed. There were no traces of speed in its movements. The brigade was jaunty and seemed to point a proud thumb at the yelling wood.

On a slope to the left there was a long row of guns, gruff and maddened, denouncing the enemy, who, down through the woods, were forming for another attack in the pitiless monotony of conflicts. The round red discharges from the guns made a crimson flare and a high, thick smoke. Occasionally glimpses could be caught of groups of the toiling artillerymen. In the rear of this row of guns stood a house, calm and white, amid bursting shells. A congregation of horses, tied to a long railing, were tugging frenziedly at their bridles. Men were running hither and thither.

The detached battle between the four regiments lasted for some time. There chanced to be no interference, and they settled their dispute by themselves. They struck savagely and powerfully at each other for a period of minutes, and then the lighter-hued regiments faltered and drew back, leaving the dark-blue lines shouting. The youth could see the two flags shaking with laughter amid the smoke remnants.—STEPHEN CRANE: *The Red Badge of Courage*, Chap. 22.[22]

ATMOSPHERE

In each of the above passages the author has, as we say, created a certain atmosphere. By atmosphere we mean the mood, the general feeling associated in the description with the scene, person, or event described. We have commented, for instance, on the atmosphere of gloom and dampness and decay in the descriptions by Poe and Dickens, or that of furtiveness and stealth and exhaustion in the description of Jidda by T. E. Lawrence, or that of ironical

[22] From *The Red Badge of Courage*, by Stephen Crane, copyright, 1925, by D. Appleton and Company. Reprinted by permission of Appleton-Century-Crofts, Inc.

jauntiness and impersonal distance in the description by Stephen Crane.

We know, however, even as we use these words to define the atmosphere of this or that piece of description, that the labels we put on the passages are too vague and loose to define really the effect given. Our defining words do not really define the atmosphere; they merely give a kind of crude indication, a not very dependable clue, to the effect we find in the actual description.

Our inability to define the atmosphere in general terms indicates the importance of the way the author himself goes about presenting it to us. The atmosphere is the general feeling he wants his work to convey, the prevailing attitude of mind which he wishes us to adopt toward his subject, but he knows that he cannot create it simply by using the loose, general words which we have used above in trying to define the effect of the passages. Therefore, he undertakes to give us such concrete details, such aspects of his object, as will stir our imaginations not only to grasp the appearance of the object (or the sound, the color, and so forth, if he is appealing to other senses than that of sight), but to adopt a certain feeling and attitude toward the object and toward the general context of the object in his work.[23]

We have said earlier that suggestive description aims not to tell us about its object but to give us the object; but it also can be said that it aims not to tell us what feelings to have about the object and what attitudes to take toward it, but to create those feelings and attitudes within us. Vividness and immediacy, not only in regard to the physical qualities of the object, but in regard to the feelings and attitudes involved, are what the writer desires.

[23] Perhaps this should be explained a little more fully. By the context of the object we mean what is around it in the piece of writing. For instance, in a story the context of a piece of description would be the events narrated, the analyses of character, and so forth, before and after the piece of description. A good author, no matter what he is writing, a story, an essay, a letter, intends some connection between the effect of a piece of description and the rest of his composition. The atmosphere of the description implies, as it were, the attitudes the author wishes the reader to take toward the whole piece of work. If we read the description of Egdon Heath at the beginning of Thomas Hardy's *Return of the Native,* the somber, brooding atmosphere of the scene implies the attitude the author wished the reader to take toward the violent, tragic human story, just as the atmosphere of the description of Eustacia Vye, the heroine of the novel, which is quoted above, implies the qualities of character and action we are to find in her.

DESCRIPTION OF FEELINGS AND STATES OF MIND

In our previous discussion we have seen how a description may evoke in the reader a certain mood or attitude which the writer wishes to communicate. There is some relation, then, between the physical details of the object described and human feelings. This leads us to another kind of description, not of objects or persons, but of feelings or states of mind. How can such an intangible, without physical existence and with no possible appeal to our senses, be described?

Strictly speaking, the literal feeling or state of mind cannot be described because it cannot be perceived through the senses. But we have seen how a character, which is also intangible, can be indicated through description. For instance, Hardy's description of Eustacia Vye's physical appearance indicates her inner nature. By a kind of parallel process we can indicate a state of mind, that of the writer himself or of some person about whom he is writing.

Our common speech recognizes the principle behind this process. For instance, if a man has an evil nature, we may say that he has a "black heart," or if a man is cheerful and optimistic we may say that he has a "sunny disposition." The abstract, general words *evil* and *cheerful* are replaced by the concrete words *black* and *sunny,* which properly belong to the physical world. Hardy is simply applying this principle in a more elaborate form when he writes of Eustacia:

Her presence brought memories of such things as Bourbon roses, rubies, and tropical midnights; her moods recalled the lotus-eaters and the march in "Athalie"; her motions, the ebb and flow of the sea; her voice, the viola.

This is a way of saying that Eustacia has a brooding, passionate, willful nature; but Hardy's words say much more than we can convey by our generalizing words. If we begin to try to elaborate in our own way, we find ourselves using such words as *sumptuous, rich, deep, stormy,*—the adjectives implied in Hardy's description; and then we realize that these words, too, are carrying us toward physical description, for words like *stormy* and *deep* have come to apply to such a thing as a personality by a kind of transference from their basic meanings (see Chapter 11).

Here is an example of the description, not of a personality, but of a state of feeling, the feeling at the moment of passing from sleep to waking:

"I was not asleep," I answered as I awoke. I said this in good faith. The great modification which the act of awakening effects in us is not so much that of introducing us to the clear life of consciousness, as that of making us lose all memory of that other, rather more diffused light in which our mind has been resting, as in the opaline depths of the sea. The tide of thought, half veiled from our perception, over which we were drifting still a moment ago, kept us in a state of motion perfectly sufficient to enable us to refer to it by the name of wakefulness. But then our actual awakenings produce an interruption of memory. A little later we describe these states as sleep because we no longer remember them. And when shines that bright star which at the moment of waking illuminates behind the sleeper the whole expense of his sleep, it makes him imagine for a few moments that this was not a sleeping but a waking state; a shooting star, it must be added, which blots out with the fading of its light not only the false existence but the very appearance of our dream, and merely enables him who has awoken to say to himself: "I was asleep."—MARCEL PROUST: *The Guermantes Way*, Part II, Chap. 1.[24]

The same use of physical description to indicate a mental state appears in the following passage:

Sterne's discovery was made. It was repugnant to his imagination, shocking to his ideas of honesty, shocking to his conception of mankind. This enormity affected one's outlook on what was possible in this world: it was as if for instance the sun had turned blue, throwing a new and sinister light on men and nature. Really in the first moment he had felt sickish, as though he had got a blow below the belt: for a second the very color of the sea seemed changed—appeared queer to his wandering eye; and he had a passing, unsteady sensation in all his limbs as though the earth had started turning the other way.—JOSEPH CONRAD: "The End of the Tether." [25]

We notice in the above quotation how the author begins by making a general statement: the discovery is repugnant, is shocking, changes Sterne's outlook. But we notice how quickly these generalities shade over into concrete presentations which are intended

[24] From *The Guermantes Way* by Marcel Proust, tr. by C. K. Scott Moncrieff. Reprinted by permission of Random House, Inc.
[25] From *Youth: A Narrative* by Joseph Conrad. Reprinted by permission of J. M. Dent and Sons, Ltd., through the courtesy of the Conrad estate.

to evoke in us a direct sense of Sterne's sensation: the blue sun, a blow below the belt, the sudden reversal of the earth's motion.

In the following passage we find a slightly different application of the same principle. Above we have been dealing with the description of a momentary feeling; here we shall be dealing with the description of a protracted situation, a state of being. A wife has discovered that her husband's conception of life, his "mansion," is oppressive and deadening for her:

But when, as the months had elapsed, she had followed him further and he had led her into the mansion of his own habitation, then, *then* she had seen where she really was.

She could live it over again, the incredulous terror with which she had taken the measure of her dwelling. Between those four walls she had lived ever since; they were to surround her for the rest of her life. It was the house of darkness, the house of dumbness, the house of suffocation. Osmond's beautiful mind gave it neither light nor air; Osmond's beautiful mind indeed seemed to peep down from a small high window and mock at her. Of course it had not been physical suffering; for physical suffering there might have been a remedy. She could come and go; she had her liberty; her husband was perfectly polite. He took himself so seriously; it was perfectly appalling. Under all his culture, his cleverness, his amenity, under his good-nature, his facility, his knowledge of life, his egotism lay hidden like a serpent in a bank of flowers.—HENRY JAMES: *The Portrait of a Lady*, Chap. 42.

The descriptions of states of feeling just considered are direct in treatment. That is, we are introduced as fully as may be into the consciousness of the person who has the feeling or experiences the state of mind, the seaman Sterne or the disappointed wife. But there is an indirect way of using description to portray feeling or state of mind, a way which presents the symptoms but does not endeavor to describe the feeling or the state of mind itself. This way is analogous, of course, to the use of description of a person's physical appearance to indicate his character, without giving any general statements about the character.

If we describe a person as having shifty eyes and a flabby mouth, the reader is very apt to draw certain conclusions about that person's character. And by the same token, if we describe a person at the moments when his lips whiten, the blood flushes his cheeks, his eyes flash, and his respiration is rapid, the reader is apt to conclude that the person is laboring under great rage or other excitement. Such descriptions of the symptoms, as it were, of a state of feeling can, when well done, be very effective in giving the reader a sense of the reality of the situation being presented. We shall draw another example from the work of Marcel Proust, who is a master in the art of presenting states of feeling by either direct or indirect methods.

I made the invalid sit at the foot of the staircase in the hall, and went up to warn my mother. I told her that my grandmother had come home feeling slightly unwell, after an attack of giddiness. As soon as I began to speak, my mother's face was convulsed by the paroxysm of a despair which was yet already so resigned that I realized that for many years she had been holding herself quietly in readiness for an uncalendared but final day. She asked me no question; it seemed that, just as malevolence likes to exaggerate the sufferings of other people, so in her devotion she would not admit that her mother was seriously ill, especially with a disease which might affect the brain. Mamma shuddered, her eyes wept without tears, she ran to give orders for the doctor to be fetched at once; but when Françoise asked who was ill she could not reply, her voice stuck in her throat. She came running downstairs with me, struggling to banish from her face the sob that contracted it.—MARCEL PROUST: *The Guermantes Way*, Part II, Chap. 1.[26]

FIGURATIVE LANGUAGE IN THE DESCRIPTION OF FEELINGS AND STATES OF MIND

It should be obvious from the examples given above that when a writer comes to describe a feeling or a state of mind he is often forced to use figurative language. For instance, when Henry James (p. 222) wishes to describe the feeling of the wife who discovers that her husband is unsympathetic and egotistical, he resorts to figurative language: the wife feels she has been imprisoned in the "house of dumbness," the "house of suffocation," and most of the passage is an elaboration of this comparison of her condition to an imprisonment. The whole question of figurative language will be discussed at some length elsewhere in this book (p. 361), but the question is of so much importance for description that we must at least touch upon it here.

We may say, for the sake of convenience, that such comparisons

[26] From *The Guermantes Way* by Marcel Proust, tr. by C. K. Scott Moncrieff. Reprinted by permission of Random House, Inc.

have two functions in description, in enriching the texture. First, they may make for vividness and immediacy. Second, they may serve to interpret the object described or an attitude toward it.

If we write of a girl's hair that it is very black and glossy, we do little to stir the imagination of the reader to a full sense of the quality of the hair. But if we write that her hair is like a raven's wing, then we have done something to set the imagination of the reader to work. The comparison just used is, unfortunately, a rather trite one; it has been used so often that its power to stir the imagination is almost gone. But when Hardy writes of Eustacia Vye's hair that "a whole winter did not contain darkness enough to form its shadow," or that it "closed over her forehead like nightfall," the imagination is stirred, and the image of Eustacia is evoked. But more than mere vividness has been gained by Hardy's comparisons. These particular comparisons also contribute to our impression of Eustacia's character—the brooding, the mystery, the sense of violence—the "nocturnal" quality, to use the word which Hardy himself uses of her later on. That is, the comparisons not only increase the vividness, but interpret the object of the comparison.

But we do often find that the function of a comparison is merely to increase vividness, to help the reader to grasp the object, or that the interpretative value of the comparison is very slight. For instance, when Ruskin describes the street leading up to the cathedral (p. 202), he writes that the house had "small porches to their doors in the shape of cockleshells." The chief function here, no doubt, is to make the impression more vivid, though we are aware of some interpretative force in *cockleshell*—an implication of quaintness, of cuteness, of childlike diminutiveness. Or when Faulkner describes Miss Emily (p. 208): "Her eyes, lost in the fatty ridges of her face, looked like two small pieces of coal pressed into a lump of dough," the chief effect is to startle us, by this caricature of a face, to visualize Miss Emily. But if we are acquainted with the story in which the sentence appears we realize that some interpretation may also be involved—the pallor, the pasty quality of the flesh, the unhuman quality of the comparison, are appropriate for this house of decay and death.

When we come, however, to Stevenson's comparison of the atoll to a basin almost submerged in water (p. 210), we have almost as pure an example as it would be possible to find of a comparison which works to aid in vividness without any interpretative force.

On the other hand, we can find many passages in which the interpretative value of the comparisons is more important than the value of vividness. For instance, when Poe refers to the "eye-like windows" of the House of Usher (p. 52) there is undoubtedly some value of vividness—that is, the comparison does help the imagination to create the house; but at the same time the chief importance of the comparison is to create an atmosphere, to interpret the scene. Or when Melville compares the vast volcanic islands to "split Syrian gourds" (p. 46), the function is primarily interpretative. By that time in the passage we already have a very strong visual impression of the islands, and in any case, split, withering gourds do not strongly suggest the picture of islands. But the gourds do strongly suggest the idea of waste and desolation—the interpretative aspect. In the last sentence of the passage from E. M. Forster (p. 205) we have an excellent case of the interpretative emphasis in a comparison: the Indian city is like "some low but indestructible form of life."

It must always be remembered, however, that the comparison which is primarily interpretative in intent must involve some basic connection between the things compared. The split gourds do bear some resemblance to the desolate islands: the cracked, parched islands, and the cracked, parched gourds.

A good comparison cannot be purely arbitrary. When T. E. Lawrence writes of the arrival at an Arabian port, "the heat of Arabia came out like a drawn sword and struck us speechless" (p. 212), we have nothing which corresponds as far as shape is concerned with the sword, but we do have the metallic glitter of sea and sand, the suddenness and violence of the heat after days at sea; and then, at the level of interpretation, we have the notion of ferocity and deadliness—the pitiless heat and the drawn blade. Or when Proust uses the comparison of various depths of the sea and of various kinds of light to describe the process of waking, there is no object which corresponds to those things; but the vague shadings and confusions of dawning consciousness provide the basis for the comparison.

It does not matter on what basis the comparison is established— by what senses or feelings—but there must be some primary connection if interpretation is to be established. A comparison, even if it does carry an appropriate interpretation, must not be so far-fetched that the reader cannot accept it. At the same time the comparison which is too trite or too obvious does not stir the imagination. There is no rule for establishing these limits. The writer must simply depend on observation of the practice of others and on his own experience.

CHOICE OF WORDS IN THE TEXTURE OF DESCRIPTION

As the selection of details and the use of figurative language helps to determine the texture of a description, so does the choice of words. The problem of diction, the choice of words, is naturally important for all writing and is discussed elsewhere in this book, but it must be touched on here in connection with description.

Inexperienced writers tend to make adjectives bear the burden in description. They do this because the adjective is the part of speech which refers to the qualities of things, and description is the kind of discourse which is chiefly concerned with the appearance of things. An inexperienced writer, therefore, tends to overload his description with adjectives, with the idea of specifying all the qualities of the thing being presented. Such a writer forgets that suggestion is often better than enumeration, and that the mere listing of qualities is not the best way to evoke an image in the reader's mind.

Let us look at the following portrait:

The woman's face was fat and shapeless, so fat that it looked soft, unresilient, grayish, and unhealthy. The features were blurred because her face was fat. But her small, black glistening eyes had a quick inquisitive motion as they moved from one face to another while the visitors stated their errand.

In that description the writer has piled up the adjectives, trying to specify each of the qualities of the woman's face and eyes. The result is a rather confused impression. Let us now take the passage as William Faulkner originally wrote it (p. 208) before we tampered with it:

Her eyes, lost in the fatty ridges of her face, looked like two small pieces of coal pressed into a lump of dough as they moved from one face to another while the visitors stated their errand.

Here the writer has managed to dispense with most of the adjectives, for the dough implies *soft, unresilient, grayish, shapeless, blurred,* and (when associated with flesh) *unhealthy,* and the coal implies *black* and *glistening.* The use of a comparison of this kind will frequently enable the writer to dispense with adjectives. But if the writer must use adjectives he should be sure that each adjective really adds something essential to the description. Rather than give the list of adjectives above, one could simply say that the face was "fat and doughy."

The discussion above really returns us to the question of selection. But it does not touch on the use of parts of speech other than adjectives. One can frequently get greater vividness by using nouns, adverbs, and verbs. For instance, notice the descriptive force of the italicized nouns in the following examples:

The very smoke coming out of their chimneys was poverty-stricken. Little *rags* and *shreds* of smoke, so unlike the great silvery *plumes* that uncurled from the Sheridans' chimneys.—KATHERINE MANSFIELD: "The Garden Party."

They crept up the hill in the twilight and entered the cottage. It was built of *mud-walls,* the surface of which had been washed by many rains into *channels* and *depressions* that left none of the original flat *face* visible; while here and there in the thatch above a rafter showed like a *bone* protruding through the *skin.*—THOMAS HARDY: "The Withered Arm."

And a wind blew there, tossing the withered tops of last year's grasses, and *mists* ran with the wind, and ragged *shadows* with the *mists,* and *mare's-tails* of clear *moonlight* among the *shadows,* so that now the boles of birches on the forest's edge beyond the fences were but opal *blurs* and now cut *alabaster.*—WILBUR DANIEL STEELE: "How Beautiful with Shoes."

We can see that in these passages, the nouns are of two kinds. First, there are those which simply point to some items in the thing described, such as *channels, depressions, mists, shadows, moonlight.* Second, there are those which involve comparisons, such as *rags, shreds, alabaster, bone,* and *skin.*

When we turn to the use of adverbs, we find that this part of speech sometimes enables a writer to get an effect with great economy by fusing the quality of a thing with its action. When Dickens writes in describing Chadband that he "moves softly and cumbrously, not unlike a bear who has been taught to walk upright" (p. 214), the adverbs *softly* and *cumbrously* give a much more vivid and immediate effect than would be possible if we broke the description up in the following fashion: Mr. Chadband is soft, heavy, and awkward-looking. When he walks his motion is not unlike that of a bear which has been taught to walk upright.

Let us take two sentences from Stephen Crane's description of a battle (p. 218) and see how the italicized adverbs used focus the main effect in each sentence:

Having stirred this prodigious uproar and, apparently, finding it too prodigious, the brigade, after a little time, came marching *airily* out again with its fine formation in nowise disturbed. . . . A congregation of horses, tied to a long railing, were tugging *frenziedly* at their bridles.

In both of these sentences the adverb is the key word. In the first, *airily,* with its implications of lightness, casualness, slight disdainfulness, and girlishness, is the key to the irony of the passage. In the second, *frenziedly* focuses the attention on the quality of the action—the important thing about the scene by the railing.

Or look at the effect of the italicized adverbs in the following passage from Katherine Anne Porter's description of Braggioni (p. 217):

His mouth opens round and yearns *sideways,* his balloon cheeks grow oily with the labor of song. He bulges *marvellously* in his expensive garments.

In the use of verbs, the same concentration of effect is possible, for frequently the right verb can imply something about the nature of the thing or person performing an action as well as about the nature of the action. In the sentence by Katherine Anne Porter just quoted, the verbs *yearns* and *bulges* are extremely important. *Yearns* implies the sentimental expression on the fat revolutionist's face, and *bulges* implies the brute heft of the man, in contrast to the sentimental song he sings. So the two verbs here really indicate the contrast in his nature, as well as in his appearance.

In the following passage, which describes a herd of wild horses corraled in a barn-lot, notice how the variety and accuracy of the italicized forms [27] give the impression of furious, aimless motion, and define the atmosphere of violence of the scene:

[27] Some of the verbs, we notice, appear in the form of participles.

"Come on, grab a holt," the Texan said. Eck grasped the wire also. The horses *laid* back against it, the pink faces *tossing* above the *back-surging* mass. "Pull him up, pull him up," the Texan said sharply. "They couldn't get up here in the wagon even if they wanted to." The wagon moved gradually backward until the head of the first horse was *snubbed* up to the tail-gate. The Texan took a turn of wire quickly about one of the wagon stakes. "Keep the slack out of it," he said. He *vanished* and *reappeared,* almost in the same second, with a pair of heavy wire-cutters. "Hold them like that," he said, and *leaped.* He *vanished,* broad hat, *flapping* vest, wire-cutters and all, into a kaleidoscopic maelstrom of long teeth and wild eyes and *slashing* feet, from which presently the horses began to *burst,* one by one like partridges *flushing,* each wearing a necklace of barbed wire. The first one crossed the lot at top speed, on a straight line. It *galloped* into the fence without any diminution whatever. The wire *gave, recovered,* and *slammed* the horse to earth where it lay for a moment, *glaring,* its legs still *galloping* in air. It scrambled up without having ceased to gallop and crossed the lot and *galloped* into the opposite fence and was *slammed* again to earth. The others were now freed. They *whipped* and *whirled* about the lot like dizzy fish in a bowl. It had seemed like a big lot until now, but now the very idea that all that fury and motion should be transpiring inside any one fence was something to be repudiated with contempt, like a mirror trick.—WILLIAM FAULKNER: *The Hamlet,* Book IV, Chap. 1.[28]

Verbs like *tossing, vanished, reappeared, leaped, slashing, slammed, whipped, whirled,* give a constant sense of seething, violent motion, and as the passage continues in the part not quoted here we find such additional verbs as *feinting, dodging, weaving, ripped, shook,* and *streaked.*

A good writer can make adjectives, nouns, adverbs, and verbs all serve his purpose. He can blend them to give his effect.

SUMMARY

Description is the kind of discourse that tells what something is like, what qualities it has, what impression it makes. It deals primarily with the appearance of the world.

We can distinguish two kinds of description, TECHNICAL and SUGGESTIVE.

Technical description may really be considered as one type of exposition, the kind of discourse concerned with explanation, with analysis and classification. But suggestive description also is related to the other forms of discourse. It frequently appears in connection with narrative of all types, and sometimes with exposition and argument.

Description, and especially suggestive description, has to do with the appearance of the world, and hence with the way the world presents itself to our senses. Any one of the senses, and the perceptions of heat and cold, of pressure and strain, may be involved in description, or any combination of them. Hence, a capacity for close observation is important for good description.

In suggestive description the writer should be concerned to give a DOMINANT IMPRESSION, the unified effect to which the details contribute, the basic mood or idea of the description.

Even if a writer knows what dominant impression he wishes to give, he must still solve certain problems of method. These may be considered under two heads, PATTERN and TEXTURE. Pattern has to do with general organization, and texture with the nature of the details and their relation to each other.

In description with an objective emphasis any one of three types of POINT OF VIEW may dictate the organization:

1. Order in the object as observed from a fixed position
2. Order in the object as observed from a shifting position
3. Order in an imaginary FRAME IMAGE

In description with a subjective emphasis either of two methods may be used to organize the details:

4. In reference to the mood or attitude
5. In reference to an interest

In addition to these types of pattern, three others may be distinguished:

6. By a listing of details with relation to a dominant mood or interest but without formal organization—IMPRESSIONISTIC PATTERN

7. In reference to a frame of narrative, argument, or exposition in which the descriptive material is absorbed—ABSORBED DESCRIPTION

8. By mixed patterns

As pattern is concerned with the organization of details, so texture is concerned with the nature of the details presented. This problem is, first, a problem of SELECTION. Selection may be considered in two aspects, VIVIDNESS and SIGNIFICANCE, but it must be remembered that the same detail may be both vivid and significant.

A detail may be vivid because it is obvious and striking, or because, though not obvious, it stimulates the reader's imagination to re-create the object described. A detail may be significant if it contributes to the dominant impression, that is, the mood, the attitude, or the idea the writer wishes to communicate.

The dominant impression may be not only of some physical object, say a scene or a person, but of the character of a person. The physical details may indicate the inner nature of the person described. By the same process, that of indicating the intangible by the tangible, feelings and states of mind may be described. This may involve the use of the physical symptoms of the feeling or state of mind and the use of figurative language. But figurative language is often important in description to indicate or to heighten the dominant impression.

The choice of words is also important in determining the texture of description. Inexperienced writers tend to rely on adjectives, but other parts of speech, nouns, adverbs, and verbs, can be used with effect. A good writer tries to use the full resources of his language and to combine its elements into a unified whole.

EXAMPLES

Following are a number of examples of description. These have already been discussed in this chapter with regard to the study of special topics.

A. A knot of country boys, gabbling at one another like starlings, shrilled a cheer as we came rattling over a stone bridge beneath which a stream shallowly washed its bank of osiers.—WALTER DE LA MARE: *Memoirs of a Midget,* Chap. 2.

B. Charmian is a hatchet faced, terra cotta colored little goblin, swift in her movements, and neatly finished at the hands and feet.—GEORGE BERNARD SHAW: *Caesar and Cleopatra,* Act IV.

C. Without being robust, her health was perfect, her needlework exquisite, her temper equable and calm; she loved and was loved by her girl-friends; she read romantic verses and select novels; above all, she danced. That was the greatest pleasure in life for her; not for the sake of her partners—those were surely only round dances, and the partners didn't count; what counted was the joy of motion, the sense of treading lightly, in perfect time, a sylph in spotless muslin, enriched with a ribbon or a flower, playing discreetly with her fan, and sailing through the air with feet that seemed scarcely to touch the ground.— GEORGE SANTAYANA: *Persons and Places,* Chap. 1.[29]

D. Leaning over the parapet he enjoyed, once more, the strangely intimate companionship of the sea. He glanced down into the water whose uneven floor was diapered with long weedy patches, fragments of fallen rock, and brighter patches of sand; he inhaled the pungent odor of sea-wrack and listened to the breathings of the waves. They lapped softly against the rounded boulders which strewed the shore like a flock of nodding Behemoths. He remembered his visits at daybreak to the beach—those unspoken confidences with the sunlit element to whose friendly caresses he had abandoned his body. How calm it was, too, in this evening light. Near at hand, somewhere, lay a sounding cave; it sang a melody of moist content. Shadows lengthened; fishing boats, moving outward for the night-work, steered darkly across the luminous river at his feet. Those jewel-like morning tints of blue and green had faded from the water; the southern cliff-scenery, projections of it, caught a fiery glare. Bastions of flame. . . .

The air seemed to have become unusually cool and bracing.—NORMAN DOUGLAS: *South Wind,* Chap. 49.[30]

E. So the day has taken place, all the visionary business of the day. The young cattle stand in the straw of the stack yard, the sun gleams on their white fleece, the eyes of Io, and the man with the side-whiskers carries more yellow straw into the compound. The sun comes in all down one side, and above, in the sky, all the gables and grey stone chimney-stacks are floating in pure dreams.

There is threshed wheat smouldering in the great barn, the fire of life: and the sound of the threshing machine, running, drumming.

The threshing machine, running, drumming, waving its steam in a corner of a great field, the rapid nucleus of darkness beside the yellow ricks: and the rich plough-land comes up, ripples up in endless grape-colored ripples, like a tide of procreant desire: the machine sighs and drums, wind blows the chaff in little eddies, blows the clothes of the men on the ricks close against their limbs: the men on the stacks in the wind

[29] From *Persons and Places* by George Santayana, copyright, 1944, 1945, by Charles Scribner's Sons.

[30] From *South Wind* by Norman Douglas. Reprinted by permission of Dodd, Mead & Company, Inc.

against a bare blue heaven, their limbs blown clean in contour naked shapely animated fragments of earth active in heaven.

Coming home, by the purple and crimson hedges, red with berries, up hill over the heavy ground to the stone, old three-pointed house with its raised chimney-stacks, the old manor lifting its fair, pure stone amid trees and foliage, rising from the lawn, we pass the pond where white ducks hastily launch upon the lustrous dark grey waters.

So up the steps to the porch, through the doorway, and into the interior, fragrant with all the memories of old age, and of bygone, remembered lustiness.—D. H. LAWRENCE: *Letters*.[31]

F. When I say they [the gondoliers of Venice] are associated with its [the city's] silence, I should immediately add that they are associated also with its sound. Among themselves they are extraordinarily talkative company. They chatter at the *traghetti* [landings], where they always have some sharp point under discussion; they bawl across the canals; they bespeak your commands as you approach; they defy each other from afar. If you happen to have a *traghetto* under your window, you are well aware that they are a vocal race. I should go even farther than I went just now, and say that the voice of the gondolier is, in fact, the voice of Venice. There is scarcely any other, and that, indeed, is part of the interest of the place. There is no noise there save distinctly human noise; no rumbling, no vague uproar, no rattle of wheels and hoofs. It is all articulate, personal sound. One may say, indeed, that Venice is, emphatically, the city of conversation; people talk all over the place, because there is nothing to interfere with their being heard. Among the populace it is a kind of family party. The still water carries the voice, and good Venetians exchange confidences at a distance of a half a mile. It saves a world of trouble, and they don't like trouble. Their delightful garrulous language helps them to make Venetian life a long *conversazione*. This language, with its soft elisions, its odd transpositions, its kindly contempt for consonants and other disagreeables, has in it something peculiarly human and accommodating.—HENRY JAMES: "Venice," *Portraits of Places*.

G. The dress of the rider and the accouterments of his horse, were peculiarly unfit for the traveller in such a country. A coat of linked mail, with long sleeves, plated gauntlets, and a steel breastplate, had not been esteemed sufficient weight of armor; there was also his triangular shield suspended round his neck, and his barred helmet of steel, over which he had a hood and collar of mail, which was drawn around the warrior's

[31] From *The Letters of D. H. Lawrence* by D. H. Lawrence, copyright, 1932, by The Viking Press, Inc.

shoulders and throat, and filled up the vacancy between the hauberk and the head-piece. His lower limbs were sheathed, like his body, in flexible mail, securing the legs and thighs, while the feet rested in plated shoes, which corresponded with the gauntlets. A long, broad, straight-shaped, double-edged falchion, with a handle formed like a cross, corresponded with a stout poniard on the other side. The Knight also bore, secured to his saddle, with one end resting on his stirrup, the long steel-headed lance, his own proper weapon, which, as he rode, projected backwards, and displayed its little pennoncelle, to dally with the faint breeze, or drop in the dead calm. –WALTER SCOTT: *The Talisman*, Bk. I, Chap. 1.

H. Say that I had walked and wandered by unknown roads, and suddenly, after climbing a gentle hill, had seen before me for the first time the valley of Usk, just above Newbridge. I think it was on one of those strange days in summer when the sky is at once so grey and luminous that I achieved this adventure. There are no clouds in the upper air, the sky is simply covered with a veil which is, as I say, both grey and luminous, and there is no breath of wind, and every leaf is still.

But now and again as the day goes on the veil will brighten, and the sun almost appear; and then here and there in the woods it is as if white moons were descending. On such a day, then, I saw that wonderful and most lovely valley; the Usk, here purged of its muddy tidal waters, now like the sky, grey and silvery and luminous, winding in mystic esses, and the dense forest bending down to it, and the grey stone bridge crossing it. Down the valley in the distance was Caerleon-on-Usk; over the hill, somewhere in the lower slopes of the forest, Caerwent, also a Roman city, was buried in the earth, and gave up now and again strange relics—fragments of the temple of "Nodens, god of the depths." I saw the lonely house between the dark forest and the silver river, and years after I wrote "The Great God Pan," an endeavor to pass on the vague, indefinable sense of awe and mystery and terror that I had received.—ARTHUR MACHEN: *Far Off Things*, Chap. 1.[32]

I. Ratmiroff gazed gloomily after his wife—even then he could not fail to observe the enchanting grace of her figure, or her movements—and crushing his cigarette with a heavy blow against the marble slab of the chimney-piece, he flung it far from him. His cheeks suddenly paled, a convulsive quiver flitted across his chin, and his eyes wandered dully and fiercely over the floor, as though in search of something. . . .

Every trace of elegance had vanished from his face. That must have been the sort of expression it had assumed when he flogged the white Russian peasants.—IVAN TURGENEV: *Smoke,* Chap. 15.

J. He was a Mr. Cornelius Vanslyperken, a tall, meagre-looking personage, with very narrow shoulders and very small head. Perfectly straight up and down, protruding in no part, he reminded you of some tall parish pump, with a great knob at its top. His face was gaunt, cheeks hollow, nose and chin showing an effection for each other, and evidently lamenting the gulf between them which prevented their meeting. Both appear to have fretted themselves to the utmost degree of tenuity from disappointment in love; as for the nose, it had a pearly round tear hanging at its tip, as if it wept.—FREDERICK MARRYAT: *The Dog Fiend,* Chap. 1.

K. Her heart seemed so full, that it spilt its new gush of happiness, as it were, like rich and sunny wine out of an overbrimming goblet.— NATHANIEL HAWTHORNE: *The Marble Faun,* Chap. 15.

L. But I eat. I gradually lose all knowledge of particulars as I eat. I am becoming weighed down with food. These delicious mouthfuls of roast duck, fitly piled with vegetables, following each other in exquisite rotation of warmth, weight, sweet and bitter, past my palate, down my gullet, into my stomach, have established my body. I feel quiet, gravity, control. All is solid now. Instinctively my palate now requires and anticipates sweetness and lightness, something sugared and evanescent; and cool wine, fitting glove-like over those finer nerves that seem to tremble from the roof of my mouth and make it spread (as I drink) into a domed cavern, green with vine leaves, musk-scented, purple with grapes. Now I can look steadily into the mill-race that foams beneath. By what particular name are we to call it? Let Rhoda speak, whose face I see reflected mistily in the looking-glass opposite; Rhoda whom I interrupted when she rocked her petals in a brown basin, asking for the pocket-knife that Bernard had stolen. Love is not a whirl-pool to her. She is not giddy when she looks down. She looks far away over our heads, beyond India.—VIRGINIA WOOLF: *The Waves,* Section 4.[33]

M. Cape Cod is the bared and bended arm of Massachusetts; the shoulder is at Buzzard's Bay; the elbow, or crazy-bone, at Cape Mallebarre; the wrist at Truro; and the sandy fist at Provincetown,—behind which the state stands on her guard, with her back to the Green Mountains, and her feet planted on the floor of the ocean, like an athlete protecting her Bay,—boxing with northeast storms, and, ever and anon,

[33] From *The Waves* by Virginia Woolf, copyright, 1931, by Harcourt, Brace and Company, Inc.

heaving up her Atlantic adversary from the lap of earth,—ready to thrust forward her other fist, which keeps guard while upon her breast at Cape Ann.—HENRY DAVID THOREAU: *Cape Cod,* Chap. 1.

N. In search of a place proper for this, I found a little plain on the side of a rising hill, whose front towards this little plain was steep as a house-side, so that nothing could come down upon me from the top; on the side of this rock there was a hollow place, worn a little way in, like the entrance or door of a cave; but there was not really any cave, or way into the rock at all.

On the flat of the green, just before this hollow place, I resolved to pitch my tent. This plain was not above an hundred yards broad, and about twice as long, and lay like a green before my door, and at the end of it descended irregularly every way down into the low grounds by the seaside. It was on the NNW. side of the hill, so that I was sheltered from the heat every day, till it came to a W. and by S. sun, or thereabouts, which in those countries is near the setting.—DANIEL DEFOE: *Robinson Crusoe.*

Narration

NARRATION is the kind of discourse concerned with action, with life in motion. It answers the question: "What happened?" It tells a story.

We ordinarily think of story-telling as being the special province of the writer of fiction, of short stories and novels, but fiction is only one type of narration, and here we shall be concerned with narration as a kind of discourse—with narration in general. Fiction involves many special problems which will not be touched on here.

Let us examine what we mean by the word *action* as used in the statement that narration is the kind of discourse concerned with action. We may discuss action under three heads, *movement, time,* and *meaning.*

MOVEMENT

Description gives us the picture of the world as fixed at a given moment, of its objects as existing at that moment. It is a portrait, a snapshot, a still life. Narration gives us a moving picture, its objects in operation, life in motion. Its emphasis is not on the thing in motion, but on the nature of the motion itself. It is concerned with a transformation from one stage to another stage. It not only answers the question, "What happened?" it also answers the question, "How did it happen?"—that is, what was the process of passing from the first stage to the last stage?

This special emphasis on movement itself means that narration does not explain a process (though it may do so) but *presents* a process. It places the event before our eyes. Narration does not *tell about* the story. It *tells* the story. Like description, narration gives the quality of immediacy.

TIME

The movement of a process, an event, is through time, from one point to another. But narration does not give us a mere segment of time, but a *unit* of time, and a unit is a thing which is complete in itself. It may be part of a larger thing, and it may contain smaller parts, but in itself it is complete. The unit of time, therefore, is the time in which a process fulfills itself. We now emphasize, not the fact of movement, but the movement from a beginning to an end. We begin a story at the moment when something is ripe to happen, when one condition prevails but is unstable, and end it when the something has finished happening, when a new condition prevails and is stable. And in between those two moments are all the moments which mark the stages of change.

But you may recall narratives which did not begin with that first moment when something was ripe to happen. For instance, a narrative may begin with a man in the very midst of his difficulties and problems, say on the battlefield or at the moment of a marital crisis or when he hears that he has lost his fortune, and then cut back to his previous experiences to explain how he came to be in such a situation. Such a narrative does not move in an orderly fashion from A to Z. It begins, instead, with G, H, I and then cuts back to A, B, and C. But we must distinguish here between two things: how the narrator treated the sequence in time and how the sequence existed in time. The narrator may have given us G, H, and I first in order to catch our interest. He may have thought that A, B, and C, would not be interesting to us until we knew what they were to lead to. But when he does finally cut back to A, B, and C, we become aware of the full sequence in time and set it up in our imaginations A, B, C . . . G, H, I. . . . In other words, we must distinguish between the *way* (G, H, I–A, B, C . . .) the narrator tells us something and the *thing* (A, B, C, D, E, F, G . . .) which he tells. The *thing* told always represents a unit of time, no matter how much the narrator may violate its natural order.

MEANING

An action, as we are using the word, is not merely a series of events but is a meaningful series. We have already implied this in saying that narration gives us a unit of time, with a beginning and an end. In other words, the events must be stages in a process and not merely a random collection held together in time. They must have a unity of meaning. Suppose we should read:

President Wilson presented his war message to Congress on April 6, 1917. War was declared. Thus the United States embarked on its first great adventure in world affairs. On April 8, 1917, just two days later, Albert Mayfield was born in Marysville, Illinois. He was a healthy baby, and grew rapidly. By the time of the Armistice he weighed 25 pounds. On December 12, 1918, the troopship *Mason,* returning to New York from Cherbourg, struck a floating mine off Ireland and sank. Two hundred and sixteen men were lost.

Several events are recounted in this passage, but as it is presented to us, nothing holds those events together. They have no significant relation to each other. They do not constitute an action, merely a sequence in time. But suppose we rewrite the passage:

President Wilson presented his war message to Congress on April 6, 1917. War was declared. Thus the United States embarked on its first great adventure in world affairs. On April 8, 1917, just two days later, Albert Mayfield was born in Marysville, Illinois. Scarcely before the ink had dried on the headlines of the extra of the Marysville *Courier* announcing the declaration of war, Albert embarked on his own great adventure in world affairs. He was a healthy baby, and grew rapidly. By the time of the Armistice he weighed 25 pounds. On December 12, 1918, the troopship *Mason,* returning to New York from Cherbourg, struck a floating mine off Ireland and sank. Two hundred and sixteen men were lost. Among those men was Sidney Mayfield, a captain of artillery, a quiet, unobtrusive, middle-aged insurance salesman, who left a widow and an infant son. That son was Albert Mayfield. So Albert grew up into a world which the war—a war he could not remember—had defined. It had defined the little world of his home, the silent, bitter woman who was his mother, the poverty and the cheerless discipline, and it had defined the big world outside.

Now we are moving toward an action. The random events are given some relationship to each other. We have unity and meaning.

We may want to go on and find out more about Albert and about the long-range effects of the war on his life, but what we have is, as far as it goes, an action in itself as well as the part of a bigger action, the story of Albert's life.

We have said that an action must have unity of meaning. This implies that one thing leads to another, or if one thing does not lead to the other, that they both belong to a body of related events all bearing on the point of the action. For instance, in the paragraph about Albert Mayfield, the declaration of war by the United States did not directly cause the floating mine to be in a particular spot off Ireland, but both events belong in the body of events contributing to the formation of Albert's character.

In seeking the unity of an action, we must often think of the persons involved. Events do not merely happen to people, but people also cause events. People have desires and impulses, and these desires and impulses are translated into deeds. Therefore, the human motives involved may contribute to the unity of an action. This human element, MOTIVATION, may provide the line which runs through the individual events and binds them together. And when motivation does not provide us with the line, we must think of the events as leading to some human response. For example, no motivation in the sense just used binds the little story of Albert Mayfield together, but the effect of the events on Albert Mayfield, his response to them, provides the unity and the meaning.

If we summarize what we mean by an action, we arrive at something like this. It is a connected sequence of events. It involves a change from one condition to another. It must have a beginning and an end. It must have unity and meaning. It must stimulate and satisfy an interest.

NARRATIVE AND NARRATION

Before we leave this preliminary discussion of narration, it may be well, as a kind of caution, to make a distinction between narration and narrative. Strictly considered, narration is a certain way of speaking or writing, a kind of discourse, and a narrative is the thing produced by its application, a discourse, either spoken or written, which presents an action. We must remember, however, that the method of narration may be used without giving us a satisfactory narrative. Suppose a woman should say:

Why, my dear, I had the pleasantest afternoon yesterday. I went down to lunch with Ethel—at the Green Room of the Millet Hotel—and we had delicious shrimp. You know, the kind they serve there. Then I went to get a facial. And guess who was there! Milly Seaver. I hadn't seen her in ages. Really, not for ages. She was looking awful well, even if she is beginning—I oughtn't say this, but it's true—to show her age just a little. You know how blondes are. She said she was getting a permanent and was in a hurry because her husband was taking her to Chicago that night on a business trip. Then I left the beauty shop and went to a movie. It wasn't very good, but I enjoyed being there in the cool, after such a hot day. But I had to come home early, before the show was over. You see, Mike, that's my biggest child, had to go to a Scout meeting. And besides, I like an early dinner for the children. Also, my new shoes weren't very comfortable, and I was glad to get home. But Milly Seaver —you really ought to see her— she's getting . . .

This rattletrap of a woman has used the method of narration, but she has used it without the distinguishing interest of narration, the presentation of an action. She has given us a sequence of events in time, but that sequence of events does not constitute an action in the real sense. The unity is a unity in time—she went down town early in the afternoon and came home late—but there is no unity of meaning in the events themselves. One may say, of course, that we get some notion of her character from the way she spends her time, and that this constitutes a meaning. But ordinarily we insist on a little more than that when we say that a sequence of events constitutes an action.

It is not profitable, however, to demand a single line of demarcation between what is narration and non-narration, between what is narrative and what is non-narrative. If we understand the extremes—the random and unrelated accumulation events at the one extreme, and the fully realized action at the other—we can use common sense to discriminate among the examples of the shadowland in between. And in our ordinary speaking and writing we shall frequently have reason to move into that shadowland where definitions are not as clear as day.

NARRATION AND THE OTHER KINDS
OF DISCOURSE

We have been discussing narration (and narrative) as a thing in itself. But it bears certain relations to the other kinds of discourse—description, exposition, and argument. What are these relations?

We can break this general question down into two other questions:

1. How does narration use other kinds of discourse?
2. How do other kinds of discourse use narration?

HOW NARRATION USES OTHER KINDS OF DISCOURSE

Let us take up the first question. A narrative may have within it descriptive, argumentative, or expository elements. In fact, any rather full narrative will almost certainly have them, but they will be, if the prevailing motive of the piece of writing is narrative, absorbed into the narrative intention.

A narrative presents us with an action. But an action implies things or persons which act and are acted upon. And the word *presents* implies that we are not told about those things or persons but are given some sense of their actual presence, their appearance, their nature. And this means that, in a greater or lesser degree, they are described. So description comes in to give us that impression of immediacy which is important for all narrative except the most bare and synoptic kind.

The same line of reasoning leads us to an awareness of the importance of exposition in narrative. A narrative involves an action, and we have defined an action as a sequence of events related to create a meaning. One thing leads to another. There is a connection of cause and effect, or at least the events are connected with each other by means of some idea. For instance, in the little example given above about Albert Mayfield and World War I, the war is the cause of the particular situation in which the boy grows up. We must understand this in order to get the point.

Exposition is the kind of discourse concerned with explanation, with making us understand something, and in so far as a narrative employs explanation to bring us to an understanding of its point, it involves exposition. Some narratives, it is true, may simply arrange their materials so that the reader is aware of the point without having to depend on any explanation, but in any rather fully developed narrative some element of exposition, even though a very slight one, is apt to appear.

Let us turn to the writing of a little narrative. Suppose we start with the following passage:

George Barton, a poor boy about twelve years old of nondescript appearance, was forced to sell the mastiff, which he had reared from a puppy and which he loved very much, for two reasons. First, having lost his job, he could no longer buy proper food for a dog of such size. Second, after it had frightened a child in the neighborhood, he was afraid that someone would poison it.

But this is not a narrative. It is concerned with an action, the fact that the boy sells his dog, but its primary concern is with the causes of the action and with what the action illustrates rather than with the immediate presentation of the action in time. Let us rewrite the passage.

George Barton owned a mastiff which he had reared from a puppy. He loved it very much. But he lost his job and could no longer buy proper food for it. Then the dog frightened a little child of the neighborhood who was eating a piece of bread. George was now afraid that someone would poison it. So he sold it.

This is a narrative. The causes of the action are given here, as before, but now they are absorbed into the movement of the action itself and appear to us in their natural sequence. When we wrote in the first example that George sold the dog for two reasons, we violated the whole nature of narrative—the movement in time—because we made, not the action itself, but the causes of the action, the thing of primary interest. The first piece of writing is expository: it explains why the boy sold the dog. The second piece of writing is narrative: it tells us what happened.

This second piece of writing is, however, a very poor, dull, and incomplete piece of narrative. It can scarcely be said, for one thing, to *present* the event at all. It gives us little sense of the immediate quality of the event. It is so bare of detail that the imagination of the reader can find little to work on. We have the basic facts given in a bare synopsis. But if we fill in the synopsis a little we can make it satisfy us somewhat better.

George Barton was a nondescript little boy, scarcely to be distinguished from the other boys living in Duck Alley. He had a pasty face, not remarkable in any way, eyes not blue and not brown but some nondescript hazel color, and a tangle of neutral colored hair. His clothes were the anonymous, drab, cast-off items worn by all the children of Duck Alley, that grimy street, scarcely a street at all but a dirt track, which ran between the sluggish, algae-crusted bayou and a scattering of shanties. His life there was unremarkable and cheerless enough, with a feeble, querulous, stooped, defeated father, a mother who had long since resigned herself to her misery, and a sullen older brother, with a mean laugh and a hard set of knuckles, who tormented George for amusement when he was not off prowling with his cronies. But this home did not distinguish George from the other children of Duck Alley. It was like many of the others. What distinguished George was his dog.

One day two years back—it was the summer when he was ten—George had found the dog. It was a puppy then, a scrawny, starving creature with absurd big paws, sniffling feebly in the garbage dump at the end of Duck Alley. No one could have guessed then that it would grow into a sleek, powerful animal, as big as a pony.

George brought it home, and defended it against the protests and jeers and random kicks of the family. "I'll feed him," he asserted. "He won't never eat a bite I don't make the money to pay for." And he was as good as his word. There was no job too hard for him, for he could look forward to evening when he would squat by the old goods box which served as a kennel and watch Jibby gnaw at the hunk of meat he had bought.

Suppose we begin the narrative in that way. We have added several elements to the bare synopsis given before. We know now why the dog is so important to the boy. There is no direct statement on this point, but we see that he lives an isolated and loveless life, and that the dog satisfies a craving of his nature for companionship and affection. We also see that now he has a reason for his own efforts, a center for his life. In other words we can imaginatively grasp his own state of mind. As we have just stated the matter, it is given as explanation, as exposition, but in the narrative itself this expository element is absorbed into situation and action. But in addition to this element, we have added little bits of description which are woven into the narrative to help us visualize the scene and George himself. The description which is absorbed into the narrative helps put the whole thing before us, helps to present it rather than tell about it.

The thing to emphasize here is that the narrative is concerned to make us sense the fullness of the process—to make us see, hear, feel, and understand the event as a single thing. Description alone might make us see or hear some aspect of the event. Exposition might make us understand its meaning, its causes or results. But narrative, when it is fully effective, makes us aware directly of the event as happening.

To return to our little narrative. Suppose we should carry on our suggested revision to the moment when George sells his dog. Would there be anything still lacking to make the narrative fully satisfying? Perhaps there would be. Perhaps the meaning of the action would not be very clear. Let us continue it at a point after George has lost his job and the dog has frightened the child.

George sold the dog to John Simpson, a boy who lived in one of the big brick houses on the hill back of town. John Simpson's father was rich. John could feed Jibby. John could take care of him. Nobody would poison Jibby up at John Simpson's house, behind the high iron fence. George comforted himself with these thoughts.

Sometimes, however, they did not comfort him enough, and he felt the old loneliness and emptiness which he had felt before Jibby came. But he was getting to be a big boy now, big and tough, and he put those feelings out of his mind as well as he could. He did not work regularly now, but hung around with the Duck Alley gang in the railroad yards. He almost forgot Jibby.

One day on the main street of town he met John Simpson and the dog, such a big, powerful, sleek dog now that he scarcely recognized him. He went up to the dog. "Hi, Jibby, hi, boy!" he said, and began to pull the dog's ears and scratch his head as he had done three years before, in the evenings, back by the goods box, after Jibby had bolted his supper. The dog nuzzled him and licked his hands. George looked up at the other boy and exclaimed, "Jeez, look at him. Look at him, will ya. Ain't he smart? He remembers me!"

John Simpson stood there and for a moment did not utter a word. Then he said, "Take your hands off that dog. He belongs to me."

George stepped back.

"Come here, Blaze," John Simpson ordered, and the dog went to him. He fondled the dog's head, and the dog licked his hands.

George turned around and walked off.

This is somewhat more complete than the previous version. If we stop with the sale of the dog, we do have an example of narration, but the reader no doubt is somewhat confused about the exact meaning of the event presented. Perhaps the reader feels sorry for the boy. Perhaps he is aware that poverty is the cause of the boy's loss of the dog. Those things may be taken as meanings of the piece of narration given. But they are not brought to focus. The reader may not be sure exactly what is intended. He is certain to feel that the narrative is rather fragmentary.

But with the addition of the next section dealing with the meeting of George and John Simpson, the reader is more certain of the direction of the narrative, of the significance. The contrast between John Simpson, who owns the dog, and George, who merely loves it, gives us a point which is clear even without any comment. And many narratives, even some examples of that highly elaborated form of narration called fiction, deliver their point without any comment.

In the new section, we may notice, however, that more is involved than the mere contrast between the two boys. The dog licks John Simpson's hands, too. How does this tie in with what we have just said? This is, as it were, a kind of betrayal of George's affection for the dog. Another question: What is George's attitude as he turns and walks off? Perhaps the reader senses the boy's resentment at the betrayal. But the writer might want more. He might want a more positive conclusion. For example, he might want to make this event a kind of turning point in George's growing up, a seemingly trivial event which had a far-reaching effect on his life. He might continue.

The next day George hunted a job. He found one at the lumberyard where he had worked before when Jibby was a puppy. He worked as steadily now as he had worked in the old days when he looked forward to getting home to feed the dog and squat by him in the dusk, or if it was winter, in the dark. But he did not love the dog now. He was through with that.

But he worked because he had learned one thing. It was a thing which he was never to forget. He had learned that even love was one of the things you cannot get unless you have the money to pay for it.

This would give us a conclusion. It would give the effect of the event on George, not merely the first reaction of resentment or hurt feelings, but the effect which would prevail over a long period of time. Neither the reader nor the writer may agree that what George learns is the truth—that money is the basis of everything, even of those things like love and loyalty and kindness—but what George learns is the "truth" for him, the thing by which he will conduct his life for a time to come.

The important thing to understand here is, however, that a point is made, whether or not the reader accepts the point as true. The narrative is complete. It is not complete merely because a summarizing statement has been made by the writer. Certainly, the summarizing statement would not make the narrative complete if the thing it says were not something which could grow reasonably out of the event for a person in George's situation. And many narratives imply rather than state their meaning. But a full narrative does involve significance, a meaning, a point, as something which grows out of the sequence of events.

We have just said that the narrative is complete. This does not necessarily mean that George will never change his mind about what is the meaning of the experience he has had. The narrative might well be part of a long story or a novel which showed how for thirty years to come George conducted his life by the hard, materialistic "truth" he had learned and then found, even in the moment of his practical success, when he had grown rich and powerful, that his "truth" was really a profound mistake and that he had to learn a new truth.

This revision might not make a good story. The event concerning the dog might be too trivial or sentimental to serve as the basis for a good piece of fiction. But it will illustrate our own statement that the significance of a narrative stems from what the narrative immediately involves. George's later experiences, including elements not involved in the little narrative given here, might make him (or the reader) revise the notion of the truth of its point. But the point, *in so far as it is already implicit in the particular narrative*, would be there, and the narrative would be complete, in terms of George's interpretation of it.

The idea of completeness as applied to narrative always involves the idea of an interpretation, stated or implied, of the events narrated. The interpretation may be made by a character in the narrative, as by George in this case, or it may be made by the reader on the basis of the presentation of the material, or it may be stated by the writer. But in all cases of fully developed narrative, an interpretation is involved. And this means that our understanding is appealed to. And a narrative may use exposition to make this appeal to our understanding, as the last paragraph of our narrative about George does.

HOW OTHER KINDS OF DISCOURSE USE NARRATION

Strictly speaking, description can scarcely be said to use narration as an aid. It is, of course, possible to find cases in which description involves movement—a man's habitual acts, for instance, in a description of a character. But we must keep in mind the distinction between an act and an action in the sense in which we have been using the word *action*. A character description might even involve an action, but our interest in action is so much more vital than our interest in mere appearance that we should probably feel that the description was incidental to the narration rather than the narration incidental to the description. An object in motion catches the eye.

The situation, however, is different in regard to exposition and argument. Frequently in extended discourses which are primarily intended to explain something to us or to convince us of something we find bits of narrative used to dramatize an attitude, to illustrate a point, to bring an idea home to us. Sermons and speeches are often full of anecdotes. The preacher tells his congregation the story of a deathbed confession. The politician tells his audience how such and such a law, which he is pledged to help repeal if elected, has ruined the life of John Doe over in Murray County. The after-dinner speaker tells the club members a joke. But the story of the deathbed confession or of the ruin of John Doe over in Murray County or the story about the two Irishmen must have a point related to the main business in hand. If it does not have such a relation, the listeners feel that the speaker has dragged it in by the tail, merely to catch their attention, that somehow he has not played fair.

What is true of the sermon or political address or after-dinner speech is true of informal essays, informational articles, character sketches, travel books, philosophical essays, essays of opinion, memoirs, historical studies, and many other types of writing. And here, too, the narrative may be used to bring directly home to the reader what argument or exposition can only give in general terms.

For instance, observe how the general statement with which the following paragraph begins takes on significance in narrative:

Undergraduate life at Cambridge [Massachusetts] has not lacked for bitter passages, which compel notice from any anatomist of society. On the one hand there has long been a snobbery moulded of New England pride and juvenile cruelty which is probably more savage than any known to Fifth Avenue and Newport. Its favorite illustration is the time-worn tale of the lonely lad who to feign that he had *one* friend used to go out as dusk fell over the yard and call beneath his own windows, "Oh, Reinhardt!" And on the other it has moments of mad, terrible loyalty —exampled by the episode which is still recalled, awesomely without names, over the coffee and liqueurs when Harvard men meet in Beacon Street or the South Seas. It is the true story of a Harvard senior at a party in Brookline, who suddenly enraged by a jocular remark made concerning the girl whom he later married, publicly slapped the face of his best friend—and then in an access of remorse walked to an open fire and held his offending hand in the flame until it shrivelled away to the wrist.—DIXON WECTER: *The Saga of American Society*, Chap. 7.[1]

Or let us take the following passage, which has the same basic pattern, the movement from a general proposition to an illustration in narrative:

There are men of all nations who feel the fascination of a life unequally divided between months of hardship and short days of riot and spending; but in the end it is the hardship that holds them. The Chinese, taking them as they come, are not like this. They frankly detest hard work. A large belly among them is an honorable thing, because it means that the owner of it does not swink for his living. I never met a Chinese outside of the caravans who was what we should call sentimental about his work. Camel pullers alone have a different spirit, a queer spirit. Time and again when the men were talking around the fire and cursing the weather, the bad taste of the water, or the dust blown into their food, I have heard one ask, rhetorically, "What is a camel puller?" . . . Then another would say, "Yes, but this is the good life—do we not all come back to it?" and be approved in a chorus of grunts and oaths. Once a veteran said the last word: "I put all my money into land in the newly opened country Behind the Hills, and my nephew farms it for me. My old woman is there, so two years ago when they had the troubles on the Great Road and my legs hurt I thought I would finish with it

[1] From *The Saga of American Society* by Dixon Wecter, copyright, 1937, by Charles Scribner's Sons.

all—defile its mother! I thought I would sleep on a warm *k'ang* and gossip with the neighbors and maybe smoke a little opium, and not work hard any more. But I am not far from the road, in my place, and after a while in the day and the night when I hear the bells of the *lien-tze* go by, *ting-lang, ting-lang,* there was a pain in my heart—*hsin-li nan-kuo.* So I said, "Dogs defile it! I will go back on the Gobi one more time and pull camels."—OWEN LATTIMORE: *The Desert Road to Turkestan,* Chap. 8.[2]

EXPOSITORY NARRATION

In the examples just given we have seen how a narrative may be used to illustrate an idea. But in addition to this ordinary use of narration in exposition or argument, there is a special type called EXPOSITORY NARRATION. This is the type found, for instance, in the account of a laboratory experiment or in the directions for making or doing something. The method of narration is used here—stage by stage a process is outlined—but the intention is not the intention of true narration. The intention here is not to present an action so that it can be grasped imaginatively but merely to explain a process. The appeal is strictly to the understanding, and therefore this type is best considered as a form of exposition. A discussion of it has already appeared in the chapter on exposition (pp. 57-58).

PATTERN IN NARRATION

In the course of time one hears and reads many different narratives—jokes, novels, short stories, anecdotes, newspaper reports—and they seem to have many different kinds of organization. But is there some fundamental principle of pattern which underlies all the particular kinds of pattern we find in narratives? If we can find such a principle, then we have taken an important step toward being able to write good narrative.

We must return at this point to a distinction we have already made in discussing time as an aspect of an action (p. 238), the distinction between events existing in time in their natural order, and the events as a narrator may re-order them by means of cutbacks and shifts when he composes his narrative. That is, the natural

[2] From *The Desert Road to Turkestan* by Owen Lattimore. Reprinted by permission of Little, Brown and Company and the Atlantic Monthly Press.

order A-Z may be shifted, to heighten interest or for other reasons, into an artificial order such as G, H, I—A, B, C—J, K, L, and so forth.

We should remember in making this distinction that it applies as well to narratives using imaginary events as to narratives using actual material. Imaginary events, as well as real events, have a natural order, their order in time. In discussing here the pattern of an action we shall be referring to the natural order and not to an artificial order which a narrator might adopt for special purposes.

We have defined an action as a meaningful sequence of events. Such a sequence may be real, that is, observed, but observed events constitute an action only in so far as we detect their meaning. Or such a sequence of events may be imaginary, made up to embody a meaning. The principle of pattern will apply equally well to either kind of action, and in seeking examples to illustrate our principle we shall sometimes draw on factual material and sometimes on imaginary material. In both kinds of examples we shall be asking what is the shape events must take in order to constitute an action.

We can begin to answer our question by saying that an action has a beginning, a middle, and an end. Let us try to analyze what is really at stake in this answer.

BEGINNING

An action does not spring from nothing. It arises from a situation. The situation, however, must be an unstable one, ready to lead to change, and containing in it the seeds of the future developments.

A situation may be very simple or very complicated. In the joke we begin, "Two Irishmen met on a bridge at midnight in a strange city. The first Irishman said . . ." We have a minimum of information here, but all we may need for the joke. The situation could not be simpler. But the principle is the same as in an enormously complicated situation, for instance, the situation from which German Nazism developed. That situation contains more elements than we can hope to enumerate. There is the conflict between capital and labor, the insecurity of the lower middle class, the fear of Bolshevism, the economic collapse and the inflation of currency, the tradition of German militarism, the demand for revenge after the defeat in World War I, the example of Italian Fascism, the personality of Hitler, his bitterness and frustration. An interaction of all these factors and many more gives us the unstable situation in which are latent the subsequent developments.

Given this material, the writer of an account of Nazism must first present the situation clearly enough for the reader to see how the rest will follow. In dealing with matters of fact, as such a writer of history would be doing, his first task would be to analyze the body of material to be sure he knew what was really significant for future developments, and his second task would be to present the material so that the reader would see the relation among the various elements. It is true that the reader may not understand the significance of the situation when it is first presented to him, but he must be given enough to go on, to rouse and sustain his interest, to show that there is a line of possible development. And he must be given enough for him to feel, when he looks back over the whole narrative, that the action is really a logical development from the situation.

The problem is essentially the same for a writer who is dealing with imaginary events. The only difference is that he does not have to analyze factual materials already given him but has to create or adapt his materials. If we glance at Act I of Shakespeare's *Romeo and Juliet*, we find a good example of a beginning. We learn that there is a feud between the houses of Capulet and Montague, that bloodshed and violence are imminent, that Romeo is an idealistic young man anxious to fall in love. Very early we have enough to account for the future events. Or if we go back to our own improvised narrative of George and the dog, the situation presenting the misery and lovelessness of the boy's life gives us enough to account for the later importance of the dog to the boy.

The beginning, the presentation of the situation, enables us to understand the narrative. Therefore, that part of the narrative is often given the name of EXPOSITION. But we must keep the word in this special sense distinct from the more general sense in which it signifies one of the kinds of discourse.

It is not to be understood, however, that the exposition of a narrative is merely a kind of necessary evil, a body of dull information which the reader must absorb before he can settle down to the real story. It need not be explanatory or descriptive material in isolation, or a colorless summary of the situation from which the action stems. Instead, the exposition may appear as an episode, a fragment of action, interesting in itself. If we think back on the opening scene of *Romeo and Juliet,* we remember that we see a street fight. We are not *told about* the feud between the rival houses of Capulet and Montague, but actually see it in operation. Not all kinds of exposition can take a direct form, but in general it can be said that all exposition which can be directly presented should have the direct form.

MIDDLE

The middle is the main body of the action. It is a series of stages in the process. It involves the points of mounting tension, or increasing complication, developing from the original situation. This mounting tension, this suspense, leads us to the point of greatest intensity or greatest suspense, called technically the CLIMAX. The climax is the focal point, the turning point of the narrative.

To return to our historical example of the rise of Nazism, we would find such points of mounting tension as the beer hall *putsch* in Munich, Hitler's imprisonment and the writing of *Mein Kampf,* the street fights against the German communists, the election of Hitler as chancellor, the Reichstag fire, the purge of the party, the claims on Sudetenland. Looking back on the events of the past twenty-five years, we can see the points of crisis, the stages at which new tensions emerged. If a historian were writing an account of those years, he might center his attention on those stages. They might provide him with natural chapter divisions.

The same principle applies in any narrative, the simple joke or the elaborate novel. If one is telling or writing about real events, one tries to focus attention on those which mark real stages of development. And if one is making up a narrative, he arranges his imaginary material in the same way. He wants to create suspense, to hold the interest of his audience. If his narrative seems to be a mere drift of events, he cannot hold their interest. He can do so only in so far as the narrative emerges in well-defined stages of increasing complication.

We can see this very clearly in the main body of *Romeo and Juliet:* Romeo meets Juliet; the marriage takes place; Romeo kills Juliet's kinsman Tybalt while trying to stop a duel; Romeo is banished, and so on. Or we can see it in the little account of the boy and the dog: George gets a job to feed the dog; the dog becomes the center of his life; he loses the job; the dog frightens the child; George sells the dog, and so on.

Just as we have a technical name for the beginning of a narrative (*exposition*), so we have one for the middle: COMPLICATION.

END

As for the end of an action, it is not simply the point where the action stops. It is, rather, the point at which the forces implicit in the situation have worked themselves out. Whether it is the gag line of the joke or Berlin shattered under British and American bombs and Russian shells, the principle is the same. The end of an action, however, is not necessarily the physical victory of one set of forces over another. It may be in the reconciliation of forces, or it may be in the fusion of previously opposing forces to create a new force. Take, for instance, the conclusion of the Constitutional Convention that defined the United States: we may regard this end as a fusion of conflicting forces. As a matter of fact, the end of an action may simply be a new awareness on the part of a person involved, directly or indirectly, in the action. We know how we can look back on an experience of our own and recognize the point at which some attitude of our own had been changed by it.

When we come to writing a narrative, we regard the end as the point where the action achieves its full meaning. It is the point where the reader is willing to say, "Oh, yes, I see what it is all about." If we look back on our narrative of the boy and the dog we see that if we had stopped with the sale of the dog, the meaning would have been very blurred. A reader would not have been quite sure what was at stake. He might have felt sorry for the boy in a vague sort of way. But the meeting with John Simpson and the dog gives us in direct terms, as a contrast, a much more sharply defined meaning. This could be an end. We, as readers, see that there is an issue, a question, raised by the narrative—the question of legal ownership of the dog opposed to the demands of affection. The narrative now has a point. If we go on to write the last paragraph we simply indicate the fact of George's awareness and the effect on him. By means of George's awareness we have made the point more explicit, but it *was* implicit at the moment when the two boys had their little encounter. The technical term for the end of a narrative is DENOUEMENT.

EXAMPLES OF NARRATIVE PATTERN

Let us look at a few examples of narrative with the idea of indicating the structure, or pattern, of each. The first is the account of how Robinson Crusoe, who fancied himself absolutely alone on his desert island, found a footprint:

It happened one day about noon, going towards my boat, I was exceedingly surprised with the print of a man's naked foot on the shore, which was very plain to be seen in the sand. I stood like one thunderstruck, or as if I had seen an apparition: I listened, I looked round me, but I could hear nothing, nor see anything. I went up to a rising ground, to look farther; I went up the shore and down the shore, but it was all one; I could see no other impression but that one. I went to it again to see if there were any more, and to observe if it might not be my fancy; but there was no room for that, for there was exactly the print of a foot, toes, heel, and every part of a foot: how it came thither I knew not, nor could I in the least imagine; but, after innumerable fluttering thoughts, like a man perfectly confused and out of myself, I came home to my fortification, not feeling, as we say, the ground I went on, but terrified to the last degree; looking behind me at every two or three steps, mistaking every bush and tree, and fancying every stump at a distance to be a man. Nor is it possible to describe how many various shapes my affrighted imagination represented things to me in, how many wild ideas were found every moment in my fancy, and what strange unaccountable whimsies came into my thoughts by the way.—DANIEL DEFOE: *Robinson Crusoe.*

A piece of narrative could scarcely be simpler than this, but we see that it follows the basic pattern. The situation is given, the time and place. The complication follows on the discovery of the print—the first reaction, the looking about and listening, the going to higher ground for a wider view, the return to verify the existence of the print. Then follows the flight and the terror consequent upon the discovery. And it is this terror, changing the whole aspect of the familiar landscape, which constitutes the denouement. Crusoe's life cannot be the same again. This fact is not specified, but it is strongly implied.

Our next example makes its point more explicitly:

And also Mohammet loved well a good Hermit that dwelled in the Deserts a Mile from Mount Sinai, in the Way that Men go from Arabia toward Chaldea and toward Ind, one Day's journey from the Sea, where the Merchants of Venice come often for Merchandise. And so often went Mohammet to this Hermit, that all his Men were wroth; for he would gladly hear this Hermit preach and make his Men wake all Night. And therefore his Men thought to put the Hermit to Death. And so it befell upon a Night, that Mohammet was drunken of good Wine, and he fell asleep. And his Men took Mohammet's Sword out of his Sheath, whiles he slept, and therewith they slew this Hermit, and put his Sword all bloody in his Sheath again. And at the Morrow, when he found the Hermit dead, he was fully sorry and wroth, and would have done his Men to Death. But they all, with one accord, said that he himself had slain him, when he was drunk, and showed him his Sword all bloody. And he trowed that they had said Truth. And then he cursed the Wine and them that drink it. And therefore Saracens that be devout drink never any Wine.—SIR JOHN MANDEVILLE: *Travels*, Chap. 16.

This, too, falls into the pattern. The exposition is a little less simple here than in our earlier example, for now we are concerned not only with the physical facts but with human motives leading up to the action—Mohammet's love of the hermit, his custom of listening to the sermons, the irritation of the men. The complication falls into three divisions—the killing of the hermit, the discovery of the deed and Mohammet's anger, the lie and the bloody sword in his own scabbard. The denouement has two divisions—Mohammet's curse on wine and the result among devout followers in later times.

Our next example is an anecdote told about an argument between the Duke of Windsor and Winston Churchill. We have here merely a clash of opinion:

The Windsors' dinner was very grand, and the guests consisted of assorted notables from up and down the coast, mostly English people of high rank who were holidaying in the South. My Lords Rothermere and Beaverbrook had been prevented from attending by colds. (Lord Beaverbrook's cold did not prevent his attendance at the Casino, where we saw him afterward.) When some of the more overpowering guests had departed, after the long and stately meal in the white-and-gold dining room, the Duke of Windsor and Mr. Churchill settled down to a prolonged argument with the rest of the party listening in silence. The Duke had read with amazement Mr. Churchill's recent articles on Spain and his newest one (out that day, I believe) in which he appealed for an alliance with Soviet Russia. "You of all people, Winston," was the gist of his argument, "you cannot wish to make friends of these murderers and thieves." At one point Mr. Churchill, who was defending his point of view stubbornly and with undiplomatic vigor, said: "Sir, I would make a friend of the devil himself, if it would save England." It resulted plainly from the statements on the two sides that the self-willed, pleasure-loving little Prince, filled to the fingertips with royal prejudice, had no conception of the deadly danger to England involved in his dalliance with Hitler, while Mr. Churchill, disliking the Bolshevik theory and practice as much as ever, was so thoroughly aware of England's peril that he would seek the alliance of Stalin at once. We sat by the fireplace, Mr. Churchill frowning with intentness at the floor in front of him, mincing no words, reminding H.R.H. of the British constitution, on occasion— "when our kings are in conflict with our constitution we change our kings," he said—and declaring flatly that the nation stood in the gravest danger of its long history. The kilted Duke in his Stuart tartan sat on the edge of the sofa, eagerly interrupting whenever he could, contesting every point, but receiving—in terms of the utmost politeness so far as the words went—an object lesson in political wisdom and public spirit. The rest of us sat fixed in silence; there was something dramatically final, irrevocable about this dispute.—VINCENT SHEEAN: *Between the Thunder and the Sun,* Chap. 1.[3]

This is scarcely a narrative at all, simply a little incident almost buried in the comment with which the author has surrounded the event. But the author has hinted at the action, and has given enough for us to grasp its natural structure and order (as contrasted with the way the author has told it, for the author has not stuck to the chronological order of event).

Situation:

Dinner with Windsors. Nature of gathering. World of pleasure and privilege. Churchill and his articles on Spain.

Complication:

Prolonged argument. The Duke's amazement at Churchill's articles, especially his demand for an alliance with Russia. The Duke's stubbornness. He eagerly leans forward from sofa, contesting every point. Churchill's remarks on relation of kingship to English constitution, the danger to England, and so forth. The Duke's statement: "You of all

[3] From *Between the Thunder and the Sun* by Vincent Sheean. Reprinted by permission of Random House, Inc.

people, Winston, cannot wish to make friends of these murderers and thieves."

Denouement:

Churchill's reply: "Sir, I would make a friend of the devil himself, if it would save England."

We do not know all that occurred at that conversation. We do not need to know it to have a notion of the action, in our sense of the word. For, in this connection, action is the word we apply to a meaningful event, and the things which merely happened and have no bearing on the meaning of the event are not, properly speaking, a part of the action. The writer has omitted them from his account.

Here is a more fully developed narrative, the story of Andrew Jackson's most famous duel, the duel with Charles Dickinson, who had made some remarks reflecting on the character of Rachel Jackson, Andrew Jackson's wife.

[*Exposition*]

On Thursday, May 29, 1806, Andrew Jackson rose at five o'clock, and after breakfast told Rachel that he would be gone for a couple of days and meanwhile he might have some trouble with Mr. Dickinson. Rachel probably knew what the trouble would be and she did not ask. Rachel had had her private channels of information concerning the Sevier affray. At six-thirty Jackson joined Overton at Nashville. Overton had the pistols. With three others they departed for the Kentucky line.

Mr. Dickinson and eight companions were already on the road. "Goodby, darling," he told his young wife. "I shall be sure to be home tomorrow evening." This confidence was not altogether assumed. He was a snap shot. At the word of command and firing apparently without aim, he could put four balls in a mark twenty-four feet away, each ball touching another. The persistent tradition on the countryside, that to worry Jackson he left several such examples of his marksmanship along the road, is unconfirmed by any member of the Dickinson or Jackson parties. But the story that he had offered on the streets of Nashville to wager he could kill Jackson at the first fire was vouchsafed by John Overton, the brother of Jackson's second, a few days after the duel.

Jackson said he was glad that "the other side" had started so early. It was a guarantee against further delay. Jackson had chafed over the seven days that had elapsed since the acceptance of the challenge. At their first interview, Overton and Dr. Hanson Catlett, Mr. Dickinson's second, had agreed that the meeting should be on Friday, May thirtieth, near Harrison's Mills on Red River just beyond the Kentucky boundary. Jackson protested at once. He did not wish to ride forty miles to preserve the fiction of a delicate regard for Tennessee's unenforceable statute against dueling. He did not wish to wait a week for something that could be done in a few hours. Dickinson's excuse was that he desired to borrow a pair of pistols. Overton offered the choice of Jackson's pistols, pledging Jackson to the use of the other. These were the weapons that had been employed by Coffee and McNairy.

As they rode Jackson talked a great deal, scrupulously avoiding the subject that burdened every mind. Really, however, there was nothing more to be profitably said on that head. General Overton was a Revolutionary soldier of long acquaintance with the Code. With his principal he had canvassed every possible aspect of the issue forthcoming. "Distance . . . twenty-four feet; the parties to stand facing each other, with their pistols down perpendicularly. When they are READY, the single word FIRE! to be given; at which they are to fire as soon as they please. Should either fire before the word is given we [the seconds] pledge ourselves to shoot him down instantly." Jackson was neither a quick shot, nor an especially good one for the western country. He had decided not to compete with Dickinson for the first fire. He expected to be hit, perhaps badly. But he counted on the resources of his will to sustain him until he could aim deliberately and shoot to kill, if it were the last act of his life.

[Complication]

On the first leg of the ride they traversed the old Kentucky road, the route by which, fifteen years before, Andrew Jackson had carried Rachel Robards from her husband's home, the present journey being a part of the long sequel to the other. Jackson rambled on in a shrill voice. Thomas Jefferson was "the best Republican in theory and the worst in practice" he had ever seen. And he lacked courage. How long were we to support the affronts of England—impressment of seamen, cuffing about of our ocean commerce? Perhaps as long as Mr. Jefferson stayed in office. Well, that would be two years, and certainly his successor should be a stouter man. "We must fight England again. In the last war I was not old enough to be any account." He prayed that the next might come "before I get too old to fight."

General Overton asked how old Jackson reckoned he would have to be for that. In England's case about a hundred, Jackson said.

He spoke of Burr. A year ago, this day, Jackson had borne him from the banquet in Nashville to the Hermitage. He recalled their first meeting in 1797 when both were in Congress. Jackson also met General Hamilton that winter. "Personally, no gentleman could help liking Hamilton. But his political views were all English." At heart a monarchist. "Why, did he not urge Washington to take a crown!"

Burr also had his failings. He had made a mistake, observed Jackson, with admirable detachment, a political mistake, when he fought Hamilton. And about his Western projects the General was none too sanguine. Burr relied overmuch on what others told him. Besides, there was Jefferson to be reckoned with. "Burr is as far from a fool as I ever saw, and yet he is as easily fooled as any man I ever knew."

The day was warm, and a little after ten o'clock the party stopped for refreshment. Jackson took a mint julep, ate lightly and rested until mid-afternoon. The party reached Miller's Tavern in Kentucky about eight o'clock. After a supper of fried chicken, waffles, sweet potatoes and coffee, Jackson repaired to the porch to chat with the inn's company. No one guessed his errand. At ten o'clock he knocked the ashes from his pipe and went to bed. Asleep in ten minutes, he had to be roused at five in the morning.

The parties met on the bank of the Red River at a break in a poplar woods. Doctor Catlett won the toss for choice of position, but as the sun had not come through the trees this signified nothing. The giving of the word fell to Overton. Jackson's pistols were to be used after all, Dickinson taking his pick. The nine-inch barrels were charged with ounce balls of seventy caliber. The ground was paced off, the principals took their places. Jackson wore a dark-blue frock coat and trousers of the same material; Mr. Dickinson a shorter coat of blue, and gray trousers.

"Gentlemen, are you ready?" called General Overton.

"Ready," said Dickinson quickly.

"Yes, sir," said Jackson.

"*Fere!*" cried Overton in the Old-Country accent.

[Denouement]

Dickinson fired almost instantly. A fleck of dust rose from Jackson's coat and his left hand clutched his chest. For an instant he thought himself dying, but, fighting for self-command, slowly he raised his pistol.

Dickinson recoiled a step horror-stricken. "My God! Have I missed him?"

Overton presented his pistol. "Back to the mark, sir!"

Dickinson folded his arms. Jackson's spare form straightened. He aimed. There was a hollow "clock" as the hammer stopped at half-cock. He drew it back, sighted again and fired. Dickinson swayed to the ground.

As they reached the horses Overton noticed that his friend's left boot was filled with blood. "Oh, I believe that he pinked me," said Jackson quickly, "but I don't want those people to know," indicating the group that bent over Dickinson. Jackson's surgeon found that Dickinson's aim had been perfectly true, but he had judged the position of Jackson's heart by the set of his coat, and Jackson wore his coats loosely on account of the excessive slenderness of his figure. "But I should have hit him," he exclaimed, "if he had shot me through the brain."—MARQUIS JAMES: *The Life of Andrew Jackson,* Chap. 8.[4]

The event narrated above is historically true. It had causes running back before the episode of the duel (Dickinson had insulted Jackson's wife), and was to have consequences long after the duel. But the writer is not immediately concerned with causes or effects. He is concerned with rendering the episode itself, the duel. We can see that in doing so he naturally gives his account in three sections, the exposition, the complication, and the denouement, as we have indicated.

The exposition describes the attitudes of the two duelists as they make ready and gives the terms of the duel. The complication seems to have a good deal of material off the point—Jackson's long conversation about politics—but we shall see that even this apparent digression is related to the point the author wishes to make in his narrative. Then the complication gives the details as the opponents face each other and Dickinson fires. The denouement falls into two related parts, Jackson's self-command when hit and his shooting of Dickinson, and his remark after the event.

Both Vincent Sheean and Marquis James are using narrative to make a point, a point more important than the event narrated. Sheean is interested in illustrating one aspect of the political background of World War II; and James, in exhibiting an aspect of Jackson's character, his iron will. But the essential narrative structure underlies both accounts. It underlies them because the action to be narrated had that natural structure, and not because the writer imposed it. The thing to remember is that events, real or imaginary, in so far as they constitute an action in our sense of the word, fall into that pattern. The writer may make shifts of order in his presen-

---

[4] From *The Life of Andrew Jackson.* By Marquis James, copyright 1938. Used by special permission of the Publishers, the Bobbs-Merrill Company, Inc.

tation, may add digressions, and may make his own comments, but the essential structure of the action remains.

PROPORTION

The relation of the parts of a narrative to each other raises the question of PROPORTION. In one way this term is misleading, for it implies a mere mechanical ratio in the size of the parts. Actually we cannot look at the question in that way. We cannot say, for instance, that the complication should be three times longer than the exposition—or five times longer than the denouement.

We must, rather, regard the question of proportion in this way: Are the parts adequate to the needs of the special narrative? What would be a satisfactory proportion for one narrative might be quite unsatisfactory for another. In other words, we have to think along these lines: Does the exposition give all the information necessary to establish the situation for the reader? Is it burdened with information which is really unnecessary and distracting? Does the complication give the reader the essential stages of the development of the action? Does it confuse the reader by presenting material which does not bear on the development of the action? Does the denouement give the reader enough to make the point of the narrative clear? Does it blur the point by putting in irrelevant material or by so extending relevant material that a clear focus is lost? But these questions cannot be answered unless we are sure of the intention of the particular narrative.

Let us, with these questions in mind, look back at the story of Jackson's duel. To answer these questions we must remember the author's basic intention. He is not writing a tract against dueling. He is not concerned with the sad death of a promising young man. He is not trying to evoke our sympathy for the young Mrs. Dickinson. All of these considerations may be present in his mind (and a little after the point at which our excerpt concludes he tells how Mrs. Jackson exclaimed, "Oh, God have pity on the poor wife—pity on the babe in her womb"), but none of them is the main intention of the narrative. That is to show an aspect of Jackson's character—his iron will.

The exposition, therefore, tells merely what we need to know to establish this point, how Jackson took a natural, casual farewell from his wife; how Dickinson was confident in his mere skill, in contrast to Jackson's deadly inner certainty. The exposition also tells us, of course, something about the procedure agreed on for the duel, but this is primarily a mechanical matter. The complication builds the suspense by details of Jackson's journey to the Kentucky line, how he discussed political questions, enjoyed his meals and his julep, talked with the guests at the inn, and slept well. These things do not bear directly on the business of the duel, and might be considered by some critics not properly part of the complication but an aside, a digression from the main line of action. But they do help to build the suspense and do indicate the quality of self-control and certainty in Jackson.

Then the details of the actual duel lead us to the climax, the moment when Dickinson's bullet strikes and Jackson reels but recovers and, with deadly deliberation, lifts his weapon.

The denouement falls into two parts, the first presenting the actual shooting of Dickinson, the second presenting Jackson's behavior after the act, his indifference to his own wound, and his final remark when it is discovered why Dickinson had missed the heart. All the way through, of course, we notice that there is a building up of suspense about the outcome of the physical event, but along with this goes the unfolding of Jackson's character, which is summarized by the grim, last remark.

The narrative of Jackson's duel is part of a full-length biography, and it might be said that we have arbitrarily chosen to limit the exposition, for instance, to the part quoted here. It is true, of course, that in the full biography there is a great deal of explanation of the quarrel leading up to the duel. But is that really a part of the exposition of the narrative when the episode is considered solely as an episode? No, for what we are concerned with here is not the causes of the duel, the character of Rachel Jackson, or her husband's attitude toward her. In the episode itself we are concerned with the single, significant flash which exhibits Jackson's will. What preceded or followed the duel is not relevant to that consideration, taken in itself. Even though this little narrative is part of a much larger narrative, the account of Jackson's entire life, we are justified in interpreting it as a unit in so far as it is dominated by one basic intention.

One word of caution should be given before we leave the topic of proportion. In many cases of narrative, one cannot draw a single hard and fast line between, say, the exposition and the complication. Instead, there may be some overlapping or an intermingling of the two elements. A certain amount of exposition is always necessary early in a narrative, but we can recall instances, especially of extended narratives, in which the complication is interrupted by the insertion of bits of exposition. A biographer, for instance, may interrupt his narrative to explain a political situation, or a novelist may give what is called a CUTBACK to an earlier scene or situation needed to explain a present action (p. 238).

TEXTURE AND SELECTION

When we turn from questions of organization to questions of detail we turn from pattern to texture. SELECTION is as important for narration as it is for description. Skillful selection permits a large action to be narrated in a relatively brief space without seeming to be stinted, as in the following account of the voyage of St. Paul to Rome:

Now when much time was spent, and when sailing was now dangerous, because the fast was now already past, Paul admonished them,

And said unto them, Sirs, I perceive that this voyage will be with hurt and much damage, not only of the lading and ship, but also of our lives.

Nevertheless the centurion believed the master and the owner of the ship, more than those things which were spoken by Paul.

And because the haven was not commodious to winter in, the more part advised to depart thence also, if by any means they might attain to Phenice, and there to winter; which is an haven of Crete, and lieth toward the southwest and northwest.

And when the south wind blew softly, supposing that they had obtained their purpose, loosing thence, they sailed close by Crete.

But not long after there arose against it a tempestuous wind called Euroclydon.

And when the ship was caught, and could not bear up into the wind, we let her drive.

And running under a certain island which is called Clauda, we had much work to come by the boat:

Which when they had taken up, they used helps, undergirding the ship; and, fearing lest they should fall into the quicksands, struck sail, and so were driven.

And we being exceedingly tossed with a tempest, the next day they lightened the ship;

And the third day we cast out with our own hands the tackling of the ship.

And when neither sun nor stars in many days appeared, and no small tempest lay on us, all hope that we should be saved was then taken away.

But after long abstinence Paul stood forth in the midst of them, and said, Sirs, ye should have hearkened unto me, and not have loosed from Crete, and to have gained this harm and loss.

And now I exhort you to be of good cheer: for there shall be no loss of any man's life among you, but of the ship.

For there stood by me this night the angel of God, whose I am, and whom I serve,

Saying, Fear not, Paul; thou must be brought before Caesar: and, lo, God hath given thee all them that sail with thee.

Wherefore, sirs, be of good cheer: for I believe God, that it shall be even as it was told me.

Howbeit we must be cast upon a certain island.

But when the fourteenth night was come, as we were driven up and down in Adria, about midnight the shipmen deemed that they drew near to some country;

And sounded, and found it twenty fathoms; and when they had gone a little further, they sounded again, and found it fifteen fathoms.

Then fearing lest we should have fallen upon rocks, they cast four anchors out of the stern, and wished for the day.

And as the shipmen were about to flee out of the ship, when they had let down the boat into the sea, under color as though they would have cast anchors out of the foreship,

Paul said to the centurion and to the soldiers, Except these abide in the ship, ye cannot be saved.

Then the soldiers cut off the ropes of the boat, and let her fall off.

And while the day was coming on, Paul besought them all to take meat, saying, This day is the fourteenth day that ye have tarried and continued fasting, having taken nothing.

Wherefore I pray you to take some meat: for this is for your health: for there shall not be an hair fallen from the head of any of you.

And when he had thus spoken, he took bread, and gave thanks to God in the presence of them all: and when he had broken it, he began to eat.

Then were they all of good cheer, and they also took some meat.

And we were in all in the ship two hundred threescore and sixteen souls.

And when they had eaten enough, they lightened the ship, and cast out the wheat into the sea.

And when it was day, they knew not the land: but they discovered a certain creek with a shore, into the which they were minded, if it were possible, to thrust in the ship.

And when they had taken up the anchors, they committed themselves unto the sea, and loosed the rudder bands, and hoisted up the mainsail to the wind, and made toward shore.

And falling into a place where two seas met, they ran the ship aground; and the forepart stuck fast, and remained unmoveable, but the hinder part was broken with the violence of the waves.

And the soldiers' counsel was to kill the prisoners, lest any of them should swim out, and escape.

But the centurion, willing to save Paul, kept them from their purpose; and commanded that they which could swim should cast themselves first into the sea, and get to land:

And the rest, some on boards, and some on broken pieces of the ship. And so it came to pass, that they escaped all safely to land.—Acts 27:9-44.

A writer does not want to present all the details of an event, either real or imaginary. He wants to present those which clarify the line of action and contribute to his point. No stage of the action should be omitted, yet no details should be included which distract from the real concern of the narrative. There is no arbitrary rule in such a matter. A writer must keep firmly in mind what his real concern is and judge for himself. For example, in the episode of Jackson's duel, it might seem at first glance that the section about Jackson's conversation on the road is unnecessary and distracts from the real concern of the narrative. But this would be so only if the duel itself were taken to be the real concern. Actually, the real intent of the author is the revelation of Jackson's character, and, therefore, the conversation on the way, illustrating his calmness and confidence, is relevant to the effect intended.

Even in a narrative dealing with fact the author may heighten the interest by leaving out merely casual material. In treating the episode of Jackson's duel Marquis James may know that, after his opponent was hit, Jackson actually said more than is given here. The author, however, presents just those remarks which contribute to our awareness of Jackson's character. In dealing with matters of fact, a writer does not want to distort the truth by omissions, but the mere fact can scarcely justify itself. The narrator should be concerned with the significant fact. When he is dealing with imaginary events, the writer has a freer hand and a greater responsibility; for now he cannot rely on the interest which mere fact as fact can sometimes evoke in the reader. With the imaginary narrative a detail can never pay its way because it is interesting in itself. It must contribute to the main business or to the vividness of the impression.

A narrative is a more or less immediate presentation of events. Therefore vividness is important, the detail which can stir the imagination. The small gesture, the trivial word, may be important here. And here the details which, strictly speaking, are descriptive may be absorbed into the narrative effect. For instance, the cut and color of Jackson's and Dickinson's clothes, the kind of woods by which the meeting took place, and the Irish accent of General Overton when he gave the command to fire contribute to the impression of reality. Marquis James is much concerned to give an immediate presentation, but if we turn back to Vincent Sheean's anecdote of the Duke of Windsor and Churchill, we find that immediacy is not very important to the author. He is chiefly concerned to present a clash of opinions. Even here, however, we get the details of the Stuart tartan which the kilted Duke wears, his posture on the sofa, and Churchill's position staring at the floor.

POINT OF VIEW

The term POINT OF VIEW implies some of the most important considerations of narration. In ordinary speech this phrase has a meaning different from the meaning of the technical term to be discussed here. In ordinary speech we say, "From my point of view, I think James was perfectly right," or, "I understand Sarah's point of view, but I don't agree with it." What we understand by point of view in these two statements is an attitude, a set of values, a body of ideas, or something of that order. We could rewrite the sentences above in these terms and not change the meaning: "According to my set of values (or my ideas, or my attitude), I think James was perfectly right." Or: "I understand Sarah's ideas (or set of values, or attitude), but I don't agree with them." But in discussing narra-

tion we shall use the term to mean the point from which the
action of a narrative is viewed.

In discussing point of view in description we mean a physical
point from which the specified or implied observer looks at the
thing described (pp. 201-03). In discussing narration we do not mean
a physical point; we mean, rather, a person who bears some relation
to the action, either as observer or participant, and whose intelligence serves as the index of the action for the reader. Point of view,
then, involves two questions: Who tells the story? What is his relation to the action?

In broad terms, there are two possible points of view, the first
person and the third person. When we read, "That summer when
we were staying at Bayport, I had the most astonishing experience
of my life," we know that we are dealing with the first-person point
of view. When we read, "When Jake Millen, at the age of sixty,
surveyed the wreck of his career, he knew that only one course
was left open to him," we know that we are dealing with a third-
person point of view. That is, in the first example, an "I," real or
fictitious, is telling us about an experience in which he himself was
involved; in the second example, an author, writing impersonally,
is telling us about an experience in which another person was
involved.

There are, however, certain shadings and variations possible
within these two broad general divisions of point of view.

What are the variations possible within the first person? The
distinctions here are to be made on the basis of the relation of the
first-person narrator to the action which he narrates. There are two
extreme positions possible here. First, the narrator may tell of an
action in which he is the main, or at least an important, participant.
That is, he tells his "own story." We are all familiar with this type
of treatment. Most autobiographies, for example, are of this kind;
for example, the life of Lincoln Steffens. Occasionally we encounter
a piece of informal history using this method, for example, T. E.
Lawrence's *Seven Pillars of Wisdom*. Many short stories and novels
create an imaginary "I" who is the main character of the story and
who tells the story. For instance, Defoe's *Robinson Crusoe,* or
Hemingway's *A Farewell to Arms.*

At the other extreme, the narrator, either real or imaginary,
recounts an action of which he is merely an observer. This, also,

is a familiar type of treatment. Memoirs tend to take this form, for frequently the writer of memoirs has not himself played a conspicuous role in affairs but has been in a position to observe important events. The account of General Eisenhower by his aide, Captain Butcher, is a good example of this type. The same type of treatment appears, of course, in fiction. Poe's "The Fall of the House of Usher" is a notable instance, and Ring Lardner's story "Haircut" is another.

Thus we may have the two types of the first-person point of view: *narrator—main character*, and *narrator—mere observer*. But in between these two extremes many variations are possible, cases in which the narrator participates directly in the action and has something at stake in its outcome but in which he is not the main character.

But what of the variations possible within the third-person point of view?

In this point of view the narrative is given by an author writing impersonally, that is, as a kind of disembodied intelligence before whom the events are played out. What is the relation of this impersonal author, this disembodied intelligence, to the action? In the first place, he does not participate in the action; he is merely an observer. The question then becomes this: How much of the action does the author observe? And here, as in dealing with the first-person point of view, we can define the two extreme positions.

One extreme we may call the PANORAMIC point of view. In this method the author may report any aspect or all aspects of an action, and may go into the head of any or all of the characters involved in the action. His eye, as it were, sweeps the entire field and he reports whatever is interesting or relevant. In an imaginary narrative there is no limit to what may be seen or reported according to this method, the most private acts and the most secret thoughts or sensations of any or all of the characters may be reported, for the author is the creator of the whole thing. But when a writer is using this method in presenting a nonimaginative narrative, say a piece of history, he is, of course, limited by what facts or plausible deductions are available to him. He cannot be as thoroughgoing in applying the method as the writer of an imaginary narrative, though within the limits of the facts available to him he may do so. Many pieces of historical and biographical writing use this method, and, of course, it is not uncommon in fiction. For instance, it appears in the following scene from Thackeray's novel *Vanity Fair*, presenting the city of Brussels when the false news comes that Napoleon has won the Battle of Quatre Bras, an engagement just before Waterloo.

We of peaceful London city have never beheld—and please God shall never witness—such a scene of hurry and alarm as that which Brussels presented. Crowds rushed to the Namur gate, from which direction the noise proceeded, and many rode along the level *chaussée*, to be in advance of any intelligence from the army. Each man asked his neighbor for news; and even great English lords and ladies condescended to speak to persons whom they did not know. The friends of the French went abroad, wild with excitement, and prophesying the triumph of their Emperor. The merchants closed their shops, and came out to swell the general chorus of alarm and clamor. Women rushed to the churches, and crowded the chapels, and knelt and prayed on the flags and steps. The dull sound of cannon went on rolling, rolling. Presently carriages with travellers began to leave the town, galloping away by the Ghent barrier. The prophecies of the French partisans began to pass for facts. "He has cut the army in two," it was said. "He is marching straight on Brussels. He will overpower the English, and be here tonight." "He will overpower the English," shrieked Isidor to his master, "and will be here tonight." The man bounded in and out from the lodgings to the street, always returning with some fresh particulars of disaster. Jos's face grew paler and paler. Alarm began to take entire possession of the stout civilian. All the champagne he drank brought no courage to him. Before sunset he was worked up to such a pitch of nervousness as gratified his friend Isidor to behold, who now counted upon the spoils of the owner of the laced coat.

The women were away all this time. After hearing the firing for a moment, the stout Major's wife bethought her of her friend in the next chamber, and ran in to watch, and if possible to console, Amelia. The idea that she had that helpless and gentle creature to protect, gave additional strength to the natural courage of the honest Irishwoman. She passed five hours by her friend's side, sometimes in remonstrance, sometimes talking cheerfully, oftener in silence, and terrified mental supplication.—WILLIAM MAKEPEACE THACKERAY: *Vanity Fair*, Chap. 32.

At the other extreme from the panoramic point of view we find what we may call the point of view of SHARP FOCUS. The author does not sweep the entire field of the action, but keeps his, and his reader's, attention focused on one character and on that character's relation to the action. Accordingly, the parts of the action not directly participated in by the selected character are not reported by the author. To use a figure of speech, the character may be regarded as a kind of prism through which the action is refracted. Here is an example of the method:

He was hungry, for, except some biscuits which he had asked two grudging curates to bring him, he had eaten nothing since breakfast-time. He sat down at an uncovered wooden table opposite two work-girls and a mechanic. A slatternly girl waited on him.

"How much is a plate of peas?" he asked.

"Three halfpence, sir," said the girl.

"Bring me a plate of peas," he said, "and a bottle of ginger beer."

He spoke roughly in order to belie his air of gentility for his entry had been followed by a pause of talk. His face was heated. To appear natural he pushed his cap back on his head and planted his elbows on the table. The mechanic and the two work-girls examined him point by point before resuming their conversation in a subdued voice. The girl brought him a plate of grocer's hot peas, seasoned with pepper and vinegar, a fork and his ginger beer. He ate his food greedily and found it so good that he made a note of the shop mentally. When he had eaten all the peas he sipped his ginger beer and sat for some time thinking of Corley's adventure. In his imagination he beheld the pair of lovers walking along some dark road; he heard Corley's voice in deep energetic gallantries, and saw again the leer of the young woman's mouth. This vision made him feel keenly his own poverty of purse and spirit. He was tired of knocking about, of pulling the devil by the tail, of shifts and intrigues. He would be thirty-one in November. Would he never get a good job? Would he never have a home of his own? He thought how pleasant it would be to have a warm fire to sit by and a good dinner to sit down to. He had walked the streets long enough with friends and with girls. He knew what those friends were worth: he knew the girls too. Experience had embittered his heart against the world. But all hope had not left him. He felt better after having eaten than he had felt before, less weary of his life, less vanquished in spirit. He might yet be able to settle down in some snug corner and live happily if he could only come across some good simple-minded girl with a little of the ready.—JAMES JOYCE: "Two Gallants," Dubliners.[5]

[5] From Dubliners by James Joyce, copyright, 1925, by The Viking Press, Inc., and now included in The Portable James Joyce, published by The Viking Press, Inc., New York.

In between the extremes of the panoramic point of view and the point of view of sharp focus there are, of course, all sorts of gradations and mixtures of the two methods. The choice of one of the methods or the mixing of the two is not a matter to be settled arbitrarily, for the method should reflect a special interest involved in the narrative. For instance, the panoramic point of view is well suited to the rendering of some large and complicated action, a battle, a mob scene, the burning of a city, where the interest lies in the sweep of events. Or the point of view of sharp focus is suited to a narrative in which the interest is primarily in the psychological analysis of the experience of some single character. A narrative may well involve both such interests, and then the writer may mix his methods according to the need of the particular moment.

But use of the panoramic point of view is not restricted to action which covers a physically broad field, like a battle. Take, for instance, this example:

One night toward the end of March Gertrude did not appear for dinner. She had never been absent at the evening meal before, though it was a common enough occurrence in the house.

"One of our sheep has strayed," the red-haired woman said. Now that spring was coming she had returned to the brown silk dress she had worn in the fall. A smile of calculated indifference was on her face. "Perhaps she is wandering by the docks and sighing for her homeland."

"What do you mean?" Marian said.

The woman pulled her salad plate closer to the edge of the table and poised her fork over it thoughtfully. "Nothing is so good as Europe, you know," she said, looking up from her plate and glancing at the entire table with the easy innocence and half-surprise of the guilty.

"You know that isn't true," Marian said sharply. "For Gertrude America appears more beautiful than any country can be in reality."

"They are very tricky," the woman said flatly.

The others at the table were listening, alternately seeming to agree with both Marian and the woman, and then suddenly and cautiously retreating into themselves, admitting to nothing except the existence of all possibilities. Florence was sitting at the end of the table and had not heard the first part of the conversation. "Where is Gertrude?" she said abruptly.

"Flown the coop," a timid young girl said.

"Have you seen her all day?" Marian asked. "I haven't."

Florence said that she had not. The meal went on.

A woman, close to seventy, with hair dyed jet black, brushed past the table and hobbled over to her own group. One of her feet was slightly malformed and it made her walk strangely, as if she were constantly trotting. She seldom ever spoke to anyone and seemed deeply engrossed in work of enormous importance.—ELIZABETH HARDWICK: *The Ghostly Lover,* Chap. 25.[6]

Here we find the event rendered as it would appear to the mere observer, in its externals only. The scene is restricted but the use of the panoramic method gives a kind of psychological distance, an impersonality, which corresponds in effect to the physical distance and impersonality one finds in the panoramic rendering of a scene which is physically large.

SCALE

The foregoing discussion leads us logically into a consideration of what may be called SCALE in narrative. As the dominant interest in a narrative or a part of a narrative may define the point of view, so it may define the scale on which it is treated. Here, too, we can think in terms of extremes of method, SUMMARY RENDERING and FULL RENDERING. The tendency in narration is to reduce the scale to that of summary in parts which are necessary only for continuity or, as it were, scaffolding, and to expand the scale in those parts which present the more significant moments. The following selection, which concludes Guy de Maupassant's story "The Diamond Necklace" illustrates the principle clearly. The main character, Mathilde Loisel, has been a vain, frivolous woman, who lived in day dreams of rich and fashionable life. When she is finally invited to a ball she borrows what she understands to be a diamond necklace from a friend, Madame Forestier. The necklace is lost at the ball, and Mathilde and her husband buy one to replace it, getting the money from usurers. At this point the selection picks up the story:

She learned the heavy cares of a household, the odious work of a kitchen. She washed the dishes, using her rosy nails upon the greasy

[6] From *The Ghostly Lover* by Elizabeth Hardwick, copyright, 1945, by Elizabeth Hardwick. Reprinted by permission of Harcourt, Brace and Company, Inc.

pots and the bottoms of the stewpans. She washed the soiled linen, the chemises and dishcloths, which she hung on the line to dry; she took down the refuse to the street each morning and brought up the water, stopping at each landing to breathe. And, clothed like a woman of the people, she went to the grocer's, the butcher's, and the fruiterer's, with her basket on her arm, shopping, haggling to the last sou her miserable money.

Every month it was necessary to renew some notes, thus obtaining time, and to pay others.

The husband worked evenings, putting the accounts of some merchant in order, and at night he often copied manuscript at five sou a page.

And this life lasted ten years.

At the end of ten years, they had restored all, all, with interest of the usurers, and the compound interest besides.

Mme. Loisel looked old now. She had become a strong, hard woman, the rough woman of the poor household. Her hair tangled, her skirts awry, her hands red, she talked in loud tones, and washed the floors with a great swishing of water. But sometimes, when her husband was at the office, she would sit by the window and remember that evening of the ball, where she had been so beautiful and so happy.

What would have happened if she had not lost the necklace? Who knows? Who knows? How life is strange and changeful! How little is needed to ruin one or to save one!

One Sunday, as she was walking in the Champs Elysées, to restore herself after the work of the week, she suddenly saw a woman with a child. It was Madame Forestier, still young, still beautiful, still charming. Madame Loisel was moved. Should she speak to her? Yes, certainly. Now that she had paid, she would tell her all. Why not?

She approached her. "Good morning, Jeanne."

Her friend did not recognize her, and was surprised to be addressed by this woman of the people. She stammered: "But, Madame—I do not know—you must be mistaken—"

"No, I am Mathilde Loisel."

Her friend uttered a cry of surprise: "Oh, my poor Mathilde! How you are changed—"

"Yes, I have seen some hard days since I saw you—some miserable ones —and all because of you—"

"Because of me? How?"

"You remember the diamond necklace you loaned me to wear to the Minister's ball?"

"Yes, very well."

"Well, I lost it."

"How is that, since you returned it to me?"

"I returned one like it. And it has taken us ten years to pay for it. You can understand that it was not easy for us who have nothing. But it is finished, and I am very glad."

Madame Forestier stopped. She said: "You say that you bought a diamond necklace to replace mine?"

"Yes. You did not know it then? They were very like."

And she smiled with a joy that was proud and naive.

Madame Forestier was touched, and seized both her hands as she said: "Oh, my poor Mathilde! My necklace was false. It was not worth over five hundred francs!"—GUY DE MAUPASSANT: "The Diamond Necklace."

We notice here that the first half of the passage covers a time of ten years, the second half a time of three or four minutes. The ten years are summarized. The meeting in the park is rendered fully, word for word, instant by instant. We can readily see the reason why the writer summarized the ten years: they are all alike, a dreary grind of misery, and what is important is their result, Mathilde's new energy and fortitude, not the single events within them. As for the last scene, we can see that it is important in itself: it is dramatic, it is the moment when Mathilde realizes her situation, it is the result of all her past experience.

In the half of the selection rendered by summary we observe, however, that certain details do give us the impression of the quality and movement of life—Mathilde's bargaining, her voice now coarse and rough, the way she scrubs the floor with great swishing sweeps of the wet mop. Narrative summary differs from the mere summary of ideas; when successful it still gives some hint of the quality and movement of life.

DIALOGUE

Narration often involves the use of dialogue—not only fiction but historical writing, biography, and other types. Dialogue sometimes seems to be an easy way to get a story told. The writer—especially an inexperienced writer—thinks that he knows how people talk and that to set down talk will be easier than to present material in the straight narrative form which he himself will have to compose. But the problem is not so simple as that. First, to compose effective dialogue is not easy, and second, the continual use of dialogue tends to give an impression of monotony.

On the first point it can be said that dialogue which is effective on the page is rarely a direct transcript of what people would say in conversation. Conversation is often stumbling, wandering, diffuse. The real point at issue in an actual conversation frequently becomes lost in mere wordiness or in the distractions of side issues and matters of incidental interest. The writer of dialogue cannot afford to duplicate such a conversation; if he does so, the reader will not be readily able to follow the line of significance. So the writer must organize the material to permit the reader to follow the development of the issue at stake. There must be an impression of give-and-take and a forward thrust of idea.

Let us examine a piece of unsatisfactory dialogue:

Gertrude collapsed into her chair, helpless with amusement; giving herself up to her laughter, she made him feel suddenly ashamed of that remembered delight.

"Oh—oh—oh—oh!" she cried. "That is the most ridiculous thing I ever heard of. You call that girl a shy arbutus. And at your age, too. You certainly are silly."

"Well! I don't think it is so funny. You don't know the girl the way I do, and furthermore she is very modest and appealing. All sorts of people think so. For example, I have heard Mrs. Buckley say—"

"The shy arbutus! As I said, it is perfectly ridiculous. I don't want to be impolite, but she isn't exactly an arbutus, and as for Mrs. Buckley's opinion, you know what a sentimental old biddy she is, and how she gushes over everything. A shy arbutus. Forgive me, Harry, but that's too funny. How old *are* you?"

He flung his cigarette at the back-log and grinned.

"I knew it was no use," he grumbled amiably. "I can't make you see her, and it's no use trying. I know Mrs. Buckley is sentimental and does gush, but I don't think I am gushy, and I have also heard Tom Barker comment on the girl. Very favorably, too. And he is a hard-headed sort of fellow. Why, you remember, don't you, how he always brings a conversation right down to common sense. There was that time we were talking about performance of that pianist—you know, the one who played at the Murdocks' house—last November—and everybody said how good she was, but Tom just said, 'Nuts, all she's got is ten quite ordinary fingers and a very extraordinary figure—but it is the fingers that have to play the piano!' That's just like old Tom. But to come back to the sub-

ject, Tom may understand the girl, but I can't make you see her, and
it's no use trying."

"I heard that pianist, and she was rather good, I thought. Whatever
Tom Barker thought. But the trouble with you is, you're in love with
this girl. It is a well known fact that a man in love is not able to exercise
his best judgment. But it's precisely when you're in love that you need
to keep your wits about you. Or the wits of your friends. Now I've come
to the conclusion that you *mustn't* marry her, Harry. There are very
good reasons."

"Well—I don't know. I don't think that being in love has done anything
to my judgment."

"*No!* It is certainly my considered opinion that to marry that girl
would be ruinous for you. You must think about your career. And more
important, about your happiness. Won't she bore you to death in three
years. She is quite dull. Now the kind of girl you want is somebody
with some spirit and mischief. A girl who has got some smartness, and
who could amuse your friends. Think of the dull parties with this girl
in the saddle."

The trouble here is that the dialogue is loaded with irrelevant
material. People do load their conversations with irrelevant material, but dialogue in narrative cannot afford that weight. It kills
the forward thrust.

Let us now look at the same piece of dialogue as it actually
occurs in a story, stripped to the essentials:

"Oh—oh—oh—oh!" she cried.

"Well!"

"The shy arbutus! . . . Forgive me, Harry, but that's too funny.
How old *are* you?"

He flung his cigarette at the back-log and grinned.

"I knew it was no use," he grunted amiably. "I can't make you see
her, and it's no use trying."

"Well—I can see this much. You *are* in love with her. Or you couldn't
possibly be such a fool. But it's precisely when you're in love that you
need to keep your wits about you. Or the wits of your friends. . . .
You *mustn't* marry her, Harry."

"Well—I don't know."

"*No!* . . . It would be ruinous."—CONRAD AIKEN: "Spider, Spider." [7]

[7] From "Spider, Spider" in *Costumes by Eros*, published by Charles Scribner's Sons. Copyright, 1928, by Conrad Aiken.

In the passage above the line of interest is clear, and the collision between Gertrude and Harry is quite definite. In the expanded version there is a blurring of the effect. This blurred effect may actually be given by the conversation of a Gertrude and Harry in real life, but that has no final bearing on the case here. The problem of the writer of dialogue is a problem of selection and logical organization.

There is also, however, the problem of giving the dialogue a realistic surface. There must be, in addition to the logical organization, an impression of real life, a sense of the pauses, the changes, the waverings of conversation. But this must be an *impression* and not a word-for-word recording. There is no rule for giving this impression, but there are certain considerations which may help a writer to give it.

First, we can notice, as in the example above, that the breaks and the italicized words are of some use in this respect. We get the impression of the sudden shift of idea or the hesitancy of a speaker. And from the italicized words we get the impression of Gertrude's voice, with the slight satirical emphasis. But these are devices that would not always apply, and in any case should be used sparingly.

Second, and more important, the writer can try to indicate the fact that each speaker has his own way of phrasing things and his own rhythm of voice. Expertness in giving such an impression can only come from close observation—an awareness of the little catch phrases a person tends to repeat, of the type of sentence structure he tends to use, of the mannerisms of speech.

Third, in addition to the individual qualities of speech, there are the qualities dependent on cultural background, race, geographical origin, and so forth, qualities which are shared by members of a group. The commonest way to indicate such qualities is by mere dialectal peculiarities, when that will apply at all. But mere peculiarity of spelling is a crude device, and in the end usually becomes monotonous. It is better for the writer to use such a device sparingly, and to focus his attention on the vocabulary, idiom, and rhythm of the class to which his speaking character belongs.

Here are some examples in which the language used by a speaker gives some impression of his social group and of his individuality:

A boy who is the son of a jockey:

I guess looking at it, now, my old man was cut out for a fat guy, one of those regular little roly fat guys you see around, but he sure never got that way, except a little toward the last, and then it wasn't his fault, he was riding over the jumps only and he could afford to carry plenty of weight then. I remember the way he'd pull on a rubber shirt over a couple of jerseys and a big sweat shirt over that, and got me to run with him in the forenoon in the hot sun.—ERNEST HEMINGWAY: "My Old Man." [8]

A Southern Negro:

"What makes you want to talk like that before these chillen?" Nancy said. "Whyn't you go on to work. You done et. You want Mr. Jason to catch you hanging around his kitchen, talking that way before these chillen?"

"Talking what way?" Caddy said.

"I cant hang around white man's kitchen," Jesus said. "But white man can hang around mine. White man can come in my house, but I cant stop him. When white man wants to come in my house, I aint got no house. I cant stop him, but he cant kick me outen it. He cant do that." —WILLIAM FAULKNER: "That Evening Sun." [9]

A pretentious, servile woman:

"Well now, that is so like you," returned Miss Knag. "Ha! ha! ha! Of club feet! Oh very good. As I often remark to the young ladies, 'Well I must say, and I do not care who knows it, of all the ready humor—hem—I ever heard anywhere'—and I have heard a good deal; for when my dear brother was alive (I kept house for him, Miss Nickleby), we had to supper once a week two or three young men, highly celebrated in those days for their humor, Madame Mantalini—'Of all the ready humor,' I say to the young ladies, 'I ever heard, Madame Mantalini's is the most remarkable—hem. It is so gentle, so sarcastic, and yet so good-natured (as I was observing to Miss Simmonds only this morning), that how, or when, or by what means she acquired it, is to me a mystery indeed.' "

Here Miss Knag paused to take breath, and while she pauses it may be observed—not that she was marvellously loquacious and marvellously deferential to Madame Mantalini, since these are facts which require no comment; but that every now and then, she was accustomed, in the

[8] From *Three Stories and Ten Poems* by Ernest Hemingway, copyright, 1923, by Charles Scribner's Sons.

[9] From "That Evening Sun," *These Thirteen* by William Faulkner, copyright, 1931, by Random House, Inc.

torrent of her discourse, to introduce a loud, shrill, clear, "hem!" the import and meaning of which was variously interpreted by her acquaintance . . .—CHARLES DICKENS: *Nicholas Nickleby,* Chap. 17.

A fatherly professor:

"You may be right, and then you may have a one-sided view. When I say that your prejudice is literary, I mean that you have read what universities are like and applied that reading here. You have condemned without participating. You know, there may be good things, even in this town. Why, I sometimes think you even like me a bit." Dr. Whitlock smiled. "You see, there is indifference, intellectual servility, a vague attempt at education. But to know these things is not enough. You have to go deeper, you must understand; your conviction must be intellectual as well as emotional. There are more than economic reasons at stake, and there may be greater social injustice in this small university town than in the smashing of a miner's strike by hired bullies."—MICHAEL DE CAPITE: *No Bright Banner,* Chap. 7.[10]

We have said earlier that logical organization, the development of the point at issue in a dialogue, is extremely important. But occasionally there is little or no point at issue, and then the intended significance of a passage may be the exhibition of the speaker's character, as in the speech by Miss Knag from *Nicholas Nickleby,* quoted above. There the wandering sentences, the interpolations, and the characteristic "hem!" indicate the quality of her mind, just as some of the remarks themselves indicate her mixture of vanity, pretentiousness, and servility.

In some instances, of course, a piece of dialogue may develop a point and at the same time contain elements which are irrelevant to that point but indicate the character of the speaker. Here is the famous passage between Falstaff and Mistress Quickly, who is trying to remind Falstaff that he had promised to marry her. Her talkativeness and fuzzy-mindedness appear here in the very way she presents the argument, the point, to Falstaff:

Marry, if thou wert an honest man, thyself and the money too. Thou didst swear to me upon a parcel-gilt goblet, sitting in my Dolphin-chamber, at the round table, by a seacoal fire, upon Wednesday in Wheeson-week, when the prince broke thy head for liking his father to

[10] Reprinted from *No Bright Banner* by Michael de Capite, by permission of The John Day Company, Inc.

a singing-man of Windsor, thou didst swear to me then, as I was washing thy wound, to marry me and make me my lady thy wife. Canst thou deny it? Did not goodwife Keech, the butcher's wife, come in then and call me gossip Quickly? coming in to borrow a mess of vinegar; telling us she had a good dish of prawns; whereby thou didst desire to eat some, whereby I told thee they were ill for a green wound? And didst thou not, when she was gone down stairs, desire me to be no more so familiarity with such poor people; saying that ere long they would call me madam? And didst thou not kiss me and bid me fetch thee thirty shillings?—WILLIAM SHAKESPEARE: *Henry IV, Part II,* Act II.

CHARACTERIZATION

Early in this discussion we pointed out the relation between persons and action. Most narratives, from news stories to novels, are about people. Things happen to people and people make things happen. To understand an action we must understand the people involved, their natures, their motives, their responses, and to present an action so that it is satisfying we must present the people. This process is called CHARACTERIZATION.

A news story gives a minimum of characterization. It merely identifies the persons involved—"Adam Perkins, age thirty-three, of 1217 Sunset Drive"—and then proceeds to give the bare facts of the event. If it deals with motive it does so in the barest possible way. If Adam Perkins has committed suicide, the news story may report that he had been in ill health and had, according to his wife, been worrying about financial reverses, but it will give no detail. On the other hand, a novel or biography usually gives very full characterization. It seeks to make us understand very fully the relation between the character and the events and the effect of events on character. In between the news story and the novel or biography, there are all sorts of narratives which present more or less fully the relationship between character and event and which try to answer the fundamental questions: Why does the character do what he does to cause the event? Why does he respond as he does to the event?

To answer these questions, the writer of a narrative must characterize the person. This is as important for narratives dealing with matters of fact, such as biography or history, as it is for narratives dealing with imaginary persons, such as novels or short stories. The difference between the two types is simply this: The biographer must interpret the facts in order to understand the character and present him, and the writer of fiction must create the details in order to present the character.

Whether the details of a character are drawn from fact or from imagination, it is important to remember that a character cannot be effectively presented as a mere accumulation of details. The details must be related to each other to build up a unified impression, the sense of an individual personality. As this impression of an individual personality relates to an action, we are concerned with motive or response. What is the main motive of a character, or what is his main response? We must be sure that we have an answer to this question before we can give an effective characterization. Then we must be sure that we have given a clear indication of this main fact of the character.

Once the main fact of the character is established in the writer's mind, he must relate other details of the character to it. That is, the character must be consistent. We know that real people are often very complicated and do things which seem inconsistent. The same person does good things and bad things, generous things and selfish things, wise things and stupid things, but even so, we usually feel that there is an explanation for such inconsistency, that the very inconsistencies can be understood in relation to a deeper consistency of character. And the object of the writer should be to contribute to this deeper understanding of character. He may present the inconsistent details, but at the same time he wants to present them as part of a comprehensible whole. There is no formula for accomplishing this, and the only way we can learn to do it is by studying human nature as we can observe it in life and in books.

Once the conception of a character is clear, we can, however, think systematically about methods of presenting it. Generally speaking, there are five methods: by appearance and mannerisms, by analysis, by speech, by reaction of other persons, by action.

Appearance and mannerisms really involve description, considered independently or as absorbed into narration, but description as an indication of the inner nature of persons. We have already seen how in Dickens's description of Chadband (p. 214) the physical oiliness of the man is taken as a lead to his "oily" personality, and how his mannerism of lifting a hand before speaking gives the suggestion of false piety and vanity, of a hypocritical preacher.

As the method of description suggests the character, that of analysis states it and explains it. This is really a kind of exposition drawn into the service of narration. It may be very obvious and systematic, as when we write:

Jack Staple's character is marked by what seems, at first inspection, to be a fundamental inconsistency: on some occasions he is kind and generous even to a fault, and at the same time he is capable of extreme cruelty. But the inconsistency disappears into a frightening consistency once we realize that the spring of his every action is a profound egotism, an egotism which can express itself as well through good as through evil. Both gratitude and fear can flatter his ego.

But in the following example, the analysis is absorbed into the account of a meeting between T. E. Lawrence, the British agent sent to Arabia in World War I to stir a revolt against Turkey, and a chieftain whom he was considering as a possible leader of the revolt:

Abdulla, on a white mare, came to us softly with a bevy of richly armed slaves on foot about him, through the silent respectful salutes of the town. He was flushed with his success at Taif, and happy. I was seeing him for the first time, while Storrs was an old friend, and on the best of terms; yet, before long, as they spoke together, I began to suspect him of a constant cheerfulness. His eyes had a confirmed twinkle; and though only thirty-five, he was putting on flesh. It might be due to too much laughter. Life seemed very merry for Abdulla. He was short, strong, fair-skinned, with a carefully trimmed brown beard, masking his round smooth face and short lips. In manner he was open, or affected openness, and was charming on acquaintance. He stood not on ceremony, but jested with all comers in most easy fashion; yet, when we fell into serious talk, the veil of humour seemed to fade away. He then chose his words, and argued shrewdly. Of course, he was in discussion with Storrs, who demanded a high standard from his opponent.

The Arabs thought Abdulla a far-seeing statesman and an astute politician. Astute he certainly was, but not greatly enough to convince us always of his sincerity. His ambition was patent. Rumour made him the brain of his father and of the Arab revolt; but he seemed too easy for that. His object was, of course, the winning of Arab independence and the building up of Arab nations, but he meant to keep the direction of the new states in the family. So he watched us, and played through us to the British gallery.

On our part, I was playing for effect, watching, criticizing him. The Sherif's rebellion had been unsatisfactory for the last few months (standing still, which, with an irregular war, was the prelude to disaster): and my suspicion was that its lack was leadership: not intellect, nor judgment, nor political wisdom, but the flame of enthusiasm, that would set the desert on fire. My visit was mainly to find the yet unknown masterspirit of the affair, and measure his capacity to carry the revolt to the goal I had conceived for it. As our conversation continued, I became more and more sure that Abdulla was too balanced, too cool, too humorous to be a prophet: especially the armed prophet who, if history be true, succeeded in revolutions. His value would come perhaps in the peace after success. During the physical struggle, when singleness of eye and magnetism, devotion and self-sacrifice were needed, Abdulla would be a tool too complex for a simple purpose, though he could not be ignored, even now.—T. E. LAWRENCE: *Seven Pillars of Wisdom*, Chap. 8.[11]

Under the topic of dialogue we have already discussed some of the ways by which speech indicates character: Miss Knag's habit of saying "hem," or the professor's special, somewhat stilted vocabulary and turn of phrase. But further, we must distinguish between what is said and the way of saying it. The ideas or attitudes expressed should spring from the character and exhibit it, and the vocabulary, rhythm, and mannerisms (if there are mannerisms) should be significant.

It is difficult to find a brief example of the method of indicating character by the reactions of other people, for usually a fully developed scene is required to make such a point. But the principle is simple and we can observe it constantly in real life: the feelings and behavior of those around a person act as a mirror of that person's character. And we often encounter it in narratives, sometimes with some such obvious signal as, "When I first met Mr. Dobbs, I felt an uneasiness which I was at a loss to explain, for he was so civil, so fatherly . . ."; but the method may be used without the signal. The reactions may form part of the narrative itself.

The method which most concerns the writer of narrative is, of course, the exhibiting of character through action. Again it is diffi-

[11] From: *Seven Pillars of Wisdom* by T. E. Lawrence. Copyright 1926, 1935 by Doubleday & Company, Inc.

cult to illustrate this method by a brief extract, for we can be sure that a single act is properly expressive of character only if we test that act against the other acts in the narrative. Any good short story or novel or biography will illustrate the matter. But in general terms, we must ask if the particular incident is vivid, significant in itself, and consistent with other incidents. Our final test here is human nature, and thorough observation is the best teacher.

SUMMARY

Narration is the kind of discourse concerned with action, with life in motion. It tells a story. An action, as we use the word here, may be discussed with reference to *movement, time,* and *meaning.*

The essence of narration is to give a sense of movement—the passing from one stage to another stage. Narration does not explain a process but places the events before our eyes to give a quality of immediacy. The movement of an action is through time, but narration gives not a mere segment of time, but rather a unit of time, and this unity is determined by the fact that the process presented in narration extends from the moment when one condition prevails but is unstable, to the moment when the process is completed by the establishment of another and stable condition. As for meaning, action does not merely involve change, but significant change. The stages of the process are related to each other in such a way that they are comprehensible and make a point. In so far as the action presented concerns human beings the comprehensibility involves MOTIVATION of events and human reaction to events.

Narration is a kind of discourse, and a NARRATIVE is the particular thing produced by the application of the method of narration. But the method of narration may be used without producing a satisfactory narrative. Events may be narrated which do not constitute an action—which are held together simply by the fact that they form a sequence in time.

The relation of narration to the other kinds of discourse may be discussed under two heads:

1. How does narration use the other kinds of discourse?
2. How do the other kinds of discourse use narration?

A narrative may, and usually does, employ the other kinds: exposition of issues involved or argument concerning them, description of characters or setting.

As for the second question, description rarely appears by itself in an extended form, and though it may use the acts, say, of a person described, it can scarcely be thought to present fully rendered actions. But both exposition and argument frequently use narration —more or less fully rendered actions—for illustrative purposes.

Is there a basic PATTERN which a narrative tends to take? This question may be approached by considering, not methods of narration, but the way in which an action appears in fact. An action arises in a situation. It moves through stages of tension to some sort of breaking point. At the breaking point a change definitely takes place to create a new situation different in meaning from the original situation in that the old tensions are relieved and a point of rest is reached. The stages of narration correspond to these divisions in an action. The beginning, the original situation, is technically called EXPOSITION. The middle, comprising the stages of mounting tension, is called COMPLICATION. The end, the definition of the new situation, is called the DENOUEMENT. The breaking point, the crisis of the action, is called the CLIMAX. These aspects of an action, even when they are not always fully presented in a narrative, as, for example, in a brief anecdote, are nevertheless always implied.

The relation of the stages of a narrative to each other raises the question of PROPORTION. But there is no mathematical ratio which can be depended upon to settle the question of proportion. Each case must be considered in terms of the material involved and the intention of the writer. The writer may, however, ask himself these guiding questions:

1. Does the exposition give all the information really necessary to establish the situation for the reader?

2. Is it burdened with information which is really unnecessary and distracting?

3. Does the complication clearly define for the reader the essential stages of the development of the action?

4. Does it confuse the reader by presenting material which does not bear on the development of the action?

5. Does the denouement give the reader enough to make the point of the narrative clear?

6. Does it blur the point by putting in irrelevant material or by so extending relevant material that a sharp focus is lost?

As the ordering of the parts of a narrative is a problem of pattern, so the rendering of the surface details is a problem of TEXTURE. Even in a narrative which deals with matters of fact, the writer cannot hope to render all details, and if he could he would simply blur the effect. He must use a principle of SELECTION. He should try to sharpen the interest of the reader by presenting only those details which have some bearing on the central concern, or which suggest the immediate quality of the event.

POINT OF VIEW, in reference to narration, means a person who bears some relation to the action, either as observer or participant, and whose intelligence serves as the index of the action for the reader. Point of view, then, involves two questions:

1. Who tells the story?

2. What is his relation to the action?

Broadly speaking, there are two possible points of view, the first person and the third person. In the first, for instance, an "I," real or fictitious, relates an event in which he himself is involved. In the second, an author, writing impersonally, relates an event in which another person is involved.

There are, however, certain shadings and variations possible within these two broad general divisions.

In the first-person point of view, two extreme positions may be distinguished.

1. The narrator may tell of an action in which he is the main, or a main, participant.

2. The narrator may tell of an action in which he has not participated, and which he has merely observed.

These two extreme positions may be called (1) NARRATOR—MAIN CHARACTER and (2) NARRATOR—MERE OBSERVER. But between them are many possible variations, corresponding to the degree in which the narrator is involved in the action.

In the third-person point of view, two extreme positions may likewise be distinguished.

1. In the PANORAMIC point of view, the writer may report any or all the aspects of an action, and may go into the head of any or all the characters involved. (In nonimaginative writing, history, for in-

stance, the writer who employs this method is limited, of course, by what facts or plausible references are available to him.)

2. In the point of view of SHARP FOCUS, the writer keeps his attention focused on one character and on that character's relation to the action. The parts of the action not directly participated in by the selected character are not reported by the writer.

Between these two extreme positions there are all sorts of gradations and mixtures possible.

In all cases the dominant interest defines the point of view.

As the dominant interest defines the point of view, so it defines the SCALE in a piece of narration. There are two extremes of scale:

1. SUMMARY RENDERING, which is used primarily in those parts necessary for continuity or scaffolding.

2. FULL RENDERING, which is used primarily in those parts of greatest interest and importance—the main scenes of a narrative.

Narration often involves the use of DIALOGUE. Dialogue sometimes appears to be an easy method of presenting an event, but in fact it is one of the most difficult. It is difficult because it is not a mere transcript of what people say; it must be carefully planned and organized to develop a point or issue. Therefore it presents a problem in selection and logical ordering. At the same time good dialogue must give an impression of naturalness, of the pauses and waverings of conversation.

Another problem in dialogue is that of giving the impression of the speech of the individual. People have different mannerisms, different idioms, different vocabularies, different rhythms, depending on personal peculiarities, educational background, geographical origin, social class, and so forth. Close observation of people and of methods used by competent writers is the only guide here.

Most narratives involve people, and to understand such a narrative we must understand the people involved, their natures, their motives, and their responses. The process of presenting this information is called CHARACTERIZATION.

Characterization does not mean the mere accumulation of details about the persons being characterized. The details must be related to each other to build up a unified impression. To do this the writer should concern himself with the main motive of a character in relation to the events, or by the main effect of the events on him. Generally speaking, there are five methods for presenting character: by description of appearance or mannerisms, by analysis of character, by speech, by reaction of other persons, and by action. The last is the most important method, for it is most closely connected with the main concern of narrative, the rendering of action.

The Paragraph

THE PARAGRAPH AS A CONVENIENCE TO THE READER

A PARAGRAPH, mechanically considered, is a division of the composition, a division set off by an indentation of its first sentence. (It may be marked in manuscript by the sign ¶.) Paragraph divisions signal to the reader that the division so set off constitutes a unit of thought.

For the reader this marking off of the whole composition into segments is a convenience, though not a strict necessity. A truly well-organized, well-written piece of prose would presumably be no worse as a piece of prose if we decided to print it with no paragraph divisions whatsoever. Printed thus, it would say precisely what it said before. The reader, however, would probably be irritated at failing to find these pointers to its organization. His reading might be made more difficult. Yet, with perhaps a little more studied attention, he could doubtless find the organization, if it were actually there. There is good reason, however, for the convention of paragraphing. Since communication of one's thoughts is at best a difficult business, it is the part of common sense, not to mention good manners, to mark for the reader the divisions of our thought, and thus make the thought structure visible upon the page.

Where should these divisions occur? How long should a paragraph be? In answering these questions, let us again begin by adopting the position of the reader. For him, a composition composed of paragraphs no longer than one or two sentences each might as well be printed without paragraph divisions at all. Segmentation on this scale would tell the reader little more about organization than the segmentation already given by the division into sentences. The opposite extreme would, of course, be quite as bad. For paragraphs of six or seven hundred words each would tell the reader little or nothing about the thought structure.

Common sense dictates that the length of the normal paragraph will lie between these extremes. But this is not to say that an *occasional* very short paragraph—even a paragraph of only one sentence—may not tell the reader a great deal. By its very shortness the importance of the paragraph would be emphasized. Similarly, an occasional long paragraph would do no damage and might serve to emphasize the unity of a long passage—always provided, of course, that the long passage actually constitutes a unit. We may sum up, then, by saying that there is no formula for ascertaining the length of paragraphs. Only common sense and the requirements of the particular occasion can determine how long any paragraph ought to be.

THE PARAGRAPH AS A UNIT OF THOUGHT

Thus far we have looked at the paragraph from the perspective of the reader's convenience. We have said that paragraphing can make visible to him the divisions of the writer's thought. But paragraphing, obviously, can be of help to the reader only if the indicated paragraphs are genuine units of thought—not faked units—not mere random bits of writing arbitrarily marked off as units. *For a paragraph undertakes to discuss one topic or one aspect of a topic.*

The preceding sentence defines the paragraph but defines it in such fashion that the reader may well question the usefulness of the definition. What, after all, is a topic? It is not easy to define; and we have probably made matters more difficult by adding "or one aspect of a topic." A discussion of "one aspect of a topic" might be thought to cover almost anything.

It ought to be admitted immediately that paragraphing is to some extent a matter of taste, not a matter of logic. Accordingly, any realistic definition must be rather loose and general. Fortunately, we do not construct paragraphs by applying definitions. In the practical problem of composition the writer will find his best approach is to remind himself that the paragraph is a *part* of the composition. Earlier in this text (p. 100) we discussed the difference between a part and a mere lump or fragment. We saw that a true part has its characteristic organization which is related to the larger organization of the whole. A paragraph thus has its "part" to play —its own particular job to do—in the larger structure of meaning.

THE STRUCTURE OF THE PARAGRAPH

The paragraph, however, has its own structure, and there are various ways of indicating that structure. One of these ways is to build the paragraph around one sentence (the TOPIC SENTENCE) which states the central thought of the whole paragraph. We may think of the topic sentence as a kind of backbone, or spine, which supports the body of the paragraph and around which the rest of the structure is formed. Here is an example.

The reader of a novel—by which I mean the critical reader—is himself a novelist; he is the maker of a book which may or may not please his taste when it is finished, but of a book for which he must take his own share of the responsibility. The author does his part, but he cannot transfer his book like a bubble into the brain of the critic; he cannot make sure that the critic will possess his work. The reader must therefore become, for his part, a novelist, never permitting himself to suppose that the creation of the book is solely the affair of the author. The difference between them is immense, of course, and so much so that a critic is always inclined to extend and intensify it. The opposition that he conceives between the creative and the critical task is a very real one; but in modestly belittling his own side of the business he is apt to forget an essential portion of it. The writer of the novel works in a manner that would be utterly impossible to the critic, no doubt, and with a liberty and with a range that would disconcert him entirely. But in one quarter their work coincides; both of them make the novel.— PERCY LUBBOCK: *The Craft of Fiction,* Chap. 2.[1]

In this paragraph the first sentence is the topic sentence. It states the thesis which the paragraph as a whole develops. It is frequently said that every paragraph contains a topic sentence,

[1] From *The Craft of Fiction,* by Percy Lubbock, through the permission of Peter Smith.

stated or implied. It might be more sensible, however, to say that some paragraphs have topic sentences and that others do not; for an implied topic sentence is one which the reader is able to construct for himself as a way of summarizing the paragraph in question. It is obvious that any composition possessing the very minimum of unity may always be summed up in some kind of sentence. The "implied" topic sentence, therefore, is an abstraction—a not very useful kind of ghost sentence. In this book, therefore, we shall mean by "topic sentence" only an actual sentence; and though insisting that every paragraph have unity, we shall admit the existence of paragraphs that do not embody a topic sentence.

The topic sentence may begin the paragraph (see the paragraph quoted above). But a topic sentence may occur elsewhere. Here, for example, is a paragraph in which the topic sentence brings the paragraph to a close.

The artistic temperament is a disease that afflicts amateurs. It is a disease which arises from men not having sufficient power of expression to utter and get rid of the element of art in their being. It is healthful to every sane man to utter the art within him; it is essential to every sane man to get rid of the art within him at all costs. Artists of a large and wholesome vitality get rid of their art easily, as they breathe easily, or perspire easily. But in artists of less force, the thing becomes a pressure, and produces a definite pain, which is called the artistic temperament. Thus, very great artists are able to be ordinary men—men like Shakespeare or Browning. There are many real tragedies of the artistic temperament, tragedies of vanity or violence or fear. But the great tragedy of the artistic temperament is that it cannot produce any art.—G. K. CHESTERTON: "On the Wit of Whistler," *Heretics*.[2]

The last sentence of this paragraph makes a generalized statement of the point developed in the preceding sentences. The topic sentence serves, in this instance, as a kind of summary. The beginning and the end of a paragraph constitute emphatic positions for the topic sentence. But topic sentences may occur at any place in the paragraph.

[2] Reprinted by permission of Dodd, Mead & Company from *Heretics* by G. K. Chesterton. Copyright, 1905, 1932, by G. K. Chesterton.

SOME TYPICAL STRUCTURAL PRINCIPLES

We do not undertake in this chapter to give an exhaustive classification of the principles of organization that govern paragraph
structure. There is value, however, in mentioning and illustrating
some of the typical principles. In this connection the reader will
find it useful to turn back to the earlier chapters of this book which
treat exposition, argument, description, and narration. A paragraph,
as we have seen, is a part of the whole composition. Since this is
true, one would expect to find that the principles which govern the
whole organization ought to apply, in some measure, to the organization of the parts (that is, to the paragraphs).

What are some of the methods by which we organize a piece
of exposition? The chapter on Exposition mentions such methods
as classification and division, comparison and contrast, illustration,
definition, chronological analysis, causal analysis, and many more.
But if we attempt to apply these principles of organization to the
paragraph—even to the paragraphs of an expository essay—we find
that they have varying degrees of applicability.

Illustration, for example, applies rather directly to paragraph
construction. (See the paragraphs quoted from Melville on p. 54,
or the sixth paragraph quoted from Della Lutes on p. 60 f.) Comparison and contrast are also methods quite applicable to paragraph
structure. Consider, for example, G. Lowes Dickinson's "Red-bloods
and Mollycoddles" (several paragraphs of which are quoted on
pp. 65 ff.). The essay as a whole makes a classification, but it is
organized in terms of comparison and contrast. The individual
paragraphs of this essay are developed on the same principle.
The first paragraph begins with a suggested definition and proceeds
to elaborate and particularize that definition by comparison and
contrast. The next paragraph emphasizes the traits of the Mollycoddle (as opposed to the Red-blood), but in illustrating the nature
of the Mollycoddle it further emphasizes his traits by means of a
series of contrasts with his opposite. The third paragraph extends
the classification from individuals to nations. Its first sentence,
which we may take as the topic sentence, reads: "Nations, like men,
may be classified roughly as Red-blood and Mollycoddle." The rest

of the paragraph illustrates this generalization through a series of contrasts of national characteristics.

There are other expository methods, however, which have less direct applicability to paragraph construction. Take, for example, the method of definition (discussed at length on pp. 83-98). As one illustration of definition (p. 96) we offered an excerpt from Newman's essay "What Is a University?" It so happens that the illustration consists of exactly one paragraph, the first paragraph of the essay.

If I were asked to describe as briefly and popularly as I could, what a University was, I should draw my answer from its ancient designation of a *Studium Generale,* or "School of Universal Learning." This description implies the assemblage of strangers from all parts in one spot;—*from all parts;* else, how will you find professors and students for every department of knowledge? and *in one spot;* else, how can there be any school at all? Accordingly, in its simple and rudimental form, it is a school of knowledge of every kind, consisting of teachers and learners from every quarter. Many things are requisite to complete and satisfy the idea embodied in this description; but such as this a University seems to be in its essence, a place for the communication and circulation of thought, by means of personal intercourse, through a wide extent of country.

It is not this paragraph, however, but Newman's whole essay that gives us his full definition of the term *university:* his first paragraph is a rather special case. What is the structure of the other paragraphs of his essay? They play their part in developing the definition of a university which the whole essay undertakes to make. But they are not themselves organized as definitions. Some provide illustrations, others make comparisons and furnish contrasts, and all take the structure of their specialized functions. Even the structure of the first paragraph might be more practically described thus: the paragraph begins by defining a university as a *Studium Generale,* and then proceeds to develop two or three basic implications of this term; that is, the structure is a generalization plus several particularizations.

We can say in general that the more complex methods of exposition and argument, such as functional analysis, chronological analysis, causal analysis, and syllogistic reasoning, rarely determine the structure of a single paragraph. Their very complexity prevents their doing so. For the paragraph as one of the smaller parts in extended composition usually has a simpler structure. It states a point and elaborates it, or it contrasts two points, or it illustrates an argument, or it makes a particular application.

Some paragraphs, however, do have a rather explicit logical structure in which the topic sentence states a conclusion which follows from premises stated in the body of the paragraph. Here is a paragraph so constructed.

A really great pitcher must have control. Charles Ramsey had wonderful speed and a curve that broke as sharply as any that I have ever seen. He dazzled opposing batters with his fireball or made them break their backs reaching for pitches that broke sharply away from the plate. Charles had nearly everything—he even fielded his position brilliantly—but he lacked control. Even on his best days his control was less than certain. Shrewd batters learned this, and waited him out, frequently successfully, for a base on balls. On his worst days he simply couldn't find the plate. A pitcher without control cannot win close games. This is why I have to scratch Ramsey from my list of great pitchers.

This is a rather simple paragraph, and on a simple enough subject; yet it is characterized by a logical structure. We can see this plainly by putting this argument in the form of a syllogism.

A great pitcher must not be lacking in control.   (major premise)
Charles Ramsey is lacking in control.   (minor premise)
∴ Charles Ramsey is not a great pitcher.   (conclusion)

Few paragraphs, however, are shaped to conform so neatly to the logical skeleton of a syllogism. We might remember that few arguments are expressed in fully developed syllogisms. They are rather a series of enthymemes, or, as we put it on page 171, a "chain of implied syllogisms, the conclusion of one becoming a premise of the next." Such a chain of reasoning is often exhibited in the characteristic paragraph organization in essays which present an argument.

The writer attempting to present a chain of reasoning will find that preliminary outlines are very helpful—indeed may be indispensable. He should turn back to Chapter 1 (pp. 26-28) and reread what has been said about outlines. (Outlining is also discussed and summarized in the Appendix on the Outline, p. 486.) A brief (p. 172) is of special utility in fashioning a close-knit fabric of argument. Such a brief as that given on page 174 states a point as a main heading, and proceeds to marshal the supporting proofs in proper degrees of subordination.

I. _____ *because*
  A. _____ _____ *because*
    1. _____ ____ *because*
      a. _____ *and*
      b. _____

This sort of brief goes far toward suggesting paragraph structure. The divisions and the more important subdivisions become paragraphs: and the sentences that constitute the headings become topic sentences.

But outlining—unless we have made specifically a paragraph outline (see Appendix on the Outline, p. 486)—does not determine paragraph structure. Outlining will not settle, for example, the problem of scale. (Are topics *a* and *b* to constitute one paragraph or four? Should *A* be developed as a short paragraph, and 1, *a*, and *b* made to constitute a long paragraph which follows it?) It will be interesting in this connection to see the comments on the partial outline of Gauss's "The Threat of Science" (Appendix on the Outline, p. 486).

Thus far we have examined paragraph structure primarily in the light of the methods of organization discussed in the chapters on Exposition and Argument. But the chapters on Description and Narration and the section on Expository Description (pp. 42-53) will suggest other ways in which paragraphs may be organized, and, on the whole, some of the simpler kinds of organization: simple time sequence, for example, or simple sequence of objects arranged in space.

Consider first a paragraph from Conrad's "The Secret Sharer."[3]

On my right hand there were lines of fishing-stakes resembling a mysterious system of half-submerged bamboo fences, incomprehensible in its division of the domain of tropical fishes, and crazy of aspect as if abandoned for ever by some nomad tribe of fishermen now gone to the other end of the ocean; for there was no sign of human habitation as far as the eye could reach. To the left a group of barren islets, suggesting ruins of stone walls, towers, and blockhouses, had its foundations set

[3] From *'Twixt Land and Sea* by Joseph Conrad. Reprinted by permission of J. M. Dent and Sons, Ltd., through the courtesy of the Conrad estate.

in a blue sea that itself looked solid, so still and stable did it lie below my feet; even the track of light from the westering sun shone smoothly, without that animated glitter which tells of an imperceptible ripple. And when I turned my head to take a parting glance at the tug which had just left us anchored outside the bar, I saw the straight line of the flat shore joined to the stable sea, edge to edge, with a perfect and unusual closeness, in one levelled floor half brown, half blue under the enormous dome of the sky.

Here we have a fixed observer. He tells us what he sees on his right hand, then on his left, and finally, turning his head, what he sees behind him. (There is even an implied look upward: "the . . . dome of the sky.") The order of composition is simple and even mechanical, though the writing itself is not mechanical. Notice, for example, the sense of finality and completeness given by the last sentence. The observer's survey comes to rest in "the straight line" of shore and sea "under the enormous dome of the sky." The paragraph thus rounds out and completes its chosen topic. It is thoroughly unified, though it does *not* contain a topic sentence.

But we may also have a scene described through the eyes of an observer who is shifting his position. The paragraph from Lawrence's *Seven Pillars of Wisdom* (p. 203) furnishes an illustration. Moreover, a scene may be described in terms of an image which provides a frame of reference for it. Thomas Hardy describes the continent of Europe under the figure of a human being (see p. 203).

The various ways in which description (and descriptive paragraphs) may be organized have been summarized on page 229 (which the writer should reread). Now these methods of description all apply to descriptive paragraphs as well as to description as a kind of discourse. In fact, the examples printed in Chapter 5 to illustrate these methods are, almost without exception, distinct paragraphs. The writer can learn from them, therefore, a great deal about paragraph development.

Some of the more subjective modes of paragraph development, however, call for a bit of further discussion. It is in these that the principle of organization is least clear; the structure of the paragraph will seem most nearly subjective—a mere matter of caprice. It will be these paragraphs, then, which will seem to the reader to stretch the very concept of the paragraph to a dangerous limit. Consider, for example, the paragraph quoted from E. M. Forster's

A Passage to India on page 205. Why did not Forster begin a new paragraph with sentence five, "Chandrapore was never . . ."? Or consider the passage quoted from Sinclair Lewis's *Main Street* (p. 207). The passage is printed as four paragraphs. Two are composed of one sentence; one, of two sentences. Only the third paragraph has more than two sentences. Would anything be lost if all four paragraphs were lumped together in one medium-length paragraph?

A defense can be offered in both instances. Forster presumably felt his description of Chandrapore was a unit—that for him at least it had a "felt unity." Lewis presumably used the ultrashort paragraphs for a special effect: to suggest someone walking down "Main Street," observing the buildings as he walks. We get a paragraph for each store. But much more is at stake than the defense of these two examples. The defense may or may not be adequate, and if the reader feels it to be inadequate, he is quite possibly right. At any rate, he is right to raise the question. For the question goes to the heart of the problem of paragraph structure. To repeat: there is no precise formula by which the length or structure of a paragraph may be determined. As we have said earlier (p. 291), the writer must use his best judgment: he must use his common sense and his taste. Unless he is very sure of his ground, he will tend to employ paragraphs of medium length. He will tend to use the more conventional paragraph structures. But in following these common-sense rules he must not conceive of paragraphs as mechanical units of even length and of homogeneous make-up. He will feel free, on occasion, to formulate paragraphs of "felt unity," relying upon his own impression of the "rightness" of the structure. For the writer must never forget that the paragraph is a part—a meaningful part—of a larger structure, and therefore cannot be formulated mechanically any more than can the larger structure of which it is a part.

LINKING PARAGRAPHS TOGETHER

Since paragraphs are parts of a whole work, elements in an ordered sequence, it is important that they be properly linked together. Even if the chain of development embodied in the series of paragraphs has been thought out carefully, the reader will still be grateful for signposts placed to direct him. The judicious use of transitional words and phrases such as *therefore, consequently, hence, thus, accordingly, on the contrary, however, nevertheless, furthermore, finally, in the same way,* and *moreover* constitutes one way of helping the reader. The writer may also make use of the co-ordinate conjunctions *for, and, but, or,* and *nor* as explicit signs of the connection between paragraph and paragraph. Since, however, we ordinarily use these conjunctions to join the parts of a sentence, or to join sentence with sentence, we employ them less frequently to tie a paragraph to a preceding paragraph. But they can be used, though the use is more appropriate to an informal than to a formal style.

If we do provide the reader with transitional words as explicit signposts, obviously we must use them accurately. We must not begin a paragraph by writing "In the same way . . ." unless what follows *is* "in the same way"; we must not write "Consequently" unless what follows is a consequence of the preceding paragraph.

An obvious device for linking paragraphs is the repetition of a key word or phrase. It is a useful device, particularly if we wish to avoid the formality of style suggested by the employment of transitional words, but wish also to avoid the abruptness occasioned by the use of *and, but,* and *or*. To illustrate: Christian Gauss, in his "The Threat of Science," effects the transition between his third and fourth paragraphs in this way. (We have italicized the key words here, and in the examples that follow.)

To the biologist the lion who kills many antelopes has "survival value." He is, this scientist will even tell us, a *good* lion.

When the scientist uses this word *good* we must be on our guard. He does not mean what the theologian . . .

The exact word or phrase, of course, need not be repeated. It may be varied. Here is Gauss's transition from paragraph six to seven.

[The] truths [of experimental science] are not really truths of a higher sort; they are not above ordinary truths, as the angels (if there still are angels) are over the earth; they are only the truths of science in what might be called *their state of innocence.*

For this reason experimental science should not be regarded as *wicked;* it is only *unmoral.* No harm will come so long . . .

Here is a series of three paragraphs from a story in *Time* magazine:

A *buzzard coasting* high in the air over Central America last week, would have seen nothing unusual. The mountainous, forest-matted *isthmus* lay quietly in the greasy November sun. Among the many human realities invisible to the buzzard were the boundary lines—the imaginary but very actual barriers that said: "This is Costa Rica; this is Guatemala; this is Nicaragua."

Far below the *coasting buzzard*, in the grey-green jungles of northern Nicaragua, more was stirring than his great bird's-eye view could catch. Snaking through the scrub, *guerrilla riflemen made short, sharp little raids* against government outposts. In and out of the piny mountain country on Nicaragua's northern flank, armed, machete-toting *men filtered mysteriously*. In Guatemala and Costa Rica dusty little *companies,* in faded denim and khaki, *marked time in the tropic heat.*

All this scattered activity added up to one gathering purpose. That purpose called itself the Caribbean Legion.[4]

Here is a series of three paragraphs from Dorothy Sayers's *The Mind of the Maker:*

It is for this reason that I have prefixed to this brief study of the creative mind an introductory chapter in which I have tried to make clear the difference between *fact and opinion,* and between the so-called "laws" based on *fact and opinion* respectively.

In the creeds of Christendom, we are confronted with a set of documents which purport to be, not expressions of *opinion* but statements of *fact.* Some of these *statements* are historical, and with these the present book is not concerned. Others are theological—which means that they claim to be statements of fact about the nature of God and the universe; and with a *limited number of these I propose to deal.*

The selected statements are those which aim at defining the nature of God, conceived in His capacity as Creator. They were originally . . .[5]

Another obvious device for linking paragraphs is the use of *this* (*these*) and *that* (*those*); but these words must be used with care. We are frequently tempted to use them vaguely, hoping that the idea or object to which they refer will be clear from the context. Frequently it is not clear, and instead of a tight and neat coupling of the two paragraphs, we have only the vague and clumsy suggestion of a tie. For example, a paragraph of "The Colors That Animals Can See"[6] ends thus:

[4] Courtesy of TIME, Copyright Time, Inc. 1948.

[5] From *The Mind of the Maker* by Dorothy Sayers, copyright, 1942, by Harcourt, Brace and Company, Inc.

[6] "The Colors That Animals Can See," from *The Personality of Animals* by H. Munro Fox.

After we have arranged these new cards, we have not long to wait. Very soon bees arrive again, and it can be seen that they fly straight on to the blue card; none goes to the red card.

Now we might be tempted to begin the next paragraph with: "This seems to indicate two things. The first is . . ." But what the author wrote was: "This behavior of the bees seems to indicate two things. . . ." A little reflection will indicate that his judgment was sound. The author intends to state clearly a process of proof. He has been wise therefore to make very precise what "this" refers to. The mistake of vague and indefinite reference can be quite serious. It is so common an error that the writer had better make sure that "this" or "that" standing at the beginning of a paragraph refer unmistakably to some specific noun.

USE OF THE PARAGRAPH TO INDICATE DIALOGUE

There is one further and special use of the paragraph. This use is conventional, though the convention is an important and inflexible one. In writing dialogue, we begin a new paragraph with each change of speaker. (A long speech by one speaker may, of course, need to be divided into two or more paragraphs: that is, the convention does not require the converse, that each new speaker be allowed only *one* paragraph.) The utility of the convention is obvious: by beginning a new paragraph each time the speaker changes, we make it much easier for the reader to keep straight who is speaking. For an illustration, see page 276.

SUMMARY

A PARAGRAPH is a unit of thought. We mark off these units of thought by indenting the first line. No precise rules govern paragraph length, but common sense dictates that very short and very long paragraphs be used rarely. A succession of very short paragraphs (or of very long paragraphs) would be of little use in indicating to the reader the divisions of the writer's thought.

Since a paragraph is a *unit* of thought, it has an ordered structure. The three great interrelated principles of order (unity, coherence, and emphasis) obviously apply to the paragraph. Now, in this text, these principles have received their fullest discussion in connection with the whole theme—in the chapters treating description, narration, exposition, and argument. But paragraphs, as meaningful parts of the whole, involve the principle of order. Paragraphs exemplify these principles in a double sense. As an individual structure the paragraph has its own unity, coherence, and emphasis. As a part of the larger structure, the paragraph contributes to the unity, coherence, and emphasis of the total composition.

The interplay between these relationships is intimate. That is why we have been able to draw from the earlier chapters, which deal with the whole theme, principles that apply to the structure of the paragraph as such. That is why these same earlier chapters furnish so many illustrations of paragraph construction. In other words, the reader should realize that when he comes to this chapter on the paragraph, he already knows a great deal about the paragraph. He has actually been studying the structural principles of the paragraph all along.

As for the part-to-whole relationship (the paragraph as related to the whole composition), a further word may be said. As parts of a larger structure, paragraphs often have specialized functions. The opening paragraph (or paragraphs), for example, must introduce the whole essay; the final paragraph (or paragraphs) must bring it to a suitable conclusion. Within the essay itself, there may be many paragraphs of specialized function: one paragraph states a particular argument; another provides an illustration; still another effects a transition between two sections of the essay.

These part-to-whole relationships, least of all, however, can be studied by considering the paragraph in isolation. Here too the reader will learn most by studying the paragraph in relation to the whole. (The reader might look, for example, at the opening paragraphs of the various essays in the selections printed at the end of this text. From such an examination he would probably learn much more about how to construct introductory paragraphs than from any general discussion.) Study of the paragraph, therefore, leads us back to the general problems of composition. The reader will provide his own best conclusion to this summary by going back to Chapter 1 and rereading pages 13-23.

The Sentence

OUR DISCUSSION in earlier chapters has dealt with rhetorical problems; that is, we have been concerned with making our expression clear and convincing to the reader. Our discussion of the whole theme and of its subdivisions, of the process of composition considered generally and considered in its various kinds (description, exposition, and so on), has been conducted from the point of view of rhetoric. We have asked: How can we select, arrange, and dispose our materials so as to make them register with maximum impact on the reader? Thus, we have applied the principles of rhetorical organization to the composition as a whole, to its parts (the paragraphs), and now are to apply them to its smallest part, the SENTENCE.

RHETORIC AND GRAMMAR

But with the sentence, this smallest rhetorical unit, we encounter another problem. It is the problem of grammar. In earlier chapters we could take the problem of grammar for granted, for, since the larger units of a composition are made up of sentences, we could assume that the demands of GRAMMAR had been met. In this chapter, although we shall still be primarily concerned with how to make our sentences effective (the rhetorical problem), we shall have to touch upon specifically grammatical problems. These have to do with the rules and conventions that govern English sentence structure. We might illustrate the relation between grammar and rhetoric in this way: The *grammar* of a game of chess, say, would be the rules of the game—what moves are possible if one is to play the game fairly and correctly. The *rhetoric* of chess, on the other hand, would be the principles which govern the playing of a winning game—what moves we ought to make and in what sequence, if we hope to play effectively and well. If we are to write English effectively, we must have a knowledge of rhetoric; but if we are to write English at all, we must have a knowledge of English grammar.

In this book the reader's knowledge of English grammar is assumed. The book is specifically a rhetoric, not a grammar. Yet, in the sentence, the two problems of grammar and rhetoric interpenetrate so thoroughly that it would be impractical, even if it were possible, to leave the grammatical aspect out of account.

A sentence is usually defined as a complete thought expressed through a subject and a predicate. Unfortunately, the definition is of little value to anyone who does not already know what "complete" means in this context, or who does not already know what predication is. The reader using this book presumably does know; and yet it may be of some value to review the definition, particularly since we shall attempt to relate the sentence to the basic principles of rhetorical structure: unity, coherence, and emphasis. A sentence has unity (is a complete thought) and its parts cohere (that is, are related to each other in a special way so as to produce that unity). But does emphasis also figure importantly in making a sentence a sentence? It does, for every complete sentence, as we shall see, must have a special focus of interest—a specific centering of emphasis, which constitutes the nucleus around which the parts cohere.

We shall need some concrete illustrations, however, if we are to make this point clear. We have said that a sentence is a complete thought; it says something about something. If one simply says, for example, "the box," we have the "something" but we do not have the "aboutness." If one should say "the large burning box in the back yard," the "aboutness" is still lacking. The box has been named, and there is even some fullness of description, but the thought is still incomplete: we feel that nothing has been "said about" this rather fully described object. If, on the other hand, one should say "the large box burns," the "aboutness" is provided. We have a sentence. The reader, however, might very well put this objection:

that there is no real difference between "the large burning box" and "the large box burns," for both connect "large box" with the idea of "burning." Why does one group of words "say" something about the box, whereas the other group does not? How is the formal difference between the two groups of words significant? By way of an answer we can say that the very *form* of "The large box burns" indicates that the matter of interest is in the fact of burning, whereas the *form* of "the large burning box" reduces the fact of burning to the naming of the box, and leaves our expectancy unsatisfied.

A sentence makes a PREDICATION. Predication means that something is said "about" the thing named—that the speaker has done more than merely point to it or name it, or characterize it. A sentence requires a SUBJECT (something named) and a predicate (a FINITE verb). But predication, as we have just seen, may be described as a way of focusing our interest. The finite verb is required in predication, for it is the function of the finite verb to supply that focus—to define what is of special importance in the speaker's statement.[1] Consider, for example, "the burning box is large" and "the large box is burning." In both sentences, "largeness" and "burning" are associated with the box, and in both there is predication. But the first sentence emphasizes the largeness as the important thing about the box; the second, the burning. On the other hand, "the large burning box," as we have noted, is not a sentence at all. "Burning," it is true, is a form of a verb. "Burning" names an action or a state of being, and it associates that action or state of being with "box." But it makes no predication, for it is not enough that we connect the thing named with some word which names an action. The verb must be "finite." In English, as well as in most other languages, *the finite verb is the signal of predication.* "The large burning box," therefore, remains unfocused. No point of emphasis is supplied, no focal point around which the other parts

[1] The reader is to be reminded here that a "finite" verb means literally a limited verb—limited with reference to person, number, tense, mood, and aspect. Thus *goes* may be used only with a singular subject in the third person, and refers only to present time, whereas the "infinite" forms like the gerund *going* and the infinitive *to go,* refer to the *general* idea of going. These infinite forms of the verb (gerunds, infinitives, and participles) may, of course, be limited as to tense: *broken* is a past participle; *to have gone* is a past infinitive; even so, the general distinction holds. The finite forms are limited and specific, and because specific, can be used to provide a focus for the sentence.

of the sentence may be made to cohere so as to give us that special kind of unity which characterizes the complete thought that is a sentence. If we hear the words "the large burning box" read aloud, we wait for the sentence to be finished—for something to be "said" about the box.

In this brief discussion of predication we have gone over ground with which the reader is expected to be familiar. Presumably he knows what a sentence is, and can distinguish between the finite verb forms and the infinite forms (infinitives, gerunds, and participles). Yet the special sense in which the sentence is related to *unity, coherence* and *emphasis,* is worth stressing. In this smallest rhetorical unit, the sentence, these fundamental principles of rhetoric coalesce with principles of grammatical construction. We organize our sentences around finite verbs. They are not only rhetorically our most vigorous and emphatic words. They constitute the core, even grammatically considered, of the sentence.

It may not be amiss at this point to say a further word about a topic mentioned earlier, the way in which we "hear" sentences. A complete sentence (i.e., "The box is burning") is always accompanied in speech by one of those changes in the pitch of the voice and one of the distinct final pauses that, together, signal to the hearer "end of utterance." This pitch-pause combination does not accompany "The burning box" or "That the box is burning," and so on. The reader might test this for himself by reading these sequences aloud. When we hear them read aloud, we wait for something else to follow. The way in which we "hear" sentences constitutes for most native speakers of English a practical means of testing any alleged sentence for completeness.

THE FIXED WORD ORDER OF THE NORMAL SENTENCE[2]

The parts of a normal English sentence are arranged in a special way. We have first the subject, then the finite verb, then the indirect object (if any), and last the direct object or any other complement of the verb (if any).

[2] For much of the material in this and the following sections of this chapter, the authors are indebted to Professor Harold Whitehall of Indiana University.

THE SENTENCE

Subject	Verb *	Indirect object	Direct object †
James	talked.		
James	told		stories.
James	was telling ‡		stories.
James	told	Roger	stories.
James	was telling	me	that he was ill.
That James was ill	caused	me	anxiety.
James	told	Roger	to stop.

* Finite verb, or finite verb plus verbals.
† Or other complement of the verb.
‡ was (finite verb) + telling (verbal—in this instance, a present participle).

The reader will notice that in these examples we have left out all modifiers, either adjectival or adverbial. The position of modifiers will be discussed later; here we are concerned with the order of the basic components of the sentence. What the reader needs to see is that the order is a *fixed* order. We cannot say, for example, "John told stories Roger," though of course we can say, "John told stories to Roger."

The reader should also observe that we have talked about the word position in the *normal* English sentence, not the average English sentence. For something more important than an average is at stake. We are concerned here with a norm, a standard pattern which is so deep-rooted in our sense of the language that most of us are quite unconscious of the fact that we observe it instinctively all the time. It is important, however, that we here see it quite consciously and explicitly, for a realization of the fact that English has a characteristic pattern of fixed word order can illuminate the deviations from this order. To sum up, in calling attention to the fixed word order we are not attempting to give the reader any new information, but rather to make him notice the pattern which he has been unconsciously observing since childhood.

VARIATIONS FROM FIXED WORD ORDER

Now, deviation from a norm is always a means of emphasis. If a man wears a red hat, he emphasizes the hat and himself. The wearing of spats on an American street, just because it deviates from the norm, calls attention to the wearer's feet, though, conversely, the *lack* of spats in a large group of people wearing spats would likewise call attention to the feet. Deviation from the fixed word positions of the sentence are emphatic as all variations from a norm tend to be emphatic. For example, compare "I do not believe that" and "That, I do not believe." The second sentence, by inverting the normal order, throws heavy emphasis on "that."

Constant emphasis, however, defeats its own end, and becomes banal and trite. Presumably the first pulp writer who wrote "Came the dawn," instead of the normal "The dawn came," was trying to secure emphasis, an emphasis which would give a certain rhetorical effect. But the writers of Hollywood in the days of silent pictures, by using "Came the dawn" over and over again, wore the caption to rags. All of which is by way of saying that we have every right to *change* the fixed word positions in order to emphasize some word, but that we vary from the normal order at our peril, and that meaningless departures from the norm make our writing empty and pretentious. Assuming, however, that we have good reason to emphasize some part of the sentence, how are the emphases secured? We have already illustrated one means, that of inversion:

That, I do not believe.
Books, he had read in plenty.

In interrogative sentences, of course, we want to emphasize the interrogative word or the verb. We regularly invert the order in English for a question.

What does he want?
When did you see him last?
Didn't you *know?*
Knew you not? (archaic)

What are some of the other means for securing emphasis?

EMPHASIS ON THE SUBJECT

Our simplest way of emphasizing the subject is to begin the sentence with "It is," "It was," and so on, or "There is," "There was," and so on. For example, compare "James told me stories" with "It was James who (that) told me stories." Or compare "A man knew seventeen languages" with "There was a man who knew seventeen languages." In each of these instances, the effect of the reformulation is to emphasize "James" and "the man" by throwing everything that follows into a subordinate clause. But it ought to be apparent that a constant and thoughtless use of "It is" and "There is" not only fails to secure emphasis but makes the sentences needlessly bumbling.

EMPHASIS ON THE OBJECTS (OR COMPLEMENTS) OF THE VERB

If we wish to emphasize the indirect object, we put it in the position of the normal subject and make the verb passive. Thus we get, not "James told me stories" but "I was told stories by James." By a similar process, we can throw emphasis upon the direct object: "Stories were told to me by James."

Now this process of converting the object of the verb (either direct or indirect) into the subject, is so familiar that the reader may well wonder that it is worth mentioning here at all, particularly in a text that is concerned with problems of rhetoric and touches upon grammatical relationships only incidentally. Yet the point involved is a very important one. If we can see that these passive constructions violate the normal English sentence pattern, it may be easier for us to see that, like all emphatic variations, they are to be used sparingly and only when we want a special emphasis on what would be, in normal order, the object of the verb. Indeed, the warning frequently given in composition books against "weak passive" constructions becomes clearer when we see that the weak passive becomes weak because it is essentially an overused, and therefore misused, *device for emphasis.*

Here are some examples of weak passives:

1. The book was picked up by me.
2. The problem of maintaining friendly relations and at the same time a proper firmness was seen.
3. The matter has been taken up for consideration, and as soon as a solution can be arrived at, settlement will be made.

Now it is apparent that in the first sentence no *emphasis* on book is intended or required. The writer has thoughtlessly drifted into the passive construction. He needs to restore the normal sentence order from which there was no good reason to depart. He should simply write "I picked up the book." (There are, of course, contexts in which *book* might deserve emphasis. One can easily imagine a story in which a character said: "But the book—not the paperweight —was picked up by *me.*")

Something more than carelessness probably accounts for the second and third examples. The real subject (what would be the subject in normal sentence order) is either vague or unknown. The writer has not troubled to define it, or else he timidly refuses to define it. Let us say that in the third sentence the true subject is "the assistant manager in charge of claims." The assistant manager shrinks from taking responsibility, or his stenographer hesitates to put him down as responsible, or feels, quite foolishly, that "we" is somehow inelegant. Thus we get the sentence as it stands, rather than "Mr. Johnson has taken the matter up and hopes to make settlement soon," or "We are considering the matter and hope to make settlement soon."

Such weak and awkward constructions have come to dominate a great deal of modern prose—especially "official" writing—writing that comes from government bureaus, business offices, and committees. The writer ought to be on his guard against its influence.

We can sum up by saying that the normal word order of the English sentence is (1) subject, (2) verb, (3) indirect object (if any), and (4) direct object or other verbal complement (if any). There is nothing inelegant about this arrangement. It constitutes the basis of a sound English style. The writer should keep to this normal pattern *unless he has a good reason for departing from it.* In checking the first draft of a piece of writing it is good practice to justify every deviation from the normal sentence pattern.

POSITION OF THE MODIFIERS

We now need to consider the position in the sentence occupied by the various modifiers—by the adjectives and adverbs, and by the phrases and clauses which function either as adjectives or adverbs. The position of some of these modifiers is rather rigidly fixed; that of others is optional, and since there is no prescribed position for them, the ordering of these "movable" modifiers is a matter of taste, emphasis, and expressiveness. We can say that the fixed modifiers are placed largely in accordance with grammatical rules; the position of the movable modifiers is assigned largely in terms of rhetorical considerations.

FIXED MODIFIERS

Let us consider first the fixed modifiers. These include most adjectives, and phrases and clauses which have the function of adjectives. Relative clauses, adjectival phrases, and adjectival infinitives *follow* the substantive which they modify. We must write, for example:

The man *to see* is Jim.
The man *I knew* was Jim.
The man *whom I mentioned* was Jim.
The house *in the country* was for sale.

We cannot write:

The *to see* man is Jim.

or:

The *I knew* man was Jim.

Single adjectives, on the contrary, just reverse this rule. The normal position of a single adjective is *before* the substantive that it modifies. For example, we would normally write:

A *bright* day dawned.
A *long black* automobile rounded the corner.
He gave an *extended, involved,* and *tortuous* argument.

Predicate adjectives, of course, do not come under this rule. We say that they modify the substantive "through the verb," and they normally come after the verb. Consider these illustrations.

The rose was *red.*
The third night seemed *long.*
The house was *for sale.*

On occasion, however, we do reverse the normal positions. Examples will readily occur to the reader. Here are a few:

Comrades *all!*
Chapter *ten.*
John the *Baptist.*
A car, *long* and *black,* rounded the corner.
A small face, *dirty,* appeared at the window.
Black is my true love's hair.

As we have seen earlier, variation from the norm is emphatic, and in all these illustrations the reversal of normal position has the effect of emphasizing the adjectives used.

One qualification of this principle, however, must be made. Some of the examples given seem to represent, not an emphatic variation, but the normal pattern: e.g., *chapter ten* and *John the Baptist*. But in expressions of this sort, as a little reflection will show, the adjective is important and normally requires stress. Furthermore, there are other expressions in which we normally encounter the adjective following the noun: first, certain fossilized expressions derived from French law, such as "body politic" and "heir apparent"; and second, expressions such as "the day following," "the funds available," which actually represent elliptical expressions which we would have to fill out as follows: "the day following (this day)," "the funds available (to us)."

These classes of exceptions, however, do not affect the general rule, that an adjective normally *precedes* its substantive, and that the reversal of this position throws emphasis upon the adjective.

We observed earlier that thoughtless use of emphatic position or overuse of emphatic position defeats its own ends. The principle applies to modifiers. John Bunyan, in his *Pilgrim's Progress*, used the phrase "the house beautiful." In the context provided by Bunyan the expression is well used. But, with it as model, the advertisers nowadays produce such absurdities as "the memorial park beautiful," "the body beautiful," and "the hair-do glamorous." Variation from the normal position of the adjective, like other emphatic devices, ought to be used sparingly and cautiously.

To sum up, the position of adjectives and adjectival phrases and clauses allows very little variation. The position of most adjectival modifiers is definitely fixed. The reader's real problem here is to avoid clumsiness and absurdity through a careless placing of such modifiers.

In this connection, relative clauses (which we must remember are adjectival modifiers) call for a further word. Relative clauses may be *unlinked* as in the sentence "The man I knew was Jim" or *linked* as in "The man whom I knew was Jim." The *link* words are the pronouns *who* (*whom*), restricted to human beings; *which*, restricted to animals and inanimate objects; and *that*, unrestricted. A relative clause which *immediately* follows the substantive modified requires no link word; otherwise it does, and the choice of the proper link word may be necessary for clarity. Compare:

1. The man in the automobile that I recognized was Jim.

with:

2. The man in the automobile whom I recognized was Jim.

Note that sentence 1 is ambiguous as sentence 2 is not.

Relative clauses occasion difficulty in still other ways. We may make a clumsy reduplication of clauses:

The man who had just come in whom I had never met was a Mr. Rogers.

Better to write:

The new arrival, whom I had never met, was a Mr. Rogers.

or:

A Mr. Rogers, whom I had never met, had just come in.

Sometimes we carelessly make a relative clause modify a general idea which is implied but not expressed. Thus:

She had been hurt and bitterly disappointed, which accounted for her strange conduct.

Better to write:

Her hurt and bitter disappointment accounted for her strange conduct.

or:

She had been hurt and bitterly disappointed, a fact which accounted for her strange conduct.

MOVABLE MODIFIERS

The attentive reader will have noticed that there is one kind of adjectival modifier, the participial phrase, that is not fixed, but is rather freely movable. Consider, for example:

Smoking a cigarette, James sauntered down the street.
James, *smoking a cigarette,* sauntered down the street.
James sauntered down the street, *smoking a cigarette.*

All three sentences are perfectly good English. There is no one correct position for this participial phrase. In choosing where to place it, we are governed by considerations of taste and emphasis.

Nearly all the *adverbs* and *adverbial modifiers*, moreover, are movable in this way. Here are sentences which will illustrate some of the various positions which adverbial modifiers may occupy.

1. *Because I respect him,* I gave him candid advice.
2. I gave him, *because I respect him,* candid advice.
3. I gave him candid advice *because I respect him.*
4. James, *with a low mumble,* took the letter.
5. I was *presumably* breaking the law.
6. I made, *with all the grace I could summon,* my amends.
7. *There, at ten o'clock,* I arrived *as I had been told.*
8. *At ten o'clock,* I arrived *there, as I had been told.*
9. *There, as I had been told,* I arrived *at ten o'clock.*

In these examples, the various arrangements of the movable modifiers make little difference to the general sense of the sentence; but they may make considerable difference in emphasis. Sentences 7, 8, and 9, for example, say much the same thing. But sentence 7 tends to stress the place; sentence 8, the time of arrival. Sentence 9 also emphasizes the place and suggests that the instructions had been primarily concerned with designating the place. Control of emphasis and of shadings of meaning is the mark of a skillful writer. He will place his movable modifiers carefully, not thoughtlessly.

The proper arrangement of the movable modifiers is necessary for nuance of meaning and exact emphasis, but in some instances proper arrangement may be necessary to prevent downright confusion. For example, consider this sentence:

The boy who sold the most tickets today will receive the prize.

Does the sentence mean that the prize will be given today? Or that the prize will be given to the boy who sold most tickets today? If we mean the former, we should write:

The boy who sold the most tickets will be given the prize today.

or:

The prize will be given today to the boy who sold the most tickets.

If we mean the latter, we should write:

The prize will be given to the boy who sold the most tickets today.

Our illustrative sentences suggest that adverbial modifiers may occur at almost any position in the sentence: at the beginning of the sentence (1, 7, 8, and 9), at the end of the sentence (3, 7, 8, and 9), between the subject and the verb (4), between the finite verb and verbal (5), between the verb and its object (6), and between the indirect object and the direct object (2). But the last two positions are somewhat special. One would hardly write:

He sang *pleasantly* the song.

though he might write:

He sang *pleasantly* the song that I had taught him.

One would hardly write:

I gave him *quickly* candid advice.

though, as we have seen, one might write:

I gave him, *because I respect him,* candid advice.

The principle would seem to be this: that if the modifier or the direct object is sufficiently weighted with words, the modifier may precede the direct object. But the whole problem of placing the movable modifier calls for taste and tact. Even an experienced writer may need to experiment with possible positions before he feels that he has placed his movable modifiers most effectively.

One further principle emerges from a consideration of our examples. Placed before or after a sentence, movable modifiers modify the sentence as a whole; placed internally, they modify the relation between the words that precede and the words that follow them. Consider the different shadings of meaning in the following sentences:

Presumably, the thief had gained entrance through a window.
The thief, presumably, had gained entrance through a window.

In the first sentence, it is the total statement that we are to presume. In the second, the presumption is limited: what we presume is that the entrant was the thief.

There is one class of adverbial modifiers, however, which is not freely movable. These are adverbs which state a direction, adverbs like *in, back, to, up,* and *down.* These adverbs (which we may call *directives*) cannot precede a verb or verbal. For example, we can write:

James gave it *back*.

but not:

James *back* gave it.

We can write:

The water had leaked *out*.

but not:

The water had *out* leaked.

or:

The water *out* had leaked.

Moreover, these directives, if used in a series of adverbial modifiers, must precede the other adverbial modifiers. Thus:

I put the cat out last night.

not:

I put the cat last night out.

But these directive adverbs *can* precede the subject of the sentence when the verb expresses explicit motion. Thus:

Back ran Jim to third base when the outfielder made his throw to the catcher.

or:

Home the little fellow darted as fast as he could run.

These last instances reveal once more our pattern of emphatic variation: *back* and *home* which, as we have seen, normally follow the verb, are emphasized when they are placed at the beginning of the sentence.

The reader already knows how to use *directives*, of course. Native speakers have *unconsciously* been using them correctly all their lives. The intention here, and elsewhere in this discussion of fixed and movable modifiers, is not to cram the reader's head with sets of rules and categories of exceptions to the rules. Most native speakers observe the rules (and their exceptions) quite automatically.

But having noted the exceptions, we are allowed to sum up the general pattern in two simple statements:

1. *Adjectival modifiers are relatively fixed: variation from the normal position constitutes a means for emphasizing the modifier.*

2. *Adverbial modifiers are rather freely movable: careful placing of the modifiers constitutes a means of controlling the finer shadings of meaning.*

Moreover, the foregoing discussion sheds real illumination on the problem of the "dangling participle."

THE DANGLING PARTICIPLE

Participles are verbal adjectives. Since they are adjectives, they must modify some substantive in the sentence. Yet, as we have seen, like adverbs, they are *movable* modifiers. This fact explains why we so easily forget that they are adjectives, and treat them as if they were truly adverbs. Here is an example:

Walking along the road, a cloud of dust obscured the neighboring fields.

Such absurdities are, as we have seen, produced by the writer's changing the construction in the course of writing the sentence. He begins with an adjectival modification and then forgets to provide a substantive for the participle to modify. The remedy, of course, is to make the construction consistent—to write:

As we walked along the road, a cloud of dust obscured the neighboring fields.

or:

Walking along the road, we encountered a cloud of dust which obscured the neighboring fields.

GENERAL PRINCIPLES OF SENTENCE STRUCTURE

PARALLELISM

Thus far we have considered the structure of the sentence from one point of view: that of the arrangement of the basic constituents of the sentence, and the arrangement of the various kinds of modifiers. But there are other principles which may determine the structure of a sentence. One of these is PARALLELISM: the adjustment of grammatical pattern to rhetorical pattern. In its simplest terms, parallelism means no more than that like meanings should be put in like constructions.

The very richness of English tempts us to violate parallelism. For example, we have two noun forms of the verb. We can use the infinitive "to swim" or the gerund "swimming." Consequently, the careless writer may blunder into a sentence like this:

To swim and *hunting* are my favorite sports.

But the distinction between infinitive and gerund awkwardly distracts the reader from what is a co-ordinate relation. We ought to write:

Swimming and *hunting* are my favorite sports.

or:

To swim and *to hunt* are my favorite sports.

It is, however, our great variety of movable modifiers that most often leads us into this kind of blundering. We write, for example:

Being lazy by nature and *because I am clumsy,* I have never liked tennis.

Such violations of parallelism easily creep into first drafts—even into the first drafts of a good writer. Careful rewriting is the answer.

We must not forget, however, that the principle of parallelism may be used positively. So used, it becomes a powerful rhetorical device. By stressing parallel constructions we emphasize the ideas expressed, and we can thus play one sort of meaning off against the other. Sentences constructed on this principle are sometimes called "balanced sentences." Here are some examples:

1. As the hart panteth after the water brooks, so panteth my soul after Thee, O God.

2. He was sick of life, but he was afraid of death; and he shuddered at every sight or sound which reminded him of the inevitable hour.

3. To examine such compositions singly, cannot be required; they have doubtless brighter and darker parts; but when they are once found to be generally dull, all further labour may be spared; for to what use can the work be criticized that will not be read?

The parallel elements may be represented in the following scheme:

1.	as	so
	hart	soul
	panteth	panteth (repetition)
	water brooks	Thee
2.	sick	afraid
	life	death
3.	singly	generally
	required	spared
	once found	all further
	be criticized	be read

CO-ORDINATION

Co-ordination may be regarded as an aspect of parallelism. We have seen that like meanings should be put in like constructions. By the same token, only sentence elements of like importance may be linked together as equals. Conversely, a less important element must be made subordinate to the more important. Consider the following sentence:

I stayed at home; I was ill.

What is the relation between the two statements? The writer has merely associated them. He has not defined the relation of one to the other. He might define the relationship in various ways:

Because I was ill, I stayed at home.
While I was staying at home, I was ill.
Although I stayed at home, I was ill.
Feeling ill, I stayed at home.
I stayed at home, quite ill.

Simple uncritical writing (that of a child, say) tends to present a succession of co-ordinate units: "Then the bear got hungry. He came out of his den. He remembered the honey tree. And he started walking toward the honey tree." The mature and discriminating writer indicates the relation of his statements, one to another, subordinating the less important to the more important, thus:

Having done this, she thought it prudent to drop a few words before the bishop, letting him know that she had acquainted the Puddingdale family with their good fortune so that he might perceive that he stood committed to the appointment.

The writer who points up relationships, instead of leaving them to be inferred by the reader, obviously makes the reader's task easier. He gives not only facts, but an integration of facts: the very pattern of subordination suggests an interpretation. If, however, the writer, by using subordination, assumes this burden of interpretation, he must not falsify his interpretation by careless and thoughtless subordination. He must think through the relation of part to part. Unless he thinks it through, he may write sentences like this:

My head was feeling heavy when I took an aspirin.

In this sentence the motive for the act is treated as if it were the matter of importance; the act itself has been relegated to the subordinate position. Rather than confuse the reader with a subordination which inverts the real relationship, the writer would have done better simply to have written:

My head was feeling heavy; I took an aspirin.

It is easy, of course, to see what the proper subordination would be:

Because my head was feeling heavy, I took an aspirin.

or:

When my head began to feel heavy, I took an aspirin.

Here are two further examples of improper subordination:

1. The workman snored loudly and he had a red face.

Alter to:

The workman, who had a red face, snored loudly.

or to:

The red-faced workman snored loudly.

2. Mr. Jones is our neighbor and he drove by in a large automobile.

Alter to:

Mr. Jones, who is our neighbor, drove by in a large automobile.

or to:

Mr. Jones, our neighbor, drove by in a large automobile.

Yet, though subordination is important as a means for tightening up a naïve and oversimple style, the writer ought not to be browbeaten into constant subordination. In certain contexts a good writer might prefer:

The workman snored loudly. He had a red face.

This form of the statement does bring into sharp focus the detail of the red face. It might even suggest a leisurely observer, looking on with some amusement. For discussion of some other effects secured by a simple and uncomplicated style, the reader might look at page 400.

We may sum up this topic as follows: Grammatical subordination must conform to the rhetorical sense; it must not mislead by inverting it. Positively, it is an important means for securing condensation. Careful subordination tends to give the sense of a thoughtful observer who has sifted his ideas and arranged them with precision.

LOOSE SENTENCES AND PERIODIC SENTENCES

We can view sentence structure in still another way. We can distinguish between those sentences in which the sense of the sentence is held up until almost the end (PERIODIC SENTENCES), and those in which it is not held up (LOOSE SENTENCES). Holding up the sense creates suspense: we do not know how the sentence is "coming out" until we have reached, or nearly reached, the end of it. Here are some examples:

1. "It was partly at such junctures as these and partly at quite different ones that, with the turn my matters had now taken, my predicament, as I have called it, grew most sensible."—HENRY JAMES.

If we convert the sentence to loose structure, we get something like this:

> With the turn my matters had now taken, my predicament, as I have called it, grew most sensible, partly at such junctures as these and partly at quite different ones.

2. "But of all those Highlanders who looked on the recent turn of fortune with painful apprehension the fiercest and the most powerful were the Macdonalds."—LORD MACAULAY

Converted to loose structure, the sentence reads:

> But the Macdonalds were the fiercest and the most powerful of all those Highlanders who looked on the recent turn of fortune with painful apprehension.

The loose sentence is the "normal" sentence in English; the structure of the periodic sentence, the "abnormal." As we have seen in this chapter, deviation from the norm always tends to be emphatic. The periodic sentence, in skillful hands, is powerfully emphatic. By inversion, by use of the "It was" construction, or by interposition of movable modifiers between subject and predicate, the sentence and its primary statement are made to end together. But like all deviations from the norm, the periodic sentence—and the balanced sentence—are somewhat artificial. Overused, such sentences would soon weary.

SENTENCE LENGTH AND SENTENCE VARIATION

How long should a sentence be? It may be as short as one word. "Go!" is a perfectly good sentence: it has a predicate with subject implied. On the other hand, a sentence may be forty or fifty words long; and by tacking on further elements with *and's* and *but's*, we could construct sentences of indefinite length. These are the possible extremes. But with the sentence, as with the paragraph, common sense and taste set reasonable limits. A succession of very short sentences tends to be monotonous. Extremely long sentences tend to bog the reader down in a quagmire of words.

This is not, of course, to say that the writer should not feel free to use a one-word sentence whenever he needs it, or even a long succession of short sentences to gain special effects (see p. 399 for an example). By the same token, he ought to feel free to use very long sentences to gain special effects. The following sentence from Lytton Strachey's *Queen Victoria* will illustrate.

Perhaps her fading mind called up once more the shadows of the past to float before it, and retraced, for the last time, the vanished visions of that long history—passing back and back, through the cloud of years, to older and ever older memories—to the spring woods at Osborne, so full of primroses for Lord Beaconsfield—to Lord Palmerston's queer clothes and high demeanour, and Albert's face under the green lamp, and Albert's first stag at Balmoral, and Albert in his blue and silver uniform, and the Baron coming in through a doorway, and Lord M. dreaming at Windsor with the rooks cawing in the elm-trees, and the Archbishop of Canterbury on his knees in the dawn, and the old King's turkey-cock ejaculations, and Uncle Leopold's soft voice at Claremont, and Lehzen with the globes, and her mother's feathers sweeping down towards her, and a great old repeater-watch of her father's in its tortoise-shell case, and a yellow rug, and some friendly flounces of sprigged muslin, and the trees and the grass at Kensington.—LYTTON STRACHEY: *Queen Victoria*, Chap. 10.[3]

Strachey is imagining what may have passed through the old Queen's dying mind as she slipped from consciousness. Moreover, he imagines the succession of memories as going backward in time, through those of adult life, to those of youth, and on back to the memories of childhood. The loosely linked series is justified on two counts: the memories are presented as those of a dying mind, and, as the memories go backward in time, they become those of a child. Thus dramatically considered, the jumping from scene to scene (as suggested by the dashes) and the loose tacking on of additional scenes (by *and's*) are justified. This sentence, which closes Strachey's book with what amounts to a recapitulation of Victoria's life, is thus used to gain a special effect.

Unless, however, the writer is striving for some special effect, he ought to look with some suspicion on very short and especially on very long sentences. Two considerations demand that he be suspicious of the extremes: the normal requirements and limitations of the human mind which dictate (1) how much we can take in

---

[3] From *Queen Victoria* by Lytton Strachey, copyright, 1921, by Harcourt, Brace and Company, Inc.

satisfactorily, and with satisfaction, "at one bite"; and (2) a need for variety.

Let us consider a particular case. Look back at the paragraph from Virginia Woolf quoted on page 235. These thirteen sentences range in length from three words to fifty-two. The fourth sentence is quite long; the seventh sentence, very long. But three short sentences lead up to the fourth sentence, and two short sentences separate the fourth and seventh sentences.

Santayana's essay on Dickens [4] will repay close study for the skill in which sentence variety is maintained. Santayana's sentences tend to be long. They are carefully constructed and are frequently quite complex. But he is careful not to tire the reader. The following passage will illustrate.

Having humility, that most liberating of sentiments, having a true vision of human existence and joy in that vision, Dickens had in a superlative degree the gift of humour, of mimicry, of unrestrained farce.

But after this sentence, we are given the simple statement:

He was the perfect comedian.

And having thus had time to catch our breaths, we are ready to go on with "When people say Dickens . . ."

Alternation of long and short sentences is but one means, however, by which to secure variety. Another, and a most important means, consists in varying the structure of the sentence. The examples from Santayana will illustrate: the sentence "He was the perfect comedian" is not only shorter than the sentence that precedes it; it represents a return to the simplest type of structure (subject + predicate + predicate complement) after the quite complex structure of the preceding sentence.

Sentences that repeat a pattern become monotonous. Here is an example:

I was twenty that April and I made the glen my book. I idled over it. I watched the rhododendron snow its petals on the dark pools that spun them round in a swirl of brown foam and beached them on a tiny coast glittering with mica and fool's gold. I got it by heart, however, the dripping rocks, the ferny grottos, the eternal freshness, the sense of loam, of

[4] "Dickens," from *Soliloquies in England and Later Soliloquies* by George Santayana.

deep sweet decay, of a chain of life continuous and rich with the ages. I gathered there the walking fern that walks across its little forest world by striking root with its long tips, tip to root and root to tip walking away from the localities that knew it once. I was aware that the walking fern has its oriental counterpart. I knew also that Shortia, the flower that was lost for a century after Michaux found it *"dans les hautes montagnes de Carolinie,"* has its next of kin upon the mountains of Japan. I sometimes met mountain people hunting for ginseng for the Chinese market; long ago the Chinese all but exterminated that herbalistic panacea of theirs, and now they turn for it to the only other source, the Appalachians.

The "I was—I idled—I gathered" formula is relieved somewhat by the long descriptive phrases and relative clauses. Even so, it is irritatingly monotonous. Here is the way in which Donald Culross Peattie actually wrote the passage:

The glen was my book, that April I was twenty. I idled over it, watching the rhododendron snow its petals on the dark pools that spun them round in a swirl of brown foam and beached them on a tiny coast glittering with mica and fool's gold. But I got it by heart, the dripping rocks, the ferny grottos, the eternal freshness, the sense of loam, of deep sweet decay, of a chain of life continuous and rich with the ages. The walking fern I gathered there, that walks across its little forest world by striking root with its long tips, tip to root and root to tip walking away from the localities that knew it once, has its oriental counterpart; of that I was aware. And I knew that Shortia, the flower that was lost for a century after Michaux found it, *"dans les hautes montagnes de Caroline,"* has its next of kin upon the mountains of Japan. Sometimes I met mountain people hunting for ginseng for the Chinese market; long ago the Chinese all but exterminated that herbalistic panacea of theirs, and now they turn for it to the only other source, the Appalachians.—DONALD CULROSS PEATTIE: *Flowering Earth,* Chap. 12.[5]

There are many ways in which to vary sentence structure. Nearly everything said earlier in this chapter can be brought to bear on this problem. We can invert the normal pattern, or rearrange the pattern to throw emphasis on what is normally the subject or complement; we can subordinate severely or rather lightly. Most of all, we can dispose the modifiers, particularly the movable modifiers, so as to vary the pattern almost infinitely. Variety is, of

[5] From *Flowering Earth* by Donald Culross Peattie. Copyright, 1939, by Donald Culross Peattie. Courtesy of G. P. Putnam's Sons.

course, never to be the overriding consideration. A sentence ought to take its characteristic shape primarily in its own right: the structure best adapted to its particular job. The writer will usually find that he is thoroughly occupied in discharging this obligation. Yet it is well to remind ourselves here again of the claims of the whole composition. We never write a "collection of sentences"—we write an essay, a theme, a total composition. The good sentence honors the claims exerted upon it by the total composition. And in our writing, and especially in our *rewriting*, we need to see that we have avoided irritating monotony of sentence length or of sentence structure.

SUMMARY

A SENTENCE is a complete thought expressed through a PREDICATE. In this chapter we are primarily concerned with the sentence as a rhetorical unit: that is, with the effectiveness of various kinds of sentences. Yet the terms UNITY, COHERENCE, and EMPHASIS, though primarily rhetorical terms, have their grammatical equivalents. A sentence is more than a vague cluster of ideas: its grammatical completeness (*unity*) requires a certain kind of *coherence* of parts (subject, predicate, complements, modifiers) organized around a point of *emphasis,* a focus of interest, which is indicated by the finite verb.

In the normal sentence the basic constituents of the sentence are arranged in a fixed order:

1. Subject + verb + indirect object (if any) + direct object or other verb complements (if any)

2a. Adjectives precede the substantive they modify. (Predicate adjectives are governed by rule 1.)

2b. Adjectival phrases and clauses follow the substantive they modify.

3a. Adverbs and adverbial modifiers (plus participial phrases) are not fixed as to position, but movable.

3b. Movable modifiers placed at the beginning or end of a sentence modify the whole sentence; placed internally, they modify the relation between the words preceding and the words following them.

Deviations from the normal pattern show EMPHASIS, and like other emphatic devices are to be used sparingly and with caution.

Sentence structure also may be viewed in terms of PARALLELISM and CO-ORDINATION.

Parallelism: like ideas demand like grammatical constructions.

Co-ordination: only elements of like importance are to be linked as equals; the less important element is to be subordinated to the more important.

Violation of these principles results in sentences that are not only ineffective and awkward but grammatically incorrect. But we can *stress* these principles, if we like, for positive rhetorical effect. The consequent variation from the normal sentence is, like all departures from the norm, emphatic. The PERIODIC SENTENCE (in which the sense of the sentence is held up until the end) is emphatic in the same way and for the same reason. These more consciously rhetorical types of sentence structure quickly lose their power when overused.

The writer will do well to master the normal pattern of sentence structure. There is nothing to be ashamed of in its sturdy simplicity. It will constitute, as it ought to constitute, the staple of his prose. But, just in proportion as the writer grasps the normal pattern *plainly as a norm,* he is enabled to use effectively departures from the norm—both for the expressiveness of the particular sentence and for general sentence variety. He can, first of all, try to place his movable modifiers with more care. He can occasionally vary the basic pattern itself in order to emphasize a particular sentence element—the more safely if he knows that his variation is for the sake of emphasis. He can occasionally experiment with the more elaborate departures from the norm such as the balanced and periodic sentences.

Style

GENERAL DEFINITION OF STYLE

WE USE the general term STYLE to indicate the manner in which something is said or done. We talk, for instance, of a pole vaulter's style; or we speak of an old style of handwriting; we talk about a coat or a dress of a certain style; and accordingly we speak of a writer's style—his manner of saying a thing—his special way of expressing an idea. But it is plain that we use the term loosely and generally. Style evidently can mean a great many different things.

A discussion of style had better begin, therefore, by making perfectly clear how the term is to be used. We have already suggested that style is used to indicate "how" a thing is said as distinguished from "what" is said. Suppose we want someone to shut the door. We can speak in a courteous or in an abrupt manner; we can make a request or a demand: we might say, "I expect you would like to close that door," or "Would you mind shutting that door," or "Shut that door now!" All three sentences have the same "content"; "what" they say is much the same; but the style, the manner, varies a great deal.

The way in which a thing is said evidently qualifies *what* is said: that is, style helps define and determine content. For the practicing writer, it is on this level that the problem of style becomes important. He cannot say accurately what he wants to say unless he also masters the "how" of saying it. This is the problem that will largely concern us in the chapters that follow. Yet we ought to mention two other senses in which we use the word *style,* if only to isolate and emphasize the basic sense.

THREE ASPECTS OF LITERARY STYLE

First, *style* can be used to designate a manner of writing characteristic of a whole age. A writer of the sixteenth century uses a different style from that of a twentieth-century writer, or, for that matter, from a writer of the late seventeenth century. The King James Version of the Bible (1611) has "the sower went forth to sow." A modern writer would normally write "the sower went out to sow." Addison, in one of his *Spectator* papers (1711), writes: ". . . several of those Gentlemen who value themselves upon their Families, and overlook such as are bred to Trade, bear the Tools of their Forefathers in their Coats of Arms." Today we would write: ". . . gentlemen who are proud of their families and look down upon people who are in business" or perhaps "upon businessmen"; and we would have to say "on," not "in their coats of arms." Some of the writing of the past, therefore, seems as quaint to us as the fashion of dress that obtained centuries ago. This aspect of style, however, need not concern us very much. We can assume that all of us who write in the twentieth century will share certain period likenesses which will set off our writing, good and bad, from the writing of earlier periods.

Second, style can be used to designate a personal and individual manner. Two tennis players, for example, though trained under the same coach, may each have his own individual style. We may mean by style, therefore, the special way in which each writer expresses himself. We can frequently recognize something written by a friend, even though it is merely read aloud to us, because we feel that the way in which it is written reflects the friend's personality: Bill Jones would put it in just this way, whereas Jim Smith would put it in that way.

Thus far we have mentioned three levels on which one encounters the problem of style. A neat summary of the three levels is provided if we consider, in each instance, what it is that shapes the style. First, and most important, there is style as shaped by the writer's specific purpose—the choice and arrangement of words as determined by the audience addressed and the purpose at hand. Second, we have style as shaped by the writer's general environment. Third, we have style as shaped by the writer's own personality. The second of these, we have said, need not concern us very much in this book. The third is a highly pervasive thing: we shall probably do well to postpone consideration of it to Chapter 13. It is with the first—the choice and arrangement of words as an adaptation to the writer's specific purpose—that the rest of this chapter will be concerned. But at this point we ought to have a concrete illustration showing how these three levels of style are related to each other. Let us return for a moment to Bill Jones.

Our friend Bill Jones may have his own personal way of saying a thing (style as expression of personality), in spite of the fact that his way of saying it will, in some respects, resemble the way in which his contemporaries say it (style as expression of a period): but Bill Jones, nevertheless, will probably write in several different styles, as he takes into account the audience he addresses and the particular occasion on which he writes. For example, he will sometimes use a colloquial style, in conversation with his fellows; at other times, when the occasion demands a certain dignity, he may prefer to use a much more formal style. We constantly make such distinctions: a letter of application for a job demands one style; a note to an intimate friend, quite another.

STYLE AS AN INTERPLAY OF ELEMENTS

In an essay entitled "Learned Words and Popular Words," Greenough and Kittredge write: "Every educated person has at least two ways of speaking his mother tongue. The first is that which he employs in his family, among his familiar friends, and on ordinary occasions. The second is that which he uses in discoursing on more complicated subjects and in addressing persons with whom he is less intimately acquainted. It is, in short, the language which he employs when he is 'on his dignity,' as he puts on evening dress when he is going to dine. The difference between these two forms of language consists, in great measure, in a difference of vocabulary."

It should be noted that Greenough and Kittredge are careful to specify "*at least two* ways of speaking his mother tongue," for if we are to be accurate, there are many more than *two* ways of speaking it, and an even larger number of ways of writing it. Indeed, we can say that between the extremes of a highly ceremonious formality, on the one hand, and utterly intimate informality, on the other, there are hundreds of intermediate shadings. In the chapters that follow we shall want to talk about some of these shadings, and how they are produced. Greenough and Kittredge are also perfectly right in saying that it is a "difference of vocabulary" which largely determines levels of style. But, important as the choice of vocabulary is, it is only one of the many elements which go to make up a style.

The real difficulty in discussing style comes just here. Style, as was pointed out in the Introduction (p. 6), is an over-all effect. It is an effect determined by the interplay of sentence structure, vocabulary, figures of speech, rhythm, and many other elements. It is not always easy for a reader to pick out the element which is most important, or even largely important, in giving the style of the writer its special quality. It is quite impossible for a writer to produce a given quality of style by mechanically measuring out so much of this element and so much of that. A modern author has put the matter in this way: "Style is not an isolable quality of writing; it is writing itself." But if style is simply writing itself, how will it be possible to give the writer any practical pointers for developing a proper style of his own? The very complexity of the interaction of form and content, element and element, may seem to render the problem hopeless.

THE PLAN OF THE FOLLOWING CHAPTERS ON STYLE

The problem of style is certainly difficult, but it is not hopeless. Granted that the separate devices cannot finally be isolated, still nothing forbids our singling out the various elements for purposes of study. In the four chapters which follow, we shall discuss some of the more important aspects of style: DICTION (the choice of words), METAPHOR (the use of comparisons and figures of speech), TONE (the manifestation of the writer's attitude toward his material and toward his audience), and RHYTHM (the pattern of stresses and pauses); we shall also, in passing, touch on various other aspects of style. Yet, even though we must, in order to treat the subject at all, try to isolate the various means by which the writer secures his effect, we must keep reminding ourselves that they are not really "isolable." Style is an over-all quality; consequently the discussion of one aspect of style necessarily overlaps other aspects.

A concrete example will serve to illustrate this necessary overlapping. Take the indignant expression "He is a dirty rat." This sentence is certainly a humble example of style, but it will serve. For it has a certain quality which differs, say, from "The man is treacherous," or "The man has evil intentions," and that quality is the result of a complex of elements. Diction is certainly involved, but so is metaphor: the "he" in question is not literally a small, gray-furred mammal. Attitude is plainly involved, for the sentence is not so much a proposition as an expression of feeling. One could argue that even rhythm may be involved. If we compare "He is a dirty rat" with "He is a contemptible little verminous animal," we sense the difference in effect: the second expression is less violent, more considered and calculated, more grandly contemptuous than the first. It is just possible that the more elaborate and formal rhythm of the second sentence has something to do with this effect.

To sum up, all four chapters that follow have to do with style. They constitute the divisions of a general discussion of this topic; but these chapters are not offered as a logical division of the topic. They are not that. They do not constitute an exhaustive classification, nor are they mutually exclusive. They overlap at points. Still, it can be claimed that they represent a practical classification.

The obvious point at which to begin any discussion of style is with DICTION. The choice of vocabulary is primary. Moreover, the chapter on diction necessarily lays the groundwork of the chapters that follow. The chapter on METAPHOR grows naturally out of it. For metaphor, and figures of speech generally, can be regarded as extensions of words—a stretching of words beyond their literal meanings, in order to gain further expressiveness. Through metaphor the writer transcends "dictionary" meanings, bending and shaping language to his particular purpose.

The chapter of TONE, like that on metaphor, grows out of the discussion of diction. For the chapter on tone extends the discussion of the ways in which a coloring of meaning, a shading of emphasis, a hint as to attitude, may be given, not merely by a particular word (a matter discussed under diction) but also by a whole phrase, or sentence, or the total composition.

The fourth chapter in this series, "The Final Integration," is, as its title suggests, something of a summary of the problems of style. It deals with general matters of over-all effect such as RHYTHM, but more especially with the way in which a successful style is made to bear the stamp of the writer's whole personality.

We have already said that these divisions of the general topic of style do not constitute a logical classification of the various aspects of style. The reader ought at the very beginning to recognize this and to expect some necessary overlapping. But the writer has it in his power to make of this necessity a virtue if he will allow the overlapping to serve as a constant reminder that "style is not an isolable quality of writing; it is writing itself."

Diction

GOOD diction is the choice of the right words. Accurate, effective expression obviously requires the right words—the words which will represent, not nearly, not approximately, but precisely and exactly what we want to say. This is a simple rule and it covers the whole problem of writing; but in application the rule is far from simple. The good writer must choose the right words, yes; but which are the right words? The criterion for judging "rightness" is not simple but highly complex.

Now diction would be no problem if there existed for each object and each idea just one word which denoted specifically that object or idea, one name and only one name for each separate thing. Unfortunately, language is not like that. Words are not strictly denotative. Some words in English, it is true, do represent the only name we have for a particular object or substance. *Lemming*, for example, is the only specific name for a certain small mouse-like rodent; *purine* is the only specific name of a compound whose chemical formula is $C_5H_4N_4$. The ideal scientific language would be a language of pure denotation. But the language of pure science (that of mathematics, say) constitutes a very special case.

DENOTATION AND CONNOTATION

Actually the writer faces quite another kind of situation: instead of one word and only one word for each thing, he ordinarily finds competing for his attention a number of words all of which denote exactly or approximately the same thing. Moreover, even those words which have exactly the same DENOTATION (that is, those which explicitly refer to the same thing) may have different CONNO-TATIONS: they may *imply* different shadings of meaning. (Every word has one *denotation*, but probably more than one *connotation*.) For example, *brightness, radiance, effulgence, brilliance* may be said to have the same denotation, but there is a considerable difference among them in what they connote. *Radiance*, for example, implies beams radiating from a source, as the words *brilliance* or *brightness* do not. *Brilliance*, on the other hand, suggests an intensity of light which *effulgence* and *brightness* do not. Again, *brightness* is a more homely, everyday word than are *radiance, brilliance*, and *effulgence*. These are only a few suggested contrasts among the connotations of these words, all of which describe a quality of light. Varying connotations in words with the same denotation may also be illustrated from words which refer to concrete objects. Compare the simple words *bucket* and *pail*. The denotations are much the same. We might apply either word to name one and the same vessel. But in present-day America, at least, *bucket* is more likely to be the ordinary word, with associations of everyday activity, whereas *pail* will seem a little more old-fashioned and endowed with more "poetic" suggestions. It will connote for some readers a bygone era of pretty milkmaids in an idyllic setting. But not necessarily, someone will exclaim, remembering the sentimental song entitled, "The Old Oaken *Bucket*." For words change from period to period and their connotations change, as a rule, much more rapidly than do their denotations.

Words, then, are not static, changeless counters, but are affected intimately, especially on the level of connotation, by the changing, developing, restless life of the men themselves who use them. Some words wear out and lose their force. Some words go downhill and lose respectability. Other words rise in the scale, and, like *mob*, which was no better than slang in the eighteenth century, acquire respectability.

In 1710 Jonathan Swift concocted the following letter to illustrate some of the faults in the English of his day:

Sir,

I *couldn't* get the things you sent for all *about Town.*—I *thot* to *ha'* come down myself, and then *I'd ha' brout 'um;* but I *han't don't*, and I *can't do't,* that's *pozz.*—Tom begins to *g'imself airs* because *he's* going with the *plenipo's.*—'Tis said, the *French* King will *bamboozl' us agen,* which *causes many speculations.* The *Jacks,* and others of that *kidney,* are very *uppish,* and *alert upon't,* as you may see by their *phizz's.*—Will Hazzard has got the *hipps,* having lost *to the tune of* five hundr'd pound, *tho* he understands play very well, *nobody better.* He has promis't me upon *rep,* to leave off play; but you know 'tis a weakness *he's* too apt to *give into, tho* he has as much wit as any man, *nobody more.* He has lain *incog* ever since.—The *mobb's* very quiet with us now.—I believe you *thot* I *banter'd* you in my last like a *country put.*—I *sha'n't* leave Town this month, &c.

Swift proceeds to comment on this letter, among other things on its diction:

The third refinement observable in the letter I send you, consists in the choice of certain words invented by some *pretty* fellows; such as *banter, bamboozle, country put,* and *kidney,* as it is there applied; some of which are now struggling for the vogue, and others are in possession of it. I have done my utmost for some years past to stop the progress of *mobb* and *banter,* but have been plainly borne down by numbers, and betrayed by those who promised to assist me.

The process of growth and decay in language is so strong that many words in the course of generations have shifted, not only their connotations, but their denotations as well; and some have even reversed their original meanings. Later in this chapter we shall have occasion to return to the history of words when we discuss the use of the dictionary. At this point, suffice it to say that the writer must take into account the connotations of a word as well as its precise denotation. He has the task of controlling words in two dimensions. Thus, in a romantic tale one might appropriately use the word *steed* rather than *horse.* But in ordinary contexts one certainly would not say or write, "Saddle my *steed*"—unless he were being deliberately playful or ironic. On the other hand there are still other contexts in which, instead of the rather neutral word, *horse,* it might be appropriate to use words like *plug* or *nag*—terms which are as derisive or humorous in tone as *steed* is poetic and "literary."

TWO DISTINCTIONS: CONCRETE-ABSTRACT AND SPECIFIC-GENERAL

There are, of course, words whose connotations are not important. Obviously this will be true of the so-called empty words like *and, if, the, however.* But even among the "full" words, some will be much richer in connotations than others. As one would expect, the richest and most colorful words will tend to be those that are CONCRETE and SPECIFIC; the most nearly neutral and colorless, those that are ABSTRACT and GENERAL. For example, *peach, pear, quince, apple, apricot* are concrete and specific. Why do we call these words both *concrete* and *specific?* Let us take the easier distinction first. *Peach, pear, quince, apple,* and *apricot* name specific members of a class of objects, the general name of which is *fruit. Peach,* therefore, is specific; *fruit,* general. Again: *ship* is a general word, but *brig, schooner, lugger, yawl,* and *brigantine* are specific: they are members of a class of which *ship* is the class name.

But why do we call *peach, pear . . . apricot* concrete? The distinction between concrete and abstract has to do with the treatment of qualities. *Concrete* comes from a Latin word that means "grown together"; *abstract,* from another Latin word that means "taken away." The word *peach* certainly implies qualities: a certain shape, a certain color, a certain sweetness. But *peach* implies these qualities as "grown together"—as we actually find them embodied in a peach. We can, however, abstract (take away) these various qualities from the actual peach, and refer to them in isolation: *sweetness, fuzziness, softness.* If we do so, we get a set of abstract words. *Sweetness,* for instance, isolates a quality common to peaches (and to many other things): the quality is thought of as an idea in itself. To give other examples: *heat* is an abstract word, but *furnace* is concrete; *force* is abstract, but *dynamo* is concrete; *insanity* is abstract, but *madman* is concrete.

Words that refer to ideas, qualities, and characteristics *as such* are usually abstract. Words that name classes of objects and actions are usually general. Words that refer to particular objects and actions are usually concrete *and* specific. (In this connection, the writer might reread the discussion of the process of abstraction on page 33.)

It ought to be plain that the two classifications just discussed are not mutually exclusive, and that consequently the same word may occupy two categories. *Peach* and *pear,* as we have seen, are concrete *and* specific. *Ship,* since it signifies an object but also names a class of objects, is both concrete and general. In the same way, abstract words may be either general or specific. *Courtesy, kindness,* and *bravery* are abstract words: they denote qualities of conduct. But in relation to *gentlemanliness,* another abstract word, they are specific; for *courtesy, kindness,* and *bravery* are specific elements of the more general virtue *gentlemanliness. Courtesy,* therefore, is abstract and specific; *gentlemanliness,* abstract and general.

This last example suggests a further point: *general* and *abstract* are not to be applied absolutely but in relation to other words. Some words are more general, or more abstract, than others. *Coat,* for example, is more specific than *garment,* for a coat is a kind of garment; but *coat* is, on the other hand, more general than *hunting jacket,* for a hunting jacket is a kind of coat.

THE MISUSE OF ABSTRACT AND GENERAL WORDS

Much writing that is woolly and clouded, difficult to read, clogged and ineffective, is writing that is filled with general and abstract words. For example: "Quite significantly, the emphasis is being placed upon vocational intelligence, which is based upon adequate occupational information for all pupils in secondary schools. . . . This emphasis upon vocational guidance for the purpose of making young people intelligent concerning the world of occupations and the requirements for entering occupations need not conflict seriously with other views of guidance that take into account everything pertaining to the education of the pupil."

There are a number of things wrong with this flabby statement, but, among other things, there is the large number of abstract words. The author might have written: "High schools today insist that the student learn enough about jobs to choose his own job wisely. Tommy and Mary Anne need to learn what various jobs pay, what training they require, and what kinds of people find them interesting. Tommy and Mary Anne can learn these things while they are learning the other things that schools are supposed to teach. Both kinds of learning are preparations for life, and one need not interfere with the other." The rewritten version still makes use of general and abstract words (*training, preparation,* and so on); but some of the cloudiest of the abstractions (*vocational intelligence, occupational information*) have been removed, and the rewritten version is not only simpler, but has more force.

We are not to assume, however, that concrete and specific words are somehow in themselves "better" than abstract and general words. They are better for some purposes; for others, not. Many subjects require general and abstract words.

For example, compare these two ways of saying the same thing. (1) "A child needs sympathy." (2) "A child does not like frowns. Cold looks cow him. He is fearful when he hears harsh words." The second account is long-winded; even so, the concrete words do not manage to give fully the meaning of the one abstract word *sympathy.*

Or, compare (1) "He lived in a house of medium size." (2) "His home did not have the suburban air of a bungalow, and it certainly had nothing of the rustic style of a lodge. It was much smaller than a mansion, but somewhat larger than a cottage." *Mansion, cottage, bungalow,* and *lodge* (not to mention *cabin, hut, villa,* and *château*) are overspecific for the writer's purpose here: he needs the simple, general term *house.* Our pronouns provide another illustration. The English personal pronouns sometimes prove to be overspecific. In some contexts, it would be most convenient if we had a pronoun which could mean either "he" or "she" ("his" or "her," "him" or "her"), without forcing us either to specify, or to use the masculine form with the understanding that it applied to either sex: "Someone has left his or her pen" (or "his pen").

The writer cannot, and need not try to, avoid abstract and general words. But he ought not to fall into the slovenly habit of using them without thought. In any case, he should remember that a sprinkling of concrete and specific words can be used to lighten the numbing weight of cumulative abstractions. To illustrate, compare (1) "A child needs sympathy. Tolerance of his mistakes and the sense of understanding and comradeship provide the proper stimulus for his developing personality. Conversely, an environment defective in sympathy and understanding can be positively thwarting; it can lead to repressions and thus lay the foundation for ruinous personality problems." (2) "A child needs sympathy. He didn't intend to smash the vase or to hurt the cat when he pulled its tail.

Tolerance of mistakes and some sense of understanding is necessary if he is to feel that he is a comrade. Acceptance as a comrade stimulates him to become a better comrade. He grows and develops toward responsibility. But he finds it hard to grow normally in a cold and repressive atmosphere. The meaningless spanking—meaningless to him, since he had no intention of breaking the vase—drives him in on himself. He becomes confused and repressed. Some of these confusions and repressions may linger into adult life."

In choosing our words, the overriding consideration, of course, will always be the particular effect which the writer wishes to secure. Description and narration, for example, thrive on the concrete and the specific. Notice the number of concrete and specific terms in the following passage:

He knew the inchoate sharp excitement of hot dandelions in young Spring grass at noon; the smell of cellars, cobwebs, and built-on secret earth; in July, of watermelons bedded in sweet hay, inside a farmer's covered wagon; of cantaloupe and crated peaches; and the scent of orange rind, bitter-sweet, before a fire of coals.—THOMAS WOLFE: *Look Homeward, Angel*, Chap. 8.

Exposition and argument, on the other hand, by their very nature, call for a diction in which general and abstract words are important.

Marx's interpretation of the past is explicit and realistic; his forecast of the future seems to me vague and idealistic. I have called it utopian, but you object to that word. I do not insist on it. I will even surrender the word "idealistic." But the point is this. Marx finds that in the past the effective force that has determined social change is the economic class conflict. He points out that this economic class conflict is working to undermine our capitalistic society. Very well. If then I project this explanation of social changes into the future, what does it tell me? It seems to tell me that there will be in the future what there has been in the past—an endless economic class conflict, and endless replacement of one dominant class by another, an endless transformation of institutions and ideas in accordance with the changes effected by the class conflict.—CARL BECKER: "The Marxian View of History." [1]

Scientific statements, for the reasons given on pages 33-36, may require a diction that is still more abstract and general. To cite

[1] From *Every Man His Own Historian: Essays on History and Politics* by Carl L. Becker. Copyright, 1935, by F. S. Crofts & Company, Inc. Permission granted by Appleton-Century-Crofts, Inc.

an extreme example, "The square of the hypotenuse of a right triangle is equaf to the sum of the squares of the other two sides." For its purpose, the diction here is admirable. The statement concerns itself, not with a triangular field or a triangular box or a triangular piece of metal. It deals with triangularity itself. The *right triangle* of this statement is an abstraction: so also are *square*, *hypotenuse*, and even *sides*, for the "sides of a right triangle" are abstractions too. They are not sides of wood or metal or plastic, but pure distances between defined points. We have here a general proposition that must hold true for all right triangles. The diction used is therefore properly abstract and general.

With terms of this extreme degree of abstraction, connotations disappear altogether. Exact science needs no colorful words. Scientific terms aspire to become pure denotations: terms that are inflexibly fixed, terms completely devoid of all blurring overtones. Science strictly conceived not only does not need connotative words; the connotations would constitute a positive nuisance.

LANGUAGE GROWTH BY EXTENSION OF MEANING

We have said that a word not only has a specific meaning (denotation) but also implied meanings (connotations). The connotations are obviously less definite than the denotation, and therefore less stable and more amenable to change. In scientific language, as we have seen, the denotations are rigidly stabilized and the hazy and shifting connotations are, in so far as possible, eliminated. In a colorful and racy use of language, just the reverse is the case. The connotations are rich and important. We are tempted to use a word, not LITERALLY (that is, adhering strictly to the denotation), but FIGURATIVELY, stressing some connotation of the word. It is through such a process that words have shifted their meanings in the past; but this process of extension of meaning is constantly at work in our own time. Let us consider an illustration of the process.

MEANINGS EXTENDED BY ANALOGY

The casual and unthinking view of language sees each word as fastened neatly and tightly to a certain specific object: "cat" means a certain kind of small, furry mammal that purrs, likes cream, and is the natural enemy of mice; "ladder" means a contraption consisting of parallel strips to which are fastened crossbars on which we rest our feet as we climb the ladder; "spade" means an instrument for digging in the earth. But words are not actually so neatly fastened to the objects for which they stand. Even when we are determined to speak forthrightly, and "call a spade a spade," we rarely do so. It is against the nature of language that we should be able to do so.

For example, Anna, who is determined to call a spade a spade, says: "I'll tell you frankly why I don't like Mary. Yesterday she saw a ladder in my stocking and a few minutes later I overheard her telling Jane that I was always slovenly. That's typical of Mary. She is a perfect cat." But obviously one is not calling a spade a *spade* when one calls a female human being a *cat,* or a special kind of unraveling in a stocking a *ladder.*

Cat and *ladder* are not being used literally here: their meanings have been extended on the basis of analogy. In the case of *ladder,* the extension of meaning is very easy to grasp: a "run," with the horizontal threads crossing the gap between the sides of the run, does resemble a ladder. *Cat* represents a slightly further extension: a cat, furry and soft, yet armed with sharp claws which it conceals but can bare in an instant, may be thought to resemble a woman who is outwardly friendly but is capable of inflicting wounding comments.

The situation we have just considered is thoroughly typical. Many common words have been extended from their original meanings in just this fashion. We speak of the "eye" of a needle, the "mouth" of a river, the "legs" of a chair, the "foot" of a bed. The hole in the end of a needle might have been given a special name; but instead, men called it an "eye" because of its fancied likeness to the human eye. So too with examples such as these: a *keen* mind, a *bright* disposition, a *sunny* smile, a *black* look. Someone saw an analogy between the way in which a *keen* blade cut through wood and the way in which a good mind penetrated the problem with which it was concerned. The smile obviously does not really shed sunlight, but it may seem to affect one as sunlight does, and in a way quite the opposite of the black look.

But the point to be made here does not concern the basis for the analogy, whether of physical resemblance (the *jaws* of a vice), similarity of function (*key* to a puzzle), similarity of effect (a *shining* example), or what not. The point to be made is rather that people normally use words in this way, extending, stretching, twisting their meanings so that they apply to other objects or actions or situations than those to which they originally applied. This is the METAPHORI-CAL process. The essence of metaphor inheres in this transfer of meaning—in the application of a word that literally means one thing to something else.

Thus far we have taken our illustrations from common words. But less common words and learned words will illustrate the same process of extension of meaning. Indeed, most of our words that express complex ideas and relationships have been built up out of simpler words. For example, we say "His generosity caused him to overlook my fault." *Overlook* here means to "disregard or ignore indulgently." But *overlook* is obviously made up of the simple words *look* and *over*. To look over an object may imply that one does not let his gaze rest upon that object: his eyes pass over it without noticing it. *Overlook*, then, in the sense of "disregard," is an extension and specialization of one of the implied meanings of *look over*. We have said "one of the meanings," for *look over* obviously implies other possible meanings. (Compare the archaic sense of *overlook* in the passage quoted from Addison, p. 330.) Consider the nearly parallel expression "to see over." From it we get the word *oversee*. This word normally means today *to direct, to supervise*—something quite different from "overlook." *Supervise* is built out of the same concepts as *oversee*, for *super* in Latin means *over*, and *-vise* comes from the Latin verb *videre* (past participle *visus*) which means *to see*. A bishop, by the way, is literally an *overseer*. For *bishop* comes originally from two Greek words: *epi*, which means *over*, and *skopein* which means *to look*. Thus, such diverse words as *overlook, oversee, overseer, supervise,* and *bishop* represent particular extensions of much the same primitive literal meaning.

THE DICTIONARY: A RECORD OF MEANINGS

The etymology (that is, the derivation and history) of a word is often highly interesting in itself, but knowledge of word origins is also of great practical usefulness. The full mastery of a particular word frequently entails knowing its root meaning. Possessing that meaning, we acquire a firm grasp on its various later meanings, for we can see them as extended and specialized meanings that have grown out of the original meaning.

Here, for example, is what *The American College Dictionary* gives for the word *litter:* [2]

> **lit·ter** (lĭt′or), *n.* **1.** things scattered about; scattered rubbish. **2.** a condition of disorder or untidiness. **3.** a number of young brought forth at one birth. **4.** a framework of canvas stretched between two parallel bars, for the transportation of the sick and the wounded. **5.** a vehicle carried by men or animals, consisting of a bed or couch, often covered and curtained, suspended between shafts. **6.** straw, hay, etc., used as bedding for animals, or as a protection for plants. **7.** the rubbish of dead leaves and twigs scattered upon the floor of the forest. —*v.t.* **8.** to strew (a place) with scattered objects. **9.** to scatter (objects) in disorder. **10.** to be strewed about (a place) in disorder (fol. by *up*). **11.** to give birth to (young): said chiefly of animals. **12.** to supply (an animal) with litter for a bed. **13.** to use (straw, hay, etc.) for litter. **14.** to cover (a floor, etc.) with litter, or straw, hay, etc. —*v.i.* **15.** to give birth to a litter. [ME *litere*, t. AF, der. *lit* bed, g. L *lectus*] —Syn. **3.** See **brood.**

The word is a noun (*n.*). Seven meanings for the noun are given. But the word is also a transitive verb (*v.t.*). Seven meanings are given for *litter* as a transitive verb. But *litter* is also an intransitive verb (*v.i.*), for which one meaning is given.[3] The word occurs in Middle English (ME *litere*), was taken from Anglo-French (t. AF), was derived from a word meaning bed (der. *lit* bed) and goes back finally to Latin bed, *lectus* (g. L *lectus*). Synonyms (words of nearly the same meaning) for the third meaning of *litter* will be found under *brood* (Syn. 3. See **brood**).

Let us consider the various meanings given for *litter*. At first glance there seems little to connect meaning 2, "a condition of disorder or untidiness" with 3, "a number of young brought forth at a birth," and even less with meaning 4, "a framework of canvas

[2] From *The American College Dictionary*, ed. by Clarence L. Barnhart, copyright, 1947, by Random House, Inc.

[3] We have said earlier (p. 336) that every word has *one* denotation, but probably more than one connotation. Are we to regard the fifteen meanings given here for *litter* as fifteen denotations, with the further consequence that we are to think of the dictionary's account as an account of fifteen different words? Probably so, particularly in view of the fact that some of the meanings are so far apart: i.e., (1) scattered rubbish and (3) a number of young brought forth at a birth. But if we think of the original meaning (*bed*) as the denotation (p. 342), then we can understand how the fifteen meanings specified are related to this root meaning, as implied meanings (connotations) of a word are related to its denotation.

. . . for the transportation of the sick and the wounded." But once we grasp the fact that *litter* comes originally from a Latin word meaning *bed*, it is fairly easy to see how the various apparently unconnected meanings of *litter* developed. Meanings 4 [4] and 5 obviously refer to special sorts of portable beds; and the term *bedding* in definition 6 provides a link to meanings 12, 13, and 14. For if beds originally consisted of straw or rushes heaped together, it is easy to see how any scattering of straw or hay might come to be called a *litter*, and the process of strewing it a process of *littering*. Meanings 1, 2, 8, and 9 are obvious further extensions, for in these meanings the emphasis has been shifted from the purpose of making a kind of bed to an aimless and untidy strewing about.

Meanings 3, 11, and 15 derive from the original meaning, bed, by another chain of development. The mother animal frequently makes a sort of rude bed in which she lies to give birth, and by association the rude bed (*litter*) comes to be used for what is found in the bed, the young animals themselves.

Let us consider one further example, this time from *Webster's Collegiate Dictionary*. Here is what the dictionary gives for the common word *sad:*

> **sad** (săd), *adj.;* SAD′DER (-ĕr); SAD′DEST. [AS. *sæd* satisfied, sated.] **1.** *Archaic.* Firmly established. **2.** Affected with or expressive of grief; downcast; gloomy. **3.** Characterized by or associated with sorrow; melancholy; as, the *sad* light of the moon. **4.** Afflictive; grievous. **5.** Dull; somber; — of colors. **6. a** Shocking; wicked; — often playfully. **b** *Slang.* Inferior. — **Syn.** Solemn, sober; sorrowful, dejected, depressed. — **Ant.** Joyous; gay.

By permission. From Webster's Collegiate Dictionary
Fifth Edition
Copyright, 1936, 1941, by G. & C. Merriam Co.

The word is an adjective (*adj.*). The forms of the comparative and superlative degrees are given; then its derivation (from Anglo-Saxon *saed*). Next, the dictionary lists five meanings, one of which it designates as archaic (1) and another as slang (6*b*). There follows a list of synonyms (words of approximately the same meaning) and of antonyms (words of opposed meaning).

Even so brief an account as this suggests a history of shifting meanings. Inspection of a larger dictionary such as *Webster's New International Dictionary* or the *Oxford English Dictionary* (*A New*

---

[4] The meanings are *not* numbered in the order of probable development.

English Dictionary), with its fuller information as to the derivation of the word and its finer discrimination of meanings (including the various earlier meanings), enables us to make out a detailed history of the meanings of the word.

Sad is closely related to the German word *satt* (full to repletion) and to the Latin word *satis* (enough) from which we get such modern English words as *satiate* and *satisfied*. But a man who has had a big dinner is torpid and heavy, not lively or restless, and so *sad* came to carry the suggestion of *calm, stable, earnest*. Shakespeare frequently uses it to mean the opposite of "trifling" or "frivolous." But a person who seems thus sober and serious *may* be so because he is grieved or melancholy, and the word gradually took on its modern meaning, "mournful" or "grieved." But we must not end this account without mentioning other lines of development. The sense of *torpid* or *heavy* was extended from animate beings, which can eat to repletion, to inanimate things which cannot—to bread, for example, that fails to rise, or to a heavy laundry iron. (The reader should look up, in this connection, the word *sadiron*.)

Meaning 5 (dull; somber;—of colors) represents still another such extension. It means the kind of color which a sobersides (as opposed to a gay and sprightly person) would wear—dull, sober colors.

Has the process of extension now ceased? Hardly. Meaning 6*a* represents a fairly late instance of it. In mock deprecation, a young fellow might be called "a sad young dog"—as if his conduct caused horror and grief. Meaning 6*b* is a later extension still, one that has not yet been approved by the dictionary as "good English." In such a phrase as "sad sack" this meaning of *sad* has temporarily gained wide currency (though in America we tend to prefer the word *sorry*: a sorry team, a sorry outfit, a sorry job). If meaning 6*b* ever establishes itself, the dictionary will presumably remove the characterization "slang." (Some terms which began as slang have found their way into the language and into good usage; but a vastly greater number have enjoyed a brief popularity, have been discarded, and are now forgotten.)

The definition of a word is, then, a somewhat more complex business than one might suppose. There is frequently not just "the" meaning, but interrelated sets of meanings, some of which are current and some of which are not; some of which are established and some of which are not; some of which have been accepted into good society and some of which are merely clinging to the fringes of society. A word which is appropriate in one context obviously might be grossly out of place in another.

THE COMPANY A WORD KEEPS: COLLOQUIAL, INFORMAL, AND FORMAL

Earlier, in discussing the connotations of words, we touched briefly upon the way in which connotations may determine the appropriateness of a word for a particular context (p. 337). The word *steed*, we saw, would be proper for some contexts, *nag* for others, and *horse* for still others. But the problem of appropriateness is important and deserves fuller treatment.

In the first place, there is what may be called the dignity and social standing of the word. Like human beings, a word tends to be known by the company it keeps. Words like *caboodle* and *gumption* are good colloquial words and perfectly appropriate to the informal give-and-take of conversation. But they would be out of place in a dignified and formal utterance. For example, a speech welcoming a great public figure in which he was complimented on his "statesman-like gumption" would be absurd. To take another example, many of us use the slang term *guy*, and though, like much slang, it has lost what pungency it may once have had, its rather flippant breeziness is not inappropriate in some contexts. But it would be foolish to welcome our elder statesman by complimenting him on being a "wise and venerable guy." The shoe, it is only fair to say, can pinch the other foot. Certain literary and rather highfalutin terms, in a *colloquial* context, sound just as absurd. We do not praise a friend for his "dexterity" or for his "erudition"— not at least when we meet him on the street, or chat with him across the table.

The fact that words are known by the company they keep does not, however, justify snobbishness in diction. Pomposity is, in the end, probably in even worse taste than the blurting out of a slang term on a formal occasion. Tact and common sense have to be used. But the comments made above do point to certain levels of usage of which most of us are already more or less aware. The various levels of diction (and their necessary overlappings) are conveniently represented in the following diagram: [5]

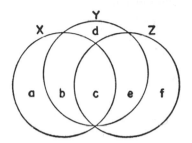

The three circles X, Y, Z, represent the three sets of language habits indicated above.
X—formal literary English, the words, the expressions, and the structures one finds in serious books.
Y—colloquial English, the words, expressions, and the structures of the informal but polite conversation of cultivated people.
Z—illiterate English, the words, the expressions, and the structures of the language of the uneducated.
b, c, and e represent the overlappings of the three types of English.
c—that which is common to all three: formal literary English, colloquial English, and illiterate English.
b—that which is common to both formal literary English and colloquial English.
e—that which is common to both colloquial English and illiterate English.
a, d, and f represent those portions of each type of English that are peculiar to that particular set of language habits.

In this matter of levels of diction, the dictionary can be of real help. It marks as such, colloquial words, slang, technical words, and so on. Yet even recourse to the dictionary is not a substitute for the writer's developing a feeling for language. In this matter the dictionary can help, but wide reading can help even more.

HOW CONNOTATIONS CONTROL MEANINGS

Thus far we have seen how connotations determine what may be called the social tone of a word. But we must go on to consider the very important way in which the connotations actually determine, though sometimes subtly, the effect of the word—that is, the way in which the connotations actually determine meaning. In our

[5] From *The American College Dictionary*, ed. by Clarence L. Barnhart, copyright, 1947, by Random House, Inc.

time especially, propaganda and advertising have made this whole matter very important.

A group of words having more or less the same denotation may range in their connotations from highly favorable to highly unfavorable. For example, we may call an agriculturist a "farmer," a "planter," a "tiller of the soil," or, in more exalted fashion, "the partner of Mother Nature"; but we can also refer to him as a "rube," a "hayseed," or a "hick." Few of our words merely *name* something. They imply a judgment about its value as well. They make a favorable or an unfavorable evaluation. Consider, for example, the following table of rough synonyms:

Favorable	Neutral	Unfavorable
highest military leadership	general staff	army brass
motor sedan, cabriolet, convertible	automobile	jallopy
special agent	informer	stool pigeon
expert advisers	technical advisers	brain trust
cherub	child	brat
Democratic (or Republican) statesman	party leader	political boss
self-control	discipline	regimentation

By choosing terms with the right connotations, one can easily color his whole account of a man or a happening or an idea. Much of the effectiveness of this method depends upon the fact that the writer ostensibly is only pointing to certain things, only naming them: the damaging (or ennobling) connotations are, as it were, smuggled in surreptitiously. This is the method frequently used by a writer like Westbrook Pegler or H. L. Mencken. Notice how heavily the following passage from one of Mencken's essays leans upon this device. (The italics are supplied by the present authors.)

"The ride of the Valkyrie" has a certain intrinsic value as pure music; played by a competent orchestra it may give civilized pleasure. But as it is commonly performed in an opera house, with a *posse* of fat *beldames* throwing themselves about the stage, it can produce the effect of a dose of ipecacua. The sort of person who actually delights in such spectacles is the sort of person who delights in plush furniture. Such half-wits are in a majority in every opera house west of the Rhine. They go to the opera, not to hear music, not even to hear bad music, but merely to see a more or less obscene *circus.*—H. L. MENCKEN: "Opera," *Prejudices: Second Series.*[6]

The power of connotations is also illustrated by our recourse to EUPHEMISMS. Certain words, even necessary words, which refer to unpleasant things, are avoided in favor of softening expressions or indirect references. "Bastard," in many contexts, is felt to be too brutal, and so "illegitimate" is substituted for it. Even a word like "died" may be avoided in favor of "deceased," or "passed away," or "went to his reward." Undertakers have taken to calling themselves "morticians," and butchers in some parts of the country prefer to be known as "meat-cutters." Whatever one may think of the substitutions, they at least testify to the strength of connotations, and the desire of men to avoid words with unpleasant or disparaging associations.

Another obvious means of influencing the reader's attitude is the use of what I. A. Richards calls "projectile" adjectives: that is, adjectives which function, not so much to give an objective description, as to express the writer's or speaker's feelings. For example, a child will say "a mean *old* teacher," whether the teacher is old or young. "Beautiful," "fine," "nice," "miserable," "great," "grand" are typical projectile adjectives. The "*miserable* wretch" may actually be smiling happily. The woman who has just been called "a *great* little wife" may be large or small. *Great* and *little* here do not measure size—they are projectile adjectives.

How some of these adjectives (and the adverbs derived from them) came to acquire their expressive force involves a study of the history of the word. In nearly every case the process has been that of extension. (See p. 347, above.) The original meaning of *fine* is "finished," "brought to perfection." But the favorable associations with which we regard carefully done workmanship came to be extended to things which were not polished or intricately made. Conversely, the favorable associations aroused by *great* as it signifies the magnitude of certain objects (a great tree, a great pile of wheat) came to be extended to objects that lack magnitude. And so we can have "a great little wife" or "a fine country of mountains and forests."

[6] Reprinted from *Prejudices: Second Series* by H. L. Mencken, by permission of Alfred A. Knopf, Inc. Copyright 1920 by Alfred A. Knopf, Inc. Copyright 1948 by H. L. Mencken.

Mention of the origin of projectile adjectives points to a third obvious device for influencing attitudes: the association of the thing in question with something pleasant or unpleasant, noble or ignoble. We express contempt by calling a man a "rat" or a "louse" or a "worm"; a certain admiration for his cleverness, by calling him a "fox"; hatred (and perhaps fear), by calling him a "snake." In general, the animal creation is a rich source of expressions of attitude toward other human beings, particularly of hostile or contemptuous attitudes. But we may use associations drawn from all sorts of areas: "He is a tower of strength," "He is as hard as flint," She is as neat as a pin."

Here follows the account of an incident as it might be reported by a relatively impartial writer:

> Democratic [or Republican] Senator Briggs expressed surprise at being met by reporters. He told them that he had no comment to make on the "Whitlow deal." He said that he had not known that Whitlow was in the employ of General Aircraft, and observed that the suggestion that he had received favors from Whitlow was an attempt to discredit him.

How might a hostile reporter describe the incident? He would perhaps give an account something like this:

> Senator Briggs, Democratic [or Republican] wheel-horse, was obviously startled to find himself confronted by newspapermen. He stubbornly refused to comment on what he called the "Whitlow deal," and professed not to have known that Whitlow was a lobbyist. The Senator complained that he was being smeared.

The second account seems to be substantially the same as the first. The "facts" are not appreciably altered. But the emotional coloring, and with it, the intended effect on the reader, have been sharply altered. The senator is now a "wheel-horse," with its suggestions of a hardened and (probably) calloused political conscience. Whitlow is a "lobbyist," and again suggestions of political corruption are insinuated. Moreover, the senator's actions and speech ("obviously startled," "stubbornly refused," "professed not to have known," and "complained") are made to suggest guilt.

Now the point in this comparison of the two accounts is not to indicate that the dryer, more objective account is necessarily "truer" and therefore to be preferred. Our estimable fictitious senator may in fact be quite guilty, and the writer of the second account may have given us the more accurate account of what actually happened in the interview. (It is even conceivable that the first account was written by a reporter who was pretty certain of the senator's guilty conduct but whose editor had ordered him to play down any suggestion of guilt. In that event, the first account would have to be regarded as the biased account.) The point to be made is this: that the coloring of attitudes in a piece of writing is extremely important, and is indeed an integral part of its "meaning."

WORN-OUT WORDS AND CLICHÉS

We began this chapter by saying that the problem of diction is that of finding the right words—the words which will say exactly what the writer wants to say. But we have seen that exactness in language cannot be secured simply and mechanically, that the exactness works on a number of levels. Words are not static. They are not changeless, inflexible counters. They have a history; they have biographies; and even, one is tempted to say, personalities. Most of all, since they are not changeless and inflexible, but to some extent plastic, changing their shape a little under the pressure of the context in which they occur, they offer a continual stimulus and challenge to the imagination of the writer.

The perfectly normal human habit of extending meanings beyond the "fixed" meaning has been discussed briefly. But it is an important topic and will be treated much more fully in Chapter 11 ("Metaphor"). In discussing a related topic, the way in which words may be used to imply value and to color an argument, we have laid the ground work for another important topic which will be discussed at large in Chapter 12 ("Situation and Tone"). We ought not, however, to conclude this chapter without noticing what we may call the degenerative disease that attacks and weakens language.

For as we have seen earlier, language changes, develops, grows, and by the same token, language wears out. We are not thinking, however, of the normal sloughing off of words that have died natural deaths, and now either do not occur in a modern dictionary at all, or if they do occur, are marked *obsolete* (*shoon* for *shoes*) or *archaic* (*e'en* for *even*). We are thinking rather of words that have been thoughtlessly used in particular contexts so often that they have lost nearly all their force. Whether we call these threadbare expressions "trite" or "hackneyed," or term them "stereotypes" and "clichés," is of little importance. Their common fault is this: they pretend to say more than the common expression says, and therefore call attention to their shabbiness.

COMMON STEREOTYPES, INCLUDING SLANG

Jargon is produced by writers who do not think out what they want to say, but find a worn groove in the language down which they let their thoughts slide. Books on rhetoric sometimes supply lists of threadbare expressions against which the reader is warned: "the more the merrier," "last but not least," "to trip the light fantastic toe." But hackneyed phrases of this sort have probably by now become too literary, too old-fashioned, to offer much temptation to a modern writer—even to a lazy one. But stereotyping continues, and much of the writing and conversation to which we are constantly exposed is a tissue of trite expressions. The sports page, for example, will yield stereotypes in abundance. Mr. Frank Sullivan amusingly exhibits some of these in the form of question and answer.

Q. If [the teams] don't roll up a score what do they do?
A. They battle to a scoreless tie.
Q. What do they hang up?
A. A victory. Or, they pull down a victory.
Q. Which means that they do what to the opposing team?
A. They take the measure of the opposing team, or take it into camp.
Q. And the opposing team?
A. Drops a game, or bows in defeat.
Q. This dropping, or bowing, constitutes what kind of blow for the losing team?
A. It is a crushing blow to its hopes of annexing the Eastern championship. Visions of the Rose Bowl fade.
Q. So what follows as a result of the defeat?
A. A drastic shakeup follows as a result of the shellacking at the hands of Cornell last Saturday.
Q. And what is developed?
A. A new line of attack.

Q. Mr. Smith, how is the first quarter of a football game commonly referred to?
A. As the initial period.

—FRANK SULLIVAN: "Football Is King." [7]

Society page editors have their own brand of stereotypes: "social function," "society bud," "gala affair." To come closer home still, there is slang. Some slang expressions may once have been pungent and colorful. The sports writer who first described the strike-out of a slugging batter by saying "he made three dents in the atmosphere" conveyed the scene sharply and humorously. When slang is thus "tailor-made" for the occasion, it may be bright and perceptive (though, if it is still fresh and vivid, it is a question whether it ought to be viewed as "slang" at all). But as most of us use it, slang is a worn and impoverished language, not sprightly and irreverently lively, but stale and dead: "the party was a washout"; "I am fed up"; "he crabbed a lot"; "he blew his top." The real sin committed here is not so much that of bringing slang's flippant associations into a serious context. We do not often commit this fault. The real sin in using slang consists in using a thin and impoverished language.

JARGON: THE DEGENERATIVE DISEASE OF PROSE

We have to step up, however, to a somewhat more exalted plane to find the stereotypes which most damage modern prose and which are calculated to do the student most harm. These are such expressions as "along the lines of," "in the last analysis," "socio-economic considerations," "the world of business affairs," "according to a usually reliable source." Such locutions puff out many an official document, many a political speech, and, it must be admitted, many a professor's lecture or article.

This wordy, woolly style is sometimes called "officialese." Former Congressman Maury Maverick has recently damned it as "gobbledygook," submitting as a horrible sample the following extract:

Whereas, national defense requirements have created a shortage of corundum (as hereafter defined) for the combined needs of defense and private account, and the supply of corundum now is and will be in-

[7] From "Football Is King," by Frank Sullivan, printed in *The Atlantic Monthly*, by permission of the author.

sufficient for defense and essential civilian requirements, unless the supply of corundum is conserved and its use in certain products manufactured for civilian use is curtailed; and it is necessary in the public interest and to promote the defense of the United States, to conserve the supply and direct the distribution and use thereof. Now, therefore, it is hereby ordered that . . .

But whether we call it officialese when it emanates from some government bureau, or gobbledygook, or simply jargon, its empty wordiness is characteristic. Here are two somewhat more respectable samples culled from *College English*—a fact which should warn us that anyone can fall into jargon, even those who undertake to teach others how to write effective English.

[1] If we start at one of the extremes of the continuum, we shall find a grouping around a point of great vitality and wide appeal. Keenly aware of the painstaking scholarship and of the high creative effort that over the centuries has accumulated the body of subject matter we call "English," a group of our ablest teachers conceive their role to be to transmit this product of human endeavor, this hard-won store of learning and of art, this rich portion of man's heritage of culture, to the oncoming generations, and to imbue them with some perception of its worth.

[2] But whether we are trained statisticians or not, we can improve the results of our examination speeches and themes. First of all, we can, without great difficulty, develop better controlled problems. There are various degrees of control possible in examination speeches and themes, and, within reasonable limits, it would seem as though the greater the control the more meaningful the test results. Complete freedom of choice of topic and material puts a premium upon accidental inspiration and upon glibness rather than thoughtfulness. A single assigned topic is palpably unfair since it may strike the interest and experience of some and yet leave others untouched.

These two passages have been somewhat unfairly taken out of context. Moreover, the topics discussed are not precisely colorful and exciting. Is it fair, then, to condemn their authors for having written jargon? How else could either writer have said what he had to say?

It is true that we have torn the passages out of context, and it is true that the subject matter is difficult. Yet even so, the symptoms of jargon are present. Consider the second excerpt: "puts a premium upon," "palpably unfair," are clearly stereotypes. Moreover, what does the author gain by specifying "without great difficulty," and "within reasonable limits"? Are these specifications necessary? Could they not be assumed? Has not the writer put them in for rhetorical purposes, that is, to "dress up" his statement, rather than to make necessary qualifications?

JARGON: SOME ANTIDOTES

But jargon, of course, involves more than stereotypes. Jargon is nearly always compounded of clusters of general and abstract words, and though there is no certain prescription against jargon, it is easy to state one or two practical antidotes.

1. The writer should try to use words that are as specific and concrete as possible; that is, he should never use a word more general and indefinite than he has to. Hazy and indefinite expressions represent the easy way out for a writer who is too timid to commit himself, or too lazy to think through what he wants to say.

2. The writer should avoid stereotypes of all kinds—prefabricated phrasings which come easily to mind but which may not represent precisely his own ideas and emotions. But note this carefully: he should never avoid an *individual* word because it seems simple and common. If the sense calls for a simple, common word, it is generally best to repeat the word, if necessary, again and again. There is little to be said in favor of what is sometimes called ELEGANT VARIATION, that is, the substitution of some synonym in order to avoid repetition. Here is an example: "Mr. Jones was a powerful *financier*. As a *tycoon* he had a deep suspicion of socialism. He shared the feelings of his associates who were also *bankers*." The variations are irritating and can be confusing. Either recast the sentence or repeat *financier*.

On the other hand, the writer should try to avoid *words strung together*—phrasings—which are common, and for that very reason, probably stereotyped. He cannot avoid all common expressions, nor should he try to avoid them, but he ought to learn to inspect them carefully before he decides to use them. If he really needs to say "along the lines of"—if something is really "in consideration of" something else and an emphasis on *consideration* is relevant—then let him use the expression by all means. But it is a good rule to remember that though he need never shy away from an individual *word* because it is common, he ought to be very shy of *phrases* that are common.

3. The writer should try to use live words, remembering that finite verbs are the most powerful words that we have. We can find an instance of the failure to do so in the second sentence of the first excerpt quoted on page 356: "Keenly aware of the painstaking scholarship and of the high creative effort that over the centuries has accumulated the body of subject matter we call 'English,' a group of our ablest teachers conceive their role to be to transmit this product of human endeavor, this hard-won store of learning and of art, this rich portion of man's heritage of culture, to the oncoming generations. . . ." This sentence is packed with ideas, but the only finite verb in it (aside from *has accumulated* and *call,* in the two relative clauses) is the verb *conceive. Aware,* a participle, is made to carry the weight of the first twenty-six words; and the whole latter part of the sentence hangs from two successive infinitives, "to be to transmit." The sentence has so little stamina that it sprawls. It sprawls because the writer has starved it of finite verbs. The author might better have written: "Our ablest teachers realize what effort has gone into the making of that body of subject matter we call 'English.' They know it is a precious thing, for it embodies the effort of painstaking scholars and of great poets and novelists. They want to transmit this heritage of culture to the oncoming generations."

Finite verbs are more powerful than strings of participles, gerunds, or infinitives. Moreover, a specific verb is usually stronger than a more general verb qualified by modifiers. Compare "He walked along slowly" with "He strolled," "He sauntered," "He dawdled," "He lagged." Frequently, it is true, we need the qualifiers. But we ought not to forget the wealth of concreteness which the English language possesses in its great number of verbs which name specifically, and therefore powerfully, specific modes of action.

4. Finally, the writer ought to remember that simple sentences in normal sentence order (see p. 307) rarely degenerate into jargon. An essay so written may be childishly simple, and it can become monotonous; but it will seldom collapse into the spineless flabbiness of jargon.

Jargon, however, is not to be dealt with summarily. It is our most pervasive kind of "bad" style, and, like style in general, it is the product of the interplay of many elements. We shall have to recur to this topic in some of the chapters that follow, particularly in the discussion of metaphor.

SUMMARY

The discussion of DICTION carried on in this chapter may be summarized rather concisely since the various aspects of diction are so closely interrelated. Words, as we have seen, are not pure DENOTATIONS, that is, words are not tied to one specific meaning and only one specific meaning. They have CONNOTATIONS as well—implied meanings, shadings of meanings, qualities of feeling which are associated with them. These implied meanings are naturally more powerful in words that refer to some specific thing or action. Connotations are generally less vivid and less important in words which are more general in their reference or which refer to some generalized quality or characteristic (abstract words).

The good writer must choose his words not only for appropriate denotations but also for appropriate connotations. His problem, of course, will vary with his purpose and with the occasion on which he writes. At one extreme is technical and scientific writing in which exact denotations are all-important and in which the writer's problem is to keep disturbing connotations out of his work. At the other extreme is that kind of writing which attempts to give the impact and quality of life itself. In such writing the connotations are of immense importance.

The dictionary is not merely a kind of logbook of precise meanings. As we have seen, words are really clusters of interrelated meanings. Some knowledge of how words grow, how meanings are extended, how language is constantly shifting and changing, will allow the writer to make a wiser use of the dictionary and of his own personal experience of language.

From the general account of language just given, several important propositions follow.

1. The writer must be careful to choose his words in terms of their appropriateness within a particular context: some words are dignified, some "literary," some pleasantly informal, and so on.

2. Few words are simple namings. They also interpret the thing in question. They may be used to beg the question or to color an argument, as the advertiser or the propagandist has learned.

3. Everything else being equal, the writer will prefer live words to dead words or drugged words. He will avoid stereotyped phrasings of all sorts. He will avoid words which have been worn smooth by overuse in certain contexts, but he may discover that even words which seem to have lost all their vigor, if put in fresh patternings, tailor-made to his specific purpose, come alive again.

4. In general, the writer will avoid wordiness, carefully choosing the right words for his purpose, and then giving these words elbow room in which to do their work.

CHAPTER 77

Metaphor

METAPHOR DEFINED

IN METAPHOR there is a transfer of meaning. We apply an old word to a new situation. Thus, as we saw in Chapter 10, we speak of the "eye" of a needle, the "legs" of a chair, the "bed" of a river. As we saw also in that chapter, language normally grows by a process of metaphorical extension. We proceed from the known to the unknown. We extend old names to new objects. But most of the illustrations of this process considered in Chapter 10 are instances of "dead" metaphor. Compare, for example, "the bed of a river" with "the dance of life." The first phrase carries no suggestion that the bed is a place of repose or that the river is sleepy! We use "bed of the river" technically, as a pure denotation from which the connotations that apply to *bed* in its usual senses are quite absent. But it is very different with the phrase "the dance of life." This metaphor is still alive. (At least Havelock Ellis, who used it as the title of one of his books, hoped that it would seem alive.) Here the connotations—the suggestions, the associations—are thoroughly relevant to Ellis's purpose. The connotations (of something rhythmic, of patterned movement, even, perhaps, of gaiety and happiness) are meant to be associated with life. We have characterized "bed of a river" as a dead metaphor, but to say "dead metaphor" is, of course, to make use of a metaphor, one based on an analogy with the animal kingdom. Animals (and vegetation, for that matter) can literally die: a metaphor cannot.

Our last metaphor, however, can illuminate the problem now being considered and may be worth a little further extension. With "dead" metaphors, we can say, *rigor mortis* has set in: they have no flexibility, no force; they have stiffened into one meaning, connotation has yielded to denotation. Metaphors that are still very much alive prove that they are alive by possessing a certain flexibility; and because they are still alive, they can be used to give color and life to a piece of writing. They can still excite the imagination.

In metaphors that are recognizably metaphors, there are, of course, varying degrees of life. The following are not very lively, but they do show that metaphor is a perfectly normal and important part of our normal speech: we say, for example, "John is a good egg," "Jane is a peach," "He ran out on the deal," "That remark threw him for a loss." Such expressions as these are rather worn and faded. But their original metaphorical character is plain enough, and we still think of them, and use them, as metaphors. The list of expressions that are badly shopworn but are still recognizably metaphors could be extended almost indefinitely: "hot as the devil," "cool as a cucumber," "independent as a hog on ice," "lazy as a dog," "crazy as a bat," and so on.

IMPORTANCE OF METAPHOR IN EVERYDAY LANGUAGE

Our preference for the concrete and the particular, as these examples show, is not only normal; it is deeply and stubbornly rooted in the human mind. Consider the following situation: it is a hot day. We can say "It is hot" or "It is very hot" or, piling on the intensives, we can say "It is abominably and excruciatingly hot." But most of us, afflicted with the heat, will resort to metaphor of some kind: "It is hot as hell," or more elaborately, "It's hot as the hinges of hell." Evidently metaphor is felt to add forcefulness, and evidently the forcefulness has some relation to freshness of expression. The "hinges of hell" are not necessarily any hotter than other parts of hell; the precise specification and additional concreteness is an attempt to freshen the worn and dulled comparison, "as hot as hell."

That is one point, then: in metaphor, force and freshness tend to go together. Indeed, we are usually attracted to metaphor in the first place because ordinary language seems trite. A second point to be made is this: metaphor tends to accompany the expression of emotions and attitudes. A strictly scientific purpose would find entirely adequate expression in the statement that it is now 97.6 degrees Fahrenheit and that the humidity is 88.

Let us consider another simple case. Suppose one feels an especial kind of happiness and tries to express his feelings. He can say, "I feel happy." Or he can try to find a word which more accurately hits off this special feeling: *merry, gay, ecstatic, cheerful, glad, jolly,* or *joyous.* There are many synonyms for *happy,* as the dictionary will quickly reveal, and they differ in their shades of meaning. For example, *jolly* suggests a kind of heartiness and good humor that goes with comfortable living; *ecstatic* suggests some kind of transcendent experience of rapture; *gay* suggests a kind of sprightliness, a nimble lightheartedness. We shall do well to consult the dictionary to learn (or remind ourselves of) the wealth of resources at our disposal. Even so, we rarely find an adjective which exactly expresses our feelings. We tend to resort to metaphor. We say "I'm happy as a June-bug" or "I feel like a million dollars" or "I'm walking on air this morning" or "I feel like a colt in springtime," or, as a poet put it once:

> My heart is like a singing bird
> Whose nest is in a water'd shoot;
> My heart is like an apple-tree
> Whose boughs are bent with thick-set fruit.

If the feeling is very special or complex, we are usually *forced* to resort to metaphor. Here are the ways in which three writers of fiction express the special kind of happiness which each of their characters experiences.

The first is the happiness of a boy at the race track as he watches the horses work out.

Well, out of the stables they come and the boys are on their backs and it's lovely to be there. You hunch down on top of the fence and itch inside you. Over in the sheds the niggers giggle and sing. Bacon is being fried and coffee made. Everything smells lovely. Nothing smells better than coffee and manure and horses and niggers and bacon frying and pipes being smoked out of doors on a morning like that. It just gets you, that's what it does.—SHERWOOD ANDERSON: "I Want to Know Why." [1]

[1] From *The Triumph of the Egg* by Sherwood Anderson. Copyright 1921 by Eleanor Anderson.

What makes this passage effective is the re-creation of the scene in our imagination. This is done through the skillful use of descriptive detail: the author summons up for us the atmosphere of the race track. But he uses metaphor too—metaphor which is charged by the atmosphere. The metaphor, it is true, is scarcely declared; but it is there under the surface. The itch "inside you" is not a real itch; and "It just gets you" is a metaphor, for all the fact that it is slang. A more explicit (and highfalutin) way of saying it—the experience seizes you, or takes hold of you powerfully—reveals the metaphor clearly.

In the next example, the principal metaphor is perfectly explicit. The experience described is that of a boy in love for the first time.

Her name sprang to my lips at moments in strange prayers and praises which I myself did not understand. My eyes were often full of tears (I could not tell why) and at times a flood from my heart seemed to pour itself out into my bosom. I thought little of the future. I did not know whether I would ever speak to her or not or, if I spoke to her, how I could tell her of my confused adoration. But my body was like a harp and her words and gestures were like fingers running upon the wires.—JAMES JOYCE: "Araby." [2]

The author uses three comparisons here: that of worship, that of a flood, and that of a harp. The second is the easiest and most obvious: the tears that well up in the boy's eyes suggest the flood metaphor. The first is the least explicit but the most pervasive: the metaphor may seem only hinted at in the phrase "strange prayers and praises"; but it is picked up once more in the phrase "confused adoration," for *adore* means literally "to pray to." This metaphor prepares for the third, the summarizing comparison: "my body was like a harp . . ." The boy responds to the loved one as a harp responds to the harpist's touch. Note that the harp comparison illuminates even "praises which I myself did not understand," for the harp as instrument cannot understand the "praise," the "adoration" which is elicited from it.

The third example describes the feelings of a shy man who has blundered into a darkened room and unexpectedly been kissed

[2] From *Dubliners* by James Joyce, copyright, 1925, by The Viking Press, Inc., and now included in *The Portable James Joyce*, published by The Viking Press, Inc., New York.

before the young woman, keeping her tryst there, has realized that he is not her lover.

At first he was tormented by shame and dread that the whole drawing-room knew that he had just been kissed and embraced by a woman. He shrank into himself and looked uneasily about him, but as he became convinced that people were dancing and talking as calmly as ever, he gave himself up entirely to the new sensation which he had never experienced before in his life. Something strange was happening to him. . . . His neck, round which soft, fragrant arms had so lately been clasped, seemed to him to be anointed with oil; on his left cheek near his moustache where the unknown had kissed him there was a faint chilly tingling sensation as from peppermint drops, and the more he rubbed the place the more distinct was the chilly sensation; all over, from head to foot, he was full of a strange new feeling which grew stronger and stronger.—ANTON CHEKHOV: "The Kiss." [3]

The man's intense emotions are treated in their vividness almost as if they were physical sensations. Notice, for example, "faint chilly tingling sensation as from peppermint drops." The comparison combines the sense of touch (chill) and taste. The sensation is slightly queer, and, to the man, troubling, and quite delightful.

SLANG AS METAPHOR

In connection with metaphor it may be profitable to consider again two abuses of language, slang and jargon, which have already been touched upon in the preceding chapter (pp. 353-56). The impulse to use slang springs from our sound general preference for the concrete and the particular. Slang expressions are originally metaphors, and the problem of the misuse of slang cannot properly be solved apart from the more general problem of the use and abuse of figurative language. That is why it does very little good to tell a writer—or for the writer to tell himself—not to use slang, for this advice is essentially negative. The writer is right in wanting to make his writing warm, colorful, and lively. What he needs to do, therefore, is not to discard figurative language in favor of abstract expressions; but rather to inspect all his figurative language, *including slang*, in order to improve it as metaphor. He will try to eliminate all metaphors which are worn and trite, or which seem preten-

[3] From Anton Chekhov: *The Party and Other Stories*. Tr. Constance Garnett. Copyright, 1917 by The Macmillan Company and used with their permission.

tious, or which are discordant with the rest of the composition. The practical result, of course, will be that in this process most of the slang will be sloughed off, but sloughed off *because it proves to be poor and ineffective metaphor,* not because it is figurative. For the good writer tries to bring his metaphors to life, and to direct and control them in that life. How to do this, of course, is a matter of craftsmanship and experience. But it is an important thing to learn, and it is our justification for devoting so much space in this text to the subject of metaphor. The writer must get firmly in mind that this discussion of figurative language has not been inserted on the supposition that the writer must learn to write a highfalutin and pretentious "literary" style. He needs, on the contrary, to master figurative language for the most practical of reasons.

JARGON AND WORN-OUT METAPHOR

But why recur to the second general abuse of language, jargon, in this chapter on metaphor? What possible connection can jargon have with metaphor? The first answer to this question can be put simply: there is an important negative relation. It is the very lack of concrete words and of metaphorical vividness and particularity that makes jargon cloudy and ineffective. A primary way to avoid jargon, then, is to use concrete language—including its extension into metaphor. The spinelessness of jargon is in part the result of the writer's timid avoidance of vigorous metaphor. Even the most timid writer, however, is not actually able to avoid all metaphor; and with this observation we can give a second answer to the question. Jargon characteristically involves stereotypes of all kinds, including stereotyped and therefore lifeless metaphor. This connection of jargon with secondhand metaphor is forcefully put by the British critic, George Orwell.

Prose [nowadays] consists less and less of *words* chosen for the sake of their meaning, and more and more of *phrases* tacked together like the sections of a prefabricated henhouse. . . . There is a huge dump of worn-out metaphors which have lost all evocative power and are merely used because they save people the trouble of inventing phrases for themselves. . . . Modern writing at its worst . . . consists in gumming together long strips of words which have already been set in order by someone else.

(The reader will notice that Orwell himself uses metaphor very effectively—"sections of a prefabricated henhouse," "dump of worn-out metaphors," "gumming together long strips of words." Orwell thus vividly suggests his two points of indictment: the lazy and careless craftsmanship of the writer of jargon, and the second-hand quality of the materials he uses.)

Orwell goes on to illustrate his point by suggesting how a modern writer of hand-me-down phrases would express the following passage from Ecclesiastes: "I returned, and saw under the sun, that the race is not to the swift, nor the battle to the strong, neither yet bread to the wise, nor yet riches to men of understanding, nor yet favor to men of skill; but time and chance happeneth to them all."

Such a writer, says Orwell, would probably turn it out like this: "Objective consideration of contemporary phenomena compels the conclusion that success or failure in competitive activities exhibits no tendency to be commensurate with innate capacity, but that a considerable element of the unpredictable must invariably be taken into account."

CONFUSED METAPHOR AND HALF-DEAD METAPHOR

Orwell has hardly exaggerated, and the faults which he points out are found just as frequently in America as in Great Britain. Consider the following passages taken from recent magazines.

In the sense that we have known it in the past, American agriculture is a dying industry. The nation's largest single business still remaining in the hands of private citizens is in the midst of a scientific revolution, and the farm as an individual production unit—the final refuge from a mechanical and goose-stepped civilization—is seeing its last days. For chemistry and technology are bringing agriculture under control.

In broad terms, one may say that the farm is being wrecked by a series of three major frontal attacks, any one of which is deadly enough to have caused a serious crisis. . . .

The authors call American agriculture a "dying industry" but in the next sentence they say that it is "in the midst of a scientific revolution" and finally, that it "is seeing its last days." They attempt to give liveliness to these statements by comparing American agriculture to a dying animal; but any sense of vigor in the metaphor is pretty well lost when we have to consider agriculture first as an animal, next as a citizen living through a revolution, and finally as a "refuge from a mechanized and goose-stepped civilization." And if the reader is able to keep the metaphorical sense at all through these confusions, that sense is completely canceled out by the short statement that follows: ". . . chemistry and technology are bringing agriculture under control." An animal or a man who is dying and has seen his last days is certainly under control, and the pyramid of metaphors thus topples to a rather absurd anticlimax.

We can reconstruct the process of composition as follows: the authors were actually not sure whether they wanted the metaphors to come alive or remain decently dead. "Dying industry" they probably used as a dying metaphor—that is, they hoped that the metaphor would be lively in the first sentence, but decently dead and forgotten by the time that the reader got to the next sentence. But, in the floridly metaphorical atmosphere of the second sentence, the metaphor implicit in "dying" comes to life too—to embarrass and distract the new metaphor.

This confusion and irresponsibility in the use of metaphor is revealed in the last sentence where the authors, still anxious to maintain a kind of rhetorical liveliness, treat the farm under the figure of a war. "The farm," they say, "is being wrecked by a series of three major frontal attacks. . . ." But let us examine the figure for only a moment. There can be only one *frontal* attack on any one position. Frontal attacks must come, as the authors have themselves indicated, in "series," one after the other. It might make sense to say that the farm is being wrecked by a frontal attack which is being carried on simultaneously with attacks on either flank. Or it might make metaphorical sense to say that the farm has already sustained two damaging frontal attacks and that the third such attack is now in progress. This last statement is perhaps what the authors intended (though actually, it is very difficult to be certain as to what they did intend); but if they did intend the latter, they have been betrayed into confusion by their desire to use the "strong" word "frontal" when actually they had in mind no conception of a frontal attack as opposed to an attack from the side or from the rear.

The first essential in providing background information would be to present a comparative view of the societies of the world, from the simple primitive tribes to the complex civilized communities. Until the student is able to place data upon his own society in a comparative framework, he cannot be said to have gained any perspective or objectivity in that field. Such a cultivated emotional detachment is the first step toward understanding.

The danger of having dead and inert metaphors come to life is well illustrated by the statement "to place data upon his own society in a comparative framework." Obviously the author does not mean "to place data upon"—though the temptation to take "place upon" as a unit is almost irresistible. He meant to say that the student must place, in a comparative framework, the data that concerns his own society. But after we have made the correction, it becomes apparent that "place" is still not the word the author wanted. He would better have said that the student must *relate* data *to* a comparative scheme, or that the student must be able to *order* it *in* a comparative framework. Further confusion is promoted by the main clause of the sentence. How can placing data, or relating it, or ordering it "in a comparative framework" be said to give perspective? One may place himself at a vantage point from which he can see objects in perspective—that is, see them at a distance, from a point of view. But the metaphor of a framework, followed closely by a metaphor of getting perspective, results in a blurring and confusion of both metaphors. The "framework" has to be taken, not as a framework at all, but as an abstraction, for it behaves with embarrassment when forced into the dance of metaphors. The last sentence of the paragraph indicates what the author meant to say: that the student must stand back from—that is, detach himself from —his material so that he can see it in perspective.

Students and professors are sometimes accused of leading a cloistered existence comfortably removed from the dust and heat of everyday life. There may be some truth in that accusation, but let us remember that in the Dark Ages it was in the cloisters rather than in the market places that the flame of the spirit was kept alive. How is it faring today at Harvard and Yale, at Dartmouth and at Cornell? Are you determined to use your education merely to get a good job, marry and settle down,— in ordinary times that would be the natural aspiration,—or are some of you chafing to defend the rights of the spirit in a rapidly materializing world? Unless you are, the shadow of Hitlerism is likely to darken the world for a long time to come.

The first part of this passage echoes—and quite properly—Milton's famous remark that he could not "praise a fugitive and cloistered virtue . . . that never sallies out to seek her adversary, but slinks out of the race, where that immortal garland is to be run for, not without dust and heat." And the contrast between the cloisters and the market place again is used soundly. But the author gets into trouble when he speaks of "the rights of the spirit in a rapidly materializing world." Mediums make (or pretend to make) spirits "materialize." Does the author mean that the world too is a spirit which is being made to materialize? Or is he trying to say that the world is rapidly becoming unspiritualized—that it is preoccupied with matter as opposed to the realm of spirit? The momentary confusion is not clarified by the sentence that follows in which "the shadow of Hitlerism" is made to threaten darkness to the world. One is tempted to see Hitlerism as a shadow which is "materializing," that is, turning the world into solid murk and darkness. Actually in this case there is little difficulty in untangling the chance associations of spiritualist mediums from the rather straightforward distinction between the realm of the spirit and the realm of the material. But would not the sentence be more effective without this confusion?

The writer of the passage which follows is attempting to describe the effect of the comic books:

> They defy the limits of accepted fact and convention, thus amortizing to apoplexy the ossified arteries of routine thought. But by these very tokens the picture-book fantasy cuts loose the hampering debris of art and artifice and touches the tender spots of universal human desires and aspirations, hidden customarily beneath long accumulated protective coverings of indirection and disguise.

But can one defy a limit? One can, of course, defy another person to set a limit. The comic books may break across boundaries, may exceed limits, and their authors may defy authorities to set any limits that they will respect. But here it is the comic books that are made to "defy limits," probably because the author was looking for a strong metaphor, and was willing to accept, without asking too many questions of it, the first strong metaphor that he found. The defiance hinted by the comic books has violent results. The comic books amortize the "ossified arteries of routine thought." To "amortize" is to cancel a mortgage. And "amortize" like "mortgage" is related etymologically to Latin *mors*, death. Even so, how can a defiance extinguish a mortgage on the arteries of thought—to the point of apoplexy? People who suffer from a hardening of the arteries are subject to strokes of apoplexy. Perhaps the writer is trying to say that the outrageous breaking of the conventions drives certain readers to apoplexy. But he has his apoplectic stroke affect the creaky and antiquated thoughts themselves. The result is a rather amazing mixup.

In the next sentence, the comic books, having by their defiance ruptured the arteries of conventional thought, proceed to cut loose the "debris of art and artifice." Or rather, it is the fantasy which cuts this debris loose. But "debris" means a scattered mass of materials. Can one cut a person loose from debris? Or does one not rather dig a victim *out of* the debris which has fallen upon him. And how can such debris be *worn*, as is evidently the case here, as a "protective covering"? The cutting loose of wreckage, the pulling off of a disguise, and the removal of a protective shell are thoroughly scrambled. And the confusion is not helped when we remember that the debris in question is composed of "art and artifice" and that the agent which cuts it loose is fantasy—something which one usually regards as associated with both art and artifice.

There is much to be said for a rich and concrete idiom. In return for it, we might be willing to disregard a few metaphorical loose ends. But there are limits, even though the comic books are said to defy limits. The writer here is evidently buried up to his ears in a debris which may be artifice but certainly is not art.

The excerpts examined are, we repeat, taken from "quality magazines"—the last and worst one, from the magazine published by Phi Beta Kappa. These are by no means the most absurd instances that could be collected. But they are absurd enough to indicate that "good" writers often manage their metaphors very poorly.

THE FUNCTION OF METAPHOR

Thus far we have given our attention to some of the abuses of figurative language. It is high time to give a more positive account of metaphor and to show some of the uses of figurative language. After all, why do we use metaphor? What purpose does it serve?

We have already assumed in earlier pages that it has its value in contributing color and liveliness, but if we are to understand why it is one of the great resources of the writer, we shall need to define more clearly what its function is. This is all the more necessary since the conventional account of the uses of metaphor is calculated to mislead. For example, we are in the habit of saying that the purpose of metaphor is (1) to illustrate or (2) to embellish; but these terms can easily suggest that figurative language is a kind of "extra" which may be usefully or gracefully "added on" to a statement, but which is never essential to the statement—never a direct part of what is being said. In accordance with this conventional view, the practical function of metaphor is to give a concrete illustration of some point which has been put more abstractly. The artistic use is to provide a pleasing decoration like an attractive wallpaper pasted onto the wall, or like a silk ribbon tied around a box of candy. But the trouble with this account is that, in either case, the figure of speech seems to be something which can be left off; and if we misconceive the purposes of metaphor by thinking of it as something external and additional, we shall never come to understand why a mastery of metaphor is absolutely essential to good writing.

WHY SCIENTIFIC STATEMENT DOES NOT REQUIRE METAPHOR

Let us begin by disposing of a special kind of writing in which metaphor is indeed unnecessary or merely an addition. If I wish to say "2 + 2 = 4" or that "the square of the hypotenuse of a right triangle is equal to the sum of the squares of the other two sides," I shall not require metaphor. Metaphor would be in the way. Such statements as these, however, are very special: the terms used in such statements are (or aspire to be) pure denotations. If such terms have connotations at all, the connotations are surely irrelevant (see p. 341). Thus the "words" employed are not words in the usual sense. They are not capable of metaphorical extension. They are very special symbols, and the purest statements of this kind are able to dispense with words altogether: thus, $2 + 2 = 4$, or $H_2SO_4 + Fe \rightarrow FeSO_4 + H_2\uparrow$.

But important as such statements are, they represent a stringently limited discourse. Most of the discourse which interests us as human beings and which we must use as writers, goes far beyond abstract relationships of this kind. Most of our discourse has to do with the "full" world of our human experience—not the colorless, soundless, abstract world of modern physics, say, or of mathematics.[4]

METAPHOR AS ILLUSTRATION

It ought to be noted, however, that even the scientific writer very often needs to go beyond this stringently limited abstract discourse, and even for him, metaphor, though frankly employed as illustration, may be highly necessary and useful. The following passage from Bertrand Russell's *The Scientific Outlook* will illustrate. The book is addressed to a general audience and Bertrand Russell is attempting to convince his reader that "what is actually experienced is much less than one would naturally suppose." He proceeds to analyze a typical experience for us. Here follows his analysis of what happens scientifically when we "see" someone.

You may say, for example, that you see your friend, Mr. Jones, walking along the street: but this is to go far beyond what you have any right to say. You see a succession of coloured patches, traversing a stationary background. These patches, by means of a Pavlov conditioned reflex, bring into your mind the word "Jones," and so you say you see Jones; but other people, looking out of their windows from different angles, will see something different, owing to the laws of perspective: therefore, if they are all seeing Jones, there must be as many different Joneses as there are spectators, and if there is only one true Jones, the sight of him is not vouchsafed to anybody. If we assume for a moment the truth of the account which physics gives, we shall explain what you call "seeing Jones" in some such terms as the following. Little packets of light, called "light quanta," shoot out from the sun, and some of these reach a region where there are atoms of a certain kind, composing Jones's face, and hands, and clothes. These atoms do not themselves exist, but are merely a compendious way of alluding to possible occurrences. Some of the light quanta, when they reach Jones's atoms, upset their internal economy. This causes him to become sunburnt, and to manufacture vitamin D. Others are reflected, and of those that are re-

[4] This is not, of course, to question the importance or the reality of such worlds. The scientist can deal with his material in this abstract way, and in no other way. His language is neither more nor less real than the language of the poet or novelist. It is merely different. In this general connection, the reader might reread the discussion of abstract and concrete words (pp. 338-39).

flected some enter your eye. They there cause a complicated disturbance of the rods and cones, which, in turn, sends a current along the optic nerve. When this current reaches the brain, it produces an event. The event which it produces is that which you call "seeing Jones." As is evident from this account, the connection of "seeing Jones" with Jones is a remote, roundabout causal connection. Jones himself, meanwhile, remains wrapped in mystery. He may be thinking about his dinner, or about how his investments have gone to pieces, or about that umbrella he lost; these thoughts are Jones, but these are not what you see.— BERTRAND RUSSELL: *The Scientific Outlook*, Chap. 3.[5]

Notice that Russell completes his analysis with the last statement of the passage; yet apparently he felt that the account might prove too technical and that his reader might fail to understand. Therefore he adds the following statement: "To say that you see Jones is no more correct than it would be, if a ball bounced off a wall in your garden and hit you, to say that the wall had hit you. Indeed, the two cases are closely analogous." Most readers will be grateful for this illustration. Most minds find abstractions so alien to them that they need a concrete statement such as the analogy provides. This is a truth which the writers of all books of scientific popularization know, and, for that matter, it is one known by every writer of directions for setting up a patent can opener. Even if the writer is able, as Bertrand Russell is able here, to state his analysis directly, the extra illustration—the concrete analogy drawn from daily experience—is helpful.

METAPHOR AS ESSENTIAL STATEMENT

We may sum up then by saying that in strict scientific statement metaphor has no place, and that in a less strict scientific discussion metaphor is optional and additional. It provides an illustration, and, as the example from Russell shows, this may be of great importance. But in most of the writing with which we are concerned —political speeches, articles on international affairs, letters to friends, expressions of opinions, attempts to persuade or convince, essays which invite other people to share our own experiences and valuations—in nearly all the ordinary writing which we shall do, metaphor

[5] From *The Scientific Outlook* by Bertrand Russell, by permission of George Allen and Unwin, Ltd.

is not subsidiary and external but a primary device by which we "say" what we want to say. Metaphor then is not to be thought of as a roundabout way—an alternative way—of communicating an experience. Often it constitutes the only possible way by which we can convey the special quality of an experience. As one authority on language puts it: we think by proceeding from the known to the unknown, by extending a familiar term to an unfamiliar fact or situation. As he defines them, metaphors are "essentially discoveries of new meanings . . . by means of old names." Seen in these terms, metaphor is not something external to thinking: it is central. By the same token, it is not vague and emotional; it has its own accuracy, for it frequently provides the only means by which a thing can be "said." Metaphor is, then, an indispensable instrument for interpreting experience.

Let us illustrate. In the sentence that follows, Helen Keller describes what tactile sensation means to a person who has always been blind and deaf: "The immovable rock, with its juts and warped surface, bends beneath my fingers into all manner of grooves and hollows." The rock, of course, does not literally bend: it is "immovable." But under her sensitive fingers, which do duty for eyes, the rock itself seems to respond dynamically to her touch. For what is being described is not the fumbling of an ordinary person who is blindfolded. We are, rather, being let into Helen Keller's "world," a world of exciting qualities which most of us do not know at all. Metaphor here is the only means by which it may be made known to us. For since this world does not exist in our experience, it cannot be pointed to: it can only be created for us. (The reader should compare with Helen Keller's account of touch, Bertrand Russell's account of sight, page 374. We do not have to choose one and reject the other. Both are true, but we must not confuse them. The two accounts are radically different in purpose, and therefore in method.)

Helen Keller's world may seem a special case. The world which Miss Keller knows through her finger tips obviously can be known by most of us who lack her sensitive finger tips only through analogy, suggestion, and imaginative insight. Yet the worlds of all of us are more special than we think, determined as they are by our values, moods, and emotional biases.

SOME ILLUSTRATIONS OF ESSENTIAL, NONDECORATIVE METAPHOR

Consider what metaphor does in the following two verses from Ecclesiastes. "It is better to bear the rebuke of the wise, than for a man to hear the song of fools. For as the crackling of thorns under a pot, so is the laughter of a fool: this also is vanity."

This comparison, as we see, uses the dry, crackling sound of burning thorn branches to describe the laughter of a fool. Now, there is a certain realistic basis for the comparison. But the metaphor is far more than a phonetic description. It makes a value judgment too: the fool's laughter, it is implied, is brittle, hollow, meaningless: it is the noise that attends the going up in smoke of something quite worthless—the rubbish of dried thorn branches. This is the justification for the last clause, "this [the fool's laughter] also is a vanity." But the metaphor does much more than to "illustrate" the vanity. It is the metaphor itself that defines vanity and realizes it for us—its specious brightness, its explosive chatter, its essential emptiness.

Let us take one further example, this time from a novel. In her *Delta Wedding* Miss Eudora Welty describes the sunset as seen by a little girl through the window of a railway coach.

In the Delta the sunsets were reddest light. The sun went down lopsided and wide as a rose on a stem in the west, and the west was a milk white edge, like the foam of the sea. The sky, the field, the little track, and the bayou, over and over—all that had been bright or dark was now one color. From the warm window sill the endless fields glowed like a hearth in firelight.—EUDORA WELTY: *Delta Wedding*, Chap. 1.[6]

Since this is a passage from a novel it is tempting to say that here surely the figurative language is merely "decorative," an attempt at a prettification of the scene. Even here, however, the metaphors have a much more important function. The sun, it is true, is compared to a conventionally pretty object, a rose. But it is here a "lopsided" rose. The "hearth" comparison is domestic rather than beautiful in its associations. Actually, the metaphors work here to create the scene and the mood. It is a particular sunset seen by a particular character at a particular time. The scene is modified by

[6] From *Delta Wedding* by Eudora Welty, copyright, 1945, 1946, by Eudora Welty. Reprinted by permission of Harcourt, Brace and Company, Inc.

the mood which it has helped to generate; and the mood itself is the reflection of a special personality. And it is this complex of scene and mood and personality which the metaphors do so much to reveal. The special quality of redness, almost unreal—the diffused rosiness of the light—the sense of warmth—the scene perceived as something framed and set apart and remote—all of these qualities are suggested by the comparison of the sun to a lopsided rose, and of the flat and endless fields to a hearth glowing in firelight. In this total pattern of statement, "lopsided" is seen to be not merely whimsical, but to contribute its own mite of precision (the apparent distortion of the red globe of the sun as it touches the horizon) to a statement that is aiming at great precision.

A few paragraphs above we admitted that the world of Helen Keller's experience is a special world which can be conveyed to us only through suggestion and analogy. Yet a little reflection will show that the world of experience of each of us is far more special than we think, for such a world is determined by our values, moods, and emotional biases. The world as seen by the little girl in *Delta Wedding* is thus special in this sense, and so too is that of the Hebrew preacher who speaks in Ecclesiastes. If we are to communicate our experience with any accuracy, figurative language is frequently the only way by which such experience can be conveyed at all. For by means of metaphor we grasp not only the object as an entity, but its "meaning," its value to us as well. The "thing" which Miss Welty wished to say was not that the sun was round or red or an immense globe of superhot elements some ninety-three million miles from the earth. What she wished to give us was the sun as it appeared to the child as she watched it from the window of the train. It is not the scientific sun—the abstraction taken from some book on astronomy—with which the author is concerned, but rather the sun as part of a total experience and of a very particular and special experience.

One more example, just to make sure that the last illustration, since it is from fiction, does not give the impression that metaphor is somehow "literary" and therefore unimportant. Here is the way in which "Bugs" Baer describes the collapse of a prize fighter: "Zale folded as gracefully as the Queen's fan and fell on his battered face alongside the ropes. His seconds carried him to his corner like three window-dressers packing a melted dummy off during a heat wave on the sunny side of Broadway." This description may be judged to be good writing or bad, but it is easy to see why Baer used figurative language. He was not trying to "tell" us about the scene: he was trying to make us *see* the scene, vividly, freshly, fully, as a somewhat cynical but highly interested observer might have seen it.

The nature and uses of metaphor can be further illustrated from passages quoted in the earlier chapter on description. For example, let us look again at the metaphor which Faulkner uses in his description of Miss Emily (p. 208): "She looked bloated, like a body long submerged in motionless water, and of that pallid hue." There is an analogy, of course, between the appearance of the bloated and unnaturally pallid woman and that of a drowned body. But the author might have found other analogies, superficially quite as apt. What specific function does the comparison serve? It serves to interpret the woman for us. It describes the woman but it gives more than mere physical description: it suggests that she has long been immersed in a thick, unnatural medium like water. Moreover, the water in which she has drowned is "motionless." There has been a kind of stagnation. She has been removed from the whole course of human activity.

Or consider Thoreau's comparison of the state of Massachusetts to a human body (p. 235). There is, it is true, some kind of resemblance between the shape of Cape Cod on the map and that of a bended arm. But the physical analogy is pretty well exhausted with this item; yet Thoreau goes on to give the state a "back" and "feet" and another "fist" with which the state "keeps guard the while upon her breast." Thoreau too is using his comparison to suggest that we are to conceive of the state as a human being and as an alert and vigilant human being.

WHAT MAKES A "GOOD" METAPHOR?

In this connection we ought to note that the physical similarity of the items compared is easily overestimated in judging the value of a metaphor. In many finely effective comparisons the degree of physical similarity is not very great. Some element of resemblance, there must be, of course. But a good comparison is not necessarily one in which there is close resemblance: for "illustration," as we have seen, is not the primary purpose of metaphor. Moreover, even a great deal of dissimilarity does not necessarily render the comparison a strained or forced one.

THE ELEMENT OF SIMILARITY IN METAPHOR

To realize this last point, let us consider one of the tritest comparisons of all: "her eyes were like stars." Far from seeming strained or overingenious, the comparison will seem to most of us entirely too simple and easy. And yet, even in this well-worn analogy, the objects compared are really very dissimilar. Certainly the human eyeball and the flaming mass of elements which make up the stars have very little in common. But if this examination, which compares the two objects as scientifically considered, seems somewhat unfair, one can go on to point out that the eyes, even those of a lovely woman, do not much resemble the glinting points of light which are the stars as we see them. The truth of the matter is that what supports this oldest and most hackneyed of comparisons is not the physical resemblances so much as the associations: the associations of stars with brilliance, with the high and celestial. It is these associations which have made the stars seem "like" the glances of the eyes of someone loved.

Thus, every comparison has a very important subjective element in it: its proper task is to interpret, to evaluate—not to point to physical analogies. Its proper function is, as we have said, to define attitude.

Let us consider a few further illustrations: Samuel Butler, in his satire, "Hudibras," gives this description of the dawn.

> And like a lobster, boyl'd, the morn
> From black to red began to turn.

We think of this as an absurd comparison, and so it is—appropriately so, for "Hudibras" is a humorous poem, and Butler is casting good-humored scorn upon his hero. Why does the comparison strike us as absurd? We are likely to say that it is absurd because the dawn doesn't in the least resemble a boiled lobster. But the colors to be seen in the shell of a boiled lobster may very closely resemble the exact shade of red to be seen on some mornings. The absurdity, then, does not come from the lack of physical resemblance: it comes rather from the absurd contrast of the associations of cooking and the associations of morning—the sense of fresh coolness and natural beauty. Butler has, for humorous effect, deliberately played the connotations of lobster-boiling against the connotations of morning. It is the clash of connotations which creates the tone (see Chapter 11) of good-humored contempt, befitting a mock epic such as "Hudibras." (Objectively considered, the sun looks quite as much like the shell of a boiled lobster as it looks like Miss Welty's lopsided rose—a figure which we have seen is *not* used for ludicrous effect.)

The principle of contrast, however, may be used for very different effects. Consider the use to which the element of contrast is put in the following passage from Aldous Huxley's *After Many a Summer Dies the Swan:*

> In the green and shadowy translucence, two huge fish hung suspended, their snouts almost touching, motionless except for the occasional ripple of a fin and the rhythmic panting of their gills. A few inches from their staring eyes a rosary of bubbles streamed ceaselessly up toward the light.

The chain of bubbles may be thought to look like a string of beads, and the rapt, motionless attitude of the staring fish may allow one fancifully to see them as participants in a religious rite, staring at the string of ascending bubbles as at a rosary. (The adjectives "suspended" and "staring" and especially the phrase "streamed ceaselessly up toward the light," tend to support the analogy.) But the effect is not absurd as Butler's is: the effect is rather that of sardonic irony. A reading of the novel would indicate how the irony fits the bitter commentary which Huxley makes on his hero's morbid grasping at life.

Here is another example of a metaphor used for ironic effect, though for a still different kind of irony:

> In the rear of this row of guns stood a house, calm and white, amid bursting shells. A congregation of horses tied to a long railing, were tugging frenziedly at their bridles. Men were running hither and thither.
> —STEPHEN CRANE: *Red Badge of Courage.*

Why "a congregation of horses" rather than "a line" or "a group" of horses? *Congregation* (from Latin *congrex*) means literally a "herding together," and (though it is a somewhat pedantic application) "congregation" is thus literally accurate here. But as we commonly use the word, "congregation" implies a group of worshipers;

people who have come together of their own will, though this particular "congregation" is frantically trying to get away. The contrast is an ironic one, but the author has not left his choice of the word to be justified by this obvious and rather brittle contrast: the metaphor points to a richer and larger contrast. The "congregation of horses" tied to the railing suggests the scene at some rural church where the congregation within is implied by the "congregation" of hitched horses without. The line of tied animals thus ironically suggests a peaceful scene in contrast to the actual battle which is raging around them.

THE ELEMENT OF CONTRAST IN METAPHOR

We think of metaphors (and related figurative expressions) as "comparisons," and yet it is plain that we might as accurately refer to them as "contrasts." For the elements of dissimilarity between the terms of a metaphor may be of just as much importance as the elements of likeness. One can go further still: in an effective metaphor there must be a *considerable degree of contrast*. If we say "the river roared like a flood" or "the dog raged like a wild beast," we feel that the metaphor in each case is weak or nonexistent. A river is too much like a flood, and a dog, though a tame beast, too much resembles a wild beast. If, on the other hand, we say, "the fire roared like a flood" or "the fire raged like a wild beast," we feel that these are metaphors (even if actually rather poor metaphors). Fire and flood or fire and beast are sufficiently dissimilar for us to feel that some metaphorical transfer occurs: in these cases there are the "new namings" which constitute metaphor.

A famous English critic of the eighteenth century, Samuel Johnson, saw this point clearly in discussing a famous poetic comparison of his time. In a poem on the battle of Blenheim, the poet had compared the English general, Marlborough, to an angel "who rides in the whirlwind and directs the storm." The general himself was not engaged in dealing blows. In a sense he was above the battle. But calm and aloof, like the angel, he directed the crushing power of his regiments. Johnson's objection to the comparison was not that the poet had not described properly Marlborough's function, but rather that the functions of Marlborough and of the angel were too nearly the same for the comparison to have any imaginative quality. Whether or not Johnson was fair to the comparison in question, the student may decide for himself by looking up Addison's poem, "The Campaign." But there is no doubt at all that Johnson was entirely right about the principle involved.

We are inclined to reject what we rather awkwardly call "far-fetched" comparisons. (The term is awkward because it suggests that the terms of a good comparison are close together, though we have seen that even "eyes" and "stars" are not really very close— see p. 379.) But if comparisons must not be too "far-fetched," neither must they be too "nearly fetched." They have to be fetched some distance if we are to have a recognizable metaphor at all.

CONSISTENCY IN METAPHOR

In this connection, it is convenient to take up the problem of consistency in metaphor. How consistent with itself need a metaphor be? The point is worth discussing because most of us have been made well aware of the absurdity of "mixed metaphors." Everyone is familiar with the Congressman's oratorical declaration: "I smell a rat. I see it floating in the air. But I shall nip it in the bud." Moreover, earlier in this chapter the absurdity of the mixed metaphors which occur in the passages on pages 367-69 has been commented upon. But it would be a mistake if the student concluded that *any* mixing of metaphors or *any* change from one metaphor to another is in itself bad.

It is perfectly true that an extended metaphor can sometimes be used for very powerful effect, and it is further true that a metaphor which suddenly, or for no apparent reason, reverses our expectations, can give us a sense of absurd confusion. But a metaphor need not be extended; and there are fine passages of prose and poetry in which the author moves rapidly from one metaphor to another. Is the following passage from *Hamlet* absurd because the metaphor is "mixed"?

> To be, or not to be—that is the question.
> Whether 'tis nobler in the mind to suffer
> The slings and arrows of outrageous fortune
> Or to take arms against a sea of troubles
> And by opposing end them. To die—to sleep—
> No more; and by a sleep to say we end
> The heartache, and the thousand natural shocks
> That flesh is heir to.

The troubles are first conceived of as missiles—"slings and arrows"— of fortune, but then they are characterized as a "sea of troubles." One can "take arms" against a contingent of bowmen, but how can one take arms against a sea? It is possible to conceive of myriad troubles as a sea; and a great armed host, with its advancing ranks and with its seemingly infinite reserves, ready to come up to replace them, may be thought of as a sea. There is a sort of link, therefore, between "slings and arrows of outrageous fortune" and "sea of troubles." Yet do we not get into an absurdity when other elements of the two figures are brought together as Shakespeare brings them together here? How can a man take arms against the sea (as one might against an army)? Only a madman would try to fight the sea, as the Irish warrior Cuchulain was fabled to have done. Perhaps so; but if so, there may be method in Hamlet's madness here (and method in Shakespeare's arrangement of metaphors). The troubles that attack Hamlet are, like the sea, infinite. He can hardly hope to conquer them. But if he advances courageously into the waves, he may "end them" nonetheless; for in swallowing *him* up, his troubles end themselves: "by the sleep [of death] . . . we end / The heartache, and the thousand natural shocks / That flesh is heir to." The figure is daring and it is difficult, but it does not involve an absurdity.

Consider another sequence of metaphors which may seem even more confusingly mixed. In the following passage Macbeth expresses his sense of the meaninglessness of life:

> . . . all our yesterdays have lighted fools
> The way to dusty death. Out, out, brief candle!
> Life's but a walking shadow; a poor player,
> That struts and frets his hour upon the stage,
> And then is heard no more: it is a tale
> Told by an idiot, full of sound and fury,
> Signifying nothing.

Here again the images may seem to have no connection with one another; but closer reading indicates that the images are knit together rather tightly.

Death is a sleep. Our bed is the dust from which we came. The sun itself is finally but a candle by which we are lighted to this bed. Macbeth, apathetic and wearied, feels ready for the bed of death, and he needs no candle to find it. He says, "Out, out, brief candle!" But the image of the candle (which one carries to light himself to bed) suggests another figure to signify the emptiness of life, the shadow. (Life has no substance; it is mere appearance.) And this figure suggests another: life is like an actor who plays a role. The actor gives us but a shadow, an appearance. Moreover, the appearance is brief: he "struts and frets" his little "hour upon the stage." With the words "And then is heard no more," we shift from a visual to an auditory figure. The actor's speech— considered coldly and in detachment, as by a spectator who has just come into the theater in the middle of the play—strikes the ear as a meaningless rant. It is like the speech of an idiot: words pour forth, there is sound and fury, but no meaning is conveyed. In this passage, then, the various metaphors are related to each other; they grow out of each other; and they enrich and develop a total meaning which is consistent with itself.

These two examples can hardly do more than suggest some of the possible justifications for certain kinds of "mixed" metaphor. The subject, moreover, is too complex for one to lay down rules which will indicate when metaphor is improperly "mixed" and when it is not. But one common-sense principle is clear enough. Looking at the problem from the standpoint of the writer, we may say that he should not arouse expectations which he does not gratify. If he leads the reader to *expect* a consistent elaboration of a figure, he becomes inconsistent at his peril.

In general, however, as writers, our best defense against absurdly mixed metaphors on the one hand, and against rigid theories of consistency on the other, is to be found in a sound conception of the function of metaphor. Let us repeat: metaphor is not a mere decoration. It is not an illustration—not a point-to-point analogical likeness. It is not an alternate naming of the thing which is chosen because it is "prettier" or "simpler." Rather it is our great instrument for interpreting the thing in question. Metaphors are new namings which seize upon the thing and interpret it lovingly, reverently, contemptuously, mockingly, coldly, or warmly as the skillful author may desire. The aptness of a comparison, therefore, cannot be determined in isolation. The author's larger purpose, and the whole context in which the comparison occurs, must be taken into account.

Because of the delicacy and the importance of these relations between the terms of a metaphor and between the metaphor and its context, we have chosen not to present the reader with the classifications of figurative language that are frequently made in rhetoric books. For many of these classifications are of no fundamental importance. We have not distinguished, for example, from metaphorical language in general, SIMILE (an explicit comparison, usually announced by *like* or *as:* "she glided into the room like a swan," "as brittle as ice") or METONYMY (the use of a part to designate the whole: "he employed twenty hands on his farm"), and so on. Such classifications, in our considered opinion, are of little importance to the practicing writer.

METAPHOR AND SYMBOL

There is, however, one further important relationship that ought to be specified: the relation of metaphor to SYMBOL. A symbol is a kind of sign. Thus, the flag is a symbol of the nation; the cross, of Christianity; the letter *a,* of a particular vowel sound (or actually in modern English, of a particular group of vowel sounds). Symbols of this sort are conventional and arbitrary signs. For example, it is conceivable that the United States of America might have adopted some other flag, and once we had agreed to think of it as *our* flag, that flag would have symbolized our nation just as much as Old Glory now does. The Greek letter, *alpha,* corresponds to our Roman letter *a,* though it has a somewhat different shape, thus α. Mathematical and scientific symbols likewise are conventional and arbitrary signs.

Now metaphor has nothing to do with this kind of conventional symbolism. In metaphor, as we have seen, words are not used literally but are extended beyond their conventional meanings. Yet there is another kind of symbol which is not conventional and arbitrary. Washing one's hands, for example, does not necessarily signify that one feels guilt. It usually means no more than that one wants to get his hands clean. But when Shakespeare has Lady Macbeth, in the sleep-walking scene in *Macbeth,* attempt to wash the imaginary blood from her hands, her action becomes a symbol of her feeling of guilt. The simple and ordinarily unimportant act turns into a revelation of character—becomes endowed with symbolic force. Likewise, in De Maupassant's story, "The Diamond Necklace" (p. 273), the paste diamonds come to stand for the vanity and emptiness for which Madame Loisel has sacrificed her youth. With this kind of symbolism, metaphor does have something in common. In metaphor, a word is extended to a new meaning; in this kind of symbolism, an object or incident is made to take on a larger meaning. In the simplest terms, we may say that metaphor has to do with the word (or the idea) and symbolism with the thing (or the action).

METAPHOR AND THE CREATIVE IMAGINATION

The distinction between such created symbols and merely arbitrary symbols can throw much light on the problem of metaphor. In the first place, most of the effective symbols in literature, since they are not arbitrary signs, are instances of the metaphorical process—that is, they represent the endowing of some concrete object or incident with further meaning. In "The Diamond Necklace," for example, the revelation that the diamonds, for which so much has been sacrificed, are really paste becomes a kind of metaphor. A writer rarely finds a symbol ready-made for him: he creates his important symbols by the same process as that by which he creates his other metaphors.

In the second place, a consideration of symbols throws light on the problems that have to do with the validity of metaphor. Some objects and incidents do seem to have a "natural" symbolic meaning. Thus, blood may seem to be a natural symbol for violence; darkness, for evil; or light, for truth. In a sense blood, darkness, and light *are* such natural symbols; yet we need to observe two things: (1) the "natural" symbolism is much more vague and general than at first sight might be supposed. Blood can be used—and has been used—to symbolize a wealth of very different things: courage or heredity or race. Moreover, darkness can be used to symbolize, not evil but goodness: at least one poet has used darkness in this way. Henry Vaughan's poem "The Night" celebrates darkness as the proper time for spiritual meditation and communion with God. Moreover, light *can* symbolize evil: i.e., the hard, hot light of the desert can be made to suggest the mocking falsity of the mirage. (2) Even the natural and obvious symbols are ineffective unless they are presented to us freshly and dramatically. The writer cannot use them merely at the conventional level and still use them effectively. The moment that the word for the object in question has become frozen at a certain level of significance, it becomes a mere sign—an alternate name—and its emotional power has all but vanished. Thus, as we have seen, the "eye of a needle" no longer suggests any association with the human eye: "eye" has become merely the conventional name for the thread-hole. No metaphorical transfer is made: the original transfer of meaning has become fixed permanently.

The ideal scientific language, it is sometimes said, would not use metaphor at all: there would be one precise term for every object, a term which would mean only one thing. For men who are irritated by the ambiguities and confusions of metaphor, such a prospect is tempting. A few years ago, Mr. Stuart Chase (in *The Tyranny of Words*) came close to recommending that we abandon metaphor altogether in favor of a strict, unambiguous use of words. (Centuries earlier, in 1667, Thomas Sprat, the historian of the Royal Society, complimented this group of new scientists on having "exacted from all their members, a close, naked, natural way of speaking; positive expressions; clear sense; a native easiness: bringing all things as near the mathematical plainness as they can.")

But such a language, though admirable for exact scientific purposes—mathematical formulae are better still (p. 342)—would be an excessively limited instrument for other purposes. Now science properly strives toward pure notation: thus, the specific gravity of iron at $20°$ C. is 7.86; granite is an igneous rock; $2 + 2 = 4$. But most that we have to say is not pure notation: we want to tell a joke or to describe a knockout or to say what it feels like to be in love. Our normal discourse is "impure" with our own interpretations, evaluations, and insights. And these interpretations are too intimately related to ourselves for us to have a precise, ready-made term for each thing that we have to say. It is better to have a language which possesses flexibility—one which can be shaped and re-formed to the most special use.

SUMMARY

METAPHOR is the use of a concrete term to signify a wider, more general relationship. Language began as metaphor. Men came to extend concrete terms by analogy to further relationships. Yet, basic as the metaphorical process is, we tend to misapprehend its real importance. We tend to think of metaphor as a kind of external decoration which may be applied or not, as the writer chooses, to the essential statement, a statement which we think of as nakedly logical.

But, just as the development of language is from the concrete to the abstract, not from the abstract to the concrete, so the normal method of composition is from the concrete to the more abstract, not from abstract schematic outlines to metaphorical expression. The compulsion to use slang, for example, is an indication of the normality of metaphor as opposed to abstract statement. For slang, though it is usually shabby and worn-out metaphor, is, nonetheless metaphor; and the impulse to use it represents a basically sound human impulse. Consequently, the most fruitful attitude toward the misuse of slang will be that which acknowledges the natural tendency toward metaphor and attempts to replace worn and inaccurate metaphor with fresh and accurate metaphor.

The misuse of metaphor is a peculiarly significant ailment of contemporary prose. It testifies, perhaps, to the fact that we have misconceived the real function of metaphor, and having misconceived it, blunder in our practice.

Since the metaphorical process is central to language, the conventional emphases on metaphor as (1) illustrative or (2) decorative go astray by suggesting that metaphor merely adds something unessential to expression. The primary function of metaphor is to interpret experience for us—to mold and control attitudes. In all discourse (except that which aspires to strict scientific notation) this interpretative element is central. Metaphor, then, is not to be thought of as a colorful but inaccurate way of saying something. What we usually have to "say" includes this aspect of interpretation, and good metaphor has therefore its own kind of accuracy.

The fact that metaphor is used primarily to control attitudes has an important bearing on the problem of the validity of metaphor.

If we misunderstand metaphor, taking it to be simply a kind of loose analogy, then the best metaphors will be those in which the items compared are physically most nearly alike; and we shall be disposed to reject all comparisons in which there is no close physical resemblance between the items compared. If, on the contrary, we see that metaphor is one of our prime instruments of interpretation, we may be prepared to admit a large interpretative (subjective) element in metaphor, and further, to understand that the element of contrast is necessary and important.

A metaphor is a kind of symbol: that is, the concrete particular comes to stand for something larger than itself. It is not, of course, an arbitrary symbol like the cross or the flag or the letter A. For when the metaphor no longer makes a transfer of meaning, it is a dead metaphor just as the arbitrary symbol is frozen to one meaning and means one, and only one, thing. But the great literary symbols (and many humbler ones in our daily experience) do not have their meaning assigned to them by an arbitrary convention. They derive their meanings from a special context—they come to mean something special and untranslatable. In this sense, they are metaphors. We may use the term *symbol* when we think of the sign itself; the term *metaphor* when we think of the process of transfer of meaning.

When men think of the neatness and logical accuracy given by scientific terms, they sometimes long for the elimination of all metaphor. But reflection indicates that such a language of terms, each frozen to one denotation, is impossible: such a language could express only "public," agreed-upon relationships. With the elimination of the possibility of metaphor we should have eliminated connotations, the whole realm of personal evaluations through language, and all those elements which make language flexible and alive. For metaphor is ultimately the power to take a given and known term and *bend* it to a fresher and richer use.

Situation and Tone

TONE AS THE EXPRESSION OF ATTITUDE

EVERY piece of discourse implies a particular situation. A man is attempting to convince a hostile audience; or a mother is attempting to coax a child into doing something which the child dislikes; or a legislator, who can assume agreement on ends, is trying to persuade his colleagues that certain procedures constitute the best means by which to secure these ends. Even technical treatises, which attempt no persuasion, imply a special situation: the writer assumes that he is writing for people whose interest in the truth is so absorbing that rhetorical persuasions would be unnecessary and even positively irritating.

But if every discourse implies a situation in which the writer is related to his audience, by the same token every piece of discourse implies a certain TONE. This term "tone" is based frankly on a metaphor. We all know how important in actual speech the tone of voice may be in indicating the precise meaning of the words themselves. For instance, the words "very well," uttered in a certain tone of voice, may imply enthusiastic agreement, but spoken in another tone of voice they may indicate nothing more than surly compliance. The "tone" of a piece of writing, in the same way, may show the writer's attitude, and in so doing may heavily qualify the literal meanings of the words themselves.

The importance of tone is easily illustrated by the misunderstandings which personal letters so often provoke. In conversation even a rather clumsy and inadequate knowledge of language can be so supplemented by the actual tone of the voice that little serious misunderstanding will occur. But when such a speaker writes a letter—where, of course, the "tone of voice" has to be implied by the words themselves—all sorts of misunderstandings can occur, and frequently do occur. The practiced writer, on the other hand, is able, even in this medium, to control what we have called the "tone."

Some of the more obvious devices for controlling tone have already been discussed in Chapter 10 (pp. 349-52). There we saw that diction itself is a most important means of expressing our ATTITUDES. We can refer to a policeman as an "officer" or as a "cop"; we can say "farmer" or "rube." There are other obvious means by which we express our attitudes: by adjectives ("projectile adjectives" we called them) which make direct valuations (*nice, good, fine, miserable,* and so on) and by simple comparisons which are also emotional and subjective, with little or no objective content ("He's a good egg," "She's a peach"). Such devices for indicating tone are so simple that they could be discussed, as they have been, in the chapter on diction. But tone is a pervasive thing which characterizes a whole composition, and diction, strictly considered, is only one of the many elements which the writer must manage in order to secure a proper tone. In the pages that follow we are to consider some of the larger problems.

THE IMPORTANCE OF TONE

In most of our writing the management of tone is an important problem, for in most of our writing our attitudes are highly relevant. An important part of what we are trying to "communicate" is the attitude itself. This is true not only of poetry and fiction, it is true also of most essays, sermons, orations, and letters. It is even true of much of what we are inclined to regard as pure exposition. For even in expository writing the author is rarely content to give us mere facts, or mere propositions. He feels that to do this is to be painfully and technically "dry."

A glance at the so-called articles of information in magazines like the *Atlantic* and *Harper's* will indicate that even here the establishment of the appropriate tone is of the highest importance. For example, a typical expository article in *Harper's* (Wolfgang

Langewiesche's "Making the Airplane Behave," May 1942) makes very special use of tone, and is thus anything but a mechanically "dry" piece of exposition. The author assumes that the reader is a reasonably intelligent person who has a fairly wide acquaintance with the modern world; specifically, that he knows how to drive an automobile, that he does not have a technical equipment in physics, but that he does have enough common sense to follow a clear illustration. The exposition does not insist on technicalities any more than the writer stands on his own dignity. His attitude toward his reader is definitely informal. The tone of his article suggests that flying is interesting and important, but that the author's attitude toward it is sprightly.

How do we know all this? Well, consider the following paragraph.

You try, for instance, steep turns in a strong wind. The ship will go in some crazy, wrong-looking attitude; but when you check your instruments you find that it is doing a correct job of flying and that the seat of your pants and your eyes would have tricked you had you been allowed to do the "co-ordinating."

The informal "you try" rather than the more formal "one tries"; the phrase "the seat of your pants" rather than the more formal "tactile pressure of the plane"; the informal "tricked" rather than the more formal "deceived"—all of these point to the tone—that is, they indicate the attitude which the author is taking toward his audience and toward his subject matter.

WHAT DETERMINES TONE?

If, however, we are to define tone as the reflection of the author's attitude, it is necessary to make a simple distinction. Tone is the reflection of the author's attitude toward what? Toward his reader? Or toward his material? For example, if one is writing about the New Deal, his attitude may be one of admiration or contempt, of approval or disapproval. That attitude will presumably color the writing and constitute one source of its tone. But there is another source to be considered: let us suppose that the writer does approve of the New Deal. When he writes to persuade a hostile audience he will probably adopt a tone quite different from that which he uses when he addresses himself to a friendly audience. Moreover, he may wish to take into account the fact that his reader is a child or an adult, a banker or a welder, a New Englander or a Midwesterner. The writer's attitude toward his reader, therefore, may be important in determining tone.

As we shall see later, there are many kinds of writing in which the distinction between attitude toward material and attitude toward audience has little importance. But in many kinds of writing where there is a strong practical purpose—political speeches, sermons, advertisements, propaganda—the writer's attitude toward his audience is of immense importance. It may be the primary determinant of the tone, and indeed of the whole strategy of the rhetorical organization.

TONE AS AN ADJUSTMENT TO THE WRITER'S AUDIENCE

Let us consider some fairly obvious instances of tone determined by the nature of the audience. Here is an advertisement for a dandruff remover. Above a picture of two young women talking, there is the caption, "It's Listerine, for you chum . . . but *quick!* Those innocent-looking flakes and scales you see on scalp, hair or dress-shoulders, are a warning. . . . This is no time to fool around with smelly lotions or sticky salves that can't kill germs. You need antiseptic action . . . and you need it quick."

The young women in the picture are clearly friends, and the opening caption is represented as the comment of one to the other. But the advice as given to a chum is meant to carry over to the reader. As the advertisement frankly goes on to address the reader, "This is no time to fool around with smelly lotions. . . . You need antiseptic action. . . ."

What is the attitude toward the reader, then? The attitude of a sprightly, intimate friend whose advice can be frank and straight from the shoulder.

Let us look at another advertisement. This one, printed in color, depicts a young woman seated on a luxurious bed looking dreamily at a handsome blanket. The caption begins "For you to whom beauty is a necessity. . . . Yours is a nature that thrives on beauty. . . . Seize it as a vital factor in your daily living. To you a blanket should be more than a source of warmth. Exquisite colors, luxuriously deep-nap, rich virgin-wool loveliness—these awaken in you an emotional response far beyond the material."

These statements, of course, are not addressed merely to the young woman pictured in the advertisement. They are addressed to the reader as well, and they make certain flattering assumptions about the reader: that she is a young woman of means who is at home with the luxurious and who has a soul which deserves and requires beauty as a necessity. Coarser natures may buy blankets simply for warmth, but you, dear and lovely reader, ought to have something more—even in a blanket.

The attitude toward the reader, of course, need not be flattering. Here follows an example of a very different tone, though like the advertisements just discussed, the tone here also is primarily conditioned by the writer's attitude toward his reader. The example is a letter written by Dr. Samuel Johnson to James Macpherson. In the 1760's Macpherson had published several volumes of poetry which he claimed to have translated from Gaelic [1] originals. Dr. Samuel Johnson refused to believe in the existence of any Gaelic originals of which the disputed poems were translations. He openly pronounced his opinion that they were Macpherson's own composition. In reply to Macpherson's demands that he retract this charge Johnson wrote the following letter:

Mr. James Macpherson:

I received your foolish and impudent letter. Any violence offered me I shall do my best to repel; and what I cannot do for myself, the law shall do for me. I hope I shall never be deterred from detecting what I think to be a cheat, by the menaces of a ruffian.

What would you have me retract? I thought your book an imposture; I think it an imposture still. For this opinion I have given my reasons to the publick, which I here dare you to refute. Your rage I defy. Your abilities, since your *Homer*,[2] are not so formidable; and what I hear of your morals, inclines me to pay regard not to what you shall say, but to what you shall prove. You may print this if you will.—SAM. JOHNSON.

A most important part of this letter is the attitude taken toward Macpherson. For Johnson might have stated the "facts" in a form

---

[1] The original Celtic language of the Scottish Highlands.
[2] Macpherson had published a translation of Homer.

as simple as this: "I continue to hold the view that the Macpherson translations are fraudulent" or "I repeat that I shall not believe in any Gaelic originals until they are produced." And if we argue that Johnson's expression of fearlessness also is a "fact" with which the letter concerns itself, even this fact might have been expressed very differently: thus, "I have no intention of expressing a retraction" or "I mean to stand my ground on this matter" or "I am sorry that I can make no retraction since I feel that there is nothing to retract."

The tone is of the utmost importance, then. How shall we characterize the tone of the letter as Johnson actually wrote it? No paraphrase of the letter will do justice to the tone; and an abstract description of the tone is clumsy as well as inadequate. For the full realization of the tone, we shall have to return to the letter itself. But one can point to some important elements of the tone: a manly contempt of threats, a confidence in truth and in his own integrity, perhaps even a trace of sardonic amusement at baffled and petty rage.

The following excerpt consists of the opening paragraphs of the first of *The Drapier's Letters*, letters which Jonathan Swift wrote to the Irish people, warning them against accepting any of the coins which one William Wood had been given a patent to mint. Swift felt that acceptance and circulation of the coins would injure the economy of Ireland.

Brethren, friends, countrymen and fellow-subjects, what I intend now to say to you, is, next to your duty to God, and the care of your salvation, of the greatest concern to yourselves, and your children; your bread and clothing, and every common necessary of life entirely depend upon it. Therefore I do most earnestly exhort you as men, as Christians, as parents, and as lovers of your country, to read this paper with the utmost attention, or get it read to you by others; which that you may do at least expense, I have ordered the printer to sell it at the lowest rate.

It is a great fault among you, that when a person writes with no other intention than to do you good, you will not be at the pains to read his advices: One copy of this paper may serve a dozen of you, which will be less than a farthing apiece. It is your folly that you have no common or general interest in your view, not even the wisest among you, neither do you know or enquire, or care who are your friends, or who are your enemies.

Swift assumes that his audience is not a learned one. He adopts the simplest language. His phrase "or get it read to you" indicates that he assumes, further, that many of the people whom he wishes to reach cannot read. But in addition to the almost painful effort to make himself completely clear, Swift implies that his readers are childishly thoughtless, taking too little care of their own interests, and confused as to their real friends. The tone is one of grave and patient admonition. Swift emphasizes the importance of what he is going to say; he appeals to his readers in terms of their deepest allegiances as "Christians, as parents, and as lovers of [their] country," and patiently makes clear how little the paper will cost such readers. He does not hesitate to tax their "folly," folly which renders them blind as to who their real friends are. The last point is, of course, of crucial importance for the effectiveness of Swift's tract. For unless his readers are willing to see that he is their real friend, he can hardly expect that they will follow his advice.

TONE AS AN ADJUSTMENT TO THE WRITER'S MATERIAL

It might seem appropriate, just at this point, to take up the matter of formality and informality of tone, for it would seem that the degree of formality of the utterance is largely determined by the kind of audience that the author addresses. In any event, the degree of formality is ostensibly an adjustment of manner to the audience addressed. For example, the writer may choose to treat his reader as a friend with whom he converses intimately and even casually. Or the author may choose to address him with a good deal more ceremony, respectful of his dignity and careful to take no liberties. Even so, by writing "the author may choose," we have indicated that formality or informality of tone is not determined automatically by the nature of the audience addressed. The occasion may determine the tone even more than the audience. A serious subject, for example, may call for a certain formality of tone, even though the writer is addressing friends with whom he moves on terms of intimacy; and actually the writer most often addresses a general reader whom he does not know personally, whom he may never see, and whom he chooses to approach formally or informally because of the nature of his subject and of his strategy for handling the subject.

With this matter of formality and informality, therefore, we have actually moved away from the audience as the determiner of tone into more general problems of tone, problems in which tone is shaped by other considerations.

But though we now turn to these more general problems of tone, we have probably been wise to begin with the problem in its easiest form, where there is a definite and particular audience to be placated, defied, cajoled, mollified, or in general induced to act in a certain way.

But what of the other kinds of writing in which the audience addressed is less special and in which the writer is less interested in an immediate result? What of fiction, poetry, formal essays, articles of information? Is tone of no importance in these? Quite the contrary, even though no matter of practical expedience is involved. The tone of such writing may be of immense importance, for the tone frequently suggests how we are to "take" what is said.

TONE AS A QUALIFICATION OF MEANING

A little reflection will show that full meaning is rarely conveyed by literal statements. We constantly find that we must "read between the lines" in order to understand a letter, or to take into account the tone of voice and the facial expressions in our conversation with a friend. To take a simple example, John tells Ben: "You have done well"; but the simple statement can convey anything from hearty commendation to hesitant and reluctant approval, depending upon the way in which John says these words. We can go further: "You have done well" can even mean, when spoken in a certain tone of voice, that Ben has not done well at all, for John may be speaking ironically.

IRONY AS A MODE OF TONE

IRONY always involves a discrepancy between the literal meaning of a statement and the actual meaning. The ironical statement says one thing on the surface, in actuality something rather different. In a lighthearted, laughingly ironical statement the literal meaning may be only partially qualified; in a bitter and obvious irony (such as we call SARCASM), the literal meaning may be entirely reversed. Between delicate ironical qualification of a statement and sarcastic reversal of a statement there are a thousand possible shadings, and it is perhaps a pity that we do not have specific terms for them.

But on second thought, our lack of the terms may be no real handi-
cap. What is important is that we be aware of the fact of ironical
qualification. Such qualification is important, even in everyday
practical writing; and if we are to learn to write, we must learn
how to qualify our statements so as to convey precisely what we
want to say, and only what we want to say.

We can say, then, that even in writing in which there is no practical problem of adjustment to a particular audience, even in writing addressed to an ideal reader, the matter of tone is of great
consequence. In fiction, for example, mastery of tone may become
almost the whole consequence; for tone, we must remember, represents the author's total attitude as it is reflected in the work; the
tone conveys the final shadings of meaning and interpretation which
he wishes to convey.

Tone may of course be handled successfully or unsuccessfully,
and a failure in tone can be thoroughly disastrous. Let us illustrate with examples both of failure and of success.

OVERSTATEMENT AND UNDERSTATEMENT

The following passage consists of the last two paragraphs of
Bret Harte's story, "The Outcasts of Poker Flat." In the story the
gambler and the prostitute rise to heroism as they try to shelter and
protect the innocent girl who has fallen into their company when
the whole party is overtaken by a severe snow storm in the mountains. The paragraphs that follow describe the last days of the two
women, the innocent girl and the prostitute.

The wind lulled as if it feared to waken them. Feathery drifts of snow,
shaken from the long pine boughs, flew like white-winged birds, and
settled about them as they slept. The moon through the rifted clouds
looked down upon what had been the camp. But all human stain, all
trace of earthly travail, was hidden beneath the spotless mantle mercifully flung from above.

They slept all day that day and the next, nor did they waken when
voices and footsteps broke the silence of the camp. And when pitying
fingers brushed the snow from their wan faces, you could scarcely have
told from the equal peace that dwelt upon them which was she that
had sinned.

Here the author, in his anxiety to stress the pathos of the scene
and the redemption of the fallen woman, is not content to let the

scene speak for itself. The wind "lulls" the two women; the moon looks down upon them; "a spotless mantle" is "mercifully flung from above." The pseudopoetic language, the suggestion that nature mercifully hides "all human stain," the general absence of restraint and reserve—all indicate that the tone here is one of SENTIMENTAL-ITY; that is, emotion in excess of the occasion. The author wants his reader to respond powerfully and sympathetically. We are to feel the pathos of the women's death.

What was Bret Harte's own attitude? One has to conclude that either he himself was "soft" (that is, that Bret Harte was taken in by his own attempt to "work up" an effect); or else that he was cynically trying to seduce his reader into an emotional response which is not itself justified by the dramatic occasion that he provided. In either case most sensitive readers will feel that the tone is sentimental. Sentimentality usually betrays itself by a conscious strain to work up the reader's feelings. Of course, in a sense, any appeal to our emotions represents an attempt "to work up" the effect. But it is one thing to do this skillfully and legitimately by presenting a scene with imaginative power, and it is quite a different thing to cram the emotion down the reader's throat. Readers may disagree on whether the response has been evoked legitimately or illegitimately (that is, sentimentally), but the principle involved is crucial. Otherwise any writer, however tawdry or mawkish, could demand our response simply by making a direct assault on our feelings.

Contrast with the passage from Bret Harte the following passage (from Hemingway's A Farewell to Arms), which describes an incident in the retreat from Caporetto in World War I. The Germans have broken through the Italian lines, and the speaker, an American serving with the ambulances attached to the Italian army, has just been picked up by the Italian battle police, who are questioning all who are separated from their units.

This officer too was separated from his troops. He was not allowed to make an explanation. He cried when they read the sentence from the pad of paper, and they were questioning another when they shot him. They made a point of being intent on questioning the next man while the man who had been questioned before was being shot. In this way there was obviously nothing they could do about it. I did not know whether I should wait to be questioned or make a break now. I was obviously a

German in Italian uniform. I saw how their minds worked; if they had minds and if they worked. They were all young men and they were saving their country. The second army was being re-formed beyond the Tagliamento. They were executing officers of the rank of major and above who were separated from their troops. They were dealing summarily with German agitators in Italian uniform. They wore steel helmets. Only two of us had steel helmets. Some of the carabinieri had them. The other carabinieri wore the wide hat. Airplanes we called them. We stood in the rain and were taken out one at a time to be questioned and shot. So far they had shot every one they had questioned. The questioners had that beautiful detachment and devotion to stern justice of men dealing in death without being in any danger of it. They were questioning a full colonel of a line regiment.—ERNEST HEMINGWAY: *A Farewell to Arms,* Chap. 30.[3]

This passage ably illustrates the effectiveness in some contexts of UNDERSTATEMENT. The speaker's comments on the actions of his captors are studiedly dry. He allows the actions to speak for themselves, his own commentary upon them being implied by the very act of refraining from the expected comment. The short sentences, the summary style, the repetitions—all point up the irony. (Understatement is a form of irony: the ironical contrast inheres in the discrepancy between what one would be expected to say and his actual refusal to say it.) Understatement then is the staple rhetorical device here, but the irony is occasionally allowed to become overt in such a passage as "if they had minds and if they worked."

Why does the author (who has on the whole avoided detailed description) give us the detail about the steel helmets? Because it points farther the ironical contrast: the men who have been under fire have not had the protection of the helmets. The men who are questioning them with that "devotion to stern justice of men dealing in death without being in any danger of it" do not need the helmets which they wear. Indeed, the steel helmets become a kind of symbol of the men who wear them: their reasoning and their justice is "steel-headed"—in a double sense.

Repetition in this passage also becomes an important adjunct of the ironical understatement. The word "questioned" (or "questioning") for example, occurs in this passage no less than seven

[3] From *A Farewell to Arms* by Ernest Hemingway, copyright, 1929, by Charles Scribner's Sons.

times. As first used, it is used innocently and normally: it merely means "interrogated," with the implication that answers are expected and that the answers given are attended to. But by the end of the passage it has become "loaded" with other meanings: it has come to mean to the speaker, and to us, "sentenced to death." That is, the "questioning" is an empty form; the answers do not matter. No one will pay attention to them anyway. But the speaker, as the narration continues, does not change his term or qualify it. He is content to continue to use the word "questioned" or "questioning," and his continuing to repeat the original word becomes thus a form of understatement.

If the tone of this excerpt from *A Farewell to Arms* can fairly be described as that of understatement, the tone of the excerpt from Bret Harte is that of OVERSTATEMENT. But we are not, of course, to conclude that understatement is always successful or that overstatement always fails. The point to be made, rather, is this: that, for the writer of fiction and poetry, tone is important, just as important as it is for the writer who wishes to produce some practical effect. True, the poet or the writer of fiction can assume a fixed audience—an ideal reader—but even so, his attitude toward his material is of the utmost importance—even if he is writing consciously only for himself. It is easy to see that the political writer, say, uses rhetorical blandishments at his peril; if he seems to play fast and loose with the truth, he may defeat his purpose by convincing his reader that he is using a specious rhetoric—trying to persuade the reader to accept a lie by playing on his emotions. But the writer of poetry and fiction, we ought to observe, does not try to win acceptance of a lie either—fiction, though not "true," is not a lie. And even though his fiction is designed to stir the reader's emotions, he is not thereby entitled to use *any* device calculated to stir the emotions. For him, too, there is a problem of integrity: the emotional response must seem to spring legitimately from the situation which he presents.

SOME PRACTICAL DON'TS

The problem of tone, then, is most important. There are obviously too many shadings of tone for us to be able to set up ar elaborate classification. But it is possible to set down a few "don'ts" which have a very general application.

1. Writing down. One must not "write down" to his audience. The sense of oversimple statement and painfully careful explanation can disgust the reader as quickly as any offense of which the writer is capable. Prose which is properly suited to an audience of eight-year-olds would prove completely tiresome, or, on the other hand, unintentionally funny, to a mature audience. Swift, for example, would have adopted a very different tone, had *The Drapier's Letters* been addressed to a lettered audience.

2. False enthusiasm. The reader is also likely to resent any hint of synthetic breeziness and false camaraderie. It is a fault into which modern advertising is tending to press the whole civilization. Bug-eyed young matrons oo-la-la-ing over the purchase of sheets or toothbrushes, and the all-too-infectious joviality of supersalesmen, more and more fill the advertisements. The writer obviously wishes to gain a kind of liveliness and warmth in his style, but an artificial concoction of informality and sprightliness can be more depressing than a rather painful dryness.

3. Sentimentality. This third fault is hardly likely to appear in most simple expository writing, but as we have seen in earlier chapters there is very little writing which is "simple expository." Sentimentality may show itself as simply gushiness or as a kind of hair-trigger emotional sensitiveness. But whatever form it takes, sentimentality always involves an implied demand, on the part of the writer, for more emotional response than the situation warrants; and it implies, on the part of the sentimental reader, a willingness to respond emotionally when the response is not actually justified.

SOME PRACTICAL APPLICATIONS

It scarcely needs to be said that the rules given on page 401 must not be applied mechanically. The problem of attitude is intimately bound up with the particular occasion presented, and what would be "writing down" in one situation might possibly be overwriting in another situation. Perhaps our best mode of procedure is to consider a series of examples of tone as growing out of particular situations.

TONE IN PERSUASION

First let us consider an example of persuasive exposition. In the passage that follows, Thomas Huxley is writing for an audience of intelligent laymen about scientific method. It is a nontechnical audience, but it is an audience capable of following an argument. Huxley takes pains to make himself clear, but he is not "writing down." In this passage he is concluding his argument that parts of England were once covered by the sea, and going on to argue that the period during which they were covered by the sea must have been a very long one.

I think you will now allow that I did not overstate my case when I asserted that we have as strong grounds for believing that all the vast area of dry land, at present occupied by the chalk, was once at the bottom of the sea, as we have for any matter of history whatever; while there is no justification for any other belief.

No less certain it is that the time during which the countries we now call south-east England, France, Germany, Poland, Russia, Egypt, Arabia, Syria, were more or less completely covered by a deep sea, was of considerable duration. We have already seen that the chalk is, in places, more than a thousand feet thick. I think you will agree with me, that it must have taken some time for the skeletons of animalcules of a hundredth of an inch in diameter to heap up such a mass as that. I have said that throughout the thickness of the chalk the remains of other animals are scattered. These remains are often in the most exquisite state of preservation. The valves of the shellfishes are commonly adherent; the long spines of some of the sea-urchins, which would be detached by the smallest jar, often remain in their places. In a word, it is certain that these animals have lived and died when the place which they now occupy was the surface of as much of the chalk as had then been deposited; and that each has been covered up by the layer of *Globigerina* mud, upon which the creatures imbedded a little higher up have, in like manner, lived and died. But some of these remains prove the existence of reptiles of vast size in the chalk sea. These lived their time, and had their ancestors and descendants, which assuredly implies time, reptiles being of slow growth.—THOMAS HUXLEY: "On a Piece of Chalk," *Discourses.*

It will of course occur to the reader that Huxley might have shortened his discussion considerably by omitting such phrases as "I think that you will now allow," "I think you will agree with me," "we have already seen," "I have said that," "it is certain that." Why did he include them? He included them because he wished to reassure his audience, to indicate to them the validity and reasonableness of the inferences he was making, and to make certain that all seemed perfectly coherent. Such phrases, indeed, tell us a great deal about the way in which Huxley envisaged his audience and about his attitude toward that audience.

Huxley evidently respects his typical hearer, even though his hearer has no technical knowledge of geology. Huxley does not water down his conclusions for him. He refuses to overwhelm him with authority. As a matter of fact, Huxley does just the reverse of this: he presents him with the evidence, and attempts to show him why certain conclusions and only certain conclusions can be fairly inferred from the evidence. Huxley, it is obvious, has complete confidence in the case that he is making; but his confidence nowhere reflects itself as arrogance.

To take up one further illustration: Why does Huxley go to the pains that he does to show that the easily detached spines of some of the sea-urchins often remain in place? It is another evidence of his respect for the intelligence of his audience. He does this obviously in order to forestall the possible objection that the remains of the sea-urchins were thrown up on the chalk at some later date. That the spines are still in place indicates that the creatures must "have lived and died when the place that they now occupy was the surface of as much of the chalk as had then been deposited."

The next passage will illustrate persuasive argument.

From 1937, when he made his "quarantine" speech in Chicago until the Japanese attack on Pearl Harbor, President Roosevelt struggled with the problem of making our bankrupt foreign position solvent. As early as 1937 it was clear that the American situation demanded an immediate, intensified expansion of our armed forces, the fortification of our strategic commitments in Alaska, Guam, the Philippines, and Panama, and the formation of arrangements for mutual aid with Great Britain, France, and China—our obvious allies in an attack which was being prepared against them and against us alike. But this prudent course was held to be politically imprudent. This is another way of saying that the American people would not agree to protect their vital interests because they had no foreign policy which disclosed their vital interests.

Thus from 1937 to 1940 President Roosevelt moved anxiously and hesitantly between his knowledge of what ought to be done and his estimate of how much the people would understand what ought to be done. I shall not attempt to answer the question whether he could have made the people understand how great was their peril because their commitments were totally unbalanced. The illusions of a century stood in the way of their understanding, and it may be that no words, but only the awful experience of total war, could even partially dispel the illusion.—WALTER LIPPMANN: *U. S. Foreign Policy: Shield of the Republic*, Chap. 4.[4]

Lippmann's general thesis is that we have lacked a meaningful foreign policy for a very long time, and that our misunderstanding of the problem has been general—not confined to one party or group. The purpose of his book is to persuade the American citizen to agree with him that the problem of foreign policy has been consistently misunderstood, and to accept now a different conception of it. But Lippmann's purpose is to win over to his thesis all American citizens, not merely those that are Republicans or those that are Democrats.

In illustrating his thesis from an episode in Roosevelt's presidency, it is not to Lippmann's purpose either to attack or to defend Roosevelt. Presumably Lippmann is sympathetic with Roosevelt's dilemma. But whether he is sympathetic or whether he is not, his primary purpose in this book is to make his general point, if possible, without alienating the reader who may be enthusiastically pro-Roosevelt or bitterly anti-Roosevelt. This purpose definitely determines the tone of this passage.

How powerfully it determines the tone can easily be demonstrated by rewriting a few of the sentences. Suppose Lippmann's attitude toward Roosevelt were more sharply critical (or that Lippmann did not mind alienating the fiercely pro-Roosevelt reader). Instead of "But this prudent course was held to be politically imprudent," he might have written: "But Roosevelt held this prudent course to be politically imprudent," or more bitterly, "But Roosevelt allowed political expediency to overrule what was the prudent course for the nation." Again, in the first sentence of the second paragraph, he might have substituted for "moved anxiously and

[4] From Walter Lippmann, *Foreign Policy: Shield of the Republic* by permission of Little, Brown and Company and the Atlantic Monthly Press.

hesitantly" the one word "vacillated." In the next sentence, he might have written, not "I shall not attempt to answer the question . . . ," but "I prefer not to try to answer the question," or "Perhaps we had better leave to Roosevelt's conscience the question." Such changes as these, plus minor changes to bring the rest of the passage into line with them, would alter the tone drastically, and with it, the total import of the whole passage.

SOME KINDS OF IRONY

In the passage that follows, the author, William Makepeace Thackeray, makes his tone clearly evident, and indeed raucously evident. The passage quoted is taken from *Vanity Fair*, Chap. 48. The author has for a moment dropped his role as narrator of the novel and describes an occasion on which he saw King George IV.

The King? There he was. Beefeaters were before the august box; the Marquis of Steyne (Lord of the Powder Closet) and other great officers of state were behind the chair on which he sate, *He* sate—florid of face, portly of person, covered with orders, and in a rich curling head of hair. How we sang, God Save Him! How the house rocked and shouted with that magnificent music. . . . Ladies wept; mothers clasped their children; some fainted with emotion. . . . Yes, we saw him. Fate cannot deprive us of *that*. Others have seen Napoleon. Some few still exist who have beheld Frederick the Great, Doctor Johnson, Marie Antoinette, etc.: be it our reasonable boast to our children that we saw George the Good, the Magnificent, the Great.

In this mock-ecstatic tribute to George IV, Thackeray makes use of an obvious sarcasm. The literal profession of his awe of the great person is completely reversed by the tone in which the profession is given. Though pretending to praise, Thackeray indicates clearly enough what his real attitude is: by his exaggerated use of capitals and italics; by his hyperbolic laudation; by the qualities which he singles out for notice—"florid of face, portly of person."

Thackeray's sarcasm is almost too obvious. It verges on the burlesque. But irony can be used in much more subtle and much more effective fashion. Notice how John Dryden uses irony in his reference to Jeremy Collier in the passage quoted below. Collier, a clergyman, had violently attacked the writers of plays, including Dryden, for their obscenity and immorality. Here follows Dryden's answer:

I shall say the less of Mr. Collier, because in many things he has taxed me justly; and I have pleaded guilty to all thoughts and expressions of mine, which can be truly argued of obscenity, profaneness, or immorality, and retract them. If he be my enemy, let him triumph; if he be my friend, as I have given him no personal occasion to be otherwise, he will be glad of my repentance. It becomes me not to draw my pen in the defense of a bad cause, when I have so often drawn it for a good one. Yet it were not difficult to prove, that in many places he has perverted my meaning by his glosses, and interpreted my words into blasphemy and bawdry, of which they were not guilty. Besides that, he is too much given to horse-play in his raillery, and comes to battle like a dictator from the plough. I will not say, *The Zeal of God's House has eaten him up;* but I am sure it has devoured some part of his good manners and civility. It might also be doubted, whether it were altogether zeal which prompted him to this rough manner of proceeding; perhaps it became not one of his function to rake into the rubbish of ancient and modern plays; a divine might have employed his pains to better purpose, than in the nastiness of Plautus and Aristophanes, whose examples, as they excuse not me, so it might be possibly supposed, that he read them not without some pleasure.

It is highly important, in view of Dryden's later sentences, that he should begin with a manly confession of his own guilt. Dryden makes his confession quietly but quite positively—"I have pleaded guilty to all thoughts . . . if he be my friend . . . he will be glad of my repentance." The next sentence—"It becomes me not to draw my pen . . ."—breathes a confidence in his own general integrity which accounts for the fact that he can afford to plead guilty, but it also looks forward to the treatment which he proposes to deal out to Collier because of the character of Collier's attack. Dryden's own counterattack is gradually developed as the paragraph goes on. It comes with deadly effect because it is made quietly and because it has been prepared for. More obvious irony would make his castigation of Collier seem heavy-handed and strained. As it is, Dryden has managed to suggest powerfully a sense of his own composure and self-confidence, and further to suggest Collier's own frenetic and bad-humored attitude.

TONE IN PUBLIC UTTERANCE AND PRIVATE UTTERANCE

John Dryden's answer to Collier is, as we have just observed, a fine example of the subtlety of tone that may be achieved by a writer who can count upon cultivated readers. The public orator will usually aim at a different kind of effect and will make use of rhetorical devices appropriate to that effect. The passage which follows is the last paragraph of the now famous speech which Winston Churchill delivered before the House of Commons on June 4, 1940, just after the British Army had been successfully removed from Dunkirk.

I have, myself, full confidence that if all do their duty, if nothing is neglected, and if the best arrangements are made, as they are being made, we shall prove ourselves once again able to defend our island home, to ride out the storm of war, and to outlive the menace of tyranny, if necessary for years, if necessary alone. At any rate, that is what we are going to try to do. That is the resolve of His Majesty's Government—every man of them. That is the will of Parliament and the nation. The British Empire and the French Republic, linked together in their cause and in their need, will defend to the death their native soil, aiding each other like good comrades to the utmost of their strength. Even though large tracts of Europe and many old and famous States have fallen or may fall into the grip of the Gestapo and all the odious apparatus of Nazi rule, we shall not flag or fail. We shall go on to the end, we shall fight in France, we shall fight on the seas and oceans, we shall fight with growing confidence and growing strength in the air, we shall defend our island, whatever the cost may be, we shall fight on the beaches, we shall fight on the landing grounds, we shall fight in the fields and in the streets, we shall fight in the hills; we shall never surrender, and even if, which I do not for a moment believe, this island or a large part of it were subjugated and starving, then our Empire beyond the seas, armed and guarded by the British Fleet, would carry on the struggle, until, in God's good time, the new world, with all its power and might, steps forth to the rescue and the liberation of the old. —WINSTON CHURCHILL: *Blood, Sweat, and Tears.*[5]

Churchill's purpose was to rally the British people in a firm determination to continue their resistance in spite of the disastrous loss of North France and the Channel ports. But he was speaking, of course, also to a world audience, an audience which also had to be given confidence in British determination to carry on the war. Notice the amount of repetition in this closing paragraph. Is it

[5] From *Blood, Sweat, and Tears* by Winston Churchill, copyright, 1941, by G. P. Putnam's Sons.

justified? Why does it not grow monotonous? Would it be particularly effective in oral delivery? Notice too that the specification of the places where the British will continue to fight makes a kind of progression, moving from France, from which the British Army had just been evacuated, to "our island," and then on to "our Empire beyond the seas." Does this progression prevent the repetition of "we shall fight" from becoming monotonous? Notice too that Churchill is willing to entertain the possibility that "this island" may be subjugated. Does the admission of the possibility undermine the sense of resolution? Or does it strengthen it?

The reader might also notice that the peroration of this speech is closely linked to the events which had just occurred at Dunkirk where the Navy had rendered splendid service. Does this linkage help give new strength to the otherwise rather worn metaphor "storm of war"? Does it help account for Churchill's putting his mention of the British Fleet in climactic position?

This speech by Churchill represents the effect sought by the orator on a high occasion. It is political in the best sense of the term, for the speaker was not only speaking to an audience but speaking consciously as the mouthpiece of a whole people. Yet the rhetorical effect sought would be quite out of place in the passage which follows, a passage which is also political, but "private" and personal. It is an excerpt from one of Thomas Jefferson's letters to his friend and former political rival, John Adams.

. . . I agree with you that there is a natural aristocracy among men. The grounds of this are virtue and talents. Formerly, bodily powers gave place among the *aristoi*. But, since the invention of gunpowder has armed the weak as well as the strong with missile death, bodily strength, like beauty, good humor, politeness, and other accomplishments, has become but an auxiliary ground for distinction. There is also an artificial aristocracy, founded on wealth and birth, without either virtue or talents; for with these it would belong to the first class. The natural aristocracy I consider as the most precious gift of nature, for the instruction, the trusts, and government of society. And, indeed, it would have been inconsistent in creation to have formed man for the social state, and not to have provided virtue and wisdom enough to manage the concerns of the society. May we not even say that that form of government is the best which provides the most effectually for a pure selection of these natural *aristoi* into the offices of government? The artificial aristocracy is a mischievous ingredient in government, and provision should be made to prevent its ascendancy. On the question what is the best provision, you and I differ; but we differ as rational friends, using the free exercise of our own reason, and mutually indulging its errors. You think it best to put the pseudo *aristoi* into a separate chamber of legislation, where they may be hindered from doing mischief by their co-ordinate branches, and where, also, they may be a protection to wealth against the agrarian and plundering enterprises of the majority of the people. I think that to give them power in order to prevent them from doing mischief is arming them for it, and increasing instead of remedying the evil. For, if the co-ordinate branches can arrest their action, so may they that of the co-ordinates. Mischief may be done negatively as well as positively. Of this a cabal in the Senate of the United States has furnished many proofs. Nor do I believe them necessary to protect the wealthy, because enough of these will find their way into every branch of the legislation to protect themselves. From fifteen to twenty legislatures of our own, in action for thirty years past, have proved that no fears of an equalization of property are to be apprehended from them. I think the best remedy is exactly that provided by all our constitutions, to leave to the citizens the free election and separation of the *aristoi* from the pseudo *aristoi*, of the wheat from the chaff. In general they will elect the really good and wise. In some instances, wealth may corrupt, and birth blind them; but not in sufficient degree to endanger society.

The tone of this passage is not formal and public, but informal and private, as befits a letter from a wise and seasoned statesman to a wise and seasoned friend. Jefferson disagrees with Adams, but there is no rancor in the disagreement. (They differ "as rational friends.") Indeed, the paragraph in question represents Jefferson's attempt to put their fundamental disagreement in its clearest light. He can appeal to the political experience shared by both of them, and this means that he need not go into detail with some of his illustrations. He can also count upon Adams' own sense of language and even on his knowledge of Greek; and so Jefferson uses the term *aristoi* (which means "the best") naturally and gracefully. Moreover, Jefferson does not need to identify "best." Adams will know that he means those "best fitted to hold office."

Jefferson does not claim too much. He can make reasonable concessions (note the last sentence in the excerpt), for this is not a lawyer's brief in which he must put the best possible face on the position he maintains, nor is it a public speech which must offer no loopholes to his opponents. It is a letter, a letter to a "rational friend," and the tone has the candor and the reasonableness of such a letter.

TONE: FAMILIAR AND FORMAL

The so-called FAMILIAR ESSAY depends upon tone for its special character. Indeed, without employing the concept of tone, it is difficult to define the familiar essay at all. For the essence of the familiar essay does not reside in subject or theme or even style, if we use style in the most general sense of that term. The essence resides in a certain geniality of tone. There are familiar essays on all sorts of subjects and they make use of long sentences or short, vivid descriptions or no descriptions at all, quotations from the classic English authors or no quotations. The one matter which they have in common is a special attitude toward the audience, and variations of tone which reflect this attitude.

THE IMPORTANCE OF TONE IN THE FAMILIAR ESSAY

In this connection consider the opening paragraphs of a celebrated familiar essay, Charles Lamb's "Mrs. Battle's Opinions on Whist."

"A clear fire, a clean hearth, and the rigour of the game." This was the celebrated *wish* of old Sarah Battle (now with God) who, next to her devotions, loved a good game at whist. She was none of your lukewarm gamesters, your half-and-half players, who have no objection to take a hand, if you want one to make up a rubber; who affirm that they have no pleasure in winning; that they like to win one game and lose another; that they can while away an hour very agreeably at a cardtable, but are indifferent whether they play or no; and will desire an adversary, who has slipped a wrong card, to take it up and play another. These insufferable triflers are the curse of a table. One of these flies will spoil a whole pot. Of such it may be said that they do not play at cards, but only play at playing at them.

Sarah Battle was none of that breed. She detested them, as I do, from her heart and soul; and would not, save upon a striking emergency, willingly seat herself at the same table with them. She loved a thorough-paced partner, a determined enemy. She took, and gave, no concessions. She hated favours. She never made a revoke, nor ever passed it over in her adversary without exacting the utmost forfeiture. She fought a good fight: cut and thrust. She held not her good sword (her cards) "like a dancer." She sate bolt upright; and neither showed you her cards, nor desired to see yours. All people have their blind side—their superstitions; and I have heard her declare, under the rose, that Hearts was her favourite suit.

What is Lamb's attitude toward his reader? Basically, the attitude assumes that the reader is a companion who is accepted on terms of friendly equality. The assumption, indeed, makes further claims still: it assumes that the reader is one of the initiate. He can be counted on to appreciate the writer's values, to respond to his jests, to understand his allusions, to take, without any urging, the writer's own attitude toward the materials with which he deals.

Because this attitude is basic, the familiar essay frequently makes use of literary allusions, quotations and semi-quotations from the classics, the more subtle forms of irony, and, in general, all the devices of indirection. Such devices can be employed because it is assumed that the reader is able to follow them, and moreover, that he will relish them. But these devices do not in themselves give us a familiar essay. Stevenson's "Pulvis et Umbra" (p. 415) is hardly an informal essay, though it contains many literary allusions; nor is Johnson's letter to Macpherson, though its tone is ironical. The informal essay requires a tone more special still.

The passage quoted from Lamb will illustrate. Lamb's implied attitude toward his reader is very different from his attitude, say, toward Mrs. Battle herself. Though Lamb obviously admires Mrs. Battle, he is capable of smiling at her too; and we are expected to join him in smiling. Mrs. Battle is presented, mock-heroically, as a warrior. She is stern; she is even grim; she lives by a strict code, insisting that her opponent live by the same, and valuing a foeman worthy of her steel. (The whist-warfare analogy, by the way, runs through the whole essay.)

In this passage she is said, in accordance with St. Paul's injunction, to have "fought a good fight"; she has the contempt of Shakespeare's battle-scarred warrior Antony for one who held his sword "like a dancer." The information that Hearts was her favorite suit is given with the air of divulging an amiable foible in an otherwise grim old warrior who might be thought to have had none.

But the irony generated in the cards-warfare contrast is directed at Sarah Battle with a difference. The speaker is careful to align himself on Sarah Battle's side. Ostensibly he agrees with her—in the zest which he takes in mimicking the excuses of her adversaries ("they can while away an hour very agreeably at a cardtable"), in joining in her detestation of those who "only play at playing at" cards ("She detested them, as I do"), in the mock-reverence with which he speaks of her ("now with God"). If, however, someone argues that the mock-reverence is not merely mock-reverence, but has an aspect of sincerity and affection, that is perfectly true. Sarah Battle is described in terms of an irony so gentle that it is finally affectionate. But this is just the point: the writer of the informal essay makes use of a complex tone: he can assume that his audience will be alive to nuance and inflection.

Compare in this matter of tone a modern example of the familiar essay—on quite another topic, and in quite another style.

I see by the new Sears Roebuck catalogue that it is still possible to buy an axle for a 1909 Model T Ford, but I am not deceived. The great days have faded, the end is in sight. Only one page in the current catalogue is devoted to parts and accessories for the Model T; yet everyone remembers springtimes when the Ford gadget section was larger than men's clothing, almost as large as household furnishings. The last Model T was built in 1927, and the car is fading from what scholars call the American scene—which is an understatement, because to a few million people who grew up with it, the old Ford practically *was* the American scene.

It was the miracle God had wrought. And it was patently the sort of thing that could only happen once. Mechanically uncanny, it was like nothing that had ever come to the world before. Flourishing industries rose and fell with it. As a vehicle, it was hard-working, commonplace, heroic; and it often seemed to transmit those qualities to the persons who rode in it. My own generation identifies it with Youth, with its gaudy, irretrievable excitements; before it fades into the mist, I would like to pay it the tribute of the sigh that is not a sob, and set down random entries in a shape somewhat less cumbersome than a Sears Roebuck catalogue.

The Model T was distinguished from all other makes of cars by the fact that its transmission was of a type known as planetary—which was half metaphysics, half sheer friction. Engineers accepted the word "planetary" in its epicyclic sense, but I was always conscious that it also means "wandering," "erratic." Because of the peculiar nature of this planetary element, there was always, in Model T, a certain dull rapport between engine and wheels, and, even when the car was in a state known as neutral, it trembled with a deep imperative and tended to inch forward. There was never a moment when the bands were not faintly egging the machine on. In this respect it was like a horse, rolling the bit on its tongue, and country people brought to it the same technique they used with draft animals.—LEE STROUT WHITE: "Farewell, My Lovely." [6]

Here we feel that we are hardly asked to be on the alert for quotations from the Bible and Shakespeare. Rather it is assumed that we are familiar with the Sears, Roebuck catalogue. (Even so, the number of literary quotations is more important than might be thought: the cliché "the American scene"; the first message sent over the telegraph wires, "What hath God wrought!"; "the tribute of a sigh" from Gray's "Elegy.") It is assumed then that the reader will be familiar with the Sears, Roebuck catalogue and with the Model T; but it is also assumed that, unlike the average Sears, Roebuck reader, he will also be conversant with epicycles and metaphysics. For unless he knows something of both, he will miss a good deal of the humor, and he may fail to realize that the "sigh that is not a sob" is a gentle noise, which for its full suspiration, requires that the tongue be held in the cheek.

Certainly, to enjoy the essay the reader must be aware that the authors lament the passing of the Model T with mock seriousness. And, if the reader objects that, as with Lamb's essay, the seriousness of the lament has its element of sincerity, one must emphatically agree. Of course it has; but to realize this is but to realize more fully the extent to which the author of the familiar essay takes his reader into his confidence. We can perhaps see the matter more clearly by discriminating the kinds of statement: direct, simple ironical, and complex ironical. In the first, the writer states his attitude directly and straightforwardly. In the second, he states it ironically and indirectly: that is, he pretends to champion a position at variance with his real position. In the third, the method is still more indirect, for here his irony partially doubles back upon itself. His attitude of affirmation and admiration is given in an indirect and

   [6] From "Farewell, My Lovely," by Lee Strout White. Copyright 1936 The New Yorker Magazine, Inc. (Formerly The F-R Publishing Corporation.)

ironic form, which, though the reader has learned to associate that form with negation, here carries an element of positive compliment.

TONE IN THE FORMAL ESSAY

A relative complexity of tone may, however, characterize essays which are not familiar at all. The familiar or informal essay always has as one of the ingredients of its tone an element of casualness and an acceptance of the reader on the same footing as the writer. Stevenson's "Pulvis et Umbra," an excerpt of which follows, will illustrate the point by contrast. For in this essay Stevenson's manner suggests a kind of formality, a mounting of the rostrum, a speaking of a set piece to an audience—all of which makes his essay a formal declamation as Lamb's essay on Mrs. Battle, or the White essay on the Model T, is not.

We look for some reward of our endeavours and are disappointed; not success, not happiness, not even peace of conscience, crowns our ineffectual efforts to do well. Our frailties are invincible, our virtues barren; the battle goes sore against us to the going down of the sun. The canting moralist tells us of right and wrong; and we look abroad, even on the face of our small earth, and find them change with every climate, and no country where some action is not honoured for a virtue and none where it is not branded for a vice; and we look in our experience, and find no vital congruity in the wisest rules, but at the best a municipal fitness. It is not strange if we are tempted to despair of good. We ask too much. Our religions and moralities have been trimmed to flatter us, till they are all emasculate and sentimentalized, and only please and weaken. Truth is of a rougher strain. In the harsh face of life, faith can be read a bracing gospel. The human race is a thing more ancient than the ten commandments; and the bones and revolutions of the Kosmos, in whose joints we are but moss and fungus, more ancient still.

There is one sense, of course, in which Stevenson takes his stand on the same level as the reader. He writes "*We* look for," "*Our* frailties are invincible," "The canting moralist tells *us* of right and wrong." Stevenson thus properly includes himself in his commentary on mankind. But his essay *is* a commentary on mankind—not a casual chat with Tom, Dick, or Harry, the writer's good friend.

The tone of formal, meditated, "public" utterance reveals itself in half-a-dozen ways. To consider only a few: (1) the vocabulary is more "literary" than Stevenson would have used in an informal essay. Thus, he writes "the battle goes sore against us" rather than "the battle goes against us" or, more colloquially still, "we begin to lose out." (2) He gives us echoes of the King James Version of the Bible. Thus, "to the going down of the sun." (cf. Joshua 10:27, "And it came to pass at the time of the going down of the sun, that Joshua commanded . . .") (3) Stevenson formalizes the rhythms to give a sense of balanced antithesis, particularly in the closing sentence of the paragraph: "The human race is a thing more ancient than the ten commandments; and the bones and revolutions of the Kosmos, in whose joints we are but moss and fungus, more ancient still."

COMPLEXITY OF TONE: WHEN, AND WHY, IT IS NECESSARY

Let us consider one more example of complexity of tone, taken this time, not from an essay either formal or informal, but from an autobiography. In the passage which follows, T. E. Lawrence describes an incident that occurred in Arabia during World War I while he was serving with the Arabs in their revolt against Turkey. The incident occurred while Lawrence was leading a raiding party of Arab tribesmen.

My followers had been quarrelling all day, and while I was lying near the rocks a shot was fired. I paid no attention; for there were hares and birds in the valley; but a little later Suleiman roused me and made me follow him across the valley to an opposite bay in the rocks, where one of the Ageyl, a Boreida man, was lying stone dead with a bullet through his temples. The shot must have been fired from close by; because the skin was burnt about the wound. The remaining Ageyl were running frantically about; and when I asked what it was, Ali, their head man, said that Hamed the Moor had done the murder. I suspected Suleiman, because of the feud between the Atban and Ageyl . . . but Ali assured me that Suleiman had been with him three hundred yards further up the valley gathering sticks when the shot was fired. I sent all out to search for Hamed, and crawled back to the baggage, feeling that it need not have happened this day of all days when I was in pain.

As I lay there I heard a rustle, and opened my eyes slowly upon Hamed's back as he stooped over his saddle-bags, which lay just beyond my rock. I covered him with a pistol and then spoke. He had put down his rifle to lift the gear: and was at my mercy till the others came.

We held a court at once; and after a while Hamed confessed that, he and Salem having had words, he had seen red and shot him suddenly. Our inquiry ended. The Ageyl, as relatives of the dead man, demanded blood for blood. The others supported them; and I tried vainly to talk the gentle Ali round. My head was aching with fever and I could not think; but hardly even in health, with all eloquence, could I have begged Hamed off; for Salem had been a friendly fellow and his sudden murder a wanton crime.

Then rose up the horror which would make civilized man shun justice like a plague if he had not the needy to serve him as hangmen for wages. There were other Moroccans in our army; [Hamed the Moor was a Moroccan] and to let the Ageyl kill one in feud meant reprisals by which our unity would have been endangered. It must be a formal execution, and at last, desperately, I told Hamed that he must die for punishment, and laid the burden of his killing on myself. Perhaps they would count me not qualified for feud. At least no revenge could lie against my followers; for I was a stranger and kinless.

I made him enter a narrow gully of the spur, a dank twilight place overgrown with weeds. Its sandy bed had been pitted by trickles of water down the cliffs in the late rain. At the end it shrank to a crack a few inches wide. The walls were vertical. I stood in the entrance and gave him a few moments' delay which he spent crying on the ground. Then I made him rise and shot him through the chest. He fell down on the weeds shrieking, with the blood coming out in spurts over his clothes, and jerked about till he rolled nearly to where I was. I fired again, but was shaking so that I only broke his wrist. He went on calling out, less loudly, now lying on his back with his feet towards me, and I leant forward and shot him for the last time in the thick of his neck under the jaw. His body shivered a little, and I called the Ageyl; who buried him in the gully where he was. Afterwards the wakeful night dragged over me, till, hours before dawn, I had the men up and made them load, in my longing to be free of Wadi Kitan. They had to lift me into the saddle.—T. E. LAWRENCE: Seven Pillars of Wisdom, Chap. 31.[7]

What is Lawrence's attitude toward Hamed? Toward the Arabs and their blood feuds? Most of all, toward himself? Is he ashamed of himself? Proud of himself? Complacent and untroubled about himself?

One's first impression is that the incident is told with detachment and an almost studied dryness; and so, in a sense, it is. But it is

[7] From: Seven Pillars of Wisdom by T. E. Lawrence. Copyright 1925, 1935 by Doubleday & Company, Inc.

evident that Lawrence is not glossing over the incident casually and briefly. He develops it, and he gives us even minute details: e.g., "bullet through his temples," "as he stooped over his saddlebags," "shot him for the last time in the thick of his neck under the jaw." Even the scene of the execution, the gully, is described carefully and precisely: "Its sandy bed had been pitted by trickles of water down the cliffs in the late rain."

The narrator evidently remembers the whole incident vividly, and knows how to make the incident vivid to his reader. Why, then, is he not much more explicit about his own feelings and attitudes? Would anything have been gained if Lawrence had added a long paragraph describing the feelings that passed through his mind as he decided that he must act as executioner? Would anything have been lost? Notice that Lawrence is willing to use the word "horror," but he does not write, "As a civilized man I was overwhelmed with horror," but rather, "Then rose up the horror which would make civilized man shun justice like a plague if he had not the needy to serve him as hangmen for wages." Why does Lawrence, in this most explicit account of his own feelings, prefer the generalized statement?

A little meditation on these questions is likely to result in some such conclusion as this: that Lawrence, far from remaining cool and detached, was indeed terribly shaken by the experience, but that, nevertheless, he preferred to make his *account* of the experience as detached and objective as was possible. He chose to give a rather restrained account of his actions, leaving his reader to infer from the actions themselves what his feelings must have been. True, Lawrence once uses the word "desperately" and he refers to "the horror which would make civilized man shun justice," had he to execute justice in his own person. But these are almost the only explicit references to his feelings; and in the account of the actual execution, there are none at all.

This restraint itself has an important effect on the tone: it implies a certain modesty (his own mental anguish is not allowed to dominate the story as if Lawrence thought his anguish the important thing in the episode); it implies a certain confidence in the reader's maturity and sensitiveness—the reader need not be "told" what Lawrence was feeling. But the restraint, here, is of still further importance: the restraint manifested in Lawrence's *account* of his action is a reflection of, and a type of, the disciplined control which he imposed on his followers and on himself in the desert. The man who relates the action is the man who acted, and his manner of writing about the event suggests his attitude toward the event itself.

There is a more general conclusion about tone which may be drawn from this example, and it is a conclusion which is well worth pointing out to the reader. It is this: that subtlety of attitude and complexity of attitude frequently (one is tempted to say usually) can only be suggested, not stated directly. The writer has to trust to the effect of the whole passage, or even the whole book—not to explicit statements of his feeling. This means that he has to place a good deal of reliance upon his audience. (A twelve-year-old reader might well decide, on reading the passage, that Lawrence was a callous man, or that he considered the Arabs to be bloodthirsty savages and therefore without the feelings of real human beings, or even that he got a positive satisfaction out of ridding the earth of Hamed, the wanton killer.) Finally, if the writer must trust to the maturity of his audience, he will do well to appeal to their imaginations—to make every detail sharp and concrete, as Lawrence does here—but he will wisely avoid writing down to them or attempting to play upon their heartstrings.

The examples of tone that we have considered in this chapter indicate how wide the range of tone is and how difficult it is to speak of tone abstractly and in general. For the tone of a piece of writing, as the various examples make plain, is intimately related to the occasion which calls forth the writing, and is as intimately related to the author's general purpose. In some instances the tone may be as elusive as the expression of personality itself; but it can be, as our examples have shown, of the utmost importance. It is not to be thought of as decoration—as a mere grace of style; it is an integral—sometimes the central—part of the meaning.

Our examples also indicate that the tone may be generated through all sorts of subtle devices; that, indeed, there is no set and specific way in which tone is indicated. Because of this fact it has been difficult to do full justice to the subject in this chapter, for it has been impossible to give examples of great length, and so, since tone is the quality of the whole context, the most important manifestations of tone—the tone of a whole novel or essay or history—could not be illustrated.

THE SPECIAL AUDIENCE AND THE IDEAL AUDIENCE

Earlier in this chapter we spoke of tone as the reflection of the author's attitude toward his audience *or* toward his material, without making any elaborate distinction between the two levels of attitude. But the reader may well ask: When should attitude toward the audience dominate, and when attitude toward the material?

Writing which demands that the author take into account his particular audience is, as we have seen, always "practical" writing —writing designed to effect some definite thing. The advertiser is trying to persuade the housewife to buy something. The politician delivers a speech which he hopes will induce citizens to vote for him. Or, to take a more exalted case (for there need be no self-interest), a statesman urges a nation (through his writing and his speeches) to adopt a certain course of action. But these cases all have one thing in common: they are designed to secure a practical end. An audience is to be won to agreement or urged to action.

If such writing is to be effective, the author must, of course, keep his audience constantly in mind. An approach that is calculated to win the suffrage of one audience may very well repel another. The age, the intelligence, the amount of education, the interest, the habits and prejudices—must all be taken into account. The skillful management of such problems is an aspect of rhetoric, and for many people rhetoric has come to mean largely the art of persuasion. Rhetoric has therefore come to have something of a bad name, as if it consisted in cold-bloodedly fitting the statement to the emotional background and even to the prejudices of the audience. Certainly rhetoric is an instrument which can be used for bad ends, and a rhetorical appeal which, in its anxiety to produce an effect, ignores truth and relevance is vicious. But the fact that it may be misused does not render the instrument vicious. It may be properly used, and it is the part of common sense for a writer to take his special audience into account as he tries to gain their conviction. One may illustrate from Churchill's speech (p. 408), but one may also cite in this connection the passage from Huxley (p. 403). For Huxley, as contrasted with the ordinary mathematician or geologist, has a "practical" end in view; and by the same token, he has a special audience. The scientist acting strictly as scientist does not argue with his reader; he "just tells him." The facts speak for themselves, and in purely technical writing they are allowed to speak for themselves. But they speak fully only to a specially trained audience. In the work from which we have quoted, Huxley is writing for an audience that is not so trained, and the tone which he adopts toward his readers quite properly takes that fact into account.

The writer, however, when he finds that he must address himself to a general reader rather than to some specific and quite special reader, may find that the problem of tone becomes difficult because he lacks a definite target at which to aim. Yet all good writing is addressed to a reader, even though that reader is an ideal reader, not a limited and special reader. One could argue, in fact, that because the ideal reader is ideal, his intelligence, his sensitivity, his general discrimination are to be honored and respected all the more. This is to say what has been said earlier, that we do not evade the problem of tone by addressing ourselves to the reader-in-general rather than to Tom, Dick, or Harry. In fact, the problem of tone here becomes more important, not less important. The writer, however, even though agreeing with what has just been argued, may find that the ideal reader remains too shadowy to furnish him something definite to shoot at. In that case it may be of practical help, as he writes, to think of some particular person, the most intelligent and discriminating person that he knows. If he can please that person and be convincing to that person, the problem of tone will probably have been taken care of quite adequately.

There is another way of solving the problem practically: we say that the author writes for a particular audience, but he also writes for himself. There is his own sense of fitness that must be satisfied. The writer himself becomes the audience at which he aims. The question which he asks himself is not, "Have I made this convincing to Tom or to Dick or to Harry?" but rather, "Have I made this convincing to myself?"; or, to put the matter more succinctly still, "Have I made this convincing?"

In writing for this "ideal" reader, then, the author can transpose all problems of tone into the problem of handling his material itself. The problem of tone alters only when the writing is addressed specifically to Tom or to Dick—not to just any reader—and in proportion as Tom or Dick differs from the ideal reader.

Let us, however, give one further illustration of the relation between these two aspects of tone, tone as modified by the special audience, and tone as modified only by the nature of the material. Let us look back at the passage quoted from *Seven Pillars of Wisdom* (p. 416). The passage, as we saw, tells us a good deal about Lawrence's character, and it makes a commentary on a number of things: to mention only a few, on the Arabs, on justice, and on capital punishment. But as we have already observed, such writing makes its points by implication, and it requires a mature reader. For the ideal reader, no alteration of tone is required, and Lawrence has managed his problem of tone in probably the most satisfactory way possible.

But let us suppose that Lawrence were relating the episode to an audience which was complacent in its contempt for the "barbarian" Arabs. Unless his attitude toward the Arabs were to be completely distorted, Lawrence would have to alter the tone to take the prejudices of his audience into account. In particular, he would have to make much more explicit the fact that the Arabs honestly faced up to their imposition of the death penalty as the more sentimental, but ultimately more callous, citizen of England or America refuses to face it.

Or suppose that Lawrence were standing for a seat in Parliament, and a garbled account of the incident were being used against him. He might be content to rely upon the relation which he has given in *Seven Pillars*. Properly read, it shows him to be anything but calloused and insensitive. But the politician cannot afford to risk what the artist can. The objectivity of his account might have to be qualified. What his feelings and attitudes were could not safely be left to inference. Lawrence would have to state them explicitly. In general, the rewritten account would be focused not on the drama of the scene itself, but on Lawrence's personal feelings and his struggle with duty.

SUMMARY

Every piece of discourse implies a particular situation, a situation which involves a certain kind of reader and an occasion that accounts for that reader's being addressed. Even technical writing assumes a special situation, one which involves a reader who need not be coaxed and who has an interest that transcends any particular occasion.

Just as every piece of discourse implies a particular situation, it also implies a particular TONE. "Tone" may be defined as the reflection in the writing itself of the author's ATTITUDE toward his audience and toward his material. (The term is a metaphor derived from the tone of the voice in which an utterance is made. The writer cannot indicate his attitude, as the speaker can, by the tone of *voice;* but by his choice and arrangement of words, the skillful writer can convey that attitude very precisely.)

But tone is not to be conceived of as a kind of surface refinement, a kind of external embellishment. On the contrary, it has to do with the central problem of meaning itself. Tone involves a qualification of the literal meaning, and in certain kinds of heavy irony it actually effects a complete reversal of the literal meaning. The management of tone, therefore, has everything to do with the meaning that the writer wishes to convey. Even in expository writing and in "practical" writing of all kinds, the problem of tone is most important.

Since the tone of a piece of writing is the result of the interplay of many elements—choice of words, sentence structure, sentence rhythm, metaphors—and since tone is always intimately related to a particular situation, it would be difficult to make a general classification of possible "tones." But it is easy to point out some general faults in the management of tone:

1. Writing down to one's reader.

2. False enthusiasm and synthetic cheeriness.

3. SENTIMENTALITY—which may be defined as the attempt to evoke an emotional response in excess of that warranted by the situation.

Moreover, though an elaborate classification of kinds of tone would be of little use, it will be profitable to mention several general methods of statement, important for their effect on tone.

1. OVERSTATEMENT (which may express proper emphasis, but which may produce mere inflation; sentimentality, false enthusiasm, and boring pomposity are kinds of overstatement).

2. UNDERSTATEMENT (in which less is said than might have been expected to be said).

3. IRONY (to which understatement is closely related). The essence of irony resides in the contrast between the surface meaning and the actual full meaning. The gradations of irony are almost infinite, ranging from a harsh SARCASM (in which the surface meaning is completely reversed) to the various kinds of gentle irony (in which

the literal meaning is only slightly qualified by the total context). It is unfortunate that we lack terms by which to point to some of the major gradations. As a result, the term "irony" is likely to be overworked as one attempts to describe the manifold, and important, ways in which the literal meaning of a statement is qualified by the context which surrounds it. Perhaps our best practical expedient is to try to define as nearly as we can the kind of irony in each particular case: playful irony, whimsical irony, sardonic irony, quiet irony, and so on.

Thus far we have approached the general problem in terms of overstatement or understatement, or in terms of literal meaning and literal meaning qualified by context. But other approaches, of course, are possible: for example, the degree of seriousness or playfulness with which the writer makes his presentation to the reader, his gravity or his gaiety. Closely related to this distinction (though by no means to be equated with it) is the distinction between his formality or his informality.

1. Formality of tone. A formal tone implies a formal relation between writer and reader and a certain regard for forms and ceremonies.

2. Informality of tone. An informal tone implies a friendly and familiar relation between writer and reader—no standing upon forms and ceremonies. (But the informal or "familiar" essay may, on occasion, embody a serious purpose; and informality of tone is certainly not in itself to be identified with lack of seriousness.)

We have used the term "tone" rather loosely to indicate the reflection of the author's attitude toward his reader *and* also toward his material. In the act of composition the two go together so closely that it is impossible to separate them, but a practical distinction is simple and obvious. In "practical writing"—writing designed to persuade or convince a special audience—the writer will find his attitude toward that special audience tends to come to the fore, and certainly it should be allowed to modify and control his method of presentation. But in imaginative writing the writer addresses himself to an ideal reader—a universal reader—and, though the *general* problem of tone becomes of even greater importance, the problem of convincing his ideal reader becomes simply a part of the problem of "convincing"—convincing all readers—convincing himself.

The Final

Integration

IN THE last three chapters we have tried to deal specifically with some of the important elements of style: diction, metaphor, and tone. In this chapter our concern is rather different. We shall be primarily interested in the interplay of elements—in the total harmony which results from the blending of the various elements. Even in the preceding chapters this interplay has come in for a great deal of attention, particularly in the chapter on tone. But before we launch into a discussion of this final integration, we must take up one element of style which thus far has been merely mentioned. It is RHYTHM, the disposition of pauses and accents.

Now rhythm is a forbidding topic. A full discussion would be highly complex and would call for a separate chapter, and a long chapter at that. Our intention here, however, is much more modest. We shall treat rhythm briefly, and as merely a part of this final chapter on style. For this last procedure there is a good deal of warrant. By its very nature, rhythm can scarcely be profitably discussed in isolation. Moreover, rhythm in itself involves a rather intricate interplay of elements.

RHYTHM

In discussing tone we pointed out that in actual conversation the tone of the voice, gesture, and facial expression supplement the words and do much to set the particular tone which the speaker intends—playfulness, seriousness, irritability, and so on. If we use the written word, however, the "tone" has to be established by the choice of words and the patterning of those words. But it will have occurred to the reader that in moving from actual conversation to the written word the speaker relinquishes still another very important element—the matter of emphasis. Consider the following simple sentence: "Are you going to town?" If we stress the word *are*, the sentence becomes an emphatic question; and if we stress it heavily, it may even suggest surprise. But if we stress *you*, the question becomes centered upon whether it is *you* who are going rather than someone else. If we stress *town*, we get a third variation; the question then emphasizes the destination.

Thus the rhythmic inflection of a sentence, with its various stresses on particular words, is a very important way in which we express our meanings. When we put the sentence on paper, we can, of course, indicate something of this stress by underlining the words to be emphasized. But mere underlining is a relatively crude substitute for the living voice, and it is the mark of a clumsy writer to have to rely upon constant underlining. The skilled writer, by his control of the rhythm of his sentences, suggests where the proper emphases are to fall; for emphasis is an element of rhythm.

RHYTHM AND CLARITY OF MEANING

Mastery of rhythm, then, is important for clarity of meaning. This is illustrated by the muddled and monotonous rhythms of technological jargon. Look back at Maury Maverick's example of gobbledygook (p. 353). Jargon of this sort is difficult to read for a variety of reasons: it is fuzzy, abstract, and dull. It lacks flavor. But it lacks clarity as well; for there are no natural emphases, no obvious points of primary stress.

Compare with the passage quoted by Maverick, the following:

Nor had Dickens any lively sense for fine art, classical tradition, science, or even the manners or feelings of the upper classes in his own time and country: in his novels we may almost say there is no army, no navy, no church, no sport, no distant travel, no daring adventure, no feeling for the watery wastes and the motley nations of the planet, and luckily, with his notion of them—no lords and ladies.—GEORGE SANTAYANA: *Soliloquies in England.*[1]

[1] From *Soliloquies in England and Later Soliloquies* by George Santayana, copyright, 1922, by Charles Scribner's Sons.

Santayana's sentence is long and relatively complex, but it is rhythmical. The heavy stresses come where they should, on words like "Dickens," "lively," "fine," "classical," "even." Moreover, phrase balances phrase: "no distant travel" balances "no daring adventure"; "watery wastes" sets off "motley nations." Even the parenthetical phrase, "with his notion of them," is prepared for. (Notice that the rhythm is destroyed if we alter the ending to read "and— with his notion of them—luckily no lords and ladies.")

We have observed that lack of rhythm is frequently a symptom of disordered discourse; an easily grasped rhythm, on the other hand, is often the sign of good order and proper disposition of words and phrases. But rhythmic quality is much more, of course, than a mere index of clarity.

Emphatic rhythms tend to accompany emotional heightening. It is no accident that eloquent prose, prose that makes a strong appeal to the feelings, tends to use clearly patterned rhythms, or that poetry is commonly written in the systematized rhythm which we call "verse." The association of formal rhythm with emotional power is based on a perfectly sound psychological fact. Fervent expression of grief, rage, or joy tends to fall into rhythmic patterns— whether it be the sobbings of a grief-stricken woman or the cursing of an irate cab driver.

RHYTHMIC PATTERNS

In verse there is a formalizing of the rhythm to a system or pattern, and we have various ways of indicating the verse pattern. A common method is to indicate unaccented syllables by this mark (˘); accented syllables, by this (´). The stanza that follows may be marked ("scanned") thus:

To skies/ that knit/ their heart/strings right,

To fields/ that bred/ them brave,

The sav/iors come/ not home/ tonight:

Themselves/ they could/ not save.

A pair of syllables, the first unaccented, the second accented, we call an iambic foot (e.g., To skies); and we would describe the verse pattern of this stanza as iambic tetrameter (that is, a line consisting of *four* iambs) alternating with iambic trimeter (a line consisting of *three* iambs).

Now prose could be marked off (scanned) in such a fashion— even though prose is not, like verse, patterned to a certain kind of foot and divided off into lines containing a certain number of feet. For example, Mr. Gorham Munson scans a sentence of Emerson's as follows: "We know/ the authentic/ effects/ of the true fire/ through every one/ of its million/ disguises." The sort of metrical analysis Mr. Munson is making would involve our knowing, not only the simpler kind of metrical feet such as the iamb ("we know" is an iamb), but many very complex feet as well. "The authentic," for example, is called a *paeon*. In order to scan prose in this fashion, we should need many more technical terms than we usually need to scan verse.

Such an analysis of prose rhythm may have considerable value. But the rhythms of prose are infinite in their kinds, and some of the rhythmic effects are so subtle that an exact description requires a very complicated scheme of representation. Such a study, however, is completely beyond the range of this book; there is little practical gain in learning the definitions of such feet as the "amphibrach" and the "cretic." The writer will probably feel that he has his hands full in trying to control diction, metaphor, and tone without adding another element, rhythm. Fortunately, there is a considerable kernel of truth in the statement made by the Duchess in *Alice in Wonderland:* "Take care of the sense and the sounds will take care of themselves."

RHYTHM AS A DEVICE OF EXPRESSION

But "the sounds" can be used as a kind of test of the sense. As we have seen, limp, weak, confused rhythms are frequently a symptom of a more general confusion; and conversely, a well-defined rhythm often points to the writer's mastery of his instrument. This generalization is not to be interpreted to mean that all unemphatic rhythms are "bad" or that all elaborate and intricate rhythms are "good." The rhythm is only one of a number of devices which the writer uses. Its goodness or badness will depend upon a number of things: the writer's purpose and the adequacy of the rhythm to that purpose.

Let us consider a passage which has been studied earlier for its tone. The fact that this passage has been analyzed in earlier pages may make clearer the specific contribution of the rhythm to the total effect. At least it should serve to warn the student not to attribute the final effect to the rhythmic pattern alone.

They were executing officers of the rank of major and above who were separated from their troops. They were dealing summarily with German agitators in Italian uniform. They wore steel helmets. Only two of us had steel helmets. Some of the carabinieri had them. The other carabinieri wore the wide hat. Airplanes we called them. We stood in the rain and were taken out one at a time to be questioned and shot. So far they had shot every one they had questioned.

In this passage the sentences are short and simple, and the rhythm of the passage supports brilliantly the ironic tone of the description. The lack of variety in the rhythmic pattern makes it seem flat, almost "expressionless," and this flatness is part of the ironic understatement. Momentous and terrible things are being described, but the description is kept studiedly dry. A more varied and complex rhythm (such as usually goes with excitement) would weaken Hemingway's effect. (See p. 399 for fuller analysis of the passage.)

In contrast to this passage, compare a paragraph of description from Thackeray's *Vanity Fair*. (See also p. 406.)

The King? There he was. Beefeaters were before the august box; the Marquis of Steyne (Lord of the Powder Closet) and other great officers of state were behind the chair on which he sate, *He* sate—florid of face, portly of person, covered with orders, and in a rich curling head of hair. How we sang, God Save Him! How the house rocked and shouted with that magnificent music. . . . Ladies wept; mothers clasped their children; some fainted with emotion. . . . Yes, we saw him. Fate cannot deprive us of *that*. Others have seen Napoleon. Some few still exist who have beheld Frederick the Great, Doctor Johnson, Marie Antoinette, etc.: be it our reasonable boast to our children that we saw George the Good, the Magnificent, the Great.

Thackeray's mockery is reflected first in the balanced phrasings as our eyes focus on the king: "*He* sate—florid of face, portly of person, covered with orders, and in a curling head of hair." Then the rhythms become staccato, expressing the sense of mock excitement: "How we sang, God Save Him! How the house rocked and shouted with that magnificent music. . . . Ladies wept; mothers grasped their children; some fainted with emotion. . . . Yes, we saw him." The sarcasm comes to a climax in the highly formalized rhythms of the concluding sentences of the paragraph: "Be it our reasonable boast to our children that we saw George the Good, the Magnificent, the Great."

One ought not claim that the rhythm alone creates the effect, or that the rhythm is even the principal device used to achieve the effect. But certainly rhythm, in conjunction with diction, metaphor, and other devices, may become powerfully expressive. In this passage the very exaggeration of the rhythmic pattern makes its function easier to discern.

Rhythm is ordinarily used more subtly, though not for that reason less effectively. Let us look at the Texan's auctioneering speech from William Faulkner's *The Hamlet*. What part, if any, does the rhythm play in producing the effect? Does it support the tone?

"Now, boys," the Texan said, "Who says that pony ain't worth fifteen dollars? You couldn't buy that much dynamite for just fifteen dollars. There ain't one of them can't do a mile in three minutes: turn them into pasture and they will board themselves; work them like hell all day and every time you think about it, lay them over the head with a single-tree and after a couple of days every jack rabbit one of them will be so tame you will have to put them out of the house at night like a cat."

Suppose that we rewrite the last few lines to read as follows:

"Work the hell out of them every day and ever so often bust a single-tree over their heads. In a little while you'll have them all tame as tame can be. You'll have to shove 'em out of the door at night just like they was a bunch of cats."

In this version the diction has not been altered from that which the Texan might be expected to use, and the rewritten version "says" just about what the original "says"; but the rhythm has been destroyed and with it much of the flavor and nearly all of the force of the Texan's auctioneering speech.

One further passage may be quoted to indicate what complex effects can be wrought by the skillful handling of rhythm in conjunction with other devices. The passage forms the opening of W. B. Yeats's *Reveries over Childhood and Youth.*

My first memories are fragmentary and isolated and contemporaneous, as though one remembered some first moments of the Seven Days. It seems as if time had not yet been created, for all thoughts connected with emotion and place are without sequence.

I remember sitting upon somebody's knee, looking out of an Irish window at a wall covered with cracked and falling plaster, but what wall I do not remember, and being told that some relation once lived there. I am looking out of a window in London. It is at Fitzroy Road. Some boys are playing in the road and among them a boy in uniform, a telegraph boy perhaps. When I ask who the boy is, the servant tells me that he is going to blow the town up, and I go to sleep in terror.[2]

The author says that his memories of childhood are "fragmentary," "isolated," "contemporaneous," and "without sequence." So they appear in his account. There is a memory of looking out of an Irish window. Then, without any transition, Yeats presents a memory of looking out a London window. Moreover, with this second instance, he drops the statement "I remember" and reverts to the present tense: "I am looking out of a window in London." The author's purpose, obviously, is to give us the sense of contemporaneity. He tries to put himself into these memories as they rise up— chaotic, disordered, fragmentary. True, he is forced to use a man's words. "Isolated" and "contemporaneous" would not be used by a child; nor would the allusion to the Biblical Seven Days of creation occur to a child. But the author has tried to suggest the movement of the child's mind in its simple, uncritical succession of events. Most of all, he has depended upon the rhythmic pattern to suggest the slow, almost tranced movement of reverie. The reader might experiment with altering the rhythm of the passage. In an altered rhythm, the sense of reverie is at once lost, and the sense of living back into one's childhood memories collapses.

RHYTHM AS A PRACTICAL TEST OF SOUND SENTENCE PATTERN

To sum up, control of rhythm is an important resource of the skilled writer. It is a powerful means for shifting tone, for establish-

[2] From W. B. Yeats: *Reveries*. Copyright, 1916 by The Macmillan Company and used with their permission.

ing a mood, for pointing a contrast, or for heightening the appeal to the emotions. The reader may feel, however, that rhythm is much too intricate an instrument for him to try to use *consciously.* It probably is. We are far from suggesting that the reader consciously try for rhythmic effects. Even so, a very practical use of rhythm can be made: the writer may learn to use rhythm in order to test his composition. As he rereads it aloud he should learn to listen for the break in the rhythm, the jangling discord, the lack of smoothness that signals to him that something in the sentence is awry. This comment applies particularly to the disposition of modifiers, prepositional phrases, and the like. The writer may find that reading his composition aloud and listening to its rhythms proves to be one of the best practical means for spotting sentence elements that are not in the best order.

Consider the following sentence:

Oriental luxury goods—jade, silk, gold, spices, vermillion, jewels—formerly had come by way of the Caspian Sea overland; and a few daring Greek sea captains, now that this route had been cut by the Huns, catching the trade winds were sailing from Red Sea ports and loading up at Ceylon.

The sentence is passable, and is not perhaps noticeably unrhythmical. But if we read this sentence in the form in which Robert Graves actually wrote it, we shall find that it is not only clearer; it is much more rhythmical and much easier to read:

Oriental luxury goods—jade, silk, gold, spices, vermillion, jewels—had formerly come overland by way of the Caspian Sea and now that this route had been cut by the Huns, a few daring Greek sea captains were sailing from Red Sea ports, catching the trade winds and loading up at Ceylon.

STYLE AS HARMONIOUS INTEGRATION

To conclude this brief note on rhythm: "Good" rhythm is rhythm which is appropriate to the passage as a whole—which contributes to the desired effect. If it functions to support that effect, it is "good." If it does not, it is "bad," no matter how soothing or lilting or beautifully harmonized it may appear in itself. The principle involved is the same principle which we have encountered earlier in discussing such topics as diction and metaphor. As we have seen, a metaphor is not to be chosen because it is beautiful in itself or is brilliant in itself. A good metaphor is rather one which "says" precisely what the composition as a whole requires at that particular point. Good diction is diction which, for the case in hand, is neither too colloquial nor too highfalutin, neither too vague nor too pedantically exact. So with rhythm. Had Hemingway used more intricate rhythms in the passage quoted on page 429, he would have impaired the effectiveness of the passage as a whole. *It is as part of the whole that any element of style is to be judged.* But what, then, of the passage from *Vanity Fair* (p. 429)? Thackeray has there used heavily formalized rhythms which are quite out of harmony with the triviality of the matters celebrated. Does this violate the principle of harmonious adaptation? Not at all, for the passage aims at a heavily ironic effect, and the absurd contrast between the exalted rhythm of the prose and the triviality of what it describes, admirably supports the ironic effect.

What has been said with reference to rhythm obviously holds for all the other elements that go to make up a style. The question to be asked is always this: Does the element in question do its particular job in the expressive pattern of the whole? In the light of this question examine the following passage, noting any disharmonious elements of whatever kind.

At latitude zero, however, the obvious is not the same as with us. Rivers imply wading, swimming, alligators. Plains mean swamps, forest, fevers. Mountains make you think of something dangerous or something just too big to get over. If you've got to go somewhere, you have to hack your way through a lot of plants and vines. "God made the country," said Cowper, in his rather too blank verse. In New Guinea he would have had his doubts; he would have longed for the man-made town.

This passage (from Huxley's "Wordsworth in the Tropics") has been garbled. The reader ought to have little difficulty in seeing that the beginning and the end of this passage are similar in style, but that the middle section is an anomalous lump. The style of the first three sentences and of the last two is characterized by condensation and thoughtful arrangement. The condensed, carefully disposed style breaks down with the fourth sentence. The fourth and fifth sentences are lumbering and clumsy, vaguely indefinite in pointing toward objects, and awkwardly colloquial. Can you rewrite the sentences so as to bring them into accord with the style of the first three and the last two? Consider diction and tone particularly, and check your rewritten sentences with what Huxley actually wrote:

At latitude zero, however, the obvious is not the same as with us. Rivers imply wading, swimming, alligators. Plains mean swamps, forests, fevers. Mountains are either dangerous or impassable. To travel is to hack one's way laboriously through a tangled, prickly, and venomous darkness. "God made the country," said Cowper, in his rather too blank verse. In New Guinea he would have had his doubts; he would have longed for the man-made town.

What anomalies of style occur in the following passage?

A large percentage of those who returned to their ordinary pursuits were conditioned to violence, since war has to be regarded as a sort of conditioning process. This large percentage of returning veterans were also disposed to be in an angry mood because of their defeat. The farm to which a majority of them had to return proved to be not so prosperous or pleasant in reality as their memories of it under war conditions had led them to believe. Men who had been bred to the law took to the plow, and others in their several ways had to bury their ambitions and go about earning a living, and by living they meant bread and meat.

The reader should compare the last sentence of this passage with the preceding sentences. The last sentence is concrete where the preceding are abstract and fuzzy. It even hints at a forceful metaphor: the soil, as it is turned over by the plow, is actually the earth covering up the plowman's ambitions. This last sentence is condensed whereas the preceding sentences are filled with distracting circumlocutions. For example, what is gained by writing "a large percentage" rather than "many"? There are contexts, to be sure, in which an exact percentage has relevance, but no figures are given here. Which is the more forceful, the simple word "many" or the phrase "a large percentage"? The student should try to rewrite the passage with a view to making the rest of the passage as concrete and specific as is the style of the last sentence. The original passage, ungarbled, reads as follows:

There were many who came home inured to ordered violence, angry at their destiny, only to find that the farm, which had remained green and fruitful in their memory, gave them a strange welcome. Men who had been bred to the law took to the plow, and others in their several ways had to bury their ambitions and go about earning a living, and by living they meant bread and meat. (JOHN A. RICE: *I Came Out of the Eighteenth Century*, Chap. 5.)

THE INSEPARABILITY OF FORM AND CONTENT

Since a good style represents an adaptation of means to a particular purpose, all the various devices of style have to be viewed as expressive devices. That is to say, even the minor ornaments of style are, strictly speaking, not ornaments but conveyors of meaning. The general point is so important that it can stand some elaboration. Mr. W. K. Wimsatt [3] provides a neat illustration. He quotes the sentence: "to read his tales is a baptism of optimism. . . ." and goes on to comment on the nasty jingle of "-ptism" and "-ptimism." The jingling effect is, as he says, nasty "just because the two combinations so nearly strive to make these words parallel, whereas they are not; one qualifies the other." That is, the style is bad because the diction (*baptism . . . optimism*) suggests a parallelism between terms that are not parallel, and the reader feels that what pretended to be an expressive element—the *-ism* link between the terms—has proved to be meaningless—even misleading. (The reader will not necessarily make this analysis, of course; he will probably merely *feel* it, hearing the *-ism* repetition as an irritating jingle.)

Mr. Wimsatt goes on to say: "The case is even plainer if we take an example of the common '-ly' jingle, 'He lived practically exclusively on milk,' and set beside it something like this: 'We are swallowed up, irreparably, irrevocably, irrecoverably, irremediably.' In the second we are not conscious of the repeated '-ly' as a jingle any more than of the repeated 'irre-.' "

Why does the second sentence not register as even more "jingling" than the first? It has not a double, but a quadruple repetition of "-ly" plus a quadruple repetition of "irre-." But it does not jingle because, to paraphrase Mr. Wimsatt, the repetitions here become a part of the structure of meaning: the words linked together by "irre-" and "-ly" *belong* together. The structure of sound effects expresses perfectly the structure of sense, which it fits like a glove.

[3] *The Prose Style of Samuel Johnson*, Yale University Press, 1941, p. 13.

Now the examples just given may be thought to be trivial, and perhaps they are; but the principle to which they point is all-important. One may state it in these terms: a good style is the perfect garment of its "content." It is perfectly adapted to its content, which it bodies forth and from which it may not be divorced.

We said in Chapter 9 that style has to do with "how" a thing is said rather than with "what" is said; and therefore this last remark, that a good style is the perfect garment of its content and cannot be separated from its content, may seem to offer a contradiction. There is no real contradiction, of course; for if we cannot separate, we can at least distinguish between the thought and the words, the content and the form, the what and the how. Moreover, the distinction between form and content is a useful one. But the distinction can be easily misused. It is proper, therefore, to see how much weight the distinction between form and content can bear.

In the first place, content and form never exist in separation. After all, we know *what* a writer says only through the way in which he has said it. Moreover, if we alter the *way* in which a thing is said, we have also altered, if only ever so slightly, *what* is said. (The alteration in what is said may sometimes be so slight that we feel justified in disregarding it; we may say that we have not changed the content, only the form.) But at this point we are interested in theory—not in the practice, but in the principle; and it is necessary to get the principle straight. Cardinal Newman has stated the principle very emphatically:

Thought and speech are inseparable from each other. Matter and expression are parts of one: style is the thinking out into language. . . . When we can separate light and illumination, life and motion, the convex and the concave of a curve . . . then will it be conceivable that the . . . intellect should renounce its own double.

In insisting on this inseparability of form and content, we may seem to be riding pure theory very hard. But if we can grasp the theory, several very important practical considerations follow from it. First, style is seen to be not a mere outward coating, a kind of veneer which overlies the content; for the style is the outward manifestation of the content. Second, the theory illuminates the difficulty of the writer as he gropes for proper expression. As writers, we usually feel that we know exactly what we want to say; we just can't quite find the precise words. But a little reflection will reveal that we know exactly what we want to say *only when we have found the precise words.* The truth of the matter is that we do not *really know* what we want to say as we chew the pen and try to get down on paper the next sentence. The process of writing is frequently, and perhaps even usually, a process of exploration. The principle of the inseparability of style and content may indicate more clearly why this is true.

A third consideration of the greatest practical importance is this: If a good style and its matter are really inseparable, it follows that bad style always reveals itself in some sort of cleavage from its "content." Let us put the matter in this way. If a style is inseparable from its content, if it is actually the bodying forth of its content, then in so far as it does this adequately we can never call it "bad"—though of course the piece of writing in question (of which style is an aspect) may be relatively trivial. But in this last instance it will be the whole piece of writing that is trivial, not the *style as such* that is bad. The term "bad" can properly be applied to style, then, only when the style does not adequately body forth what we guess must have been the content that the writer had in mind.

To sum up: there are no devices of style that are "good," absolutely and in themselves. They become good only in so far as they are used to promote the fullest, best, most adequate expression of what is to be said. One is tempted to say, conversely, that there are no really "bad" devices—provided always that they are "English"— that is, arrangements of words which the genius of the language permits. But, and this is the point of crucial importance, *any* device, any patterning which violates the larger pattern, which works at cross purposes to it, or which is irrelevant to it—any such patterning, by "sticking out," by calling attention to itself, warns the writer to reconsider. It warns him to reconsider not only how he shall "say it" but also *what it is precisely that he has to say.* For in a good style the two are inseparable, and the very fact of their separation signals that revision is in order. To use the example already given above: the *-ly* parallel in "He lives practically exclusively on milk" *sticks out,* whereas the much heavier reiteration of the *-ly,* and the *irre-* in "We are swallowed up, irreparably, irrevocably, irrecoverably, irremediably" does not stick out: these latter repetitions become part of the pattern of meaning and seem an inevitable part of it.

STYLE AS AN EXPRESSION OF PERSONALITY

Thus far we have primarily considered style as related to the writer's purpose, but there are other important relations to be considered, and one of them, the relation of style to the writer's personality, requires careful attention. The relation of style to personality comes up appropriately at this point, for we have just said that a good style does not call attention to itself: style and content are inseparable, and the very cleavage between them is a symptom of something's having gone wrong.

But this last point suggests further that a good style is not pretentious or affected: that it is natural and sincere, that it is the authentic expression of the writer's mind. This matter of unaffected naturalness is so important that many writers on style have emphasized it. One celebrated essay on style gives the following advice: "Be natural, be simple, be yourself: shun artifices, tricks, fashions. Gain the tone of ease, plainness, self-respect. To thine own self be true. Speak out frankly that which you have thought out in your own brain and have felt within your soul" (Frederic Harrison, "On English Prose").

This, it goes without saying, is good advice; but it does not take us very far. In the first place, like so much advice which urges us to "be ourselves," it assumes that we know what that self is. But writing is precisely the field in which it is most difficult to know oneself. One "finds himself" in a style only through exploration, and perhaps painful experiment.

In the second place, there is danger that Harrison's comment may confuse the real issue by seeming to associate "truth to self" with simplicity, plainness, and ease. If we took his advice literally, we might be tempted to throw out any style which was not thoroughly simple. Pomposity is always bad, of course; but some very fine prose is rich and complex—which is quite another thing (see "Complexity of Tone: When, and Why, It Is Necessary," p. 416).

Yet, having made these qualifications, it is proper to point out that a "good style" always does express the personality of the writer.

Such self-expression is usually unconscious, however; and the student may well allow it to remain unconscious, not asking "Does this express me?" but rather "Does this say what ought to be said?" Indeed, the reader can be assured that the writer's personality always does find expression in any good style. For the style of a piece of writing is the shaping, directing, organizing force made manifest in the writing itself. The way in which the topic is approached, the kind of analyses to which it is subjected, the emphases, heavy or light, that it receives, are revealed in the style, and through the style. The style, so conceived, becomes an index of the mind and personality of the writer. A metaphor may serve to illustrate: The style of a work is not a sort of veneer glued over the outside. On the contrary, it is like the pattern of the grain in a piece of wood. It is a pattern that goes all the way through: a manifestation of the growth and development of the structure of the tree itself.

The writer does not need to strive for individuality as such, since individuality must obtain in any genuine piece of work. (The grain pattern of no two trees is just alike, and human personalities are at least as various as trees.) Individuality in style is important, then, *not because it is valuable in itself, but as a symptom of the presence of something else: genuineness.*

The distinct impress which a personality gives to a style is easily demonstrated. The very structure of sentences and the handling of rhythms is tempered by the mind and personality of the writer. A child, for example, obviously will tend to use short sentences linked together by *and's* and *but's* and interspersed with very few subordinate clauses. Such a style thus reflects the simple, relatively uncritical response to the child's experience.

Let us go on to consider a more elaborate example, not a "natural" and naïve simplicity, but the carefully fashioned simplicity of a conscious artist. In the stories of Ernest Hemingway, the style is simple, even to the point of monotony. Most of the sentences are simple or compound. The paragraphs tend to be based upon simple sequence. In part, of course, this simplicity of style derives from the fact that Hemingway's typical characters are unsophisticated, and that they are characteristically treated in simple, fundamental situations. The uncomplicated style of the stories, therefore, is a matter of dramatic propriety: that is, the author is merely having his characters talk in the way in which they would talk.[4] But this is not the whole explanation. In part, the uncomplicated style is a reflection of the sensibility of the author himself. The short, simple rhythms, the succession of co-ordinate clauses, and the general lack of subordination—all suggest a dislocated and ununified world. Hemingway is apparently trying to suggest in his style the direct experience—things as seen and felt, one after another, and not as the mind arranges and analyzes them. Consider the following paragraphs from his story, "In Another Country":

In the fall the war was always there, but we did not go to it any more. It was cold in the fall in Milan and the dark came very early. Then the electric lights came on, and it was pleasant along the streets looking in the windows. There was much game hanging outside the shops, and the snow powdered in the fur of the foxes and the wind blew their tails. The deer hung stiff and heavy and empty, and small birds blew in the wind and the wind turned their feathers. It was a cold fall and the wind came down from the mountains.

We were all at the hospital every afternoon, and there were different ways of walking across the town through the dusk to the hospital. Two of the ways were alongside canals, but they were long. Always, though, you crossed a bridge across a canal to enter the hospital. There was a choice of three bridges. On one of them a woman sold roasted chestnuts. It was warm, standing in front of her charcoal fire, and the chestnuts were warm afterward in your pocket. The hospital was very old and very beautiful, and you entered through a gate and walked across a courtyard and out a gate on the other side. There were usually funerals starting from the courtyard. Beyond the old hospital were the new brick pavilions, and there we met every afternoon and were all very polite and interested in what was the matter, and sat in the machines that were to make so much difference.

The doctor came up to the machine where I was sitting and said: "What did you like best to do before the war? Did you practise a sport?"

I said: "Yes, football."

"Good," he said. "You will be able to play football again better than ever."

My knee did not bend and the leg dropped straight from the knee to the ankle without a calf, and the machine was to bend the knee and make it move as in riding a tricycle. But it did not bend yet, and in-

[4] This is not to say, of course, that Hemingway is simply giving a kind of transcript of actual conversation. See p. 276.

stead the machine lurched when it came to the bending part. The doctor said: "That will all pass. You are a fortunate young man. You will play football again like a champion."—ERNEST HEMINGWAY: "In Another Country." [5]

A style which involves subordination and complicated shadings of emphasis—a style which tends toward complex sentences with many qualifying clauses and phrases—implies an exercise of critical discrimination. It implies the sifting of experience through the intellect. But Hemingway, apparently, is primarily concerned with giving the immediate impact of experience rather than with analyzing and evaluating it in detail. His very style, then, seems to imply that the use of the intellect, with its careful discriminations, may blur the rendering of experience and may falsify it; and this style, taken with his basic concern for simple, and frequently, "tough" characters, seems to imply a distrust of the intellect in solving man's basic problems.

Compare with Hemingway's style that of the following passage from Henry James's *The Turn of the Screw*. An English governess is telling the story, and in this passage she is reflecting upon the housekeeper's (Mrs. Grose's) account of a former servant of the house.

I forebore, for the moment, to analyze this description further than by the reflection that a part of it applied to several members of the household, of the half-dozen maids and men who were still of our small colony. But there was everything, for our apprehension, in the lucky fact that no discomfortable legend, no perturbation of scullions, had ever, within anyone's memory, attached to the kind old place. It had neither bad name nor ill fame, and Mrs. Grose, most apparently, only desired to cling to me and to quake in silence. I even put her, the very last thing of all, to the test. It was when, at midnight, she had her hand on the schoolroom door to take leave. "I have it from you then—for it's of great importance—that he was definitely and admittedly bad."

The passage is, first of all, in character. The governess is a carefully educated woman. Her choice of words reflects her education; but it reflects also a certain primness, a certain fastidiousness. For example, she refines the phrase "no discomfortable legend," by add-

[5] From *Men Without Women* by Ernest Hemingway, copyright, 1927, by Charles Scribner's Sons.

ing an elaboration of it, "no perturbation of scullions." The structure of the sentences too reflects the governess's manner. In telling the story, she is re-creating events which have already happened. As she relates them, she tries to render them faithfully and exactly, but she is not being carried along by the rush of events. She has the advantage of looking back on them, and that reflection displays itself in the style. The sentences are "arranged," thought out with some care: for example, she says, "But there was everything, *for our apprehension*, in the lucky fact that. . . ." Or, she can write "I even put her, *the very last of all*, to the test."

Perhaps we ought to leave our analysis of the style at this level, and say merely that it reflects precisely the character and personality of James's chosen narrator, the governess. Yet one is tempted to try to penetrate a little deeper and find in the style something of the sensibility of James himself: if so, we should find in James's prose just the reverse of what we found in Hemingway's. We could say of this passage (and of most of Henry James's work) that the style does imply an exercise of critical discrimination, the sifting of experience through the intellect. The sentence rhythms are complex, there is a high degree of subordination, there are complicated shadings of emphasis. It is the prose of a mind which is arranging its world, by delicate adjustments and careful discriminations, into a perspectived pattern.

FURTHER EXAMPLES OF THE EXPRESSION OF THE WRITER'S PERSONALITY

These generalizations on Hemingway and James are based, of course, on each man's work as a whole, and the validity of the generalizations would require for demonstration extended passages rather than the short excerpts that we have quoted. Indeed, it is always difficult to make a convincing case for the impress of a writer's personality on his style if one has only a short excerpt to exhibit. The short passages which follow, however, may serve further to suggest some of the more obvious ways in which an author's style may reflect his personality.

Here is Donald Culross Peattie's definition of a weed. The definition is a thoroughly accurate one. (Compare it with the dictionary definition: "a plant occurring obtrusively in cultivated ground to the exclusion or injury of the desired crop.") But how lively an account it is; and how much it tells us about the personality of Peattie!

What is a weed? I have heard it said that there are sixty definitions. For me, a weed is a plant out of place. Or, less tolerantly, call it a foreign aggressor, which is a thing not so mild as a mere escape from cultivation, a visitor that sows itself innocently in a garden bed where you would not choose to plant it. Most weeds have natal countries, whence they have sortied. So Japanese honeysuckle, English plantain, Russian thistle came from lands we recognize, but others, like gypsies, have lost all record of their geographic origin. Some of them turn up in all countries, and are listed in no flora as natives. Some knock about the seaports of the world, springing up wherever ballast used to be dumped from the old sailing ships. Others prefer cities; they have lost contact with sweet soil, and lead a guttersnipe existence. A little group occurs only where wool waste is dumped, others are dooryard and pavement weeds, seeming to thrive the more as they are trod by the feet of man's generations. Some prized in an age of simpler tastes have become garden *déclassés* and street urchins; thus it comes about that the pleasant but plebeian scent of Bouncing Bet, that somewhat blowsy pink of old English gardens, is now one of the characteristic odors of American sidewalk ends, where the pavement peters out and shacks and junked cars begin. —DONALD CULROSS PEATTIE: *Flowering Earth*, Chap. 12.[6]

The writer, as this passage indicates, evidently possesses a great deal of botanical information. He is undoubtedly familiar with the various "flora" and knows which plants are listed in them and which are not. But this passage is not intended to be a technical description; rather it is a more desultory and amiable account of weeds. Peattie is a man of perception, with senses that are keen ("the pleasant but plebeian scent of Bouncing Bet," "the characteristic odors of American sidewalk ends"). He evidently has a sense of humor. He is aware of current politics ("foreign aggressor"). He has a sense of history.

In short, in this passage we get something of the play of an informed and sensitive mind—a mind which special knowledge has not made stuffy—and of a personality which savors, with evident enjoyment, the varied and amusing world with which it is thoroughly familiar. In this connection notice how the general metaphor which treats the weed as a human being who has broken bounds

[6] From *Flowering Earth*, by Donald Culross Peattie. Copyright, 1939, by Donald Culross Peattie. Courtesy of G. P. Putnam's Sons.

runs through the whole passage, and how this metaphor is varied through the passage to express the varying aspects of weeds in general and of certain weeds in particular. One weed may be like a "foreign aggressor" to be resisted; another, like an immigrant or colonist from another land; still another, like a gypsy whose original homeland is lost in obscurity. Some weeds, like groups of immigrants, remain near the seaports where they made their first entry. But the migration of other weeds has been from country to city. They have moved in from the provinces and have become citified and now lead a "guttersnipe" existence. Still other weeds are like human beings who have come down in the world from a higher class of society, and having lost pride of class and dignity, are now happily and frowsily plebeian. The general comparison of the weed to the human migrant is flexible enough to provide quite specific illustrations of the various kinds of weeds. The metaphor not only renders the abstract definition concrete, but it suggests Peattie's own attitude toward weeds—an attitude which is one of genial and good-humored amusement.

Notice too how the diction unobtrusively but powerfully supports the variations of the basic metaphor. "Foreign aggressor" is pointed up by the use of the word "sortied." (A "sortie" suggests a military raid.) "Guttersnipe existence" sharpens the hint given by "others prefer cities." "Plebeian" and "somewhat blowsy" support and extend the suggestions made by "*déclassé.*"

The diction, of course, has been chosen to do something more. Though Peattie is willing to use a technical term like *flora,* most of his words are specific and concrete. Moreover, he does not hesitate to use colloquial expressions like "knock about" and even the slang expression "peters out." Peattie is not at all like the fabled scholar who knew all the pedantic terms but could not address a dog in his own dialect. His diction is accommodated to the wholesome vulgarity of his subject. Weeds interest him, and to that interest he brings not only a fund of knowledge but all the resources of a rich personality.

The familiar essay, as we should expect, furnishes obvious examples of the reflection of personality in the style. (The familiar essay is sometimes called the "personal essay.") Here is the first paragraph of Charles Lamb's essay, "Mackery End, in Hertfordshire":

Bridget Elia has been my housekeeper for many a long year. I have obligations to Bridget, extending beyond the period of memory. We house together, old bachelor and maid, in a sort of double singleness; with such tolerable comfort, upon the whole, that I, for one, find in myself no sort of disposition to go out upon the mountains, with the rash king's offspring, to bewail my celibacy. We agree pretty well in our tastes and habits—yet so, as "with a difference." We are generally in harmony, with occasional bickerings—as it should be among near relations. Our sympathies are rather understood, than expressed; and once, upon my dissembling a tone in my voice more kind than ordinary, my cousin burst into tears, and complained that I was altered. We are both great readers in different directions. While I am hanging over (for the thousandth time) some passage in old Burton, or one of his strange contemporaries, she is abstracted in some modern tale, or adventure, whereof our common reading-table is daily fed with assiduously fresh supplies. Narrative teazes me. I have little concern in the progress of events. She must have a story—well, ill, or indifferently told—so there be life stirring in it, and plenty of good or evil accidents. The fluctuations of fortune in fiction—and almost in real life—have ceased to interest, or operate but dully upon me. Out-of-the-way humors and opinions—heads with some diverting twist in them—the oddities of authorship please me most. My cousin has a native disrelish of anything that sounds odd or bizarre. Nothing goes down with her that is quaint, irregular, or out of the road of common sympathy. She "holds Nature more clever. . . ."

Lamb begins his essay by pointing some contrasts between himself and his cousin, Bridget. They have come to know intimately, and to be reconciled to, and even to enjoy, their differences. Their tastes in literature illustrate the basic difference very well. Bridget demands in her reading a chain of narrative, a plot; but "Narrative teazes" him. He is for out-of-the-way humors and opinions, foibles, crotchets, and oddities. But notice that the prose that *tells us this* provides in itself a nice instance of Elia's taste. For his first sentence hints at a narrative, but the narrative does not develop. Indeed, with the playful phrase, "double singleness," there comes the "diverting twist" which Elia tells us he relishes. So also is the humorous collocation of King Jephthah's daughter bewailing her virginity, and the comfortable bachelor Elia, reading "for the thousandth time" some passage from Burton's *Anatomy of Melancholy*.

The structure of the sentences, with their asides and their abrupt and whimsical shifts, reflects the very traits of the personality which these sentences undertake to describe: thus, "She must have a story —well, ill, or indifferently told—so there be life stirring in it, and plenty of good or evil accidents. The fluctuations of fortune in fiction—and almost in real life—have ceased to interest, or operate but dully upon me." In short, the *way* in which Elia writes about his traits of character is an exemplification of those very traits: the style mirrors its content.

The reflection of personality in style comes out clearly if we compare the varying accounts of two writers who have the same topic. In the two passages that follow, James Boswell and Lord Macaulay discuss the personal eccentricities of the eighteenth-century critic and man of letters, Samuel Johnson. First, Boswell's account:

He had another particularity, of which none of his friends ever ventured to ask an explanation. It appeared to me as some superstitious habit, which he had contracted early, and from which he had never called upon his reason to disentangle him. This was his anxious care to go out or in at a door or passage by a certain number of steps from a certain point, or at least so that either his right or his left foot (I am not certain which) should constantly make the first actual movement when he came close to the door or passage. Thus I conjecture: for I have, upon innumerable occasions, observed him suddenly stop, and then seem to count his steps with a deep earnestness: and when he had neglected or gone wrong in this sort of magical movement, I have seen him go back again, put himself in a proper posture to begin the ceremony, and, having gone through it, break from his abstraction, walk briskly on, and join his companion. A strange instance of something of this nature, even when on horseback, happened when he was in the isle of Sky. Sir Joshua Reynolds has observed him to go a good way about, rather than cross a particular alley in Leicester-fields; but this Sir Joshua imputed to his having had some disagreeable recollection associated with it.

That the most minute singularities which belonged to him, and made very observable parts of his appearance and manner, may not be omitted, it is requisite to mention, that while talking or even musing, as he sat in his chair, he commonly held his head to one side towards his right shoulder, and shook it in a tremulous manner, moving his body backwards and forwards, and rubbing his left knee in the same direction, with the palm of his hand. In the intervals of articulating he made various sounds with his mouth, sometimes as if ruminating, or what is called chewing the cud, sometimes giving a half whistle, sometimes making his tongue play backwards from the roof of his mouth, as if clucking like a hen, and sometimes protruding it against his upper gums in front, as if pronouncing quickly under his breath, *too, too, too:* all this accompanied sometimes with a thoughtful look, but more frequently with a smile. Generally when he had concluded a period, in the course of a dispute, by which time he was a good deal exhausted by violence and vociferation, he used to blow out his breath like a Whale. This I supposed was a relief to his lungs; and it seemed in him to be a contemptuous mode of expression, as if he had made the arguments of his opponent fly like chaff before the wind.

I am fully aware how very obvious an occasion I here give for the sneering jocularity of such as have no relish of an exact likeness: which to render complete, he who draws it must not disdain the slightest strokes. But if witlings should be inclined to attack this account, let them have the candour to quote what I have offered in my defense.— JAMES BOSWELL: "1764: Ætat 55," *Life of Johnson.*

His life during the thirty years which followed was one hard struggle with poverty. The misery of that struggle needed no aggravation, but was aggravated by the sufferings of an unsound body and an unsound mind. Before the young man left the university, his hereditary malady had broken forth in a singularly cruel form. He had become an incurable hypochondriac. He said long after that he had been mad all his life, or at least not perfectly sane; and, in truth, eccentricities less strange than his have often been thought grounds sufficient for absolving felons and for setting aside wills. His grimaces, his gestures, his mutterings, sometimes diverted and sometimes terrified people who did not know him. At a dinner table he would, in a fit of absence, stoop down and twitch off a lady's shoe. He would amaze a drawing-room by suddenly ejaculating a clause of the Lord's Prayer. He would conceive an unintelligible aversion to a particular alley, and perform a great circuit rather than see the hateful place. He would set his heart on touching every post in the streets through which he walked. If by any chance he missed a post, he would go back a hundred yards and repair the omission. Under the influence of his disease, his senses became morbidly torpid, and his imagination morbidly active. At one time he would stand poring on the town clock without being able to tell the hour. At another he would distinctly hear his mother, who was many miles off, calling him by name. But this was not the worst. A deep melancholy took possession of him, and gave a dark tinge to all his views of human nature and of human destiny. Such wretchedness as he endured has driven many men to shoot themselves or drown themselves. But he was under no temptation to commit suicide. He was sick of life, but he was afraid of death; and he shuddered at every sight or sound which reminded him of the inevitable hour. In religion he found but little comfort during his long and frequent fits of dejection; for his religion partook of his own character. The light from heaven shone on him, indeed, but not in a direct line, or with its own pure splendor. The rays had to struggle through a disturbing medium; they reached him refracted, dulled and discolored by the thick gloom which had settled on his soul; and, though they might be sufficiently clear to guide him, were too dim to cheer him.—THOMAS BABINGTON MACAULAY: "Samuel Johnson."

Lord Melbourne, a contemporary of Macaulay's, once said that he wished that he could be as cocksure of anything as Macaulay was of everything. If this is not the prose of a cocksure man, it is at least the prose of a thoroughly assured man. Macaulay has a tidy mind; he values clarity; he enjoys clean balances and antitheses. One judges that he has small patience with mysteries and mystifications. Certainly, he sees Johnson's character as plain as a pikestaff. Johnson suffered from an "unsound body and an unsound mind." His struggle aggravated his misery. His eccentricities are the product of his hereditary malady. Johnson was "sick of life." If he did not rid himself of a life he was "sick of," it was because he was "afraid" of death.

Now this is not the place in which to discuss whether or not Macaulay has oversimplified Johnson's personality. The passage has been quoted, not to throw light upon Johnson's personality, but upon Macaulay's. But some comparison with Boswell's account of Johnson's eccentricities may be of help here. Boswell agrees that Johnson was sick, but he does not say patly that he was "sick of life" (which, in Macaulay's sentence so neatly balances "afraid of death"). Moreover, Boswell, in mentioning the alley which Johnson avoided, takes pains to refer to Reynolds's conjecture that Johnson avoided it because it was for him associated with some painful memory. Boswell does not say that he agrees with Reynolds, and he frankly calls one of Johnson's eccentricities a "superstitious habit," and another a "magical movement." Still, Boswell is more tentative than Macaulay in his explanations of Johnson's conduct, just as he presents a richer and more detailed description of the eccentricities.

One must not, of course, build too much upon two rather brief passages. Even these passages, however, do present some contrasts between Boswell's personality and Macaulay's. Macaulay's is obviously the more methodical mind, the more practical mind, the more "brilliant" mind. Boswell, one would suppose, has more geniality, more sympathy, more sense of the rich sensuous detail of life, more humility before the mystery of human personality. This last comment requires the admission, of course, that Boswell, in the passage in question, is writing about his hero, Johnson. This is true enough. But the passage does not breathe uncritical hero-worship. Boswell is willing to characterize the odd action he describes as "a ceremony," and he is not unduly squeamish about his great friend's dignity when he writes "sometimes giving a half whistle, sometimes making his tongue play backwards from the roof of his mouth, as if clucking like a hen."

Boswell is neither the uncritical devotee nor the meticulous cataloguer. We get a better characterization of his interests if we read the last paragraph of his selection. Here the conscious artist is speaking. Boswell is fascinated with Johnson; he means to make us see him, even if the minuteness of the details may prompt some readers to laugh. He is the sort of man who will not be satisfied with a formula which will explain Johnson or satisfied with any mere summary of Johnson's traits. Macaulay (in the best, as well as in the worst sense) is the man who is fascinated by summaries, who sees the value of summaries, and means to give us the neatest and most pithy summary possible.

IMPROPER INTRUSION OF THE WRITER'S PERSONALITY

The writer's own personality, then, is reflected in his writing, even though that reflection may well be unconscious. This fact offers an opportunity to consider briefly a further point which is of the utmost concern to the writer. If personality ultimately cannot be kept out of one's writing, how is the expression of the writer's personality to be controlled?

Consider the following passage from one of Dickens's novels.

She was dead. Dear, gentle, patient, noble Nell was dead. Her little bird—a poor slight thing the pressure of a finger would have crushed—was stirring nimbly in its cage; and the strong heart of its child mistress was mute and motionless for ever.

Where were the traces of her early cares, her sufferings, and fatigues? All gone. Sorrow was dead indeed in her, but peace and perfect happiness were born; imaged in her tranquil beauty and profound repose.

And still her former self lay there, unaltered in this change. Yes. The old fireside had smiled upon that same sweet face; it had passed, like a dream, through haunts of misery and care; at the door of the poor schoolmaster on the summer evening, before the furnace fire on the cold wet night, at the still bedside of the dying boy, there had been the same mild lovely look. So shall we know the angels in their majesty, after death.

The old man held one languid arm in his, and had the small hand tight folded to his breast, for warmth. It was the hand she had stretched out to him with her last smile—the hand that had led him on, through all their wanderings. Ever and anon he pressed it to his lips; then hugged it to his breast again, murmuring that it was warmer now; and, as he said it, he looked, in agony, to those who stood around, as if imploring them to help her.—CHARLES DICKENS: *The Old Curiosity Shop*, Chap. 71.

Many things could be said about this passage: its obvious sentimentality (cf. p. 398), the strain evidenced by the writer as he tries to squeeze the last drop of feeling from the scene, its shameless parading of all the clichés of tenderness, its invitation to the reader to abandon himself to the sweet sadness of little Nell's death. Yet the passage does express Dickens's own feelings, and it would probably be idle to argue that it is not a "sincere" expression of values that Dickens held very dearly. (That is, it is unlikely that Dickens was cold-bloodedly attempting to stir the reader's feelings. Dickens, too, probably felt the scene deeply, and far from cynically playing upon our feelings, is himself being swept along by his own emotions.) Even so, the passage reveals what may be called a disturbing intrusion of the author's own personality into the scene. The feeling of tenderness is not absorbed and objectified: it spills over chaotically. Compare this death scene with the following:

Snag was a crippled Negro who had caddied for my uncle when he won his first golf tournament. Cap'm John had been fond of Snag. He was fond of all Negroes, and I remember how pleased both he and Snag would be over any golf shot the two of them contrived to make. . . .

But Snag used to swim in the river. He believed it would help his undeveloped leg. He had a mongrel dog, and the two of them would swim on warm mornings up at a great sweeping bend of levee and wilderness beyond the golf course. It was on an empty Sunday morning that Snag was killed. He hadn't seen the oil tanker when she came around the bend. They were out in the middle, then, just two black specks on the yellow vastness. Then the long blast came like a mighty trumpet. They said that the nigger must have misjudged their swing. They were already well on the turn when they saw him and they said that they eased the wheel to straighten out and pass the nigger on starboard. They said that he must have just put it to a guess and he guessed wrong, because they said that he had two-thirds of the river to swim in but that he had turned back and so they put the wheel hard to starboard and then he turned back again—the two of them, the nigger and the dog, swimming back and forth each time in a shorter arc until they could see his face stretched like laughter in the sunshine with all the white teeth, or like a grimace of joyous surprise, recognition, and with men even running forward, waving from the swinging cliff (she was high, empty) and the long trumpet blast right up to the moment he was struck and they wasted the life preserver. He was struck by the great bulging side, nearly amidship, as the wall of steel swung gatelike and fast with the wheel hard over. They saw only the hand and the vanishing gleam of teeth and then nothing.—s. s. FIELD: "Goodbye to Cap'm John." [7]

In its intention, this passage is not, to be sure, quite on the same level with that of Dickens. It is more modest in its claim on our emotions; it presumably aims at a less intense effect. Yet the man who remembers the story from his boyhood, and narrates it here, is obviously fond of Snag, and feels a sense of sorrow at his death. Moreover, the student will probably find the passage quite moving. How is the emotion which we feel kept from spilling over into sentimentality? Why does it not become excessive? In part, because the scene has been realized for us vividly in its detail; because the writer does not seem at our elbow nudging us to "emote," or suggesting what we ought to feel; because he has left us free to draw our own interpretations, confident that if the scene is fairly presented, the reader may be relied upon to respond fully and properly to it. In short, Field does not *intrude* his own personality into the scene: his relevant emotion is absorbed into the scene itself.

The sensitive artist's ability to express emotion without cramming it down our throats—without intruding his own personality into the work—may be further illustrated by excerpts from a story by Katherine Anne Porter and a story by Ernest Hemingway. In

[7] From "Goodbye to Cap'm John," by S. S. Field, published by *The Southern Review*, Vol. I (1936). Courtesy of Louisiana State University Press.

Miss Porter's story two little girls have been watching a race which their uncle's horse, Miss Lucy, has just won.

The little girls sat down, feeling quite dizzy, while their father tried to pull their hats straight, and taking out his handkerchief held it to Miranda's face, saying very gently, "Here, blow your nose," and he dried her eyes while he was about it. He stood up then and shook them out of their daze. He was smiling with deep laughing wrinkles around his eyes, and spoke to them as if they were grown young ladies he was squiring around.

"Let's go out and pay our respects to Miss Lucy," he said. "She's the star of the day."

The horses were coming in, looking as if their hides had been drenched and rubbed with soap, their ribs heaving, their nostrils flaring and closing. The jockeys sat bowed and relaxed, their faces calm, moving a little at the waist with the movement of the horses. Miranda noted this for future use; that was the way you came in from a race, easy and quiet, whether you had won or lost. Miss Lucy came last, and a little handful of winners applauded her and cheered the jockey. He smiled and lifted his whip, his eyes and shriveled brown face perfectly serene. Miss Lucy was bleeding at the nose, two thick red rivulets were stiffening her tender mouth and chin, the round velvet chin that Miranda thought the nicest kind of chin in the world. Her eyes were wild and her knees were trembling, and she snored when she drew her breath.

Miranda stood staring. That was winning, too. Her heart clinched tight; that was winning, for Miss Lucy. So instantly and completely did her heart reject that victory, she did not know when it happened, but she hated it, and was ashamed that she had screamed and shed tears of joy when Miss Lucy, with her bloodied nose and bursting heart, had gone past the judges' stand a neck ahead. She felt empty and sick and held to her father's hand so hard that he shook her off a little impatiently and said, "What is the matter with you? Don't be so fidgety."—KATHERINE ANNE PORTER: "Old Mortality." [8]

In Hemingway's story, the boy is watching a race that has been "fixed."

They weren't at the post hardly any time at all when the gong started and you could see them way off across the infield all in a bunch starting on the first swing like a lot of little toy horses. I was watching them

[8] From *Pale Horse, Pale Rider* by Katherine Anne Porter, copyright, 1939, by Katherine Anne Porter. Reprinted by permission of Harcourt, Brace and Company, Inc.

through the glasses and Kzar was running well back, with one of the bays making the pace. They swept down and around and came pounding past and Kzar was way back when they passed us and this Kircubbin horse in front and going smooth. Gee it's awful when they go by you and then you have to watch them go farther away and get smaller and smaller and then all bunched up on the turns and then come around towards you into the stretch and you feel like swearing and goddamming worse and worse. Finally they made the last turn and came into the straightaway with this Kircubbin horse way out in front. Everybody was looking funny and saying "Kzar" in a sort of sick way and them pounding nearer down the stretch, and then something came out of the pack right into my glasses like a horse-headed yellow streak and everybody began to yell "Kzar" as though they were crazy. Kzar came on faster than I'd ever seen anything in my life and pulled up on Kircubbin that was going as fast as any black horse could go with the jock flogging hell out of him with the gad and they were right dead neck for neck for a second but Kzar seemed going about twice as fast with those great jumps and that head out—but it was while they were neck and neck that they passed the winning post and when the numbers went up in the slots the first one was 2 and that meant Kircubbin had won.

I felt all trembly and funny inside, and then we were all jammed in with the people going down stairs to stand in front of the board where they'd post what Kircubbin paid. Honest, watching the race I'd forgot how much my old man had bet on Kircubbin. I'd wanted Kzar to win so damned bad. But now it was all over it was swell to know we had a winner.

"Wasn't it a swell race, Dad?" I said to him.

He looked at me sort of funny with his derby on the back of his head. "George Gardner's a swell jockey, all right," he said. "It sure took a great jock to keep that Kzar horse from winning."—ERNEST HEMINGWAY: "My Old Man." [9]

Both passages attempt to suggest, first the excitement of the observer, and then the subsequent disappointment: in the case of the little girl, at the realization that the horse has been pushed beyond its strength and injured; in the case of the boy, at the realization that the race has been "fixed"—that the horse that should have won has been held back and cheated of its victory. Each passage reflects the dramatic character (the "personality") of the observer. This fact is, of course, primary. But it is possible to see that each passage

[9] From *Three Stories and Ten Poems* by Ernest Hemingway, copyright, 1923, by Charles Scribner's Sons.

also reflects the personality of the author. We have already commented upon the way in which the style of a typical Hemingway story is related to Hemingway's own personality (p. 440). This excerpt from "My Old Man" provides a good instance of our generalization. But what of Miss Porter's style? Can a comparable generalization be made?

Probably so. Hers is the prose of a sensitive observer. It is feminine prose (in the best sense of that term) as Hemingway's is masculine prose. But the details, rich as they are, and "naturally" as they are presented (through the eyes of the little girl), are not chaotic. They are ordered to a pattern; they are meaningful in terms of a generalization about life. This is not to say that the little girl is made to appear too wise for her years. It is rather to say that the scene is being described as remembered by a woman; that the experience of the little girl receives the benefit of subsequent maturity; that, though the scene is focused upon the child, the passage describing it is not being written by a child.

Are we to conclude, then, that both passages are autobiographical: that Miranda is taken from Miss Porter's childhood and that the boy observer in Hemingway's "My Old Man" is the boy Hemingway, or at least derives from some comparable boyhood experience of Hemingway's? Not necessarily. For the point to be made here concerns *how* a writer uses his materials—not *where* they may have come from.

PERSONALITY CONTROLLED AND OBJECTIFIED IN THE WORK

In both passages before us the intelligence and sensitivity of the writer, his interests and values, are subordinated to the work in question. It would be more accurate to say that they are here completely *absorbed* into the story of Miranda and into the story of the boy at the race track. If there is a moral here for the writer, it is one that applies not merely to the writer of fiction. Even the essayist who writes in the first person may profit by using a comparable means of objectification and control. He may actually find it helpful to objectify and dramatize the "I" who speaks, not at all to disguise or suppress his personality, but rather to realize that personality most fully. Even Charles Lamb preferred to write as "Elia" rather than as Charles Lamb, Esq.

STYLE CULTIVATED BY READING

Thus far in this chapter we have discussed style (1) as related to the writer's immediate purpose and (2) as related to the writer's personality. But there is a third aspect of style which ought to be discussed at least briefly: (3) style as related to the writer's linguistic environment. The first aspect of style is, of course, all-important. It is the aspect of style which concerns the writer immediately as he looks down upon the paper before him and grapples with the problem of putting his meaning adequately into words. The second aspect (style as the expression of the writer's innermost self) involves a double problem: on the one hand, that of the writer's personal integrity, and on the other, that of his originality. The third aspect of style has to do with the writer's inheritance, his relation to his linguistic tradition generally. Specifically and practically, it has a great deal to do with his reading.

One cannot learn how to write unless he learns how to read. In stressing this we are not forgetting the importance of originality or urging the writer's falling into slavish imitation. For it is only through reading that we discover ourselves and find our own individual style.

A little reflection will show why reading is of paramount importance for writing. In the first place, we inherit language. We learn words by imitating our parents. We imitate their words, and we learn to associate meanings with these spoken sounds. As we grow, the meanings of these words are enriched, and we acquire fresh words. Moreover, we learn, again by imitation, how to arrange these words in patterns so that more precise meanings can be conveyed. A child who can merely babble a few isolated words may be able to make its wants known. When it says "water," the mother understands that it wants a drink of water. As it grows, it acquires grammatical patterns. But it learns further expressive patterns as well. The devices of style are expressive patternings. Parallelism and antithesis, for example, express relationships: they point (or should point) to elements that line up together and to others that balance each other in opposition. Stylistic arrangements *of all sorts* are thus acquired by imitation: for the process of learning by imitation is not interrupted as we learn to read.

A writer who has read nothing but the local newspaper will begin by writing in the style of the local newspaper. How could he do otherwise? Anyone who can read and write has been thoroughly exposed to models of a sort. Strictly speaking, there is no such thing as a "natural" style. The only question, then, is not whether one shall or shall not be exposed to models of style. It is rather whether his experience shall include a wide range of models or be restricted to a narrow one. Ironically, it is the writer least acquainted with a variety of styles who usually turns out to be least individual in his own style. It is easy to see why this must be true. If our acquaintance with style is limited to that of the newspapers, a few popular magazines, and an occasional novel, our knowledge of the expressive possibilities of the language is so restricted that we have little range in which to make our own personalities felt.

Imitation, then, does not necessarily run counter to originality. For we must remember the terms in which our problem is set for us: we can always be as "original" as we please by using our own peculiar grammar, by assigning our own meaning to words, or, for that matter, by simply inventing a new language. The penalty for such originality is that we should not be understood. The only originality that counts, therefore, is an originality that does not deny the necessary conventional element in language. That element—though we may want to argue about its ultimate limits—is always very great. Therefore, since we can win only a cheap and worthless originality by violating the permissible modes of expression, the way to a truly individual style is through acquaintance with the whole realm of possibilities. For we do not invent words and expression: the only area in which we may display originality is in the way in which we may dispose and reorder them.

In the next chapter the importance of reading will be discussed more generally. Suffice it to say here that learning how to write goes hand in hand with learning how to read, and that a rich background in reading, far from fettering the writer to worn and dull conventionality, is his richest resource for discovering his own characteristic style.

How far back should the reading go? Can the (to our ears) quaint and obsolete style of Sir Thomas Malory aid us who are committed to the idiom of the twentieth century? Can the eighteenth-century prose of Joseph Addison be of any real utility to us in forming a style? Has not prose changed so much since the nineteenth century that a nineteenth-century style, even that of Charles Lamb, for example, seems quaint and out of place today? These are some of the questions that the student may be tempted to ask at this point.

A proper answer to these questions might take some such form as this. It is perfectly true that language changes and that writers of an earlier century can rather easily be identified through the period style which they write. It is also perfectly true that it would be absurd for a twentieth-century writer to affect the prose style, say, of a seventeenth-century writer. Naturally he will derive most direct help from writers who are attempting to solve the typical problems of style that face a writer of our time. But even the writers of the remote past may prove to be of more direct value than a superficial opinion would indicate. For we must remember that reading is not undertaken for the sake of carbon-copy imitation. Not even the twentieth-century writer is to be read as a model to be followed slavishly. We read in order to enlarge our resources, in order to strengthen our hold on the language and its range of expressive devices; we read other writers in order to provide ourselves with the equipment which will give us the means to be more truly ourselves. Seen in these terms, imitation and originality do not war against each other; a writer may possibly find that he can learn from the prose of two centuries ago as well as from that which was written last year.

SUMMARY

A very important element in style is RHYTHM. Rhythm depends upon the relationship of stressed and unstressed syllables. Poetry tends to employ a formalized rhythm which we call verse. Prose rhythms are much less formalized, and for that reason somewhat more difficult to describe accurately. But rhythm is frequently one of the most important expressive devices which the writer possesses. The writer is not advised to try consciously for special rhythmic effects. He ought, however, to learn to recognize rhythmic defects in his own prose as symptoms of poor or defective arrangement of sentences and sentence elements.

Style involves an over-all harmony among the various expressive elements: sentence structure, diction, metaphor, rhythm, and all the rest. There are, therefore, no devices that are good in themselves, absolutely and intrinsically. Moreover, if we are to speak strictly, we shall have to regard as a bad style only that style which is at odds with itself, a style which lacks harmony among its various expressive factors. By the same token, we have to say that style and matter, form and content, are inseparable. We know what is said only through the way in which it is said; and to alter the way in which a thing is said is always to alter, if only ever so slightly, what is said. Three practical considerations follow from our realization of this inseparability of style and matter. (1) Style is not a mere veneer, a decorated surface laid over the content. (2) The writer's real difficulty in composition is finally to know what he wants to say—not, as we are tempted to think, merely how to say it. (3) Bad style always shows itself in some disharmony or cleavage between what is said and what we guess the author actually meant to say. The elements at fault call attention to themselves —"stick out."

These last considerations bear upon another aspect of style: the sincerity of the writer. We properly take originality to be a symptom of a good style. If we see that the style is not a veneer, but rather the informing principle of content, we can understand why good style is always indelibly impressed with the personality of the writer. But the reader needs to be warned against any excessive striving for originality as such. It is not enough to urge him to be his unique self, for frequently he finds that true self only through a process of exploration. Originality, the impress of personality, like good rhythm, fortunately can be left to take care of itself if the writer manages to take care of what he can consciously control in his composition.

Thus far we have considered the relation of style to the writer's purpose and to the writer's own inner self. A third matter has to be considered: the relation of a writer to his linguistic environment. This amounts, in practice, to what the writer can learn from his reading, since language itself is inherited along with all of its expressive devices. The writer who strives to avoid all imitation locks himself into a narrow prison. His way to freedom and to true originality consists rather in extending his knowledge of the language and of various styles. Intelligent reading goes hand in hand with the discipline of writing.

A MORE CONCRETE SUMMARY

If some of the matters discussed in this chapter seem rather abstract, perhaps it may be helpful to discuss them under the following metaphor. We are familiar with "styles" of dress, and Lord Chesterfield, in a well-known pronouncement on style, defined style as "the dress of thoughts." It probably seems natural to most of us to think of style as a garb in which our thoughts are clothed.

Buffon, however, made a comment on style quite as famous as that of Chesterfield. He said that "the style is the man himself." His statement and Chesterfield's, then, seem to stand in flat contradiction. Is there a way out of the apparent contradiction? There is, for both Chesterfield and Buffon are making use of the same metaphor, though they use different aspects of it. Chesterfield is presumably thinking of the writer's power to choose a proper style and of his need to choose wisely. A man does not choose to wear a dinner jacket for work in the garden, nor does he choose a suit of overalls to wear to a formal dinner. There must be an accommodation of style to the occasion, and Chesterfield's statement insists upon the necessity for careful choice. Buffon, on the other hand, is stressing the fact that in a proper style the words do not cover up and disguise the man; instead the style becomes an expression of the man. The two pronouncements thus can be reconciled; for if words may be thought of as a kind of dress, still a proper kind of dress ought to reflect the personality of the wearer. In other words, Buffon is not recommending that the writer walk about naked, for, since, in terms of our clothes analogy, the words are the clothing, that would be to have the writer give up words altogether. Nor is Chesterfield, one may assume, recommending that the writer shrivel away into a kind of tailor's dummy—that is, become merely an animated suit of clothes.

Our clothes metaphor, then, properly understood, will carry us a step further. It will even account for the fact that we do not know what we want to say until, through exploration, we have found how we are to say it. We may fit the problem to the metaphor in this fashion. It is true that a man's "word-clothing" is not like his naked skin, something that he is born with and cannot and need not change. He acquires language: language is not natural but always in some sense artificial. Nevertheless, this also needs to be remembered: the "man" who is to be measured and clothed, in this case, cannot turn over his measurements to a journeyman clerk who selects from the shelves the ready-made articles, guaranteed to fit. On the contrary, an intricate and careful tailoring is required; for we must remember that the "man" to be fitted (the "thing" to be said) is only a vague and nebulous ectoplasm *until he assumes the garments which define him and realize him.* For the thoughts, of which the words are the dress, are not defined with any precision until they have assumed their dress—until they are expressed in words.

Lastly, even the problem of reading can be fitted to the clothes metaphor. In suggesting that the writer may, by intelligent reading, learn how to write, one is not suggesting that he go into a museum and choose a sixteenth-century doublet, an eighteenth-century peruke, and Dickens's nineteenth-century greatcoat. To acquire past styles in this sense would be merely to outfit oneself for a fancy-dress party. But the person who is acquainted with no styles except those of the newspaper and an occasional magazine is like a man who goes shopping in a shop so meagerly furnished that it can offer him only one shoddy suit, size 28, and one overcoat, size 42. He cannot clothe himself properly unless he has a variety of items from which to choose, a variety large enough to allow him to display real discrimination and thus dress himself not only comfortably, but also in a fashion which will express his own individual personality.

CHAPTER 11

Reading: What Does It Mean to a Writer?

A LARGE part of the material we write about is drawn from our personal experience and observation. Reporters, feature writers, essayists, and fiction writers draw heavily on actual life, as do, at times, even more technical writers, philosophers, for instance. The most important or vivid events, experienced or witnessed, are not worth much to us, however, unless we think about them. We have to see their significance before they are worth recording. And in one sense, it can even be said that they cannot be recorded at all unless we think about them, for the only thing that we can record is what we think of something, how it strikes us, how we interpret it. We cannot record the thing in its absolute purity without reference to our own response to it.

So our experience and observation are extremely important to us. But what of experience and observation that come to us second-hand, through reading? What can reading do for us? It can do many things for us, but for immediate purposes, we may list three. It can help us think. It can give us things to think about. And it can help us to express our thoughts.

Reading can help us think by giving us examples of thinking, good or bad. Obviously, the example of good thinking helps us. It gives us a model. It shows the principles of thinking in operation. But the example of bad thinking is useful, too. At least, it is useful if we read critically enough to spot it as bad. The bad thinking gives us the challenge to define the real issue, assess the evidence offered, correct the bad logic. And it may even awaken us to our own failures in thinking by showing us how some method we have employed leads to confusion. In reading, the student must try to break down what he reads into its logical divisions and state for himself the relation among these divisions. In other words, he must try to define the structure of the whole discourse.

Reading may be about anything. Every subject that conceivably interests man has been written about somewhere. So reading is the great mine of material for our thinking. It extends our limited individual experience in time and space, back into the past and outward into other places than our own. We can find out what Athens was like at the time of Plato or what London was like at the time of George III. Reading tells us what our own time and place are like. And it can put us inside the being of other people. The poem, the novel, the play, the memoir, the autobiography or biography, the philosophical treatise, the essay—almost any form of writing—can do this. Characteristically, it is the job of poetry, fiction, and drama—imaginative literature—to draw us fully into the flow of the experience of others. But in so far as our imagination, or the imagination of the writer, works on the material, any form of writing can do this. We feel that we know Macbeth or Becky Sharp better than we know our next-door neighbor, and Socrates or George Washington better than we know Calvin Coolidge. Writers have made this possible for us, Shakespeare, Thackeray, Plato, and the historians of the American Revolution.

Reading gets us out of our own time and place, out of ourselves, but it can in the end return us to ourselves and help us to define ourselves. It places us in relation to human history and human effort. It locates us on a map, as it were, of human experience, and sets up points of reference by which we can inspect ourselves. Reading ends by giving us ourselves as material for thinking.

It also gives us our own immediate world. We thought that we had that already, the home and family, the daily occupations, the familiar street, but when we come back to that world from our reading we find that it has a new look, a deeper interest, and a brighter gloss. After Sinclair Lewis's *Main Street*, Edgar Lee Masters' *Spoon River Anthology*, Thomas Wolfe's *Look Homeward, Angel*, or Sherwood Anderson's *Winesburg, Ohio*, the American small town never looks the same. After Thoreau's *Walden*, the back pasture or the creek never looks the same. Or after Charles A. Beard's *The Making of the American Constitution,* the report in the morning paper about the latest action of Congress does not look the same. Reading gives us our immediate world, because it gives us a new way of looking at that world. We can see new material in it.

Reading can help us to express our thoughts. Every selection or example in this book shows us, by its success or failure, something about the process of getting our meaning into words. With this topic, however, we return to our first topic—and also to a topic discussed on page 435, the inseparability of "form" and "content." For the way of thinking and the way of saying meet at one level and become the same thing. Can we say that we have thought something through until we have the words for it? In a kind of rough-and-ready way, we do distinguish between our idea and the words we put it into, and the distinction is useful, just as, in reading, the attempt to put the writer's idea into our own words is a useful check on our understanding. But words are the instrument of thought and there are no two ways of saying exactly the same thing. The difference may be slight in a given case, so slight that it doesn't matter, but the principle does matter. When we read we are constantly being affected by the slight qualifications of meaning and these slight qualifications are in the end of enormous importance.

When we write, if we are writing conscientiously, we keep trying to locate the right word or phrase. The thing doesn't "feel" right to us as it stands. We don't know exactly how we want to put it (in other words, we don't quite have our idea), but we are dissatisfied and keep fumbling for the right expression. We may even try to phrase to ourselves the grounds of our dissatisfaction—using words to diagnose our bad use of words—and this may help us. But we do not have the right expression until we have it, and we may have to get it by a process of trial and error, checking each try by our "feel," our hunch, continually asking ourselves the question: "Is this really what I want to say?" Sometimes we have to arrive at the right expression by some such process of elimination. For instance, when asked how he managed to get the right word, the poet A. E. Housman replied that he didn't bother so much about getting the right word; he bothered about getting rid of the wrong one.

Is there some sort of a system for reading which will help the writer? There is no foolproof system. For one thing, different kinds of writing may call for different systems of reading. What may work for fiction may not, and probably will not, work for writing that is primarily expository. Moreover, a system which works for one person may not work for another. In the end the student may have to develop his own system. But any system must take into account such questions as these:

1. What is the material?
2. What understanding do I already have of such material? That is, do I have any basis for comparison and criticism?
3. What is the author's motivation? Is he trying to inform me, convince me, persuade me, or make me participate in a total, imaginative experience—the experience of a novel, say, or of a poem or play?
4. What is the author's basic idea or theme?
5. How is this idea developed in the structure of the work? In other words, what is the author's method of thinking?
6. What are the tone and style of the work? Do I understand the intention and the effect of the language as used in his work?
7. What enlightenment does the work give me? New facts? New ideas? New methods of thought? New sense of character? Deeper awareness of human experience?

Number 1 is the easiest question. The book, or whatever it is, is about something. The material (as opposed to the author's interpretation of that material—the idea or theme) may be tribal life in Polynesia, co-operative marketing, the theory of relativity, the program of the Republican Party, socialism, the nature of the good. It is fairly easy to identify the material—the "raw material"—the author worked with. Number 2 also seems easy, but it is sometimes harder than it looks. To answer these questions, the reader must look honestly into his own knowledge. It is easy to delude oneself. A person hears about something and in the end assumes that he knows something about it. But he merely has the words, and perhaps has one accidental or arbitrary interpretation. He must ask: What do I know about Polynesia? What do I know about the ways in which the good has been conceived? What are some of the problems involved in defining it? Certainly, we want to read about subjects we do not know about, and for any subject there must always be the first acquaintance. We have to start somewhere. The point is simply this: the reader must try to know where he stands, what is his own background and equipment for dealing with a subject.

Number 3 seems relatively easy, and usually is. Often an author will state quite flatly what he intends to do—to inform the reader about tribal life in Polynesia, to persuade the reader to vote the Republican ticket. But all cases are not so simple. Sometimes there are concealed motives. For instance, what seems to be a piece of history may actually be written from a point of view that would imply your adopting some attitude or line of action, here and now. The life of Abraham Lincoln might work as an appeal to support the Republican Party in the next election, or the life of George Washington might work as an argument against political co-operation with Great Britain. In both of these examples, the apparent motive would be to inform but the real motive would be to convince or persuade. Try to see whether the author has something up his sleeve.

When we deal with fiction, poetry, or drama—the kinds of writing which are art forms—the question of the author's motivation becomes even more complicated. In one sense such kinds of writing are primarily for our enjoyment. That is their distinguishing characteristic. But a great deal hinges on the word *enjoyment* here. We recognize immediately some difference between the kind of enjoyment found in a who-dun-it and that found in Shakespeare's *Romeo and Juliet*. The who-dun-it gives us the pleasure of the puzzle, the excitement of action. That is all the author commits himself to provide. *Romeo and Juliet* gives us the pleasure of a fuller acquaintance with life, a sense that experience can be rich and meaningful, a deeper understanding of human motives and problems (including our own). This does not mean that the thrill of suspense and the excitement of action are lacking, for those qualities may be present in serious literature, but it does mean that those qualities are not present for their own sakes but are part of a larger intention. The who-dun-it gives us mere entertainment. When we finish reading it we are through with it. *Romeo and Juliet* gives us artistic enjoyment, and we are never through with it. We can come back to it over and over again and find fuller significance in it and renewed enjoyment.

This is not the occasion to try to analyze the elements involved in the enjoyment of literature. But we can say here that it is a mistake to think of such enjoyment as something cut off from our other interests in the world. It involves those other interests, makes use of them, and returns us to them with more insight. On the practical side, a novel, for instance, may give us certain facts about the life and background presented, certain information about social conditions and psychology, ideas on a number of subjects. Such things have their own interest without relation to the novel in which they appear. Such things, nevertheless, are the material of fiction, and, as material, can be judged on their own merits. The picture of a social situation may be false or the ideas involved may be trivial. Or a novel which is sound in such matters may still be a very poor novel. It may not capture the sense of life in motion, the pattern of human beings acting and reacting on each other. It might not appeal to the imagination. But sound facts, true information, just and adequate pictures of the social situation are important in a work of art, even if their presence does not insure the goodness of the work as art. For our experience of a work of art is not cut off from our other and more general interests: The experience of a work of art stems from these interests.

In regard to question 4, sometimes an author will state very explicitly his main idea, or theme. This idea is to be distinguished sharply from the mere material. It is what the author *thinks about* the material, his interpretation of it, the line of action that he proposes be taken in regard to it. But sometimes he is not explicit. The reader must arrive at it by the course of the discussion. Furthermore, even if an author does state the idea, it is sometimes a good thing for the reader to put it into his own words, to state it as it would appear to him, and to try to see how it might apply to other instances and situations than those used by the author. The whole point here is for the reader to be sure that he really has the idea in its fundamental significance and in its implications.

The business of stating the theme of one of the literary art forms ordinarily is much more difficult than that of stating the theme of a piece of exposition or argument. To do this well requires a good deal of experience in reading poetry, drama, or fiction, and this is no place for such a special study. But when we read such works we can ask ourselves questions such as these: What does the author think is bad or good in human conduct? What does he think constitutes success or failure? What does he think about the relation between the individual and the group he lives with? Do his characters seem to be responsible for their own lives or do they seem to be the victims of outside forces? Is the general effect of his work brisk, humorous, satirical, serious, sad, tragic? An attempt to answer such questions may provide us with the material from which we can phrase the statement of the theme of a novel. We want, in the end, to get a statement which will indicate the author's basic view of the world, his set of values, and how they work out in human experience. In other words, we must ask: What is the essential meaning, the significance, of the novel?

Once we get such a statement framed, we shall probably consider it very poor and bare compared to, for instance, the novel itself. And the better the novel, the poorer and barer the statement of theme will appear. The theme is not the novel, the poem, or the play. The novel, poem, or play is the vital working out of the theme in its complexities of experience. If the work of art is good, it will give us the feeling of meaning in experience, and will return us, filled with that sense, to our own living.

When we think we have some grasp of the theme of the work in hand, we should try to answer question 5, to see in some detail how the theme is developed in the structure of that work. How does one idea lead to another, what is the handling of explanation or argument? Why are things put in this particular order? Do illustrations really illustrate the point intended by the author? Is the work consistent, or does it contain self-contradictions? Are the author's conclusions the only conclusions which could be derived from the evidence he presents? Questions such as these—and the writer can frame others of the same sort—will give some notion of the structure of the whole.

By a parallel process we can investigate the structure of the play, poem, or piece of fiction. Poetry raises many special considerations; fiction is a little easier to handle. We can ask, for example, about the logic of the plot. Does one situation or event really lead to the next? Do the motives of the characters adequately account for the behavior of the characters? What idea does a character or event seem to embody? How do the different ideas relate to each other? How do they lead us to the theme?

As for question 6, we seem to come to this late in the day. How do we get anything from a piece of writing if we do not really understand the language? But there are degrees of understanding. After we think we have understood well enough to get the main drift—to state, for instance, the theme and to work out something of the structure of the whole composition—we can return to a closer inspection of the language itself. Upon this inspection we may find that we had not really understood many things. We may have even missed the basic notion of the whole work. So we may have to revise our answers to earlier questions.

When we read we are constantly being affected, whether we know it or not, by the slight qualifications of meaning in the language, and these slight shadings are in the end of enormous importance. Attention to such matters in our reading leads us to a skill in our own use of language. What questions can we ask ourselves to sharpen our own sensitivity to language?

For one thing, we can ask as a general question of any phrase or passage that seems interesting or important: Why is it this way and no other? Any writer can try to state to himself the exact significance of a word or phrase as it appears in the particular context. He can ask himself how this may differ from other uses which he has encountered. He might try to imagine what other words the writer may have originally used and discarded. Why would he have discarded them? Was the original version inaccurate, that is, was its dictionary content wrong in some degree for the purpose in hand? Was it vague, so that the reader couldn't be sure of any particular meaning? Was it ambiguous, so that the reader had a choice of different meanings and could not decide between them? Was the tone inappropriate to the occasion, or inconsistent with the rest of the composition? The writer ought to try to define the tone of the whole composition and see how individual items, words, phrases, or images, contribute to this tone.

But we should never forget that we cannot deal with any part of a piece of writing in isolation. Words modify sentences, paragraphs modify other paragraphs. As readers, we are dealing with an elaborate tissue of interrelations, and the whole point of our effort is to understand this fact in a practical way. And a practical way, as opposed to a theoretical way, is the way of recognition and use. To gain this practical understanding the student will find theorizing helpful. We theorize when we try to state why a thing works the way it does, and why it succeeds or fails. But the end of your effort is not to say why. It is to appreciate and do.

The answer to the last question, number 7, really summarizes all the other answers. But it does more. It puts what the writer has gained from the present work into the context of what he has gained from all his past reading and experience. It may be that he has gained nothing—for several possible reasons. The work may be bad or trivial in itself. Or the work may be good in itself, but be a thing which is too elementary for the writer's present stage of maturity. Or the writer may simply not be prepared to profit from the work; his background may not qualify him to grasp it. Or it may be that the writer simply hasn't given enough time and effort to it. But if you discover that you have failed to gain anything from something you have read, try honestly to understand why.

The questions have been numbered, one to seven, but this does not mean that there is any order of importance here. All are important, and if you as reader cannot answer one, you probably cannot answer others. They are all interrelated, and in the end have to do with the unit which is the work. As there is no order of importance here, so there is no necessary order in which the questions should be considered. With one reservation: perhaps numbers 1 and 2 should always be first and second, and number 7 last. But the others may have to be considered in different orders at different times. Occasionally, for instance, the reader might have to work hard at the language before he could get at the theme and organization. Or he might find the reverse true. Fumble with the thing until you find a key. If one approach fails, try another. The random touch may spring the secret latch. Or long after, when you have decided that you cannot come to grips with the thing, its significance will suddenly dawn upon you.

There is one more general remark of great importance. This has to do with the speed and amount of reading. The superstition is current, particularly in schools and colleges, that speed and amount of reading are valuable in themselves. But do not believe a word of it.

It is true that there is some correlation between speed and expertness in reading. And there is some correlation between a person's intellectual resources and the amount of reading he has done. But more important than speed or amount is the quality of the reading itself. If one does not read thoughtfully, he might as well not read at all. Even if the reader amasses information from his reading, this is still true, because information without thought is dead lumber. Only thought can erect that lumber into a useful structure. Different kinds of reading demand different speeds, and the right speed for you is the speed that allows you to get the most out of your reading. Familiar material presented in familiar patterns permits a relatively high degree of speed. A certain amount of familiar materials presented in familiar patterns comes to anyone in the course of his work. In dealing with it use what speed you can. But this kind of reading does not do the reader as much good as reading which involves unfamiliar materials presented in unfamiliar patterns. Then we have to put our minds to it and stretch our capacities. It is the hard reading—and since hard, therefore slow—that develops our own possibilities. And as a corollary to this, the amount of reading is not in itself important. A thing worth reading at all, except for mere entertainment, is probably worth reading more than once, and it is certainly worth thinking about. And it is better to read one good thing well than a dozen things in a routine, mechanical way.

If this is true for reading in general, it is especially true for the reading of poetry, fiction, and drama. There are two reasons for this. The first has to do with the handling of the material, and the second with the handling of the language. By and large, the writer of exposition or argument uses a direct method. He tries to say quite explicitly and directly what he means, to present his facts or ideas straight. This is not usually true of poetry, fiction, or drama. Or rather, what the author "means" here is different from what he means in the other type of writing. Here he is trying to capture the quality of experience, the flow of event, the colors, forms, and smells of the physical world, states of being, modes of character and motivation, as well as to give facts or ideas. Facts and ideas, as we have said, are involved here; but we do not read poetry, fiction, or drama for the facts and ideas *as such*. We read them to experience imaginatively how the facts and ideas relate to the other elements—how, for instance, ideas grow out of other elements of experience and are embodied in them. This means that the language of the art forms is of primary importance, because here the language is not *about* something but *is* something. There is a kind of parallel with painting. What is the picture without line and color—the medium in which it appears? Or what is music without the organization of sound—its medium?

Appendixes

Causal Analysis

THERE are four methods which are helpful in investigating a situation to determine a cause. They are called the methods of AGREEMENT, of DIFFERENCE, of AGREEMENT AND DIFFERENCE, and of VARIATION. After examining them the student may feel that he has always been acquainted with them, for they merely describe how his mind *does* work when it is working straight on problems of this kind. But studying the methods may sharpen his awareness of the processes of his own reasoning.

1. AGREEMENT. If we have two or more situations from which we get the effect X, and find that these situations have only one constant factor, E, then that constant factor may be taken as the cause of X. Let us set this up as a chart:

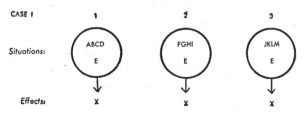

CASE I   1   2   3

Situations: ABCD / E   FGHI / E   JKLM / E

Effects: X   X   X

Here E is the cause of X.

The method here stated is sound in theory but in some cases is difficult to apply. Even in the laboratory, where the experimenter can create his situation with a degree of control, it is hard to be sure that only one factor E is constant. But it is especially difficult to apply this method to a complicated event outside of the laboratory. The investigator rarely finds a set of situations in which *only* one factor is constant. Ordinarily he will encounter a set of situations such as may be indicated by the following chart:

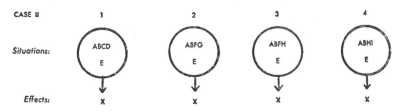

We can notice two things about this set of situations.

First, several factors occur in more than one situation. For instance, factor F occurs in situations 2 and 3; factor H occurs in situations 3 and 4.

Second, three factors (A, B, and E) occur in all situations.

When the investigator sees that certain factors are repeated, as is true of F and H, he must inquire whether they are repeated in *all* situations. If they are not repeated in all situations he can discard them. So F and H can be discarded. When the investigator sees that two or more factors, as is true of A, B, and E, are repeated in all situations, there are two lines of thought open to him.

First, he may explore the possibility that A, B, and E are to be taken as components of the cause—that no one by itself would be sufficient to bring about the effect.

Second, he may explore the possibility that one or two of the factors which are present in all of his available instances might not occur in other instances when the effect does not occur and therefore are not relevant to the effect.

At this point the investigator has to make a judgment as to which of the two lines of thought he will follow. He must judge whether or not all of the constant factors (A, B, and E) are relevant to the effect. He can do this only in terms of his knowledge of the field which he is investigating.

Let us take an example. Suppose we wish to learn why a certain school lost most of its football games over a period of years. We find certain things true every year. Most of the players every year are Catholic, for it is a Catholic school. Let us call this constant factor A. The same coach had been employed for a number of years (factor B). The school has very high academic standards and no one is permitted to participate in any athletic event who does not have an average grade of "fair" (factor E). The question is: Do we have a complex of factors here (A, B, and E) which are all necessary components of the cause?

Common sense and our experience with athletics at once make us rule out factor A—for we know that Catholicism bears no relation to the matter of football losses. But we cannot so readily rule out factors B and E, the matter of the coach and the matter of the high academic average required. At this point we have to make further investigation. We have to look into the coach's previous record, we have to pass a judgment on the type of instruction he gives now, and so forth. Or we must try to learn how many good players have been disqualified by the rule requiring a certain scholastic average, and so forth. We may satisfy ourselves that both of these factors (B and E) contribute to the defeats. Or we may decide that only one is the cause.

In any event, this is not a foolproof formula. Knowledge and experience are required to apply it. Even when it is applied we cannot be absolutely sure that we have determined the cause of X. We have merely indicated a certain degree of probability.

2. DIFFERENCE. If we have two situations, identical save that one involves the factor E and the effect X, and the other does not involve the factor E and the effect X, then E may be taken as the cause of X or an indispensable factor in the cause. Let us put it as a chart:

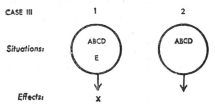

If we can be quite sure that the first situation resembles the second in all significant factors except E and X, then we may take E as the cause of X or an indispensable factor in the cause. But it is often difficult to find such clear-cut instances, and we have to draw on our judgment and experience to decide what factors are relevant. For instance, we might get the following case:

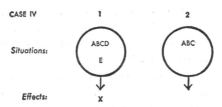

Here D as well as E is missing from the second situation. The following possibilities suggest themselves. First, D may be irrelevant, and E is the cause. Second, D may be relevant and in conjunction with E constitutes the cause. If we can control the situation, we may test the second possibility by setting up the factors ABCE. If we still get X, then we know that D is irrelevant. But if we cannot control the situation, we must consult our judgment and experience in deciding about the relevance of D.

3. AGREEMENT AND DIFFERENCE. This is, of course, a combination of the two previous methods. Therefore the method involves both *positive* and *negative* instances. In the positive instances we apply the method of agreement, and then check the negative instances against the positive instances by the method of difference.

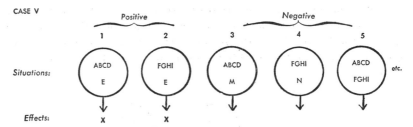

In situations 1 and 2 we have the ordinary method of agreement. But when we come to the negative situations, we notice that there is none which fulfills the requirement of the strict method of difference; i.e., the negative situation differing from the positive situation only in that it does not have the factor which appears to be the cause. But here, though situation 3 has all the factors of situation 1 except E, the factor of cause, it does have a new factor, M. And so on with the other cases: they would always involve, in differing combinations and sometimes with new factors, the various factors, except E, which were present when X took place.

We can set up a simple example of the method. Let us assume

that in a family of five people three suffer from an attack of food poisoning. The problem is to determine what item of the restaurant meal was the cause. John, Mary, and Sue are ill.

John ate beans, potatoes, beef, and ice cream.

Mary ate a salad, a soup, and ice cream.

Sue ate sweet potatoes, broccoli, ham, and ice cream.

So much for the positive cases. Since ice cream is the only item common to the meals eaten by the victims there is a strong probability that it is the cause. But we can check this against the negative cases, i.e., cases of persons who were *not* ill.

Mildred ate beans, potatoes, beef, and lemon pie.

Thomas ate a salad, sweet potatoes, and ham, with no dessert.

These negative cases include most of the dishes eaten by the victims—with the exception of ice cream. So the argument for ice cream becomes even stronger. Few situations, however, are as simple as the one given above, and in making our analysis we are often called upon to rule out many common factors which we judge to be unrelated to the effect (for instance, we might rule out the color of the plates used in all the above meals).

4. VARIATION. If one factor in a situation varies whenever a certain other factor varies, there is a causal connection between the factors.

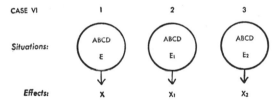

For instance, as the temperature rises mercury expands, as the supply of a commodity increases, its price goes down, or as the amount of advertising of a product increases, its sale increases. These are illustrations of the principle, but in them are great differences in the degree of complication. In the first instance, the relation between the variation of temperature and the variation in the mercury is regular and constant. We depend on the fact, and our thermometers operate on that principle. But an economist cannot depend on the relation between supply and price with the same certainty, nor can a sales manager be sure that an increase in his advertising appropriation will pay off in the market. Here too many unpredictable factors may be involved in the situation.

In applying the method of variation, we must remember that it does not matter whether the variation is direct or inverse. For instance, we have direct variation with temperatures and mercury: as the temperature increases the mercury increases in volume. And we have inverse variation with supply and price: as the supply increases the price decreases.

The Syllogism:
Distribution of Terms

IN STUDYING the syllogism we are led to what is called the DISTRIBUTION OF TERMS. A term is said to be distributed when it refers to every member of the class which it names. Let us return to our first syllogism (p. 159):

All men are mortal. (major premise)
Socrates was a man. (minor premise)
∴ Socrates was mortal. (conclusion)

The premise, "All men are mortal," contains two terms. The first, *men,* is obviously distributed, as the word *all* indicates, but the second term, *mortal,* is not distributed; that is, it is not used, in that premise, to refer to every member of the class which it names, only to those (mortals) who are also men. It does not exhaust the class *mortal creatures.* The premise really says: "All men are some of the class of mortal creatures," or, "The class *men* is included in, but does not exhaust, the class *mortal creatures.*"

We may ask about the term Socrates. Is it distributed or undistributed? It is distributed, for there is only one member, Socrates himself, of the class Socrates. This comes clear if we substitute some such term as "Frenchmen" in a similar statement: "Frenchmen are men." We would mean, of course, "*All* Frenchmen are men."

To determine whether a term is distributed we must look at the meaning of the proposition in which it appears. If we take the proposition, "Graduates of Hawkins School are honest," we see that the real meaning is, "*All* graduates of Hawkins School are *some* of the class of honest people."

There are four basic types of propositions in which we must inspect the question of distribution of terms. Here the underscoring of a letter in a proposition indicates distribution, and the shading of an area in the accompanying chart indicates distribution.

1. All x̲ is y

All x̲ is referred to here but only some of y, the part overlapped by x̲: i.e., all x̲ is (some) y.

2. No x̲ is y̲

All x̲ is referred to here, and all y̲, for there is no overlap; i.e., no (part of all) x̲ is any part of (all) y̲.

3. Some x is y

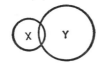

Here some of x overlaps some of y; i.e., some x is (some) y.

4. Some x is not y̲

All y̲ lies outside some of x: i.e., some x is not (any part of all) y̲.

To distinguish distributed from undistributed terms is very important, for the distribution of terms may affect the validity of a syllogism. But before discussing that topic we must glance at what is meant by validity in this connection. It does not mean the same thing as the truth of the conclusion. We may have a valid conclusion which is not true. For instance:

All legless creatures that crawl are snakes.
Worms are legless creatures that crawl.
∴. Worms are snakes.

This syllogism is valid. That is, given the premises we must grant the conclusion. But the validity of the conclusion does not mean that it is true. In fact, we know it to be untrue. But it is untrue, not because the reasoning is wrong (the syllogism is valid), but because one of the premises is not true. So when we use the word *valid* we are referring to the correctness of the reasoning from the given set of premises, whatever they are, true or untrue.

As we have said, the distribution of terms may affect the validity of a syllogism. We can set up two rules for distribution which must be observed if a syllogism is to be valid:

I. The middle term must be distributed at least once.

II. No term can be distributed in the conclusion if it is undistributed in its premise.

Let us examine some cases which violate the first rule.

CASE I

All sergeants are soldiers.
Some soldiers are corporals.
∴ All sergeants are corporals.

This is obviously untrue in fact, as we know from our information about military organization. But, above and beyond that, the syllogism is not valid, as we can see if we set it up. (The middle term is represented by M, the major term by A, and the minor term by B. Numbers in parentheses indicate the type of proposition.)

All B is M. (1)
Some M is A. (3)
∴ All B is A.

Here the middle term is not distributed as we can readily tell by looking at our table of the types of propositions. This means that the major term (A) and the minor term (B) do not, for certain, have any members in common. All we can be certain of is that both A and B fall within M.

The following syllogism with a changed content still illustrates the same formal defect:

CASE II

All Marines are soldiers.	All B is M. (1)
Some soldiers are corporals.	Some M is A. (3)
∴ All Marines are corporals.	∴ All B is A.

The fact that *some* Marines are corporals, that a partial truth may be involved in the conclusion, does not alter the case, for the proposition to be proved concerns *all* Marines.

If we shift the positions of the terms in the major premise of Case I, the syllogism remains invalid.

CASE III

All corporals are soldiers.   All $\underline{A}$ is M.   (1)

All sergeants are soldiers.   All $\underline{B}$ is M.   (1)

∴ All sergeants are corporals.   ∴ All B is A.

Again the middle term is undistributed, as we can see from consulting the table of types of propositions. If we drew a chart of this we would have a figure identical to that of Case I.

There are other possible combinations which violate the first rule about the distribution of terms, but the cases given are the most common. In all cases, it is only necessary to inspect the premises carefully to determine the situation.

The second rule about the distribution of terms declares that no term can be distributed in the conclusion if it is not distributed in its premise. That is, you cannot argue necessarily from a "some" to an "all." Since there are two terms in a conclusion, the major and the minor, two possibilities of error are open here. We may have ILLICIT distribution in the major term or in the minor term. The following syllogism illustrates illicit distribution in the major:

All banks are financial institutions.   All M is A.   (1)

Some building and loan organizations are not banks.   Some B is not $\underline{M}$.   (4)

∴ Some building and loan organizations are not financial institutions.   ∴ Some B is not $\underline{A}$.   (4)

Here the major term ("financial institutions"—A) is not distributed in the premise, but it is distributed in the conclusion. The error results from assuming that the major term is distributed in the major premise—that is, from assuming that it says, "All banks are *all* financial institutions," and therefore that whatever is true of banks will be true of all financial institutions. Actually, the major premise says, "All banks are *some* financial institutions," and therefore what may be true of those financial institutions which are banks may not be true of those which are not banks.

The same principle applies in the case of the illicit minor:

No member of the Jones family is a drunkard.   No $\underline{A}$ is $\underline{M}$.   (2)

All drunkards are irresponsible people.   All $\underline{M}$ is B.   (1)

∴ No irresponsible person is a member   ∴ No $\underline{B}$ is $\underline{A}$. (2)
    of the Jones family.

Here the minor term ("irresponsible people"—B) is not distributed in the premise, but is distributed in the conclusion. Therefore the conclusion is not valid.

To the two rules concerning distribution of terms we may add two rules concerning negative premises or conclusion.

III. From two negative premises nothing can be inferred.

IV. If one premise is negative the conclusion must be negative.

Here is a syllogism with both premises negative:

No royalist is a democrat.   No $\underline{M}$ is $\underline{A}$. (2)
No true American is a royalist.   No $\underline{B}$ is $\underline{M}$. (2)
∴ No true American is a democrat.   ∴ No $\underline{B}$ is $\underline{A}$. (2)

The trouble here is that no necessary common ground is established for the major and the minor premise.

Here is a violation of rule IV:

No true American is a royalist.   No $\underline{M}$ is $\underline{A}$. (2)
Our children are true Americans.   All $\underline{B}$ is $\underline{M}$. (1)
∴ Our children are royalists.   ∴ All B is A. (1)

When we pause to think that the major premise says that all members of class M lie outside of class A, and that the minor premise says that all members of class B lie within class M, we see immediately the absurdity of affirming that members of class B lie necessarily within class M. But occasionally such an argument can be so buried that the absurdity does not appear without some analysis.

The Outline, Summary, and Précis; Notes; Research Paper; and Book Report

THE OUTLINE[1]

THE OUTLINE has two uses. It can help the writer to organize his own thoughts and lay a plan for his work before he begins the actual composition. It can help the reader define the basic meaning and structure of what he reads. The two uses have much in common, for both mean that the maker of the outline is dealing with the structure of a discourse. In fact, once an outline is completed, an observer might not be able to tell whether it was designed by a writer or a reader.

There are several common types of outlines: (1) the suggestive outline, (2) the topic outline, (3) the sentence outline, and (4) the paragraph outline. Variations may be worked out for special purposes.

1. THE SCRATCH OUTLINE

The scratch outline is a set of notes and jottings which may come in handy either for writing or for understanding and remembering what one has read. It is probably not highly organized. For instance, the writer, in making a preliminary survey of his subject, may simply put down the various topics and ideas that come to him in the order in which they come. As some line of thought begins to emerge he may indicate this, too. But

[1] The form of outline called the brief is discussed in the chapter on argument (p. 172).

his primary purpose is not to define the form and order from the beginning. It is to assemble suggestive material. Some of it he may not use because, in the end, it may seem superfluous or irrelevant. The scratch outline embodies the early exploration of a subject, and may be meaningless to everybody except the maker of the outline. When such an outline is made by a reader, there is naturally some indication of the order of topics in the thing read; but even here the outline does not undertake to record the details of relations among the parts. It is merely a jog to the reader's mind, a record of the first acquaintance with the thing read.

2. THE TOPIC OUTLINE

The topic outline does indicate the order of treatment of individual topics and does indicate in a systematic fashion, by heads and subheads, the relation among the parts in degree of importance. But as the name indicates, it proceeds, not by sentences, but by listing topics. There is, however, one exception: the outline is to be introduced by a statement of the theme of the composition in the form of a fully rounded sentence. Let us set up a topic outline of the first section of "The Threat of Science," by Christian Gauss, which follows:

THE THREAT OF SCIENCE

CHRISTIAN GAUSS [2]

There is a wide-spread belief fostered occasionally by scientists themselves that if we will but allow science fullest freedom it will eventually make us all healthy and wealthy and wise. There is little doubt that up to a certain point it can make us healthy and wealthy. If we pass over, for the moment, the question whether the health which science can give us is only physical (and not moral) health, we will all readily admit that a clearer understanding of the processes of nature and the sources of physical power can certainly save us from many ills. Science can and has eliminated many diseases and much useless motion. No one under a scientific dispensation will waste his time and effort in praying for rain or in attempting, as they did in Homer, to stop the flow of blood by

[2] "The Threat of Science:" Originally printed in *Scribner's Magazine* and later incorporated in *A Primer for Tomorrow*, copyright, 1935, by Charles Scribner's Sons. Reprinted here by permission of the author and *Scribner's Magazine*.

incantation. It can increase and has increased immeasurably our mastery of nature. It makes us far more efficient. Whether it can really increase our mastery of human nature and thus make us wise and good is a different question. Scientists sometimes tell us that it can. In any attempt to predict our future under science this is really a much more important question than the first, for if without changing your man you place at his disposal a ton of TNT or only a sawed-off shotgun and an armored car, you may make life far more dangerous than if you had left your untutored savage with only his primitive battering-ram and his relatively harmless bow and arrow.

The academic mind is inclined to call a man wise if he understands things like the Bohr atom and the Einstein theory. That, too, is a mistake. He is not really wise; he is only intelligent. The normal, ordinary human being must express himself by his acts. Even a recluse is involved in countless enterprises and relationships with others. If we say a man is wise we mean that whatever his theoretical beliefs, in the conduct of his life he chooses sane courses of action. If the scientist cannot help him to do this it is as much a superstition to expect unaided science to give us a safe and happy future as it was for our ancestors to believe in witch-doctors or to pray for rain.

There are times when the discouraged student of religion, of history, and of letters is tempted to rise up and call his brother who works in the laboratory blessed. Among scholars the experimental scientist is a privileged character. He is allowed to live and work in a world that knows not sin nor evil. Like Adam and Eve he lives in a Garden of Eden. Trinitrotoluol is not evil because it explodes. Hydrogen sulphide is not unclean because it smells badly. The lion is not wicked because he kills the antelope. He is only leonine. That is what lions do for a living. To the biologist the lion who kills many antelopes has "survival value." He is, this scientist will even tell us, a good lion.

When the scientist uses this word *good* we must be upon our guard. He does not mean what the theologian, the moralist, the artist, or even the ordinary man means by that word. His lion, for instance, is frankly predatory. To Dante he was the personification of pride, the most deadly of all the sins, and quite evidently he fiercely seeks his own. If the biologist should invent a science for lions, a leonine science (and knowing his ingenuity I do not put it beyond him), it would make life easier for lions. It would increase their number, eliminate waste motion in their technic of pouncing upon antelopes. In the biologist's way of looking at things, it would make them better lions but from any outside non-scientific point of view, that of antelopes, for instance, it would not make lions better. It would change only their outward habits, not their inner natures.

So it is perhaps with our science in general, and if it is to be the only force operative upon humanity then to the end of time we shall have to carry with us into no matter how roseate a future only the same old Adam.

If to avoid confusion we must be on our guard when he uses the word *good*, much the same is true when he uses certain other words like *pure*, even when he uses them in his really fine phrase, pure science.

In the first instance pure science, of course, means disinterested, not applied, science. The more competent scientists when on their guard never pretend that it means anything more. It is a really noble conception, science divorced from any consideration of its useful or profitable applications. The ordinary man must be cautious, however, and not conclude that science because "pure" somehow gives us a higher kind of truth than that revealed by just plain ordinary religion or art or philosophy. The devotees of these latter studies are assumed, sometimes even by scientists, to have been laggard and never to have pushed their subjects to this twenty-four carat stage of ultimate purity. There may be an error in all this, for it must be remembered and emphasized that science becomes pure only when it has been divorced also from any consideration of social and moral welfare. The pure scientist might conceivably in his laboratory seek to discover that least stable combination of chemical elements which under given conditions would constitute the world's most powerful explosive. This deadly formula would then be available for those who apply to more practical uses the findings of pure science. Its truths are not really truths of a higher sort; they are not above ordinary truths, as the angels (if there still are angels) are over the earth; they are only the truths of science in what might be called their state of innocence.

For this reason experimental science should not be regarded as wicked; it is only unmoral. No harm will come so long as we all remember that it has little relation to what the ordinary man regards as beautiful, or holy, or good. Such extraneous considerations of beauty and holiness and goodness are really impurities in science at its highest stage. They are, however, probably still aspects of truth and it might in one sense almost be said that pure science gives us impure truth, or perhaps rather, truth mutilated; truth from which certain elements that under ideal conditions enter into its fulness have of necessity been cut off.

Statement: This essay is a discussion of the pretensions and limitations of science as a means to social, moral, esthetic, or religious truth.

  I. Question whether science can make men healthy, wealthy, and wise.
     A. Increase of health and wealth by science.

    B. Wisdom not a matter of mastery over nature but over human
       nature.
II. Nature of wisdom.
    A. Academic notion of wisdom.
      1. Understanding of Bohr atom or Einstein theory.
      2. Intelligence, not wisdom.
    B. True wisdom a sane course of action in life.
III. Science not concerned with general values.
    A. Scientific goodness in a thing the fulfillment of its nature.
      1. TNT good when it explodes.
      2. Lion good when it kills antelope.
    B. Science pure as divorced from any consideration of useful or
      profitable applications.
      1. Example explosive discovered by pure science but used later
        for destructive purposes.
      2. Beauty, holiness, goodness impurities in science as such.
    C. Truth of pure science a mutilated truth.

When you check this outline by the essay, you will see that headings I and II correspond to single paragraphs in the text, but that
III corresponds to four paragraphs. That is, the outline is not an
outline of paragraphs but by topics. The last four paragraphs of
the section are really concerned with one topic, the limitations of
science in regard to certain human values—beauty, holiness, goodness. This notion is developed, (A) by reference to what science
means by goodness, (B) by what it means by purity, and (C) by a
statement of the kind of truth which science can give—a mutilated
truth, incomplete in regard to social, moral, and esthetic values.
Here even the subheads, A, B, and C, do not correspond to paragraphs in the text. Topic III, A really involves two paragraphs,
and topic III, B involves the better part of one paragraph, the last.
Topic III, C involves only the last part of the last paragraph. Not
infrequently we find that a topic which looms very important in
the outline will correspond to only part of a paragraph in the text.
The outline indicates the relative importance of a topic and not
the amount of space devoted to it. Sometimes, however, after we
have finished an outline we may feel that the author has failed to
use proper proportion or emphasis. And in this instance we may
feel that the author would have been well advised to develop
such an important point as III, C in a separate paragraph. But that

is his problem, not ours. We have to face such a problem only when we are writing from our own preliminary outline.

3. THE SENTENCE OUTLINE

The sentence outline is the most complete and formal type. Here every entry is in the form of a complete sentence. As with the topic outline, the entries in the sentence outline should correspond to the content and the order of arrangement in the text. The sentence outline differs from the topic outline in indicating more fully the content of each item and the relation among the items. To fulfill these requirements, the sentences should be very precise and to the point. Vague statements defeat the very purpose of the sentence outline and make such an outline look like merely an inflated topic outline. For the sentence outline should really take us deeper into the subject, defining the items more closely and indicating the structure more fully. By and large, the topic outline will serve for fairly simple material, the sentence outline for more complicated material.

Here is an example of the sentence outline as applied to the following first two paragraphs of Mill's essay, "On Liberty."

ON LIBERTY

JOHN STUART MILL [3]

The subject of this Essay is not the so-called Liberty of the Will, so unfortunately opposed to the misnamed doctrine of Philosphical Necessity; but Civil, or Social Liberty: the nature and limits of the power which can be legitimately exercised by society over the individual. A question seldom stated, and hardly ever discussed, in general terms, but which profoundly influences the practical controversies of the age by its latent presence, and is likely soon to make itself recognized as the vital question of the future. It is so far from being new, that, in a certain sense, it has divided mankind, almost from the remotest ages; but in the stage of progress into which the more civilized portions of the species have now entered, it presents itself under new conditions, and requires a different and more fundamental treatment.

The struggle between Liberty and Authority is the most conspicuous feature in the portions of history with which we are earliest familiar, particularly in that of Greece, Rome, and England. But in the old times

[3] From Chapter 1 of *On Liberty*, by John Stuart Mill.

this contest was between subjects, or some classes of subjects, and the government. By liberty was meant protection against the tyranny of the political rulers. The rulers were conceived (except in some of the popular governments of Greece) as in a necessarily antagonistic position to the people whom they ruled. They consisted of a governing One, or a governing tribe or caste, who derived their authority from inheritance or conquest; who, at all events, did not hold it at the pleasure of the governed, and whose supremacy men did not venture, perhaps did not desire, to contest, whatever precautions might be taken against its oppressive exercise. Their power was regarded as necessary, but also as highly dangerous; as a weapon which they would attempt to use against their subjects, no less than against external enemies. To prevent the weaker members of the community from being preyed upon by innumerable vultures, it was needful that there should be an animal of prey stronger than the rest, commissioned to keep them down. But as the king of the vultures would be no less bent upon preying on the flock than any of the minor harpies, it was indispensable to be in a perpetual attitude of defence against his beak and claws. The aim, therefore, of patriots, was to set limits to the power which the ruler should be suffered to exercise over the community; and this limitation was what they meant by liberty. It was attempted in two ways. First, by obtaining a recognition of certain immunities, called political liberties or rights, which it was to be regarded as a breach of duty in the ruler to infringe, and which, if he did infringe, specific resistance, or general rebellion, was held to be justifiable. A second, and generally a later expedient, was the establishment of constitutional checks; by which the consent of the community, or of a body of some sort supposed to represent its interests, was made a necessary condition to some of the more important acts of the governing power. To the first of these modes of limitations, the ruling power, in most European countries, was compelled, more or less, to submit. It was not so with the second; and, to attain this, or when already in some degree possessed, to attain it more completely, became everywhere the principal object of the lovers of liberty. And so long as mankind were content to combat one enemy by another, and to be ruled by a master, on condition of being guaranteed more or less efficaciously against his tyranny, they did not carry their aspirations beyond this point.

Statement: This essay is a discussion of the nature of civil liberty, and of the development of effective checks upon the power which the state may exercise over the individual.

    I. The nature of the power exerted by society over the individual is and has been a very important question.

A. This question influences the present age by its *latent* presence.
   1. The question is seldom stated.
   2. It is rarely discussed in general terms.
B. This question, however, is likely to be regarded as the vital question of the future.
C. It has in the past divided mankind.
   1. The struggle between liberty and authority is the salient feature in the history of Greece.
   2. The struggle between liberty and authority is the salient feature in the history of Rome.
   3. The struggle between liberty and authority is the salient feature in the history of England.
II. In the past the contest between liberty and authority was a contest between subjects and their rulers.
   A. Rulers were regarded as necessarily antagonistic to the governed.
      1. The rulers did not hold their power at the pleasure of the governed.
      2. Subjects did not venture to contest their supremacy.
   B. The rulers' power was regarded as necessary but also as dangerous.
      1. Their power might be used against external enemies.
      2. Their power, however, might be used against their subjects.
III. It was highly important, therefore, to set limits to the power which the ruler might exercise over the subject.
   A. This limitation of the ruler's power took two forms.
      1. The subjects tried to obtain a recognition of certain immunities, infringement of which justified
         a. specific resistance, or
         b. general rebellion.
      2. The subjects attempted to set up constitutional checks.
   B. The first mode of limitation was successfully secured in most European countries.
   C. The second mode of limitation has proved much more difficult to secure.

4. THE PARAGRAPH OUTLINE

In the paragraph outline each sentence corresponds to a paragraph in the text. In dealing with a very obviously organized piece of writing, the paragraph outline may be practically composed of the topic sentences, or adaptations of the topic sentences, of the paragraphs. (It is possible, of course, to make a paragraph outline of entries which are not complete sentences, but such a paragraph outline would have little utility. It would consist of little more than suggestive notes for paragraphs.) In dealing with other kinds of writing, however, it is necessary to summarize for each paragraph the content and intention. The paragraph outline has a very limited utility. On the one hand, in dealing with work composed by someone else, the paragraph outline often misses the real logical organization; for, as we have seen, paragraphs do not necessarily represent logical stages. On the other hand, in dealing in a preliminary way with material which one himself intends to write about, not only may the outline fail to indicate the logical organization desired, but it may be arbitrary and misleading. It is very hard to predict the paragraph-by-paragraph development of any relatively extensive or complicated piece of work. To try to do so sometimes cramps and confuses the writer in the actual process of composition. The paragraph outline is chiefly valuable as a check on your own writing. Before you attempt to make a paragraph outline of one of your own compositions, you must first decide whether each of your paragraphs has a real center and function.

Here is a sample of a paragraph outline designed to schematize the first three paragraphs of "Should the Scientists Strike?" (p. 179 ff.).

I. Though the scientists have done much to bring plenty to our modern world, some of the scientists themselves must be aghast to realize the tremendous destructive power of the atomic bomb which they have created.
II. Certainly the scientists themselves, as well as laymen, have testified to the destructive power of the atomic bomb.
III. Efforts are being made to curb the use of atomic energy for war.

Each of these three sentences sketches out the matter to be developed in the corresponding paragraph of the essay. These headings might be developed somewhat more elaborately; but for the purpose of laying out the order of the paragraphs and suggesting what is to be covered in each paragraph, they probably are developed as far as is useful.

The writer ought to compare this fragment of a paragraph outline with the corresponding part of the brief on page 179 ff. He will notice that the paragraph outline does not correspond with the brief at all points. II, A becomes paragraph one. All the material under subheadings 1 and 2 become the second paragraph; and II, B, with its subheadings 1 and 2, becomes the third paragraph. The paragraph outline, in short, is a way of outlining what sections of the sentence outline (in this case a sentence outline which is also a brief) are to be grouped together in particular paragraphs.

SUMMARY AND PRÉCIS

A SUMMARY summarizes. It gives in compact form the main points of a longer discourse. If it misses any fundamental points or introduces material not found in the text summarized (no matter how relevant or interesting) or gives a false notion of how the points are related to each other, it fails as a summary.

A summary is a digest or reduction of a longer discourse, but it is a discourse itself. It is composed of complete sentences, and observes the principles of unity, coherence, emphasis, and proportion. This means that the connection among sentences must be obvious in itself or indicated by suitable transitions. If the summary is composed of more than one paragraph the connection between paragraphs must be clear.

Any such reduced and complete statement is a summary. The general organization of a summary is a matter to be decided by reference to the purpose for which it is intended. For instance, a summary may follow the order of the original text and thereby give some notion of the approach used by its author. Or a summary may, on the other hand, be organized by a new method. Suppose, for example, an article agitating for the reform of the public school system in a certain city begins with an illustrative anecdote, then moves forward by analyzing certain particular situations, and ends by an appeal for reorganization. The summary might change this method. It might very well begin with a statement of the appeal for reform, and then proceed to give the analysis of particular situations as reasons for reform. The summary might read as follows:

Summary of "DO WE GIVE OUR CHILDREN A BREAK?"
by William Becker

The conditions in our public schools are deplorable on several accounts. It is well known that the record in college of graduates of our high schools falls below the average for graduates of schools in cities of comparable size. Local businessmen, industrialists, and editors are not satisfied with the general or vocational training of job-holders from our schools. And the schools are not doing their part in maintaining the moral health of the young, as is witnessed by the alarming and disproportionate increase in juvenile delinquency. It is time to have a general overhauling of our system.

Before we can remedy the situation, however, we must diagnose the causes. First, the school system has become a political football: members of the school board are chiefly concerned with building their political fences, and many appointments to supervisory and teaching positions are not made on merit. Second, parents have been uninterested in the schools, and many with influence have been more concerned to get special favors for their children than to raise the educational level. Third, local salaries are deplorably low, below the national average, and far below those paid in neighboring cities. No one of these causes can be taken in isolation, and any serious attempt to improve our schools must attempt to deal with all of them.

The organization of the original article might have provided more interesting reading and have been better adapted to catch the attention of a general audience, but the method used here is more systematic and states the logic of the case in a clearer form. Organize a summary in the way that will serve your own purpose best. At times you will wish to follow the author's organization; at other times the author's organization will be irrelevant to your purposes and your own organization will be more appropriate.

The question of the scale of a summary, like the question of organization, is to be determined by the purpose the summary is intended to serve. What do you need to have at your disposal in this capsule form? Occasionally a summary of one brief paragraph would give an adequate digest of a whole book. Or, the summary of an essay might require a number of paragraphs. In general, the important thing to remember is that a summary means a very drastic reduction.

The form of summary known as the PRÉCIS (pronounced *pray-see*) is more standardized than the general kind of summary we have been discussing. It undertakes to retain the basic order of the original text, the same proportions of part to part, and the same tone. Like any summary, however, it is committed to presenting the fundamental points of the original and indicating the relation among them. This closer relation to the original text does not mean a dependence on quotation and paraphrase. Material should be restated for economy and emphasis. The scale of the précis, like that of any outline, may vary according to the purpose it is to serve, but since it is committed to maintain the relative proportions of an original, it can never be as drastic in its reduction as a general summary may be.

Here is a précis of the first section of "The Threat of Science," by Christian Gauss, of which we have already given a topic outline.

There is a widespread belief that science may make us healthy, wealthy, and wise. It may make us healthy and wealthy by increasing our mastery over nature, but the question is whether it can make us wise by increasing our mastery over human nature. The academic notion of wisdom is that of understanding things like the Bohr atom, but such an understanding means intelligence, not wisdom, for wisdom implies a sane course of action in life. The scientist's use of words like *good* and *pure* should not trick us into believing that he is dealing with the values we ordinarily indicate by such words. For him the good thing is simply the thing that fulfills its essential nature, as TNT does when it explodes or the lion does when it kills an antelope. And by pure science he means science divorced from any useful or profitable application. The pure scientist may, for instance, discover an explosive later used for the most immoral purposes. Therefore, the truths of science are not necessarily of a higher sort than those arrived at by other means. Considerations of the beautiful, the holy, or the good are impurities for science, that is, are irrelevant to its special business. But they remain considerations for man in his total living, and the truth or science is really truth mutilated.

Here the original passage runs about 1,200 words, and the précis a little over 200. The précis itself might be reduced a little more if that seemed desirable.

NOTES

Notes may be taken on any subject, from any source, for any purpose, and by many methods.

Some people take casual notes on all sorts of things, experiences and observations, conversations and thoughts, as well as books they have read. The casual note-taker records anything that strikes him as interesting. He is merely providing a jog to his memory and a sort of record for himself. But notes on a wide range of subjects and from a wide range of sources may be drawn by a person who has a special interest. The novelist may keep notes on little turns of phrase he hears, gestures or facial expressions he observes, little episodes he witnesses, his own experiences, or ideas he has. At the moment he takes the note he may see no specific use for it, but he knows that in the future it may, in some form, be usable. The anthropologist living with an Indian tribe will probably keep very careful notes on customs, rituals, language, games, and so forth. At the time he takes the note he may not see the importance of the particular item, but he knows that this is the sort of material which he must analyze and try to fit into a comprehensible pattern.

Either casual note-taking or note-taking in terms of some general interest, like the novelist's or anthropologist's, is a good habit. It sharpens the powers of observation and reflection, and can sometimes give a keener pleasure to experience.

We have said that there are many methods of note-taking, but fundamentally the method is dictated by the purpose for which the notes are taken. The main thing is to have some method, to be systematic, and to keep in mind your purpose. Good lecture notes are difficult to take. For one thing, many lectures are not carefully organized and may be conversational and informal in tone. But as you become acquainted with the general subject of a course you will see the relevance of information or ideas and will have some notion of what is important. A good lecturer will, of course, help you to establish this relevance, but no lecturer will do all of your thinking for you.

When you are listening to a lecture, you should try to understand the basic line of the lecturer's thought rather than try to put down everything he says. Good notes may be very brief. Sometimes it may be a good procedure to jot down during the lecture only the main topics or ideas, and afterwards, while the lecturer's development of them is still fresh, to go back and fill in from memory. Experiment to find out what will work best for you with a particular lecturer.

Here is a sample of notes that might be taken on a lecture on "The Differences between British and American Pronunciation."

Many American pronunciations represent <u>earlier</u> <u>forms</u> of British pronunciation.

So-called broad a became standard in late 18th cent. in England. Gives other examples. See G. P. Krapp's English Lang. in America. Some American pronunciations represent local dialects of Great Britain. Standard in England not rigidly fixed at time of settlement of America. (Sir Walter Raleigh spoke "broad Devon" to his dying day—Aubrey.) Southern half of Great Britain prominent in early colonization.

Eastern New England and east Anglican counties.

South Atlantic states and counties of southwestern England—Devon, Dorset, etc.

Examples: from early New England town records "evidence of spelling."

This fragment would represent "fresh notes"—not yet carefully organized. But, even so, the student has been able to suggest an organization by means of underscoring, parentheses, the notation "Examples," and so on.

When you are dealing with textbooks or collateral reading various methods may be useful, the sentence outline, the general summary, or the précis. The whole point is to get the main ideas or pieces of information on record and to establish the relation among them. There are three basic questions to ask:

1. What important information does your author give?
2. What use or interpretation does he make?
3. How does he justify his interpretation?

The outline, summary, or précis will help you to answer these questions. But there are other questions which you must ask yourself:

4. How does this author's information relate to other information on the subject which I already have from other sources?
5. How do his uses or interpretations compare with uses or interpretations of such material by other writers?
6. How do I assess his work? Is he logical? Does he present adequate evidence? Is his organization clear? And so on?

And so with these questions you depart from the outline or summary. You may do so by following the presentation of your author's material by answers to these questions or by marginal or parenthetic commentary, putting in your own queries, comparisons, and judgments at the appropriate points.

When you take notes for a book report or a research or critical paper, you are working for a special purpose, and the nature of the purpose determines the kind of notes you will take. So we shall discuss note-taking for these in the course of discussing their purposes and forms.

THE RESEARCH PAPER

The research paper draws its material from many sources. Its aim is to assemble facts and ideas and by studying them to draw new conclusions as to fact or interpretation, or to present the material in the light of a new interest. For instance, a military historian who wanted to understand why General Lee lost the Battle of Gettysburg would study the written records of orders and events, the correspondence and memoirs of witnesses, the actual terrain, and the interpretations of other historians. In the light of that evidence, he would try to frame an explanation. Or a literary critic who wanted to understand why a certain novelist often used certain themes would study the facts of the novelist's life as found in whatever sources (letters, memoirs, public records, biographies), the kind of education he received, the kind of ideas current in his particular place and time, and so forth. Such material would be his evidence. The researcher might discover new facts, and new facts can easily upset old theories. But he might have to depend on facts which were already available but available in scattered sources. Then his task would be to collect those facts into a new pattern of interpretation.

The difference between the book written by the professional historian or literary critic and the term paper written by a student may appear so great that they seem to have no relation. But the basic method should be the same: to collect the facts and interpret them. The term paper can be intelligent, well informed, interesting, and original in its conclusions, and the student should try to make it so. But first of all he should try to make his work systematic. If it is not systematic it will probably not have the other qualities. The first step toward making his paper systematic is to learn how to investigate his subject. The historian going to the order book of a general, the documents of a politician, the terrain of a battlefield; the anthropologist observing the Indian tribe; or the literary scholar studying the manuscripts or letters of an author is using what are called primary sources. He goes to original source of information for his facts. But the college student must usually use secondary sources. He reads the report of the anthropologist or he studies an edition of a poet prepared by a scholar. But even here there are degrees. He should try to use material which is as close as possible to the original source of information. He should not depend on digests or commentaries of the anthropologist's report, but should go to the report itself. He should not merely read what has been said about a novelist, but should read the novelist's actual work. He should not rely on interpretations of the Declaration of Independence, but should study the actual text. Get as close to the facts as possible. No matter how good your reasoning is, it is useless if the facts on which it works are not dependable.

The research paper, we have said, draws its material from many sources. It is not a digest of one book or article. But how do you get at the useful sources?

Special reference books give a good starting point, standard encyclopedias and dictionaries, and such compilations as the *American Yearbook*, the *Statesman's Yearbook*, and the *World Almanac*. In addition to such general reference works, there are those devoted to special fields, for example, the *Dictionary of National Biography* (limited to the British), the *Dictionary of American Biography, Living Authors, Who's Who* (British), *Who's Who in America*, the *Encyclopedia of the Social Sciences*, the *Catholic Encyclopedia*, the *Cambridge History of English Literature*, the *Cambridge History of American Literature*, the *Oxford Companion to English Literature*, the *Oxford Companion to American Literature*, Bartlett's *Familiar Quotations*, and the *Reader's Guide to Periodical Literature*. Reference books are so numerous and sometimes so specialized that it is often helpful to consult the *Guide to Reference Books*, by I. G. Mudge, to know where to go in the first place.

The reference book will give an introduction to a subject and certain basic facts. Best of all for the student, it will usually offer a list of other works, books or articles less limited in scope than the treatment in the reference book itself. With this as a starting point the student can make up his own *working bibliography* for his subject. As he reads into his subject he will encounter references to other works, and can gradually extend the range of his working bibliography. The subject catalogue of the library will also provide new items.

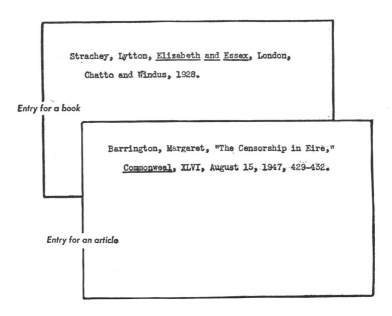

Strachey, Lytton, Elizabeth and Essex, London, Chatto and Windus, 1928.

Entry for a book

Barrington, Margaret, "The Censorship in Eire," Commonweal, XLVI, August 15, 1947, 429–432.

Entry for an article

The working bibliography should be kept on convenient cards of uniform size, with only one entry to a card. This allows the student to arrange them in alphabetical, or other order (by topics, for example), according to his need. The entry on the card should contain all the basic information about a book or article; the author's name with the last name first, the title of the work, the volume number if any, the place of publication, the publisher, the date of publication. If the work appears in a periodical or collection, that fact should be indicated with volume number, the date, and the pages occupied by the work.

This form is to be retained in making up the final bibliography to be attached to your finished paper. There the order will be alphabetical by authors. Your final bibliography may be shorter than your working bibliography, for the final bibliography should contain no entry from which you have not taken material for the actual paper, whereas certain items in your working bibliography will be dropped as more valuable items come to light.

The professional scholar may want to work through all the material on his subject, but the student preparing a term paper scarcely has the time for such a program. And many items in the bibliographies he encounters are antiquated or trivial. So to save his time and energy, he should try to select the items which will best repay his attention. There is no rule for this. Selected bibliographies sometimes appear in textbooks and other works. Sometimes an author will refer with special respect to another work on his subject. But the student can always take his working bibliography to an instructor and ask for comment.

Unless you take notes on your reading you will probably not be able to remember much of the relevant material and will certainly not be able to organize it well when you come to write your paper. If you have taken your notes carefully, you will be able to lay out before you the whole subject and put it in order. The paper will almost write itself. But if the notes are to give you the most help, they must have a convenient mechanical form.

Notes can be put on note cards (usually 3" by 5"), on small or half sheets, or on full sheets. What you use does not much matter, so long as the size is manageable and uniform. As already mentioned, not more than one note, however brief, should be on a single card or sheet. This rule should be strictly adhered to, even when the notes are on the same topic; for when you take the notes, you cannot be sure in what order you will eventually use them. Only if each note is independent can you arrange them in the order desired when you come to write your paper. Each note should carry at the top, at left or toward the center, some indication of the precise content, not the general subject of your investigation, but some subtopic. And at the top right, or at the bottom, the note should carry an adequate reference to the source from which it is drawn. Presumably the full bibliographical information about that source is already in your working bibliography, and so some skeleton notation will be adequate here. (When you are taking notes not related to a working bibliography, say when you are doing general reading, you should record full bibliographical information with the note.) Below is a specimen card or sheet:

```
American success worship    Chesterton, What I Saw
                                 in America, pp. 107-10.

American worship of success not materialistic.  Fact
of worship means a mystic rather than a materialist.
Frenchman who saves money to retire and enjoy his
omelet more of a materialist.  American does not work
for the enjoyment of things, but for some ideal vision
of success.  He does not want the dollar for what it
will buy but as a symbol.  Phrase "making good" il-
lustrates the fact; carries a moral connotation by
a "sort of ethical echo in the word" good (p. 108).
Not necessarily an admirable morality, but a morality
implied, and idealism of a kind.
```

When we look at the actual note on the card we see that several other phrases might have been used to indicate the topic discussed. For instance, "American business mysticism," or "American materialism." All that is needed is a word or phrase which will remind the note-taker of the content. We notice, too, that after the direct quotation there is a parenthesis with the page number. The note-taker apparently feels that this is a telling phrase worth remembering and perhaps using. If he quotes it, he will want the exact page reference.

As for the bibliographical indication at the upper right, he might have reduced it simply to "Chesterton" if there was no Chesterton other than G. K. Chesterton on his bibliography and no other book by that author. This, like the topic indication, is for his own convenience and need tell no more than he himself has to know to identify the source.

So much for the mechanics of note-taking. As for the process, you should make your notes relevant, accurate, and clear. To make them relevant you must keep constantly in mind the main purpose of your investigation. You are studying a particular subject with particular limits. You are not concerned with anything only casually associated with the subject. If, for instance, when your subject is the economic backgrounds of the American Revolution, you are reading a general history of the period, you should not be distracted by military strategy of the French and Indian Wars or an analysis of Puritan theology. Your job is to follow your main purpose through a body of various materials, and often what is major for you will be minor in the work you are investigating.

It is possible to take notes prematurely. Therefore, it is always best to become acquainted with a work before you take notes from it. In your first reading you may indicate material for possible notes, and pass on. When you have finished the work, or those parts relevant to your interest, you can then better assess the material for possible notes. In this way you will get from any particular work only the most pertinent notes, and you will avoid duplication.

The note itself may be direct quotation or summary. If direct quotation is used, it is sometimes valuable to record the context of the quotation. What leads the author to make his statement? What point does he try to establish by it? You do not want to misinterpret your author by implication. For instance, suppose a critic should write:

Although Herman Melville has created in Captain Ahab of *Moby Dick* a character of intense interest and monumental proportions, he has in general little sense of the shadings of personality and motive. Most of his creations are schematic, mere outlines without flesh. He lacks that basic gift of the novelist, a sense of character.

If you, assembling material for a paper on Melville as a novelist, should merely quote, "Herman Melville has created in Captain Ahab of *Moby Dick* a character of intense interest and monumental proportions," you would have a misleading note. An accurate note would run something like this:

Even though William —— believes that Melville in general lacks a sense of character, he admits that Captain Ahab is a "character of intense interest and monumental proportions."

But this principle of context holds good for the note by summary as well as the note by quotation.

When you are taking notes by summary, the kind of summary to be used depends on the special case. In one case, the author's method of reasoning may be very important, and then the summary should be of a form to indicate the logical structure of the original text. In another case, where mere facts or scattered opinions are involved, the summary need record merely these facts and opinions. As for the scale of the summary, there is no guiding principle except the note-taker's need. Try to forecast what you will need when you actually come to write your paper, not merely what you will want to incorporate in the paper but what you will need to understand your subject fully.

Once your notes are taken, how do you use them? This again depends on the kind of subject you are dealing with. Some subjects suggest a chronological order, others a logical order. For instance, if you are doing a paper on Keats's development as a poet you might first arrange your notes chronologically—notes on early poems, notes on middle poems, notes on late poems. But if your subject is an analysis of the themes of Keats's poems, you might try to arrange your notes by themes, running various classifications until you had one that seemed to make sense. Or you might find, sometimes, that two levels of organization were necessary. For instance, certain themes of Keats's poems might be characteristic of certain periods. Then having established one type of classification (by theme) you might run another type (by chronology). Notes are flexible. You can use them as a device to help your thinking, or to help you organize your material.

Notes record questions and issues. The different authors you have consulted have had individual approaches to the general subject, different interests, different conclusions. As you work over your cards you can locate these differences and try to see what they mean to you in your special project. Ask yourself if there is any pattern of disagreement among the authors you have consulted. List the disagreements. Are they disagreements of fact or of interpretation? Compare the evidence and reasoning offered by the authors who are in disagreement. Can you think of any new evidence or new line of reasoning on disputed points? Can you think of any significant points not discussed by your authors? What bearing would such points have on their conclusions? Again, use your notes as a device to help your thinking.

By working over your notes and thinking about ideas suggested in them you will probably strike on some vague general plan for your paper. But do not commit yourself to the first plan that comes into your head. Consider various possibilities. Then when you have struck on the most promising, try to work up an outline on that basis. You will undoubtedly start with a sort of rough suggestive outline, the barest shadow of the paper you want to write. By checking back on your material you can begin to fill in the outline and determine the relation among the facts and ideas you wish to present. So you will arrive at a more fully organized outline. Perhaps a topic outline will serve your purpose, but at some stage a sentence outline will probably be helpful, for to make it you will have to state clearly exactly what you mean.

Once you have an outline prepared you can begin the actual composition. Use your outline as a guide, but do not consider yourself bound by it. As you write, new ideas will probably come to you, and if they are good ideas you should revise your outline to accommodate them. The outline is not sacred. Like your notes, it is simply a device to help you think. And remember that your paper should be a fully rounded composition, unified and coherent, emphasizing matters according to the scale of their importance. The outline is only a start toward creating a balanced, fluent, well-proportioned discussion.

Your paper should be more than a tissue of facts and quotations from your notes. It should represent your handling of a subject and not a mere report on what other writers have said. Naturally, a large part of your material will be derived from other writers, but you should always ask yourself just what a fact or idea means in terms of your own purpose. It should find a place in your pattern, and if there is no proper place for it, it should be excluded. In the end, you will always find that some of your notes are not usable. A writer who has studied his subject always has more material than he can well use.

Full credit should be given for the source of every fact or idea derived from another writer. In your own text you will want to acknowledge any important item as a matter of help to your reader. It is easy to introduce a statement or a quotation by a clear explanatory phrase or sentence. We are all accustomed to such introductory remarks as these:

Charles A. Beard has proved that . . .
James Truslow Adams maintains that . . .
An excellent statement of this view is given by James Truslow Adams in his *Epic of America:* . . .

As Sinclair Lewis shows in *Main Street*, the culture of the American town is . . .
On the other hand, such a liberal as Henry A. Wallace holds that . . .
As Thomas Wolfe observed . . .

Some facts or ideas can simply be stated in your text if the fact or idea is not specially to be associated with the particular writer from whom you derived it. But in all cases, authority should be given in a footnote.

Exactly what demands a footnote? First, every direct quotation is identified in a footnote. Second, every statement of fact is referred to its source in a footnote. Third, every opinion or interpretation drawn from another writer should be referred to its source in a footnote, *even if the opinion or interpretation is one which you have independently come upon in your own thinking.* In cases where a group of facts or opinions treated together in one paragraph are drawn from the same source, one note at the end of the paragraph will serve for all the material. In cases where more than one source is involved for a single item in the text, one note will serve to acknowledge the several sources.

Variation in certain details is permissible in the form of footnotes—*but not* in the same paper. Learn one of the standard forms and use it consistently in all your work. Here are a few general principles:

1. The author's name appears in direct form, not with the last name first, as in the bibliography.

2. The title of a book or periodical is underlined in typescript or writing. This corresponds to italics in print. Even a relatively short piece of writing which has independent publication is considered a book. Sometimes a piece of writing, a poem for instance, first appears independently as a little book and is later included in a collection of the author's work. Practice varies in treating such items, but it is permissible to treat it as a book. Thus, we would underscore the title of T. S. Eliot's Four Quartets, but we might quote "Burnt Norton" (which is one of the four poems included) or we might underscore it, thus: Burnt Norton.

3. The title of an item in a periodical appears in quotation marks.

4. When an item is first mentioned in a footnote full bibliographical information is given. Later references use a brief identifying form, to be described later.

Here are examples of various types of footnotes. Observe carefully the form of punctuation, the nature of the material included, and the order of the items presented.

FOOTNOTES FOR BOOKS:

One author:

(1) [1] Gerald G. Walsh, *Dante Alighieri: Citizen of Christendom*, Milwaukee, Bruce Publishing Company, 1946, p. 17.

[But the punctuation might be handled in this fashion: Gerald G. Walsh, *Dante Alighieri: Citizen of Christendom* (Milwaukee: Bruce Publishing Company, 1946), p. 17.]

More than one author:

(2) [1] William Buell Meldrum and Frank Thomson Gucker, Jr., *Introduction to Theoretical Chemistry*, New York, American Book Company, 1936, p. 133.

Translation:

(3) [1] Anton Chekhov, *The Party and Other Stories*, tr. Constance Garnett, London, Chatto and Windus, 1919.

FOOTNOTES FOR ITEMS FROM COLLECTIONS:

(4) [1] Wendell L. Willkie, "Freedom and the Liberal Arts," in *The Humanities after the War*, Norman Foerster, ed., Princeton, Princeton University Press, 1944, p. 5.

[Here the abbreviation *ed.* is for editor: Norman Foerster is the editor of the collection.]

FOOTNOTES FOR ITEMS FROM PERIODICALS:

(5) [1] Henry Albert Phillips, "The Pith of Peru," *National Geographic*, LXXXII, August 1942,[4] 169.

[Here the Roman numerals give the volume number of the periodical. The last number, 169, is the page reference. Notice that the abbreviation *p.* is omitted for periodicals after the volume number.]

(6) [1] Arthur Mizener, "The Desires of the Mind," *Sewanee Review*, LX, Summer 1947, 462.

[For a quarterly magazine, as in this case, the season instead of the month is given, if that is the practice of the magazine itself.]

[4] Although some authorities still prefer a comma between month and year, the trend in current usage is toward omission of the comma.

(7) ¹ Peter F. Drucker, "The Industrial Revolution Hits the Farmer," *Harper's*, No. 1074, November 1939, 593.

[When, as here, the magazine carries an issue number and not a volume number, the issue number appears: "No. 1074."]

FOOTNOTES FOR ITEMS FROM THE BIBLE:

(8) ¹ Psalms 23:6-8.

[Here the first number is for chapter, the others for verses, inclusive.]

(9) ¹ II Cor. 6:9.

[Here the abbreviation *Cor.* is for Corinthians. Certain books of the Bible have such standard abbreviations. The Roman numeral indicates Second Corinthians.]

All the forms given above indicate the first reference to a work. For subsequent references, three forms may be used. When the source in a footnote is the same as that indicated in the footnote immediately preceding, the abbreviation *ibid.* (for *ibidem:* in the same place) is used, with a new page reference, if that is needed. For example:

(10) ¹ Arthur Mizener, "The Desires of the Mind," *Sewanee Review*, LX, Summer 1947, 462.

² *Ibid.* 464.

When the reference repeated does not immediately precede, either of two basic forms may be used. If the author has only one work referred to in the footnotes, his last name may be used, followed by the page reference, or his last name with the abbreviation *op. cit.* (for *opere citato:* in the work cited), with the page reference. The first practice is simpler, and is becoming more common than the other. For example:

(11) ¹ Arthur Mizener, "The Desires of the Mind," *Sewanee Review*, LX, Summer 1947, 462.

² Wendell L. Willkie, "Freedom and the Liberal Arts," in *The Humanities after the War*, Norman Foerster, ed., Princeton, Princeton University Press, 1944, p. 5.

³ Mizener, 464.

If the author has more than one work referred to in the footnotes, then his last name will not be enough, and an abbreviated title will be necessary.

(12) ¹ Mizener, "Desires," 464.   *Or:*   ¹ Walsh, *Dante*, p. 19.

[Notice that the abbreviation *p.* is omitted in the Mizener reference, for the reference is to a periodical, while it is used in the Walsh reference, which is to a book. In other words, the short form follows the practice of the long form in this respect.]

When material is not drawn directly from its original source but from some intermediary source, acknowledgment should be made to both sources. For instance, the following note indicates that the writer has used a quotation from Stephen Spender which appeared in a book by Moody E. Prior:

(13) ¹ Stephen Spender, *The Destructive Element*, Boston, Houghton Mifflin Company, p. 11, quoted Moody E. Prior, *The Language of Tragedy*, New York, Columbia University Press, 1947, p. 343.

We have already referred to the abbreviations *ibid.* and *op. cit.* But there are a number of other abbreviations found in notes and bibliographical forms. You will not find a use for all of them in your own writing, but you will sooner or later encounter them in works which you read. Some of the Latin abbreviations are now commonly replaced by English forms or may be omitted altogether (as with *op. cit.*). In using such abbreviations, the main thing is to be consistent. For instance, do not use *vide* (for *see*) in one place and *ff.* (for *seq.*) in another.

c. (*circa*)   About a certain date (to be used to indicate an approximate date, when the real date cannot be determined).

cf. (*confer*)   Compare (English form: see).

ch. or chaps.   Chapter(s).

col. or cols.   Column(s).

ed.   Edited by, or edition.

et al. (*et alii*)   And others (when a book has several authors, the first, with *et al.*, may replace the full list).

f. or ff.   One or more pages following the page indicated.

ibid. (*ibidem*)   In the same work (referring to a work cited in a note immediately preceding).

infra   Below (indicating a later discussion).

l. or ll.   Line(s).

loc. cit. (*loco citato*)   In the place cited (when there is an earlier reference to the source).

MS.   Manuscript.

n.d.   No date (when publication date cannot be determined).

no.   Number (as when listing the number of the issue of a periodical or series).

n.p.   No place (when place of publication cannot be determined).

op. cit. (opere citato) In the work cited (used with author's name to indicate source already referred to).

p. or pp. Page(s).

passim In various places (when the topic referred to appears at more than one place in a work cited).

q.v. (quod vide) Which see (English form: see).

see Used to suggest that the reader consult a certain work referred to.

seq. (sequentes) Following (English form: F. or ff.).

supra Above (when the topic referred to has already been discussed).

tr. Translated by.

vide See (English form: see).

vol. or vols. Volume(s) (but vol. and p. are not used if figures for both are given, as in listing a periodical reference; in such cases, use Roman numerals for volume and Arabic for page: II, 391).

After you have prepared a draft of your paper and established all your footnotes, you are ready to set up your final bibliography. This may differ from your working bibliography, in that it contains only items which are actually referred to in your paper, not items which have been consulted but not used.

The form for such a bibliography permits certain minor variations. For instance, the place without the publisher is sometimes given; and there may be differences in punctuation. For example, the following entry can be punctuated in two ways:

Barnes, Harry Elmer, *The Genesis of the World War,* New York, Alfred A. Knopf, 1926.

Or:

Barnes, Harry Elmer. *The Genesis of the World War.* New York: Alfred A. Knopf, 1926.

But in all forms the author's name comes first, with the last name first, followed by the full title of the work, the periodical or series if any, the place of publication, the publisher (if this form is used), and the date of publication. The items may be arranged in either of two ways. First, in a straight alphabetical order, according to the last name of the author or, if there is no author, by the main word of the title. Second, alphabetically within certain groups determined by the material dealt with: "Books," "Periodicals," "Documents," and so forth. Here are some examples of entries as they might appear in the bibliography of a paper on Woodrow Wilson:

(Periodical)   Baker, Ray Stannard, "Our Next President and Some Others," *American Magazine*, LXXIV, June 1912, 131-143.

(Book)   Barnes, Harry Elmer, *The Genesis of the World War*, New York, Alfred A. Knopf, 1926.

(Document)   *Congressional Record*, XLIX-LI, Washington, 1913-1914.

(Document)   *Legislative Manual, State of New Jersey*, 1912, Trenton, 1912.

(Book)   McAdoo, Eleanor R. W., *The Woodrow Wilsons*, New York, Macmillan Company, 1937.

(Book)   Wilson, Woodrow, *The Public Papers of Woodrow Wilson*, Baker, Ray Stannard, and Dodd, William Edward, eds., New York, Harper and Bros., 1925-1927.

(Periodical)   Wilson, Woodrow, "Democracy and Efficiency," *Atlantic Monthly*, LXXXVII, March 1901, 289-299.

(Collection)   Wilson, Woodrow, "Leaderless Government," in *Report of the Ninth Annual Meeting of the Virginia State Bar Association*, Richmond, 1897.

Notice that an over-all alphabetical order is given, by author when an author is specified, and by leading word when there is no author ("Congressional" and "Legislative"). In this short bibliography all types of sources are grouped together—books, collections, periodicals, and documents. In a long bibliography such types might be set up as separate, each group in alphabetical order.

At this stage you should have an outline and a draft of your paper, with all quotations properly inserted, all acknowledgments for facts and opinions (either quoted or summarized) indicated in footnotes, and a final bibliography attached for all works actually referred to in your footnotes. Now is the time to check carefully to see if there is any need for revision. Try to answer the following questions to see if all is in order.

1. Does my paper have a guiding purpose? That is, is there a subject properly fixed and limited? Have I stated it clearly?

2. Is my paper really a discussion of the subject and not a mere tissue of quotations and summaries? Does it really go somewhere? What is my own contribution to the discussion of the subject? Have I offered evidence and arguments for my point of view? Have I indicated how my point of view differs from the points of view held by other writers? If my paper is primarily exposition and not

argument, have I added new facts to the discussion, or have I made the pattern of facts clearer than before?

3. Is my paper well organized and proportioned? Is there a clear introduction? Does the discussion really constitute the main body of the paper? Is my conclusion an accurate statement of what I have accomplished? Is it brief and pointed? Are my transitions clear? Have I introduced irrelevant material?

4. Is my style clear and grammatical? Are my paragraphs well organized? Is my punctuation correct?

5. Is my outline a satisfactory one for my paper as it now stands?

6. Am I sure that all my quotations and summaries are accurate?

7. Am I sure that my footnote references are accurate?

8. Is my final bibliography accurate?

9. Are my footnotes and bibliography in the proper form? Is the form I have used consistent?

If your paper is deficient on any of these counts, revise it. In checking on the paper or in making revisions, it is wise not to try to do everything at once. Take one question and follow it through the whole paper, say the matter of organization, or the matter of punctuation. You cannot do everything at once, and you will get your best results by concentrating on one consideration at a time.

THE BOOK REPORT

The book report is to be sharply distinguished on one hand from the research paper and on the other hand from the book review or the critical essay. It is to be distinguished from the research paper primarily because it deals with one book in its entirety, and from the review or critical essay because it merely reports on a book, presents that book, and does not compare it with other books or attempt to make judgments as to its value. But the book report may include a certain amount of background material about the author himself, his other work and his reputation, or the circumstances of the composition of the book being reported on. Such material is to be used as a means of presenting the book in question. It is not to become an end in itself, and in proportion it should be subordinated to the actual presentation of the book. Some book reports do not require this background material at all. The nature of the assignment determines its inclusion.

To write a good book report you need to answer the following questions:

1. Who is the author? (What is his nationality and origins? What is his period?)
2. What other work has he done?
3. What is his reputation?
4. Are there any important or enlightening circumstances connected with the composition of this book?
5. What kind of book is this? (Is it fiction, history, literary criticism, biography, poetry, drama, or what?)
6. What is the subject of this book?
7. What material does it treat?
8. What is the theme of the book—the author's basic interpretation of the material?
9. What method of organization does he employ?
10. What is the tone and style of the book?

You will notice that the first four questions involve background information. If your report is to present such information, you do not need to make a full-dress research paper on that part of the assignment. You can merely consult a few standard reference works to get the basic facts, or look into one or two good biographies or historical or critical works. In doing this, however, it is wise to take your notes as if for a research paper so that your material will be conveniently available and can be put into order.

The kind of book you are dealing with determines to a considerable extent the kind of treatment you can appropriately give it. For instance, if you are dealing with a biography, you should identify the character who is the subject of the work, summarize his career as given by the author (including the basic pieces of evidence which he employs to support his interpretation of the character), give some idea of his method of organization, and comment on his tone and style. This last consideration may involve such questions as these: Is he writing a scholarly treatise or a popular biography? Is his work adapted to the audience he has in mind? Does he give interesting anecdotes and colorful personal touches, or does he devote himself to facts and historical or psychological analysis? If you are dealing with a book on public policy—say on the reconstruction of Germany or international relations—the important considerations would be somewhat different. You would primarily be concerned to present the author's picture of the situation provoking the discussion, state the policy which he recommends, and offer the arguments for that policy. You might even be led to present the philosophical or political assumptions on which he bases his policy. The kind of audience he has in mind would still be important, and you should define it; but in general in this type of book, questions of tone and style, except in so far as mere clarity is concerned, would not be important. Or if you are dealing with a novel, the emphasis in your report would again be different. It would now be important to define the kind of world your author is interested in. Does he write of drawing rooms or village parlors, or farms or battlefields? What kind of characters and issues interest him? What is the outline of his plot? How do the motivations of his characters fit the plot? What is the theme of his book? And here questions of tone and style might become very important. But in all cases, remember that the book report *presents* a book, primarily in its own terms. It does not compare, criticize, or evaluate.

Index

INDEX

Abstract words: *see* Diction
Adjectives: position of, in sentence, 311-18; "projectile," 351, 391; use and misuse of, 226-7
Adverbs: conjunctive, 19; position of, in sentence, 311-18; to establish continuity, 19; use and misuse of, 227-8
Advertising, appeal of, 393-4
Analogy: as type of induction, 158-9; word meanings extended by, 342-4
Analysis: **98-119;** and expository (technical) description, 101-19; and structure, 99-100; causal, 111-19, **App. 1;** chronological, 110; conceptual, 99; functional, 105-10; physical, 99; relation among parts, 100; *see also* Exposition
Argument: 30, 35, 38, **125-94,** 196; as appeal to emotions, 125; as appeal to the understanding, 125, 127-8; based on conflict, 125; extended, and the brief, 172-83; subject matter of, 128-31; *see also* Proposition, Reasoning
Attitude, of the writer toward the reader: 5, 183-9, **390-1;** *see also* Tone
Attribute and subject, 155
Audience: influenced by authority, 154; influenced by tone, 393-4; special and ideal, 420-2; *see also* Reader

Authority: and the audience, 154; tests of, 151-4
Axioms, 159

Begging the question, 134, 168
Bibliography, preparation of, **App. 3**
Body of a discourse, 23-4
Book report, App. 3
Brief, 172-83

Capital letters, misuse of, 22
Catch words, misuse of, 22
Cause: *see* Analysis, causal
Central idea, 11
Characterization, 281-5
Classification and division, 67-83
Clauses, relative, 313
Clichés, 353-60
Climax, 253
Coherence: within the sentence, 305; within the theme, 15-19
Communication, as motivation of the writer, 3-4, 29
Comparison: as basis of metaphor, 378-89; as method of exposition, **61-2;** function of, in description, 223-6
Complication, of a narrative, 254
Concrete words: *see* Diction
Conclusion from evidence, 155
Conclusion: of a brief, 173; of a discourse, 23, 25
Condition: distinguished from cause, 114 *note;* of an event, 113-14; sufficient and necessary, 115

Conflict, as basis of argument, 125
Conjunctions, 19, 300
Connotation, 335-42, 345 note, 349-53, 372
Content and form, inseparability of, 435-8
Continuity: and transition, 19; intrinsic, 18
Contrast: as basis of metaphor, 381-9; as method of exposition, **61-7**
Co-ordination, 320-2
Cross division, 71
Cutback, 238, 250, 264

Deduction, 159-67
Definition: **83-98;** and the common ground, 87-9; extended, 91-98; of terms, 97, 133-4; parts of, 84; principles of, 89-91; process of, 85-7
Denotation, **335-42,** 345 note
Denouement, 254
Derivation of words, 97-8, 344
Description: 30, 35, 38, **195-236;** absorbed, 207-9; generalized, 48; objective, 50-3; of feelings and states of mind, 220-6; subjective, 50-3; see also Expository (technical) description, Pattern, Suggestive description
Dialogue, **275-81,** 302
Diction: 2, **335-60;** abstract-general, 338-42; colloquial, 348-9; concrete-specific, 338-42; formal, 348-9; in description, 197-200, 226-9; informal, 348-9
Dictionary: a record of meanings, 344-8; sample entries from, 345, 346
Differentia, 85
Discourse: divisions of a, 23-5; kinds of, **29-37;** objective and subjective, 31-7; outlining, 26-8
Discussion (argument) of a brief, 173
Division and classification, 67-83
Divisions of a discourse, 23-5

Emotions, appeal to, 125, 127-8, 183-4
Emphasis: general problem of, 19-23; in the paragraph, 291; within the sentence, 305-7; see also Variation, emphatic

Enthusiasm, false, 402
Enthymeme, 171, 296
Equivocation, 167
Essay: familiar, 411-15; formal, 415
Euphemisms, 351
Evidence, kinds of, 148-54
Exaggeration, as a fault of style, 22
Exclamation points, misuse of, 22
Explanation: see Exposition
Exposition: 30, 35, **38-124,** 126, 195; and narration, 242-50; methods of, 41-120; see also Analysis, Expository Description, Expository Narration
Exposition (beginning) of a narrative, 251-3
Expository description (technical description): and analysis, 101-20; and generalized description, 48; as method of exposition, **42;** distinguished from suggestive description, **42-50;** in relation to the objective-subjective distinction, 53-5; uses of, 55-6
Expository narration: **57,** 250; and analysis, 105, 111
Expression, as motivation of the writer, 3-4

Fact, as evidence, 148-51
Fallacies, 167-70
Figurative language: in description of feelings and states of mind, 223-6, 362-3, 374-6; see also Diction, Metaphor
Figures of speech: see Metaphor
First person: see Point of view
Fixed word order: of basic sentence elements, 307-8; of the modifiers, 311-18
Focus, 270-2
Form and content, inseparability of, 435-8
Footnotes, in research paper, App. 3
Frame image, 203-4

Generalization: see Induction
Genus (genera), 70-1, 86-7
Gobbledygook, 355-6, 426
Grammar, in relation to rhetoric, 304-7
Ground, common, 87-9

Harmony: *see* Style
History of the question, 134-5

Identification, as method of exposition, 41
Ignoring the question, 168-9
Illustration: as method of exposition, **57-61;** metaphor employed as, 373-4
Imagination, creative, and metaphor, 386-7
Impression, dominant, 200
Impressionism: *see* Pattern
Individuality, in style, 438-57
Induction (generalization), 155-9
Intention: **29-37;** and the kinds of discourse, 30; artistic, 33-7; scientific, 32-3
Interest: and descriptive pattern, 205-7; in exposition, **38-40;** special, in determining cause, 113
Introduction: of a brief, 173; of a discourse, 23-24
Irony, 397, 406-7
Irrelevancy, 15
Issues, of a proposition, 135-46
Italics, misuse of, 22

Jargon: 354-9, 366-7, 426; *see also* Cliché, Slang

Language: growth of, by extension of meaning, 342-8; habits, diagram of, 349; *see also* Diction, Words
Logic: *see* Reasoning

Meaning, 239-40
Medium, as aspect of writing, 2
Metaphor, 344, **361-89;** and the creative imagination, 386-7; and symbol, 385-6; as essential statement, 374-8; as illustration, 373-4; confused and half-dead, 367-70; consistency in, 382-5; defined, 361; function of, 371-4; "good," 378-85; in description of feelings and states of mind, 223-6; in everyday language, 362-71
Modifiers: 311-18; fixed, 312-14; movable, 314-18
Mood, to create pattern, 204-5

Motivation: in narration, 240; of the writer, 2, 3
Movement, 237-8

Narration: 30, 35, 38, **237-89;** and narrative, 240-1; and other kinds of discourse, 242-50; *see also* Expository narration, Meaning, Movement, Pattern, Time
Non sequitur, 169-70
Notes, and note-taking, App. 3
Nouns: 227; *see also* Subject

Object, of a verb, 307-8, 310
Objectivity: **31-2;** and the four kinds of discourse, 35; and scientific intention, 32-3, 36-7; in expository description, 50-5
Occasion: as aspect of writing, 3; as factor in effective persuasion, 185-7
Opinion, as evidence, 148, 151
Order, principles of: *see* Coherence, Emphasis, Unity
Organization of material: 16, 63-7, App. 3; emphasis in, 19; problems of, 11
Outline: as aid to reasoning, 296-7; of a discourse, **26-8,** App. 3
Overstatement, 398-401

Paragraph: **290-303;** as convenience to the reader, 290-1; as device of emphasis, 22; as unit of thought, 291-2; dialogue in, 302; linking, 299-302; structure of, 292-9
Parallelism, 318-20
Participles, dangling, 318
Passive voice, use and misuse of, 310
Pattern: and interest, 205-7; and mood, 204-5; from fixed point of view, 201-2; from moving point of view, 202-3; impressionistic, 207; in description, **200-11;** in narration, **250-62;** rhythmic, 427-8
Personality: controlled and objectified, 454; expressed in style, 438-54; intrusion of, 449-54
Persuasion, 125, **183-9,** 403-6
Point of view: **267-73;** and pattern, 201-3; of first person, 268-9; of sharp focus, 270-2; of third person, 201, 268, 269; panoramic, 269-73

Position, as device as emphasis, 20
Précis, App. 3
Predication, 305-7
Premise, minor and major, 160, App. 2
Proportion: as device of emphasis, 20; in divisions of a discourse, 25-6; in narration, 262-4
Proposition: 131-48; clear, 133-4; of fact, 131, 146-8; of policy, 131; single, 132-3; statement of, 131-4; unprejudiced, 134; see also Argument

Question: begging the, 134, 168; history of the, 134-5; ignoring the, 168-9; stock, 142; see also Proposition

Reader: appeal to, 4; nature of, 5; relationship to writer, 5; see also Audience
Reading: as aspect of style, 455-7; importance of, 461 ff.
Research paper: App. 3
Reasoning: 7-8, 127-8, 154-72; about cause and effect, 117-19; by either-or, 165-6; by if-then, 166-7; see also Argument
Refutation, 170
Relevancy, 15
Repetition: as device of emphasis, 22; as linking device, 18
Resolution, as formal statement of a proposition, 131-2
Rhythm: 2, 307, 425-32

Sarcasm, 397
Scale, in narrative, 273-5
Scanning, 427
Scientific intention (scientific statement), 32-7, 341-2, 372-3, 387
Selection: in description, 42-53, 200, 211-19; in narration, 264-7
Senses, and suggestive description, 197-200
Sentence: 304-28; length and variation, 323-7; loose and periodic, 322-3; parts of, 306; position of modifiers in, 311-18; structure, principles of, 318-23; topic, 292-3; word order in, 307-11, 358

Sentimentality, 399, 402, 450
Significance, in selection of descriptive details, 215
Similarity, in metaphor, 379-81
Simile, 385
Situation and tone, 390-424
Slang: 354-5, 365-6; see also Metaphor, Tone
Species, 70-1, 86-7, 90
"Specific-general" distinction, 338-9
Stereotypes: 354; see also Jargon, Slang
Structure, and analysis, 99-100
Style: 329-34; as device of emphasis, 20-2; as expression of personality, 438-54; as harmonious integration, 432-5; as interplay of elements, 331-2; Buffon on, 459; Chesterfield on, 459; cultivation of, by reading, 455-7; definition of, 329; see also Diction, Metaphor, Rhythm, Tone
Subject: as aspect of writing, 2; locating, 11-12, 39-40
Subject, of a sentence: 306, 308; emphasis on, 309-10
Subjectivity: 31-2; and the four kinds of discourse, 35; and artistic intention, 33-7; in expository description, 50-5
Suggestive description: and the senses, 197-200; distinguished from expository (technical) description, 42-50; in relation to the other kinds of discourse, 195-7; in relation to the objective-subjective distinction, 53-5; uses of, 55-6
Summary, App. 3
Syllogism: 159-67, App. 2; implied, 170-2
Symbol, and metaphor, 385-6

Technical description: see Expository description
Term: changed use of, 97; in definition, 84; see also Words
Testimony, 150-1
Texture: in description, 211-19; in narration, 264-7
Thinking: see Reasoning
Third person: see Point of view
Time, in narration, 238

Tone: 5, 6, **390-424;** and audience, 393-4; and material, 396-7; as expression of attitude, 390; as qualification of meaning, 397-401; complex, 416-19, 438; familiar and formal, 411-16; importance of, 391; in persuasion, 403-6; in private and public utterance, 407-11; see also Connotation
Topic: see Subject
Topic sentence, 292-3
Transference, authority by, 152
Transitional words and phrases, 18-19, 299-300

Understanding: appeal to, 127-8; see also Reasoning
Understatement, 398-401

Uniformity, principle of, 115
Unity: in the sentence, 305; in the theme, 13-15

Variation: elegant, 357; emphatic, 308-11, 313, 317
Verbs: 227-8; finite, 306 note, 307, 358; infinite, 306 note, 307
Verification of facts, 149-50
Vividness, 33-5, 50-6, 212-15, 338-42, 362-5

Words: derivation, 97-8, 344; worn-out, 353-9; see also Diction, Language, Term
Writer: motivation of, 3; relationship with reader, 5
Writing, background for, 7-8
"Writing down," 402